Microsoft®
Office XP

ESSENTIALS

Microsoft® Office XP

ESSENTIALS

MARIANNE FOX
COLLEGE OF BUSINESS ADMINISTRATION
BUTLER UNIVERSITY

LAWRENCE C. METZELAAR
COLLEGE OF BUSINESS ADMINISTRATION
BUTLER UNIVERSITY

LINDA BIRD
SOFTWARE SOLUTIONS

KEITH MULBERY
UTAH VALLEY STATE COLLEGE

DAWN PARRISH WOOD
SOFTWARE SUPPORT

Prentice
Hall

Upper Saddle River, New Jersey

LIBRARY OF CONGRESS CATALOGING-IN-PUBLICATION DATA

Essentials Microsoft Office XP / Marianne Fox . . . [et al.].
    p. cm.—(Essentials 2002 series)
    ISBN 0-13-092781-3
    1. Microsoft Office.   I. Fox, Marianne B.   II. Series.
HF5548.4.M525 E84 2002
005.369—dc21   2001004498

Publisher and Vice President: Natalie E. Anderson
Executive Editor: Jodi McPherson
Managing Editor: Monica Stipanov
Assistant Editor: Jennifer Cappello
Editorial Assistant: Dayna Hilinsky
Developmental Editors: Joyce J. Nielsen and Jan Snyder
Media Project Manager: Cathleen Profitko
Executive Marketing Manager: Emily Williams Knight
Manager, Production: Gail Steier de Acevedo
Project Managers: April Montana
Associate Director, Manufacturing: Vincent Scelta
Manufacturing Buyer: Natacha St. Hill Moore
Design Manager: Pat Smythe
Interior Design: Kim Buckley
Cover Design: Pisaza Design Studio, Ltd.
Production Assistant to Design and Media: Christopher Kossa
Manager, Print Production: Christy Mahon
Full-Service Composition: Impressions Book and Journal Services, Inc.
Printer/Binder: Courier Companies, Inc. Kendallville

Credits and acknowledgments borrowed from other sources and reproduced, with permission, in this textbook appear on the appropriate page within the text.

Microsoft, Windows, Windows NT, MSN, The Microsoft Network, PowerPoint, Outlook, FrontPage, Hotmail, the MSN logo, and/or other Microsoft products referenced herein are either trademarks or registered trademarks of Microsoft Corporation in the United States and/or other countries. Screen shots and icons reprinted with permission from the Microsoft Corporation. This book is not sponsored or endorsed by or affiliated with Microsoft Corporation.

Microsoft is a registered trademark of Microsoft Corporation in the United States and/or other countries. Pearson Education is independent from Microsoft Corporation, and is not affiliated with Microsoft in any manner. This text may be used in assisting students to prepare for a Microsoft Office User Specialist (MOUS) Exam. Neither Microsoft, its designated review company, nor Pearson Education warrants that use of this text will ensure passing this exam.

10 9 8 7 6 5 4 3 2 1
ISBN 0-13-092781-3

Dedications

Marianne Fox and Lawrence C. Metzelaar

We would like to dedicate this book to all who use it, in appreciation of your desire to learn how to learn and your selection of our book to support those efforts.

Linda Bird

I would like to dedicate this book to my family: Lonnie, a published author and my best supporter; and Rebecca and Sarah, our family's incredible readers (and future authors).

Keith Mulbery

I would like to dedicate this book to my parents—Kenneth and Mary Lu—and grandparents—Herman, Billie, and Orpha—for their support and encouragement. I further dedicate this book to the memory of Grandpa (Raymond) Mulbery. Through them, I learned the value of hard work, a passion for my work, and the importance of education.

Dawn Parrish Wood

I would like to dedicate this series of books to my supportive and loving family. I especially want to thank my husband, Kenneth, who encourages me to achieve the highest level of success to which I am able, and helps me to be the best person I can be. To my girls, Micaela and Kendra, who allow me to write while being "Mommy." To my parents, Norman and Wilma, for teaching me that integrity and hard work are not optional in life. To my mother-in-law, Elizabeth, for all of her help with the girls when deadlines are tight.

Acknowledgments

Marianne Fox and Lawrence C. Metzelaar

We want to express our appreciation to the entire *essentials* 2002 team—other authors, editors, production staff, and those in marketing who start and end the process of developing and delivering a quality text. Special thanks go to those with whom we were most involved on a day-to-day basis: **Monica Stipanov**, managing editor; **Joyce Nielsen**, developmental editor; and **April Montana**, project manager. They continue to have our respect and gratitude for the prompt, professional, and always pleasant way in which they manage the creative process.

We also thank several colleagues at Butler University for supporting the collaborative process that was critical to the success of the *essentials* 2002 series: the dean of the College of Business Administration, **Dr. Richard Fetter;** and the executive director of Information Resources, initially **Sondrea Ozolins** and then **Ken Sorenson.** Their combined support enabled us as series editors to host a launch meeting at Butler University and to coordinate a listserv used by authors and editors to ensure consistency and quality across all titles in the series.

Linda Bird

No book is ever the result of a sole individual, but rather the result of a hard-working team of talented individuals. Although most of these persons worked behind the scenes, I would like to publicly acknowledge their professionalism, hard work, and dedication to producing a top-quality publication.

First, I'd like to thank Executive Editor **Jodi McPherson** for providing the opportunity to be involved in the project; Managing Editor **Monica Stipanov** for her quick and valuable feedback and overseeing the entire project; and Project Manager **April Montana** for using her knowledge to direct the book through the production process. I also want to express my appreciation to Developmental Editor **Joyce Nielsen** and Copy Editor **Susan Hobbs,** who served as a top-notch editorial team and helped to ensure the quality of the book.

I'd also like to thank the other *essentials* authors for their valuable feedback, their willingness to share ideas, and their friendship: **Larry Metzelaar** and **Marianne Fox** (*essentials Excel 2002*), **Keith Mulberry** (*essentials Word 2002*), and **Dawn Wood** (*essentials Access 2002*).

Most of all, I would like to thank my family: **Lonnie, Rebecca,** and **Sarah,** who were my best fans and cheerleaders throughout the entire writing process.

Keith Mulbery

This book is a result of collaborative effort from the *essentials* team. First, I'd like to express sincere appreciation to **Monica Stipanov** and **April Montana** at Prentice Hall for their professionalism and dedication to the *essentials* series. They have been a reliable force throughout the years for ensuring continuity, accuracy, and pedagogical strength throughout the series. The team at Impressions converted the manuscript and individual screen shots into actual pages. The *essentials* series would not be the popular series it is today without the Prentice Hall marketing team: **Emily Knight** and **Jason Smith**.

A special thanks to **Larry Metzelaar** and **Marianne Fox** for providing a positive direction as series editors. I appreciate the valuable advice provided by Developmental Editor **Jan Snyder**. Her suggestions definitely strengthened the content of this book. In addition, Copy Editor **Nancy Sixsmith** ensured the grammatical accuracy of the manuscript—thanks for catching those sneaky little typos that almost slipped by!

Some final acknowledgments: **Nancy Bartlett**, Director of Human Resources at Utah Valley State College, gave me permission to use AAEO documentation as data files; **Rick Bradshaw** took me to Cold Stone Creamery for ice cream to relieve stress; my colleagues at Utah Valley State College gave me their support and ideas; and my students provided valuable feedback while working through previous editions of this book.

Dawn Parrish Wood

I would also like to thank all the staff members involved with the series for their extremely hard work and timeliness in the project. A special thanks to **Jan Snyder** for using an extra fine-tooth comb to look over the books so we could produce the highest quality product for the students and instructors. Another thanks to **Monica Stipanov** and **Jennifer Cappello** for having such confidence in my work.

About the Series Editors

Marianne Fox—Series editor and coauthor of *essentials Excel 2002 Level 1, Level 2,* and *Level 3.* Marianne Fox is an Indiana CPA with B.S. and M.B.A. degrees in Accounting from Indiana University. For more than 20 years, she has enjoyed teaching full-time—initially in Indiana University's School of Business; since 1988 in the College of Business Administration at Butler University. As the co-owner of an Indiana-based consulting firm, Marianne has extensive experience consulting and training in the corporate and continuing education environments. Since 1984, she has co-authored more than 35 computer-related books; and has given presentations on accounting, computer applications, and instructional development topics at a variety of seminars and conferences.

Lawrence C. Metzelaar—Series editor and coauthor of *essentials Excel 2002 Level 1, Level 2,* and *Level 3.* Lawrence C. Metzelaar earned a B.S. in Business Administration and Computer Science from the University of Maryland, and an Ed.M. and C.A.G.S. in Human Problem

Solving from Boston University. Lawrence has more than 30 years of experience with military and corporate mainframe and microcomputer systems. He has taught computer science and Management Information Systems (MIS) courses at the University of Hawaii, Control Data Institute, Indiana University, and Purdue University; currently, he is a full-time faculty member in the College of Business Administration at Butler University. As the co-owner of an Indiana-based consulting firm, he has extensive experience consulting and training in the corporate and continuing education environments. Since 1984, he has co-authored more than 35 computer-related books; and has given presentations on computer applications and instructional development topics at a variety of seminars and conferences.

About the Series Authors

Linda Bird—Author of *essentials PowerPoint® 2002 Level 1* and *Level 2*. Linda Bird specializes in corporate training and support through her company, Software Solutions. She has successfully trained users representing more than 75 businesses, including several Fortune 500 companies. She custom designs many of her training materials. Her clients include Appalachian Electric Power Co., Goodyear, Pillsbury, Rockwell, and Shell Chemical. Her background also includes teaching at Averett College and overseeing computer training for a business training organization.

Using her training experience as a springboard, Linda has written numerous books on PowerPoint, Word, Excel, Access, and Windows. Additionally, she has written more than 20 instructor's manuals and contributed to books on a variety of desktop application programs. She has also penned more than 150 magazine articles, as well as monthly how-to columns on PowerPoint and Excel for *Smart Computing* magazine.

Linda, a graduate of the University of Wisconsin, lives near the Great Smoky Mountains in Tennessee with her husband, Lonnie, and daughters, Rebecca and Sarah. Besides authoring books, Linda home-educates her daughters. If she's not writing, you can probably find her trekking around the mountains (or horseback riding) with her family.

Keith Mulbery—Author of *essentials Word 2002 Level 1 and Level 2* and coauthor of *Level 3*. Keith Mulbery is an associate professor in the Information Systems Department at Utah Valley State College, where he teaches computer applications courses and assists with curriculum development. Keith received his B.S. and M.Ed. (majoring in Business Education) from Southwestern Oklahoma State University. Keith has written several Word and WordPerfect textbooks. His previous book, *MOUS essentials Word 2000*, received the Utah Valley State College Board of Trustees Award of Excellence in January 2001. In addition, he was the developmental editor of *essentials Word 2000 intermediate* and *essentials Word 2000 advanced*. Keith also conducts hands-on computer application workshops at the local, state, and national levels, including at the National Business Education Association convention.

Dawn Parrish Wood—Author of *essentials Access 2002 Level 1*, *Level 2*, and *Level 3*. Dawn Parrish Wood is an independent contractor, and provides software training through her own business, Software Support. She teaches customized courses to local businesses and individuals in order to upgrade employee skills and knowledge of computers. Dawn has written materials for these specialized courses for her own use. She also provides software consultation to local businesses. Previously, she was the computer coordinator/lead instructor for the Business & Industry Services division at Valdosta Technical Institute in Valdosta, Georgia. The majority of the coursework she taught was in continuing education. Prior to teaching, she worked as a technical support representative and technical writer for a software firm. She lives in Valdosta, Georgia, with her husband, Kenneth, and their two daughters, Micaela (4 1/2 years) and Kendra (2 1/2 years). Both girls have been her superlative students, learning more on the computer every day.

Contents at a Glance

Table of Contents

Introduction

Essentials courseware from Prentice Hall Information Technology is anchored in the practical and professional needs of all types of students.

The *essentials* series has been conceived around a "learning-by-doing" approach that encourages you to grasp application-related concepts as you expand your skills through hands-on tutorials. As such, it consists of modular lessons that are built around a series of numbered, step-by-step procedures that are clear, concise, and easy to review. The end-of-chapter exercises have likewise been carefully graded from the routine Checking Concepts and Terms to tasks in the Discovery Zone that gently prod you into extending what you've learned into areas beyond the explicit scope of the lessons proper. Following, you'll find out more about the rationale behind each book element and how to use each to your maximum benefit.

Key Features

❑ **Step-by-Step Tutorials.** Each lesson in a project includes numbered, bold step-by-step instructions that show you how to perform the procedures in a clear, concise, and direct manner. These hands-on tutorials let you "learn by doing." A short paragraph may appear after a step to clarify the results of that step. To review the lesson, you can easily scan the bold numbered steps. Accompanying data files eliminate unnecessary typing.

❑ **End-of-Project Exercises.** Check out the extensive end-of-project exercises (generally 20 to 25 percent of the pages in each project) that emphasize hands-on skill development. You'll find three levels of reinforcement: Skill Drill, Challenge, and Discovery Zone. Generally, each exercise is independent of other exercises, so you can complete your choices in any order. Accompanying data files eliminate unnecessary typing.

Skill Drill   Skill Drill exercises reinforce project skills. Each skill reinforced is the same, or nearly the same, as a skill presented in the project. Each exercise includes a brief narrative introduction, followed by detailed instructions in a step-by-step format.

Challenge   Challenge exercises expand on or are somewhat related to skills presented in the lessons. Each exercise provides a brief narrative introduction, followed by instructions in a numbered-step format that are not as detailed as those in the Skill Drill section.

Discovery Zone   Discovery Zone exercises require advanced knowledge of topics presented in lessons, application of skills from multiple lessons, or self-directed learning of new skills. Each exercise provides a brief narrative introduction. Numbered steps are not provided.

Two other sections precede the end-of-project exercises: **Summary** and **Checking Concepts and Terms**. The Summary provides a brief recap of tasks learned in the project, and guides you to topics or places where you can expand your knowledge. The Checking Concepts and Terms section includes Multiple Choice and Discussion questions that are designed to check your comprehension and assess retention. Projects that introduce a new work area include a Screen ID question.

❑ **Notes.** Projects include two types of notes: "If you have problems..." and "To extend your knowledge..." The first type displays between hands-on steps. These short troubleshooting notes help you anticipate or solve common problems quickly and effectively. Many lessons in the projects end with "To extend your knowledge..." notes that provide extra tips, shortcuts, and alternative ways to complete a process, as well as special hints. You may safely ignore these for the moment to focus on the main task at hand, or you may pause to learn and appreciate the additional information.

❏ **Task Guide.** The Task Guide, which follows the Overview of Windows, lists common procedures and shortcuts. It can be used in two complementary ways to enhance your learning experience. You can refer to it while progressing through projects to refresh your memory on procedures learned. Or, you can keep it as a handy real-world reference while using the application for your daily work.

❏ **Illustrations.** Multiple illustrations add visual appeal and reinforce learning in each project. An opening section titled "Visual Summary" graphically illustrates the concepts and features included in the project and/or the output you will produce. Each time a new button is introduced, its icon displays in the margin. Screen shots display after key steps for you to check against the results on your monitor. These figures, with ample callouts, make it easy to check your progress.

❏ **Learn-How-to-Learn Focus.** Software has become so rich in features that cater to so many diverse needs that it is no longer possible to anticipate and include everything that you might need to know. Therefore, a learn-how-to-learn component is provided as an "essential" element in the series. Selected lessons and end-of-project exercises include accessing onscreen Help for guidance. References to onscreen Help are also included in selected project summaries and "To extend your knowledge…" notes.

How to Use This Book

Typically, each *essentials* book is divided into seven to eight projects. A project covers one area (or a few closely related areas) of application functionality. Each project consists of six to eight lessons that are related to that topic. Each lesson presents a specific task or closely related set of tasks in a manageable chunk that is easy to assimilate and retain.

Each element in the *essentials* book is designed to maximize your learning experience. Following is a list of the *essentials* project elements and a description of how each element can help you:

❏ **Project Objectives.** Starting with an objective gives you short-term, attainable goals. Using project objectives that closely match the titles of the step-by-step tutorials breaks down the possibly overwhelming prospect of learning several new features of an Office XP application into small, attainable, bite-sized tasks. Look over the objectives on the opening page of the project before you begin, and review them after completing the project to identify the main goals for each project.

❏ **Key Terms.** Key terms introduced in each project are listed, in alphabetical order, immediately after the objectives on the opening page of the project. Each key term is defined during its first use within the text, and is shown in bold italic within that explanation. Definitions of key terms are also included in the Glossary.

❏ **Why Would I Do This?** You are studying Office XP applications so you can accomplish useful tasks. This brief section provides an overview of why these tasks and procedures are important.

❏ **Visual Summary.** This opening section graphically illustrates the concepts and features that you will learn in the project. One or more figures, with ample callouts, show the final result of completing the project.

 ❏ **If You Have Problems…** These short troubleshooting notes help you anticipate or solve common problems quickly and effectively. Even if you do not encounter the problem at this time, make a mental note of it so that you know where to look when you (or others) have difficulty.

 ❏ **To Extend Your Knowledge…** Many lessons end with "To extend your knowledge…" comments. These notes provide extra tips, shortcuts, alternative ways to complete a process, and special hints about using the software.

Typeface Conventions Used in This Book

Essentials 2002 uses the following conventions to make it easier for you to understand the material.

- ❏ Key terms appear in ***italic and bold*** the first time they are defined in a project.

- ❏ Monospace type appears frequently and looks `like this`. It is used to indicate text that you are instructed to key in.

- ❏ *Italic text* indicates text that appears onscreen as (1) warnings, confirmations, or general information; (2) the name of a file to be used in a lesson or exercise; and (3) text from a dialog box that is referenced within a sentence, when that sentence might appear awkward if the dialog box text were not set off.

- ❏ Hotkeys are indicated by underline. Hotkeys are the underlined letters in menus, toolbars, and dialog boxes that activate commands and options, and are a quick way to choose frequently used commands and options. Hotkeys look like this: File, Save.

Accessing Student Data Files

The data files that students need to work through the projects can be downloaded from the Custom PHIT Web site (www.prenhall.com/customphit). Data files are provided for each project. The filenames correspond to the filenames called for in this book. The files are named in the following manner: The first character indicates the book series (e=essentials); the second character denotes the application (w=Word, e=Excel, and so forth); and the third character indicates the level (1=Level 1, 2=Level 2, and 3=Level 3). The last four digits indicate the project number and the file number within the project. For example, the first file used in Project 3 would be 0301. Therefore, the complete name for the first file in Project 3 in the *Word Level 1* book is ew1-0301. The complete name for the third file in Project 7 in the *Excel Level 2* book is ee2-0703.

Instructor's Resources

- ❏ **Customize Your Book (www.prenhall.com/customphit).** The Prentice Hall Information Technology Custom PHIT Program gives professors the power to control and customize their books to their course needs. The best part is that it is done completely online using a simple interface.

  Professors choose exactly what projects they need in the *essentials* Office XP series, and in what order they appear. The program also allows professors to add their own material anywhere in the text's presentation, and the final product will arrive at each professor's bookstore as a professionally formatted text.

  To learn more about this new system for creating the perfect textbook, go to www.prenhall.com/customphit, where you can go through the online walkthrough of how to create a book.

- ❏ **Instructor's Resource CD-ROM.** This CD-ROM includes the entire *Instructor's Manual* for each application in Microsoft Word format. A computerized testbank is included to create tests, maintain student records, and provide online practice testing. Student data files and completed solutions files are also on this CD-ROM. The *Instructor's Manual* will contain a reference guide of these files for the instructor's convenience. PowerPoint slides, which give more information about each project, are also available for classroom use.

- ❏ **Test Manager.** Prentice Hall Test Manager is an integrated, PC-compatible test-generation and classroom-management software package. The package permits instructors to design and create tests, maintain student records, and provide online practice testing for students.

Prentice Hall has also formed close alliances with each of the leading online platform providers: WebCT, Blackboard, and our own Pearson CourseCompass.

❏ **WebCT and Blackboard.** This custom-built distance-learning course features exercises, sample quizzes, and tests in a course-management system that provides class administration tools as well as the ability to customize this material at the instructor's discretion.

❏ **CourseCompass.** CourseCompass is a dynamic, interactive online course-management tool powered by Blackboard. It lets professors create their own courses in 15 minutes or less with preloaded quality content that can include quizzes, tests, lecture materials, and interactive exercises.

Training and Assessment (www.prenhall.com/phit)

Prentice Hall
TRAIN Generation it

Prentice Hall's Train Generation IT is a computer-based training software a student can use to preview, learn, and review Microsoft® Office application skills. Delivered via intranet, network, CD-ROM, or the Web, Train IT offers interactive, multimedia, computer-based training to augment classroom learning. Built-in prescriptive testing suggests a study path based on not only student test results, but also the specific textbook chosen for the course.

Prentice Hall
ASSESS Generation it

Prentice Hall's Assess Generation IT is separate computer-based testing software used to evaluate a student's knowledge about specific topics on Word, Excel, Access, and PowerPoint®. More extensive than the testing in Train IT, Assess IT offers more features for the instructor and many more questions for the student.

Word

KEITH MULBERY

PART

1

Getting Started
with Word

Objectives

In this project, you learn how to

- ✔ Explore the Word Screen
- ✔ Use Menus and Toolbars
- ✔ Enter Text in a Document
- ✔ Save a Document
- ✔ Correct Spelling and Grammatical Errors
- ✔ Print a Document
- ✔ Get Help
- ✔ Close a Document and Exit Word

Key terms in this project include

- ❏ Click and Type feature
- ❏ close
- ❏ defaults
- ❏ document window
- ❏ end-of-document marker
- ❏ exit
- ❏ Formatting toolbar
- ❏ full menu
- ❏ grayed-out
- ❏ Help
- ❏ horizontal scrollbar
- ❏ hypertext links
- ❏ icons
- ❏ insertion point
- ❏ menu
- ❏ menu bar
- ❏ Office Assistant
- ❏ ruler
- ❏ saving
- ❏ ScreenTip
- ❏ short menu
- ❏ shortcuts
- ❏ Standard toolbar
- ❏ status bar
- ❏ submenu
- ❏ task pane
- ❏ title bar
- ❏ vertical scrollbar
- ❏ view buttons
- ❏ word-wrap feature

Why Would I Do This?

Word-processing software is possibly the most commonly used type of software. People around the world—students, office assistants, managers, and business professionals—use word-processing programs such as Microsoft Word for a variety of tasks. You can create letters, research papers, newsletters, brochures, and other documents with Word. You can even create and send e-mail and produce Web pages with Word.

After creating your documents, you need to edit and format them. These tasks are a snap with Word. But first, you need to learn your way around the Word window and understand how to create, save, and print your documents. In this project, you learn all of that, plus how to use the built-in Help feature. Let's get started!

Visual Summary

In this project, you learn about the Word interface—the screen and common tools—and how to create a short document, as shown in Figure 1.1.

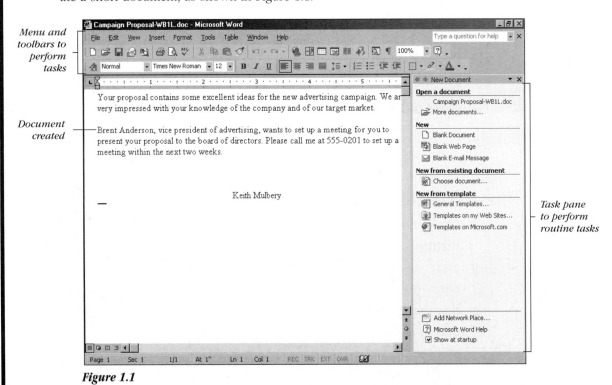

Menu and toolbars to perform tasks

Document created

Task pane to perform routine tasks

Figure 1.1

Lesson 1: Exploring the Word Screen

Starting Word is the first step to learning and using the software. Your exciting experience with Word all begins with the Start button on the taskbar. After you start Word, you learn your way around the Word screen.

To Start Word and Explore the Word Screen

1 **Click the Start button on the left side of the Windows taskbar.**
The Start menu appears. Use this menu to start programs, get help, choose computer settings, and shut down your computer.

2 **Move the mouse pointer to the Programs menu item.**
The Programs menu appears on the right of the Start menu, as shown in Figure 1.2.

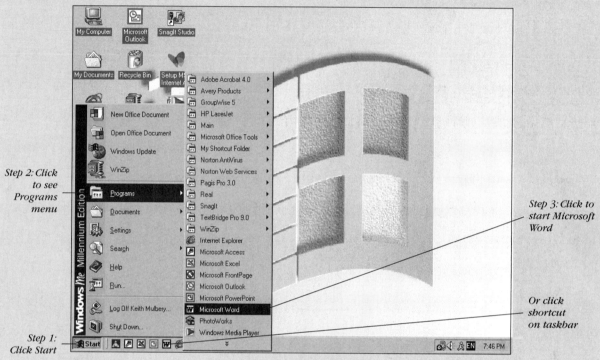

Step 2: Click to see Programs menu

Step 3: Click to start Microsoft Word

Or click shortcut on taskbar

Step 1: Click Start

Figure 1.2

3 **Move the mouse pointer to Microsoft Word on the Programs menu, and click it once.**

If you have problems...

If you don't see Microsoft Word on the Programs menu, ask your instructor for further assistance.

Word is loaded into the computer, and a blank document appears (see Figure 1.3). The Word window consists of a large area on which you place your text, graphics; and many different buttons, icons, and menus. They are all designed to help you create the perfect document for any occasion.

(Continues)

To Start Word and Explore the Word Screen (Continued)

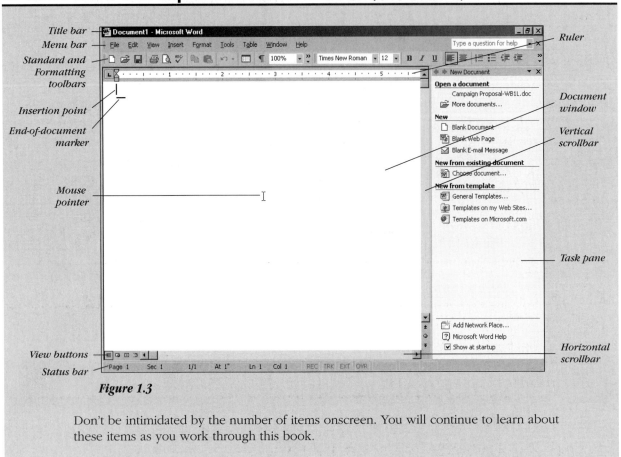

Figure 1.3

Don't be intimidated by the number of items onscreen. You will continue to learn about these items as you work through this book.

Table 1.1 lists the default screen elements and gives a brief description of each element.

Table 1.1 Elements of the Microsoft Word Screen

Element	Description
Insertion point	Shows your location in the document.
End-of-document marker	Indicates the end of the document. Appears only in Normal view.
Title bar	Shows the name of the file you are currently working on. If you haven't saved the document, Word displays a document number, such as Document2. Word also shows the name of the program, such as Microsoft Word.
Menu bar	Lists the categories of menus that contain options from which to choose.
Standard toolbar	Contains a row of buttons that perform routine tasks such as opening, saving, and printing a file. Other toolbars are available for specific types of tasks.
Formatting toolbar	Contains a row of buttons that perform functions to enhance the appearance of your documents.

Table 1.1 Elements of the Microsoft Word Screen

Element	Description
Ruler	Shows the location of tabs, indents, and left and right margins.
Document window	Displays text and formats for documents you create.
Vertical scrollbar	Moves up and down in a document.
View buttons	Switch between different view modes. These options are also available on the <u>V</u>iew pull-down menu.
Horizontal scrollbar	Adjusts horizontal view (left to right).
Status bar	Displays the current page number and location of the insertion point. Also displays active modes, such as Overtype.
Task pane	A window pane that displays frequently used features. It displays different tasks, based on what you are doing—such as options for creating a new document, document recovery, and styles and formatting.

To extend your knowledge...

Using the Word Shortcut Icon

If you see the Word icon on the Windows taskbar, you can click it to immediately start Word, instead of using the Start menu.

Lesson 2: Using Menus and Toolbars

Word's commands are organized in menus. The menu bar lists nine command categories, such as <u>F</u>ile. When you click a menu category name, you see a **menu**—a list of commands that relate to the category. Word's menus appear as short or full menus. The **short menus** display a list of commonly used commands (see Figure 1.4).

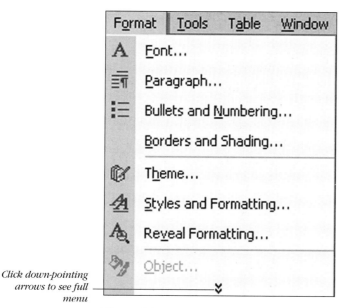

Click down-pointing arrows to see full menu

Figure 1.4

After a few seconds, or when you click the down-pointing arrows, you see the ***full menu***, which includes all commands in that menu category (see Figure 1.5). When you select a command from the full menu, Word adapts the short menu by including that command the next time you display the menu.

Additional options appear

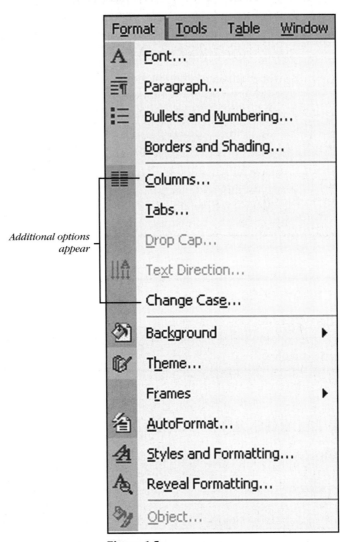

Figure 1.5

To Use the Menu Bar

❶ Click File on the menu bar.
The File menu displays, listing the last four to nine documents used on your computer (see Figure 1.6). Your list will show different document names.

To Use the Menu Bar

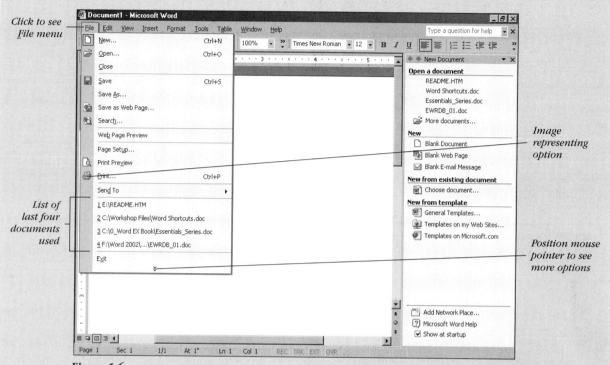

Click to see File menu

List of last four documents used

Image representing option

Position mouse pointer to see more options

Figure 1.6

You see images on the left side of some menu options. These images, called *icons*, represent various tasks. For example, the Print icon looks like a printer. Notice that some of the icons in the menu also appear on the toolbar.

2 **Move the mouse pointer to the bottom of the File menu, where you see the arrows.**

You now see the full menu, which contains additional options, such as Send To and Properties. The following table describes the different types of menu options that you encounter as you study the other menus.

Characteristic	*Description*	*Example*
… (ellipsis)	Displays a dialog box with specific task-related options.	Print…
▶ (triangle)	Displays a *submenu*, a menu of more specific options, to the side of the current menu.	Send To ▶
No symbol	Performs the task immediately without providing additional options.	Exit
✔ (check mark)	Indicates that an option is turned on or active.	✔ Standard
Gray option name	Indicates that the option is currently unavailable (*grayed-out*).	Cut

(Continues)

To Use the Menu Bar (Continued)

❸ Click File again on the menu bar to close the menu.
If you decide not to select a menu bar option, close the menu by clicking the menu name.

You can close the task pane if it's visible onscreen. If the task pane does not appear on the right side of your screen, as shown in Figure 1.3, skip the next two steps of this exercise.

❹ Choose View.
You see a check mark to the left of Task Pane, indicating that it is visible.

❺ Choose Task Pane to deselect it.
The task pane is no longer visible.

To extend your knowledge...

Closing Menus

You can also close a menu by pressing Esc twice; by pressing Alt once; or by clicking outside of the menu, such as in the document window.

Selecting Menus from the Keyboard

You can use the keyboard to select from the menu bar. Notice that one letter (often the first) of each menu bar option is underlined. For example, F is underlined in File. To choose a particular menu, press Alt and the underlined letter. For example, pressing Alt+F displays the File menu.

When the menu displays, press ↓ or ↑ to highlight an option; then press ⏎Enter to select that option. You can also press the underlined letter to immediately select the option of your choice. For example, press C for Close on the File menu.

The menus also display keyboard ***shortcuts***, such as Ctrl+S for Save (refer to Figure 1.6). By using keyboard shortcuts, you can keep your hands on the keyboard and maybe save a little time.

The Standard and Formatting toolbars are rows containing icons or buttons to perform various tasks. For example, click the Save button to save a file. Clicking the Save button is often faster than opening the File menu and choosing the Save command.

Currently, the Standard and Formatting toolbars share one row. In the next exercise, you learn how to separate them to see all icons on both toolbars at the same time. Plus, you learn about ScreenTips.

To Use Toolbars

❶ Move the mouse pointer to the New Blank Document button on the Standard toolbar.
When you position the mouse pointer on an icon, Word displays the icon's name in a little box, called a ***ScreenTip***. You should see the ScreenTip *New Blank Document (Ctrl+N)* now.

 ### If you have problems...

If the menus and ScreenTips do not show the shortcut keys, choose Tools, Customize; click the Options tab; and click the *Show ScreenTips on toolbars* check box. Make sure that the *Show shortcut keys in ScreenTips* check box is selected, and click Close.

To Use Toolbars

② **Click View on the menu bar to see the View menu.**

③ **Choose Toolbars.**

You see a list of different toolbars, plus the Customize option (see Figure 1.7). The check marks indicate the active toolbars.

Active toolbars indicated by check marks

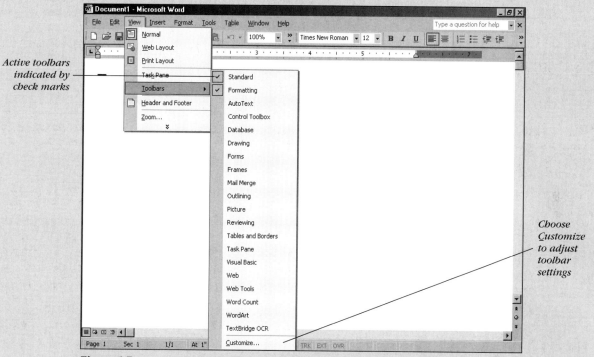

Choose Customize to adjust toolbar settings

Figure 1.7

④ **Click Customize at the bottom of the menu.**

The Customize dialog box appears, in which you can adjust the way the toolbars appear on your screen (see Figure 1.8).

(Continues)

To Use Toolbars (Continued)

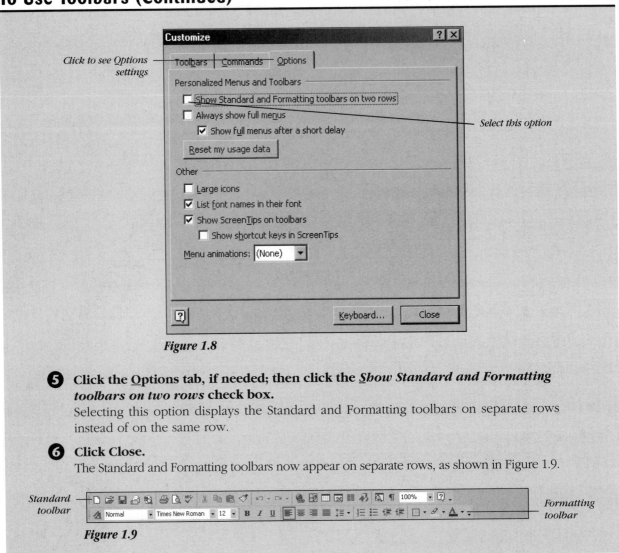

Figure 1.8

⑤ Click the Underline Options tab, if needed; then click the _Show Standard and Formatting toolbars on two rows_ check box.

Selecting this option displays the Standard and Formatting toolbars on separate rows instead of on the same row.

⑥ Click Close.

The Standard and Formatting toolbars now appear on separate rows, as shown in Figure 1.9.

Figure 1.9

To extend your knowledge...

Customizing the Toolbar

Instead of choosing View, Toolbars, Customize, you can right-click anywhere on the toolbar and choose Customize.

Lesson 3: Entering Text in a Document

You can begin entering text for your document as soon as you start Word. When you begin a new document, Word's **defaults**, predefined settings such as margins and font size, control the original format of the document. The document window is where you type and format your documents, and the *insertion point* should appear below the ruler. The insertion point, sometimes called a *cursor*, is the thin vertical blinking line that indicates where you are about to insert text.

In this lesson, you enter text using the default settings.

To Enter Text in a Document

❶ Type the following text, including the misspelled words and grammatical error, in the document window:

Your proposal contain some excelant ideas for the new advertising campagn. We are very impressed with your knowledge of the company and of our target market.

Don't press ⏎Enter when you reach the end of a line. When you enter more text than can fit on the current line, the ***word-wrap feature*** continues text to the next line when it runs out of room on the current line.

 ### If you have problems...

If the document area is gray instead of white, the Word document window isn't active and you need to start a new document. Click the New Blank Document button on the left side of the Standard toolbar.

❷ Press ⏎Enter twice when you reach the end of a single-spaced paragraph.

Pressing ⏎Enter tells Word to go to the next line. Pressing ⏎Enter a second time leaves one blank line between paragraphs.

❸ Continue by typing the following paragraph:

Brent Anderson, vice president of advertising, wants to set up a meeting for you to present your proposal to the board of directors. Please call me at 555-0201 to set up a meeting within the next two weeks.

Figure 1.10 shows what your document should look like.

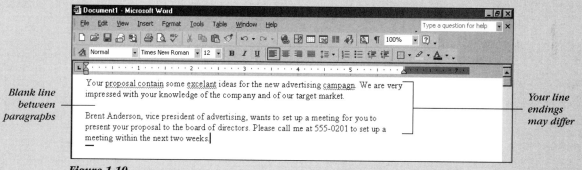

Blank line between paragraphs

Your line endings may differ

Figure 1.10

❹ Leave the text you typed onscreen to continue with the next exercise.

 ## To extend your knowledge...

Correcting Mistakes

If you make a mistake as you type, press ⬅Backspace to delete text to the *left* of the insertion point, or press Del to delete text to the *right* of the insertion point. After deleting incorrect letters, type the correct letters.

Seeing Dots and Symbols

You might see dots between words and a paragraph (¶) symbol at the end of the paragraphs. You learn about these marks in Project 3, "Formatting Text." For now, click the Show/Hide ¶ button on the Standard toolbar to hide the symbols.

The ***Click and Type feature*** lets you double-click in any area of the document, and type new text in Print Layout View. Depending on where you double-click, you can type text at the left margin, tabbed in from the left margin, centered between the margins, or flush with the right margin.

To Use Click and Type

❶ **Choose <u>V</u>iew and then choose <u>P</u>rint Layout from the <u>V</u>iew menu.**
The end-of-document marker disappears in Print Layout view. However, you can use the Click and Type feature.

❷ **Position the mouse pointer about one-half inch below your last paragraph and centered between the left and right edges of the screen.**
Figure 1.11 shows the mouse pointer. The horizontal lines below the mouse pointer indicate that text will be centered when you double-click.

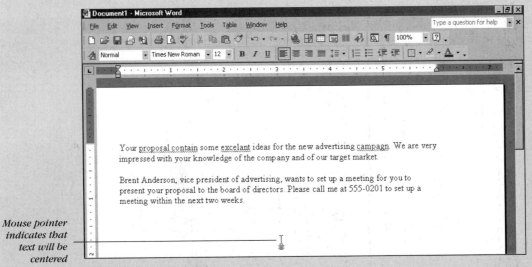

Mouse pointer indicates that text will be centered

Figure 1.11

 ## If you have problems...

If you don't see the horizontal lines by the mouse pointer, you might be in Normal view instead of Print Layout view. Click the Print Layout View button above the left side of the status bar.

If Click and Type is still not working, you need to activate it. To do this, choose <u>T</u>ools and choose <u>O</u>ptions from the <u>T</u>ools menu. Click the Edit tab, click the *Enable <u>c</u>lick and type* check box, and click OK.

❸ **Double-click in the center point, and type your name.**
Your name is centered between the left and right margins.

❹ **Leave the document onscreen to continue with the next lesson.**

Lesson 4: Saving a Document

After creating part of a document, you should save it. **Saving** is the process of storing a document with a unique filename in a particular location, such as a data disk or hard drive. Currently, the document you created exists only in the computer's random access (RAM) memory. RAM is temporary; it is cleared when you shut off your system, or if the system crashes or locks up on you. Therefore, you should save your documents to use them in the future.

In this lesson, you save the two-paragraph document with the name *Campaign Proposal-WB1L*. When saving lesson files in this book, you assign realistic filenames, such as *Campaign Proposal*, followed by a code. *WB* stands for the Word Basic (Level I) book, *1* represents the project number, and *L* represents a file you save within a lesson.

To Save a Document

1 **Insert a new formatted disk into the appropriate disk drive if you plan to save to a floppy disk or Zip disk.**

2 **With your new Word document open, choose File, Save As.**
The Save As dialog box appears (see Figure 1.12). The first step in saving your document is to choose a location where you want to keep it.

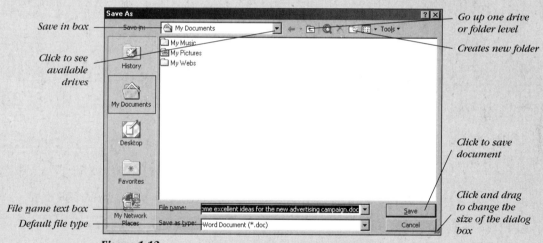

Figure 1.12

By default, Word saves documents in the My Documents folder on the hard drive.

3 **Click the drop-down arrow on the right side of the *Save in* text box.**
You see a list of available storage devices on your computer system (see Figure 1.13). You may choose to save to a floppy disk, a hard drive, a Zip disk, or a network drive. If you want to save the file in a different folder, select the folder from the *Save in* list, or click the Create New Folder button to create and name a new folder. Ask your instructor if you are not sure about the location for saving the files you create.

(Continues)

To Save a Document (Continued)

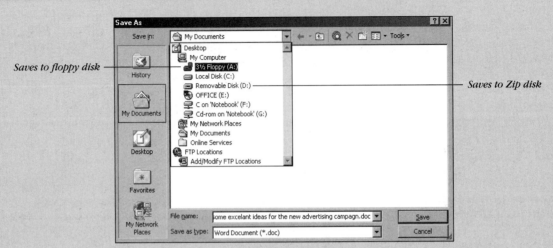

Saves to floppy disk ⎯⎯⎯⎯⎯⎯⎯

Saves to Zip disk

Figure 1.13

4 Select the drive and folder in which you want to save the current document.

If you have problems...

If the *Save in* option displays Desktop and you don't see a list of drives, ask your instructor how to proceed.

5 Press Alt+N to make the *File name* text box active.
Now, you can type over the suggested filename.

6 Type Campaign Proposal-WB1L in the *File name* text box.
When you type a filename, it replaces the default name suggested by Word. You can assign long filenames based on Windows limitations, including upper- and lowercase letters, numbers, some symbols, and spaces.

7 Click Save in the bottom-right corner of the dialog box.

8 Leave your document onscreen to continue with the next lesson.

If you have problems...

If you try to save to a floppy disk and get an error message, make sure that you have correctly inserted a disk in the disk drive, and make sure that you have selected the correct drive. Some network drives may prohibit users from storing files in these locations.

To extend your knowledge...

Using Save versus Save As

The first time you save a document, you can use either Save or Save As. Either way, you see the Save As dialog box. After you save a document, however, Save and Save As have two different effects.

If you modify a document and use Save, Word saves the changes under the same filename without displaying the Save As dialog box. Use Save to save a document under the same filename and then continue entering text and formatting it.

At other times, you might want to assign a different name to a modified document, so you have the original document as well as the modified document. Use Save As to save the document with a different filename or to a different location. For example, you might want to save a document in two different locations: on a Zip disk and on your hard drive. To do this, click the *Save in* drop-down arrow, and choose the drive and folder in which to save the modified document. Furthermore, you might want to save a document in a non-Word format. To do this, click the *Save as type* drop-down arrow, and choose the file type, such as *Plain Text (*.txt)*.

Saving Methods

You can also press Ctrl+S, or click the Save button on the Standard toolbar to save a document. Note that the toolbar does *not* contain a button for Save As, although the Save button displays the Save As dialog box if you have *not* saved the document yet.

Lesson 5: Correcting Spelling and Grammatical Errors

A wavy red underline below a word indicates that the word is not in Microsoft's main dictionary. You see these wavy red lines below misspelled words and proper nouns. For example, you see a wavy red underline below *excelant*.

A wavy green underline below a word or phrase indicates a potential grammatical error. For example, you see a wavy green underline below *proposal contain*.

You can correct spelling and grammatical errors by right-clicking the text above the wavy underline and choosing the correct spelling or grammar from the menu that appears.

To Correct Spelling and Grammatical Errors

❶ Right-click *proposal contain* in the first paragraph in the *Campaign Proposal-WB1L* document.
You see a shortcut menu that displays possible corrections, as shown in Figure 1.14.

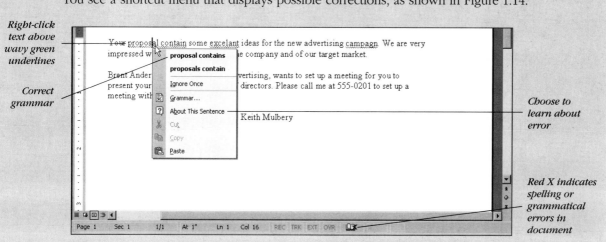

Figure 1.14

❷ Select *proposal contains* from the menu.
Word replaces the grammatical error with the correct grammar you select from the menu.

(Continues)

To Correct Spelling and Grammatical Errors (Continued)

3 Right-click *excelant*.
Word displays a list of suggested spellings (see Figure 1.15).

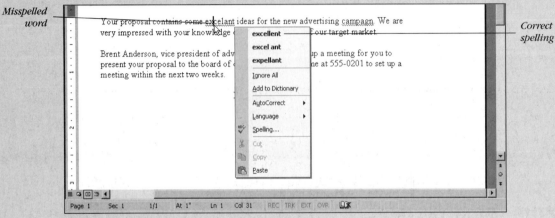

Misspelled word

Correct spelling

Figure 1.15

4 Choose *excellent* from the menu that appears.
Word replaces *excelant* with *excellent*.

5 Right-click *campagn* and choose *campaign* from the menu.
Word replaces *campagn* with *campaign*. Notice that the red X changes to a red check mark on the status bar, indicating that the document does not contain any spelling or major grammatical errors.

6 Click the Save icon on the Standard toolbar.

To extend your knowledge...

Spelling and Grammar Dialog Box

Instead of looking through your document to find text with wavy red or green underlines, you can use the Spelling and Grammar dialog box to find and correct these types of errors.

Click the Spelling and Grammar button on the Standard toolbar. Figure 1.16 shows a sample error in the dialog box.

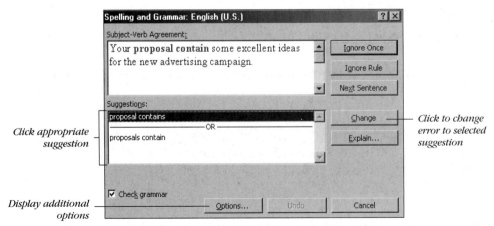

Click appropriate suggestion

Click to change error to selected suggestion

Display additional options

Figure 1.16

The top of the Spelling and Grammar dialog box tells you the type of error, such as Subject-Verb Agreement. You see the error in a different color and suggestions to choose from. You can ignore the detected word or phrase if it is really correct.

Lesson 6: Printing a Document

Before printing a document, you should preview it to make sure it looks the way you want it to look. If the document is formatted correctly, you can then print it. If not, you can correctly format the document before printing it.

To Use Print Preview

❶ **Click the Print Preview button on the Standard toolbar.**
You see a preview of what the printed document will look like (see Figure 1.17).

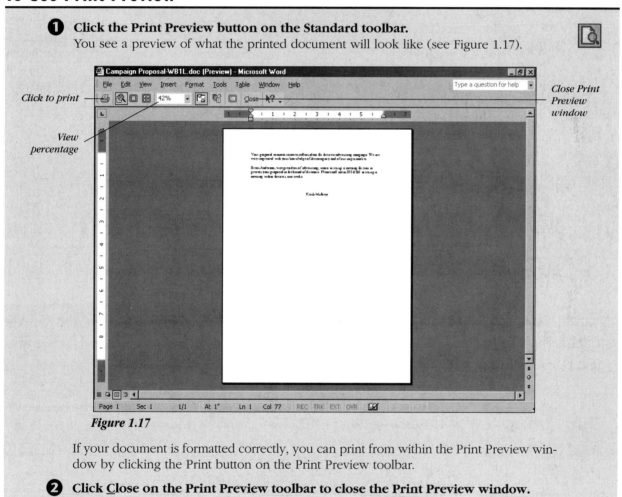

Figure 1.17

If your document is formatted correctly, you can print from within the Print Preview window by clicking the Print button on the Print Preview toolbar.

❷ **Click Close on the Print Preview toolbar to close the Print Preview window.**

To extend your knowledge...

Print Preview Options

You can press ↵Enter to move text down or display the Ruler to change margins to balance text on a page if needed. The Print Preview toolbar contains buttons for magnifying the page onscreen, displaying one page, displaying multiple pages, or shrinking the document to fit.

After previewing a document and adjusting the format, if needed, you are ready to print it. You can quickly print the entire document by clicking the Print button on the Standard toolbar. If you need to specify print settings, such as the number of copies to print, you need to display the Print dialog box.

To Print a Document

1 **Make sure the printer is turned on, has paper, and is online.**
Ask your instructor if you need further assistance in using the printer.

2 **Click File and then choose Print from the menu.**
The Print dialog box appears (see Figure 1.18).

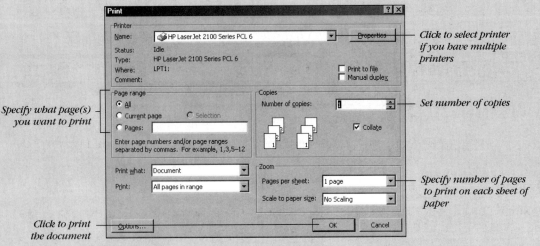

Click to select printer if you have multiple printers

Specify what page(s) you want to print

Set number of copies

Specify number of pages to print on each sheet of paper

Click to print the document

Figure 1.18

3 **Ask your instructor which printer name is correct for the system you're using. If needed, click the down arrow to the right of the *Name* text box and choose the correct printer name from the list.**

4 **Click OK to print your document.**
Word sends a copy of the document to the printer. After you print a document, make sure the text looks good on paper. Check the format. You might need to adjust the formatting and print the document again.

5 **Leave your Word document onscreen to continue with the next lesson.**

To extend your knowledge...

Print Keyboard Shortcut

You can press Ctrl+P to display the Print dialog box.

Clicking the Print Button

Clicking the Print button on the Standard toolbar sends the entire document to the printer without displaying the Print dialog box. Although this is a fast way to print a document, it doesn't give you the opportunity to select print options.

Print Options

The Print dialog box contains many useful options. For example, you can print only the page that contains the insertion point (Current page) or a range of pages, such as pages 3–10 (Pages). Furthermore, you can print several copies of the document (Number of copies), print miniature copies of pages on a single sheet of paper (Pages per sheet), or adjust the document text size to fit on a particular type of paper (Scale to paper size).

Lesson 7: Getting Help

When you work with Word, you might need to know about a specific feature or how to perform a certain task. Although you are learning a lot about Word by completing this book, you might run across a situation in which you need assistance. Word contains an onscreen assistance feature called Help. **Help** provides information about Word features and step-by-step instructions for performing tasks.

You can get quick assistance by using Word Version 2002's Ask a Question text box, which is located to the right of the menu bar. Figure 1.19 shows the Ask a Question box to the right of the menu bar.

Figure 1.19

In this lesson, you want to find out how to recover a document when Word locks up and you haven't saved it recently.

To Get Help from the Ask a Question Box

❶ Type How do I recover a document? **in the Ask a Question text box, and then press** ⤶Enter.

Figure 1.20 shows the options that appear for the topic you entered in the Ask a Question text box.

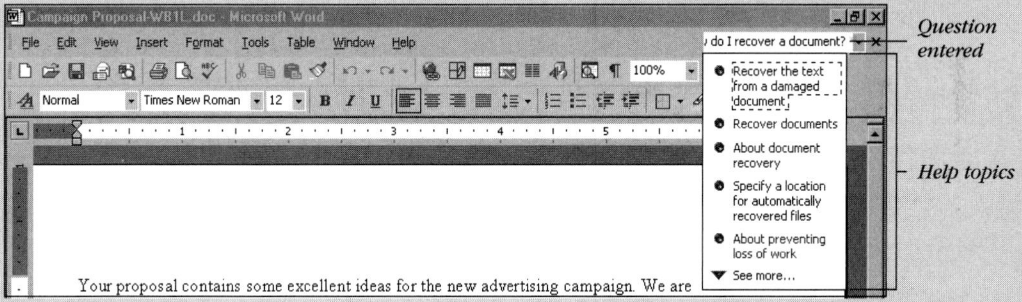

Figure 1.20

❷ Choose *Recover documents*.

The Microsoft Word Help window appears (see Figure 1.21).

(Continues)

To Get Help from the Ask a Question Box (Continued)

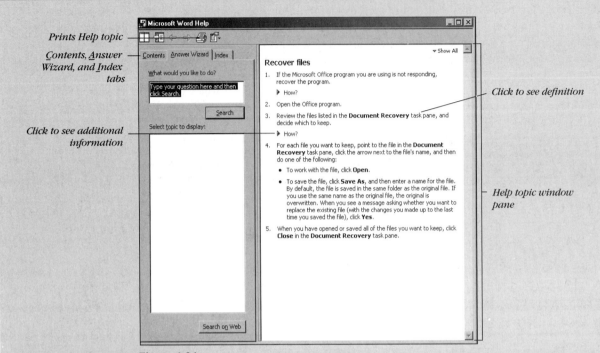

Prints Help topic

Contents, Answer Wizard, and Index tabs

Click to see additional information

Click to see definition

Help topic window pane

Figure 1.21

The left side contains tabs for different ways of accessing Help: Contents, Answer Wizard, and Index. The right side contains information about the topic you selected. The Help window covers part or all of the document. Don't worry about this; the document window enlarges when you close the Help feature. Keywords and phrases appearing in a different color—usually blue—are called ***hypertext links***. When you click a hypertext link, you see additional information.

 If you have problems...

If you don't see the Navigation pane, click the Show button on the Help toolbar.

❸ **Click the blue words *task pane* on the right side of the window.**
A definition appears in green letters.

❹ **Click *How?* below step 1 in the Help window.**
When you click a hyperlink preceded by a triangle, Word displays additional information, such as specific steps or explanations. If you click the hyperlink again, the additional information is hidden again.

❺ **Click the Print button on the Microsoft Word Help toolbar to display the Print dialog box.**

❻ **Click OK to print the Help topic.**
Word sends the Help topic to the printer so that you'll have a hard copy of the information as you perform the step-by-step instructions, if needed.

❼ **Click the Close button—the X in the top right corner of the Help window—to close the Microsoft Word Help window.**

❽ **Keep the document onscreen to continue to the next lesson.**

To extend your knowledge...

Help Index

The Index feature lets you type a topic and search through the alphabetical index of topics. The first step is to enter keywords (particular words that might be found in the Help topics) and then click the Search button. Alternatively, you can scroll through the list of keywords in the index to find what you're looking for.

You see a list of topics in the *Choose a topic* list box. Double-click the topic listed in the *Or choose keywords* list box.

What's This? Feature

The What's This? Feature displays a ScreenTip about a screen item. To use this feature, choose Help, What's This, or press ◆Shift+F1. When the pointer resembles a question mark with an arrow, click the mouse pointer on the screen item that you don't understand. Word then provides a ScreenTip that describes that feature. Press ◆Shift+F1 to turn off the What's This? feature. If you click within text with the What's This? mouse pointer, the task pane appears with information describing the formats of the text you click in.

Office Assistant

You might see the **Office Assistant**, which is an animated image, onscreen. The Office Assistant offers suggestions and lets you click it and type in questions or topics like you do in the Ask a Question text box. You can display or hide the Office Assistant by choosing the option you want from the Help menu.

Help on the Web

If you can't find the information you need within Word, you can access resources available on the World Wide Web. Assuming you have Internet access, you can choose Help, Office on the Web to view information on Microsoft's Web site for Word.

Lesson 8: Closing a Document and Exiting Word

When you finish working on your documents, you should properly *close* the files (that is, remove them from the screen). When you finish using Word, you should *exit* (close down) the Word software. If you simply turn off the computer, you might lose valuable work and create problems within the computer itself. Because you saved the document in Lesson 4 and have not made any changes to it, you can close the document without having to save again.

To Close a Document and Exit Word

1 **Choose File, Close from the menu.**
The file closes immediately. If you haven't saved the document after modifying it, Word displays a dialog box that asks if you want to save the changes. Click Yes to save the file before closing it, or click No to close the document without saving the changes.

2 **Choose File, Exit from the menu to close Word.**
If other Word files are open, they close immediately if you saved them. If other files have been modified since you last saved them, Word prompts you to save them before the program closes. After Word closes, you see the Windows Desktop if no other programs are running.

This concludes Project 1. You can reinforce and expand your knowledge and skills by completing the end-of-project activities that follow the summary.

Summary

You are now familiar with some of the Word screen components. You can also use the menu bar and toolbars to access commands easily. You can enter text, check the spelling and grammar, and save and print the document.

You can extend your learning by studying the menu bar and toolbars to see how commands are organized. Use the Office Assistant and the Help feature to learn more about the exciting things you can do with Word. Remember to use the index at the back of this book; it's an excellent way to find the *exact* pages that discuss particular topics. These sources provide a vast array of information to help you become comfortable with and proficient at using Word.

Checking Concepts and Terms

Multiple Choice

Circle the letter of the correct answer for each of the following.

1. How can you tell if a word is misspelled onscreen? [L5]

   a. Green underline

   b. Red wavy underline

   c. Red check mark on Spelling and Grammar Status icon on the status bar

   d. Word blinks onscreen

2. What happens when you choose a menu option that displays a triangle? [L2]

   a. You see a submenu.

   b. A dialog box appears.

   c. Word immediately performs the command.

   d. The menu closes.

3. Which of the following does *not* happen when you use the Save command? [L4]

   a. Word saves an existing document with the same filename.

   b. The document closes.

   c. The Save As dialog box appears if you haven't saved the document before.

   d. You are able to use the document in the future.

4. If you want to scroll through an alphabetical list of Help topics, which Help feature do you use? [L7]

   a. Index

   b. Contents

   c. Office Assistant

   d. Answer Wizard

5. Which of the following can you do in the Print Preview window? [L6]

   a. See the amount of space for the margins.

   b. Type and edit text.

   c. Look at the overall format of the document.

   d. All of the above.

Screen ID

Label each element of the Word screen shown in Figure 1.22.

A. Ask a Question box
B. end-of-document marker
C. Formatting toolbar
D. insertion point
E. menu bar
F. mouse pointer
G. Standard toolbar
H. status bar

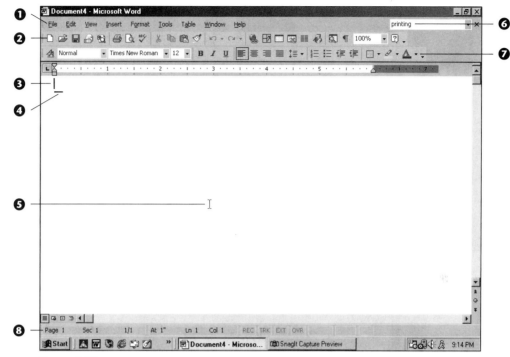

Figure 1.22

1. _____   5. _____

2. _____   6. _____

3. _____   7. _____

4. _____   8. _____

Discussion

1. Explain how the menus are adaptive. Provide an example of options on a short and long menu. [L2]

2. Explain the difference between Save and Save As. Provide an example of a situation when you would use each command. [L4]

3. Display the Microsoft Word Help window. Explore the Contents, Answer Wizard, and Index tabs. Explain how each tab of options is organized and when you would use each tab. [L7]

Skill Drill

Skill Drill exercises reinforce project skills. Each skill reinforced is the same, or nearly the same, as a skill presented in the project. Detailed instructions are provided in a step-by-step format.

1. Exploring Menus and ScreenTips

You want to study Word's menus. The more you study the screen components, the more you understand the structure and logic of using Word. Plus, you want to display shortcuts in the ScreenTips until you learn them.

1. Start Word.
2. Press Alt+A to display the Table menu. (You press A because **a** is underlined in Ta̲ble.)
3. Click the arrows to display the full Ta̲ble menu.
4. Try choosing Table Pr̲operties.
   Nothing happens because the option is grayed-out. It is available only when you perform a specific task first.
5. Press Alt once to close the Ta̲ble menu without choosing any options.
6. Choose T̲ools from the menu bar.
7. Choose C̲ustomize from the T̲ools menu.
8. Click the O̲ptions tab, if needed.
9. Look at the *Show s̲hortcut keys in ScreenTips* option. If it is selected, click Close. Otherwise, click the *Show s̲hortcut keys in ScreenTips* check box to select it and then click Close.
10. Position the mouse pointer on the second button on the Standard toolbar to see the Screen-Tip *Open (Ctrl+O)*.
11. Position the mouse pointer on the capital B icon on the Formatting toolbar to see the Screen-Tip *Bold (Ctrl+B)*.
12. Choose F̲ile, C̲lose to close the document. Click N̲o if you are prompted to save the document. Choose F̲ile, E̲xit if you need to end your work session.

2. Displaying Different Toolbars

You want to see some of the other Word toolbars. You can display and hide toolbars, as needed.

1. Choose V̲iew and then choose T̲oolbars to display the Toolbars submenu.
2. Click Drawing to display the Drawing toolbar. (The toolbar appears at the bottom of the Word screen.)
3. Position the mouse pointer over the blue A button on the Drawing toolbar. (You should see the ScreenTip *Insert WordArt.*)
4. Repeat Steps 1 and 2 to hide the Drawing toolbar.
5. Click the right mouse button on any icon on the Standard toolbar.
6. Choose Word Count from the list of toolbars to display the Word Count toolbar.
7. Click the Re̲count button on the Word Count toolbar that appears.
   The Word Count toolbar displays that you have 0 words in the current document.
8. Right-click anywhere on the Word Count toolbar, and choose Word Count to hide that toolbar.

3. Creating, Spell-Checking, Saving, and Printing a Document

You need to compose a short note to your immediate supervisor, telling her that you need to come in later on Friday because you have a special test in the morning. You create and save the first note; then, you change the supervisor's name and save the modified document with a new filename.

1. Type `Dear Ms. Turner:`, and press `Enter` twice.
2. Type the following paragraph, including the errors:

   `This Friday I have a specal test in my history class at the local community college. These test is scheduled during a specific time, which is controlled by the instructer. I would appreciate being able to come in to work at 11:30 instead of my usual 8:30 time. Thank you for working around my college class scedul.`

3. Press `Enter` twice after the last paragraph, type `Sincerely yours,` press `Enter` four times, and type your name.
4. Choose File, Save As.
5. Click the *Save in* drop-down arrow, and choose the drive in which you have been instructed to save documents.
6. Type `Turner Note-WB1SD3` in the File name text box, and click Save to save the document.
7. Right-click *specal*, and choose *special* from the suggested spellings.
8. Right-click *These test*, and choose *This test* from the suggestions.
9. Right-click *is scheduled*, and choose Ignore Once to ignore the passive voice message.
   You might see wavy lines below *is controlled*. If so, you need to ignore it. If you don't see wavy lines below the phrase, skip the next step.
10. Right-click *is controlled*, and choose Ignore Once.
11. Continue right-clicking words with the wavy red or green underlines, and then choose the correct suggestions.
12. Choose File, Print, and then click OK to print the document.
13. Keep the document onscreen to continue with the next exercise.

4. Saving a Document Under a Different Name

You need to send the same message to the branch manager. Instead of typing the same text, you edit the existing document and save it with a different name.

1. In the open *Turner Note* document, click to the left of Ms. Turner on the first line, and press `Del` until you have deleted her name.
2. Type `Mr. Baxter`, the branch manager's name. Make sure that there is still a colon after the name.
3. Choose File, Save As to assign a new name to the modified document.
4. Make sure that the correct drive is displayed in the Save in option. Change it if necessary.
5. Type `Baxter Note-WB1SD4` in the File name text box, and click Save.
6. Click the Print button on the Standard toolbar to print the document without displaying the Print dialog box.
7. Choose File, Close to close the document.
8. Choose File, Exit if you need to exit Word now. Leave Word open if you are continuing with the next exercise.

5. Using the Office Assistant and the Help Index

You want to continue studying various topics in the Help Index and then print a Help topic.

1. Click the Office Assistant if it's displayed. If it's not displayed, choose Help, Show the Office Assistant, and then click it.

2. Click the Options button to display the Office Assistant dialog box.

3. Click the Use the Office Assistant check box to deselect it. Then, click OK.

4. Press F1 to display the Microsoft Word Help window.

5. Click the Index tab on the left side of the Microsoft Word Help window.

6. Type **save** and click the Search button.

7. Click the topic, *Save a document* to display information on the right side of the window.

8. Scroll through the topic to continue reading information about saving documents.

9. Click the Close button in the top-right corner of the Microsoft Word Help window to close it.

10. Continue working in Word if you want to complete the Challenge exercises, or choose File, Exit to close Word.

Challenge

Challenge exercises expand on or are somewhat related to skills presented in the lessons. Each exercise provides a brief narrative introduction, followed by instructions in a numbered-step format that are not as detailed as those in the Skill Drill section.

1. Creating, Modifying, Saving, and Printing a Letter

You want to write a short note to your word processing instructor to let him or her know your goals for learning Microsoft Word.

1. In a new document window, type today's date, and press Enter four times.

2. Type your instructor's name and address on separate lines. Press Enter twice after the address.

3. Type the greeting, press Enter twice, and type a first paragraph about yourself.

4. Save the document on your data disk as `Introduction Letter-WB1CH1`.

5. Type a second paragraph that describes why you are learning Word. Then, complete the rest of the letter with a complimentary closing and your name.

6. Check the spelling and grammar in the document by right-clicking words and phrases that have a wavy red or green underline, and choosing the correct word or phrase.

7. Save the modified document under the same name.

8. Preview, print, and close the document.

2. Creating, Saving, and Printing Two Copies of a Study Guide

You want to create a list of the terminology you studied in this project. After creating the document, you want to print two copies.

1. Create the study guide shown in Figure 1.23, pressing Tab once or twice to type the definitions.

```
Jorg Carsten
Project 1 Terminology

Close          Process of removing a document from the screen.

Default        Standard setting, such as margins, determined by software.

Exit           Process of "turning off" the software.

Help           Feature that provides online assistance about tasks and commands.

ScreenTip      Little yellow box that tells name of toolbar icon.

Menu           List of commands.

Ruler          Measurements for visualizing vertical or horizontal distance.

Status Bar     Row that shows location in document, among other things.

Toolbar        Row of icons or buttons that provide quick way to execute commands.
```

Figure 1.23

2. Save the study guide with these specifications:
- `Terminology List-WB1CH2` is the filename.
- It should be saved to a Zip disk or personal network drive.

3. Preview the document and then print two copies of it.

3. Using Help and Printing a Help Topic

You want to print a list of keyboard shortcuts for reference. A friend told you that you can find a Help topic that provides step-by-step instructions for displaying and printing such a list.

1. Search for `keyboard shortcuts` in the Ask a Question box.
2. Choose the option that will display information about printing a list of shortcuts.
3. Print the Help topic that provides the step-by-step instructions.
4. Refer to your printout, and complete the steps to list the keyboard shortcuts.
5. Save the document that results as `Keyboard Commands-WB1CH3`, and obtain a printout of the first two pages of the keyboard shortcuts.

4. Finding Information in the Help Index

The Help Index provides an alphabetical listing of various topics. You want to find information in the Help Index to learn more about the status bar components.

1. Display the Office Assistant.
2. Click Options, deselect the option that uses the Office Assistant, and then click OK.
3. Access Microsoft Word Help without using the Office Assistant.
4. Type `status bar` as a keyword in the Index.
5. Display the topic that tells you about items on the status bar.
6. Print the topic.
7. Close the Help window.

Discovery Zone exercises require advanced knowledge of topics presented in *Essentials* lessons, application of skills from multiple lessons, or self-directed learning of new skills.

1. Saving a File with a Password

You need to create a highly confidential document. You want to save the document so that the user must enter a password to open the document. Use the Help Index or Office Assistant to find out how to save a document with a password. Print the specific step-by-step help instructions.

Compose a document that briefly discusses the difference between <u>S</u>ave and Save <u>A</u>s. Type two paragraphs. Save the document on your data disk as `Saving Documents-WB1DZ1` with the password `Secret`. Print the document.

2. Customizing Grammar Checking

Create a new blank document and type the following paragraph, including the errors and two spaces between *comitee meeting*.

`The next comitee  meeting will be held on tusday in the conference room. Mr. Chen will discusses the budget implications for our project. Before the meeting begins you should reviewe the attached agenda, budget and polcies.`

Display the Spelling and Grammar dialog box. Before correcting errors, select the Grammar & Style writing style, and set the *Comma required before last list item* to *always*. You may need to explore the Options and Settings buttons to find these options.

Start the Spelling and Grammar check. Correct all spelling and punctuation errors. Ignore any passive-voice detections. When you're done, type your name a double-space below the paragraph, save the document as `Committee Meeting-WB1DZ2`, and then print it.

3. Using the Language Bar

You remember reading about a new feature called the Language bar in Word Version 2002. Because you want to know more about it, use the Help feature to display information.

Specifically, find out how to show and hide the Language bar. Print the Help topic, and practice showing and hiding it. Ask your instructor if you have the devices to use this feature. If so, experiment with the Language bar and then hide it.

Working with a Document

Objectives

In this project you learn how to

- ✔ Open a Document
- ✔ Scroll in a Document
- ✔ Insert Text
- ✔ Select Text
- ✔ Delete and Change Text
- ✔ Change View Modes
- ✔ Create Envelopes
- ✔ Create Labels

Key terms in this project include

- ❏ AutoComplete
- ❏ folders
- ❏ Full Screen view
- ❏ Insert mode
- ❏ Normal view
- ❏ opening
- ❏ Overtype mode
- ❏ Print Layout view
- ❏ scrolling
- ❏ selecting
- ❏ selection bar
- ❏ Smart Tag
- ❏ zoom

Why Would I Do This?

Now that you are familiar with the Word screen and know the basics for creating, saving, and printing a document, you are ready to expand your knowledge to modify a document. In Project 1, "Getting Started with Word," you created a two-paragraph document, and corrected spelling and grammatical errors. In this project, you insert, select, and delete text to create a business letter. In addition, you create an envelope for your printed letter.

Visual Summary

Figure 2.1 shows the business letter you create.

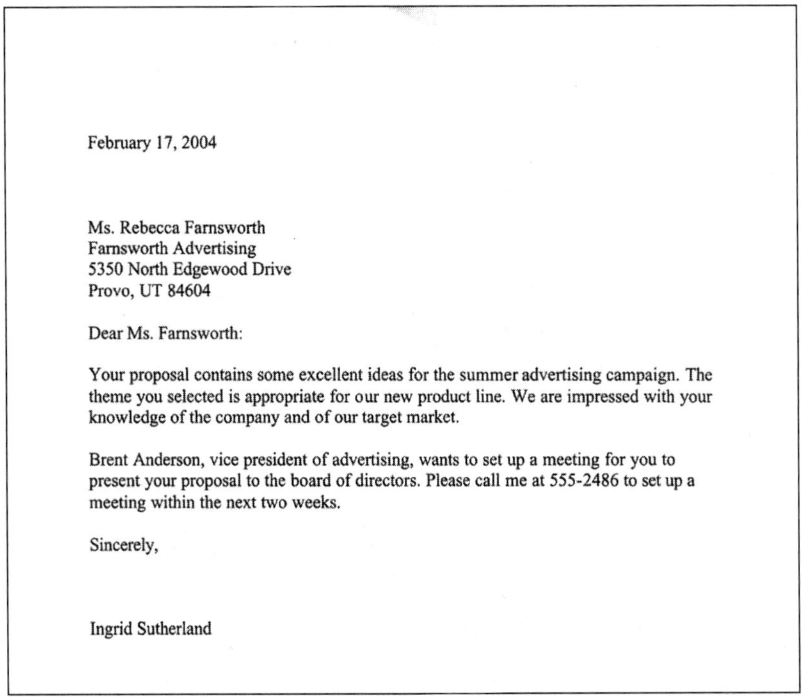

February 17, 2004

Ms. Rebecca Farnsworth
Farnsworth Advertising
5350 North Edgewood Drive
Provo, UT 84604

Dear Ms. Farnsworth:

Your proposal contains some excellent ideas for the summer advertising campaign. The theme you selected is appropriate for our new product line. We are impressed with your knowledge of the company and of our target market.

Brent Anderson, vice president of advertising, wants to set up a meeting for you to present your proposal to the board of directors. Please call me at 555-2486 to set up a meeting within the next two weeks.

Sincerely,

Ingrid Sutherland

Figure 2.1

Figure 2.2 shows the envelope you create for the business letter.

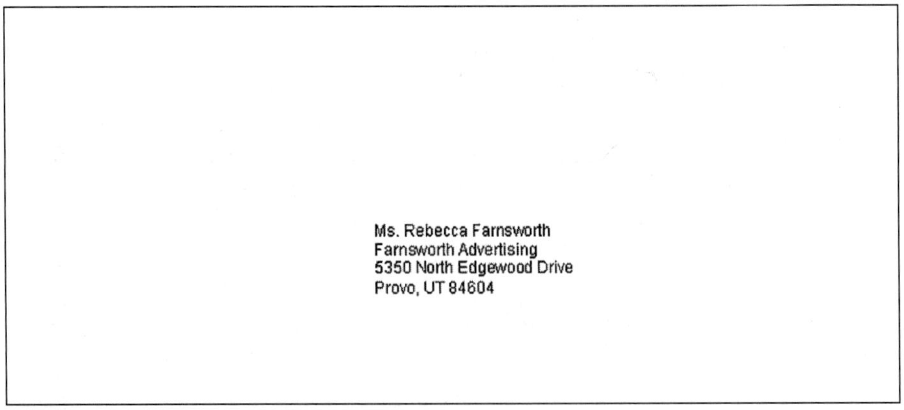

Ms. Rebecca Farnsworth
Farnsworth Advertising
5350 North Edgewood Drive
Provo, UT 84604

Figure 2.2

Lesson 1: Opening an Existing Document

One of the greatest benefits of using a computer is the capability to save documents and then use them again later. Using documents that were previously created saves valuable time in retyping and reformatting the document.

Opening is the process of displaying a previously saved document. After you open a document, you can make changes, add new text, format text, save it, and print it.

To Open an Existing Document

1 If Word is not already running on your system, start the program, as described in Project 1.

2 Click the Open button on the Standard toolbar.
The Open dialog box appears, as shown in Figure 2.3. Notice that it looks similar to the Save As dialog box you saw when you saved a document in Project 1.

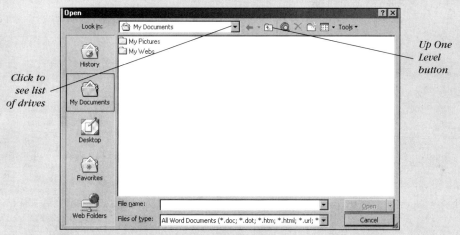

Figure 2.3

3 Click the arrow to the right of the *Look in* box.
The Look in list is identical to the Save in list you saw in Project 1. It lists the available storage drives, such as 3½ Floppy (A:).

4 Select the drive and folder containing the student files for this book.

If you have problems...

If you don't know where the data files are located, ask your instructor where the files are stored (for example, the hard drive or school network). You might need to download the student data files from the Prentice Hall Web site. See the Introduction of this book for more information.

5 Double-click the folder that contains the Project 2 files.
Data files are stored in categories called ***folders***. Each folder name correlates to a project in this book. For example, all files you need to open for this project are stored in the same folder.

(Continues)

To Open an Existing Document (Continued)

6 Click *ew1-0201* in the file list to select it.

7 Click <u>O</u>pen in the bottom-right corner of the dialog box.
Word accesses the document from its storage device and displays it in a document window. The filename *ew1-0201* appears on the title bar (see Figure 2.4).

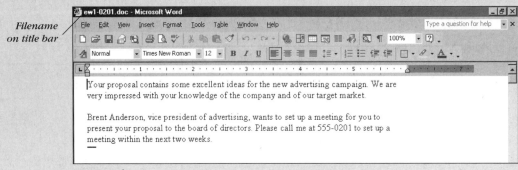

Filename on title bar

Figure 2.4

8 Choose <u>F</u>ile, Save <u>A</u>s.
The Save As dialog box displays.

9 Click the arrow to the right of the *Save <u>in</u>* box, and choose the drive and folder where you save documents.
You need to change the *Save <u>in</u>* location if you opened the file from a read-only network drive. You need to save files to a data disk, Zip disk, or personal network drive.

10 In the File <u>n</u>ame box, type Proposal Letter-WB2L and then click <u>S</u>ave.
From now on, you are instructed to open and save files without specific instructions to display the Open or Save As dialog boxes.

11 Keep the document onscreen to continue with the next lesson.

To extend your knowledge...

Displaying the Open Dialog Box

You can also display the Open dialog box by choosing <u>F</u>ile, <u>O</u>pen, or by pressing Ctrl+O.

Opening Recently Used Files

The <u>F</u>ile menu lists the last four documents that were used on your computer. If this menu lists the name of the document you want to work with, you can choose it from the menu to open that document. If the current disk does not contain the file, you see an error message.

You can customize the number of recently used files that are listed. Choose <u>T</u>ools, <u>O</u>ptions. Click the General tab. Specify how many filenames you want to list in the *Recently used file list* box and then click OK.

Opening Files from the Task Pane

If the task pane is displayed on the right side of the screen, you can click a filename to open a recently used file. You can also click *More documents* to display the Open dialog box and navigate through the storage devices to find the file you want to open.

Lesson 2: Scrolling in a Document

To make changes and corrections quickly and easily, you need to know the various ways of *scrolling*, or moving around in a document. For example, you can use either the mouse or the keyboard to move the insertion point in Word. Table 2.1 shows useful keyboard shortcuts for moving around in a document.

Table 2.1	**Keyboard Shortcuts for Working in a Document**
Key(s)	**Moves the Insertion Point**
←	one character to the left
→	one character to the right
↑	up one line
↓	down one line
Home	to the beginning of the line
End	to the end of the line
PgUp	up one window or page
PgDn	down one window or page
Ctrl + Home	to the beginning of the document
Ctrl + End	to the end of the document
Ctrl + ←	one word to the left
Ctrl + →	one word to the right
Ctrl + ↑	up one paragraph
Ctrl + ↓	down one paragraph
Ctrl + PgUp	to the top of the previous page
Ctrl + PgDn	to the top of the next page

The *Proposal Letter-WB2L* document should be open on your screen. In the next exercise, you practice scrolling through the letter using both the mouse and the keyboard.

To Scroll Through the Document

① Press Ctrl + End **to move the insertion point to the end of the document.**

② **Position the mouse pointer to the immediate left of the word *proposal* on the first line in the first paragraph; then, click the left mouse button.**
When the mouse pointer is shaped like an I-beam, click within the document to place the insertion point at that location. This is a fast way of positioning the insertion point when you want to add new text within an existing paragraph.

③ Press Ctrl + ↓ **to position the insertion point on the blank line between paragraphs.**

④ Press Ctrl + ↓ **again to position the insertion point at the beginning of the next paragraph.**
Every time you press ↵Enter, you create a paragraph. Word treats blank lines as paragraphs as well as regular text paragraphs.

(Continues)

To Scroll Through the Document (Continued)

You might see an icon called a ***Smart Tag***, which displays options when you click it. In this case, the Smart Tag might let you add Brent's name to the Microsoft Outlook Contacts folder.

5 **On the vertical scrollbar, click the down scroll arrow two times.**
Clicking items on the vertical scrollbar, such as the down scroll arrow or the up scroll arrow, does not move the insertion point. Using the vertical scrollbar merely lets you see different parts of the document. The insertion point remains where you last positioned it (see Figure 2.5).

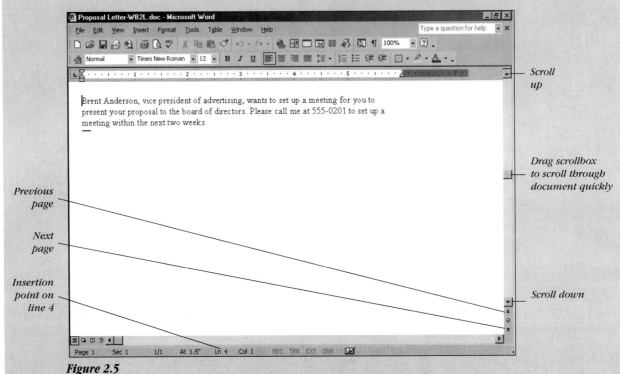

Scroll up

Drag scrollbox to scroll through document quickly

Previous page

Next page

Insertion point on line 4

Scroll down

Figure 2.5

6 **Click and drag the scrollbox to the top of the vertical scrollbar. You can now see the top of your document again.**
If your document contains more than one page, you see a ScreenTip noting the page number, such as Page: 3, as you click and drag the scrollbox.

7 **Press Ctrl + Home to move the insertion point to the top of the document.**
Take a minute now to practice some of the other keyboard shortcuts listed in Table 2.1.

In most cases, you save changes to your document before continuing to the next lesson. Because you just practiced scrolling in the document, you don't need to save the document because no changes were made.

8 **Keep the document onscreen to continue with the next lesson.**

To extend your knowledge...

Select Browse Object

Clicking the Select Browse Object button displays a palette (see Figure 2.6), so you can choose the object you want to quickly move the insertion point to.

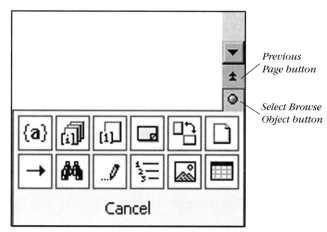

*Previous
Page button*

*Select Browse
Object button*

Cancel

Figure 2.6

The default object is Page, which lets you move the insertion point to the top of the previous page or to the top of the next page. When you select a different browse object, such as Heading, the double arrows appear in blue. When you click the Next button, Word takes you to the next object, such as the next heading.

Click the Select Browse Object button, and choose Page to change the browse mode back to Page.

Using the Go To Option

You can move the insertion point to a specific location by using the Go To option in the Find and Replace dialog box. Click Edit, Go To, or press Ctrl+G to display the Go To options. Then type the page number in the *Enter page number* text box. See Figure 2.7 for an example of the Go To options.

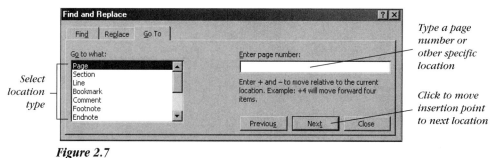

*Select
location
type*

*Type a page
number or
other specific
location*

*Click to move
insertion point
to next location*

Figure 2.7

Lesson 3: Inserting Text

You can insert text within existing text when ***Insert mode*** is active. When you insert text, the new text is inserted at the insertion point's location. Existing text moves over to allow room for the new text. You can tell if you're in the Insert mode if OVR is grayed-out on the status bar.

In this lesson, you use Insert mode to insert text to complete the letter. You need to insert the date, inside address, salutation, and signature block to have a fully formatted letter. You will use the Auto-Complete feature to help you insert the current date. ***AutoComplete*** displays a ScreenTip with text, such as a date, when you type parts of certain words that are stored within Word.

To Insert the Date with AutoComplete

❶ **In the *Proposal Letter-WB2L* document, press** Ctrl+Home **to move the insertion point to the beginning of the first paragraph in the document.**
You need to insert the date at the beginning of the document.

❷ **Start typing the name of the current month. For example, if the current month is February, type** Febr**.**
You should see a ScreenTip that shows the rest of the month, as shown in Figure 2.8.

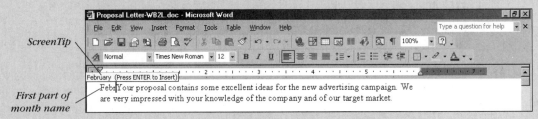

ScreenTip

First part of month name

Figure 2.8

If the current month is March, April, May, June, or July, the ScreenTip won't appear to finish the month name. After you type the full month name and press Spacebar, however, you should see a ScreenTip showing the full date.

❸ **Press** ↵Enter**.**
Word inserts the rest of the month name that was displayed in the ScreenTip instead of moving the insertion point to the next line.

❹ **Press** Spacebar**.**
Now you see a ScreenTip that shows the current date, such as *February 17, 2004 (Press ENTER to Insert)*.

❺ **Press** ↵Enter**.**
Word inserts the rest of the current date.

Now you need to insert the inside address, salutation, additional words, and complimentary closing.

To Insert Text

❶ **Press** ↵Enter **four times.**
You need to add space after the date before you insert the inside address.

❷ **Type the following text, pressing** ↵Enter **once after each line:**
Ms. Rebecca Farnsworth
Farnsworth Advertising
5350 North Edgewood Drive
Provo, UT 84604

Word moves the existing paragraphs down to make room for the new lines of text you insert. Your letter should look like Figure 2.9.

To Insert Text

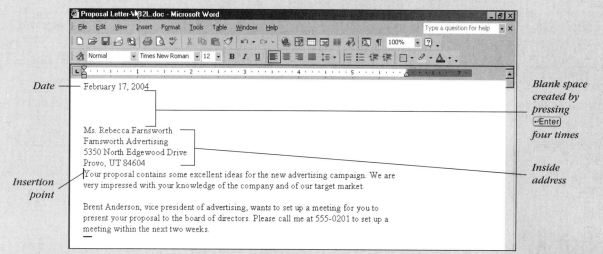

Date — February 17, 2004

Blank space created by pressing ⏎Enter four times

Ms. Rebecca Farnsworth
Farnsworth Advertising
5350 North Edgewood Drive
Provo, UT 84604

Inside address

Insertion point

Figure 2.9

❸ Press ⏎Enter **again to leave one blank line between the inside address and the salutation.**

❹ Type Dear Ms. Farnsworth: **and press** ⏎Enter **twice.**
You should now have one blank line between the salutation and the first line of the first paragraph.

If you have problems...

If the Office Assistant appears to ask if you want help to create the letter, click Cancel.

You need to add a sentence between the existing sentences in the first paragraph.

❺ Click to the left of *We* in the first paragraph.
Before inserting new text, make sure that you position the insertion point where you want the new text to appear. In this case, make sure the insertion point is to the immediate left of *We*.

❻ Type the following sentence, pressing Spacebar **after the period.**
The theme you selected is appropriate for our new product line.

Because Insert mode is active, the new text appears at the insertion point. The existing text simply word-wraps differently.

❼ Press Ctrl+End, **and press** ⏎Enter **twice to move the insertion point to the end of the letter.**
You need to type the signature block at the end of the letter.

❽ Type Sincerely **and then press** ⏎Enter **four times to allow enough room to sign your printed letter.**

❾ Type your name.
The letter is now complete. Compare your letter with the one shown in Figure 2.10.

(Continues)

To Insert Text (Continued)

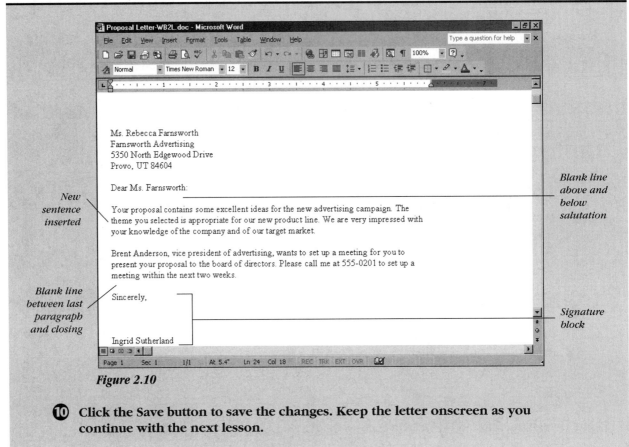

Figure 2.10

🔟 **Click the Save button to save the changes. Keep the letter onscreen as you continue with the next lesson.**

Lesson 4: Selecting Text

Making changes to a Word document is a simple process, especially when you can select text to change it. For example, you might want to delete an entire sentence or group of sentences. Instead of deleting characters one by one with ⬅Backspace or Del, you can select and delete text.

Selecting is the action of defining an area of text so you can do something to it, such as delete or format it. When you select text, Word displays it in white with a black background. In this lesson, you learn how to select text.

To Select Text

❶ **In the *Proposal Letter-WB2L* document, double-click the word *proposal* in the first paragraph to select it and the space after it.**

❷ **Deselect the word *proposal*, press and hold down Ctrl, and click anywhere in the first sentence of the first paragraph.**
This action selects the entire sentence, along with any additional blank spaces after the period.

❸ **Triple-click anywhere inside the first paragraph.**
This action selects the entire paragraph (see Figure 2.11).

To Select Text

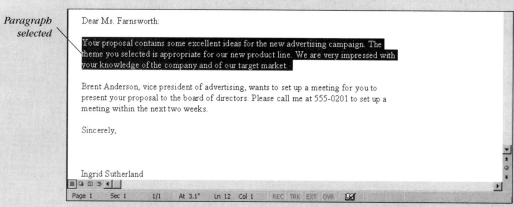

Paragraph selected

Figure 2.11

If you have problems…

If the paragraph is not selected, make sure that you click three times in quick succession, and that you don't move the mouse as you click.

4 **Click anywhere inside the document window to deselect the text.**

5 **Click at the beginning of the inside address and hold down the mouse button while you drag the mouse down to the middle of the second paragraph. Then, release the mouse button.**

Clicking and dragging is a fast way to select a specific block of text, as shown in Figure 2.12.

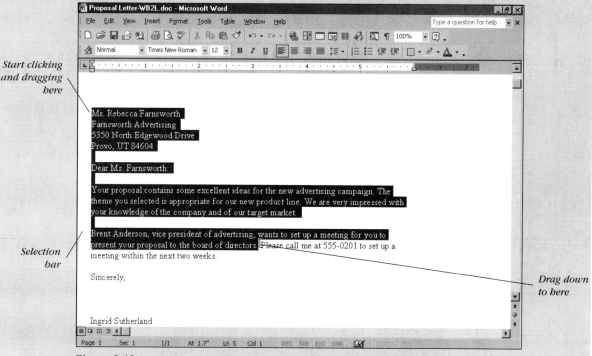

Start clicking and dragging here

Selection bar

Drag down to here

Figure 2.12

(Continues)

To Select Text (Continued)

If you have problems...

If you click and drag too fast, you might end up selecting too much text. If this happens, try this method instead of clicking and dragging: Click at the point where you want to start selecting text, press and hold down ⬆Shift, and click at the point where you want to end the selected text. This selects from the insertion point to the place where you ⬆Shift+click.

6 **Click in the document window to deselect the text.**

7 **Keep the document onscreen to continue with the next lesson.**

To extend your knowledge...

Selecting by Clicking the Selection Bar

You can also select text by clicking the **selection bar** (refer to Figure 2.11 in the previous exercise), the space in the left margin area where you see a right-pointing arrow. Click once to select the current text line. Double-click to select the current paragraph, and triple-click to select the entire document.

Selecting Multiple Items at the Same Time

In Word Version 2002, you can now select two different areas in the document at the same time. To do this, select one area (such as a heading); press and hold down Ctrl as you select another area. This feature is similar to selecting nonconsecutive ranges in Excel.

Selecting Text with the Keyboard

You can also use the arrow keys on the keyboard to select text. You might find this method more convenient when selecting a small section of text, or if you prefer to keep your hands on the keyboard. First, you position the insertion point where you want to start selecting text. Press ⬆Shift and then use the arrow keys to select text. Release ⬆Shift to stop selecting text. Press any arrow key to deselect the text.

If you want to select the entire document, press Ctrl+A.

Lesson 5: Deleting and Changing Text

As you read the first draft of your letter, you may decide that you don't like the way a particular sentence sounds, or you may find that you have simply entered the wrong information. Word lets you delete text that you don't want, enter new text, and correct existing text. In this lesson, you learn how to make basic corrections to text in a document.

To Delete and Change Text

1 **In the *Proposal Letter-WB2L* document, double-click the word *new* on the first line of the first paragraph.**
You want to replace the word *new* with *summer*.

2 **Type summer.**
When you select text and type new text, the new text replaces the selected text.

To Delete and Change Text

3 **Position the insertion point at the beginning of the word *very* in the second sentence of the first paragraph.**

4 **Press Ctrl+Del to delete the word to the right of the insertion point.**

5 **Position the insertion point before the first 0 in the phone number.**
This phone number is incorrect. You need to replace it with the correct phone number.

6 **Double-click the OVR indicator on the status bar.**
The OVR indicator appears darker. You are now in the ***Overtype mode***, which overwrites (or replaces) existing text as you type new text.

7 **Type 2486 to insert the correct phone number and replace the old number, as shown in Figure 2.13.**

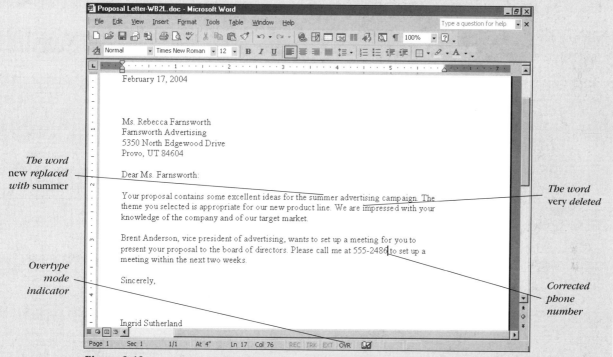

The word new replaced with summer

Overtype mode indicator

The word very deleted

Corrected phone number

Figure 2.13

If you have problems…

If you forget to turn off Overtype mode, you might accidentally delete text and replace it with other text, instead of simply inserting new text. Double-click the OVR indicator on the status bar to turn off Overtype mode.

8 **Double-click the OVR indicator to return to Insert mode.**

9 **Save the document, and keep it onscreen to continue with the next lesson.**

To extend your knowledge…

Deleting Text

You can delete the word to the left of the insertion point by pressing Ctrl+◆Backspace. To delete larger sections of text, select the text first and then press Del.

Insert and Overtype modes

In addition to clicking OVR on the status bar, you can press `Insert` on the keyboard to toggle between Insert and Overtype modes.

Lesson 6: Changing View Modes

When you work with a document, you might want to adjust the way it appears on the screen. For example, you can adjust the document to display the layout with the margins, or you can maximize the amount of screen space devoted to seeing text. In addition, you can adjust the way spacing or the size of the characters appears on your screen without changing the size of the printed characters. This lesson teaches you how to use view options to focus on particular elements of your document, such as layout or text.

Normal view shows text without displaying space for margins, page numbers, or other supplemental text. Normal view is appropriate when you are simply typing and editing text, and you want to use the screen space for displaying text without seeing the margins.

To Change View Options

1 Press `Ctrl`+`Home` to move your insertion point to the top of the document.

2 Click the Print Layout View button to the left of the horizontal scrollbar.
Print Layout view shows you what the document will look like when it's printed. This view shows margin space, graphics locations, headers, footers, and page numbers. Although your document does not contain headers, footers, or page numbers, you can look at the margins (see Figure 2.14).

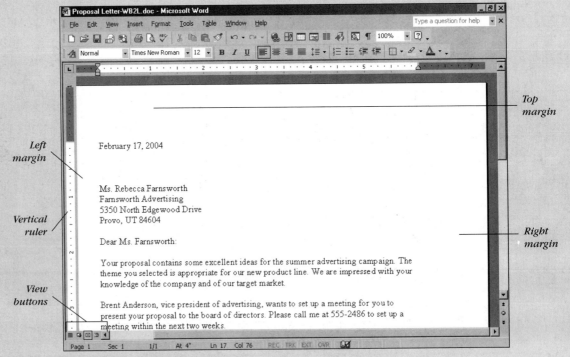

Figure 2.14

Notice that the end-of-document marker does *not* appear in Print Layout view.

3 Click the Normal View button to change back to the regular view.

To Change View Options

The end-of-document marker appears again in Normal view. Although you can see more text in Normal view, you still want to see more text on your screen.

4 **Choose View, and click the down arrows at the bottom of the menu to display the full View menu.**

5 **Choose Full Screen.**
Full Screen view uses the entire screen to display the document text, as shown in Figure 2.15. In this view, you do *not* see the title bar, menu bar, toolbars, or other Word elements. However, you do see the end-of-document marker.

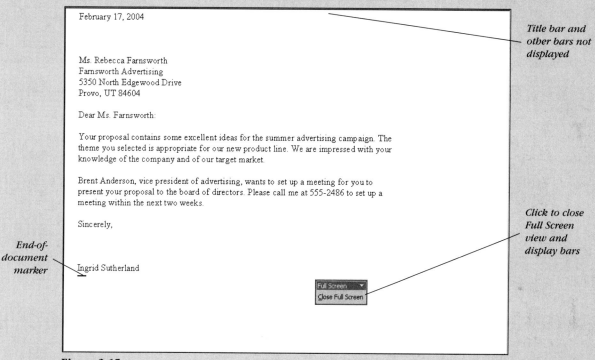

Title bar and other bars not displayed

Click to close Full Screen view and display bars

End-of-document marker

Figure 2.15

6 **Click Close Full Screen or press Esc to close the Full Screen view.**

7 **Click the Zoom drop-down arrow.**
You see the Zoom menu (see Figure 2.16), which lets you change the *zoom*, or magnification percentage, of your document onscreen.

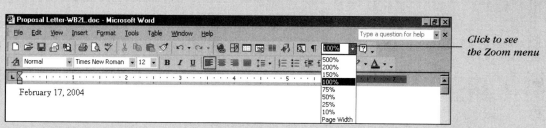

Click to see the Zoom menu

Figure 2.16

(Continues)

To Change View Options (Continued)

8 **Choose 150%.**

The document is now displayed at 150% of its regular screen size, as shown in Figure 2.17. Changing the zoom does not, however, change the size of the text when it is printed.

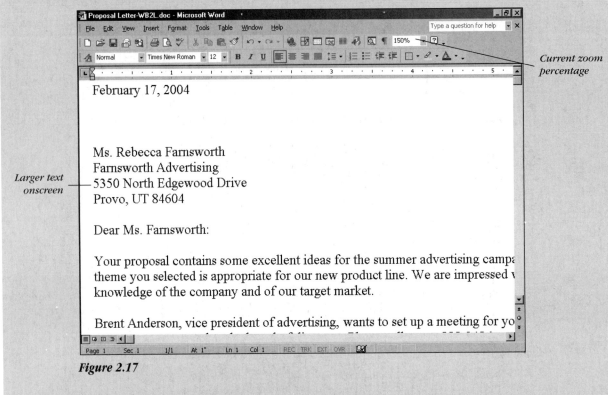

Figure 2.17

9 **Click the arrow to the right of the Zoom box again, and choose 100%.**

10 **Click the Print button on the Standard toolbar to print the document.**

11 **Keep the document onscreen to continue with the next lesson.**

To extend your knowledge...

Setting Specific Zoom

You can click inside the Zoom box and type the exact percentage. For example, you can type **93** if you want. You don't have to type the percent sign. Press ⏎Enter after you type the zoom value.

Using the Zoom Dialog Box

Choose View, Zoom to display the Zoom dialog box, which provides preset options and a Percent option that allows you to specify the exact magnification (see Figure 2.18).

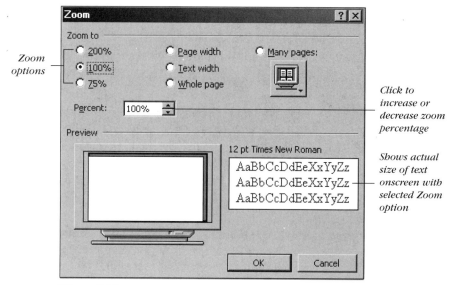

Figure 2.18

The options shown in Figure 2.18 appear when Print Layout view is active. The options will differ slightly if you have Normal view active.

Using Zoom Options

When you select the Print Layout view, you can select Whole Page, Two Pages, and Text Width from the Zoom menu. Viewing the whole page or two pages is nice because it allows you to see the overall layout, such as spacing and margins. These options are not available when you use the Normal view. Text Width displays text from the left to the right side of the monitor.

Working in Full Screen View

Although you can't see the menu bar, you can still access the menus. Simply press Alt and the hotkey to display the desired menu. For example, press Alt+V to display the View menu.

The keyboard shortcut for closing Full Screen view is Alt+C.

Lesson 7: Creating Envelopes

You have a printed copy of your letter, but you need an envelope to mail it in. Use Word's Envelope feature to quickly create and print an envelope for your letter. The Envelope feature creates the address from the existing letter, and lets you select the envelope type and other options. In this lesson, you create and print an envelope for the *Proposal Letter-WB2L* document that is displayed on your screen.

To Create an Envelope

1 Choose **Tools, Letters and Mailings.**

2 Choose **Envelopes and Labels.**
The Envelopes and Labels dialog box appears.

3 Click the **Envelopes** tab if it's not already selected.

(Continues)

To Create an Envelope (Continued)

The Envelopes and Labels dialog box shows the envelope options (see Figure 2.19). Word copies the inside address from your letter to the *Delivery address* section in the dialog box.

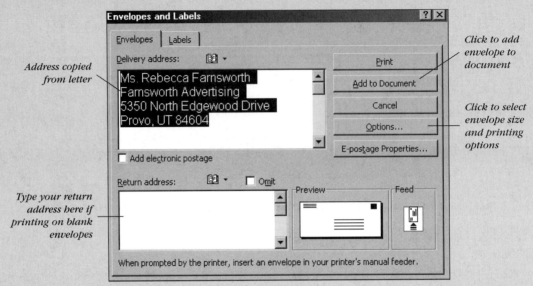

Address copied from letter

Click to add envelope to document

Click to select envelope size and printing options

Type your return address here if printing on blank envelopes

Figure 2.19

❹ **Click Add to Document.**
Clicking this button inserts a new page at the beginning of the document, before the letter. The envelope is on page zero.

❺ **Click the Print Layout View button.**

❻ **Click the Zoom drop-down arrow and choose 75%.**
The envelope text now looks like it's placed on an envelope onscreen (see Figure 2.20).

To Create an Envelope

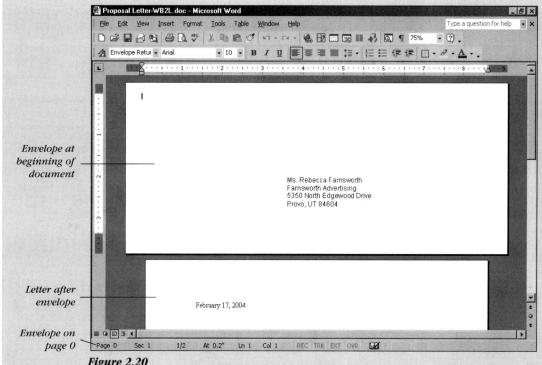

Envelope at beginning of document —

Ms. Rebecca Farnsworth
Farnsworth Advertising
5350 North Edgewood Drive
Provo, UT 84604

Letter after envelope —

February 17, 2004

Envelope on page 0 —

Figure 2.20

7 **Click the Save button on the Standard toolbar.**
You have now saved the envelope settings as part of the document.

8 **Click File, Print to display the Print dialog box.**

9 **Click the *Current page* option button; then click OK.**
You will probably see a message instructing you to manually insert the envelope into the printer. Ask your instructor for assistance, if needed. If you don't have an envelope to print on, simply insert a regular sheet of paper into the printer.

10 **Close the document.**

To extend your knowledge...

Creating Envelopes

You can select a variety of envelope options by clicking Options in the Envelopes and Labels dialog box. For example, you can select a different envelope size, add a barcode, and specify how you want to insert the envelope into the printer.

Lesson 8: Creating Labels

Instead of printing addresses on envelopes, you might want to print addresses on labels. Word's Label feature provides a variety of label formats, such as address, data disk, file folder, name badge, and video label. The label choices correspond to brand-name label product numbers, such as Avery 5160 Address labels. In this lesson, you select an address label format and enter data into some labels.

To Create Address Labels

1 **Click the New Blank Document button on the Standard toolbar to start a new document, and change the Zoom to 100%.**

2 **Choose Tools, Letters and Mailings, Envelopes and Labels.**
The Envelopes and Labels dialog box appears.

3 **Click the Labels tab.**
You can type an address into the Address text box, start a new label document, and select different label formats (see Figure 2.21).

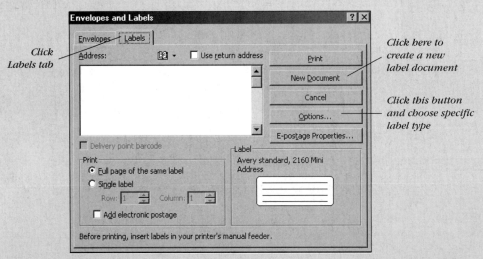

Figure 2.21

4 **Click Options.**
Before creating a label document, you should specify which label format and printer settings you want (see Figure 2.22). Most Avery-brand label products are listed.

To Create Address Labels

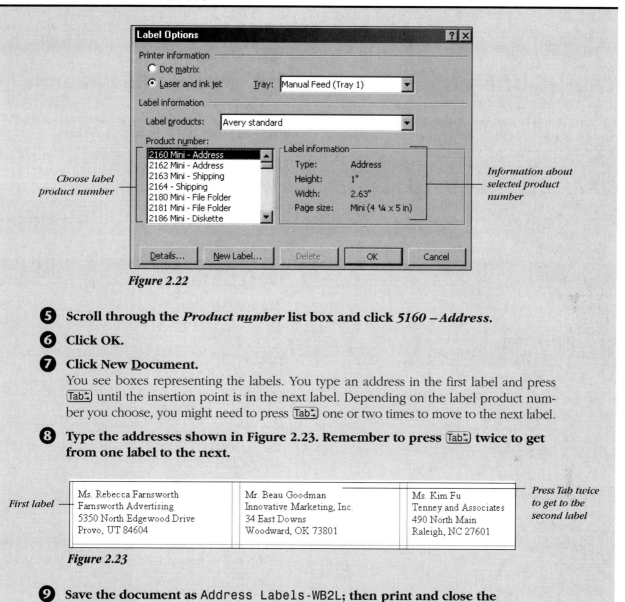

Choose label product number

Information about selected product number

Figure 2.22

5 Scroll through the *Product number* list box and click *5160 – Address*.

6 Click OK.

7 Click New Document.

You see boxes representing the labels. You type an address in the first label and press Tab until the insertion point is in the next label. Depending on the label product number you choose, you might need to press Tab one or two times to move to the next label.

8 Type the addresses shown in Figure 2.23. Remember to press Tab twice to get from one label to the next.

First label

Ms. Rebecca Farnsworth Farnsworth Advertising 5350 North Edgewood Drive Provo, UT 84604	Mr. Beau Goodman Innovative Marketing, Inc. 34 East Downs Woodward, OK 73801	Ms. Kim Fu Tenney and Associates 490 North Main Raleigh, NC 27601	*Press Tab twice to get to the second label*

Figure 2.23

9 Save the document as Address Labels-WB2L; then print and close the document.

To extend your knowledge...

Creating Return Address Labels

You can create a sheet of personal address labels for yourself quickly and easily. Simply type your name and address in the Address box, choose the label format you want, and click the *Full page of the same label* option button. When you click New Document, Word creates an entire sheet of labels for you!

Summary

In this project, you learned some very important word processing tasks. You learned how to open a document that you previously saved and how to efficiently navigate through it. You also learned how to select, insert, and delete text. In addition, you learned how to change the view options to see your document from different perspectives. Finally, you created an envelope and mailing labels.

Now you're ready to reinforce your knowledge by completing the end-of-project exercises. In addition, experiment with features. For example, create labels for videos. Furthermore, you can expand your knowledge and skills by using Help to find out more about the topics covered in this project.

Checking Concepts and Terms

Multiple Choice

Circle the letter of the correct answer for each of the following.

1. What feature would you use to adjust the percentage of a document that displays onscreen? [L6]

    a. Print Layout

    b. Zoom

    c. Full Screen

    d. Normal view

2. Which menu lists the most recently used documents? [L1]

    a. Edit

    b. Format

    c. Open

    d. File

3. Which method should you use to select one sentence within a paragraph? [L4]

    a. Double-click the sentence.

    b. Double-click the selection bar by the sentence.

    c. Press Ctrl+A.

    d. Hold Ctrl while you click in the sentence.

4. What option is the most efficient for moving the insertion point from page 3 of your document to the top of page 12? [L2]

    a. Press Ctrl+PgDn nine times.

    b. Click the Next Page button nine times.

    c. Display the Go To dialog box, type **12**, and click the Go To button.

    d. Press ↓ repeatedly until you're on page 12.

5. When you create labels, which of the following steps should you perform first? [L8]

    a. Type names and addresses.

    b. Choose the label product number.

    c. Click the New Document button in the dialog box.

    d. Press Tab to separate addresses into separate labels.

Screen ID

Label each element of the Word screen shown in Figure 2.24.

A. Normal view button

B. Overtype mode

C. Print Layout view button

D. Select Browse Object button

E. Zoom

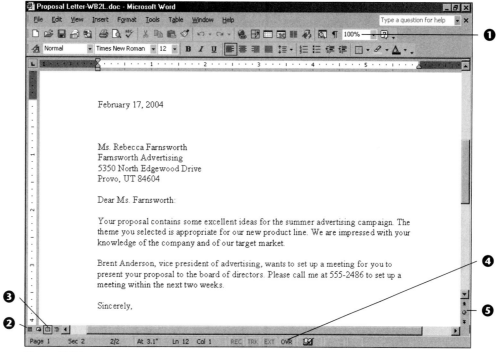

Figure 2.24

1. _____   4. _____

2. _____   5. _____

3. _____

Discussion

1. What is the advantage of knowing and using the keyboard to scroll through a document? [L2]

2. What is the difference between Normal view and Print Layout view? Provide an example of when you might use each view. [L6]

3. Explain why selecting and typing text might be preferable to using the Overtype mode to change existing text. [L5]

Skill Drill exercises reinforce project skills. Each skill reinforced is the same, or nearly the same, as a skill presented in the project. Detailed instructions are provided in a step-by-step format.

1. Opening a Document

You know you can perform the same tasks with different methods. Because you want to learn the different methods and see which you like best, you decide to practice another way of opening a document.

1. In Word, press Ctrl+O to display the Open dialog box.
2. Click the *Look in* drop-down arrow, and choose the drive and folder that contains the data files for this book.
3. Click *ew1-0202*, and press ↵Enter to open the document.
4. Choose File, Save As.
5. Click the *Save in* drop-down arrow, and choose the drive that contains your data disk or Zip disk.
6. Type `Chambers Letter-WB2SD` in the *File name* box and then click Save.
7. Choose File, Close to close the document.
8. Choose File, and look at the bottom of the menu.
9. Select *1 Chambers Letter-WB2SD.doc* from the bottom of the menu.
   The menu might display the path and filename, such as *1 C:\My Documents\Chambers Letter-WB2SD.doc*.
10. Keep the document onscreen to continue with the next exercise.

2. Scrolling in the Document

To become efficient in scrolling through a document, you want to practice different methods.

1. Press Ctrl+Home to move the insertion point to the beginning of the document.
2. Click and drag the vertical scrollbox until the ScreenTip shows *Page: 1*; then release the mouse button.
3. Click the Previous Page button.
4. Click the Next Page button.
5. Press Ctrl+End to move the insertion point to the end of the document.
6. Press Ctrl+G to display the Go To option.
7. Type `0` in the *Enter page number* box, click Go To, and then click Close.
8. Drag the scroll box down to see the letter.
9. Click at the beginning of the first paragraph in the letter.
10. Press Ctrl+↓ twice to move the insertion point to the beginning of the second paragraph.
11. Leave the document onscreen to continue with the next exercise.

3. Selecting, Changing, and Deleting Text

You want to use the same letter to send to someone else. Instead of typing a new letter, you decide to select and delete the original envelope, and select and replace the inside address and salutation.

1. With the *Chambers Letter-WB2SD* document onscreen, select the entire inside address on the letter (not envelope).

2. Type the following new address while the old address is selected:

```
Mr. Aaron Chambers
McClure and Associates
305 West Main Street
Toledo, OH 43615
```

3. Make sure that you still have one blank line between the inside address and the salutation.

4. Select Ms. Farnsworth in the salutation; then type **Mr. Chambers**.

5. Click the Normal View button to the left of the horizontal scrollbar and then press Ctrl+Home.

6. Position the mouse pointer in the left margin—the selection bar area. The mouse pointer is an arrow pointing to the right.

7. Click and drag to select the envelope, including the lines that mention the section break. Press Del to delete the entire envelope page.

8. Click to the right of the hyphen in the phone number.

9. Double-click OVR on the status bar, type **7356**, and double-click OVR again.

10. Save the document, and keep it onscreen to continue with the next exercise.

4. Inserting Text

You need to insert new text within the document. Because you don't want to delete existing text, you use Insert mode.

1. Click to the left of *vice president* in the second paragraph, type **senior**, and press Spacebar.

2. Click at the beginning of the second paragraph, and type the following paragraph:

```
As you are probably aware, we are expecting sales from the summer
campaign to generate a 25 percent increase over last summer's campaign.
The economy is very favorable, and we have many new products to hit
the market.
```

3. Press Enter twice after the paragraph to have a blank line between paragraphs.

4. Click to the left of *economy*, and type **regional**. Make sure that you have a space before and after the new word.

5. Click to the left of the date, and press Ctrl+Del four times to delete the date.

6. Start typing the name of the current month. When you see the full month name in the Screen-Tip, press Enter.

7. Press Enter to see a ScreenTip showing the current date.

8. Press Enter to insert the date shown in the ScreenTip.

9. Save the document, and keep it onscreen to continue with the next exercise.

5. Viewing the Document

You want to review view options to look at the overall format and to adjust the magnification onscreen.

1. With *Chambers Letter-WB2SD* onscreen, click the Print Layout View button to the left of the horizontal scrollbar.

2. Choose View, Zoom to display the Zoom dialog box.

3. Click the Percent increment button to *125%*, and click OK.

4. Click the Normal View button to the left of the horizontal scrollbar.

5. Click the Zoom drop-down arrow, and choose 75%.

6. Keep the document onscreen to continue with the next exercise.

6. Creating an Envelope

After creating the letter, you need to create an envelope for it. You create the envelope and add it to the document window.

1. With the *Chambers Letter-WB2SD* onscreen, choose Tools, Letters and Mailing, Envelopes and Labels.

2. Click the Envelopes tab, and click the Add to Document button.

3. Save the document with the envelope.

4. Print the envelope and letter.

5. Close the document.

Challenge

Challenge exercises expand on or are somewhat related to skills presented in the lessons. Each exercise provides a brief narrative introduction, followed by instructions in a numbered-step format that are not as detailed as those in the Skill Drill section.

1. Editing a Discount Message

You work for Mega Music, a regional retail store that sells CDs, cassettes, and movies. To promote your store to the college students, you are offering a special sale to them. A coworker created a document announcing the discount; you need to open, edit, and save the document.

1. Open *ew1-0203*, and save it as `Mega Music-WB2CH1`.

2. Use Overtype, and retype the title in capital letters.

3. Delete the text *or copy your official class schedule* from the second paragraph.

4. Change the street address number to `2286` and insert `North` between the street number and name.

5. Insert a line between the CD and VHS movies lines, and type `15% off on all cassette tapes`.

6. Select the four lines about the discount percentages, and press `Tab` once.

7. Insert the word `movie` between the words *your collection* in the last paragraph.

8. Save, print, and close the document.

2. Editing a Memo about Parking Rules

You composed a memo to inform employees about a new parking rule. You need to open it and make a few changes before sending it out.

1. Open *ew1-0204* and save it as `Parking Memo-WB2CH2`.

2. Select Normal view and then change the zoom to Page Width.

3. Delete the asterisk on the Date line, and use AutoComplete to enter today's date.

4. Delete the asterisk on the From line, and type your name. Make sure that the date and your name line up with the word *New* on the Subject line.

5. Press `Tab` to line up *All Employees* with the other items in the memorandum heading.

6. Use the most efficient method for changing *8:30* to `8:45`.

7. Select the last sentence in the memo, and replace it with `We appreciate your cooperation during this construction period.`

8. Select and change these words to all caps: *Date, To, From,* and *Subject.* If needed, adjust the second column in the heading.

9. Save, print, and close the document.

3. Editing a Memo about MOUS Certification

As the Office Manager, you are pleased to announce rewards for employees who pass MOUS certification tests. You created a memo this morning announcing the reward, but you need to edit it before sending it to your employees.

1. Open *ew1-0205*, and save it as `Certification Reward-WB2CH3`.

2. Select Robert's full name, and type your name to replace his name.

3. Use AutoComplete to insert the current date in the appropriate location in the memo heading.

4. Add the following text in the respective locations:
   - `special` before *fund* in the first paragraph
   - `by calling 555-EXAM` at the end of the first sentence in the second paragraph
   - `You are reimbursed only if you pass the exam, so be sure to study and practice!` at the end of the second paragraph

5. Delete *computer applications* in the second paragraph.

6. Select and change the following text, as indicated:
   - *test* to `measure` in the first paragraph
   - *$175* to `$200` in the third paragraph
   - *one month* to `two weeks` in the third paragraph

7. Check the current MOUS exam prices at www.mous.net on the Internet.

8. Save, print, and close the document.

4. Editing a Letter Requesting Donations

You belong to a campus organization that is sponsoring a track meet for underprivileged children in your area. As president of the organization, you are responsible for writing letters to local retail stores to solicit donations for the event. You want to receive cash and food donations. The money will help defray the cost of sponsoring the event, and the food donations will help your members prepare a cookout after the event.

1. From a blank document window, insert the date and the following inside address:
   ```
   Mr. John Davis
   Fresher Groceries, Inc.
   344 NW First
   Racine, WI 53402
   ```

2. Insert and correctly format the salutation.

3. Type a three-paragraph letter that describes what your organization is sponsoring and the type of donations you seek. End with a statement showing appreciation for any donation the retailer might provide.

4. Include an appropriate closing with your name. Type your organization name on the line below your typed name.

5. Save the document as `Donation Letter-WB2CH4`.

6. Create an envelope without a return address. Insert the envelope in the document.

7. Save the document, and print both the envelope and the letter. Then, close the document.

5. Creating Mailing Labels for Family Names

One of your family members asked you to create mailing labels for her annual holiday newsletter. She wants you to save the label document so that she can use it again next year.

1. Start a new blank document.

2. Select *Avery 5260 - Address* and start a new document.

3. Enter the names and addresses of your family members and friends. You should enter enough addresses to fill the sheet of labels. Correctly format the addresses.

4. Save the document as `Personal Address Labels-WB2CH5`.

5. Print and close the document.

iscovery Zone

Discovery Zone exercises require advanced knowledge of topics presented in *essentials* lessons, application of skills from multiple lessons, or self-directed learning of new skills.

1. Using Help to Learn About Open Options

You noticed the drop-down arrow by the Open button in the Open dialog box. Two options caught your attention: Open Read-Only and Open as Copy. Use the Help feature to find out what each option does. Print the Help topics that you find.

Create a document in which you describe Open Read-Only and Open as Copy options. Write one paragraph for each option. In each paragraph provide an example of when you might use that particular option.

Save your document as `Open Options-WB2DZ1` and then print it.

2. Creating a Sheet of Disk Labels

As an assistant for a computer consulting company, you are responsible for preparing data disks to contain documents that the clients will use during the consultations.

From a new document window, create a sheet of labels using the Avery 6460 Remove 'Em laser diskette labels. Type the following text for the label, and make sure that the same text repeats on each label. Place the labels in a new document window; don't print from within the Envelopes and Labels dialog box.

```
Introduction to Word
Computer Essentials Training
April 5, 2004
Trainer: your name
```

Save the sheet of labels as `Disk Labels-WB2DZ2`, and print the labels on a regular sheet of paper.

3. Creating a Small Envelope with a Barcode

One of your college professors said he would mail your final grade to you if you provide a self-addressed stamped envelope. You only have $6\frac{1}{2}$ inch $\times$ $3\frac{5}{8}$ inch-sized envelopes.

Create the envelope in the Envelopes and Labels dialog box. Use your name and address in the Delivery address section and your professor's name and address in the Return address section. If needed, use Help to learn how to select an envelope size and how to insert a barcode on the envelope. Make these adjustments before adding the envelope to your document. Save the document as `Instructor Envelope-WB2DZ3` and print the envelope.

Formatting Text

Objectives

In this project, you learn how to

- ✔ Apply and Modify Character Formats
- ✔ Change the Font, Size, and Color
- ✔ Apply Character Effects and Spacing
- ✔ Copy Formats with Format Painter
- ✔ Highlight Text
- ✔ Insert Symbols
- ✔ Display Formatting Marks
- ✔ Insert Nonbreaking Spaces and Hyphens

Key terms in this project include

- ❑ character effects
- ❑ character formats
- ❑ character spacing
- ❑ designer font
- ❑ em dash
- ❑ en dash
- ❑ font
- ❑ font size
- ❑ Format Painter
- ❑ formatting marks
- ❑ hard return
- ❑ headings
- ❑ highlight
- ❑ kerning
- ❑ nonbreaking hyphen
- ❑ nonbreaking space
- ❑ position
- ❑ sans serif font
- ❑ scale
- ❑ serif font
- ❑ spacing
- ❑ WYSIWYG

Why Would I Do This?

In the previous project, you used basic editing techniques such as deleting and inserting text. You are now ready to learn how to make document text look better. In this project, you learn to change the appearance of your text by adding bold, italic, and underlining. You also learn how to change the font, font size, and font color of your text to add emphasis and draw the reader's eyes to specific parts of your document. These and other features make your documents look more professional.

Visual Summary

Although the most important part of a document is accuracy of content, unformatted text doesn't entice someone to read the document. Lack of using fonts, sizes, symbols, and highlighting creates a dull image. Figure 3.1 shows unformatted text.

Microsoft Office Professional

Microsoft Office Professional contains several powerful application software programs to help people improve their professional and personal productivity. The core applications are Word, Excel, PowerPoint, and Access.

Microsoft Word is a powerful word processing program. You can use it to create a variety of documents such as letters, reports, newsletters, and fliers. Furthermore, you can create dynamic tables, drawings, and graphics. Various formatting options help you achieve a professional image. For example, you can insert a nonbreaking space in "May 15" to prevent the text from word-wrapping between the month and date.

Microsoft Excel is the leading spreadsheet software. You can use Excel to create budgets, sales forecasts, mortgage payments, and other financial spreadsheets. Excel's power lies in its "what-if" ability. After you set up formulas, you can change input data and see what type of effect the change has on a particular result.

Microsoft PowerPoint is a presentation graphics program. People around the world use this software to create dynamic, professional presentation slide shows. You can insert images, tables, and sound to enhance your slide shows. Animated transitions and specialized drawing tools help complete your presentation.

Microsoft Access is a powerful database management program. It is effective for storing, retrieving, organizing, and printing data. Companies use database software to keep track of inventory, client information, and suppliers. You can even create a database to store names, addresses, phone numbers, and e-mail addresses of your family and friends!

Figure 3.1

Formatted text, on the other hand, enhances the document. In other words, it "brings the document to life." Text formats help focus the reader's eyes and stress important aspects. Figure 3.2 shows the impact of formatted text.

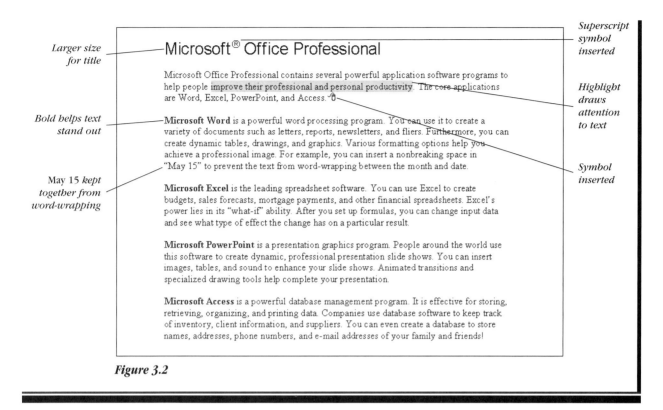

Figure 3.2

Lesson 1: Applying and Modifying Character Formats

In the last project, you learned how to select and delete text. In addition to deleting selected text, you can enhance the appearance of text by applying bold, italic, underline, or color. These text formats, known as ***character formats***, emphasize ideas as well as improve readability and clarity.

Table 3.1 shows the toolbar buttons and keyboard shortcuts that you use to apply these character formats.

Table 3.1 Character Format Buttons and Keyboard Shortcuts

Button	Button Name	Keyboard Shortcut
B	**Bold**	Ctrl + B
I	**Italic**	Ctrl + I
U	**Underline**	Ctrl + U

To Apply Character Formats

❶ Open *ew1-0301*, and save it as `Office Software-WB3L`**.**
Currently, the document looks very plain. However, after you apply character formats, the document will look a lot better.

❷ Click and drag across *Microsoft Word* at the beginning of the second full paragraph.
You want the software name to stand out from the rest of the paragraph.

(Continues)

To Apply Character Formats (Continued)

3 **Click the Underline button on the Formatting toolbar.**
The selected text, *Microsoft Word*, is now underlined, so it stands out from the regular text. After underlining the text, you need to deselect it.

4 **Click inside the selected text to deselect it.**
Notice how underlined text differs from regular text (see Figure 3.3).

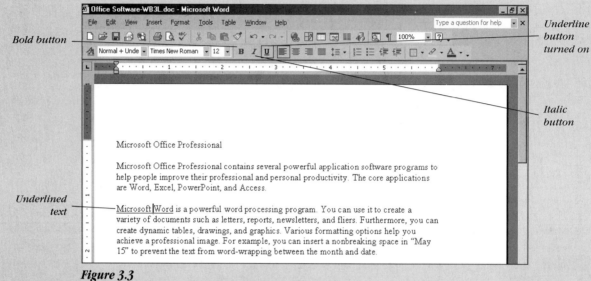

Figure 3.3

You can remove formatting if you don't want the character format after all.

5 **Select the underlined *Microsoft Word*.**
You remove formatting the same way you applied it.

6 **Click the Underline button to remove the underline format.**
If you want to apply a different character format, keep the text selected.

7 **Click the Bold button.**
The selected text, *Microsoft Word*, is now bold.

8 **Deselect the text.**

9 **Save the document, and keep it onscreen to continue with the next lesson.**

To extend your knowledge...

Using Bold, Italic, and Underline

Although both bold and italic character formats emphasize text, use bold for stronger emphasis and italic for lesser emphasis.

Some reference manuals specify that you apply bold and underline to report ***headings***—descriptive words or phrases placed between sections to help readers understand the organization of your document.

Lesson 2: Changing the Font, Size, and Color

Font refers to the overall appearance—style, weight, and typeface—of a set of characters. You can choose from literally thousands of fonts. Fonts are available from a variety of sources. For example, printers come with built-in fonts they can produce. You can also purchase font software from companies such as Adobe. Fonts range in appearance from very professional to informal fun fonts. Figure 3.4 illustrates some examples of different fonts.

Arial	K E Y S T R O K E
Arial Rounded MT Bold	Kids
Bauhaus Md MT	Parisian BT
Bookman Old Style	Snell BT
Broadway BT	Tango BT
Comic Sans MS	Technical
Courier New	Times New Roman
Hobo BT	Typo Upright BT
Kabel Bk BT	Westminster

Figure 3.4

When choosing a font, consider the font's readability, its suitability to the document's purpose, and its appeal to the reader. Most fonts are classified as serif or sans serif. A ***serif font***, such as Times New Roman, has tiny lines at the ends of the characters that help guide the reader's eyes across the line of text. Serif fonts should be used for text-intensive reading, such as paragraphs.

A ***sans serif font***, such as Arial, does not have the tiny lines or extensions on the characters. Although a sans serif font has a crisp, clean look, it is difficult to read in large blocks of text, such as paragraphs. Use sans serif fonts for titles, headings, and other short blocks of text.

A ***designer font*** is a special font used in creative documents, such as wedding announcements, fliers, brochures, and other special-occasion documents. Examples of designer fonts include Broadway BT, Comic Sans MS, and Keystroke.

In addition to choosing the font, you should also consider the font size. ***Font size*** is the height of the characters, which is typically measured in points. One vertical inch contains about 72 points. You should use between 10-point and 12-point size for most correspondence and reports. Point sizes below 10 are difficult to read for detailed text, and point sizes above 12 are too big for regular paragraphs. However, you might want to use a larger font size for titles and headings so that they are emphasized.

Currently, your document is formatted in 12-point Times New Roman. You want to apply 24-point Arial to the title to make it stand out. In addition, you want to apply a font color to the bold *Microsoft Word* in the second paragraph.

To Change the Font, Font Size, and Font Color

❶ In the open `Office Software-WB3L` document, position the mouse pointer to the left side of the title *Microsoft Office Professional*.

(Continues)

To Change the Font, Font Size, and Font Color (Continued)

② **Click the mouse pointer in the selection bar area to select the title.**
You must select text to apply a different font, font size, and font color.

③ **Click the Font drop-down arrow on the Formatting toolbar.**
The Font menu displays the available fonts for the current printer (see Figure 3.5); your font list probably looks different. You can scroll through the list to see all the available fonts.

Times New Roman ▾

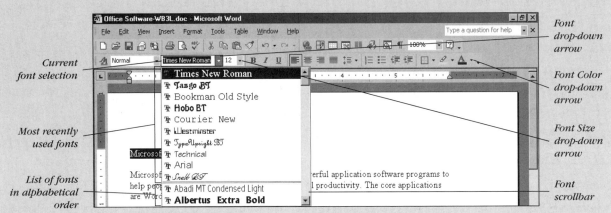

Figure 3.5

④ **Scroll down through the menu, and choose Arial.**
The title appears in Arial font. The Font button displays the font, *Arial*, for the currently selected text.

⑤ **Click the Font Size drop-down arrow.**
You see a list of different font sizes, ranging from 8 to 72.

12 ▾

⑥ **Choose *20* from the Font Size list and then click inside the text to deselect it.**
The title is now bigger at 20-point size. Notice that the Font Size button on the Formatting toolbar displays the font size, *20*, at the insertion point's location (see Figure 3.6).

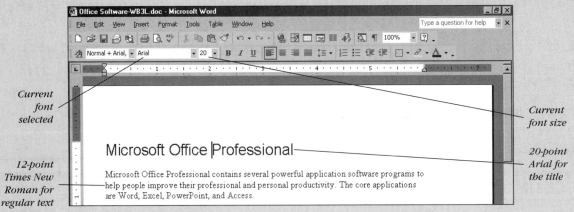

Figure 3.6

To Change the Font, Font Size, and Font Color

Titles are typically printed in a larger point size, but be careful that the title isn't too over-powering compared with the regular document text.

7 **Select the bold *Microsoft Word* at the beginning of the second paragraph.**
To apply a font color, you must select the text first.

8 **Click the Font Color drop-down arrow on the Formatting toolbar.**
The Font Color palette appears, so you can choose a color for the selected text. As you move your mouse over each color, you see a ScreenTip that tells you the exact color name, such as Blue, Light Blue, and Sky Blue.

If you have problems...

If you click the Font Color button (instead of the drop-down arrow), you immediately apply the default color, which is the last color someone selected. If this happens, select your text, and make sure you click the Font Color drop-down arrow to see the palette. The new color you choose replaces the previous color.

9 **Position the mouse pointer on the blue color, the third color from the right on the second row (see Figure 3.7).**

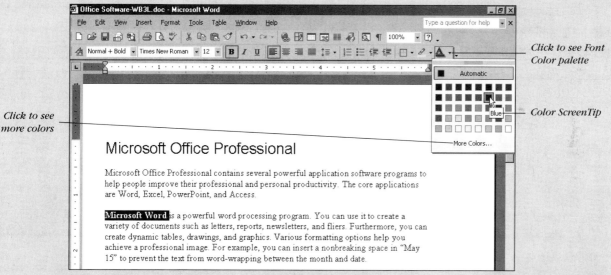

Figure 3.7

10 **Click Blue on the color palette to apply blue color to the selected text; then, deselect the text.**
Microsoft Word stands out more with the blue font color.

11 **Save the document, and keep it onscreen to continue with the next lesson.**

To extend your knowledge...

Keyboard Shortcuts for Changing Font Size

Select text and press Ctrl+[to decrease the font size one point at a time, or press Ctrl+] to increase the font size one point at a time.

Font and Font Size Keyboard Shortcuts

If your mouse isn't working, you can still access Font and Font Size on the Formatting toolbar. Press Ctrl+◆Shift+F to activate the Font button. Press Ctrl+◆Shift+P to activate the Font (point) Size button. For either list, press ↑ or ↓ to scroll through the list. You see only the font name or font size on the respective button as you press the scrolling keys on your keyboard. Press ↵Enter to select the font or size you want.

Lesson 3: Applying Character Effects and Spacing

In addition to changing the font face and font size, you might want to apply other font or character attributes. **Character effects** are special formats that you apply to characters. Font effects include strikethrough, superscript, subscript, emboss, and other special effects. You can even apply onscreen text effects or specify character spacing.

You can choose some character effects by using keyboard shortcuts. Table 3.2 shows the available keyboard shortcuts.

Table 3.2	**Special Effects Keyboard Shortcuts**
Keyboard Shortcut	**Effect**
Ctrl+◆Shift+=	Superscript
Ctrl+=	Subscript
Ctrl+◆Shift+D	Double Underline
Ctrl+◆Shift+W	Underline Words Only
Ctrl+◆Shift+K	Small Caps
Ctrl+◆Shift+A	All Caps
Ctrl+◆Shift+H	Hidden Text
Ctrl+Spacebar	Removes Character Effects

In this lesson, you insert the ® symbol, apply the superscript character effect, and set character spacing between letters in the title.

To Apply Character Effects

❶ In the *Office Software-WB3L* document, type **(r)** immediately after *Microsoft* in the title.
When you type the closing parenthesis, Word changes *(r)* to ®, the registered trademark symbol.

❷ Select only the ® symbol.
The symbol typically appears in superscript. You must select it to apply the superscript character effect.

❸ Choose F**o**rmat, **F**ont to display the Font dialog box.

To Apply Character Effects

The Font dialog box (see Figure 3.8) contains options for selecting the font, font style, size, font color, underline options, and character effects.

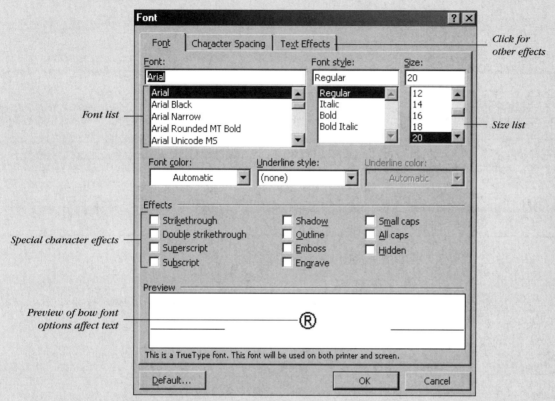

Figure 3.8

4 **Click the *Superscript* check box.**
A check mark appears in the check box to let you know the option is selected. The Preview window shows you that superscript text appears in smaller size and above the baseline.

5 **Click OK and deselect the text.**
Figure 3.9 shows the superscript symbol.

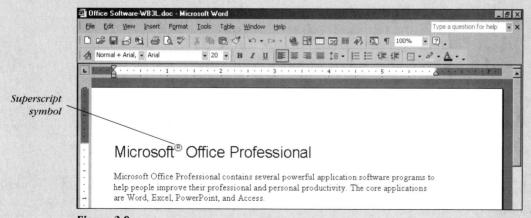

Figure 3.9

6 **Save the document, and keep it onscreen to continue with the next exercise.**

To extend your knowledge…

Font Dialog Box Keyboard Shortcut

The keyboard shortcut for accessing the Font dialog box is Ctrl+D.

Text Effects

You can select onscreen text effects to draw attention to selected text. Click the Text Effects tab in the Font dialog box. You can choose effects such as Blinking Background, Las Vegas Lights, and Marching Red Ants. These effects are for onscreen reading only; they do not appear on printouts.

The Font dialog box contains a set of options to adjust the character spacing. **Character spacing** is the amount of space between printed characters. Although most character spacing is acceptable, some character combinations appear too far apart or too close together in large-sized text. In the next exercise, you increase the character spacing between *f* and *t* in *Microsoft* and between *f* and *f* in *Office* so that the characters are properly spaced apart.

To Adjust Character Spacing

1   In the *Office Software-WB3L* document, select *ft* in *Microsoft* in the title.
The characters are too close together and need to be separated.

2   Choose F**o**rmat, **F**ont to display the Font dialog box.

3   Click the Cha**r**acter Spacing tab.
You have four options for adjusting the character spacing (see Figure 3.10).

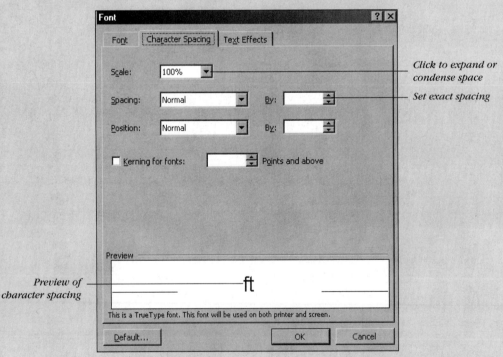

Figure 3.10

Scale increases or decreases the text horizontally as a percentage of its size. **Spacing** controls the amount of space between two or more characters. **Position** raises or lowers text from the baseline without creating superscript or subscript size. **Kerning** automatically adjusts spacing between characters to achieve a more evenly spaced appearance.

To Adjust Character Spacing

④ **Click the Spacing drop-down arrow, and choose Expanded.**
The *Spacing By* option displays *1 pt*, which increases the amount of space between characters by 1 pt.

⑤ **Click the Spacing By spin button to display *1.5 pt* and click OK.**
The selected letters have a little space between the characters now. Let's also adjust the character spacing between *f* and *f* in *Office*.

⑥ **Select *ff* in *Office* in the title.**

⑦ **Choose Format, Font.**
The Font dialog box displays the Character Spacing options.

⑧ **Click the Spacing drop-down arrow, choose Expanded, click the Spacing By increment button to *1.5 pt*, and click OK.**

⑨ **Deselect the text onscreen.**
Figure 3.11 shows the improved character spacing between the two sets of letters.

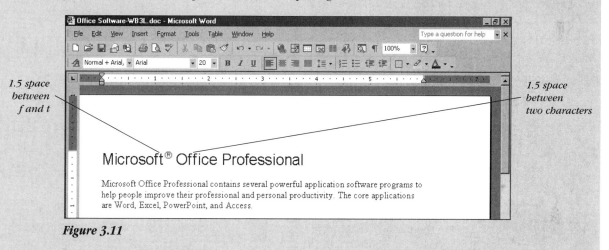

1.5 space between f and t

1.5 space between two characters

Figure 3.11

⑩ **Save the document, and keep it onscreen to continue with the next lesson.**

Lesson 4: Copying Formats with Format Painter

Similar headings and text within a document should have the same formatting. However, selecting every heading individually and clicking the desired format buttons (such as bold, underline, and font color) can be time-consuming.

By using the **Format Painter**, you can copy existing text formats to ensure consistency. As an added bonus, using the Format Painter takes fewer mouse clicks to format text than formatting each instance individually. In this lesson, you use Format Painter to copy formats (bold and blue color) from the first software name to the other software names.

To Copy Formats Using Format Painter

① **In the *Office Software-WB3L* document, click anywhere inside the bold, blue *Microsoft Word*.**
You need to click inside formatted text so that Word knows what formats you want to copy.

(Continues)

To Copy Formats Using Format Painter (Continued)

2 **Double-click the Format Painter button on the Standard toolbar.**
When you double-click the Format Painter button, the mouse pointer turns into a paintbrush next to the I-beam (see Figure 3.12).

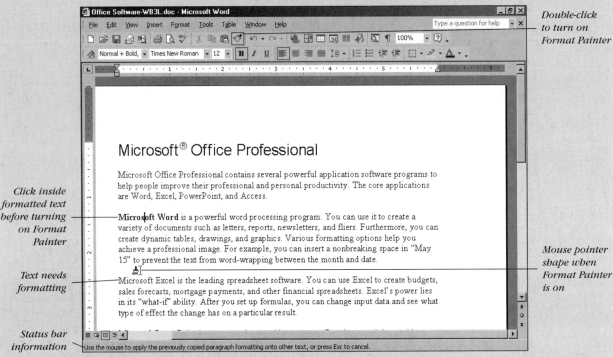

Double-click to turn on Format Painter

Click inside formatted text before turning on Format Painter

Text needs formatting

Status bar information

Mouse pointer shape when Format Painter is on

Figure 3.12

If you have problems...
Be careful where you click and drag with the Format Painter turned on; Word immediately formats any characters you select. If you accidentally format text, immediately click the Undo button to remove the format.

3 **Select *Microsoft Excel* at the beginning of the next paragraph.**
The second software name now has the same text enhancements as the first heading. Using Format Painter saves you from having to click two separate buttons (Bold and Font Color) to format the text.

If you have problems...
If the insertion point was *not* in formatted text when you turned on Format Painter, it won't copy any formats. If this happens, turn off Format Painter by clicking the Format Painter button again, click inside the formatted text you wish to copy, and then use Format Painter to copy the formats.

4 **Repeatedly click the scroll-down arrow on the vertical scrollbar until you see the last two paragraphs.**
You need to select the software names at the beginning of these two paragraphs.

5 **Select *Microsoft PowerPoint* and then select *Microsoft Access* to apply the text enhancements to these two software names.**

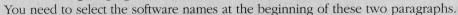

To Copy Formats Using Format Painter

After formatting the last text, turn off the Format Painter.

6 **Click the Format Painter button to turn off this feature.**

7 **Click inside the text to deselect it.**

The software names at the beginning of each paragraph are now formatted consistently (see Figure 3.13).

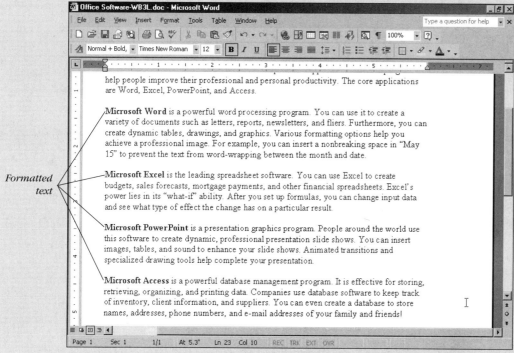

Formatted text

Figure 3.13

8 **Save the document and keep it onscreen to continue with the next lesson.**

To extend your knowledge...

Single- and Double-Clicking the Format Painter Button

If you single-click the Format Painter button, you can copy the formats only one time; then, Word turns off Format Painter.

If you double-click the Format Painter button, you can continue formatting additional text. To turn off Format Painter when you're done, click the Format Painter button once.

Formatting Headings

Instead of using Format Painter, you can create a paragraph style and apply it to your document headings. The benefit of a style over using Format Painter is that you can quickly edit the style formats, and all text formatted by that style is immediately updated. With Format Painter, you have to reapply the formats to the headings. Use the Help feature to learn how to create and apply paragraph styles.

Lesson 5: Highlighting Text

People often use a highlighting marker to highlight important parts of textbooks, magazine articles, and other documents. You can *highlight* text to draw the reader's attention to important information within the documents you create.

After reviewing the *Office Software-WB3L* document, you decide to highlight the phrase *improve their professional and personal productivity.*

To Highlight Text

❶ In the *Office Software-WB3L* document, press `Ctrl`+`Home` to position the insertion point at the beginning of the document.

❷ Select the phrase *improve their professional and personal productivity* in the first paragraph.

You want to highlight this phrase so it will stand out.

If you have problems...

If you have trouble clicking and dragging to select text, you can use keyboard shortcuts. First, position the insertion point at the beginning of the word *improve*; press and hold down `⇧Shift` while you click after the *y* in *productivity.*

---

❸ Click the Highlight button on the Formatting toolbar.

Word uses the default highlight color to highlight the text you selected. After you click the Highlight button, the text is deselected (see Figure 3.14)

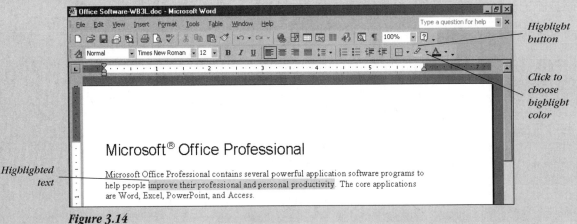

Highlight button

Click to choose highlight color

Highlighted text

Figure 3.14

❹ Save the document, and keep it onscreen to continue with the next lesson.

To extend your knowledge...

Using the Highlight Feature

You can click the Highlight button before selecting text. When you do this, the mouse pointer resembles a highlighting pen. You can then click and drag across text you want to highlight. The Highlight feature stays on, so you can highlight additional text. When you finish, click the Highlight button to turn it off. To remove highlight, select the highlighted text, click the Highlight drop-down arrow, and choose None.

Printing Highlighted Text

If you have a color printer, you see the highlight colors on your printout. If you're using a black-and-white printer, the highlight appears in shades of gray. Make sure that you can easily read the text with the gray highlight. If not, select a lighter highlight color, and print it again.

Lesson 6: Inserting Symbols

Although the keyboard contains some keys that produce symbols, such as the plus sign (+), hundreds of other symbols are not on the standard keyboard. For example, you might want to insert an ***em dash***, a dash the width of a lowercase m, to indicate a pause or change in thought, or an ***en dash***, a dash the width of a lowercase n, to indicate a series, such as pages 9–15.

You can display the Symbol dialog box to insert these special dashes, a copyright symbol, or a paragraph mark. In addition, you can select from a variety of specialized symbols such as a plane, data disk, spider web, and book. In this lesson, you insert the mouse symbol in the first paragraph.

To Insert a Symbol

❶ In the *Office Software-WB3L* document, position the insertion point at the end of the first paragraph.
This is where you want to insert the symbol.

❷ Choose Insert, Symbol.
The Symbol dialog box appears (see Figure 3.15).

Click to select a font

Click to see other characters

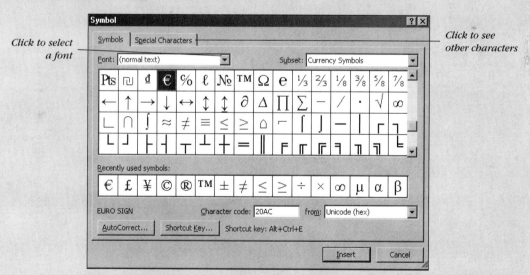

Figure 3.15

The dialog box has two tabs: Symbols and Special Characters. The Symbols tab provides access to hundreds of special symbols; the Special Characters tab provides access to standard characters, such as the em dash.

❸ Click the Font drop-down arrow, and choose Wingdings if it is not already selected.
Some of the most interesting and diverse symbols are located in Wingdings, Wingdings 2, Wingdings 3, and Webdings. Figure 3.16 shows the Wingdings symbols.

(Continues)

To Insert a Symbol (Continued)

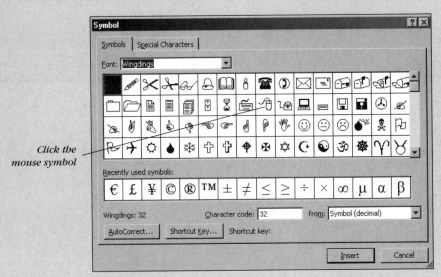

Figure 3.16

❹ **Click the mouse symbol in the middle of the second row.**
This is the symbol that looks like an aerial view of a mouse.

❺ **Click Insert to place the symbol at the insertion point.**
The Cancel button changes to the Close button after you insert a symbol.

❻ **Click Close to close the Symbol dialog box.**
Figure 3.17 shows the symbol in the paragraph.

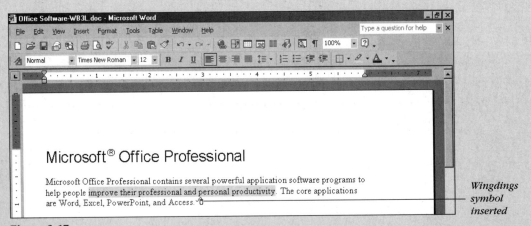

Figure 3.17

❼ **Save the document, and keep it onscreen to continue with the next lesson.**

To extend your knowledge...

Using Common Symbols

If you're asked to insert a common symbol—such as an em dash, copyright symbol, or registered symbol—you can insert them from the Special Characters section of the Symbol dialog box (see Figure 3.18), or you can use the keyboard shortcuts, if available.

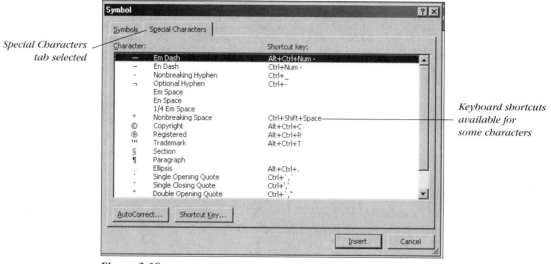

Figure 3.18

Lesson 7: Displaying Formatting Marks

The document onscreen looks basically like what its printout looks like. This feature is known as "What You See Is What You Get" (**WYSIWYG**). Although you see most formatting, you don't see everything. For example, you might not know at a glance whether you pressed (Tab⇆) or (Spacebar) to indent text. Although either method might be acceptable in the short run, the spacing might look different if you print your document on a different system.

To help you see how your document is formatted, display formatting marks. **Formatting marks** are nonprinting symbols and characters that indicate spaces, tabs, hyphen types, page breaks, and hard returns. A **hard return** is where you press (↵Enter) to start a new line instead of letting text word-wrap to the next line. Table 3.3 shows common formatting marks and what they indicate.

Table 3.3	Formatting Marks
Symbol	**Description**
·	space
°	nonbreaking space
-	hyphen
—	nonbreaking hyphen
→	tab
¶	end of paragraph

To Show and Hide Formatting Marks

❶ Click the Show/Hide ¶ button on the Standard toolbar.
You now see nonprinting formatting marks within your document, as shown in Figure 3.19.

(Continues)

To Show and Hide Formatting Marks (Continued)

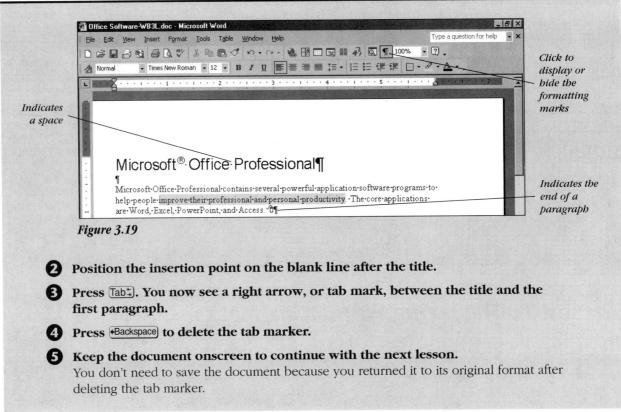

Figure 3.19

② **Position the insertion point on the blank line after the title.**

③ **Press [Tab↹]. You now see a right arrow, or tab mark, between the title and the first paragraph.**

④ **Press [⬅Backspace] to delete the tab marker.**

⑤ **Keep the document onscreen to continue with the next lesson.**
You don't need to save the document because you returned it to its original format after deleting the tab marker.

To extend your knowledge...

Displaying Formatting Marks

If you don't see all three types of formatting marks, you need to display the Options dialog box to change the default. To view all formatting marks, choose <u>T</u>ools on the menu bar and choose <u>O</u>ptions. When the Options dialog box appears, click the View tab and then click the <u>A</u>ll check box in the Formatting marks section. Click OK to close the dialog box.

Lesson 8: Inserting Nonbreaking Spaces and Hyphens

By now you know that the word-wrap feature wraps a word to the next line if it doesn't fit at the end of the current line. Occasionally, word-wrapping between certain types of words is undesirable; that is, some words should be kept together. For example, the date *March 31* should stay together instead of word-wrapping after *March*. Other items that should stay together include names, such as *Ms. Stevenson*, and page references, such as *page 15*. To prevent words from separating due to the word-wrap feature, insert a ***nonbreaking space*** or a hard space.

As you review your document, you notice that the words *May* and *15* word-wrap between the two words. You want to keep *May 15* together on the same line.

To Insert a Nonbreaking Space

1 In the *Office Software-WB3L* document, click the Show/Hide ¶ button on the Standard toolbar if the formatting marks are not already displayed.

2 Position the insertion point after *May* at the end of the fourth line in the second paragraph.

You need to delete the regular space after *May* and replace it with a nonbreaking space to keep *May 15* together (see Figure 3.20).

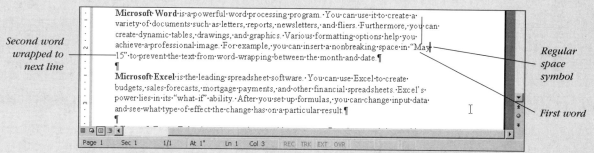

Figure 3.20

3 Press Del to delete the regular space.

This brings *May15* together without any space between the two words.

4 Press Ctrl+⇧Shift+Spacebar.

Word now keeps *May 15* together. Notice the difference in the nonbreaking space symbol and the regular space symbol (see Figure 3.21).

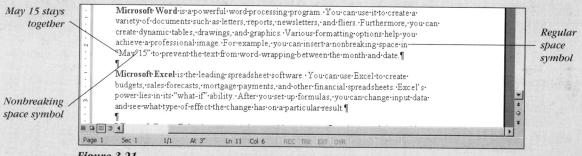

Figure 3.21

5 Click the Show/Hide ¶ button on the Standard toolbar to hide the symbols.

6 Save the document and close it.

To extend your knowledge...

Nonbreaking Hyphens

Hyphens cause another word-wrap problem. Words containing hyphens can word-wrap at the hyphen location, causing undesirable results. Certain hyphenated text, such as phone numbers, should stay together.

To keep hyphenated words together, replace the regular hyphen with a nonbreaking hyphen. A ***nonbreaking hyphen*** keeps text on both sides of the hyphen together. To insert a nonbreaking hyphen, press Ctrl+⇧Shift+-.

When you display the formatting symbols, a regular hyphen looks like a hyphen. A nonbreaking hyphen appears as a wider hyphen. However, the nonbreaking hyphen looks like a regular hyphen when printed.

Inserting Nonbreaking Spaces and Hyphens from the Symbols Dialog Box

Instead of using the keyboard shortcuts, you can insert nonbreaking spaces and hyphens from the Special Characters page of the Symbols dialog box.

Summary

In this project, you used character formats such as bold to emphasize text. You also selected fonts, font sizes, font colors, and character spacing to enhance the visual effectiveness of documents. By using Format Painter, you can save time by copying text formats to other text in your document. Furthermore, you can highlight text to draw attention to important ideas. You can prevent word-wrapping between words by using nonbreaking spaces and hyphens. Finally, you can display the nonprinting symbols to help you see spacing, tabs, and hard returns.

For additional information, use the Help feature to learn more about these topics. In addition, complete the following end-of-project exercises to reinforce and build on the skills you acquired in this project.

Checking Concepts and Terms

Multiple Choice

Circle the letter of the correct answer for each of the following.

1. All of the following have keyboard shortcuts except _____. [L1]

   a. underline

   b. font color

   c. bold

   d. italic

2. How many points are in a vertical inch? [L2]

   a. 10

   b. 12

   c. 24

   d. 72

3. Which effect only appears onscreen and not on a printout? [L3]

   a. Blinking background

   b. Superscript

   c. Strikethrough

   d. Emboss

4. What nonprinting format symbol represents a nonbreaking space? [L7]

   a. •

   b. ¶

   c. →

   d. °

5. Look at Figure 3.4, and identify an example of a serif font. [L2]

   a. Arial Rounded MT Bold

   b. Courier New

   c. Keystroke

   d. Westminster

Screen ID

Label each element of the Word screen shown in Figure 3.22.

A. Font Color button

B. Format Painter button

C. Highlight button

D. Nonbreaking space symbol

E. Paragraph symbol

F. Tab symbol

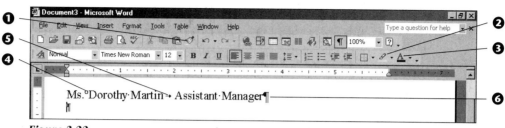

Figure 3.22

1. _____   4. _____

2. _____   5. _____

3. _____   6. _____

Discussion

1. Find two examples of documents (for example, the minutes of a meeting, the letter to stockholders in a company's annual report, or a magazine article) that use character formats. Identify the types of character formats and evaluate their effectiveness. If the character formats are not effective, provide suggestions for improving the document. [L1–8]

2. What is the purpose of displaying formatting marks? Provide an example when you should have the formatting marks displayed. [L7]

3. Explain how em dashes, en dashes, and nonbreaking hyphens differ. Provide an example of the use of each. [L6, 8]

Skill Drill exercises reinforce project skills. Each skill reinforced is the same, or nearly the same, as a skill presented in the project. Detailed instructions are provided in a step-by-step format.

1. Using Character Formats and Font Attributes to Enhance a Newsletter

You work for an apartment complex manager. She just finished typing the October newsletter and wants you to enhance its appearance.

1. Open *ew1-0302*, and save it as `October Newsletter-WB3SD`.
2. Click and drag across the first two lines of text.
3. Click the Font drop-down arrow; and choose Arial Rounded MT Bold, Kabel Dm BT, or Tahoma.
4. Deselect both lines and select the first line only.
5. Click the Font Size drop-down arrow, and choose 18.
6. Select the first heading, *Water Hoses*.
7. Click the Bold button.
8. Click the Font Color drop-down arrow, and choose Pink.

9. Click inside the *Water Hoses* heading to deselect it.

10. Save the document, and keep it onscreen to continue with the next exercise.

2. Using Format Painter to Format Other Headings

To save time applying character formats and font attributes to other headings, you want to use Format Painter to copy the formats from the *Water Hoses* heading to the other headings.

1. In the open *October Newsletter-WB3SD* document, make sure that the insertion point is inside the *Water Hoses* heading and then double-click the Format Painter button.

2. Scroll down to see *Thermostat Settings* at the top of the screen.

3. Click and drag across *Thermostat Settings* with the Format Painter mouse pointer.

4. Click and drag across *Sidewalk Salt* and then click and drag across *Laundry Room Hours.*

5. Click the Format Painter button to turn off this feature.

6. Save the document, and keep it onscreen to continue with the next exercise.

3. Applying Character Effects and Character Spacing

You decide to apply the Small Caps character effect to the second line to add some contrast to the headings. In addition, you notice that some characters are too close together in the main title and need to be separated.

1. In the *October Newsletter-WB3SD* document, select *October 2004 Newsletter.*

2. Choose Format, Font. If needed, click the Font tab.

3. Click the Font tab, if necessary, to see the Font options.

4. Click the Small caps check box and then click OK.

5. Click and drag across *rt* in *Apartment* in the main title.

6. Choose Format, Font.

7. Click the Character Spacing tab.

8. Click the Spacing drop-down arrow, and choose Expanded.

9. Click the Spacing By increment button to 1.3 and then click OK.

10. Click inside the document to deselect the text.

11. Save the document, and keep it onscreen to continue with the next exercise.

4. Highlighting Text and Inserting a Symbol in the Newsletter

You want to highlight a sentence so that it stands out for your tenants. In addition, you want to insert a thermometer symbol as a visual effect.

1. In the *October Newsletter-WB3SD* document, press and hold down Ctrl while you click the mouse button on the sentence *Please disconnect these hoses by October 15.* in the second paragraph.

2. Click the Highlight button.

3. Click on the right side of the *Thermostat Settings* heading.

4. Choose Insert, Symbol.

5. Click the Symbols tab, if needed, to display symbol options.

6. Click the Font drop-down arrow and choose Webdings.

7. Click the scroll-down arrow nine times.

8. Click the thermometer symbol, which is the second symbol from the left (fourth row down).

9. Click Insert and then click Close.

10. Select the thermometer symbol, and click the Bold button to remove bold from the symbol.

11. Save the document. and keep it onscreen to continue with the next exercise.

5. Inserting a Nonbreaking Space and En Dashes

The newsletter is almost done. However, you need to insert a nonbreaking space to keep *7 a.m.* together. In addition, you want to insert en dashes in the times to look professional.

1. In the *October Newsletter-WB3SD* document, press Ctrl+End to position the insertion point at the end of the document.

2. Click the Show/Hide ¶ button to see the nonprinting symbols, if they are not already displayed.

3. Click to the immediate right of 7, and press Del to delete the regular space symbol.

4. Press Ctrl+⇧Shift+Spacebar to insert a nonbreaking space.

5. Click after *Monday* on the previous line, and press Del to delete the regular space symbol.

6. Choose Insert, Symbol.

7. Click the Special Characters tab.

8. Click En Dash, click Insert, and then click Close to insert an en dash between *Monday* and *Thursday*.

9. Click after *Friday* on the next line and press Del to delete the regular space symbol.

10. Press Ctrl+- (the minus key on the numeric keypad) to insert an en dash without having to access the Symbol dialog box.

11. Save the document, print it, and then close it.

Challenge

Challenge exercises expand on or are somewhat related to skills presented in the lessons. Each exercise provides a brief narrative introduction, followed by instructions in a numbered-step format that are not as detailed as those in the Skill Drill section.

1. Enhancing an Apartment Complex Newsletter

You need to update the apartment newsletter for December. You want to change some text, apply character formats, insert symbols, and add highlighting.

1. Open *ew1-0302*, and save it as *December Newsletter-WB3CH1*.

2. Make the following edits:
   - Change *October 2004* to December 2004.
   - Change *Winter will soon be* to Winter is now.
   - Select and delete the heading and paragraph about *Water Hoses*.
   - Select and delete the heading and paragraph about *Laundry Room Hours*.

3. Add this heading and section below the first paragraph:

Christmas Trees

Only artificial trees are permitted in apartments. We know many residents prefer live trees, but they pose a fire hazard; therefore, our insurance company will not permit live trees in apartments. If you want the aroma of a live Christmas tree, we suggest you purchase pine-scented fragrances at the local discount store and spray your artificial tree.

4. Make sure that you have a blank line above and below the new heading and a blank line after the new paragraph you typed.

5. Add this heading and section at the end of the document:

Open House

Be sure to stop by the office on December 20 for the annual Holiday Party. From 5:30 p.m. to 8:00 p.m., enjoy refreshments while visiting with the management team and your neighbors.

6. Apply 18-point Arial bold Green font color to the title, and apply 14-point Arial italic Red font color to the secondary title.

7. Select the *Christmas Trees* heading, and apply 12-point Arial bold italic. Use the Format Painter to copy these formats to the other headings.

8. Highlight in yellow the following text:
   - the first sentence of the first paragraph
   - *December 20* in the last paragraph
   - *5:30 p.m. to 8:00 p.m.* in the last paragraph

9. Insert nonbreaking spaces within *5:30 p.m.* and *8:00 p.m.*

10. Insert the symbol of a house on the right side of the heading *Open House*. The house symbol is located on the third row, ninth column in Webdings font symbols. Remove the bold and italic format from the symbol.

11. Delete the word *degrees* in the second paragraph in the *Thermostat Settings* section. Insert the degree symbol to the immediate right of *60*. This symbol is located in the normal font symbol palette.

12. Save, print, and close the document.

2. Enhancing a Letter to a Student Organization

You prepared a response to a student organization that is interested in holding a fundraiser for a charitable contribution. You work with the student organizations to inform them of the required sales tax forms for their vendors. You now want to enhance the letter to make certain points stand out.

1. Open *ew1-0303*, and save it as `Tax Letter-WB3CH2`.

2. Emphasize the subject line by making it bold and applying Arial Narrow font to *Sales Tax Forms for the Gift and Craft Fair.*

3. Use Bright Green highlight on the phrase *must return the master forms to the tax commission's office by December 15.*

4. Display the formatting marks. Insert nonbreaking spaces and hyphens in the appropriate locations. (Hint: You need at least one of each.)

5. Italicize and bold the last sentence in the third paragraph; then, apply Red font color to the sentence.

6. Save, print, and close the document.

3. Creating a Health Benefits Memo

You work in your company's Benefits Office. You need to prepare a memo to inform employees of a few changes and of upcoming seminars that further explain the changes.

1. From a new window, create the document shown in Figure 3.23, applying character formats and Arial font as shown.

2. Apply Red font color to *Changes in Benefits.*

3. Use Format Painter to copy formats from the first heading to the other heading.

4. Display the formatting marks. Make sure that you have two paragraph marks at the end of the *TO*, *FROM*, and *DATE* lines. Make sure that you have three paragraph marks after the *SUBJECT* line.

5. Correct all spelling and typographical errors.

6. Select the dates at the bottom of the memo, press Tab to indent them, and apply Red font color to them.

7. Highlight the last sentence in Turquoise.

8. Insert nonbreaking spaces and hyphens, if needed.

9. Save the document as `Health Benefits Memo-WB3CH3`; then print and close it.

TO: Full-Time Employees

FROM: Student Name, Benefits Office

DATE: March 1, 2004

SUBJECT: Health-Care Plan Options

It's that time of year again when we update all employees' health benefit records. This memo provides some information about changes and seminars.

Changes in Benefits

The co-pay on prescription drugs has increased slightly. Generic prescriptions are now $5, and brand-name prescriptions are $10. We had to compromise with the service provider to keep the premiums as low as possible.

We've selected another provider for dental benefits. Employees will still receive the same value and services with no out-of-pocket premiums. The deductibles are also the same. However, to receive full coverage, employees must select a dentist on the provider's list. The list will be distributed at the upcoming seminars.

Seminars

Additional information will be provided through seminars for all employees. At the end of each one-hour seminar, you will receive enrollment forms for the fiscal year starting on July 1. Please attend one of the following seminars:

March 10 @ 1:15 p.m.
March 12 @ 8:30 a.m.
March 16 @ 3:30 p.m.

All seminars are held in the Lincoln Conference Room. Refreshments will be served.

Figure 3.23

4. Enhancing an Advertisement Flier

In Project 2, you created an announcement to college students about your Mega Music store's special discount. Now, you want to create and enhance a flier to go on bulletin boards around the campus.

1. Open *ew1-0304*, and save it as **Mega Music Flier-WB3CH4**.
2. Select the entire document, and apply 20-point Comic Sans MS font.
3. Select the first two lines in the document, and apply 28-point Arial Rounded MT Bold in Violet font color. (If you don't have Arial Rounded MT Bold, ask your instructor for an alternative sans serif font face.)
4. Apply an appropriate highlight color to the three lines that list the discount percentages.
5. Delete the asterisk, and insert the Webdings symbol that looks like two masks—the symbol that you often see for theatrical events. The symbol is on the ninth row of symbols. Select the symbol and apply 72-point size with Violet font color.

6. Insert the telephone symbol from the Wingdings symbols at the beginning of the phone number on the last line of the document.

7. Delete *to* between *9 a.m. to 9 p.m.* and insert an en dash. Delete any spaces before and after the en dash.

8. Save, print, and close the document.

5. Formatting Text in a Software Information Sheet

Your supervisor wants you to apply some different formatting to the information sheet about Microsoft Office Professional. He recommends using different fonts, font color, and other character formats.

1. Open *ew1-0301*, and save it as `Office Software Sheet-WB3CH5`.

2. Select the entire document, and apply Bookman Old Style font.

3. Apply these formats to the title: 16-point Albertus Medium or Arial bold font (or a font of your instructor's choice), Dark Blue font color, and Yellow highlight color.

4. Press Tab⇥ to indent the first line of each paragraph except the first paragraph.

5. Use Overtype mode to change *newsletters, and fliers* to `fliers, and newsletters` in the Microsoft Word paragraph.

6. Make the following changes:
   - *May 15* to `November 21`
   - *financial spreadsheets* to `financial statements`
   - *Excel's power lies in its* to `Business people appreciate Excel's powerful`

7. Insert a nonbreaking hyphen and a nonbreaking space in the appropriate locations.

8. Apply bold, Arial, Dark Blue font color to *Microsoft Word*. Use the Format Painter to duplicate the character formats for *Microsoft Excel*, *Microsoft PowerPoint*, and *Microsoft Access*.

9. Insert ® after *Microsoft* in the title. Make it appear in superscript.

10. Save, print, and close the document.

Discovery Zone exercises require advanced knowledge of topics presented in *essentials* lessons, application of skills from multiple lessons, or self-directed learning of new skills.

1. Enhancing a Restaurant Review Article

You are the newly appointed restaurant critic for your college newspaper. Your first article is to introduce your column and define your grading scale. Open *ew1-0305*, and save it as `Restaurant Review-WB3DZ1`. Change * to your name and ** to your e-mail address, such as `name@college.edu`.

Apply 10-point Comic Sans MS font to the entire document. Apply 14-point Arial, Plum font color, and Blinking Background text effect to the title. Use the Help feature to learn more about text effects. Use your judgment in adjusting character spacing as needed within the title. Also activate kerning for point sizes above 12. Insert any necessary nonbreaking spaces or hyphens in the correct locations.

Use Figure 3.24 to finish formatting the document. Pay close attention to detail. Use the Symbol dialog box to locate and insert é in the last sentence. Save, print, and close the document.

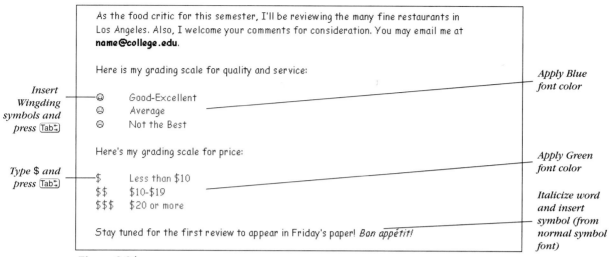

As the food critic for this semester, I'll be reviewing the many fine restaurants in Los Angeles. Also, I welcome your comments for consideration. You may email me at **name@college.edu**.

Here is my grading scale for quality and service:

Insert Wingding symbols and press Tab⇥ — ☺ Good-Excellent
☺ Average
☺ Not the Best

Apply Blue font color

Here's my grading scale for price:

Type $ and press Tab⇥ — $ Less than $10
$$ $10-$19
$$$ $20 or more

Apply Green font color

Stay tuned for the first review to appear in Friday's paper! *Bon appétit!*

Italicize word and insert symbol (from normal symbol font)

Figure 3.24

2. Creating a Notice for a Professor's Door

You are a student worker for a department on your college campus. You were asked to create a notice to tape to a professor's door. Create the notice shown in Figure 3.25 by using the formats specified.

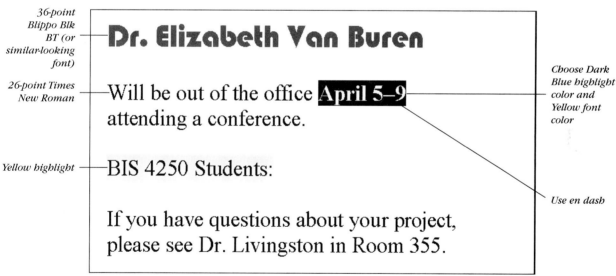

36-point Blippo Blk BT (or similar-looking font) — **Dr. Elizabeth Van Buren**

26-point Times New Roman — Will be out of the office **April 5–9** attending a conference.

Choose Dark Blue highlight color and Yellow font color

Use en dash

Yellow highlight — BIS 4250 Students:

If you have questions about your project, please see Dr. Livingston in Room 355.

Figure 3.25

Apply a custom color to the title using these settings: Hue 238, Sat 128, Lum 133, Red 194, Green 72, and Blue 121. Use Help, if needed, to learn how to create a custom font color.

Save the document as `Office Door Notice-WB3DZ2`, and print it. Fold the note in half, just below the last text line.

3. Experimenting with the Software Announcement

You want to experiment with the *Office Software-WB3L* document you formatted within the lessons. Open the document, and save it as `Office Software-WB3DZ3`.

Experiment with different fonts for the main title. Try Outline, Emboss, and Engrave character effects (individually). Decide which effect looks the best, and apply it again.

Experiment with different highlight colors and font color combinations on the text *Microsoft Word* that is currently bold. Use Format Painter to copy the formats to the other headings.

Select the paragraphs, and choose another serif font face.

Find and insert these symbols in front of their respective paragraphs:

video camera	PowerPoint
line chart	Excel
miniature letter	Word
three computer monitors	Access

Select each symbol and remove the bold formatting. Save, print, and close the document.

Editing Documents

Objectives

In this project, you learn how to

- ✔ Insert and Modify Date and Time Fields
- ✔ Change the Case of Text
- ✔ Cut, Copy, and Paste Text
- ✔ Copy Between Document Windows
- ✔ Undo and Redo Actions
- ✔ Use AutoCorrect
- ✔ Use the Thesaurus

Key terms introduced in this project include

- ❑ action
- ❑ active document window
- ❑ AutoCorrect
- ❑ case
- ❑ copy
- ❑ cut
- ❑ date or time field
- ❑ object
- ❑ Office Clipboard
- ❑ paste
- ❑ Paste Options Smart Tag
- ❑ Redo
- ❑ synonyms
- ❑ Undo

Why Would I Do This?

Editing is an important step when preparing documents for yourself or for others. For example, you might have the perfect paragraph, but it's not in the best location. Or, you might have several documents that contain information that you need to pull together into a new document. Furthermore, you might need to change capitalization style for text without retyping it, or you might need to edit words by choosing synonyms.

In this project, you learn how to insert and modify the date and time, change capitalization style, rearrange text, and copy text from one document to another. In addition, you learn how to use Undo, AutoCorrect, and Thesaurus during the editing process.

Visual Summary

Figure 4.1 shows a document that contains a capitalized paragraph, a paragraph in the wrong location, and a word that needs to be changed.

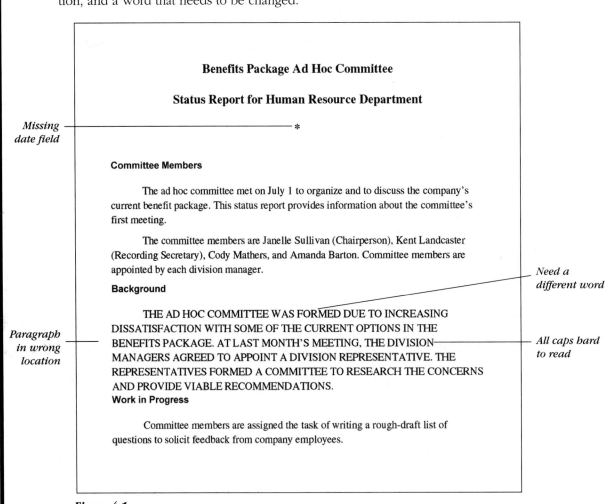

Benefits Package Ad Hoc Committee

Status Report for Human Resource Department

Missing date field ————————————————— *

Committee Members

The ad hoc committee met on July 1 to organize and to discuss the company's current benefit package. This status report provides information about the committee's first meeting.

The committee members are Janelle Sullivan (Chairperson), Kent Landcaster (Recording Secretary), Cody Mathers, and Amanda Barton. Committee members are appointed by each division manager.

Background

THE AD HOC COMMITTEE WAS FORMED DUE TO INCREASING DISSATISFACTION WITH SOME OF THE CURRENT OPTIONS IN THE BENEFITS PACKAGE. AT LAST MONTH'S MEETING, THE DIVISION MANAGERS AGREED TO APPOINT A DIVISION REPRESENTATIVE. THE REPRESENTATIVES FORMED A COMMITTEE TO RESEARCH THE CONCERNS AND PROVIDE VIABLE RECOMMENDATIONS.

Work in Progress

Committee members are assigned the task of writing a rough-draft list of questions to solicit feedback from company employees.

Paragraph in wrong location

Need a different word

All caps hard to read

Figure 4.1

Figure 4.2 shows the document after it has been edited.

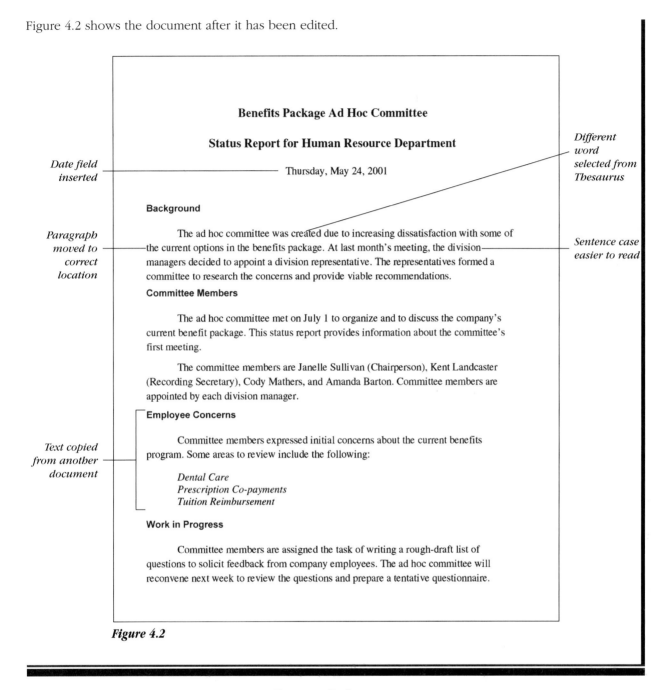

Date field inserted

Paragraph moved to correct location

Text copied from another document

Different word selected from Thesaurus

Sentence case easier to read

Benefits Package Ad Hoc Committee

Status Report for Human Resource Department

Thursday, May 24, 2001

Background

The ad hoc committee was created due to increasing dissatisfaction with some of the current options in the benefits package. At last month's meeting, the division managers decided to appoint a division representative. The representatives formed a committee to research the concerns and provide viable recommendations.

Committee Members

The ad hoc committee met on July 1 to organize and to discuss the company's current benefit package. This status report provides information about the committee's first meeting.

The committee members are Janelle Sullivan (Chairperson), Kent Landcaster (Recording Secretary), Cody Mathers, and Amanda Barton. Committee members are appointed by each division manager.

Employee Concerns

Committee members expressed initial concerns about the current benefits program. Some areas to review include the following:

Dental Care
Prescription Co-payments
Tuition Reimbursement

Work in Progress

Committee members are assigned the task of writing a rough-draft list of questions to solicit feedback from company employees. The ad hoc committee will reconvene next week to review the questions and prepare a tentative questionnaire.

Figure 4.2

Lesson 1: Inserting and Modifying Date and Time Fields

Previously, you learned that AutoComplete can help you enter some month names and the current date, such as September 24, 2004. However, you might want to use other date formats, such as 9/24/04 or 24 September 2004. In addition, you might want to insert the time in a document. In these situations, you need to use the Date and Time dialog box to insert other date or time formats.

Furthermore, you might need to insert a date or time that always displays the current date—not the date or time that you insert it. In this case, you need to insert a ***date or time field***, a placeholder for a date or time that needs to change to reflect the current date or time when opened or printed.

In this lesson, you insert and modify a date field.

To Insert Date and Time Fields

① **Open *ew1-0401*, and save it as** `Status Report-WB4L`.
You want to delete the asterisk below the second title and replace it with a date field.

② **Delete the asterisk, and leave the insertion point in that location.**

③ **Choose Insert, Date and Time.**
The Date and Time dialog box appears, showing you the available formats (see Figure 4.3).

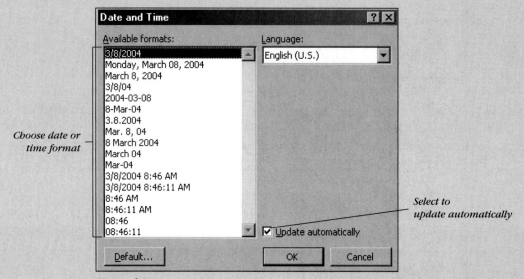

Choose date or time format

Select to update automatically

Figure 4.3

Your dates and times are different from those shown in the figures in this book. When choosing date or time options, choose the format that resembles the format specified in the instructions or in the figures.

④ **Choose format *8 March 2004* in the *Available formats* list box.**

⑤ **Click the *Update automatically* check box, if it's not already selected.**
If you want to create a date or time field that automatically updates the date, you must make sure that the *Update automatically* check box is selected.

⑥ **Click OK, and position the insertion point inside the date.**
Figure 4.4 shows the current date with a shaded background, which indicates that it is a date field.

To Insert Date and Time Fields

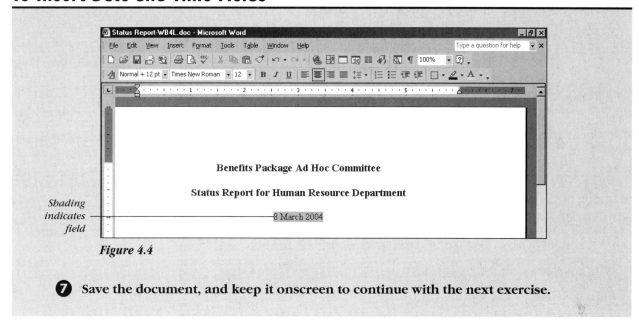

Figure 4.4

7 **Save the document, and keep it onscreen to continue with the next exercise.**

To extend your knowledge...

Updating Date and Time Fields

When you open the document on another date, the date field should reflect that particular date, not the date that you inserted the date field. If the date or time does not update automatically, click inside the field and press F9, or right-click within the field and choose *Update Field* from the shortcut menu.

After inserting a date or time field, you might want to choose a different format. You can easily modify the format of the date or time field. In addition to changing the field's characteristics, you can also change how it is formatted, such as fonts, and so on. In the next exercise, you modify the field to look like *Monday, March 08, 2004*.

To Modify a Date or Time Field

1 **In the open *Status Report-WB3L* document, right-click within the date.**
Right-clicking within the date field displays a shortcut menu (see Figure 4.5).

(Continues)

To Modify a Date or Time Field (Continued)

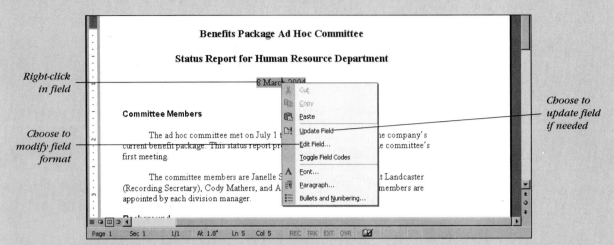

Figure 4.5

❷ Choose _Edit Field_.

The Field dialog box appears so that you can select a different date or time field format (see Figure 4.6).

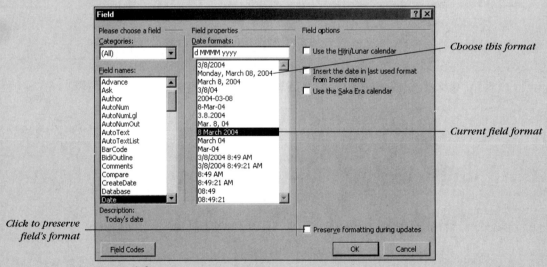

Figure 4.6

❸ Choose _Monday, March 08, 2004_ format.

❹ Click the _Preserve formatting during updates_ check box and then click OK.

Clicking the _Preserve formatting during updates_ check box maintains any formatting you have applied to the date or time field. Otherwise, you lose the field's formats.

The date should now appear as _Monday, March 08, 2004_.

❺ Save the document and keep it onscreen to continue with the next lesson.

To extend your knowledge...

Creating Date and Time Field Codes

If you don't see any fields that display the date or time exactly as you want, you can create your own format from within the Field dialog box. Click the Field Codes button, and enter the date or time codes exactly as you want the date or time to appear. For more information, type `Date-Time Picture field switch` in the Ask a Question text box to display Help topics to create advanced date and time fields.

Lesson 2: Changing the Case of Text

It's frustrating to discover that you typed an entire paragraph (or more) in all capital letters before realizing that you forgot to turn off Caps Lock! Instead of deleting and retyping everything you worked so hard to type, you can select the text and change its *case*. **Case** refers to the capitalization style, such as lowercase or uppercase, of text.

In this lesson, you notice that a full paragraph is capitalized. You need to change the case of the text to be consistent with the other paragraphs.

To Change the Case of Text

❶ In the open *Status Report-WB4L* document, scroll down to see the capitalized paragraph.
The third paragraph is formatted in all capital letters. You want to select a different case style.

❷ Select the third paragraph, which is currently formatted in all capital letters.
You must select the text that you want to change to a different case.

❸ Choose Fo**rmat, Change Cas**e**.**

If you have problems...

If you don't see the *Change Case* option, position the mouse pointer on the downward-pointing arrows at the bottom of the F**o**rmat menu to see the full menu.

The Change Case dialog box appears (see Figure 4.7).

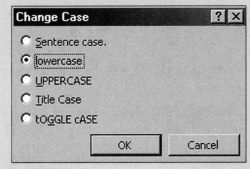

Figure 4.7

(Continues)

To Change the Case of Text (Continued)

The *Sentence case* option capitalizes only the first letter of each sentence. The *lowercase* option changes the selected text to lowercase letters. The *UPPERCASE* option changes the selected text to all capital letters. The *Title Case* option capitalizes the first letter of each word. The *tOGGLE cASE* option reverses the capitalization of selected text. For example, it changes uppercase letters to lowercase and lowercase letters to uppercase.

4 **Click *Sentence case* and click OK.**
Now, only the first letter of each sentence is capitalized. After changing the case, you should read the text and individually capitalize the first letter of proper nouns.

5 **Deselect the paragraph.**
Figure 4.8 shows how your paragraph should look after changing the case.

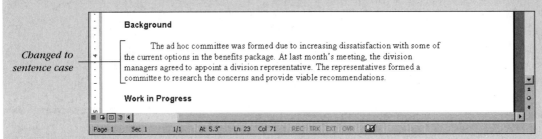

Changed to sentence case

Background

The ad hoc committee was formed due to increasing dissatisfaction with some of the current options in the benefits package. At last month's meeting, the division managers agreed to appoint a division representative. The representatives formed a committee to research the concerns and provide viable recommendations.

Work in Progress

Page 1   Sec 1   1/1   At 5.3"   Ln 23   Col 71   REC TRK EXT OVR

Figure 4.8

6 **Save the document, and keep it onscreen to continue with the next lesson.**

To extend your knowledge...

Using Title Case

After you use the *Title Case* option from the Change Case dialog box on headings, you should change the first letter of small words to lowercase, such as *in* and *the* in the middle of the heading.

Using Keyboard Shortcuts

You can press `⬆Shift`+`F3` to change selected text to uppercase, lowercase, or sentence caps. Keep pressing this shortcut to cycle through the case options until the text appears in the case you want.

To quickly change selected text to all capitals, press `Ctrl`+`⬆Shift`+`A`.

Lesson 3: Cutting, Copying, and Pasting Text

After you create a document, you might decide to rearrange sentences and paragraphs to improve the clarity and organization of the content. You might want to move a paragraph to a different location, rearrange the sentences within a paragraph, or move sentences from different paragraphs to form one paragraph.

Here is the general process of moving text:

1. Select the text or ***object***, a non-text visual item such as an image or chart, which you want to move.
2. ***Cut*** or remove the selected item from its current location, and place it in the **Office Clipboard**, a temporary holding place for up to 24 items you cut or copy.
3. Position the insertion point where you want the text to appear.

4. *Paste* the item in its new location. Pasting inserts the item that you cut or copied to the Office Clipboard.

In some cases, you need to duplicate, or ***copy***, text or an object. Instead of removing the text, you use the Copy command instead of the Cut command in Step 2. The Copy command leaves the original text or object in its location while making a duplicate in the Clipboard.

In this lesson, you move the Background section from its current location so that it's above the Committee Members section.

To Move Text

❶ In the ***Status Report-WB4L*** **document, click the Show/Hide ¶ button to display the nonprinting symbols.**

❷ Select the heading ***Background***, **the paragraph below it, and the paragraph symbol above** ***Work in Progress***, **as shown in Figure 4.9.**

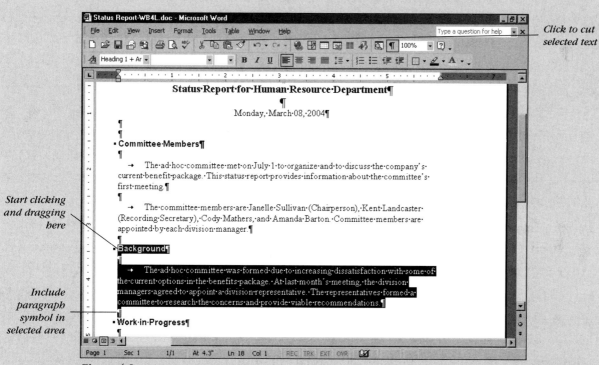

Click to cut selected text

Start clicking and dragging here

Include paragraph symbol in selected area

Figure 4.9

If you have problems...

If you're having problems selecting this text, place the insertion point at the beginning of the word *Background*, and press Ctrl+⇧Shift+↓ four times.

The Background section is selected, so you can move it. You must select text and any blank lines you want to cut. Make sure that the paragraph symbol between the paragraph and the next heading is selected.

❸ **Click the Cut button on the Standard toolbar.**
The Background section is removed from the document. It is stored in the Office Clipboard.

(Continues)

To Move Text (Continued)

④ **Position the insertion point to the left of the letter *C* in the heading *Committee Members*.**
After cutting the text, you need to place the insertion point where you want the text to appear. In this document, you want to place the Background section before the Committee Members section.

⑤ **Click the Paste button on the Standard toolbar.**
When you paste the Background section in its new location, the Committee Members section moves down to accommodate it (see Figure 4.10).

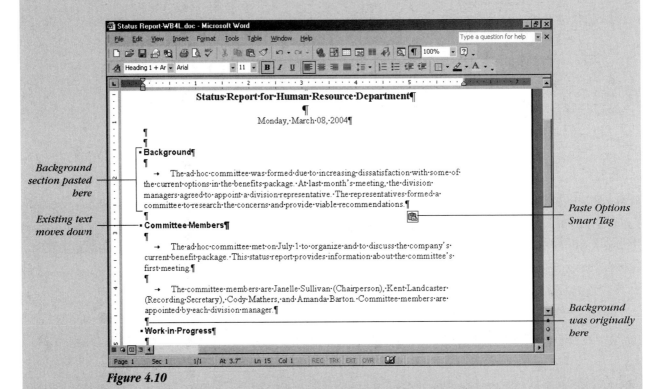

Background section pasted here

Existing text moves down

Paste Options Smart Tag

Background was originally here

Figure 4.10

The ***Paste Options Smart Tag*** that appears lets you choose the formatting style for the text you paste. You learn more about this button in the next lesson.

⑥ **Save the document, and keep it onscreen to continue with the next lesson.**

Table 4.1 shows various methods for cutting, copying, and pasting items.

Table 4.1	Cut, Copy, and Paste Methods		
Method	**Cut**	**Copy**	**Paste**
Toolbar	✂	📋	📋
Menu	Edit, Cut	Edit, Copy	Edit, Paste
Keyboard	Ctrl+X	Ctrl+C	Ctrl+V
Shortcut Menu	Right-click, Cut	Right-click, Copy	Right-click, Paste

To extend your knowledge...

Dragging and Dropping Text

You can also move text by dragging it into place. To move text, point inside the selected text, and drag it to a new location. When you release the mouse button, the text is moved from its original location to the new location. If you hold down Ctrl while dragging, you copy the selected text rather than cut it.

Using the Office Clipboard Task Pane

Choose Edit, Office Clipboard to display the Office Clipboard task pane to see the items you copy or cut (see Figure 4.11).

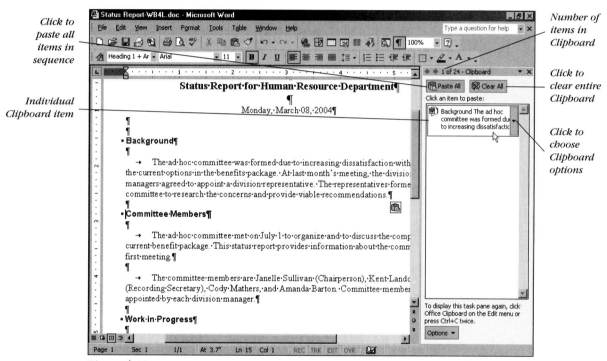

Click to paste all items in sequence

Individual Clipboard item

Number of items in Clipboard

Click to clear entire Clipboard

Click to choose Clipboard options

Figure 4.11

When you position the mouse pointer on a Clipboard item, a border appears around it with a down-pointing arrow on the right side. You can click the item to immediately paste it at the insertion point's location in the document. When you click the down-pointing arrow that appears when you place your mouse pointer to the right of the item, you can choose Paste to paste the item in the document, or choose Delete to remove the item from the Clipboard. Click Clear All to clear the Clipboard items.

Collecting and Pasting

You can use the Office Clipboard task pane to compile items from different sources and then paste them at one time to create a new document. The key to collecting items is to copy them in the order you want them to appear, such as first, second, and so on. When you click Paste All, the Clipboard pastes all its items in the sequence in which you copied or cut them. This is a great way to use documents obtained from team members to create a final document to submit to your supervisor.

Lesson 4: Copying Between Document Windows

In business, people often reuse information from previous reports and documents as they prepare new reports. In addition, people often work in teams, write their individual assignments, and send their documents to a team leader to collate. In these situations, you can open two or more documents and easily copy information from one document window to another. This process saves you from having to retype the information.

In this lesson, you copy some information from another document and paste it in your current document.

To Copy and Paste Between Document Windows

❶ With the *Status Report-WB4L* document onscreen, open *ew1-0402*, and make sure the formatting marks are displayed.
The *ew1-0402* document is in the *active document window*. The **active document window** is the window that contains a document with the insertion point; the title bar is blue or another color. The title bars for other document windows are a lighter color or gray.

❷ Select the heading *Employee Concerns*, the paragraph below it, and the three indented lines. Make sure that you select the paragraph mark representing the blank line below *Tuition Reimbursement*.
Figure 4.12 shows the text that you should select.

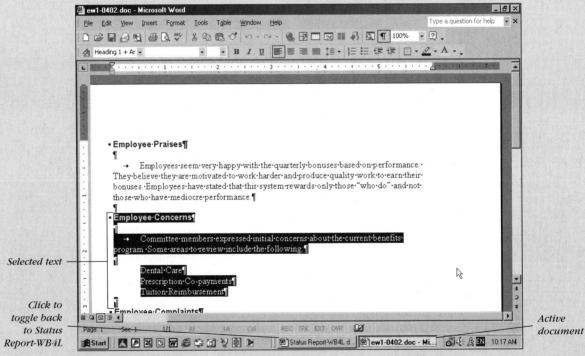

Figure 4.12

❸ Click the Copy button.
This copies the selected text to the Office Clipboard.

❹ Click the *Status Report-WB4L.doc* button on the Windows taskbar.
You can go back and forth between open documents by clicking their respective buttons on the taskbar. Now, *Status Report-WB4L* is the active document.

❺ Position the insertion point to the left of the *Work in Progress* heading, and click the Paste button.
Figure 4.13 shows the text pasted before *Work in Progress*.

To Copy and Paste Between Document Windows

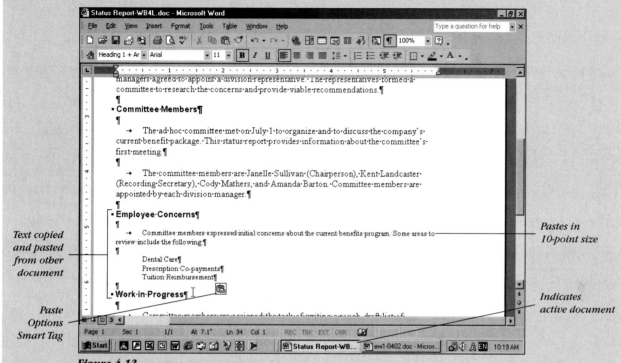

Text copied and pasted from other document

Paste Options Smart Tag

Pastes in 10-point size

Indicates active document

Figure 4.13

Notice that the paragraph and indented items appear in 10-point size, even if the original text was in 12-point size. You can use the Paste Options button to select the formatting for the pasted text.

6 **Click the Paste Options Smart Tag at the bottom-right corner of the pasted text.**
Figure 4.14 shows your options for formatting the pasted text.

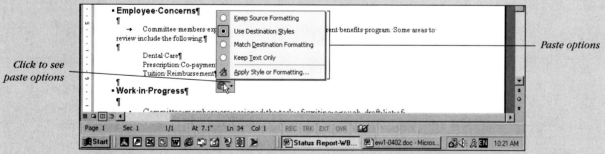

Click to see paste options

Paste options

Figure 4.14

In some instances, you want the pasted text to match the formatting in the destination document—the document in which you pasted the text. However, in this situation, the regular text would be formatted like the heading if you choose this option. Therefore, let's keep the original formatting, which was in 12-point size.

7 **Click the *Keep Source Formatting* option.**

(Continues)

To Copy and Paste Between Document Windows (Continued)

The pasted paragraph and indented items are formatted with their original 12-point size (see Figure 4.15).

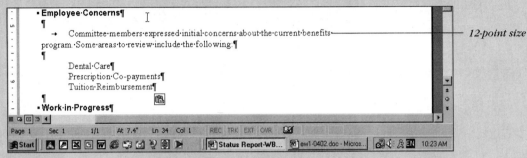

Figure 4.15

 If you have problems...

If the original formatting and the destination formatting don't format the pasted text to match the rest of the destination document's format, you might have to select the pasted text and manually apply the formats you want.

8 **Click the *ew1-0402.doc* button on the taskbar to toggle back to that document.**

9 **Choose File, Close to close *ew1-0402.***
If you are prompted to save that document, click No. The *Status Report-WB4L* document is now the only open document.

10 **Save the document, and keep it onscreen to continue with the next lesson.**

Lesson 5: Undoing and Redoing Actions

Sometimes, you make a mistake in formatting, deleting, or typing text and then immediately realize your mistake. When this happens, use the *Undo* feature to reverse the actions you took. **Undo** reverses actions in sequential order—starting with the last action you performed. Using Undo again reverses the second-to-the-last action, and so on.

For example, assume that you paste a paragraph in the wrong location. Using the Undo feature removes the pasted text. If you accidentally click the Underline button, using the Undo feature removes the underline. Undo works for almost every action you perform within a document: formatting, deleting, sorting, placing graphics, and so on. Some actions cannot be reversed with Undo, however. For example, if you choose Save instead of Save As, you can't undo the saving process.

In this lesson, you delete a sentence in the first paragraph and then use Undo to restore the deleted text. In addition, you use Undo to remove italics from text.

To Undo Actions

1 **In the *Status Report-WB4L* document, press and hold Ctrl while clicking the first sentence.**
This is the sentence you want to delete.

2 **Press Del.**

To Undo Actions

The sentence is not in the Clipboard because you deleted it instead of cutting it. Figure 4.16 shows the document after deleting the sentence.

Undo button reverses actions

Tab and sentence deleted

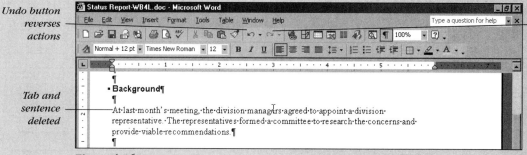

Redo button reverses Undo actions

Figure 4.16

3 **Click the Undo button on the Standard toolbar.**
The Undo feature reserves your last action. In this case, your last action deleted a sentence. Clicking the Undo button restores the deleted text.

4 **Select the three indented lines of text in the Employee Concerns section; then, click the Italic button.**

5 **Deselect the text to see the italic format.**
After italicizing the text, you realize immediately that you don't want it italicized.

6 **Click the Undo button.**
Undo reverses the last action by removing the italics from the text.

If you have problems...

If Undo doesn't undelete the text or remove the italic format, you probably performed another action on the document. Any change you make to the document, such as adding a space, is called an ***action***.

7 **Save the document, and keep the document onscreen to continue with the next exercise.**

To extend your knowledge...

Undo Keyboard Shortcut

The keyboard shortcut for undo is Ctrl+Z.

Undo List

Clicking the Undo button reverses the last action. If you need to restore previous actions, click the Undo button again. Each time you click the Undo button, you work backward—reversing the actions you took.

You can reverse a series of actions by clicking the Undo drop-down arrow. When you select an action from the list, Word reverses the most recent actions, including the one you select. Figure 4.17 shows that the last four actions will be undone.

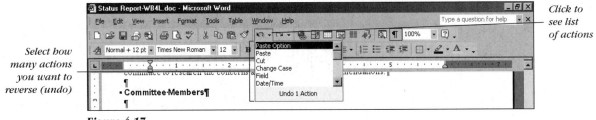

Select how
many actions
you want to
reverse (undo)

Click to
see list
of actions

Figure 4.17

If you decide that you preferred the action before undoing it, you can restore that action by using the **Redo** command to reverse the Undo command. The Redo button is grayed-out if you have not used the Undo feature in a document.

In the next exercise, you change your mind and want to reverse the last Undo action; that is, you want to restore the italic format the fastest way possible—by using Redo instead of selecting and italicizing text again.

To Redo an Action

❶ **Click the Redo button.**
The indented text in the Employee Concerns section is italicized again, because Redo reverses the last Undo action.

❷ **Deselect the italicized items.**

❸ **Save the document, and keep it onscreen to continue with the next lesson.**

Lesson 6: Using AutoCorrect

AutoCorrect corrects errors "on-the-fly," which means that it corrects errors as you type them. For example, it changes *teh* to *the*. It also corrects other types of errors, such as capitalization at the beginning of a sentence. It even helps you change manually typed symbols to unique symbols, such as changing :) to ☺. You can even insert AutoCorrect entries to change abbreviations to fully expanded text, such as changing *uvsc* to *Utah Valley State College*.

In this lesson, you type a sentence at the end of the document. Although you type it with errors, AutoCorrect corrects the errors for you.

To Use AutoCorrect

❶ **In the *Status Report-WB4L* document, press Ctrl+End, and click the Show/Hide ¶ button to turn off the formatting marks.**

❷ **Type teh and press Spacebar.**
When you press Spacebar, AutoCorrect changes *teh* to *the* and then capitalizes the first letter of the sentence.

❸ **Type ad hoc comittee will reconvene next week to reveiw the questons and prepare a tenative questionaire.**
Your sentence should look like the one shown in Figure 4.18.

To Use AutoCorrect

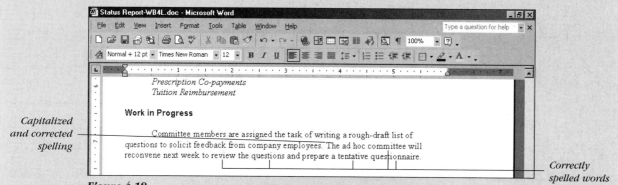

Capitalized and corrected spelling

Correctly spelled words

Figure 4.18

Now let's look at AutoCorrect to see what words are detected and corrected for you.

4 **Choose Tools, AutoCorrect Options to display the AutoCorrect dialog box.**

If you have problems...

If you don't see AutoCorrect Options on the Tools menu, click the down-pointing arrows to display the full Tools menu.

5 **Click the scroll-down arrow on the right side of the dialog box to scroll through the list until you see the word *committee* in the second column.**

The first column shows misspelled words, and the second column shows the correct spellings, as shown in Figure 4.19.

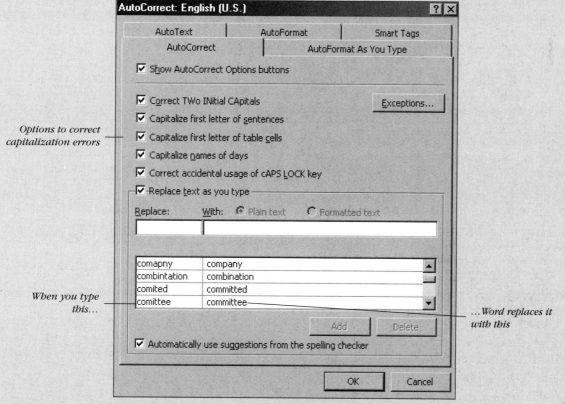

Options to correct capitalization errors

When you type this...

...Word replaces it with this

Figure 4.19

(Continues)

To Use AutoCorrect (Continued)

6 **Click the AutoText tab.**
The AutoText section of the AutoCorrect dialog box contains frequently used text. When you start to type text that matches one of the AutoText entries, you see a ScreenTip that prompts you to press ⏎Enter to complete the text automatically so you don't have to type the rest of it.

7 **Click the scroll down arrow to see *Ladies and Gentlemen:*.**
When you start to type text stored as AutoText, you see a prompt to press ⏎Enter to complete the text for you.

8 **Click Cancel to close the dialog box.**

9 **Press ⏎Enter twice and type Ladi.**
You should see the following ScreenTip: *Ladies and Gentlemen: (Press ENTER to Insert).*

10 **Press ⏎Enter.**
Ladies and Gentlemen: appears automatically without your having to type the rest of it.

11 **Click the Undo button twice to remove the *Ladies and Gentlemen:* text.**

12 **Save the document and keep it onscreen to continue with the next lesson.**

To extend your knowledge...

Adding AutoCorrect Entries

You can add words you typically misspell or abbreviations in AutoCorrect. Assume that you typically misspell *business* as *busenes*. With the AutoCorrect dialog box, type busenes in the *Replace* text box, and type business in the *With* text box. After entering the two words, click *Add* to add the entry.

Learning More About AutoText

Use the Help feature to learn more about AutoText. After reading the Help information, you can experiment with adding AutoText entries.

Lesson 7: Using the Thesaurus

Finding the perfect word to communicate your ideas clearly is sometimes difficult. You might type a word, but you then realize that it doesn't quite describe what you're thinking. It might not have the impact for which you were searching. The Thesaurus tool helps you choose words to improve the clarity of your documents. You can select **synonyms** (words with similar meanings) from Word's Thesaurus feature and get your point across with greater ease.

To Use Thesaurus

1 **In the *Status Report-WB4L* document, click in the word *formed* on the first line in the first paragraph.**
You should click within the word that you want to look up in Thesaurus.

2 **Choose Tools, Language, Thesaurus.**
The thesaurus appears with a list of possible replacement words (see Figure 4.20).

To Use Thesaurus

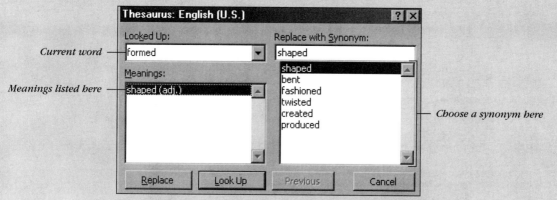

Current word ——
Meanings listed here ——
Choose a synonym here

Figure 4.20

If a word has multiple meanings, you can click a meaning and then see different synonyms on the right side of the dialog box.

If you have problems...

You see an error message if Thesaurus is not loaded on your computer. If you have the Microsoft Office installation CD, insert it and follow the prompts to install Thesaurus.

❸ Click *created* in the Replace with Synonym box and then click Replace.
Word replaces *formed* with *created*, the synonym you select.

❹ Right-click *agreed* in the first paragraph.
A shortcut menu appears with a Synonyms option. Choosing a synonym from this menu might be preferable to using the Thesaurus dialog box.

❺ Choose Synonyms.
Figure 4.21 shows a list of synonyms for the current word.

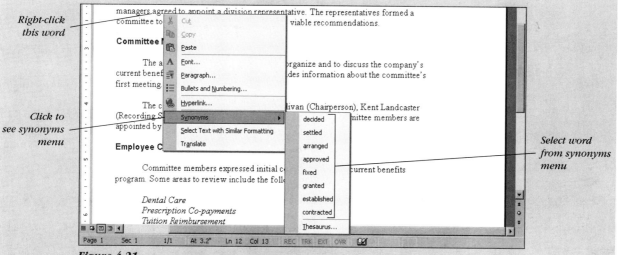

Right-click this word
Click to see synonyms menu
Select word from synonyms menu

Figure 4.21

❻ Choose *decided*.
Word replaces *agreed* with *decided*.

❼ Save the document and close it.

Summary

You now know how to perform several essential tasks to enhance text and improve the clarity of your document. You learned how to quickly change the case of selected text instead of retyping it. In addition, you moved text to a different location and copied text from one document to another. You'll probably find the Undo and Redo features handy to reverse actions you made in a document. Furthermore, you inserted a date field, saw first-hand how AutoCorrect corrects some commonly misspelled words, and used Thesaurus to find a synonym.

You can extend your learning by exploring some of the other Date and Time field options, AutoCorrect options, and the Office Clipboard task pane. For more information, refer to the online Help feature and complete the end-of-projects tasks assigned by your instructor.

Checking Concepts and Terms

Multiple Choice

Circle the letter of the correct answer for each of the following.

1. What Change Case option capitalizes the first letter after a punctuation mark, such as the period, question mark, or exclamation mark? [L2]

   a. Sentence case

   b. Title Case

   c. tOGGLE cASE

   d. UPPERCASE

2. What is the keyboard shortcut for cutting text? [L3]

   a. Ctrl+C

   b. Ctrl+X

   c. Ctrl+Z

   d. ⬆Shift+F3

3. What feature reverses the last action you performed on the document? [L5]

   a. Redo

   b. Paste

   c. Undo

   d. Format Painter

4. AutoCorrect does all of the following tasks except which one? [L6]

   a. Corrects some misspelled words as you type.

   b. Capitalizes the first letter of a sentence if you don't.

   c. Changes some keyboard symbols to other symbols, such as a smiley face.

   d. Places red wavy lines below grammatical errors.

5. What is the first step for duplicating text? [L4]

   a. Click the Paste button.

   b. Click the Copy button.

   c. Position the insertion point where you want the duplicate text to appear.

   d. Select the original text that you want to duplicate.

Screen ID

Label each element of the Word screen shown in Figure 4.22.

A. Clipboard item

B. Copy button

C. Cut button

D. Paste button

E. Pastes entire Clipboard contents in sequence

F. Redo button

G. Removes items from Clipboard

H. Undo button

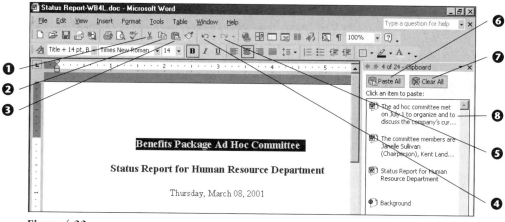

Figure 4.22

1. _____   5. _____

2. _____   6. _____

3. _____   7. _____

4. _____   8. _____

Discussion

1. What is the purpose of AutoCorrect? How does it improve your efficiency? [L6]

2. Practice using the drag-and-drop method for moving text. Explain how it might be helpful to use this feature. Discuss any disadvantages you experience in using the drag-and-drop feature compared to using the Cut and Paste commands. [L3]

3. What is the purpose of a date or time field? Discuss situations in which you should insert a date or time field instead of typing it yourself. [L1]

Skill Drill

Skill Drill exercises reinforce project skills. Each skill reinforced is the same, or nearly the same, as a skill presented in the project. Detailed instructions are provided in a step-by-step format.

1. Inserting Date and Time Fields

You are working on a memo to send to a colleague. However, you're not sure if you have time to finish it today. Because you are worried that you might forget to change the date if you finish it a few days from now, you insert a date field.

1. Open *ew1-0403*, and save it as `Newsletter Memo-WB4SD`.
2. Select the date in the memo (but don't select the paragraph symbol), and press `Del`.
3. Choose Insert, Date and Time.

4. Click the *March 4, 2004* format. (The exact date will differ on your computer.)

5. If the *Update automatically* check box is not selected, click it.

6. Click OK.

7. Right-click within the date field and choose *Edit Field*.

8. Click the *3/4/2004 2:50 PM* format and then click OK. (The exact date and time will differ, but choose the same format.)

9. Save the document and keep it onscreen to continue with the next exercise.

2. Changing the Case

You just finished composing a status report memo to your manager. After proofreading the memo, you decide to change the case of some text to either uppercase or sentence case.

1. In the open *Newsletter Memo-WB4SD* document, change Andy Barton's name to your name.

2. Double-click the word *Subject*.

3. Choose Format, Change Case.

4. Click the UPPERCASE option and then click OK.

5. Select the first heading, *News articles*.

6. Press ⇧Shift+F3 three times to choose the Title Case capitalization style.

7. Use the same process to apply the Title Case style to the other two headings.

8. Save the document and keep it onscreen to continue with the next exercise.

3. Using Undo and Redo

As you continue editing your memo, you realize that you want to undo some actions you take. Therefore, you use Undo and Redo, as needed.

1. In the open *Newsletter Memo-WB4SD* document, select and bold *Winter Newsletter* on the fourth line of the document.

2. Click the Undo button to remove bold from *Winter Newsletter*.

3. Click the Undo button again to change the case style of the last heading that you formatted in Skill Drill 2.

You realize that you "accidentally" clicked Undo too many times and did not want to reverse the case action.

4. Click the Redo button to reverse the last Undo action. In other words, you are restoring the Title Case capitalization style to the last heading.

5. Save the document and keep it onscreen to continue with the next exercise.

4. Moving Text to a Different Location

As you read through the memo, you decide to move the Art Work section below the News Articles section. In addition, you notice that a sentence should also be moved to a different location.

1. In the *Newsletter Memo-WB4SD* document, click at the beginning of the heading *Art Work*.

2. Click the Show/Hide ¶ button to see the nonprinting symbols if they are not already displayed.

3. Select the *Art Work* heading and the paragraph below it. Make sure that you include the ¶ symbol below the paragraph.

4. Click the Cut button to remove the selected text from its location.

5. Position the insertion point to the left of the *Classified Advertisements* heading.

6. Click the Paste button to paste the text between the News Articles and Classified Advertisement sections.

7. Select the sentence that begins with *The residents have expressed...*, which is the last sentence in the Classified Advertisement section.

8. Press Ctrl+X to cut the sentence.

9. Position the insertion point at the beginning of the sentence that begins with *We are currently accepting...* in the same paragraph, and press Ctrl+V to paste it as the second sentence in the paragraph.

10. Press Spacebar, if necessary, to have a space between sentences.

11. Save the document, and keep it onscreen to continue with the next exercise.

5. Copying Text from One Document to Another

Your assistant sent you a document that contains some information you need in your current document. Therefore, you want to copy it so that you don't have to type the data yourself.

1. Leave the *Newsletter Memo-WB4SD* document open.

2. Open *ew1-0404*, the document that contains text you want to duplicate in your newsletter memo.

3. Select the second paragraph and the blank line below it.

4. Press Ctrl+C to copy it to the Clipboard.

5. Close *ew1-0404*.

6. Position the insertion point below the paragraph in the Classified Advertisement section.

7. Press ↵Enter, and click the Paste button to paste the text you had copied from the other document.

8. Make sure that you have one blank line above the pasted paragraph. Make adjustments as needed.

9. If the pasted paragraph appears in 10-point size, click the Paste Options Smart Tag and choose *Keep Source Formatting* to maintain its 12-point size.

10. Save the document, and keep it onscreen to continue with the next exercise.

6. Using AutoCorrect and Thesaurus

You need to add a sentence to the document. As you quickly type it, you make some mistakes. AutoCorrect will correct them for you. Furthermore, you want to find an appropriate synonym for a word in the document.

1. In the *Newsletter Memo-WB4SD* document, position the insertion point at the end of the first paragraph in the News Articles section.

2. Type the following sentence exactly as shown with mistakes:

    ```
    some topiks for artecles include informing residents ofthe new recycling
    program and trafic issues during home football games in september and
    october.
    ```

3. Check to make sure that AutoCorrect corrected the misspelled words as you typed them.

4. Right-click *currently* in the first paragraph in the Classified Advertisements section, choose Synonyms, and choose *presently*.

5. Save the document, print it, and close it.

Challenge

Challenge exercises expand on or are somewhat related to skills presented in the lessons. Each exercise provides a brief narrative introduction, followed by instructions in a numbered-step format that are not as detailed as those in the Skill Drill section.

1. Correcting Errors in a Letter

You work as an assistant for a real estate company. One of the agents wrote a letter to condominium owners who expressed interest in selling their condominiums. The agent asked you to make the necessary corrections.

1. Open *ew1-0405*, and save it as `Condominium Letter-WB4CH1`.
2. Insert the date as a field in this format: *April 15, 2004* at the top of the document.
3. Double-click the Spelling and Grammar Status button on the status bar to display the first spelling or grammatical error, and correct it. Continue doing this until you correct all errors.
4. Choose an appropriate synonym for *maximum* in the last paragraph.
5. Select the appropriate case for the third paragraph. Manually capitalize any letters that should remain capitalized.
6. Select the four items below the third paragraph, press Tab⇄, and italicize them.
7. Apply bold to the first paragraph.
8. Select *Sincerely*, and capitalize it.
9. Delete the first sentence in the first paragraph.
10. Click the drop-down arrow to the right of the Undo button. Select Undo actions, starting with bolding text to the latest action.
11. Save, print, and close the document.

2. Enhancing and Editing a Welcome Letter

You live in a townhouse condominium complex in Amarillo, Texas. You are also on the welcome committee that greets new residents as they buy a townhouse. You have prepared a welcome letter, and you need to enhance and correct it.

1. Open *ew1-0406* and save it as `Welcome New Owners-WB4CH2`.
2. Insert today's date as a field in this format: *January 15, 2004*.
3. Select Title Case for each of these headings: lawn care, snow removal, and workout room.
4. Select *Lawn Care*, and make it bold and underlined. Use Format Painter to copy these formats to the other two headings.
5. Open *ew1-0407*, and copy the *Swimming Pool* paragraph and the blank line below it. Paste the text at the beginning of the Lawn Care paragraph in the *Welcome New Owners-WB4CH2* document. (The paragraphs should remain separate with one blank line between them.) Close *ew1-0407*.
6. Use the Paste Options Smart Tag to format the pasted text consistently with the original text. If these options don't provide the format you want, manually format the paragraph.
7. Apply Arial Narrow, bold, and Green font color to the first occurrence of Madison Village. Use Format Painter to apply these formats to the other Madison Village occurrences.
8. Move the *Snow Removal* paragraph below the *Workout Room* paragraph.
9. Check the spacing between paragraphs, and make the necessary adjustments.
10. Delete the *Snow Removal* paragraph; then undo the action.
11. Save, print, and close the document.

3. Correcting Errors and Enhancing Minutes from a Meeting

You are the secretary for a condominium association. You need to enhance the minutes and correct errors in them.

1. Open *ew1-0408*, and save it as `Association Minutes-WB4CH3`.
2. Type the following sentence *exactly* as shown at the end of the *Minutes* paragraph, and let AutoCorrect correct errors for you: `teh minutes were aproved as corected.`
3. Enhance the title by applying boldface, Arial, and Violet font color to it.

4. Enhance the headings by applying 11-point Arial, bold, and Violet font color. Use Format Painter to help copy the formats from one heading to the other headings.

5. Use the appropriate Change Case option on the headings, as you did in the lesson; make sure that they are consistently formatted. You need to manually change prepositions, such as *to,* to lowercase.

6. Move the Condominium Dues section above the Parking Regulations section. You should have one blank line between paragraphs.

7. Choose an appropriate synonym for the word *additional* in the *Condominium Dues* paragraph.

8. Save, print, and close the document.

4. Editing an Author Guideline Document

You are an assistant to a project manager for a textbook series. The project manager gave you a rough-draft document that will be e-mailed to the authors so that they will know what to include in their projects.

1. Open *ew1-0409*, and save it as `Author Guidelines-WB4CH4`.

2. Use the Change Case feature to change the paragraph headings to Title Case format.

3. Rearrange the paragraphs based on the order in which items are mentioned in the first sentence of the first paragraph. Make sure that you have one blank line between paragraphs after rearranging them.

4. Use Thesaurus to find a synonym for *useful* in the first sentence in the *Project Overview* paragraph.

5. At the end of the document, modify the date field to display the date and time in this format: *4/30/2004 9:15 PM.*

6. Move the first sentence in the first paragraph so that it's the last sentence in the first paragraph.

7. Save, print, and close the document.

Discovery Zone exercises require advanced knowledge of topics presented in *essentials* lessons, application of skills from multiple lessons, or self-directed learning of new skills.

1. Creating AutoCorrect Entries

You really like the way AutoCorrect can correct some errors as you type. Because you find yourself typing your name and a club name several times a day, you want to create AutoCorrect entries that allow you to type an abbreviation and automatically expand it to the full text.

Use onscreen Help to learn how to create and use AutoCorrect entries. Then, create the following two entries:

- ccc for College Computer Club
- your initials for your full name

Be careful when creating the entry for your name. Some names may expand state abbreviations or simple words, which you don't want to do. For example, a person named *Ingrid Smith* should not create an AutoCorrect entry named *is.*

Create the document shown in Figure 4.23, using your initials for Vice President and Activities Director instead of *zxy*.

---

ccc Officers

The ccc officers for the 2003-04 academic year are listed below:

President   Vicki Kamoreaux

Vice President   xyz

Secretary   Tyler Jorgenson

Treasurer   Gloria Rokovitz

Activities Director   zxy

Figure 4.23

Word should automatically expand the abbreviations as you type them. Select the title, and use the keyboard shortcut for changing the case to uppercase. Make two more copies of the list, so you have three copies of the list on one piece of paper. Save the document as `Club Officers-WB4DZ1` and print it.

2. Compiling an Information Sheet by Using the Office Clipboard

You have a master file of workshop descriptions that your training company provides to business people in the area. You need to prepare a custom workshop program for one of your clients. In a new document window, type the title in 16-point Arial font, bold, and Small Caps effect. Triple-space after the title, select 12-point, Bookman Old Style font; and type the paragraph shown in Figure 4.24.

COMPUTER WORKSHOPS FOR BRADSHAW AND ASSOCIATES

We are pleased to provide the workshops you requested for individuals in your organization. According to our agreement, you may send up to 15 individuals to each session listed below. The workshops are scheduled for May 18 in your conference room. If you have additional questions, please call Taralyn VanBuren at 555-7843.

Figure 4.24

Save the document as `Workshops for Bradshaw-WB4DZ2`. Open *ew1-0410*. Refer to Lesson 3, "Cutting, Copying, and Pasting Text," and onscreen Help to learn about the Office Clipboard and how to use it to collect and paste several items at once.

Display the Office Clipboard task pane. Clear any existing items in the Clipboard, and copy the paragraphs to the Clipboard in this order: *Upgrade to Word 2002, Automating Your Work,* and *Collaborating on Documents.* Paste the entire Clipboard contents below the introductory paragraph in *Workshops for Bradshaw-WB4DZ2.* Make sure that you have one blank line between paragraphs, and ensure that the pasted paragraphs have the same font and font size as the introductory paragraph. Save the document, and print it.

Change *Bradshaw and Associates* to `The Rowley Group`. Save the modified document as `Workshops for Rowley-WB4DZ2`. Delete the paragraphs about the workshops. Clear the Office Clipboard. Click *ew1-0410* on the taskbar to go back to this document, and copy these paragraphs in this order to the Clipboard: *Basic Formatting with Word, Graphics Jamboree, Integrating Excel Data into Word,* and *Organizing Items in Tables.* Paste the entire Office Clipboard contents at the bottom of The Rowley Group document. Adjust the font and font size, if necessary, to be consistent with the first paragraph. Save the document and print it. Close all open documents.

Formatting Paragraphs

Objectives

In this project, you learn how to

- ✔ Set Line and Paragraph Spacing
- ✔ Select Text Alignment
- ✔ Indent Text
- ✔ Insert Bulleted and Numbered Lists
- ✔ Create an Outline Numbered List
- ✔ Add Borders and Shading
- ✔ Set and Modify Tabs
- ✔ Reveal and Clear Formats

Key terms introduced in this project include

- ❏ alignment
- ❏ bar tab
- ❏ border
- ❏ bullet
- ❏ bulleted list
- ❏ double indent
- ❏ double-spaced
- ❏ first line indent
- ❏ hanging indent
- ❏ leader
- ❏ left indent
- ❏ line break
- ❏ line spacing
- ❏ outline numbered list
- ❏ paragraph spacing
- ❏ Reveal Formatting task pane
- ❏ reverse text effect
- ❏ right indent
- ❏ shading
- ❏ single-spaced
- ❏ soft return
- ❏ tabs

Why Would I Do This?

So far, you created documents using the default settings. Although these settings are acceptable for some basic documents, you probably want to have control over the format settings used for different types of documents. In this project, you learn a lot of common paragraph-formatting techniques that can make your documents look professional. You can use these formats to control a single paragraph or groups of paragraphs.

Visual Summary

In this project, you format paragraphs and text in an annual report. Figure 5.1 shows the paragraph formats applied to text on the first page of the report.

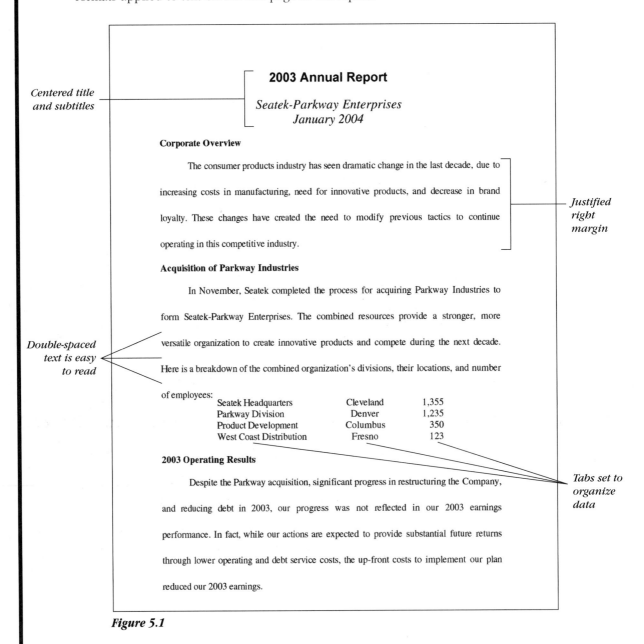

Centered title and subtitles

2003 Annual Report

Seatek-Parkway Enterprises
January 2004

Corporate Overview

The consumer products industry has seen dramatic change in the last decade, due to increasing costs in manufacturing, need for innovative products, and decrease in brand loyalty. These changes have created the need to modify previous tactics to continue operating in this competitive industry.

Justified right margin

Acquisition of Parkway Industries

In November, Seatek completed the process for acquiring Parkway Industries to form Seatek-Parkway Enterprises. The combined resources provide a stronger, more versatile organization to create innovative products and compete during the next decade. Here is a breakdown of the combined organization's divisions, their locations, and number

Double-spaced text is easy to read

of employees:

Seatek Headquarters	Cleveland	1,355
Parkway Division	Denver	1,235
Product Development	Columbus	350
West Coast Distribution	Fresno	123

2003 Operating Results

Despite the Parkway acquisition, significant progress in restructuring the Company, and reducing debt in 2003, our progress was not reflected in our 2003 earnings performance. In fact, while our actions are expected to provide substantial future returns through lower operating and debt service costs, the up-front costs to implement our plan reduced our 2003 earnings.

Tabs set to organize data

Figure 5.1

Figure 5.2 shows the last part of the document with additional paragraph formats.

In March 2003, Grant S. Keeper joined Seatek as its Chief Financial Officer. Grant has an impressive record in the industry over the past 33 years. Grant adds strength to our management team, particularly as the Company faces the important challenge of improving the financial and operating performance. Mr. Keeper has stated:

Indented from the left and right margins

Border encompasses paragraph

> 2004 is the year we take the bull by the horns. Everyone at Seatek-Parkway must pull together and work toward our mutual success. I'm counting on every employee to focus on our common goals to improve the financial status of the Company.

Shading behind text

Goals for 2004

Fully implementing our strategic action plan will take several years to complete and 2004 will be no less critical than 2003. In pursuing the second year of our plan, we have established several key goals for 2004:

Bulleted list

- Pursue innovative marketing techniques.
- Increase usage of existing computer systems by hiring in-house training personnel and establishing a continuing schedule of training classes.
- Implement an electronic project management program in all business units and corporate headquarters.
- Reduce the travel expenditures for the Company by closely evaluating each request for viability.

Single-spaced

With the changes occurring in the Company, we need to make sure that we continue to assess the interaction and activities among the merged divisions. Therefore, it is imperative to continually set and review goals using the following steps:

Numbered list

1. Assess the situation.
2. Set measurable goals.
3. Communicate goals to all employees.
4. Implement programs to strive to meet goals.
5. Monitor programs and record results.
6. Evaluate programs in relation to goals.
7. Continue or adjust programs as needed.

Figure 5.2

Lesson 1: Setting Line and Paragraph Spacing

Line spacing is the amount of vertical space from the bottom of one text line to the bottom of another. You use line spacing to control the amount of space between text lines in Word.

When you create a new document, Word makes the document text ***single-spaced***, which means that text lines are close together with a small space to separate the lines. Although some documents, such as letters, should be single-spaced, other documents look better ***double-spaced***. For example, a long report is typically easier to read if it is double-spaced.

If you click inside a paragraph and change the line spacing, only that paragraph is affected. To change line spacing for multiple paragraphs, you must select them first. In this lesson, you change the line spacing to double for most of the document.

To Change Line Spacing

1 Open *ew1-0501*, and save it as Annual Report-WB5L.

2 **Position the insertion point at the beginning of the** *Corporate Overview* **heading.**
Before setting the line spacing, you must select the paragraphs that you want to format. In this document, you want to double-space most paragraphs, except the titles and some text at the end of the document.

3 **Leaving the insertion point in that location, click and drag the vertical scroll box down to see the second page.**

4 **Press and hold down** ⟨◆Shift⟩ **and click after the colon that ends the first paragraph below the** *Goals for 2004* **heading.**
The paragraphs that you want to format are selected.

5 **Click the Line Spacing button.**
Figure 5.3 shows the Line Spacing menu.

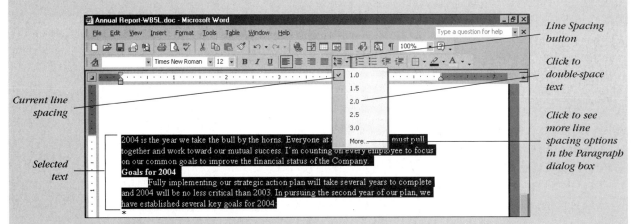

Figure 5.3

6 **Click** *2.0* **on the Line Spacing menu.**
The text is now double-spaced. When you double-space text, Word leaves one blank line between lines within a paragraph. Each soft return and each hard return in the selected area are doubled. A ***soft return*** occurs when Word word-wraps text to the next line within a paragraph as you type it.

7 **Press** ⟨Ctrl⟩+⟨Home⟩ **to return the insertion point to the beginning of the document, and deselect the text.**

8 **Click the Show/Hide ¶ button on the Standard toolbar.**
Although hard returns create blank lines between the titles, the blank lines within and between paragraphs are caused by the double-spacing (see Figure 5.4).

To Change Line Spacing

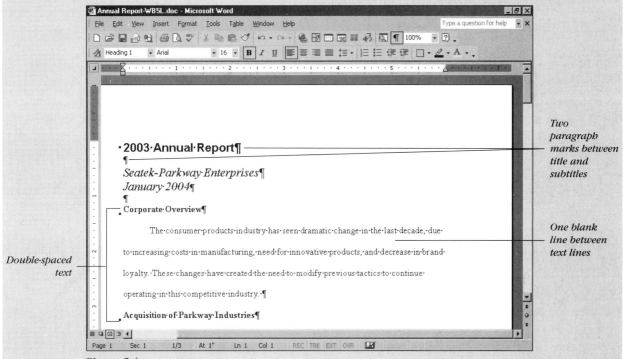

Figure 5.4

Now, you want to single-space the quoted paragraph to set it off from the regular paragraphs. The quoted text is probably the last paragraph on page 2 of your document.

9 **Scroll down, and click inside the paragraph that starts with** *2004 is the year we take the bull by the horns.*
Instead of selecting single-line spacing from the Line Spacing menu, you use a keyboard shortcut to save time.

10 **Press** Ctrl+1.
This keyboard shortcut single-spaces the current paragraph or group of selected paragraphs.

11 **Save the document, and keep it onscreen to continue with the next exercise.**

To extend your knowledge...

The Paragraph Dialog Box

The Paragraph dialog box also contains an option for choosing the line spacing. To display the Paragraph dialog box, choose F̲ormat, P̲aragraph or right-click within a paragraph and choose P̲aragraph.

Line Spacing Keyboard Shortcuts

Use the following keyboard shortcuts to change line spacing for selected text: Ctrl+1 for single-spacing, Ctrl+2 for double-spacing, and Ctrl+5 for 1.5 spacing.

Table 5.1 lists and describes the line-spacing options available in the Paragraph dialog box.

Table 5.1 Line-Spacing Options	
Spacing Option	**Description**
Single	Places a text line immediately beneath the previous line.
1.5 lines	Leaves one-and-one-half the amount of space of single-spacing.
Double	Doubles the amount of space between lines.
At least	Specifies the minimum amount of spacing between lines. Word adjusts the spacing as needed to make room for larger fonts or graphics.
Exactly	Specifies an exact spacing measurement. Word cannot adjust the line spacing to make room for larger elements.
Multiple	Specifies how much Word can adjust the line spacing (up or down) by a particular percentage. For example, 1.25 increases the space by 25 percent; .75 decreases the space by 25 percent. You can also enter full values, such as **3** to triple-space text.

You might want to keep text single-spaced by adjusting the spacing between paragraphs (that is, change the space created by paragraph marks each time you press ⏎Enter). For example, you might want to have single-spaced paragraphs with the equivalent of double-spacing between paragraphs.

You can achieve this effect by setting the ***paragraph spacing***, which controls the amount of space before or after the paragraph. Access the Paragraph dialog box, and change the Before or After spacing. For example, changing the After spacing to 12 points creates a double-space after the paragraph. In the next exercise, you choose 12-point paragraph spacing for the single-spaced paragraph to leave space after it.

To Change Paragraph Spacing

❶ In the open *Annual Report-WB5L* document, make sure that the insertion point is inside the single-spaced paragraph that begins with *2004 is the year....*
You need space between this paragraph and the following heading. Depending on your screen display and current printer, you might see *Goals for 2004* at the top of page 3. Nevertheless, you need a blank space in case you add or delete text later.

❷ Choose F̲ormat, P̲aragraph.
The Paragraph dialog box contains the options for changing paragraph formats, such as paragraph spacing (see Figure 5.5).

To Change Paragraph Spacing

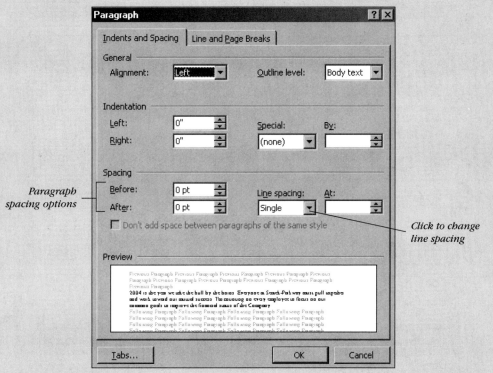

Figure 5.5

❸ **In the Spacing section, click the *After* spin button to increase the spacing to *12 pt*.**
Choosing *12 pt* spacing after paragraph is the equivalent of one blank line after the paragraph.

❹ **Click OK.**
The blank line above the paragraph is due to the double-space setting, and the space after the paragraph is due to the 12-pt after-paragraph spacing (see Figure 5.6).

(Continues)

To Change Paragraph Spacing (Continued)

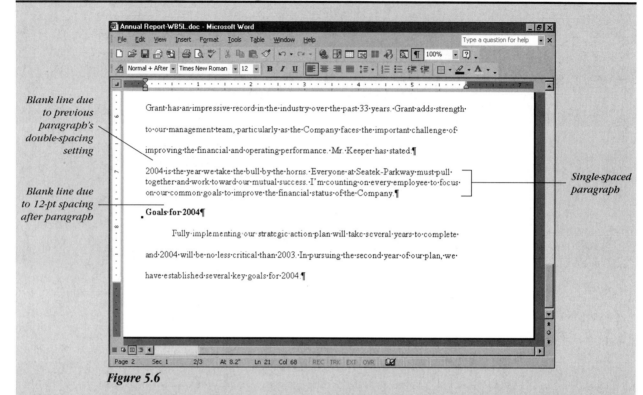

Blank line due to previous paragraph's double-spacing setting

Blank line due to 12-pt spacing after paragraph

Single-spaced paragraph

Figure 5.6

You need only one hard return *before* the quoted text because double-spacing is in effect until the beginning of the quoted paragraph. You need either two hard returns or a 12-point spacing after paragraph for the quoted paragraph because single-spacing is in effect until you reach the beginning of the following paragraph.

5 **Save the document, and keep it onscreen to continue with the next lesson.**

Lesson 2: Selecting Text Alignment

Alignment refers to the placement of text between the left and right margins. The default alignment is Align Left, which aligns text with the left margin. Table 5.2 lists and describes the four alignment options.

Table 5.2 Alignment Options

Button	Option	Keyboard Shortcut	Description
≣	Align Left	Ctrl+L	Aligns text on the left margin only. The left side is perfectly aligned, and the right side is ragged.
≣	Center	Ctrl+E	Centers text between the left and right margins.
≣	Align Right	Ctrl+R	Aligns text at the right margin only. The right side is perfectly aligned, and the left side is ragged.
≣	Justify	Ctrl+J	Aligns text along the left and right margins, so both sides are perfectly aligned. Inserts extra space between words to justify text.

In this lesson, you justify the paragraphs to make them look more formal. The smooth edges on the left and right sides provide a cleaner look for the document. Also, you need to center the title between the margins.

To Change the Alignment

❶ **In the *Annual Report-WB5L* document, choose E̲dit, Select A̲ll.**
Because you want to justify the text in the whole document, you must first select the entire document.

❷ **Click the Justify button on the Formatting toolbar.**
When you justify text, Word inserts a small amount of space between the characters, so the text aligns at both the left and right margins. Notice, however, that you see one space symbol between words, even in justified text. Justified text creates a more formal appearance than left-aligned text.

❸ **Press Ctrl+Home to deselect the text, and position the insertion point at the top of the document within the main title.**
Now, you need to center the title between the margins. To change the alignment for a single paragraph, click within that paragraph (such as a title followed by a hard return), and click the alignment button. Only that paragraph's alignment changes.

❹ **Click the Center button on the Formatting toolbar to center the title between the left and right margins.**

❺ **Select the two-line italicized subtitles and then click the Center button on the Formatting toolbar to center them.**

❻ **Deselect the text.**
Figure 5.7 shows the centered titles and justified paragraphs.

(Continues)

To Change the Alignment (Continued)

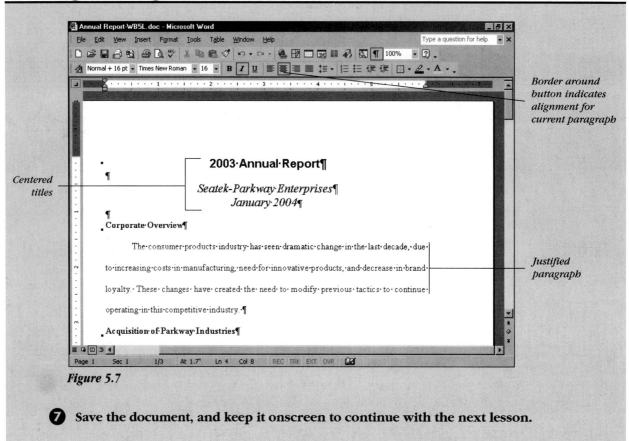

Figure 5.7

7 Save the document, and keep it onscreen to continue with the next lesson.

To extend your knowledge...

Aligning New Text

In the previous exercise, you changed the alignment for existing text by selecting it first. You can also select alignment before typing a document. For example, you can select Center alignment, type a document title, press ⏎Enter two or three times, and select Justify alignment. All new text from that point forward is automatically justified without selecting it first.

Lesson 3: Indenting Text

By now, you know to press Tab↹ to indent the first line of a paragraph. This format is typical in formal reports, letters, and legal documents. Sometimes, however, you might want to indent an entire paragraph from the left margin, right margin, or both margins. A *left indent* indents a paragraph a specified amount of space from the left margin, whereas a *right indent* indents a paragraph a specified amount of space from the right margin.

As you review the annual report, you see a quotation from the Chief Financial Officer, Grant Keeper, at the top of the third page. Often, you see a paragraph of quoted text indented from both margins, which is called a *double indent*. In this lesson, you indent the paragraph from both margins.

To Indent Text

❶ In the *Annual Report-WB5L* document, position the insertion point within the single-spaced paragraph that begins with *2004 is the year...*.
This quotation needs to be indented from both margins. Because you are formatting a single paragraph, you don't need to select it first. Simply position the insertion point within the paragraph that you want to format.

❷ Choose F*o*rmat, *P*aragraph to display the Paragraph dialog box.
You need to change the settings in the Indentation section.

❸ In the Indentation section, click the *Left* spin button until you see *0.5"* in the *Left* text box.

❹ Click the *Right* spin button until you see *0.5"* in the *Right* text box, and click OK.
The quotation paragraph is indented from the left and right margins (see Figure 5.8).

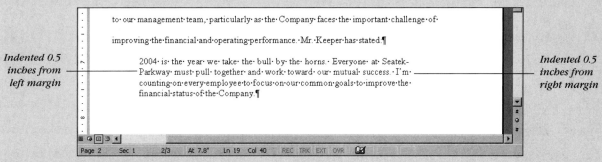

Figure 5.8

❺ Click the Show/Hide ¶ button to turn off the formatting marks.

❻ Save the document and keep it onscreen to continue with the next lesson.

To extend your knowledge...

Indent Markers on the Ruler

The ruler contains markers that you can also use to indent text. Figure 5.9 shows the ruler indent markers as well as indent buttons on the Formatting toolbar.

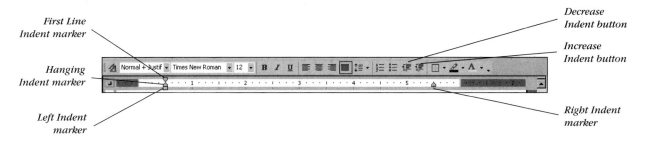

Figure 5.9

Indent and Decrease Indents

Click the Decrease Indent button to decrease (bring text to the left) indented text one-half inch. The keyboard shortcut for decreasing indented text is Ctrl+⬆Shift+M.

Click the Increase Indent button to increase the indent one-half inch. The keyboard shortcut for indenting text from the left side is Ctrl+M.

You can also set indents on the ruler. Click and drag the Left Indent marker to set the amount of space to indent text from the left margin.

Click and drag the Right Indent marker to set the amount of space to indent from the right margin.

First Line Indent

A *first line indent* automatically indents the first line of each paragraph. You can specify how much to indent the text. To set a first line indent, click the *Special* drop-down arrow in the Paragraph dialog box, and choose *First line*. Set the amount of space for the indent, such as 0.5″, in the *By* text box. Alternatively, you can click and drag the First Line Indent marker on the ruler.

Hanging Indent

A *hanging indent* keeps the first line of a paragraph at the left margin and indents the rest of the lines of that paragraph from the left margin. Bibliographic entries are typically formatted with a hanging indent.

You can create a hanging indent by choosing *Hanging* from the *Special* drop-down list in the Paragraph dialog box, by clicking and dragging the Hanging Indent marker on the ruler, or by pressing Ctrl+T. If you accidentally indent a hanging indent too far, press Ctrl+◆Shift+T to reduce the hanging indent.

Sorting Paragraphs

You might need to sort indenting paragraphs in a document. For example, if the bibliographic entries are not alphabetized by authors' last names, you need to sort them. Select the paragraphs you want to sort; choose T<u>a</u>ble, <u>S</u>ort; and then click OK.

Lesson 4: Inserting Bulleted and Numbered Lists

In word processing, a *bullet* is a special symbol used to attract attention to something on the page. People often use a *bulleted list* to itemize a series to make it stand out and be easy to read. For example, the objectives and terminology appear in bulleted lists on the first page of each project in this book. Use bulleted lists for listing items that can go in any order; use a numbered list for a list of items that must be in sequential order.

In this lesson, you create a bulleted list of goals for the coming year, and a numbered list to indicate sequence for setting and evaluating goals.

To Create a Bulleted List

❶ In the *Annual Report-WB5L* document, go to the top of the third page.

❷ Scroll down and delete the asterisk (*) after the first paragraph; keep the insertion point on the blank line.
This location is where you want to create a bulleted list that itemizes the company's goals for the upcoming year.

❸ Click the Bullets button on the Formatting toolbar.
Word indents the bullet, which is a round dot, and then indents from the bullet for you to type text.

To Create a Bulleted List

If you have problems...

Word creates a bulleted list based on the last bullet type selected. If you see a different bullet shape, such as a check mark, choose Format, Bullets and Numbering, click the rounded bullet list from the palette, and click OK.

4 **Type** `Pursue innovative marketing techniques.` **and press** ⏎Enter.

When you press ⏎Enter, Word inserts another bullet, followed by an indent (see Figure 5.10).

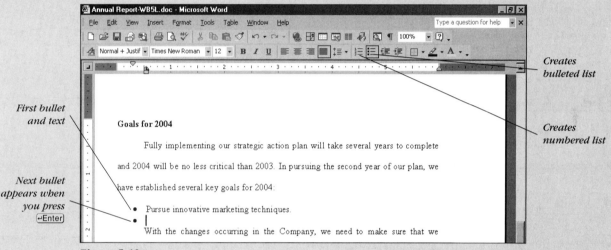

First bullet and text

Next bullet appears when you press ⏎Enter

Creates bulleted list

Creates numbered list

Figure 5.10

The bulleted list is single-spaced because you didn't select the asterisk when you selected other paragraphs to double-space in Lesson 1. The paragraph following the asterisk was already double-spaced for you.

5 **Type the following paragraphs, pressing** ⏎Enter **after each one.**

Increase usage of existing computer systems by hiring in-house training personnel and establishing a continuing schedule of training classes.

Implement an electronic project management program in all business units and corporate headquarters.

Reduce the travel expenditures for the Company by closely evaluating each request for viability.

Your document should look like Figure 5.11.

(Continues)

To Create a Bulleted List (Continued)

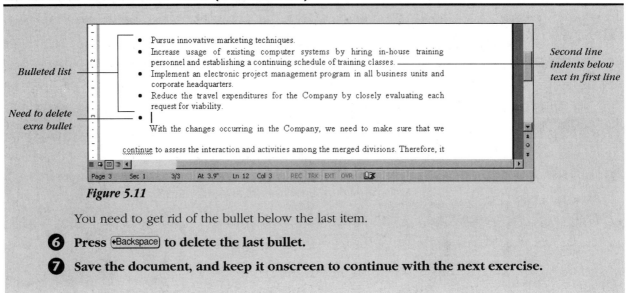

Bulleted list

Need to delete extra bullet

Second line indents below text in first line

Figure 5.11

You need to get rid of the bullet below the last item.

6 Press ⟨+Backspace⟩ **to delete the last bullet.**

7 Save the document, and keep it onscreen to continue with the next exercise.

In the next exercise, you want to create a numbered list from the items at the end of the document.

To Create a Numbered List

1 In the *Annual Report-WB5L* document, select the single-spaced items at the end of the document.

There are six single-spaced items that need to be formatted as a numbered list.

2 Click the Numbering button on the Formatting toolbar and then deselect the text.

Word inserts numbers for each selected paragraph (see Figure 5.12).

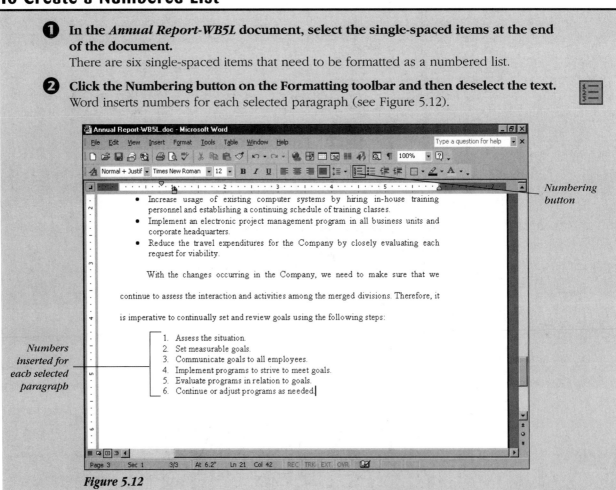

Numbering button

Numbers inserted for each selected paragraph

Figure 5.12

To Create a Numbered List

While reviewing the list, you notice that a step is missing.

3 **Click at the end of the fourth numbered paragraph, and press** ⏎Enter.
Word inserts a blank line and number to type a new numbered paragraph. The remaining numbered paragraphs are renumbered to accommodate the new numbered paragraph.

4 **Type** Monitor programs and record results.
Figure 5.13 shows the updated numbered list.

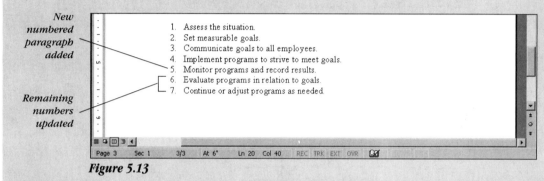

New numbered paragraph added

Remaining numbers updated

1. Assess the situation.
2. Set measurable goals.
3. Communicate goals to all employees.
4. Implement programs to strive to meet goals.
5. Monitor programs and record results.
6. Evaluate programs in relation to goals.
7. Continue or adjust programs as needed.

Figure 5.13

5 **Save and close the document.**

To extend your knowledge...

Creating Numbered Lists from Scratch

You can create a numbered list from scratch. To do this, click the Numbering button, and type the text for the first numbered paragraph; press ⏎Enter to continue creating a numbered list, similar to creating a bulleted list from scratch.

Bullet and Numbering Styles

You can choose other bullet and number styles for new or existing lists. For existing lists, select the items; then, choose F**o**rmat, Bullets and **N**umbering. When the Bullets and Numbering dialog box appears (see Figure 5.14), click the style you want and then click OK.

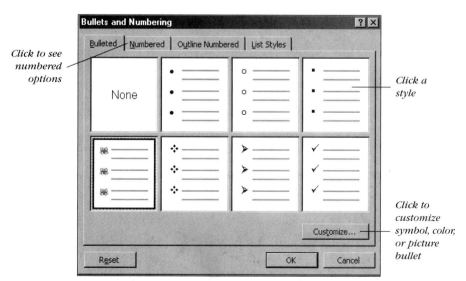

Click to see numbered options

Click a style

Click to customize symbol, color, or picture bullet

Figure 5.14

You can customize your bulleted list or choose another symbol. To do this, click an existing bullet in the Bullets and Numbering dialog box and then click the Customize button. The Customize Bulleted List dialog box contains options for customizing your bulleted list (see Figure 5.15).

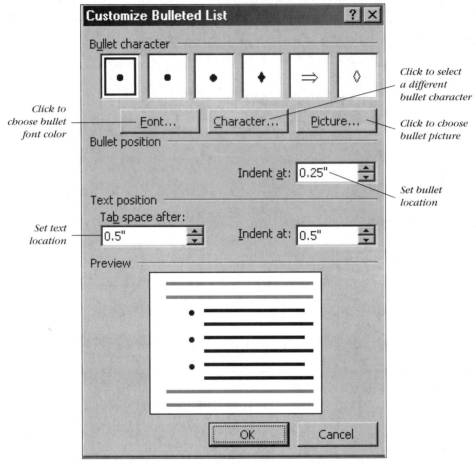

Figure 5.15

By default, bullets are indented 0.25″ from the left margin; however, you can place bullets at the left margin by changing the indent to 0″. You can also set the amount of space for indenting text after the bullet.

Click Font to select a font color for the bullets. Click Character to choose a bullet character from the Symbols dialog box as you did in Lesson 6, "Inserting Symbols," of Project 3, "Formatting Text."

Lesson 5: Creating an Outline Numbered List

Numbered lists are appropriate for formatting a sequence of steps or procedures. However, you might need an ***outline numbered list***, which is a numbered list with subcategories like an outline. In this lesson, you create an outline numbered list to show key administrators for selected divisions of Seatek-Parkway Enterprises.

To Create an Outline Numbered List

❶ **Click the New Blank Document button to create a new document.**

❷ **Type** Seatek-Parkway Enterprises, **and press** ⏎Enter **twice.**
You are ready to create the outline numbered list.

To Create an Outline Numbered List

❸ Choose F̲ormat, Bullets and N̲umbering.
The Bullets and Numbering dialog box contains options for starting a numbered outline.

❹ Click the O̲utline Numbered tab at the top of the dialog box.
The O̲utline Numbered tab provides various outline styles to choose from (see Figure 5.16).

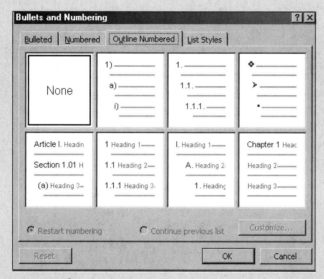

Figure 5.16

❺ Click the first style to the right of None and then click OK.
Word starts the numbered outline similar to a regular numbered list.

❻ Type Manufacturing, **and press** ↵Enter.
Word inserts the next number, but you want to have subdivisions within the first number.

❼ Press Tab↹ **to create a lower-level entry.**
Pressing Tab↹ creates a lower-level entry within an outline.

❽ Type East Coast Plant, **and press** ↵Enter.

❾ Press Tab↹, **type** Fred Barton, **and press** ↵Enter.

❿ Type Liz Keone, **press** ↵Enter, **and press** ⬆Shift+Tab↹.
Pressing ⬆Shift+Tab↹ creates a higher-level entry.

⓫ Type the rest of the entries shown in Figure 5.17 to complete the outline. Press Tab↹ **and** ⬆Shift+Tab↹ **as needed to create higher-level or lower-level entries.**

(Continues)

To Create an Outline Numbered List (Continued)

Seatek-Parkway Enterprises

1) Manufacturing
    a) East Coast Plant
        i) Fred Barton
        ii) Liz Keone
    b) West Coast Plant
        i) Betty Ann Bartley
        ii) Paul Knaphus
2) Advertising
    a) Benjamin Womble
    b) Iris Eccles

Figure 5.17

12 **Save the document as** Company Outline-WB5L, **and close it.**

To extend your knowledge...

Viewing Outlines

You can click the Outline View button or choose View, Outline to display the Outline toolbar. The Outline toolbar contains buttons for promoting or demoting entries, moving entries up or down within the outline, and showing certain outline levels. Figure 5.18 shows the Outline toolbar.

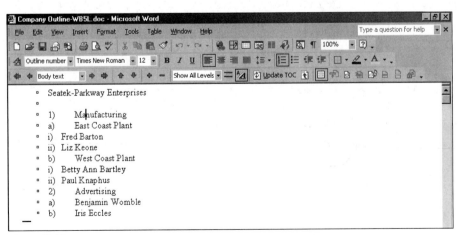

Figure 5.18

Refer to online Help to learn more about working with outlines.

Lesson 6: Adding Borders and Shading

You can draw attention to an entire paragraph by putting a border around it. A ***border*** is a line that surrounds a paragraph or group of paragraphs. You can select the setting, line style, color, and width. To further enhance a border, you can also apply ***shading***, a background color behind the text. Unlike a highlight color that places a color behind the text only, shading fills in the space between lines also.

In this lesson, you add a border with shading for the double-indented paragraph.

To Add a Border and Shading

1 Open *Annual Report-WB5L*, and click inside the double-indented paragraph on page 2.

2 Choose Format, Borders and Shading; and click the Borders tab, if needed.
The Borders and Shading dialog box appears so that you can select the border's characteristics (see Figure 5.19).

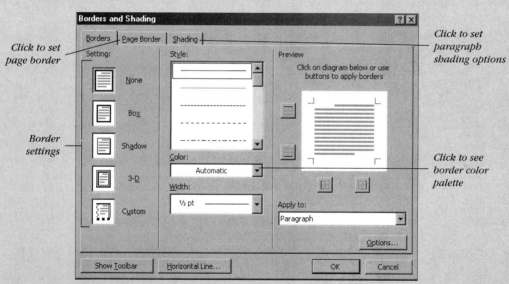

Figure 5.19

3 Click Box in the Setting section to select the primary format of the border.

4 Click the Color drop-down arrow.
A color palette appears, so you can choose the color you want for the border.

5 Click Blue (the third color from the right on the second row).
The color palette closes, and you see the blue color displayed.

6 Click the Shading tab at the top of the dialog box.
You see shading options (see Figure 5.20).

(Continues)

To Add a Border and Shading (Continued)

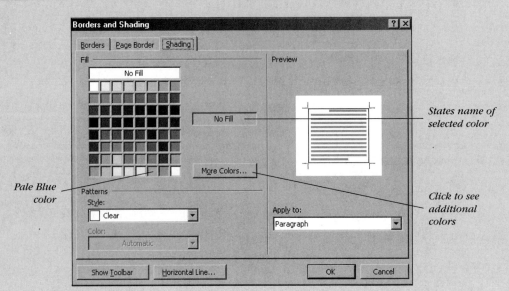

Figure 5.20

⑦ Click Pale Blue, the third color from the right on the last row, and then click OK.
Word applies a blue shadow border with Pale Blue shading around the selected paragraph, as shown in Figure 5.21.

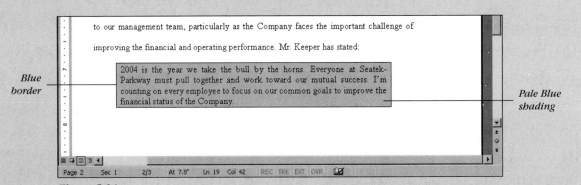

Figure 5.21

⑧ Save the document, and keep it onscreen to continue with the next lesson.

To extend your knowledge...

Choosing Border and Shading Colors

Choose complementary colors for the border and shading. Typically, you should choose a darker border color and a lighter shading color. If the shading color is too dark, the text will be difficult to read.

You can create a ***reverse text effect***, which is an appearance that uses a dark background with a lighter colored font. For example, choose Blue shading color and Yellow font color.

Choosing a Page Border

You can also create a border for the entire page. Click the Page Border tab at the top of the Borders and Shading dialog box, and choose the options you want. Instead of using line page borders, you might want to select a creative page border. Click the Art drop-down arrow to display fun image borders, such as hearts and stars (see Figure 5.22).

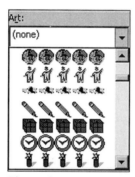

Figure 5.22

You might get an error message, saying that the art borders are not installed. If this happens, insert the Microsoft Office XP installation CD, and perform a custom installation to install the art borders.

With page borders, you can choose the pages you want to place the border on. Click the *Apply to* drop-down arrow and choose from *Whole document, This section, This section—First page only,* or *This section—All except first page.* If your document contains section breaks, which you'll learn about in Project 6, you can apply different page borders to each section.

In addition, click Options to customize the page border. For example, you can set the page border margins.

Lesson 7: Setting and Modifying Tabs

You can set *tabs*—markers that specify the position for aligning text—to create organized lists. You can set left, center, right, and decimal tabs. In addition, you can set a *bar tab*, a marker that produces a vertical bar between two columns when you press Tab.

When you start a new document, Word uses the default tab settings. Every time you press Tab, the insertion point moves over one-half inch. You can use the Ruler to set tabs at any location. Table 5.3 shows the different tab and indent alignments you can set on the ruler.

Table 5.3 Tab Alignment Buttons

Symbol	Type	Description
L	Left Tab	Aligns text at the left side of the tab setting, and continues to the right—similar to Left alignment.
⊥	Center Tab	Centers text on the tab setting; half of the characters appear on the left side and half of the characters appear on the right side of the tab setting.
⌐	Right Tab	Aligns text at the right side of the tab setting—similar to Right alignment.
⊥.	Decimal Tab	Aligns text at the decimal point.
|	Bar Tab	Inserts a vertical line at the tab setting; useful for separating tabular columns.
▽	First Line Indent	Sets the amount of space for indenting the first line of a paragraph.
△	Hanging Indent	Sets the indent for all lines of a paragraph except the first line.

In this lesson, you set tabs to create a list of the organization's divisions, locations, and employees.

To Set Tabs on the Ruler

1 **In the open *Annual Report-WB5L* document, delete the asterisk (*) that is above the *2003 Operating Results* heading on the first page.**
This is where you want to create a tabulated list.

 If you have problems...
If you don't see the Ruler below the Formatting toolbar, choose View, Ruler.

Each mark on the Ruler is one-eighth of an inch.

2 **Click below the 1″ marker on the Ruler.**
You should see a symbol that looks like an L, indicating a left tab setting (see Figure 5.23).

To Set Tabs on the Ruler

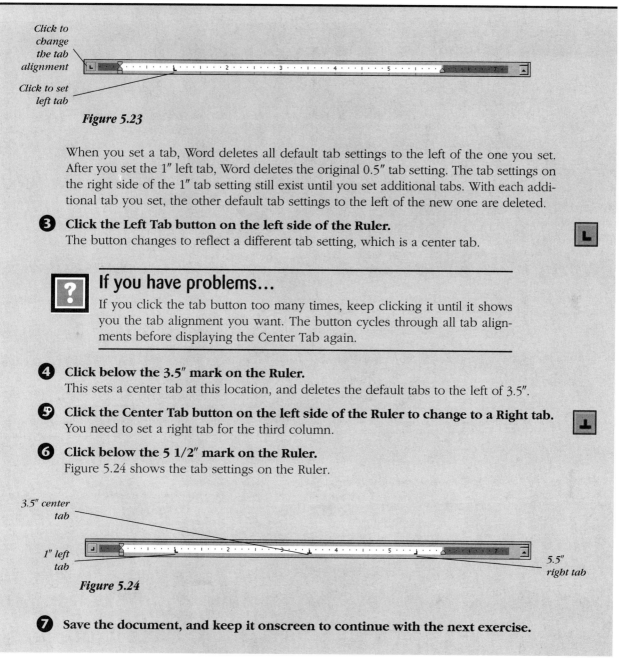

Click to change the tab alignment

Click to set left tab

Figure 5.23

When you set a tab, Word deletes all default tab settings to the left of the one you set. After you set the 1″ left tab, Word deletes the original 0.5″ tab setting. The tab settings on the right side of the 1″ tab setting still exist until you set additional tabs. With each additional tab you set, the other default tab settings to the left of the new one are deleted.

❸ Click the Left Tab button on the left side of the Ruler.
The button changes to reflect a different tab setting, which is a center tab.

? If you have problems...

If you click the tab button too many times, keep clicking it until it shows you the tab alignment you want. The button cycles through all tab alignments before displaying the Center Tab again.

❹ Click below the 3.5″ mark on the Ruler.
This sets a center tab at this location, and deletes the default tabs to the left of 3.5″.

❺ Click the Center Tab button on the left side of the Ruler to change to a Right tab.
You need to set a right tab for the third column.

❻ Click below the 5 1/2″ mark on the Ruler.
Figure 5.24 shows the tab settings on the Ruler.

3.5″ center tab

1″ left tab

5.5″ right tab

Figure 5.24

❼ Save the document, and keep it onscreen to continue with the next exercise.

You are ready to type the tabulated text. When you press ⏎Enter), you create a hard return, which is treated as a new paragraph. However, you might want to change the tab settings for the entire list after typing it. With hard returns, you'd have to select the tabulated text before adjusting tabs.

Instead of pressing ⏎Enter) to insert additional lines of tabulated text, you can insert a *line break* between lines. A **line break** continues text on the next line, but treats the text as a continuation of the previous paragraph instead of a separate paragraph. You insert a line break by pressing ⬆Shift)+⏎Enter).

In the next exercise, you type the tabulated text with a line break between lines.

To Type Tabulated Text with Line Breaks

① In the *Annual Report-WB5L* document, click the Show/Hide ¶ button.

② Press (Tab↹), and type `Seatek Headquarters`.
Typically, you press (Tab↹) before typing text in the first column.

③ Press (Tab↹), and type `Cleveland`.
Cleveland appears in the second column.

④ Press (Tab↹), and type `1,355`.
The value appears in the third column.

⑤ Press (⬆Shift)+(⏎Enter).
Word inserts a line break symbol and positions the insertion point on the next line. The new line is treated as part of the same paragraph.

⑥ Type the rest of the tabulated list, pressing (⬆Shift)+(⏎Enter) after each line.

```
Parkway Division          Denver       1,235

Product Development       Columbus      350

West Coast Distribution   Fresno        123
```

Figure 5.25 shows how the tabulated text appears.

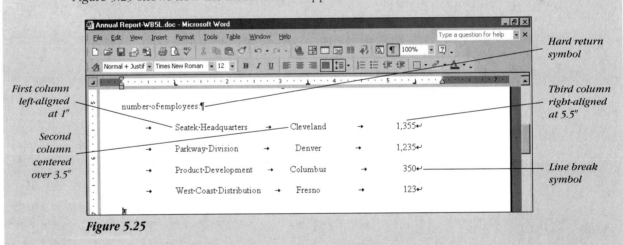

First column left-aligned at 1"

Second column centered over 3.5"

Hard return symbol

Third column right-aligned at 5.5"

Line break symbol

Figure 5.25

⑦ Save the document, and keep it onscreen to continue with the next exercise.

After typing tabulated text, make sure that the tabulated columns are balanced. You should have the same amount of space before the first column and after the last column. Furthermore, you should balance the space between the columns. Currently, the third column is too far to the right. In this lesson, you move the third tab marker to 5" to balance the tabulated text.

To Move Tab Settings

① In the *Annual Report-WB5L* document, click inside the tabulated text.
You want to single-space the tabulated text.

② Click the Line Spacing button on the Formatting toolbar and choose *1.0*.
Because you inserted line breaks instead of hard returns within the tabulated text, the tabulated text is treated as one paragraph and is now single-spaced.

To Move Tab Settings

If you have problems...
If the entire list is not single-spaced, you probably have hard returns within the tabulated text instead of line breaks. If so, press Del to delete the ¶ symbols, and press ⬆Shift + ⏎Enter to insert line breaks.

3 **Click the 5.5″ tab marker, and drag it to the left to the 5″ position.**
When you release the mouse, the entire third column moves to the left. Aligning the third column at 5″ provides a one-inch space on the right side, which balances the one-inch space before the first column. Now, you need to move the second column to balance the internal space.

4 **Click the 3.5″ tab marker to 3 5/8″ position.**
The internal space between columns is balanced (see Figure 5.26).

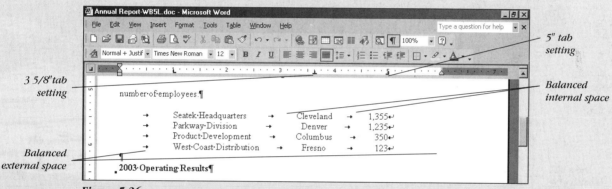

Figure 5.26

5 **Click the Show/Hide ¶ button to hide the nonprinting symbols.**

6 **Save the document, and keep it onscreen to continue with the next lesson.**

To extend your knowledge...

Setting Exact Measurements

You can set a more precise measurement by pressing Alt as you click and drag the tab marker along the Ruler. When you do this, Word displays the amount of space between the left margin and the tab setting and the amount of space between the tab setting and the right margin (see Figure 5.27).

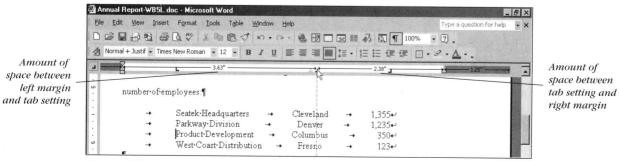

Figure 5.27

The Tabs dialog box is another way to clear and set tabs. Using the Tabs dialog box has an advantage in that you can set *leader* options that produce dots, a dashed line, or a solid line between the current column and the next column. Leaders guide the reader's eyes from one column to the next. Figure 5.28 shows the Tabs dialog box.

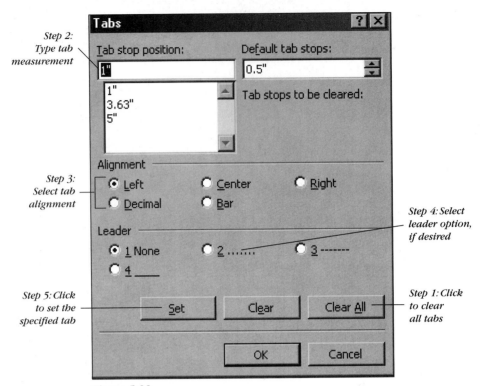

Figure 5.28

Using Line Breaks in Numbered Lists

If you want a blank line between items in a numbered list, you can't press ⏎Enter twice because Word removes the number when you press ⏎Enter the second time. Therefore, you can use paragraph spacing or insert line breaks to create blank lines between numbered items.

Lesson 8: Revealing and Clearing Formats

While double-checking a printed document, you might notice a formatting problem. However, identifying the exact problem might not be obvious. For example, did you double-space text, press ⏎Enter an extra time, or set paragraph spacing? You can detect the exact format of text by displaying the ***Reveal Formatting task pane*** that shows the font characteristics, alignment, indentation, spacing, and tabs.

In this lesson, you reveal formatting to see how you formatted different text.

To Reveal Formatting

1 In the *Annual Report-WB5L* document, make sure the insertion point is inside the tabulated text.

2 Choose F**o**rmat, Re**v**eal Formatting.
The Reveal Formatting task pane appears (see Figure 5.29).

To Reveal Formatting

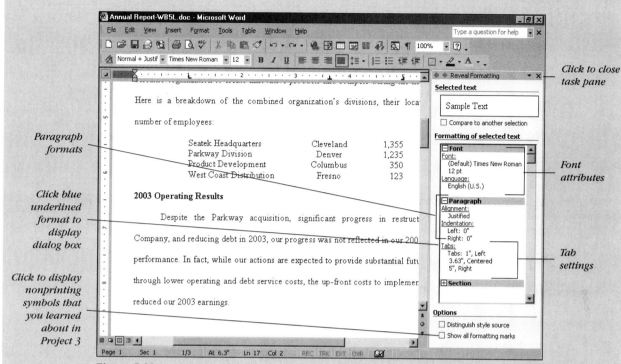

Figure 5.29

The task pane window shows character formats, paragraph formats, and tab settings. It does not show nonprinting symbols, such as hard returns, nonbreaking spaces, and regular spaces. Clicking the *Show all formatting marks* check box displays the nonprinting symbols in the document window, not the task pane.

③ Click the blue underlined *Tabs* link in the Reveal Formatting task pane.
The Tabs dialog box appears so that you can change the tab settings.

④ Click Cancel to close the dialog box without changing any formats.
Next, view the formats for the paragraph with the border and shading.

⑤ Scroll to the bottom of page 2, and click inside the paragraph that contains the pale blue shading.
The Reveal Formatting task pane shows that the paragraph is justified with 0.5" left and right indentation, 12 pt spacing after the paragraph, single solid blue line, and a pale blue shading.

⑥ Click the task pane's Close button.

You can remove formats if you want to return text to its original unformatted condition. That way, you can start fresh by reformatting it. In the next exercise, you see how the Clear Formats option works.

To Clear Formats

① In the *Annual Report-WB5L* document, make sure that the insertion point is in the shaded paragraph.

② Choose Edit, Clear, Formats.

(Continues)

To Clear Formats (Continued)

All formatting is removed from the paragraph. It is no longer indented, justified, shaded, or enclosed in a border (see Figure 5.30).

Formats removed from paragraph

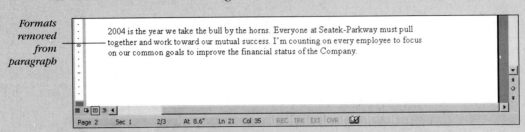

2004 is the year we take the bull by the horns. Everyone at Seatek-Parkway must pull together and work toward our mutual success. I'm counting on every employee to focus on our common goals to improve the financial status of the Company.

Page 2   Sec 1   2/3   At 8.6"   Ln 21   Col 35   REC TRK EXT OVR

Figure 5.30

If the paragraph had character formats, such as bold, the bold would not have cleared. Character formats are cleared if you *select* text before using the Clear option.

3 **Click the Undo button to restore the formats to the paragraph.**

4 **Save, print, and close the document.**

Summary

In this project, you learned some exciting methods to format paragraphs. You made text easier to read by using double-spacing and paragraph spacing, inserting bulleted and numbered lists, and adding a border with shading. You also learned how to set tabs, change the alignment, and indent text. All of these formatting techniques dramatically improve the professionalism of the document you create.

Although these features are a great way to start improving your documents, Word offers a lot more enhancements. Use the Help feature to learn more about formatting options, especially those found in the Paragraph, Borders and Shading, and Tabs dialog boxes. There are no limits to what you can do with these features!

Checking Concepts and Terms

Multiple Choice

Circle the letter of the correct answer for each of the following.

1. What term refers to the way text lines up at the left and right margins? [L2]

    a. line spacing

    b. margins

    c. justified text

    d. alignment

2. What feature keeps the first line of a paragraph at the left margin and indents the rest of the paragraph? [L3]

    a. indent

    b. double indent

    c. hanging indent

    d. double-spacing

3. What format is most appropriate for emphasizing a list of items in sequential order? [L4]

a. bulleted list
b. numbered list
c. border
d. highlight

4. What type of tab produces a vertical line between columns? [L7]

a. left
b. dot leader
c. bar
d. hanging indent

5. Which type of formatting does not appear in the Reveal Formatting task pane? [L8]

a. Nonbreaking Space
b. Indentation
c. Font
d. Alignment

Screen ID

Label each element of the Word screen shown in Figure 5.31.

A. center-aligned text
B. Decrease Indent
C. double-spaced text
D. Increase Indent
E. justified text
F. numbered list

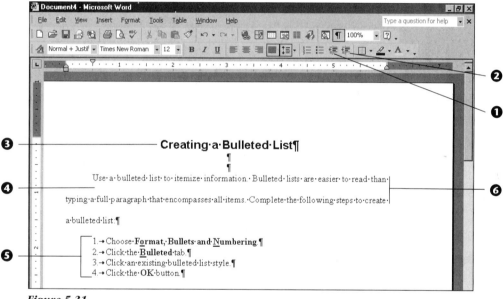

Figure 5.31

1. _____
2. _____
3. _____
4. _____
5. _____
6. _____

Discussion

1. What is the difference between line spacing and paragraph spacing? [L1]

2. Why would you clear formats from a paragraph? [L8]

3. What is the purpose of displaying the Reveal Formatting task pane? [L8]

Skill Drill exercises reinforce project skills. Each skill reinforced is the same, or nearly the same, as a skill presented in the project. Detailed instructions are provided in a step-by-step format.

1. Setting Text Alignment

You created a short report for a class. After creating the text, you decide to center the title and justify the rest of the document.

1. Open *ew1-0502*, and save it as `Internet Report-WB5SD`.
2. Choose <u>E</u>dit, Select A<u>l</u>l.
3. Click the Justify button on the Formatting toolbar.
4. Click in the document window to deselect text.
5. Position the insertion point within the title *Using the Internet,* and click the Center button on the Formatting toolbar.
6. Select the subtitle *Internet Protocol*; then click the Center button on the Formatting toolbar.
7. Repeat step 6 for these two subtitles: *Domain Names* and *Problems.*
8. Save the document and keep it onscreen to continue with the next exercise.

2. Changing Line Spacing and Paragraph Spacing

You decide to change the line spacing in your document to double-spacing to improve its readability. Then, you want to single-space a list of domain names. Finally, you want to add a little space above the centered headings by increasing the spacing before paragraph.

1. In the *Internet Report-WB5SD* document, position the insertion point at the beginning of the first paragraph.
2. Select the paragraphs you want to format by pressing Ctrl+⬆Shift+End.
3. Press Ctrl+2 to double-space the selected paragraphs.
4. Position the insertion point before the text *.edu* on page 2.
5. Hold down ⬆Shift and click at the end of the *.org* paragraph to select the paragraphs about domain names.
6. Click the Line Spacing button on the Formatting toolbar, and choose *1.0.*
7. Position the insertion point in the centered heading, *Internet Protocol.*
8. Choose F<u>o</u>rmat, <u>P</u>aragraph.
9. Click the Spacing <u>B</u>efore spin button to *6 pt*, and click OK.
10. Click in the heading *Domain Names*; then, repeat steps 8 and 9 to increase spacing before paragraph.
11. Click in the *Problems* heading.

12. Choose Format, Paragraph; click the Spacing Before spin button to *18 pt*; and click OK. When you changed the line spacing for the *org* paragraph, you eliminated the blank space between that paragraph and the following heading. Therefore, setting 18 pt paragraph spacing before the heading creates the visual space of one blank line plus the other 6 pt space you used for the other headings.

13. Save the document, and keep it onscreen to continue with the next exercise.

3. Creating a Bulleted List and Indenting Text

The list of domain conventions is difficult to read. You determine that including a bullet before each convention will improve both the appearance and readability of the list. In addition, you want to indent the left side of the bulleted list so that the bullets are indented the same amount of space as the paragraphs. Finally, you want to double-indent the last paragraph.

1. With the *Internet Report-WB5SD* onscreen, position the insertion point before the text *.edu* on page 2.

2. Select the list of domains.

3. Click the Bullets button on the Formatting toolbar.

4. Click the Increase Indent button on the Formatting toolbar to indent the bulleted lists from the left side.

5. Press Ctrl+End to position the insertion point in the last paragraph.

6. Choose Format, Paragraph.

7. Click the Left spin button until you see *0.5"*.

8. Click the Right spin button until you see *0.5"*.

9. Click the *Line spacing* drop-down arrow, and choose *Single*.

10. Click OK.

11. Save the document, and keep it onscreen to continue with the next exercise.

4. Applying Borders and Shading

You believe the bulleted list would look nicer with a border and paragraph shading.

1. In the *Internet Report-WB5SD* document, select the bulleted list.

2. Choose Format, Borders and Shading.

3. Click the Borders tab, if needed, and click the Shadow setting.

4. Click the Color drop-down arrow, and click Orange.

5. Click the Shading tab.

6. Click Tan, the second color from the left on the last row.

7. Click OK, and deselect the bulleted list.

8. Save the document, and keep it onscreen to continue with the next exercise.

5. Revealing and Clearing Formats

You want to study the formats that you applied to various paragraphs. Therefore, you display the Reveal Formatting task pane. In addition, you clear formats from a paragraph.

1. In the *Internet Report-WB5SD* document, select the bulleted list.

2. Choose Format, Reveal Formatting to see the Reveal Formatting task pane.

3. Click the task pane's scroll-down arrow to display the Bullets and Numbering section.

4. Click *List* in the task pane to display the Bullets and Numbering dialog box.

5. Click the arrowhead-shaped bulleted list style and then click OK.

6. Click *Alignment* in the task pane to display the Paragraph dialog box.

7. Click the *Alignment* drop-down arrow, choose *Left*, and click OK.

8. Click in the *Problems* heading to see the information shown in the task pane.

9. Click the *Show all formatting marks* check box at the bottom of the task pane to see non-printing symbols such as the ¶ marks.

10. Click the task pane's Close button.

11. With the insertion point still in the *Problems* heading, choose Edit, Clear, Formats to remove formats from that heading.

12. Click the Undo button to restore the heading's formats.

13. Save, print, and close the document.

Challenge exercises expand on or are somewhat related to skills presented in the lessons. Each exercise provides a brief narrative introduction, followed by instructions in a numbered-step format that are not as detailed as those in the Skill Drill section.

1. Editing a Welcome Letter

You composed a letter to welcome new members to an organization of which you are president. You use several of the formatting techniques you learned in this project to improve the appearance of the letter.

1. Open *ew1-0503*, and save it as `Welcome Letter-WB5CH1`.

2. Change Ken's name to your name in the signature block.

3. Select the entire document, and choose Justify alignment.

4. Delete the asterisk, and create the following bulleted list:
   ○ `Having administrative professionals be guest speakers at meetings.`
   ○ `Participating in the regional and national conferences.`
   ○ `Shadowing an administrative professional for a day.`
   ○ `Finding internships for members of the organization.`

5. Select the bulleted list, display the Bullets and Numbering dialog box, and choose the check mark bulleted list.

6. Select the salutation through the last paragraph. Set 12-point spacing after paragraph.

7. Select the Date, Time, and three Where lines. Set 1.5″ left and right indents, 0 pt spacing after paragraph, and a blue paragraph border. Click on the last Where line, and set a 12 pt after paragraph spacing. Indent all text after the colons so they align at 2.5″.

8. Select the entire document, and display the Reveal Formatting task pane.

9. Click *Font* on the task pane to display the Font dialog box.

10. Select Bookman Old Style and 12 point size.

11. Save, print, and close the document.

2. Formatting an Invitation to a Halloween Party

You are having a Halloween party at your home, and decide to create your own invitations. You create the text first and then want to improve it by changing fonts, changing text alignment, creating a fun bulleted list, and adding a page border.

1. Open *ew1-0504*, and save it as `Halloween Party-WB5CH2`.

2. Apply triple-spacing to the entire document.

3. Make the first line of the invitation (`Hey! It's a Halloween Party!`) larger (at least 30-point) and bolder by using the Font dialog box. Because this is a fun invitation, try a different font—such as Chiller, Dauphin, Desdemona, or Copperplate Gothic Bold. Ask your instructor for an alternative font if you don't have any of the fonts specified previously. Adjust the font size if the title takes up two lines.

4. Apply your font choice to the last line of the invitation so both lines have the same appearance. Apply 16-point size to the last line.

5. Pick another font for the body of the invitation. Select one that coordinates with the one you used for the title.

6. Select the When, Where, Why, and RSVP lines. Display the Bullets and Numbering dialog box. Customize the bulleted list by choosing a Halloween-type symbol, such as the spider or spider web, from the Webdings font. Select orange font for the bullets. Also set 1.5″ left indent for the bulleted list.

7. Center the first line of the invitation. Left-align the body of the invitation and the bulleted list. Center the last line of the invitation.

8. Select a Halloween theme page border from the Art drop-down list. Select an appropriate page border color.

9. Make adjustments in internal spacing (line or paragraph) and font sizes to spread the text out, so it's not all clustered together.

10. Save, print, and close the document.

3. Creating and Formatting a Reference Page (Bibliography)

Your supervisor gave you a rough-draft sheet of references. She asked you to correctly format the reference page.

1. In a new document window, type the title `Works Cited`, centered between the left and right margins. Triple-space after the title. Then, change to left alignment.

2. Create the following references using hanging indents and italicize the book titles. Keep the entire list single-spaced for now (no blank lines between reference entries).
   Boettcher, David. "Motivating Customer Service Associates." *Contemporary Managerial Report* 25 Jan. 2003: 86.
   Reudter, Rodolph. *Managerial Failures in the Food Services Industry.* Proc. of the Regional Managerial Professionals Conference, Oct. 2003, State University. Las Vegas, 2004.
   Faamausili, Jon. "Practical Tips for Managing Employees." *City Daily Times* 15 Jan. 2004: B15.
   Corrado, Vicente. *The Performance Appraisal: More Than a Critical Review.* Boston: Book Group Publishing Company, 2002.

3. Insert nonbreaking spaces if needed to keep appropriate words together.

4. Select the four reference entries, and set 16-point spacing after paragraph.

5. Use the Sort command to sort the selected paragraphs in alphabetical order.

6. Adjust spacing after the title if needed to maintain the triple-space. (Check the paragraph spacing for the blank lines to make sure that it is 0 points before the first reference entry.)

7. Select the title, apply Small Caps effect, and choose 14-point Arial Rounded MT Bold (or Arial with bold).

8. Save the document as `Works Cited-WB5CH3`, print it, and close the document.

4. Creating a Memo with Tabulated Text

You want to send a memo to your company's employees about upcoming Word workshops. You want to align the colons in the heading, so you plan to set appropriate tabs. In addition, you create a tabulated list of workshops, dates, and times.

1. In a new document window, press ⏎Enter three times, and save the document as `Word Workshops-WB5CH4`.

2. In the Tabs dialog box, clear existing tabs, and set a 0.81″ right tab and a 0.95″ left tab.

3. Type the following heading with these specifications:
   - Press Tab⇆ before typing the first column for each line.
   - Type the bold capitalized words. Turn off bold after typing the colon, press Tab⇆, and type the second column.

    ○ Press `⏎Enter` twice after typing each of the first three lines of the heading; press `⏎Enter` three times after typing the subject line.

TO:	All Employees
FROM:	your name
DATE:	February 2, 2004
SUBJECT:	Word Workshops

4. Type the following paragraph:

    The Computer Services Department has completed the installation of the new computer systems and Microsoft Office XP software. We are offering the following training sessions to help you become more proficient in Word 2002. All sessions will be held in Room 415. Please call Extension 5840 to register for workshops you'd like to attend.

5. Double-space, clear existing tabs, and set the following tabs: 1″ left, 3.38″ center, and 5″ right.

6. Type the following tabulated text, inserting line breaks between lines:

New Features	February 9	3:30 p.m.
Section Formats	February 23	9:00 a.m.
Table Formats	March 8	12:00 p.m.
Excel Integration	March 22	10:00 a.m.
Styles & Templates	April 5	3:30 p.m.
Advanced Formats	April 19	10:30 a.m.

7. Select the tabulated text and move the second tab to the left about 1/8″.

8. Save, print, and close the document.

5. Setting Tabs to Create a Table of Contents

You recently completed a report, and now want to create a table of contents that provides leaders between the headings in the first column and the page numbers.

1. In a new document window, type `Table of Contents`.

2. Triple-space, set tabs, and type the table of contents with hard returns instead of line breaks, as shown in Figure 5.32.

TABLE OF CONTENTS

The Personal Interview	1
Introduction	1
Pre-interview Impression Effects	1
Pre-interview Impressions	1
Self-Fulfilling Prophecy	2
The Bias of Information Processing	2
Perception of the Interview	3
The Unfavorable Information Effect	3
Interviewer Decision Styles	3
The Attribution Theory and Attribution Bias	3
Stereotypes	4
Non-Verbal Communications	4
Physical Characteristics	5

Figure 5.32

3. Center the title, and apply 14-point Arial bold to the title.

4. Save the document as `Table of Contents-WB5CH5`.

5. Print and close the document.

6. Balancing Tabulated Text in a Letter

You work as an assistant to a product manager at a major publishing company. Your supervisor typed a letter to a new author, and asked you to type in contact data as tabulated text within the letter. You must use your own judgment to perfectly balance the tabulated text between the left and right margins, and to balance the internal space between columns.

1. Open *ew1-0505*, and save it as `Author Letter-WB5CH6`.

2. Select the first three full paragraphs, and apply 12-point spacing after paragraph.

3. Delete the asterisk, and set tabs for the following data. Set a center tab for the second column and a right tab for the last column to help you balance the tabulated text when you are through. Type the following single-spaced tabulated text with line breaks between lines:

Esther Israelsen	Acquisitions Editor	(201) 555-9040
Sunther Chaney	Product Manager	(201) 555-9050
Gaylen Sainsbury	Developmental Editor	(435) 555-4321
Tiffany Truong	Technical Editor	(419) 555-6742
Ira Wesemann	Production Manager	(201) 555-9187

4. Modify the tab settings for the first and last columns to balance the tabulated text between the left and right margins.

5. Modify the middle tab setting to balance space between the tabulated columns.

6. Make sure that there is one blank line after the last tabulated line.

7. Insert a nonbreaking space and a nonbreaking hyphen with the phone number in the last paragraph.

8. Save, print, and close the document.

Discovery Zone exercises require advanced knowledge of topics presented in *essentials* lessons, application of skills from multiple lessons, or self-directed learning of new skills.

1. Creating a Health Information Sheet

As part of an assignment in a health class, you create an information sheet on osteoarthritis to share with your classmates.

Open *ew1-0506*, and save it as `Osteoarthritis-WB5DZ1`. Use one of these sans serif fonts for the title and two headings: Arial Rounded MT Bold, AvantGarde with bold font style, Kabel Dm BT, or Arial with bold. Use Bookman Old Style font for the paragraph and bulleted items. When creating the page border, select the fourth style from the bottom of the Style list. Use a Pale Blue shading and other formats, as indicated in Figure 5.33.

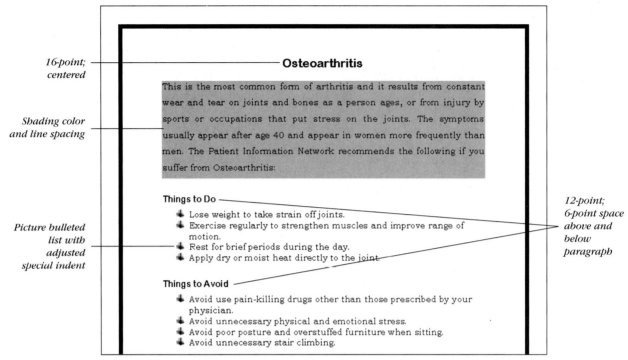

16-point; centered

Shading color and line spacing

Picture bulleted list with adjusted special indent

12-point; 6-point space above and below paragraph

Figure 5.33

Save, print, and close the document.

2. Formatting a Course Description Document

Refer to Figure 5.34 to create a course description document. Create the customized bulleted list using the disk symbol found in the Wingdings font. Save the document as `Course Descriptions-WB5DZ2` and print it.

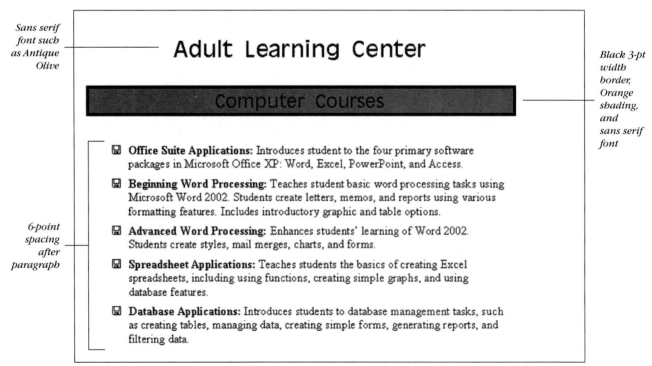

Sans serif font such as Antique Olive

Black 3-pt width border, Orange shading, and sans serif font

6-point spacing after paragraph

Figure 5.34

3. Preparing an Outline Numbered List for Teachers

As a student assistant in your college's administration office, you have been asked to type an outline numbered list of teaching responsibilities. In a new document window, type **Teaching Responsibilities** centered, boldface, and in 14-point Arial. Make sure that the rest of the document is left-aligned.

Create the outline numbered list using the style and format shown in Figure 5.35.

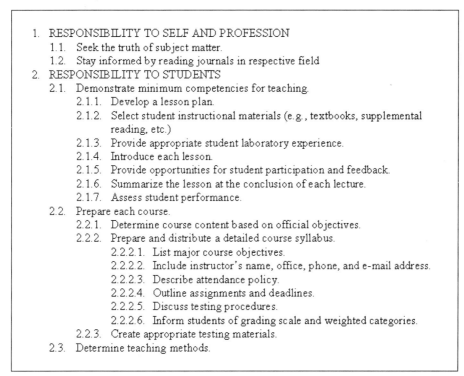

1. RESPONSIBILITY TO SELF AND PROFESSION
    1.1. Seek the truth of subject matter.
    1.2. Stay informed by reading journals in respective field
2. RESPONSIBILITY TO STUDENTS
    2.1. Demonstrate minimum competencies for teaching.
        2.1.1. Develop a lesson plan.
        2.1.2. Select student instructional materials (e.g., textbooks, supplemental reading, etc.)
        2.1.3. Provide appropriate student laboratory experience.
        2.1.4. Introduce each lesson.
        2.1.5. Provide opportunities for student participation and feedback.
        2.1.6. Summarize the lesson at the conclusion of each lecture.
        2.1.7. Assess student performance.
    2.2. Prepare each course.
        2.2.1. Determine course content based on official objectives.
        2.2.2. Prepare and distribute a detailed course syllabus.
            2.2.2.1. List major course objectives.
            2.2.2.2. Include instructor's name, office, phone, and e-mail address.
            2.2.2.3. Describe attendance policy.
            2.2.2.4. Outline assignments and deadlines.
            2.2.2.5. Discuss testing procedures.
            2.2.2.6. Inform students of grading scale and weighted categories.
        2.2.3. Create appropriate testing materials.
    2.3. Determine teaching methods.

Figure 5.35

After you select the appropriate outline style, customize it to adjust the formats based on the following specifications:

Level 1:	Aligned at 0″	Indent at 0.25″
Level 2:	Aligned at 0.25″	Indent at 0.65″
Level 3:	Aligned at 0.65″	Indent at 1.15″
Level 4:	Aligned at 1.15″	Indent at 1.75″

Type the outline list shown in the figure; choose the Outline view mode; and then demote the last entry, *Determine teaching methods*. Move down *List major course objectives*.

For the first first-level entry, set a 12-pt spacing after paragraph. For the second first-level entry, set a 12-pt before and 12-pt after paragraph spacing.

Save the document as **Teaching Responsibilities-WB5DZ3**. Print and close the document.

Formatting Documents

Objectives

In this project, you learn how to

- ✔ Set Margins
- ✔ Insert Section and Page Breaks
- ✔ Center Text Vertically
- ✔ Insert Page Numbers
- ✔ Prevent Text from Separating Between Pages
- ✔ Create Headers and Footers
- ✔ Navigate with the Document Map

Key terms introduced in this project include

- ❑ automatic page break
- ❑ Document Map
- ❑ footer
- ❑ header
- ❑ manual page break
- ❑ margins
- ❑ orphan
- ❑ section break
- ❑ suppress
- ❑ vertical alignment
- ❑ widow

Why Would I Do This?

By now you know how to format paragraphs or small sections of text. Now you are ready to format entire documents and control pagination. In this project, you set margins, insert section and page breaks, center text vertically, insert page numbers, and create headers and footers. Finally, you keep bulleted text from spanning page breaks and use navigation features to get around a long document.

Visual Summary

Figure 6.1 shows a title page that is centered vertically and horizontally.

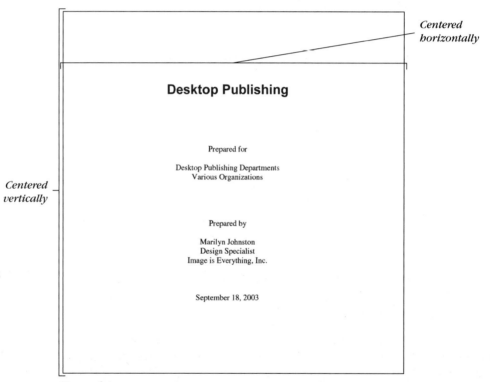

Centered horizontally

Centered vertically

Desktop Publishing

Prepared for

Desktop Publishing Departments
Various Organizations

Prepared by

Marilyn Johnston
Design Specialist
Image is Everything, Inc.

September 18, 2003

Figure 6.1

Figure 6.2 shows the second page in a report that contains a header, different margins, a bulleted list, and a page number.

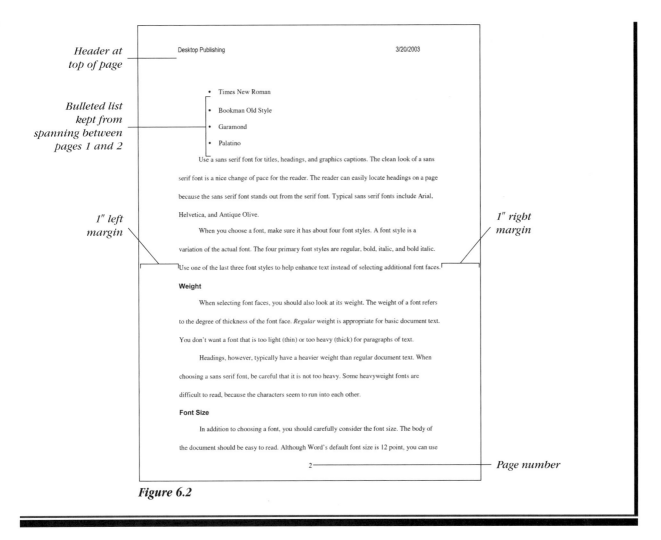

Header at top of page

Bulleted list kept from spanning between pages 1 and 2

1″ left margin

1″ right margin

Page number

Figure 6.2

Lesson 1: Setting Margins

A document's ***margins*** determine the amount of white space around the text. New documents have 1″ top and bottom margins and 1.25″ left and right margins. These margin settings are acceptable for many documents. However, you should change margins when doing so improves the appearance of your document. General or company reference manuals specify certain margin settings for particular documents.

In this lesson, you set a larger top margin and smaller left and right margins in a document.

To Set Margins

❶ **Open *ew1-0601*, and save it as** `Desktop Publishing-WB6L`.
The report is currently formatted by the default margins.

❷ **Press** `PgDn` **twice to see paragraphs in the document.**
You want to see how the current margins affect line endings.

❸ **Choose** <u>F</u>**ile, Page Set<u>u</u>p; click the *Margins* tab if needed to see the margin options.**
The Page Setup dialog box appears with options for setting the margins, selecting paper sizes, and specifying the layout (see Figure 6.3).

(Continues)

To Set Margins (Continued)

Click the Margins tab

Margin settings

Choose the document part for applying the settings

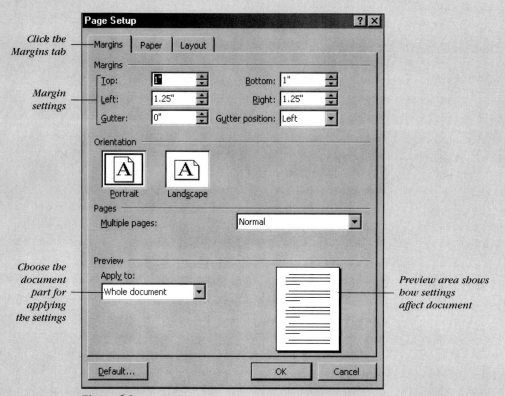

Preview area shows how settings affect document

Figure 6.3

4 **Type 1.5 in the _Top_ text box.**
Because the _Top_ text box is selected when you first open the Page Setup dialog box, you can type the margin setting; the number you type replaces the original setting. You don't have to type the inch mark ("); Word assumes that you are setting margins in inches.

5 **Click the _Left_ spin button to decrease the left margin to 1".**
The left margin setting is now smaller.

6 **Click the _Right_ spin button to decrease the right margin to 1".**
The right margin setting is now smaller. Notice that the margin settings will be applied to the entire document because the default _Apply to_ option is _Whole document_. This is why the insertion point can be anywhere in the document when you change margins.

7 **Click OK.**
Each line in the paragraph contains more text because decreasing the left and right margins increases the space for text (see Figure 6.4).

To Set Margins

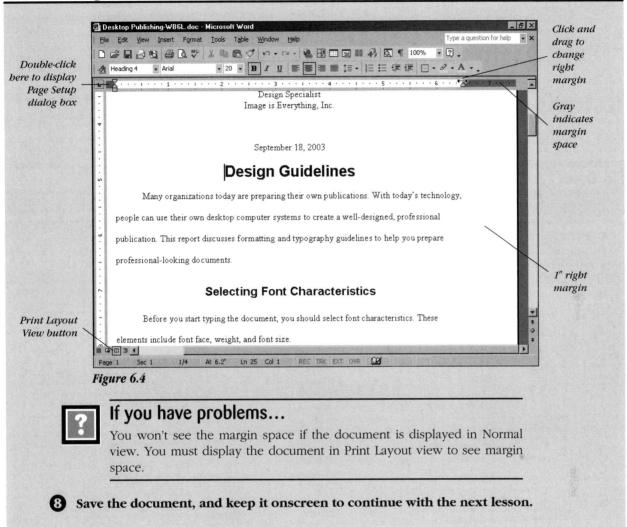

Double-click here to display Page Setup dialog box

Click and drag to change right margin

Gray indicates margin space

1" right margin

Print Layout View button

Figure 6.4

If you have problems...

You won't see the margin space if the document is displayed in Normal view. You must display the document in Print Layout view to see margin space.

8 **Save the document, and keep it onscreen to continue with the next lesson.**

To extend your knowledge...

Displaying the Page Setup Dialog Box

Double-click the empty gray space on the far left or far right side of the ruler to display the Page Setup dialog box.

Setting Margins on the Ruler

When you display the document in Print Layout view, you can set the margins on the ruler. You can set the left and right margins on the horizontal ruler and the top and bottom margins on the vertical ruler.

As shown in Figure 6.4, the white area on the ruler displays the typing area between the margins, and the dark gray area represents the margins. To change the margins, click and drag the margin markers on the ruler. You see a two-headed arrow as you click and drag the margin markers.

Lesson 2: Inserting Section and Page Breaks

When you set some formats, such as margins, Word applies those formats to the *entire* document. However, you might need to apply different formats throughout the document. Therefore, you need to insert **section breaks**, which are markers that divide the document into sections that you can format separately.

In this lesson, you insert a section break so that you can format the title page differently from the rest of the document.

To Insert a Section Break

❶ In the *Desktop Publishing-WB6L* document, click the Normal View button.
The first page contains information for a title page and regular document text. You need to start the document text on a new page. More importantly, you need to be able to format the title page differently from the document text.

❷ Position the insertion point to the left of *Design Guidelines*, which is below the date on the first page.
You want the document title to start a new section.

❸ Choose Insert, Break.
The Break dialog box contains options for inserting page and section breaks (see Figure 6.5).

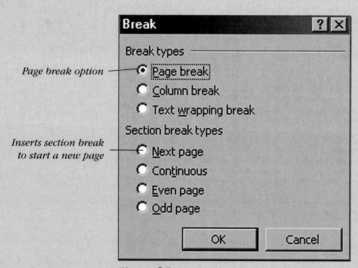

Page break option ⎯

Inserts section break to start a new page ⎯

Figure 6.5

❹ Click the *Next page* option, and click OK.
Figure 6.6 shows the section break, indicated by a double-dotted line and *Section Break (Next Page)*.

To Insert a Section Break

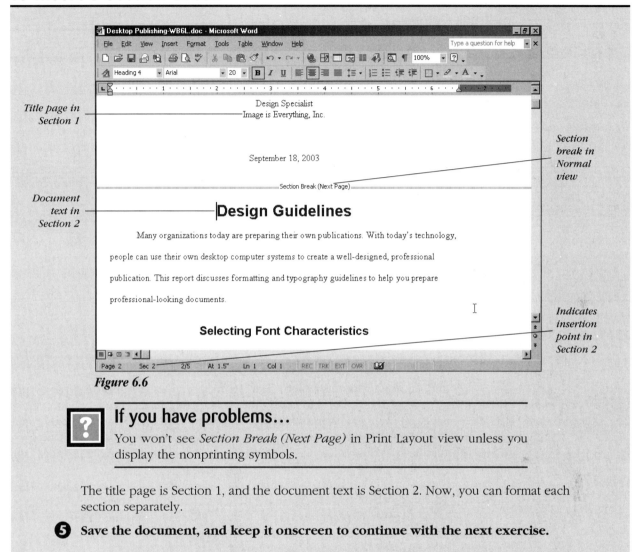

Title page in Section 1

Section break in Normal view

Document text in Section 2

Indicates insertion point in Section 2

Figure 6.6

If you have problems...

You won't see *Section Break (Next Page)* in Print Layout view unless you display the nonprinting symbols.

The title page is Section 1, and the document text is Section 2. Now, you can format each section separately.

5 **Save the document, and keep it onscreen to continue with the next exercise.**

Table 6.1 lists and describes the options in the Break dialog box.

Table 6.1 Break Options

Option	Description
Page break	Inserts a hard page break (starts a new page) within the same section.
Column break	Starts a new column within columnar text.
Text wrapping break	Stops entering text on the current line and continues text on the next blank line; treats next line as part of paragraph. Useful for positioning text below a picture or table.
Next page	Inserts a section break by starting a new page. Allows you to apply different formats to different sections.
Continuous	Starts a new section on the *same* page. Useful for creating different formats, such as margins, on the same page of a newsletter.
Even page	Starts a new section by forcing text to appear on the next available even-numbered page. If the next page is an odd-numbered page, Word leaves that page blank.
Odd page	Starts a new section by forcing text to appear on the next available odd-numbered page. Useful for making sure all new sections or chapters start on the right-hand side of a double-sided document.

When a page is full and cannot contain any more data, Word inserts an ***automatic page break***, which ends the current page and starts the next page. Automatic page breaks change when you add or delete data on a page. You can create a ***manual page break*** to start a new page instead of continuing to enter data until Word inserts an automatic page break. Manual page breaks, which are appropriate for ensuring the start of a new page, stay where you insert them unless you specifically delete them.

In the previous exercise, you created a new section page break so that you can apply different formats to each section—title page section and document section. However, in some cases, you might want to create a page break within the same section and continue the same formats. Therefore, you insert a manual page break instead of a section break.

In this exercise, you insert a manual page break to start *Setting the Spacing* on a new page within the same section as the previous text.

To Insert a Manual Page Break

1 In the ***Desktop Publishing-WB6L*** **document, click to the left of** *Setting the Spacing*, **which is near the top of page 4.**
You want the heading *Setting the Spacing* to start at the top of a new page.

2 **Choose** Insert, Break.

3 **Make sure that the** *Page break* **option is selected and then click OK.**
Word inserts a manual page break, designed by a dotted line and the words *Page Break* in Normal view. *Setting the Spacing* is now positioned at the top of a new page (see Figure 6.7) within the same section—Section 2.

To Insert a Manual Page Break

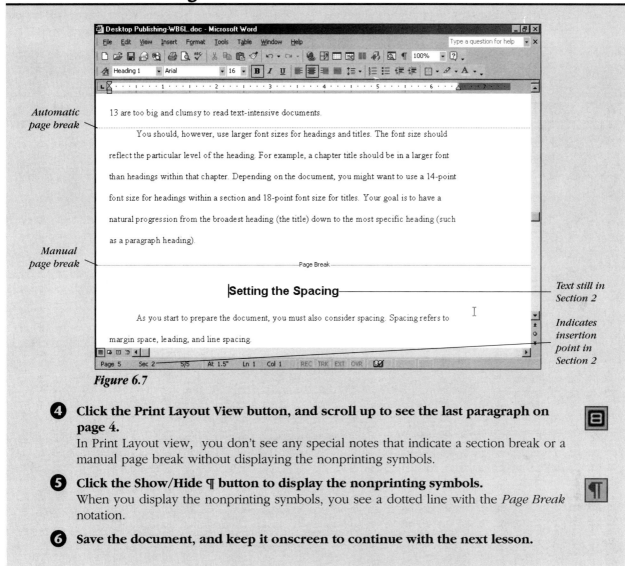

Automatic page break

Manual page break

Text still in Section 2

Indicates insertion point in Section 2

Figure 6.7

❹ Click the Print Layout View button, and scroll up to see the last paragraph on page 4.
In Print Layout view, you don't see any special notes that indicate a section break or a manual page break without displaying the nonprinting symbols.

❺ Click the Show/Hide ¶ button to display the nonprinting symbols.
When you display the nonprinting symbols, you see a dotted line with the *Page Break* notation.

❻ Save the document, and keep it onscreen to continue with the next lesson.

To extend your knowledge...

Manual Page Break Keyboard Shortcut

You can insert a manual page break quickly by pressing Ctrl+↵Enter.

Lesson 3: Centering Text Vertically on a Page

Typically, the first page in a document or research paper is the title page. The standard format is to center it horizontally and vertically. In Project 5, "Formatting Paragraphs," you applied Center alignment to center text horizontally (left to right).

In addition to aligning text horizontally, you might need to select ***vertical alignment***, which controls how text aligns between the top and bottom margins. The default vertical alignment is Top, which starts text at the top margin and continues down a page. When formatting a title page, you should choose Center vertical alignment to center the text between the top and bottom margins.

In this lesson, you vertically center text on the title page in your document.

To Center Text Vertically on a Page

❶ In the *Desktop Publishing-WB6L* document, click the Show/Hide ¶ button to hide the nonprinting symbols.

❷ Press Ctrl+Home to position the insertion point at the beginning of the document.

❸ Choose File, Page Setup.
The Page Setup dialog box appears with the margin options displayed. You need to display the layout options.

❹ Click the *Layout* tab.
The layout options appear. Notice that the default *Vertical alignment* option is *Top* (see Figure 6.8)

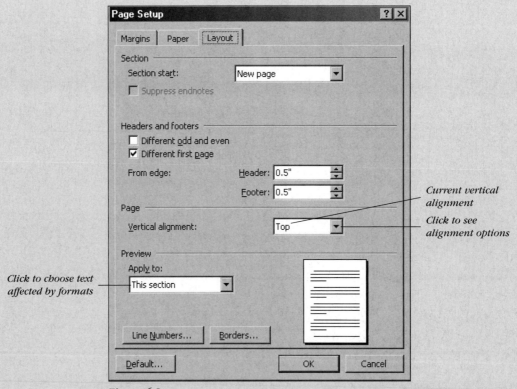

Click to choose text affected by formats

Current vertical alignment

Click to see alignment options

Figure 6.8

❺ Click the *Vertical alignment* drop-down arrow.

❻ Choose *Center*.
The *Vertical alignment* option now displays *Center*. The center vertical alignment format applies to the current section only, indicated by *This section* as the *Apply to* option.

To Center Text Vertically on a Page

 If you have problems...

If the *Apply to* options are only *Whole document* and *This point forward*, you need to make sure you have a section break—not a hard page break—after the title page. Using a hard page break does not let you vertically center the title page only; Word would vertically center the entire document.

7 **Click OK.**

8 **Click the Zoom drop-down arrow on the Standard toolbar, and choose *Two Pages*.** 100%

The title page is now centered vertically on the page within Section 1, whereas the rest of the document text in Section 2 is aligned at the top margin (see Figure 6.9).

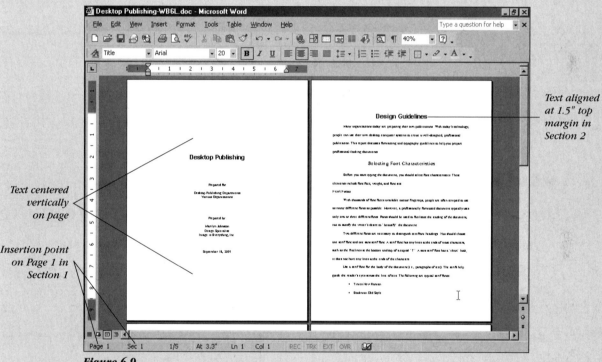

Text aligned at 1.5" top margin in Section 2

Text centered vertically on page

Insertion point on Page 1 in Section 1

Figure 6.9

9 **Press** Ctrl+PgDn **two times to see pages 3 and 4.**

Text in this section has a top vertical alignment, which you can easily see on page 4.

10 **Save the document, and keep it onscreen to continue with the next lesson.**

When you select options in the Page Setup dialog box, you specify the amount of text to which you wish to apply the formats. Table 6.2 lists and describes the *Apply to* options.

Table 6.2	Page Setup Apply to Options
Option	**Description**
Whole document	Applies formats to the entire document, regardless of where the insertion point is when you access the dialog box.
This point forward	Applies formats from the current page to the end of the document.
This section	Applies formats to the current section only; other sections retain their formats.
Selected text	Applies formats to only the text you selected prior to accessing the Page Setup dialog box.
Selected sections	Applies formats to the sections you selected in the document.

To extend your knowledge...

Page Setup Options for Different Sections

You might be instructed to specify different page setup options for different sections of a document. Make sure that you click in the specified section before accessing the Page Setup dialog box. Then, ensure that the *Apply to* option is *This section*.

Lesson 4: Inserting Page Numbers

Page numbers are essential in long documents. They serve as a convenient reference point for the writer and the reader. Without page numbers in a long document, you would have difficulty trying to find text on a particular page or trying to tell someone else where to locate a particular passage in the document.

Use the Page Numbers feature to automatically insert page numbers throughout your document. You select the page-number position (top or bottom of the page) and the alignment (left, center, right, inside, or outside). Word not only inserts page numbers but also updates the numbers when you add or delete pages. In this lesson, you insert page numbers in your report.

To Insert Page Numbers

❶ In the *Desktop Publishing-WB6L* document, press Ctrl+Home, and make sure that you are displaying the document in Print Layout View with the Two Pages zoom option.
Although your document is divided into two sections, Word applies page numbering to the *entire* document, continuing page numbers from one section to the next. To prevent a page number from appearing on the title page, you must position the insertion point on that page before you access the Page Numbers feature so that you can instruct Word *not* to number the first page of each section.

❷ Choose Insert, Page Numbers.
The Page Numbers dialog box appears so you can choose the position and alignment of the page numbers (see Figure 6.10).

To Insert Page Numbers

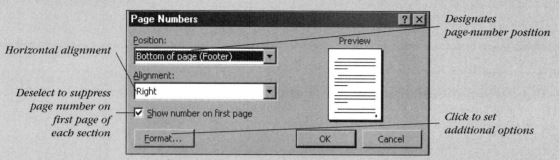

Horizontal alignment

Deselect to suppress page number on first page of each section

Designates page-number position

Click to set additional options

Figure 6.10

❸ **Click the *Alignment* drop-down arrow, and choose *Center*.**
This option centers the page numbers between the left and right margins, similar to the Center alignment you used in Project 5 to center text horizontally between the margins.

❹ **If the *Show number on first page* check box is checked, click the check box to deselect this option.**
By deselecting *Show number on first page*, you **suppress**, or "hide" the page number on the first page of each section in the document. The page is still counted as page 1, but the page number does not appear.

❺ **Click OK.**
Word does not show a page number on the title page or the next page because each page is the first page in its respective section.

If you were displaying the document in Normal view, Word automatically switches to Print Layout view so that you can see page numbers. Normal view does not display page numbers.

❻ **Click the Zoom drop-down arrow, and choose 100%.**

❼ **Scroll to the bottom of page 3.**
In Print Layout view, you see the page number at the bottom of the third page. It is centered between the left and right margins, as shown in Figure 6.11.

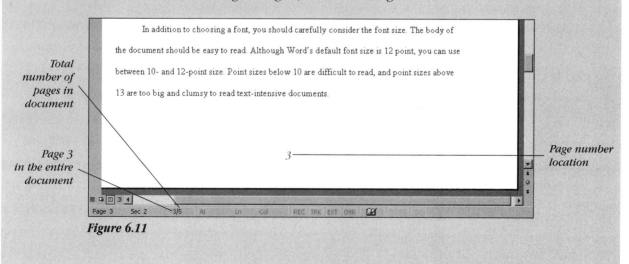

Total number of pages in document

Page 3 in the entire document

Page number location

Figure 6.11

The page numbers actually appear, starting with the second page within Section 2. Word, however, counts the title page as page 1 and the first page of Section 2 as page 2. Typically, you should count the first page of the body of the report as page 1. Therefore, in the next exercise, you position the insertion point at the beginning of Section 2 and restart the section page numbers at 1 again.

To Restart Page Numbers in Section 2

1 **Position the insertion point at the top of page 2, the first page of the body of the document.**

The first page of the body of the report—not the title page—should count as page 1. Therefore, you must change the page number value back to 1 on this page.

2 **Choose Insert, Page Numbers.**

The alignment should still be *Center*, and the *Show number on first page* is still deselected.

3 **Click the *Format* button to display additional options.**

The Page Number Format dialog box appears. The default *Page numbering* option is *Continue from previous section* (see Figure 6.12).

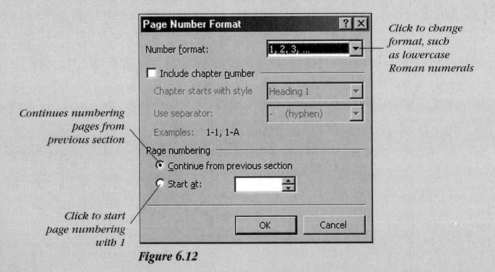

Click to change format, such as lowercase Roman numerals

Continues numbering pages from previous section

Click to start page numbering with 1

Figure 6.12

4 **Click the *Start at* option, and make sure that it displays 1.**

Changing the *Start at* option to **1** starts counting the first page of the current section as page 1, instead of continuing page numbering from the previous (title page) section.

5 **Click OK to close the Page Number Format dialog box; then click OK in the Page Numbers dialog box.**

The first page in Section 2 is counted as page 1 within its section (see Figure 6.13).

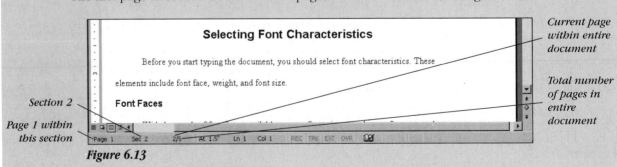

Current page within entire document

Total number of pages in entire document

Section 2

Page 1 within this section

Figure 6.13

To Restart Page Numbers in Section 2

6 **Scroll to the bottom of page 2 within Section 2.**
The page number is page 2 in Section 2. It is the third page in the entire document, as indicated by *Page 2 Sec 2 3/5.*

7 **Save the document, and keep it onscreen to continue with the next lesson.**

To extend your knowledge...

Modifying Page Numbering

You might decide to change one or more page-numbering options. For example, you might want to choose a different page number alignment, start at a different page number, or use a different numbering format such as lowercase Roman numerals.

To change page-numbering, position the insertion point at the beginning of the section you want to change, and access the Page Numbers dialog box. Make the changes you want, and click OK.

Lesson 5: Preventing Text from Separating Across Page Breaks

To achieve a professional appearance, certain types of text should not separate between pages. For example, your document should not contain widows or orphans. A ***widow*** is the last line of a paragraph that appears by itself at the top of a page. An ***orphan*** is the first line of a paragraph that appears by itself at the bottom of a page. However, you don't have to worry about widows and orphans because Word's Widow/Orphan Control feature is a default option. Word also typically keeps a heading from being the last line on a page with the following paragraph on the next page.

However, Word lets other text separate between pages. For example, it does not keep bulleted lists or tabulated text together on a page. Your document has a bulleted list that spans across the bottom of page 1 and the top of page 2 in Section 2.

Word can identify widows and orphans because lines within a paragraph end in a soft return. The Widow/Orphan Control can't keep bulleted list items together, however, because each line ends with a hard return instead of a soft return.

In this lesson, you select the bulleted list and use the *Keep with ne*x*t* option in the Paragraph dialog box.

To Keep Text from Separating Across Page Breaks

1 **In the *Desktop Publishing-WB6L* document, click the Normal View button and change the zoom to 100%, if needed.**
Because the bottom and top margin spaces don't appear in Normal View, you can more easily select text that spans across page breaks.

2 **Scroll through the document so you see the bottom of page 1 and the top of page 2 in Section 2.**
Two bulleted items appear at the bottom of page 1, and the remaining bulleted list continues on the next page.

(Continues)

To Keep Text from Separating Across Page Breaks (Continued)

③ Click and drag to select the entire bulleted list, which spans both pages.
You need to select the text that you want to keep from separating across pages (see Figure 6.14).

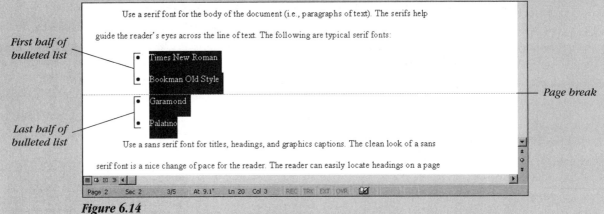

First half of bulleted list

Last half of bulleted list

Page break

Figure 6.14

④ Choose Format, Paragraph.
The Paragraph dialog box is displayed.

⑤ Click the *Line and Page Breaks* tab.
The *Widow/Orphan control* check box is selected. Although it keeps at least two lines of a paragraph together on each page, it does not keep lines together that end with a hard return. You need to select the *Keep with next* check box (see Figure 6.15).

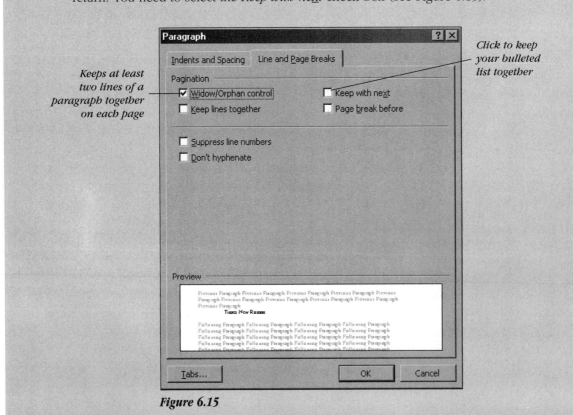

Keeps at least two lines of a paragraph together on each page

Click to keep your bulleted list together

Figure 6.15

To Keep Text from Separating Across Page Breaks

If you have problems...

Don't select the *Keep lines together* option to attempt to keep bulleted lists from separating across page breaks. This option keeps an entire paragraph together—not individual lines created by hard returns.

6 **Click the *Keep with next* check box, and then click OK.**
Word now keeps the entire bulleted list together. Because the bulleted list can't fit at the bottom of page 1, the bulleted list appears at the top of page 2 (see Figure 6.16).

Entire bulleted list on same page

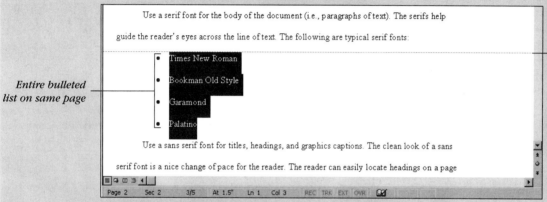

Automatic page break

Figure 6.16

If You Have Problems...

If the entire bulleted list does not appear at the top of page 2, switch to Print Layout view and then back to Normal view.

7 **Deselect the bulleted list.**

8 **Save the document, and keep it onscreen to continue with the next lesson.**

Lesson 6: Creating Headers and Footers

A **header** contains standard data (text and graphics) in the top margin of most document pages. A **footer** contains standard data in the bottom margin of most document pages. You can insert text, page numbers, dates, filenames, and logos in headers and footers. Headers and footers are typically used in long documents, such as reports, legal briefs, medical transcripts, and proposals.

Each section in a document can have different information in a header. For example, the header in your textbook changes to reflect the project number and topic.

In this lesson, you create a header containing the title of the report.

To Create Headers

1 **In the *Desktop Publishing-WB6L* document, press Ctrl+Home to position the insertion point at the top of the document.**

(Continues)

To Create Headers (Continued)

2 **Choose View, Header and Footer.**
Word switches to the Print Layout view. The header area is outlined at the top of the document window, and the Header and Footer toolbar appears (see Figure 6.17).

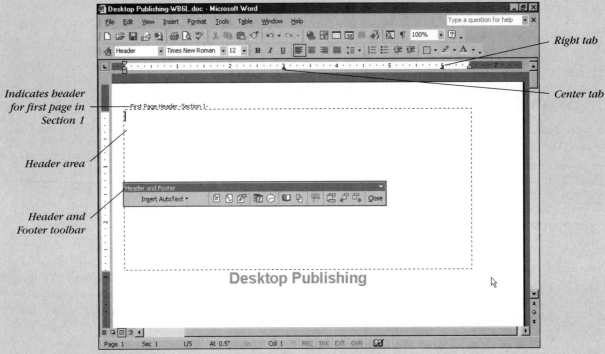

Indicates header for first page in Section 1

Header area

Header and Footer toolbar

Right tab

Center tab

Figure 6.17

Word displays information that the header will appear on the first page in Section 1. You want to display the header on all pages.

3 **Click the Page Setup button on the Headers and Footers toolbar.**
The Page Setup dialog box appears with the layout options displayed. Notice that the *Different first page* option is selected, which means that the header on the first page of each section is different from the rest of the pages.

4 **Click the *Different first page* check box to deselect it, and then click OK.**
Deselecting this option causes the header you're about to type to appear on all pages, not just the first page in the section. The note about the header window now displays *Header-Section 1-*.

5 **Type** Desktop Publishing.
You want to insert the date at the right side of the header.

6 **Press** Tab **twice—once to get to the center point and again to align text at the right side of the header.**

7 **Click the Insert Date button on the Header and Footer toolbar.**
Word inserts a date field right-aligned at the 6″ mark.

8 **Click Close on the Header and Footer toolbar.**
When you click Close, the Header and Footer toolbar disappears, and the insertion point is inside regular document text. The header does not appear in Normal view.

To Create Headers

⑨ Click the Print Layout View button, click the Zoom drop-down arrow, and choose *Two Pages*.

The header appears on the title page. Notice that the page number now displays on the title page because you deselected the *Different first page* option for the header. However, the *Different first page* option is still in effect (see Figure 6.18).

Header on page 1 in Section 1

No header on page 1 in Section 2

Page number appears on title page

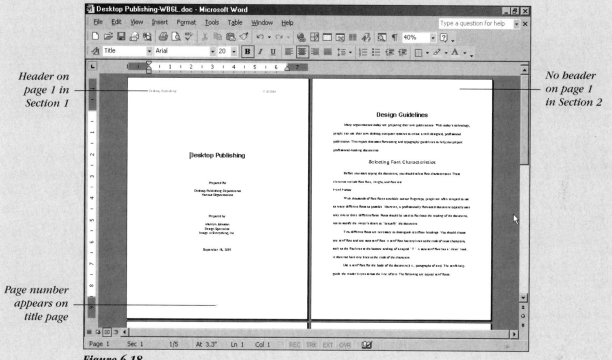

Figure 6.18

⑩ Press Ctrl+PgDn two times to see the header continue on the rest of the pages in Section 2.

⑪ Save the document, and keep it onscreen to continue with the next lesson.

Table 6.3 lists and describes the Header and Footer toolbar buttons.

Table 6.3 **Header and Footer Toolbar Buttons**		
Button	**Button Name**	**Description**
Insert AutoText ▾	Insert AutoText	Inserts items such as the filename, filename and path, and creation data.
[#]	Insert Page Number	Inserts a code to display the page number.
[⊞]	Insert Number of Pages	Inserts a code to display the total number of pages in a document.
[⊞]	Format Page Number	Lets you choose the page-number format, such as the number format and whether you want continuous page numbers or new page numbers for a section.
[🕮]	Insert Date	Inserts a code to display the current date.
[◔]	Insert Time	Inserts a code to display the current time.
[▯]	Page Setup	Displays the Page Setup dialog box, so you can set different headers and footers for odd- and even-numbered pages and different headers and footers for the first page in a section.
[▤]	Show/Hide Document Text	Shows or hides the document text.
[▦]	Same as Previous	Links the header or footer to the same header or footer in the previous section when clicked. Click to set different headers and footers for the current section.
[▤]	Switch Between Header and footer window.	Switches between the header and Footer
[◀]	Show Previous	Shows the previous header or footer.
[▶]	Show Next	Shows the next header or footer.
Close	Close Header and Footer	Closes the header or footer window, and hides the Header and Footer toolbar.

To extend your knowledge...

Creating a Footer

You can create a footer by clicking the Switch Between Header and Footer button on the Headers and Footers toolbar.

Suppressing a Header or Footer on the First Page

If you don't want a header or footer to appear on the first page, make sure that the *Different first page* option is selected in the Page Setup dialog box; then click the Show Next button on the toolbar to go to the next page within the section. The header you create will appear on all pages except the first page in the section.

Creating Multiple or Odd/Even Headers and Footers

Use the Help feature to learn how to create multiple headers or different headers for odd and even pages.

Lesson 7: Navigating Through a Document

You learned how to scroll and how to use the Go To feature in Project 2, "Working with a Document." Although those navigation features are helpful, you are now ready to learn additional navigation features for longer documents.

The **Document Map** feature displays a window that lists the structure of headings in your document. You can quickly display a particular section by clicking the heading in the Document Map. Furthermore, you use the Select Browse Object button to browse by footnotes or sections.

To Navigate Through Documents

1 In the *Desktop Publishing-WB6L* document, press Ctrl+Home, and click the Normal View button.

2 Click the Document Map button on the Standard toolbar.
The Document Map appears on the left side of the document window (see Figure 6.19).

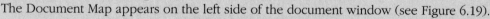
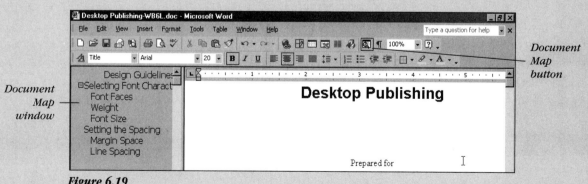

Figure 6.19

3 Click *Setting the Spacing* in the Document Map window.
Word takes you to that section immediately (see Figure 6.20).

(Continues)

To Navigate Through Documents (Continued)

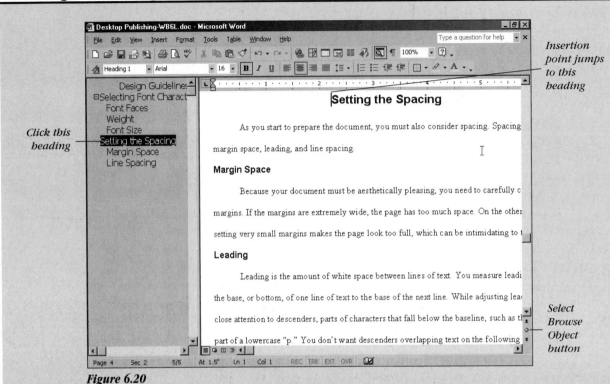

Figure 6.20

④ Click the Document Map button to turn off this feature.
Now, you want to scroll by jumping from heading to heading.

⑤ Click the Select Browse Object button below the vertical scrollbar buttons.
The Select Browse Object palette appears (see Figure 6.21).

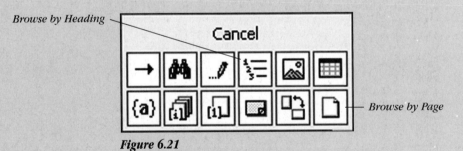

Figure 6.21

⑥ Click the Browse by Heading button.
Word moves the insertion point to the next heading: *Margin Space*. Notice that the Previous and Next buttons turn blue, indicating that you are browsing by any object *except* by page. When you position the mouse on top of these buttons, the ScreenTip displays *Previous Heading* and *Next Heading*, respectively.

⑦ Click the Next Heading button.
The insertion point jumps to the next heading, *Leading*.

⑧ Click the Next Heading button again.
The next heading is *Line Spacing*.

⑨ Click the Select Browse Object button, and click the Browse by Page button.

To Navigate Through Documents

This changes the browse back to the original default, which is browsing by page. The Previous and Next buttons are black again.

 10 **Save the document, and close it.**

 ## To extend your knowledge...

Select Browse Object Options

As you position the mouse pointer over a button on the Browse Object palette, the top of the palette displays the name of the button, such as *Browse by Edits.*

Summary

You learned a lot of valuable document-formatting features. You can set margins, center text vertically, insert page numbers, create headers, and insert section and page breaks. In addition, you learned how to keep bulleted lists from separating across page breaks, and how to navigate quickly through your documents using the Document Map and the Select Browse Object options.

You can now expand your knowledge and skills of these and related features by using Help. For example, you might want to learn more about section breaks and the other buttons on the Header and Footer toolbar. In addition to using Help, complete the following exercises to reinforce and expand your skills.

# Checking Concepts and Terms

Multiple Choice

Circle the letter of the correct answer for each of the following.

1. What is the keyboard shortcut for inserting a manual page break? [L2]

  a. ⏎Enter

  b. Ctrl+⏎Enter

  c. Ctrl+Break

  d. Pause+Break

2. The *Vertical alignment* option is found in which tab of the Page Setup dialog box? [L3]

  a. Margins

  b. Line and Page Breaks

  c. Paper Source

  d. Layout

3. Which option should you use to keep a selected numbered list together? [L5]

    a. <u>W</u>idow/Orphan control

    b. <u>K</u>eep lines together

    c. Keep with ne<u>x</u>t

    d. Page <u>b</u>reak before

4. Which of the following is a default setting for page numbers? [L4]

    a. The number is positioned at the top of the page within a header.

    b. The page numbers continue from one section to another.

    c. The page numbers appear as lowercase Roman numerals.

    d. Page numbers appear left-aligned.

5. What types of items can you put into a header or footer? [L6]

    a. page numbers

    b. text

    c. date

    d. all of the above

Discussion

1. Describe a section page break and when you need section breaks in a document. [L2]

2. Look at the location of page numbers in this textbook. What position and alignment options would you choose to produce this effect? [L4]

3. What type of formatting is different in bulleted lists that the Widow/Orphan Control can't help keep the items from separating between page breaks? [L5]

Skill Drill

Skill Drill exercises reinforce project skills. Each skill reinforced is the same, or nearly the same, as a skill presented in the project. Detailed instructions are provided in a step-by-step format.

1. Setting Margins

You created an information report for your business communication class. After reviewing the instructor's guidelines, you realize that you need to change the left and right margins.

    1. Open *ew1-0602*, and save it as `Interview Paper-WB6SD`.
    2. Choose <u>F</u>ile, Page Set<u>u</u>p.
    3. Click the *Margins* tab, if needed, to see the margin options.
    4. Press [Tab⁺⁺] two (or three) times, and type 1 in the <u>L</u>eft box.
    5. Press [Tab⁺⁺], and type 1 in the <u>R</u>ight box.
    6. Click OK.
    7. Save the document, and keep it onscreen to continue with the next exercise.

2. Inserting a Section Break and Centering Text Vertically

You need to replace a manual page break with a section break, so you can vertically center the title page without centering the rest of the document.

1. In the *Interview Paper-WB6SD* document, click the Normal View button.
2. Scroll down on the first page, and click on the page break line between the title page and the next page.
3. Press Del to remove the hard page break.
4. Choose Insert, Break. Click the *Next page* option, and click OK to insert a section break.
5. Press Ctrl+Home to position the insertion point on the title page.
6. Choose File, Page Setup, and click the *Layout* tab.
7. Click the *Vertical alignment* drop-down arrow, and choose *Center*.
8. Check to see that the *Apply to* option displays *This section*; then click OK.
9. Click the Print Layout View button.
10. Click the Zoom drop-down arrow, and choose *Whole Page*.

    You can see that the title page is centered vertically.
11. Press Ctrl+End to see the last page.

    This page is not vertically centered because the vertical alignment is Top.
12. Save the document and keep it onscreen to continue with the next exercise.

3. Using the Document Map and Inserting Manual Page Breaks

You need to use the Document Map to navigate quickly through the document. In addition, you want to insert manual page breaks to create page breaks within the same section.

1. In the *Interview Paper-WB6SD* document, change the zoom to 100%.
2. Click the Document Map button on the Standard toolbar.
3. Click *Pre-interview Impression Effects* in the Document Map window to move the insertion point there.
4. Press Ctrl+↵Enter to insert a manual page break.
5. Click *Perception in the Interview* in the Document Map window; then press Ctrl+↵Enter to insert a manual page break.
6. Click the Document Map button to remove the Document Map from the screen.
7. Save the document, and keep it onscreen to continue with the next exercise.

4. Inserting Page Numbers

You decide to insert page numbers in your document so your readers can easily locate specific sections of the paper. You want page numbers to begin with the main document, and not the title page. In addition, you need to keep a heading from being isolated at the bottom of a page.

1. In the *Interview Paper-WB6SD* document, position the insertion point at the top of the document (the title page).
2. Make sure that you are displaying the document in Print Layout view with the Two Pages zoom option. (If the Document Map appears, turn it off.)
3. Choose Insert, Page Numbers.
4. Click the *Alignment* drop-down arrow, and choose *Center*.
5. Click the *Show number on the first page* check box to deselect this option (if it is selected) and then click OK.
6. Click the Zoom drop-down arrow and choose 100%. Scroll to the bottom of page 3 to check the placement of the page number.
7. Position the insertion point at the top of page 2, the first page of the body of the document.
8. Choose Insert, Page Numbers, and deselect the *Show number on the first page* check box, if needed.
9. Click Format to display additional options.
10. Click the *Start at* option, and type 1.
11. Click OK and then click OK in the Page Numbers dialog box.
12. Notice that the page number indicator is *Page 1* on the status bar.

5. Keeping a Heading with the Following Paragraph

While reviewing the latest version of the document, you notice that a heading is the last line of a page with the following paragraph at the top of the next page. Although you want to keep the heading with the paragraph, you don't necessarily want to insert a manual page break because the heading does not always need to be at the top of a page; it just needs to be kept with its paragraph.

1. In the *Interview Paper-WB6SD* document, click the Normal View button.
2. Scroll through the document so you see the bottom of page 2 and the top of page 3 in Section 2.
3. Drag across the heading *The Bias of Information Processing* and the first two lines of the following paragraph.
4. Choose F*o*rmat, *P*aragraph to display the Paragraph dialog box.
5. Click the *Line and P*age Breaks* tab.
6. Click the *Keep with *n*ext* check box, and click OK. If the heading does not appear at the top of page 3, click the Print Layout View button and then click the Normal View button again.
7. Repeat this process with any other headings that have separated incorrectly.
8. Save the document, and keep it onscreen to continue with the next exercise.

6. Creating a Header

You decide to create a header to appear in the second section of your document.

1. In the *Interview Paper-WB6SD* document, click the Normal View button.
2. Display the first page in Section 2.
3. Choose *V*iew, *H*eader and Footer.
4. Click the Page Setup button on the Header and Footer toolbar.
5. Deselect the *Different first page* option and then click OK to use the same header on the first and subsequent pages in the header.
6. Click the Same as Previous button on the Header and Footer toolbar to disconnect the header from the (non) header in Section 1.
7. Type `The Personal Interview`, press ⓉⒶⒷ twice, and type your name.
8. Select the header text, and choose 11-point Arial.
9. Click the Close button on the Header and Footer toolbar.
10. Save the document, print it, and close it.

Challenge

Challenge exercises expand on or are somewhat related to skills presented in the lessons. Each exercise provides a brief narrative introduction, followed by instructions in a numbered-step format that are not as detailed as those in the Skill Drill section.

1. Formatting a Status Report

You composed a status report for division managers concerning an upcoming Information Technology Training Conference. You open it, and make a few changes before sending it out.

1. Open *ew1-0603*, and save it as `Status Report-WB6CH1`.
2. On the blank line above the title, create the title page shown in Figure 6.22.

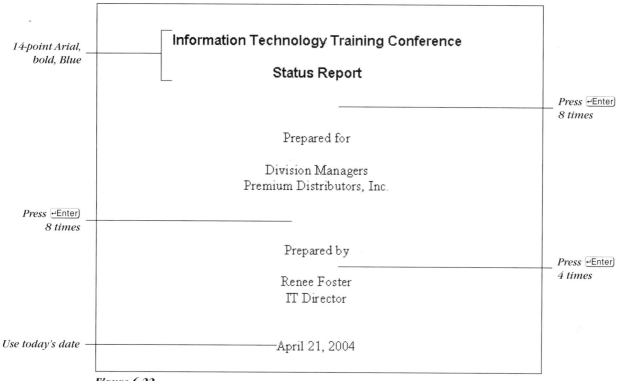

14-point Arial,
bold, Blue

Information Technology Training Conference

Status Report

Press ⏎Enter
8 times

Prepared for

Division Managers
Premium Distributors, Inc.

Press ⏎Enter
8 times

Prepared by

Press ⏎Enter
4 times

Renee Foster
IT Director

Use today's date

April 21, 2004

Figure 6.22

3. Apply bold to the two-line title only; the rest of the title page should *not* be bold.

4. Change Renee's name to your name.

5. Apply Center alignment for the text you typed on the title page.

6. Insert a section break after the date. Then, vertically center text in the first section only (that is, the title page).

7. Select text, starting with the first full paragraph to the end of the document, and apply Justify alignment.

8. Select the bulleted list, and use the feature that prevents a page break within this text.

9. Insert page numbers in the bottom center of the pages. Do not display a page number on the title page. Make sure that the page number value starts at 1 on the first page of the body of the report.

10. Save the document, print it, and close it.

2. Formatting the Annual Report

The top corporate officials have reviewed the annual report you worked on. After making the revisions they requested, you want to reformat it to look more professional by controlling page breaks and creating a footer with identification information.

1. Open *ew1-0604*, and save it as `Annual Report-WB6CH2`.

2. Set 1″ left and right margins.

3. Use the appropriate feature to keep any tabulated list or bulleted list from separating across page breaks.

4. Create a *footer* that displays `Seatek-Parkway Enterprises` at the left side, the page number in the center, and `2003 Annual Report` on the right side of the footer.
Hint: Use the Header and Footer toolbar to insert the page number *within* the footer.

5. Edit the footer by moving the center tab to 3.25″ and the right tab to 6.5″.

6. Display the Document Map, and use it to display each heading within the report; then, remove the Document Map.

7. Save, print, and close the document.

3. Formatting a Document for Lab Assistants

You work for the College of Business Lab Center. Your supervisor typed a memo and job description list for the lab assistants. You need to finish formatting the document for your supervisor.

1. Open *ew1-0605*, and save it as **Lab Assistant-WB6CH3**.
2. Insert a section break at the beginning of the title *College of Business*.
3. Vertically center text in the first section.
4. Create a footer with this information: **Lab Assistant Rules** at the left side, automatic page number in the center, and automatic date at the right side. Use the Header and Footer toolbar to insert automatic components.
5. Insert a manual page break before *Classroom Lab Assistant Expectations*.
6. Set 1″ left and right margins for Section 2.
7. Save, print, and close your document.

4. Formatting a Job Screening Guidelines Document

As the Human Resources Director at Woodward State College, you are responsible for informing and training screening committees on equal opportunity regulations. These rules are important to ensure fair and legal hiring practices at your college. You need to format a document to distribute to hiring committees.

1. Open *ew1-0606*, and save it as **Screening Guidelines-WB6CH4**.
2. Set 1″ left and right margins, and a 1.25″ bottom margin.
3. Insert section page breaks at the beginning of *Applicant Evaluation* and *Referral, Selection, and Protection* headings.
4. Select all items except the last item in the first bulleted list, and set **8 pt** spacing after paragraph.
5. Repeat the last step to format the other bulleted lists.
6. Select the entire document and turn on the Widow/Orphan Control.
7. Select the *Human Resources Director…* heading and the first bulleted item on the next page; use the feature to keep the heading and first bulleted item from separating across a page break. (Do *not* insert a section or manual page break.)
8. Insert page numbers in the bottom center of all pages.
9. Save, print, and close the document. (To save paper, consider changing the *Pages per sheet* option in the Print dialog box to **2 pages**.)

Discovery Zone exercises help you gain advanced knowledge of project topics and/or application of skills. These exercises focus on enhancing your problem-solving skills. Numbered steps are not provided, but you are given hints, reminders, screen shots, and/or references to help you reach your goal for each exercise.

1. Customizing the Contents of a Footer

You want to try some other formatting for the personal interview paper you created. You want to create a footer with filename and page number fields. Open *ew1-0602*, and save it as **Personal Interview-WB6DZ1**.

Delete the page break after the title page, and insert a section page break. In addition, insert section page breaks for the other two centered titles. Use appropriate vertical alignment for the title page.

Starting on the first page of Section 2, make sure that the *Headers and footers* options are deselected in the Page Setup dialog box. Then, create a footer starting in Section 2 that is not the same as the previous section. Insert a filename field (left side), your name (centered), and *Page X of Y* page-numbering format field (right side). Within the footer, change the page number to start the page number at 1 with the first page of Section 2.

If you need assistance, study the Header and Footer toolbar options to create this effect. Apply 11-point Arial Narrow font face to the footer.

Check for headings isolated at the bottom of pages and then use the appropriate feature to keep the headings with their following paragraphs.

Save, print, and close the document. (To save paper, consider changing the *Pages per sheet* option in the Print dialog box to **2 pages**.)

2. Creating and Printing a Booklet with Page Numbers

You want to create a double-sided booklet for the screening committee document. Use Help to learn about creating and printing booklets in Word Version 2002.

Open *ew1-0606*, and save it as **AAEO Booklet-WB6DZ2**. Set 0.75″ left and right margins; 1″ top and bottom margins; and landscape orientation. Set the option to lay out the document as a booklet with 0.75″ inside and outside space.

Insert page numbers at the bottom of all pages, except the first page of the first section. Select the alignment option that places odd page numbers on the right side, and places even page numbers on the left side.

Insert section page breaks for the three centered headings. Apply the Widow/Orphan Control to the entire document and then use the appropriate feature to prevent headings from being isolated at the bottom of a page, while the following paragraph appears on the next page. (**Hint:** You might want to choose the Two Pages zoom to see how text flows from page to page.) In addition, apply **8 pt** spacing after paragraph for all bulleted items except the last item in each bulleted list. Keep the *Administrators are responsible for* heading on the same page as its entire bulleted list using a page break.

The title should be the only text on the first page. Add appropriate, relevant information to make the first page. Use other formats as needed for the title page.

Save the document. If your printer has duplexing capabilities, print the document. If your printer does not have duplexing capabilities, choose the appropriate option in the Print dialog box to manually duplex the document. Your document should be printed on both sides of the paper. Collate the booklet and then close the document.

Creating and Formatting Tables

Objectives

In this project, you learn how to

- ✔ Create a Table
- ✔ Enter Text into a Table
- ✔ Insert Rows and Columns
- ✔ Delete Rows and Columns
- ✔ Adjust Column Widths and Row Height
- ✔ Format Cells
- ✔ Apply Shading and Borders
- ✔ Move and Position a Table

Key terms introduced in this project include

- ❏ cell
- ❏ column
- ❏ column headings
- ❏ column width
- ❏ gridlines
- ❏ row
- ❏ row height
- ❏ table
- ❏ table alignment

Why Would I Do This?

Sometimes, you might want an easy way to organize a series of data in a columnar list format. Although you can align text with tabs, you have more format control when you create a table. A **table** is a series of rows and columns that neatly organizes data. Each **row** presents data going horizontally (across the table from left to right), and each **column** presents data going vertically in the table. The intersection of a row and column is called a **cell**.

You can create tables to store customer names and addresses, phone lists, personal inventories, calendars, project forms, and so on. After you complete this project, you'll probably think of additional ways you can use tables in your own documents.

Visual Summary

Figure 7.1 shows the structure of a table in Word.

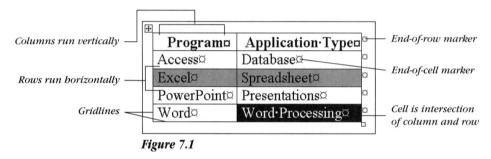

Figure 7.1

Figure 7.2 shows a table that you create within a business letter in this project.

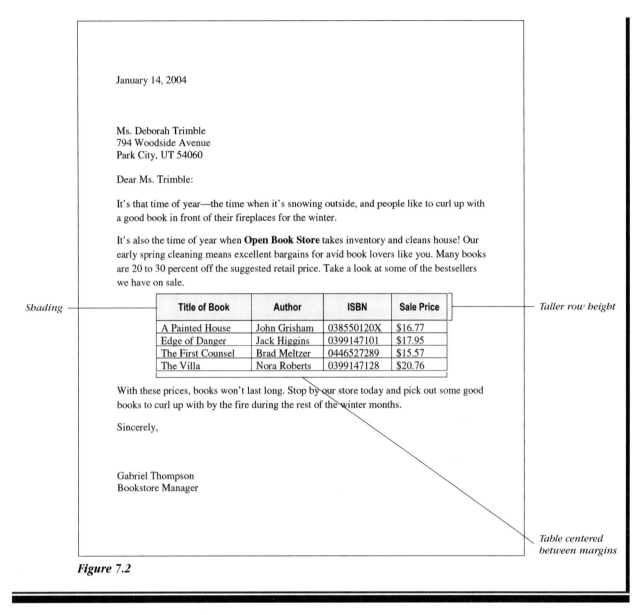

Figure 7.2

Lesson 1: Creating a Table

You can create a table between paragraphs in a letter, memo, or report; or you can create a table as a separate document. Before you create a table, plan what data you want to include and how you want to organize it. Doing so helps you create an appropriate table structure from the beginning, but you can always change the table later.

In this lesson, suppose that you work for a local bookstore named Open Book Store. Your manager, Gabriel Thompson, asked you to insert a table that lists some books that are on sale. You need to create a table that lists book titles, authors, ISBN numbers, and sale prices.

To Create a Table

❶ Open *ew1-0701*, and save it as Book Letter-WB7L.

❷ Scroll down through the document, and position the insertion point on the blank line above *Sincerely.*

(Continues)

To Create a Table (Continued)

You need to position the insertion point where you want to create the table.

❸ Click the Insert Table button on the Standard toolbar.
Word displays a table grid. You click and drag through the grid to specify how many columns and rows you want in your table.

❹ Position the mouse pointer on the fourth cell down in the fourth column.
The grid shows that you are creating a table with four rows and four columns (see Figure 7.3).

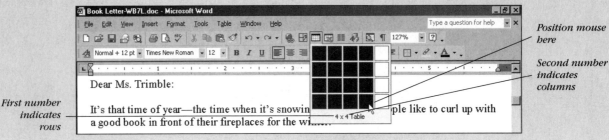

Figure 7.3

❺ Click the mouse button in the cell on the grid.
You now have a new table in your document. By default, Word creates evenly spaced columns between the left and right margins. Your table contains *gridlines*, which are lines that separate cells within the table (see Figure 7.4).

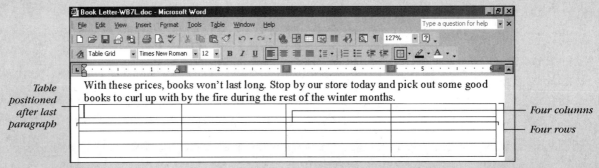

Figure 7.4

If you have problems...

If you accidentally choose the wrong number of columns and rows for the table, click the Undo button to remove the table. Then, click the Insert Table button again to create the table.

❻ Save the document, and keep it onscreen to continue with the next lesson.

To extend your knowledge...

Creating a Table

You can also create a table by choosing Table, Insert, Table and then specifying the number of columns and rows you want in the Insert Table dialog box (see Figure 7.5).

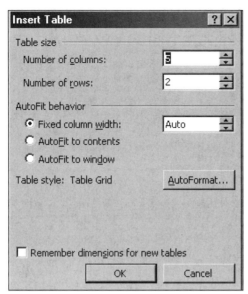

Figure 7.5

Lesson 2: Entering Text in a Table

After creating a table, you are ready to enter text into the cells. Type directly in the cell, letting the text word-wrap within the cell. When you are ready to type in the next cell, press Tab⇄.

You are now ready to type book titles, author names, ISBN numbers, and sale prices in your table. The insertion point is in the first cell, so you can start typing the first item now.

To Enter Text in a Table

❶ In the *Book Letter-WB7L* document, type the following book title in the first cell of the table: From the Corner of His Eye
The book title wraps within the same cell, making the first row taller.

 ## If you have problems...

Do not press ⏎Enter within the cell. Let Word word-wrap the text within the cell. Inserting a hard return can cause problems when you adjust the column widths later. If you think you pressed ⏎Enter within a table, display the nonprinting symbols to identify the paragraph marks and then delete them.

❷ Press Tab⇄ to move the insertion point to the next cell to the right on the same row.

❸ Type Dean R. Koontz **in the cell.**

❹ Press Tab⇄, and type 0553801341.

❺ Press Tab⇄, and type $16.17.
You are ready to type text on the next row. When you press Tab⇄ in the last cell on a row, Word moves the insertion point to the first cell on the next row.

(Continues)

To Enter Text in a Table (Continued)

6 Press Tab and then type the data in the last three rows of the table, as shown in Figure 7.6. Do not press Tab after typing $15.57 in the last cell.

From the Corner of His Eye	Dean R. Koontz	0553801341	$16.17
A Painted House	John Grisham	038550120X	$16.77
Edge of Danger	Jack Higgins	0399147101	$17.95
The First Counsel	Brad Meltzer	0446527289	$15.57

Figure 7.6

If you have problems...

If you accidentally press Tab in the last cell and create a new row at the end of the table, click the Undo button to remove the extra row.

7 Save the document, and keep it onscreen to continue with the next lesson.

Table 7.1 lists different methods for moving around in a table.

Table 7.1 Moving the Insertion Point in a Table

To Move to the	Press
Next cell to the right	Tab
Cell to the left	⇧Shift + Tab
First cell in column	Alt + PgUp
Last cell in column	Alt + PgDn
First cell in current row	Alt + Home
Last cell in current row	Alt + End

To extend your knowledge...

Sorting Table Data

You can rearrange the rows within a table by using the Sort command. To do this, select the rows you want to arrange (minus the headings on the first row), choose Table, Sort. Specify how you want to sort the table, and click OK. Refer to Help for more information on sorting table data.

Lesson 3: Inserting Rows and Columns

After creating the table, you might decide to add another row or column. For example, you might realize that you left out information in the middle of the table, or you might want to create a row for **column headings**—text that appears at the top of each column describing that column.

In this lesson, you insert a row at the top of the table to type in column headings and a row at the end of the table for an additional book.

To Insert a Row

1 In the *Book Letter-WB7L* document, position the insertion point within any cell on the first row of the table.

Remember that rows go across, not down. If the insertion point is not on the first row, the new row might not be inserted in the correct location.

2 Choose T**a**ble, **I**nsert to display the Table Insert menu options for inserting columns and rows (see Figure 7.7).

White box represents new row or column

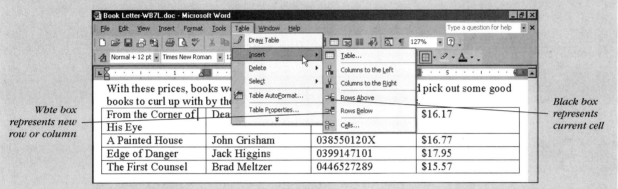

Black box represents current cell

***Figure** 7.7*

3 Choose Rows **A**bove.

Word inserts a new row above the current one. The new row is currently selected.

4 Click in the first cell, and type the following data in cells on the first row:

```
Title of Book    Author    ISBN    Sale Price
```

Your table now contains all the data you want to include (see Figure 7.8).

Text on new row

Original first row is now second row

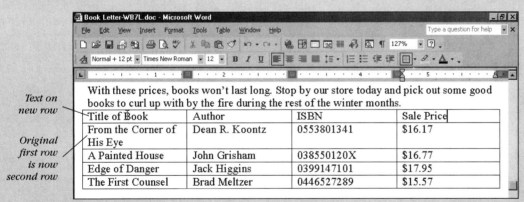

***Figure** 7.8*

5 Click in the last cell on the last row—the cell containing *$15.57.*

You want to add a row below the last row for another book that's on sale.

6 Press Tab.

Pressing Tab in the last cell on the last row creates a new row below the original last row.

7 Type the following information on the last row:

```
The Villa    Nora Roberts    0399147128    $20.76
```

(Continues)

To Insert a Row (Continued)

Your table contains data on the new row at the bottom of the table (see Figure 7.9).

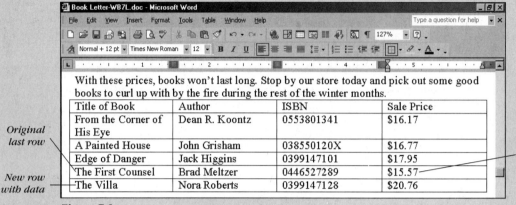

Original last row

New row with data

Press Tab *here to create new row*

Figure 7.9

8 **Save the document, and keep it onscreen to continue with the next lesson.**

To extend your knowledge...

Inserting Columns

Use the Table, Insert menu to insert a new column to the left or right of the column containing the insertion point. For example, if the insertion point is in the second column and you insert a column to the left, the new column becomes the second column, and the original second column becomes the third column. When you insert a column, the existing columns decrease in width to make room for the new column.

Lesson 4: Deleting Rows and Columns

After creating a table, you might decide that you no longer need a particular row or column. You can delete a row or column just as easily as you insert rows and columns. In this lesson, you realize that your bookstore only has one copy of *From the Corner of His Eye*, and will not receive more for another month. Therefore, you decide to remove this book from your list of sale items.

To Delete a Row

1 **In the *Book Letter-WB7L* document, position the insertion point in the second row of the table—the row that contains *From the Corner of His Eye*.**
You must first position the insertion point in any cell on the row that you want to delete.

2 **Choose Table, Delete.**
The Delete options include Table, Columns, Rows, Cells.

3 **Choose Rows.**
Word deletes the row containing the insertion point (see Figure 7.10).

To Delete a Row

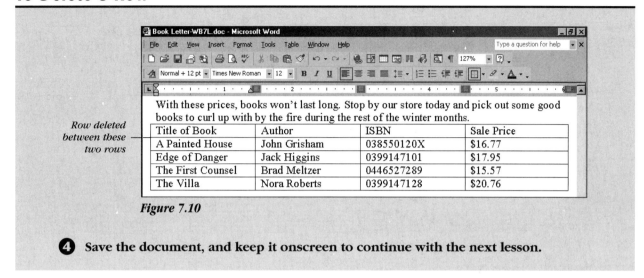

Title of Book	Author	ISBN	Sale Price
A Painted House	John Grisham	038550120X	$16.77
Edge of Danger	Jack Higgins	0399147101	$17.95
The First Counsel	Brad Meltzer	0446527289	$15.57
The Villa	Nora Roberts	0399147128	$20.76

Row deleted between these two rows

Figure 7.10

④ Save the document, and keep it onscreen to continue with the next lesson.

To extend your knowledge...

Deleting Cell Contents

Instead of deleting a row or column, you might want to keep the table structure but delete the text in the cells. To delete just the text, select the cells containing the text you want to delete and then press Del. This process leaves empty cells in which you can type new text.

Lesson 5: Adjusting Column Width and Row Height

When you create a table, Word creates evenly spaced columns. ***Column width*** is the horizontal space or width of a column. You may, however, need to adjust the column widths based on the type of data you type in the column. For example, the columns in your table should be narrower.

Furthermore, you might want to adjust the row height. ***Row height*** is the vertical distance from the top of the row to the bottom of the row. By default, Word expands the row height when text word-wraps within a cell on that row. To make the column headings on the first row stand out, you want to make this row taller.

To Adjust Row Height and Column Widths

① In the *Book Letter-WB7L* document, click the Print Layout View button, and change the zoom to 100%.

② Position the mouse pointer on the gridline that separates the first and second rows of the table.
As Figure 7.11 shows, the mouse pointer turns into a two-headed arrow, indicating that you can adjust the height by clicking and dragging the gridline.

(Continues)

To Adjust Row Height and Column Widths (Continued)

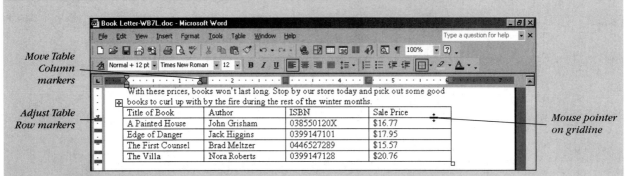

Figure 7.11

? If you have problems...

You won't see the two-headed mouse arrow in Normal view. You must be in Print Layout view to see the two-headed arrow on the table gridlines.

❸ Click and drag the gridline down to make the row about twice its original height, as shown in Figure 7.12.

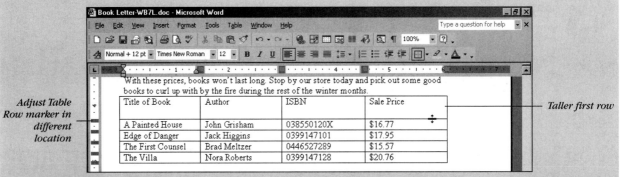

Figure 7.12

You now need to decrease the column widths.

❹ Position the mouse pointer on the vertical gridline on the right side of the Sale Price column.

The mouse pointer is a two-headed arrow, indicating that you can change the column width (see Figure 7.13).

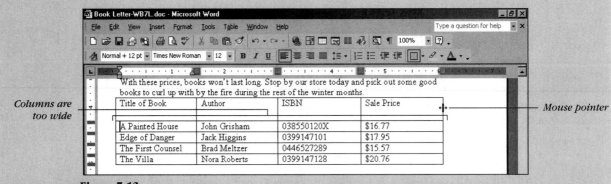

Figure 7.13

To Adjust Row Height and Column Widths

5 **Double-click the gridline.**
Double-clicking a vertical gridline adjusts the column width based on the text in that column. The fourth column is now narrower.

6 **Double-click the vertical gridline between the third and fourth columns to decrease the width of the third column.**

7 **Double-click the vertical gridline between the second and third columns.**
The columns look better than they did when they were wider (see Figure 7.14).

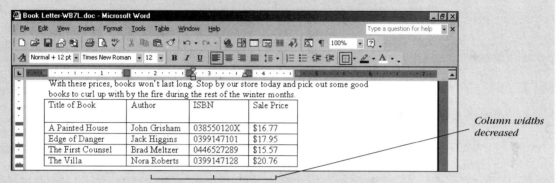

Column widths decreased

Figure 7.14

8 **Save the document, and keep it onscreen to continue with the next lesson.**

To extend your knowledge...

Decreasing Widths Before Increasing Other Widths

Before making a column *wider*, adjust other columns that need to be *narrower*. If you make one wider and then decrease other column widths, you might have to increase the first column width again.

Using the Markers to Adjust Width and Height

You can click and drag the Adjust Table Row marker to change the row height and the Move Table Column marker to change a column width (refer to Figure 7.11 in the previous exercise).

Adjusting Exact Column Widths

If instructed, you can specify an *exact* measurement for column widths. To do this, click inside a cell within the column for which you want to adjust its width. Choose T̲able, Table P̲roperties. Then, click the Col̲umn tab, click the *Preferred w̲idth* check box, and set a specific setting (see Figure 7.15).

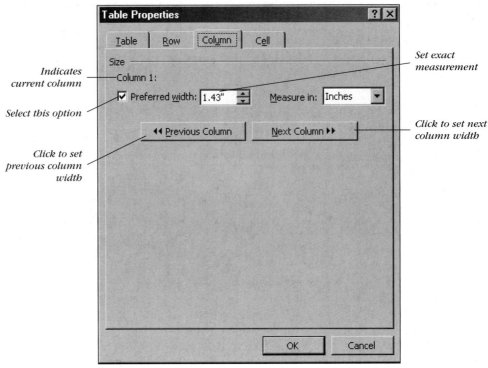

Figure 7.15

If you want to set the same width for all columns, click the <u>T</u>able tab in the Table Properties dialog box and set the Preferred <u>w</u>idth there.

Setting a Specific Row Height

Instead of clicking and dragging a horizontal gridline to change row height, you can display the Table Properties dialog box and set an exact row height under the *<u>R</u>ow* tab. Click the *<u>S</u>pecify height* check box and then type the exact height in the text box.

Lesson 6: Formatting Cells

After creating a table, entering data, and adjusting the structure, you need to format data within the cells. You can use many common formatting techniques you already know, such as bold, font color, font, font size, bullets, and more.

In this lesson, you make the first-row text stand out by choosing center alignment, boldface, and center vertical alignment. In addition, you set cell margins for the cells in the first column.

To Apply Cell Formats

❶ In the *Book Letter-WB7L* document, click and drag across the text in the first row of the table.
You must select the text in the first-row cells to format them simultaneously.

❷ Click the Font button and choose Arial Narrow, click the Bold button, and then click the Center button on the Formatting toolbar.
The text on the first row is now bold and centered horizontally in Arial Narrow font.

❸ Choose Table, Table P<u>r</u>operties, and click the *Cell* tab, if needed.
Figure 7.16 shows the Cell options in the Table Properties dialog box.

To Apply Cell Formats

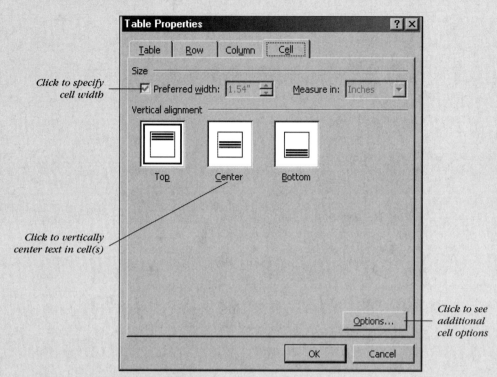

Click to specify cell width

Click to vertically center text in cell(s)

Click to see additional cell options

Figure 7.16

4 **Click *Center*, click OK, and deselect the text.**

Figure 7.17 shows the first-row text centered vertically within the respective cells.

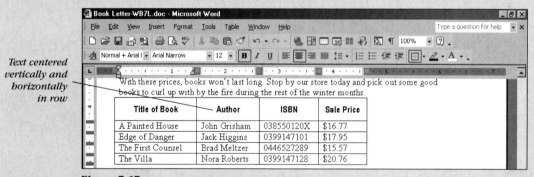

Text centered vertically and horizontally in row

Title of Book	Author	ISBN	Sale Price
A Painted House	John Grisham	038550120X	$16.77
Edge of Danger	Jack Higgins	0399147101	$17.95
The First Counsel	Brad Meltzer	0446527289	$15.57
The Villa	Nora Roberts	0399147128	$20.76

Figure 7.17

Now, you want to adjust cell margins for the first column.

5 **Select the entire first column—the column containing the book titles.**

6 **Choose Table, Table Properties.**

7 **Click the Options button.**

(Continues)

To Apply Cell Formats (Continued)

The Cell Options dialog box appears (see Figure 7.18) so that you can adjust cell margins and wrap options.

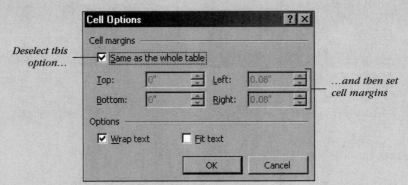

Deselect this option...

...and then set cell margins

Figure 7.18

8 **Click the *Same as the whole table* check box to deselect it.**
After deselecting the check box, the four margin setting options are available.

9 **Click both the *Left* and *Right* spin buttons to display *0.16"*.**
Increasing the left and right cell margins helps balance the text within the cells.

10 **Click OK to close each open dialog box; then deselect the column.**
The first-column text looks balanced after increasing the cell margins (see Figure 7.19).

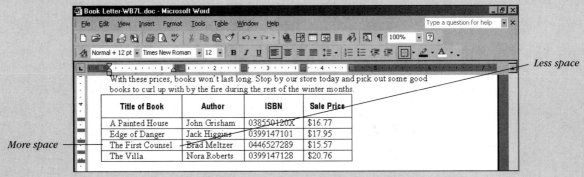

Less space

More space

Figure 7.19

11 **Save the document, and keep it onscreen to continue with the next lesson.**

To extend your knowledge...

Selecting a Row

Instead of clicking and dragging across a row, you can position the mouse pointer to the left side of a row (in the selection bar area). When the mouse pointer is an arrow pointing to the top right, click to select the row.

Lesson 7: Applying Shading and Borders

You can also enhance the appearance of a table by selecting shading and border options. Shading refers to the background color within a cell or group of cells. Table shading is similar to the High-light feature that places a color behind text. Border refers to the line style around each cell in the table. The default line style is a single line.

In this lesson, you enhance the table by shading the first row, so it stands out.

To Select Table Shading

① **In the** *Book Letter-WB7L* **document, choose** **V**iew, **T**oolbars, Tables and Borders.
The Tables and Borders toolbar appears onscreen (see Figure 7.20).

Figure 7.20

② **Select the text on the first row of the table.**

③ **Click the drop-down arrow to the right of the Shading Color button on the Tables and Borders toolbar.**
You see the Shading Color palette, as shown in Figure 7.21.

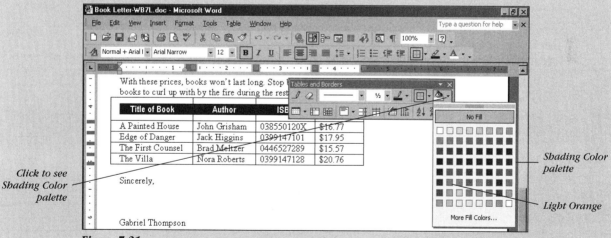

Figure 7.21

When you position the mouse pointer on a color, Word displays a ScreenTip that tells you the exact name of the color, such as Sky Blue.

④ **Click the Light Orange color.**

⑤ **Deselect the row to see the color and then close the Tables and Borders toolbar.**
The first row contains a Light Orange shading color, as shown in Figure 7.22.

(Continues)

To Select Table Shading (Continued)

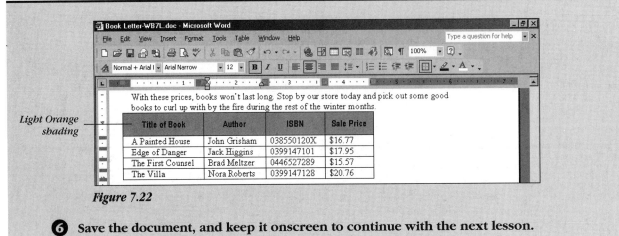

Light Orange shading

Figure 7.22

6 Save the document, and keep it onscreen to continue with the next lesson.

To extend your knowledge...

Table Borders

In Project 5, "Formatting Documents," you learned how to insert a border around a paragraph. Although you see borders for your table, you can customize the borders. To do this, click inside the table, and choose Table, Table Properties. Click the Table tab and then click the Borders and Shading button. You'll see options similar to those you used for paragraph borders. When choosing shading colors, be sure to specify whether you want to apply the shading to the entire table or the selected cells.

Remember that some colors do not print well or might cause text to be difficult to read on a black-and-white printout.

Lesson 8: Moving and Positioning a Table

After creating a table, you might decide to move it to a different location. You might also want to change the *table alignment*, the location of a table between the margins. In this lesson, you move the table above the last paragraph, make sure there is a blank line before and after the table, and choose center table alignment.

To Move the Table

1 In the *Book Letter-WB7L* document, adjust the view to see the table and the first two paragraphs.

2 Make sure the insertion point is inside the table; then position the mouse pointer on the table marker.
You should see a four-headed arrow, indicating that you can move the entire table.

3 Click and drag the table marker to the blank line above the last paragraph.
As you drag the table marker, you see a dotted line, indicating where you're moving the table. When you release the mouse, Word moves the table to that location (see Figure 7.23).

To Move the Table

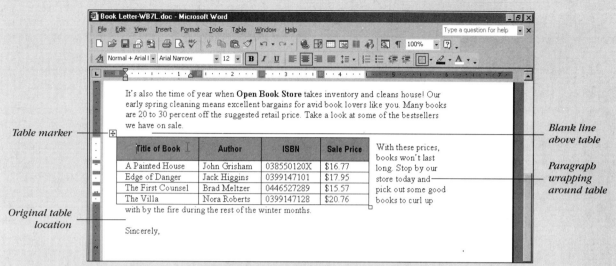

Figure 7.23

The last paragraph might word-wrap around the table. You need to take off the word-wrapping, and also center the table between the left and right margins.

④ Right-click in the table, and choose Table Properties.
When you right-click in a table, a shortcut menu appears. You can choose options from this menu or from the Table menu on the menu bar.

⑤ Click the Table tab.
Figure 7.24 shows the table options.

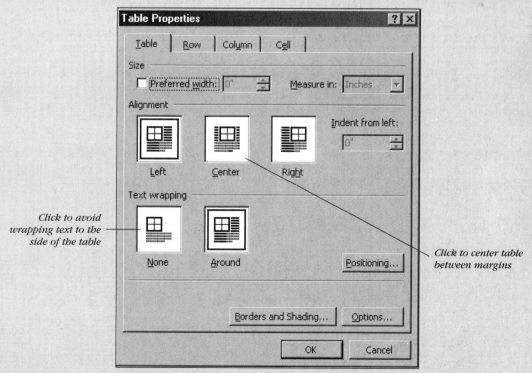

Figure 7.24

(Continues)

To Move the Table (Continued)

6 **Click the _Center_ alignment option.**
This option centers the table between the left and right margins.

7 **Click _None_ in the text-wrapping options and then click OK.**
This option prevents text from wrapping on the left or right side of the table.

8 **If necessary, press ⏎Enter at the end of the paragraph above the table.**
Figure 7.25 shows the centered table with text that does not wrap around the table.

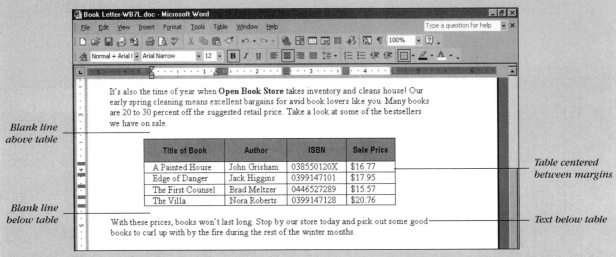

Blank line above table

Blank line below table

Table centered between margins

Text below table

Figure 7.25

9 **Save, print, and close the document.**

Summary

After completing these lessons, you know how to create a table, adjust the structure, and format the data. You can create exciting tables that look professional by centering text, shading cells, and positioning the table. In addition, you know how to move a table to a new location.

You probably noticed a lot of different buttons on the Tables and Borders toolbar. To learn more about these buttons, point to the button to see the ScreenTip displaying the button's name. Then, access onscreen Help to learn about these additional table buttons.

Checking Concepts and Terms

Multiple Choice

Circle the letter of the correct answer for each of the following.

1. If the insertion point is in the last cell on the first row, what key(s) should you press to go to the first cell on the next row? [L2]

   a. Ctrl + G

   b. ⬆Shift + Tab

   c. Alt + Home

   d. Tab

2. Assume that you created a table with the names of the months in the first column. Each row lists data for that particular month. The insertion point is in the first cell on the third row. This row list goals for April. You realize that you left out the goals for March. What should you do? [L3]

   a. Choose Table, Insert, Columns to the Left.

   b. Choose Table, Insert, Columns to the Right.

   c. Choose Table, Insert, Rows Above.

   d. Choose Table, Insert, Rows Below.

3. What happens when you press Tab when the insertion point is in the last cell in the last row? [L3]

   a. Word inserts a new row above the current row.

   b. Word inserts a new row below the current row.

   c. The insertion point appears in the paragraph below the table.

   d. The insertion point stays in the cell because it's already in the last cell of the table.

4. Refer to Figure 7.25 in Lesson 8. If the insertion point is in the cell that contains *$15.57*, and you choose Table, Delete, Rows, what happens? [L4]

   a. You delete just the *$15.57* text.

   b. You delete the Sale Price column.

   c. You delete the entire fourth row.

   d. You delete the entire third row.

5. All of the following help make the first row stand out, except _____. [L6,7]

   a. shading

   b. boldface

   c. taller height

   d. smaller font size

Discussion

1. Look through magazines, brochures, reports, and other documents that contain tables. Discuss the types of data conveyed in the tables. Evaluate the effectiveness of the table designs and formats. Provide suggestions for improving the tables. [L1–8]

2. Why should you adjust column widths instead of using the default column widths? [L5]

3. Describe the difference between table alignment and text alignment. [L8]

Skill Drill

Skill Drill exercises reinforce project skills. Each skill reinforced is the same, or nearly the same, as a skill presented in the project. Detailed instructions are provided in a step-by-step format.

1. Creating a Table of Seminars

As the assistant to David Zaugg, you need to create a table that lists upcoming seminars for employees in the Dallas area.

1. Open *ew1-0702*, and save it as `Dallas Seminars-WB7SD`.
2. Position the insertion point between the first and second paragraphs.
3. Choose Table, Insert, Table.
4. Type 4 in the *Number of columns* box, press Tab, and type 5 in the *Number of rows* box. Then, click OK.
5. Type the data shown in Figure 7.26.

October 17	8:00-10:00 a.m.	Working with Difficult Customers	Baker Room
October 17	1:30-3:30 p.m.	Communicating with Subordinates	Texas Ballroom
October 18	8:00-10:00 a.m.	Resolving Customer Complaints	Suite 495
October 18	9:30-11:30 a.m.	Climbing the Corporate Ladder	Texas Ballroom
October 18	3:30-5:30 p.m.	Analyzing Data	Suite 495

Figure 7.26

6. Save the document, and keep it onscreen to continue with the next exercise.

2. Adjusting the Table Structure

You need to add a row at the top of the table to enter column headings to identify the data. You also need to add a row at the bottom of the table. Your supervisor, David Zaugg, just informed you that one seminar was canceled; therefore, you need to delete that row.

1. With the *Dallas Seminars-WB7SD* document onscreen, position the insertion point in any cell on the first row.
2. Choose Table, Insert.
3. Choose Rows Above.
4. Click in the first cell.
5. Type the following data in cells on the first row:
   Date   Time   Topic   Room
6. Click in the last cell on the last row—the cell containing *Suite 495*—and press Tab.
7. Type the following data in the cells on the new row:
   October 19   9:30-11:30 a.m. Working with Managers   Suite 495
8. Click in the cell containing *Climbing the Corporate Ladder*.
9. Choose Table, Delete, Rows to delete the row.
10. Save the document, and keep it onscreen to continue with the next exercise.

3. Adjusting Column Width and Row Height

You need to adjust the column widths in the table. Most columns are too wide. In addition, you want to increase the height of the first row.

1. In the *Dallas Seminar-WB7SD* document, position the mouse pointer on the vertical gridline on the right side of the last column, and double-click to decrease its width.
2. Double-click the vertical gridline between the Date and Time columns.
3. Double-click the vertical gridline between the Time and Topic columns.
4. Double-click the vertical gridline between the Topic and Room columns.
5. Click the Print Layout View button.
6. Click and drag the horizontal gridline between the first and second rows down to double the height of the first row.
7. Save the document, and keep it onscreen to continue to the next exercise.

4. Formatting Table Cells

You want the column headings to stand out, so you plan to add bold, centering, and shading to the first row. In addition, you want to right-align text in the second column.

1. In the *Dallas Seminars-WB7SD* document, select the first row by positioning the mouse pointer between the left gridline and the text in the first cell, and double-click.
2. Choose T<u>a</u>ble, Table P<u>r</u>operties.
3. Click the *C<u>e</u>ll* tab.
4. Click the *<u>C</u>enter* vertical alignment option and then click OK.
5. Click the *<u>T</u>able* tab and then click the <u>B</u>orders and Shading button.
6. Click the *<u>S</u>hading* tab in the Borders and Shading dialog box.
7. Click Light Green (fourth from the left on the last row) on the palette.
8. Make sure the *App<u>l</u>y to* option is *Cell*.
9. Click OK to close each open dialog box.
10. Click the Bold and Center buttons on the Formatting toolbar.
11. Deselect the first row.
12. Click and drag to select the times (but not the column heading) in the second column.
13. Click the Align Right button on the Formatting toolbar.
14. Deselect the text.
15. Save the document and keep it onscreen to continue with the next exercise.

5. Moving the Table

You want to move the table to a different location within the memo. In addition, you need to make sure you have one blank line above and below the table.

1. In the *Dallas Seminar-WB7SD* document, scroll down to see the table and the last two paragraphs.
2. Click in the table, and position the mouse pointer on the table marker.
3. When you see the four-headed arrow, click and drag the table marker straight down, and position the table between the second and third paragraphs.
4. Click at the end of the second paragraph, and press ⏎Enter.
5. Make sure you have one blank line above and below the table.
6. Save, print, and close the document.

hallenge

Challenge exercises expand on or are somewhat related to skills presented in the lessons. Each exercise provides a brief narrative introduction, followed by instructions in a numbered-step format that are not as detailed as those in the Skill Drill section.

1. Creating an Alternative Book Sales Letter

Gabriel Thompson, manager of Open Book Store, has asked you to create another sales letter with different book choices. As you create the table, Gabriel provides continual input for changes.

1. Open *ew1-0701*, and save it as `Book Letter2-WB7CH1`.
2. Between the second and third paragraphs, create a table with the data shown in Figure 7.27.

Shreve, Anita	Where or When	April 1999	240
Connelly, Michael	Blood Work	September 1998	528
McFarland, Dennis	Singing Boy	February 2001	320
Shreve, Anita	Last Time They Met, The	April 2001	320
Diamant, Anita	Red Tent, The	September 1997	321
Connelly, Michael	Darkness More than Night, A	January 2001	432

Figure 7.27

3. Insert a row at the top of the table and enter the following information:

   `Author     Book Title     Publication Date     Pages`

4. Format the first row with bold, center horizontal alignment, 0.4″ row height, center vertical alignment, and Pale Blue shading.
5. Decrease all column widths to fit the data.
6. Center-align the text in the third and fourth columns.
7. Make sure you have one blank line above and below the table.
8. Center the table itself between the left and right margins.
9. Save and print the document.
10. Delete the publication date column, and insert a new column on the far right side of the table.
11. Enter the following data in the last column:

    ```
    Sale Price
    $11.70
    $6.75
    $20.00
    $19.96
    $19.96
    $15.57
    ```

12. Save the revised letter as `Book Letter 3-WB7CH1`, print it, and close the document.

2. Creating a Table in a Flier

The Life and Learning Center at a college is sponsoring two series of workshops: one series to improve student success and one series on effective writing. You were asked to create and format a table in the flier that will be distributed on campus.

1. Open *ew1-0703*, and save it as `Workshops-WB7CH2`.

2. Create a table with two columns and six rows. Place the table between the *Free Workshops* and *Sponsored By* text lines. Use the following information to create the table:

```
Student Success Series      Effective Writing Series
Taking Notes                Using Proper Punctuation
Using Textbooks Effectively  Writing Creatively
Improving Concentration      Correcting Common Mistakes
Managing Time                Streamlining Prose
Taking Tests                 Proofreading Carefully
```

3. Select the table, and apply 16-point Times New Roman.

4. Emphasize the *first row* by applying these formats: Arial Narrow, bold, 0.5″ row height, and centered vertically and horizontally.

5. Apply Yellow font color and Blue shading for the first row.

6. Double-click the vertical gridlines to adjust the column widths.

7. Center the table between the left and right margins.

8. Add some blank lines between *Workshops* and the table, and between the table and *Sponsored By*.

9. Center the document vertically.

10. Insert a row after the fourth row. Type the following information in the new row:

```
Overcoming Test Anxiety       Revising Globally
```

11. Apply the Pencil art page border to the document. You might need to custom-install Office XP if the art page borders are not available.

12. Save, print, and close the document.

3. Creating a Table of People Involved in a Book Project

You are an assistant for a book publisher. Your supervisor wants you to create a table that lists the key people involved with an Office XP book.

1. In a new document window, type the title `Office XP Book Project`, and triple-space after the title.

2. Apply these formats to the title: center-align, bold, 16-point Antique Olive or Arial Rounded MT Bold, and Dark Blue font color. Choose Arial Black if you don't have Antique Olive or Arial Rounded MT Bold fonts.

3. Create a table after the hard returns. Use the information shown in Figure 7.28.

Name	Job Title	Phone Number
Monica Stewart	Author	801.555.8237
Susan Layne	Developmental Editor	580.555.7033
Justin Fields	Project Editor	201.555.4387
Melody Devereaux	Proofreader	419.555.2031
Louisa Jayaraman	Indexer	734.555.2499
Andy Ottley	Layout Technician	201.555.8108
Geoff Scovel	Usability Tester	801.555.1634

Figure 7.28

4. Insert a row above the developmental editor, and enter the following data:

   `Nick Lopez        Acquisitions Editor    201.555.8642`

5. Insert a row below the project editor, and enter the following data:

   `Josie Rynbrandt    Copy Editor            201.555.8265`

6. Apply Pale Blue shading to the entire table.

7. Set a 0.25″ row height for the entire table.

8. Apply a vertical center alignment to the cells within the table.

9. Horizontally center the text in the third column.

10. Center-align and bold the text on the first row.

11. Adjust the column widths, as needed.

12. Center the table between the left and right margins. (Make sure you center the *table*, not the text.)

13. Select the first column, set a **1.75″** cell width, and **0.21″** left and right cell margins.

14. Save the document as `Book Project-WB7CH3`, print it, and close it.

4. Creating Tables for Candle Scents and Prices

You work for Heavenly Scents Candles, a company that makes and distributes a variety of candle fragrances. You just wrote a letter to a customer who is interested in your candles. Now, you need to create two tables: one to list candle fragrances, and one for sizes and pricing.

1. Open *ew1-0704*, and save it as `Candle Letter-WB7CH4`.

2. Create the first table below the first paragraph. Use the information shown in Figure 7.29.

Standard Scents	Exotic Scents
Cinnamon	Pina Colada
Peach	Raspberry Delight
Mulberry	Mango
Vanilla	Passion Fruit

Figure 7.29

3. Add a row at the bottom of the table for **Apple Spice** and **Tropical Mist**, two popular standard and exotic scents.

4. Delete the row containing *Peach* and *Raspberry Delight* because you ran out of those scents and won't have any more for another month.

5. Apply these formats to the first row: centered vertically and horizontally, bold, 11-point Arial, Violet font color, Yellow shading color, and 0.35″ row height.

6. Apply a Light Yellow shading color to the rest of the table.

7. Adjust the column widths.

8. Create another table after the second paragraph, using the information shown in Figure 7.30.

Size	Price
8 ounce	$9.95
16 ounce	$17.95
26 ounce	$19.95
28 ounce	$22.95

Figure 7.30

9. Insert a column between the two existing columns in the second table. Enter this data:

```
Description
Round Jar
Round Jar
Octagon Jar; 2 Wicks
Square Jar; 2 Wicks
```

10. Apply these formats to the first row of the second table: centered vertically and horizontally, bold, 11-point Arial, Yellow font color, Violet shading color, and 0.35″ row height.

11. Apply Lavender shading color to the rest of the second table.

12. Adjust column widths as needed for the second table.

13. Center-align the data in the first and third columns of the second table.

14. Right-align the dollar values in the last column.

15. Center both tables between the left and right margins.

16. Make sure you have one blank line above and below each table.

17. Select the second table, and apply a 1.5-point Box border with Violet border to the outside of the table. (This process applies a thicker outside border and removes the cell borders inside the table.)

18. Replace the regular hyphens with nonbreaking hyphens in the phone number.

19. Save, print, and close the document.

Discovery Zone

Discovery Zone exercises help you gain advanced knowledge of project topics and/or application of skills. These exercises focus on enhancing your problem-solving skills. Numbered steps are not provided, but you are given hints, reminders, screen shots, and/or references to help you reach your goal for each exercise.

1. Sorting and Aligning Decimals in a Table

Gabriel Thompson wants you to make a few more changes to your latest book letter that you completed in Challenge 1. Open *Book Letter 3-WB7CH1*, and save it as `Book Letter 4-WB7DZ1`.

Set a `0.75"` cell width for the entire last column. Also, select left alignment and a decimal tab for the prices within the last column. (Make sure the cells are selected first.)

Sort the table by author in ascending order and then further sort by title. Study the options in the Sort dialog box, and select the appropriate options based on the table data.

Save, print, and close the document.

2. Enhancing the Candle Letter Tables

You want to further enhance the tables you created in Challenge 3. Open *Candle Letter-WB7CH4*, and save it as `Candle Letter-WB7DZ2`.

Use Help to learn how to create captions for tables. Create a caption for each table that reflects the table content. Keep the caption brief. Use the option to place the caption above the tables. After creating the captions, center them above their respective tables.

Select the first table, and apply these border options: Grid setting, ninth line style, Pink line color, and applied to the table. Also, choose a Rose shading color for the table. Italicize the fragrance names, but not the column headings. Apply the same border style to the bottom of the first row. *Hint:* Look at the buttons in the Preview section of the dialog box to apply a border to a certain part of the cell.

Select the second table, and apply these border options: Box setting, Yellow line color, 3 pt width, and applied to table. Also, add a Yellow bottom border to the first row only.

Save, print, and close the document.

3. Creating a Table of Potential Computer Systems

Your supervisor asked you to research six different computer systems and provide the following details in a table: brand name and model number, hard-drive capacity, RAM, megahertz, other features (such as CD-ROM or DVD; Jazz or Zip drive), and price. Choose one major computer retailer to complete your research. You might want to conduct Internet research by looking at the retailer's Web site. Choose models with similar features so the comparison will be appropriate.

Write a memo to your supervisor that explains where you got the research, and create a table that compares the computer systems. Apply appropriate formatting that you learned in this project. For example, select shading and borders; set column widths and row height; and choose fonts, font sizes, and font color to make the table look good. Use Help to learn how to select landscape page orientation. Explore the Tables and Borders toolbar.

Save your document as `Computer Memo-WB7DZ3`, print it, and close it.

Inserting and Formatting Graphics

Objectives

In this project, you learn how to

- ✔ Insert an Image
- ✔ Move and Delete an Image
- ✔ Size an Image
- ✔ Wrap Text Around an Image
- ✔ Apply Borders and Fills
- ✔ Copy Images with the Clip Organizer
- ✔ Download and Insert an Online Clip
- ✔ Create a Watermark
- ✔ Create WordArt

Key terms introduced in this project include

- ❑ clip art
- ❑ Clip Organizer
- ❑ fill
- ❑ Insert Clip Art task pane
- ❑ keyword
- ❑ sizing handles
- ❑ tight wrap
- ❑ watermark
- ❑ WordArt
- ❑ wrapping style

Why Would I Do This?

Some of the most exciting features of Word are its graphic capabilities. You can insert ***clip art***, graphic images, or drawings in any document. Clip art and images provide visual appeal for a variety of documents. People use clip art, images, drawings, and scanned photographs to enhance brochures, newsletters, and announcements.

Visual Summary

Figure 8.1 shows various visual elements in a document that you complete in this project.

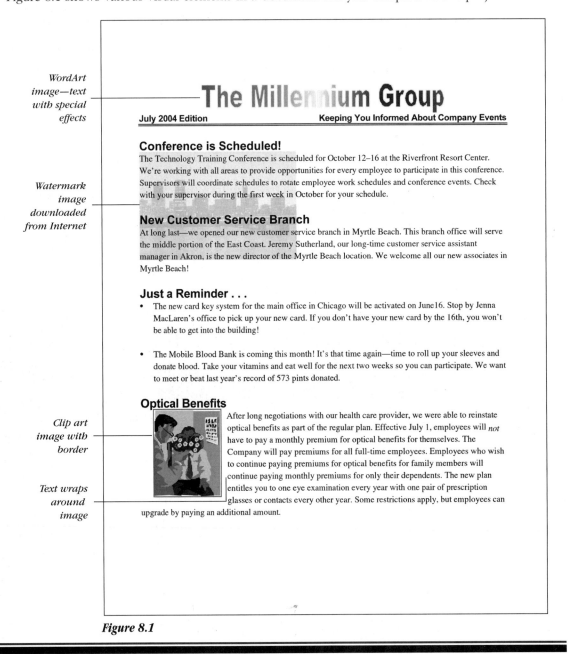

WordArt image—text with special effects

Watermark image downloaded from Internet

Clip art image with border

Text wraps around image

Figure 8.1

Lesson 1: Inserting an Image

Office XP comes with an enormous number of clip art images. You can find images representing people, animals, special occasions, and more! Depending on how Office XP was installed on your computer, you may have just a few or all of these images. You can also obtain clip art from the Microsoft Design Gallery Live, Microsoft's online clip gallery, or you can purchase clip art packages at a computer supply store.

Be sure to read about the legal uses of clip art images, whether you're using Microsoft's clip art or other clip art you purchased. Although clip art is often acceptable for education or non-profit use, it may not be legal to use in some advertising situations.

In this lesson, you insert clip art in a company newsletter by using the ***Insert Clip Art task pane***, a window pane in which you search for and select clip art, photographs, movies, and sounds.

To Insert an Image

1 Open *ew1-0801,* **and save it as** `July Newsletter-WB8L`.

2 **Press** Ctrl+End **to position the insertion point at the end of the document.** You want to insert an image after the last paragraph.

3 **Choose Insert, Picture, Clip Art.**

If you have problems...

If you see the Add Clips to Organizer dialog box, click the Later button to see the Insert Clip Art task pane.

The Insert Clip Art task pane appears so that you can search for clip art and other media (see Figure 8.2).

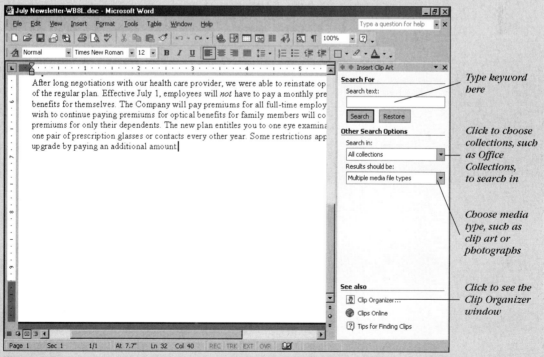

Figure 8.2

(Continues)

To Insert an Image (Continued)

You want to select an image that depicts an optometrist. To display clips, you type a **keyword**, a word or phrase that describes the type of clip you're looking for. You can type very specific keywords, such as `optometrist`, or general keywords, such as `medicines`.

4 **Type** `medicine` **in the *Search text* box.**
The keyword *medicine* provides more results than *optometrist*.

5 **Click the *Search in* drop-down arrow, select *Office Collections*, deselect the other options, and then click the drop-down arrow to close the menu.**
The Office Collection refers to the clips that are stored on your computer when you installed the software. Although you could leave all options selected, doing so would slow down the search process.

6 **Click the *Results should be* drop-down arrow, and deselect all check boxes except *Clip Art*, which should be selected, and then click the drop-down arrow to close the *Results should be* list.**
You should check the media types you want to find to expedite the search process.

7 **Click the Search button in the task pane.**
Word searches through the clips to find ones that contain the keyword you typed for the media you selected (see Figure 8.3).

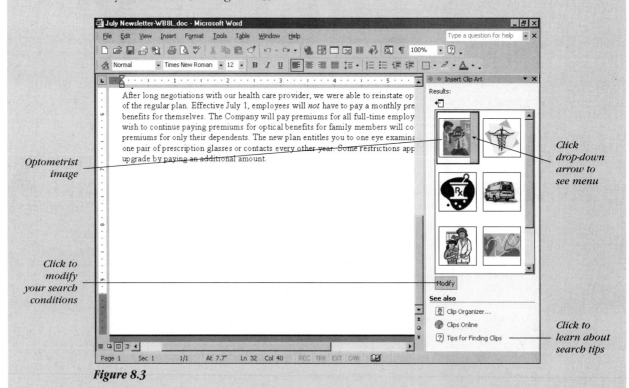

Optometrist image

Click to modify your search conditions

Click drop-down arrow to see menu

Click to learn about search tips

Figure 8.3

8 **Position the mouse pointer on the optometrist image and then click the down-pointing arrow to the right of the image.**
A menu of options appears (see Figure 8.4).

To Insert an Image

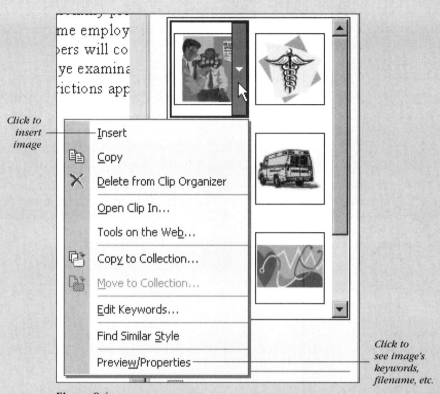

Click to
insert
image

Click to
see image's
keywords,
filename, etc.

Figure 8.4

9 **Click Insert from the menu and then click the task pane's Close button.**
Word inserts the image at the insertion point location, causing the last line of the paragraph to align with the bottom of the image (see Figure 8.5).

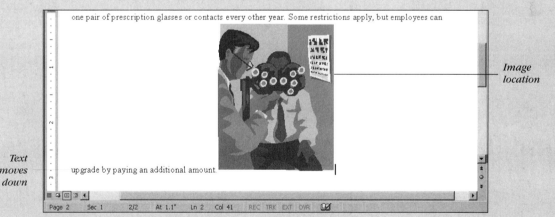

Image
location

Text
moves
down

Figure 8.5

10 **Save the document, and keep it onscreen to continue with the next lesson.**

To extend your knowledge...

Using the Clip Organizer

Instead of entering keywords and searching for clips, you can display the **Clip Organizer**, which is a gallery of clips organized on your hard drive with access to download and organize clips from Microsoft's Web site.

To use the Clip Organizer, click *Clip Organizer* at the bottom of the Insert Clip Art task pane. Within the Clip Organizer window, click *Office Collections*, and click a category such as *Business*. Figure 8.6 shows a sample palette of clip art you can choose from.

Figure 8.6

Using Other Images

You can insert almost any type of image by choosing Insert, Picture, From File. Some image file types you can use include Joint Photographic Experts Group (.jpg), Windows Bitmap (.bmp), Graphics Interchange Format (.gif), and Windows Metafile (.wmf). Word can insert these types of files without any special conversion.

If you want to insert other types of graphics files, such as a WordPerfect (.wpg) graphics image, you must install the graphics filters from the installation CD first.

Scanning a Picture

If you have a scanner attached to your computer, you can scan a picture to use as an image within Word. Choose Insert, Picture, From Scanner or Camera. Type `insert picture` in the Answer Wizard section of the Help window and then click *Insert a picture directly from a scanner or digital camera* for more information about inserting an image into your document by using a scanner.

Lesson 2: Moving and Deleting an Image

After inserting an image, you might want to move it around on the page until you are satisfied with its location. If you want to move an image to another area that you currently see onscreen, you can click and drag the image there.

In this lesson, you move the image below the *Optical Benefits* heading, and position it at the left margin.

To Move an Image

1 **In the** *July Newsletter-WB8L* **document, click the Normal View button.**
Because you want to drag the image from the second to the first page, you need to display the document in Normal view.

2 **Click the image to select it.**
When you click an image, the Picture toolbar appears. Word displays ***sizing handles***—little black boxes that appear around the image so you can adjust the image's size and move it elsewhere (see Figure 8.7).

Picture toolbar

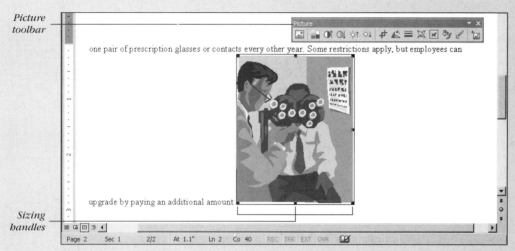

Sizing handles

Figure 8.7

If you have problems...

If you don't see the Picture toolbar, choose View, Toolbars, Picture to display the Picture toolbar.

---

3 **Click the scroll up button about six times to see the last heading and paragraph on page 1.**
You can see the beginning of the paragraph without the bottom and top margin space in Normal view. Without the margin space, it is easier for you to click and drag the image to the correct place.

4 **Click and drag the image to the beginning of the paragraph immediately below** *Optical Benefits.*
A shadow cursor follows your mouse pointer, letting you know where the image will appear when you release the mouse button.

If you have problems...

If you can't see the part of the document to which you want to move the image, do *not* click and drag. Doing so might cause your screen to scroll so quickly through the document that you won't be able to stop at the place you want to drop the image.

Instead, click the image and then click the Cut button. Position the insertion point where you want the image to appear and click the Paste button. The cutting and pasting process is easier than clicking and dragging the image from page to page.

(Continues)

To Move an Image (Continued)

The image appears at the beginning of the paragraph, as shown in Figure 8.8.

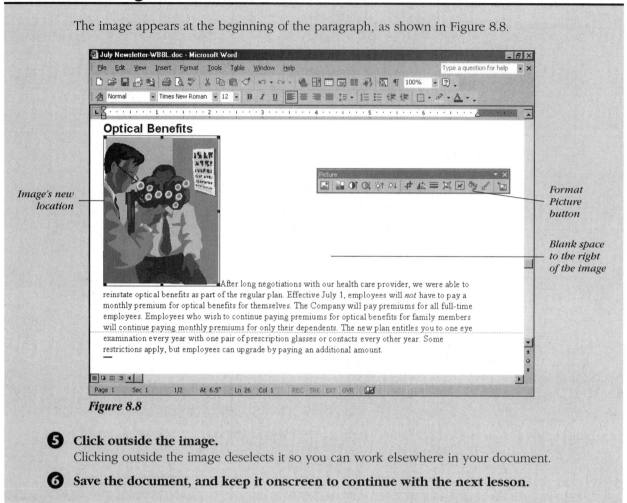

Figure 8.8

⑤ Click outside the image.
Clicking outside the image deselects it so you can work elsewhere in your document.

⑥ Save the document, and keep it onscreen to continue with the next lesson.

To extend your knowledge...

Deleting an Image

If you want to delete an image, click it to select it. Then, press Del.

Lesson 3: Sizing an Image

When you insert an image in a document, it comes in at a predetermined size. Most of the time, you need to adjust the image's size so it fits better within the document.

In this lesson, you decide on a specific size for the image. You want it to be 1.6″ tall and 1.29″ wide. To set a specific size, you need to access the Format Picture dialog box.

To Change the Image's Size

1 **In the *July Newsletter-WB8L* document, click the image to select it.**
The Picture toolbar should appear. If it doesn't, right-click the Standard toolbar, and choose Picture.

2 **Click the Format Picture button on the Picture toolbar.**
The Format Picture dialog box appears. You use this dialog box to select the format settings for your images.

3 **Click the Size tab.**
You see the options for setting the size of your image, as shown in Figure 8.9.

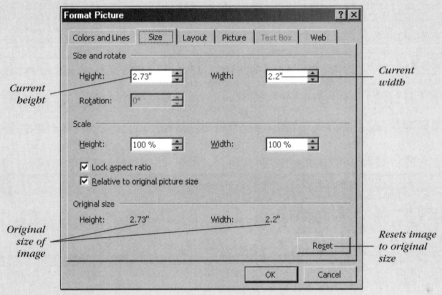

Figure 8.9

4 **Highlight 2.73″ in the *Height* box.**

5 **Type 1.6 and click OK.**
You don't need to set the width because it automatically adjusts when you click OK to maintain a proportionate size. Figure 8.10 shows the smaller image.

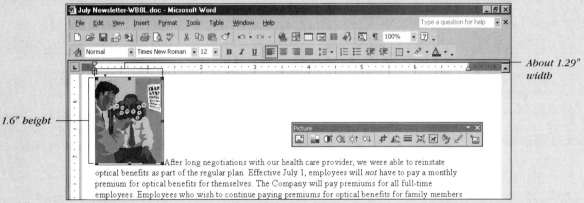

Figure 8.10

6 **Click outside the image, save the document, and keep it onscreen to continue with the next lesson.**

To extend your knowledge...

Using the Sizing Handles

If you don't need an exact size, you can click and drag the sizing handles to adjust the image's size. Table 8.1 describes how to use the sizing handles.

Table 8.1	Adjusting the Image's Size with the Sizing Handles
Desired Result	**Do This:**
Increase the width	Click and drag either the middle-left or middle-right sizing handle away from the image.
Decrease the width	Click and drag either the middle-left or middle-right sizing handle toward the image.
Increase the height	Click and drag the upper-middle or bottom-middle sizing handle away from the image.
Decrease the height	Click and drag the upper-middle or bottom-middle sizing handle toward the image.
Adjust the height and width at the same time	Click and drag a corner sizing handle at an angle to adjust the height and width. Hold down ◆Shift to maintain the image's proportions.

Displaying the Format Picture Dialog Box

You can also double-click an image or right-click an image and choose Format Picture to display the Format Picture dialog box.

Lesson 4: Wrapping Text Around an Image

When you first insert an image, Word treats it as a character on the line of text; therefore, the text line allows a lot of empty space on the left or right side of the image. You probably want to allow text to wrap differently. **Wrapping style** refers to the way text wraps around an image. You can have text appear on top of or behind an image, wrap tightly around the outer edges of the image itself, or wrap above or below the image.

In this lesson, you choose a square wrap style to let the paragraph wrap on the right side of the image.

To Wrap Text Around an Image

❶ In the *July Newsletter-WB8L* document, click the image to select it.

❷ Click the Text Wrapping button on the Picture toolbar.
A list of text-wrapping options appears (see Figure 8.11).

To Wrap Text Around an Image

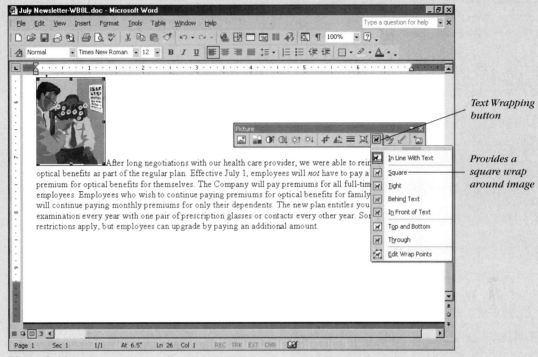

Text Wrapping button

Provides a square wrap around image

Figure 8.11

❸ **Choose Square from the menu.**

Text now wraps square around the right side of the image (see Figure 8.12).

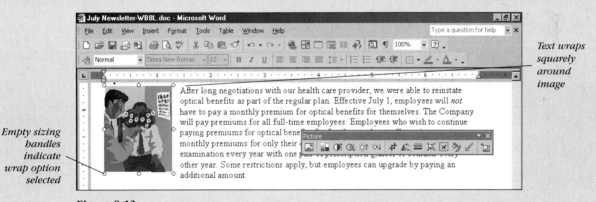

Text wraps squarely around image

Empty sizing handles indicate wrap option selected

Figure 8.12

❹ **Deselect the image, save the document, and keep it onscreen to continue with the next lesson.**

To extend your knowledge...

Selecting Wrap Style and Alignment

You can display the Format Picture dialog box and then click the Layout tab to select a wrapping style, the image's horizontal alignment, or advanced options (see Figure 8.13).

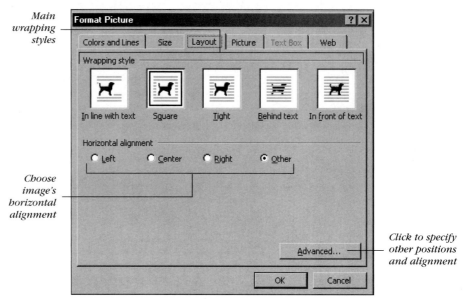

Main wrapping styles

Choose image's horizontal alignment

Click to specify other positions and alignment

Figure 8.13

The Horizontal alignment options are available for any wrapping style except *In line with text*.

Top and Bottom Wrap

If you want to place an image between paragraphs without text wrapping on either the left or right sides, you need to choose *Top and Bottom* as the wrap option. You can choose this option by clicking the Text Wrapping button on the Picture toolbar or by clicking the Advanced button within the Layout tab of the Format Picture dialog box.

Tight Wrap

The **tight wrap** option wraps text around the edge of the image itself—contouring around the image—instead of the square boundary of the image.

Lesson 5: Applying Borders and Fills

You can apply a *border* or *fill* to an image. A border is a line style that creates a frame around an object. **Fill** refers to a shading color that appears in the background of a text box or around the image within its square boundaries.

In this lesson, you apply a border around the optometrist image in your newsletter.

To Apply a Border

❶ In the *July Newsletter-WB8L* document, click the optometrist image.

❷ Click the Format Picture button on the Picture toolbar.
The Format Picture dialog box appears.

❸ Click the Colors and Lines tab in the dialog box.
You see options for selecting border lines and fill colors (see Figure 8.14).

To Apply a Border

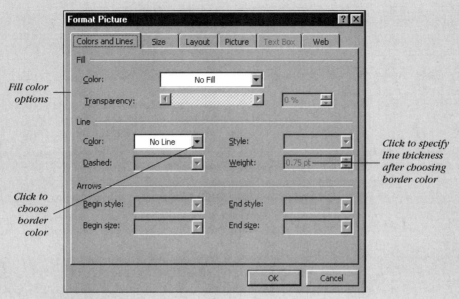

Fill color options

Click to choose border color

Click to specify line thickness after choosing border color

Figure 8.14

④ **Click the Teal color, the fifth color on the second row.**
You see a ScreenTip that displays the color, such as *Teal*, when you position the mouse pointer over a color.

⑤ **Click the Weight spin button to display *1.25 pt*.**
Choosing 1.25 pt provides a thicker border line.

⑥ **Click OK and then deselect the image.**
The image is enclosed in a 1.25 pt Teal-colored border (see Figure 8.15).

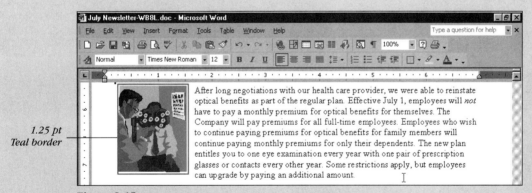

1.25 pt Teal border

Figure 8.15

⑦ **Save the document, and keep it onscreen to continue with the next lesson.**

To extend your knowledge...

Using the Line Style Button

You can apply a border line by clicking the Line Style button on the Picture toolbar. When you click this button, you see a list of point sizes that indicates the thickness of the line. Word applies a black line around the image.

Lesson 6: Copying Images with the Clip Organizer

Microsoft provides additional clips on its Web site—Microsoft Design Gallery Live. The Web site contains several thousand clips to choose from. From within the Clip Organizer, you can view online clips or link to the Web site, download images to the Clip Organizer, and then insert the images in your documents.

In this lesson, you look at the Web Collections clips—clips found on Microsoft's Web site—and then copy a clip art image to your computer.

To Copy an Image with the Clip Organizer

❶ In the *July Newsletter-WB8L* document, position the insertion point at the beginning of the first paragraph after the *Conference is Scheduled!* heading.
This is the location where you eventually insert a downloaded clip.

❷ Make sure you have a live connection to the Internet.
If you are using a computer with a direct Internet connection, you can continue with the next step. If you are using a home computer, you need to connect to your Internet Service Provider (ISP), such as America Online, before continuing to the next step.

❸ Choose **I**nsert, **P**icture, **C**lip Art to display the Insert Clip Art task pane.

If you have problems...
Although the task pane contains the *Clips Online* option, do not use it. You must have the Clip Organizer window open in order to download to it.

❹ Click *Clip Organizer* at the bottom of the task pane and then click its Maximize button.
The Clip Organizer dialog box appears. You can organize clips, choose from the Office Collections clips that are stored on your computer, or choose Web Collections to see online clips.

❺ Double-click *Web Collections* in the Collection List, and then double-click *Design Gallery Live.*
You see a list of categories, similar to the categories shown in Figure 8.6 at the end of Lesson 1.

❻ Scroll through the list and click *Office.*
You see office clips that are in the Microsoft Design Gallery Live Web site (see Figure 8.16).

To Copy an Image with the Clip Organizer

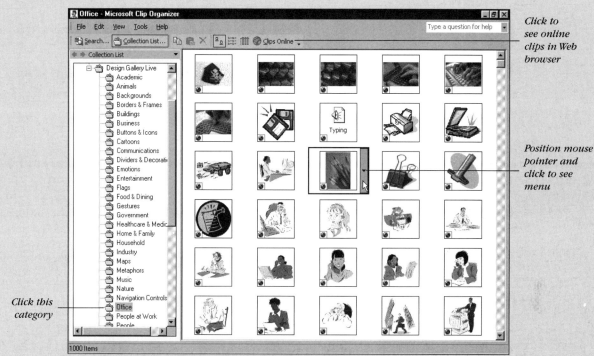

Click to see online clips in Web browser

Position mouse pointer and click to see menu

Click this category

Figure 8.16

If you have problems...

Depending on your Internet connection, you might see icons instead of the actual images. If this happens, read the rest of this exercise without completing the steps. You can study the steps and figures to see what happens when you have a higher-speed Internet connection.

7 **Position the mouse pointer on the photograph clip of pencils, and click the drop-down arrow.**

A menu appears so that you can choose what to do. For example, you can copy the image to the Clipboard and then click the Paste button in the document window to paste the clip there.

8 **Click *Copy to Collection*, choose Favorites, and then click OK.**

Choosing *Copy to Collection* displays a dialog box so that you can copy the image from the online Web site to your hard drive. This gives you access to the clip without being connected to the Internet.

9 **Scroll up through the Collection List, and click *Favorites*.**

You see the image stored in this location within the Clip Organizer. Next time you need this image, you don't have to have a live Internet connection; you can simply select it from your Favorites list.

10 **Keep the document and Clip Organizer window open to continue with the next lesson.**

Lesson 7: Downloading and Inserting an Online Clip

If your computer can't load the images in the Web Collections category of the Clip Organizer, you need to click the *Clips Online* button to actually go to the Design Gallery Live Web site, search for images, and download them.

In the next exercise, you go to the Microsoft Design Gallery Live and download a photo of a city to the Clip Organizer.

To Download an Image from the Web Site

❶ Click the Clips Online button at the top of the Clip Organizer window.
Your Internet browser window opens. If you see the End-User License Agreement, read it to learn about acceptable uses of the clips, and then click the Accept button.

? If you have problems...
If you use another browser instead of Internet Explorer, the images might not download correctly. Make sure that Internet Explorer is the default browser.

The Microsoft Design Gallery Live Web page appears (see Figure 8.17).

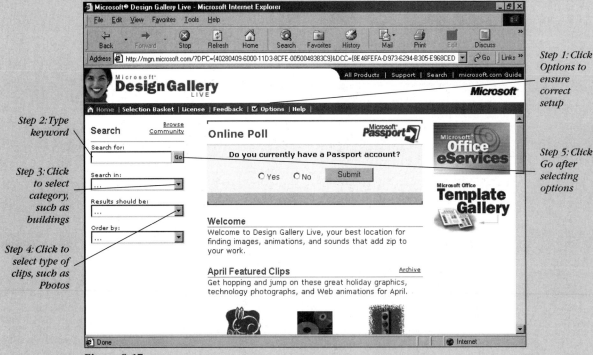

Figure 8.17

Web pages constantly change; therefore, the gallery might look different from the figures shown in this book.

To Download an Image from the Web Site

Before searching for a photograph of a city, you need to ensure that the correction option is selected in order to download correctly.

② **Click the *Options* link in the top middle section of the Web page.**
You need to specify the appropriate file type to download.

③ **Scroll down to see *Specify preferred file type to download* options, click the *MPF (Media Package File)* option, and then click the *Update* button.**
The MPF option is required to download to Office XP applications, such as Word 2002.

④ **Type cities in the *Search for* text box.**
You want to find images of cities.

⑤ **Click the *Search in* drop-down arrow, and choose *Buildings*.**

⑥ **Click the *Results should be* drop-down arrow, and choose *Photos*.**

⑦ **Click the Go button to the right of the *Search for* box.**
You should see photos of cities.

⑧ **Click the photo of the city with the waterfront and orange skyline background.**
The image appears in a separate preview window, along with keywords formatted as hypertext links that display another Web page of images when clicked (see Figure 8.18).

Clip appears in preview area

Download icon

Clip's keywords

Figure 8.18

⑨ **Click the download icon to download the image.**
The picture is downloaded into the Clip Organizer (see Figure 8.19).

(Continues)

To Download an Image from the Web Site (Continued)

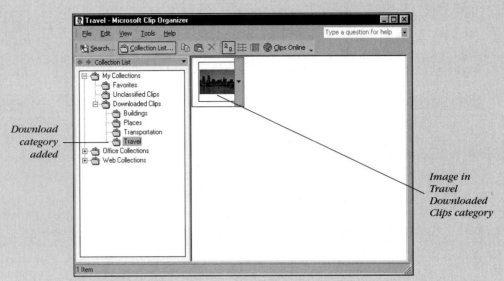

Download category added →

Image in Travel Downloaded Clips category

Figure 8.19

If you have problems...

If the image does not download to your Clip Organizer, save it as an image. Right-click the preview image in your Web browser; choose Save Picture As; choose a storage location, filename, and file type—such as gif or bmp; and then click the Save button. You can then choose Insert, Picture, From File to insert the image file.

⑩ **Keep the Clip Organizer onscreen to continue with the next exercise.**

To extend your knowledge...

Searching for Online Clips from the Insert Clip Art Task Pane

Instead of clicking the Clips Online button and searching for clips, you can use the Insert Clip Art task pane to search for online clips from the Microsoft Design Gallery Live. To do this, type your keyword in the *Search text* box; click the *Search in* drop-down arrow, and choose only *Web Collections*; click the *Results should be* drop-down arrow, and choose the type of clip you want; and click the Search button.

You are ready to insert the downloaded photograph into your document.

To Insert the Downloaded Image

❶ **Make sure you can see the image in the *Travel Downloaded Clips* category in the Collection List.**

If you have problems...

If you saved the image instead of downloading it in the last exercise, close the Clip Organizer. Choose Insert, Picture, From File; locate the gif or bmp

To Insert the Downloaded Image

image you saved; and click In_s_ert. The image is inserted in your document. Save the document and skip the rest of the steps in this exercise.

2 **Click the drop-down arrow for the city photograph you downloaded and then choose _C_opy.**
The drop-down arrow in the Clip Organizer does not have an Insert option, so you must copy the image and then paste it into the document.

3 **Click the Minimize button to minimize the Clip Organizer and then close the Insert Clip Art task pane.**

4 **Click the Paste button on the Formatting toolbar.**
The image is pasted at the insertion point's location (see Figure 8.20).

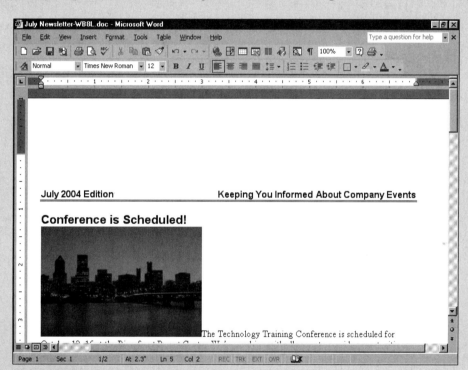

Figure 8.20

5 **Save the document, and keep it onscreen to continue with the next lesson.**

Lesson 8: Creating a Watermark

A ***watermark*** is a "washed-out" graphic object or text that typically appears behind text. People use watermarks as an imprint for a logo that helps people to remember and identify a company's image. You can also use watermarks as visual effects for creative documents, such as fliers, brochures, and newsletters.

In this lesson, you format the photograph as a watermark.

To Create a Watermark from an Image

1 In the *July Newsletter-WB8L* document, click the photograph to select it.

2 Click the Color button on the Picture toolbar.
A list of color options appears.

3 Choose <u>W</u>ashout.
The image appears washed-out, which is how watermarks appear.

4 Click the Text Wrapping button and choose Behin<u>d</u> Text.
Figure 8.21 shows the watermark image behind the text.

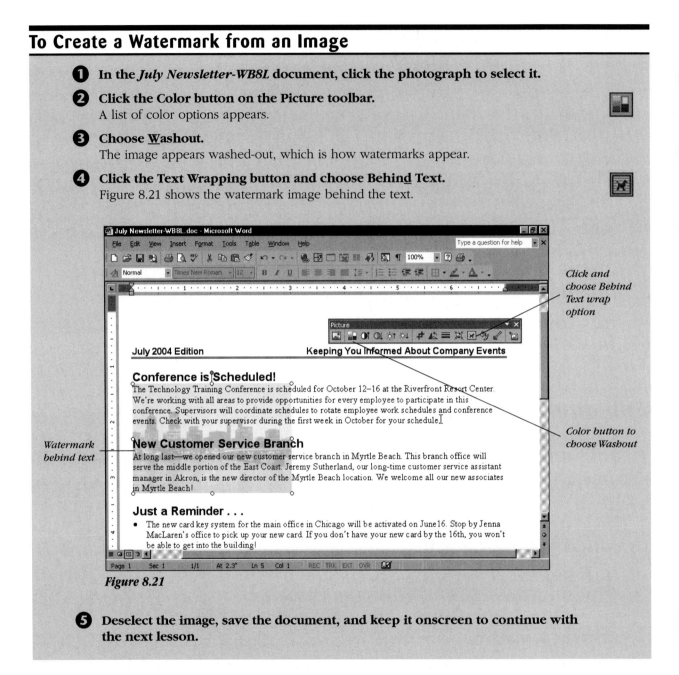

Figure 8.21

5 Deselect the image, save the document, and keep it onscreen to continue with the next lesson.

To extend your knowledge...

Creating a Watermark in a Header

You can create a watermark within a header. After displaying the header window, insert the image and set a larger width—typically one that spans the image from the left to the right margins. Click the Color button, and choose <u>W</u>ashout. Click the Text Wrapping button, and choose Behin<u>d</u> Text. Adjust the contrast using the buttons on the Picture toolbar.

Lesson 9: Creating WordArt

Another exciting graphic feature is WordArt. **WordArt** shapes text into designs for you. You can use WordArt to create unique banners and titles for fliers, brochures, and other advertising documents. Because WordArt is a graphic object, you can use similar options to those you used to customize your clip art.

In this lesson, you create a WordArt object for the title of your newsletter.

To Create WordArt

1 In the *July Newsletter-WB8L* document, position the insertion point at the top of the document.

2 Choose **I**nsert, **P**icture, **W**ordArt.
The WordArt Gallery dialog box appears so that you can select a WordArt style (see Figure 8.22).

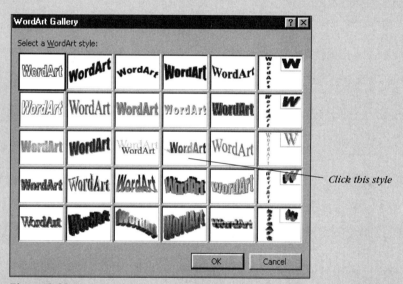

Figure 8.22

3 Click the fourth style on the third row and then click OK.
The Edit WordArt Text dialog box appears, so that you can enter text and select the font and font size (see Figure 8.23).

(Continues)

To Create WordArt (Continued)

Select WordArt font

Type text here

Click to select a font size

Figure 8.23

4 **Type** `The Millennium Group` **in the text area.**
You need to choose a smaller font size for your title.

5 **Click the Size drop-down arrow and choose 28; then click OK.**
The WordArt appears where you positioned the insertion point prior to creating the WordArt.

6 **Click the WordArt.**
The WordArt is selected, and the WordArt toolbar appears so that you can customize it (see Figure 8.24).

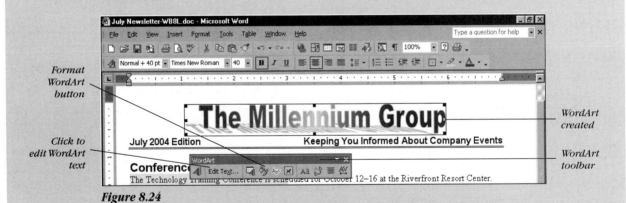

Format WordArt button

Click to edit WordArt text

WordArt created

WordArt toolbar

Figure 8.24

7 **Deselect the WordArt object, save the document, print it, and then close the document.**

To extend your knowledge...

Customizing WordArt

If you need to edit your WordArt object later, double-click the WordArt object to change the text, font, or font size.

Use the WordArt toolbar to customize the WordArt's appearance. For example, you can rotate the object, select a different style from the gallery, or choose a different shape. Table 8.2 lists the functions of different WordArt toolbar buttons.

Table 8.2 | WordArt Buttons

Button	Button Name	Description
	Insert WordArt	Displays the WordArt Gallery dialog box, so you can choose a style and then type WordArt text.
Edit Text...	Edit Text	Displays dialog box to edit text, font, and font size.
	WordArt Gallery	Displays Gallery to choose a different style.
	Format WordArt	Displays the Format WordArt dialog box to change size, layout, and so on.
	WordArt Shape	Displays palette of various shapes for WordArt.
	Text Wrapping	Displays list of text-wrapping options, such as Top and Bottom.
	WordArt Same Letter Heights	Adjusts WordArt letters so they are the same height.
	WordArt Vertical Text	Changes WordArt to a vertical object.
	WordArt Alignment	Displays palette of alignment options, such as Stretch Justify.
	WordArt Character Spacing	Lets you adjust spacing between characters.

You should be able to create exciting graphics in your documents now. You can insert clip art and images from the Insert Clip Art task pane, Clip Organizer, or Microsoft Design Gallery Live. After inserting an image, you can change the image's size and location, apply a border, and adjust the way text wraps around the image. Finally, you learned how to create watermarks and design exciting WordArt objects to make headings and banners.

Although much information about graphics is included here, Word provides many more choices for customizing pictures, watermarks, and WordArt. You can learn a lot by exploring the different options on the toolbars and by using onscreen Help.

Checking Concepts and Terms

Multiple Choice

Circle the letter of the correct answer for each of the following.

1. All of the following are graphic image types except _____. [L1]

   a. .jpg
   b. .gif
   c. .doc
   d. .bmp

2. You can use the sizing handles to do all of the following except _____. [L2–4]

   a. adjust the image's width
   b. move the image to a different location
   c. increase the height of the image
   d. adjust the text-wrapping around the image

3. Which wrap option contours text around an image in your document? [L4]

   a. Square
   b. Tight
   c. Top to Bottom
   d. Through

4. What two options should you select to format an image as a watermark? [L8]

   a. Tight wrap and WordArt Gallery
   b. Through wrap and fill color
   c. Washout and Behind Text wrap
   d. More Brightness and Square wrap

5. What term refers to interesting, colorful shapes for text? [L9]

   a. WordArt
   b. Microsoft Design Gallery Live
   c. watermark
   d. clip art

Discussion

1. Look through several magazines, newsletters, and brochures. Evaluate the use of clip art. Notice which types of clip art or images are used, how are they placed, and so on. [L1–9]

2. Review the license agreements for different clip art programs. What are some commonalities? [L1]

3. Create a variety of WordArt images, and print them on a color printer and a black-and-white printer. What warnings or suggestions do you have about using various WordArt images? [L9]

Skill Drill exercises reinforce project skills. Each skill reinforced is the same, or nearly the same, as a skill presented in the project. Detailed instructions are provided in a step-by-step format.

1. Inserting and Sizing a Bitmap Image

The local Parent Educator Association (PEA) has asked you to create this month's newsletter about school activities for parents. You have been given the basic text, but you decide that graphic elements will enhance the newsletter's appearance and encourage parents to read it.

1. Open *ew1-0802*, and save it as **PEA Newsletter-WB8SD**.
2. With the insertion point aligned at the right at the beginning of the document, choose Insert, Picture, From File.
3. Choose the drive and folder that contains files for this project, click *PEA.bmp*, and click the Insert button.
4. Click the image to display the sizing handles.
5. Click the Format Picture button on the Picture toolbar.
6. Click the Size tab.
7. Select the current *Height* setting, type **1.5**, and click OK.
8. Deselect the image.
9. Save the document, and keep it onscreen to continue with the next exercise.

2. Inserting an Image from the Clip Organizer

You want to insert clip art by the *New School Buses* section of the newsletter. The Clip Organizer contains an image of a school bus in the Transportation section of the Office Collections category.

1. In the open *PEA Newsletter-WB8SD* document, position the insertion point at the beginning of the *New School Buses* heading.
2. Choose Insert, Picture, Clip Art.
3. Click the *Clip Organizer* link at the bottom of the Insert Clip Art task pane.
4. Double-click *Office Collections* in the Collection List, double-click the *Transportation* category, and double-click the *Land* category.
5. Click the drop-down arrow for the school bus image, and choose Copy.
6. Minimize the Clip Organizer.
7. Click the Paste button on the Formatting toolbar to paste the image.
   If text is pasted instead of the image, click the Undo button, display the Office Clipboard, and click the clip art object in the Office Clipboard task pane to paste it in the document.
8. Deselect the image and close the Clip Organizer.
9. Save the document, and keep it onscreen to continue with the next exercise.

3. Adjusting the Size, Wrap, and Border Options

After inserting the image, you need to reduce its size and select a text-wrapping option for it. You want the text to wrap on the right side of the image.

1. In the *PEA Newsletter-WB8SD* document, click the school bus image to select it.
2. Click the Format Picture button on the Picture toolbar.
3. Click the Size tab.
4. Select the width, type **1"**, and click OK.

5. Click the Text Wrapping button on the Picture toolbar, and choose Square.

6. Click the Format Picture button.

7. Click the Colors and Lines tab.

8. Click the *Line Color* drop-down arrow, and choose Gold.

9. Click the *Weight* spin button to display *1.5 pt*, and then click OK.

10. Deselect the image, save the document, and keep it onscreen to continue with the next exercise.

4. Creating a WordArt Banner

The newsletter needs a title or banner. Instead of typing the banner in a larger font size, you decide to create a WordArt banner for a better visual effect.

1. In the open *PEA Newsletter-WB8L* document, position the insertion point at the top of the document.

2. Choose Insert, Picture, WordArt.

3. Click the third style on the third row, and click OK.

4. Type `Maple Elementary` in the Text area.

5. Make sure that the font is Times New Roman.

6. Click the Size drop-down arrow, choose 40, and click OK.

7. Click the WordArt to select it.

8. Click the Text Wrapping button on the WordArt toolbar, and choose Square.

9. Drag the WordArt to the left of the triangle image you inserted in the first exercise. The top of the uppercase letters in the WordArt should align with the top of the triangle.

10. Deselect the WordArt.

11. Save, print, and close the document.

Challenge

Challenge exercises expand on or are somewhat related to skills presented in the lessons. Each exercise provides a brief narrative introduction, followed by instructions in a numbered-step format that are not as detailed as those in the Skill Drill section.

1. Creating an Announcement for Pictures with Santa

The management at the local mall will have a picture day with Santa. You have been asked to create a flier with two pages per sheet with the announcement.

1. Open *ew1-0803*, and save it as `Santa Photo-WB8CH1`.

2. Delete the asterisk, and keep the insertion point there.

3. Display the Insert Clip Art task pane, and search for holiday clip art in the Office Collections.

4. Insert the Santa clip art.

5. Apply the In Front of Text wrap style, and center-align the image.

6. With the image selected, press ↑ about six times to bring the image higher on the page.

7. Apply the art page border that looks like poinsettias.

8. Choose *2 pages per sheet* as the *Multiple pages* option in the Page Setup dialog box.

9. Copy the document, press ↵Enter below the last line, and paste to get a duplicate announcement on the same sheet of paper.

10. Save, print, and close the document.

2. Creating an Independence Day Announcement with a Watermark

You are in charge of promoting your local town's Independence Day celebration. You decide to create an eye-catching flier you can print and post around town. You want it to have a watermark and appropriate page border.

1. Open *ew1-0804*, and save it as `July 4 Celebration-WB8CH2`.

2. Apply the Fireworks Art border to the page. It is the 28th border option in the A<u>r</u>t border drop-down list.

3. Position your insertion point at the top of the document, and search for clips with these specifications:

- `Fireworks` keyword
- Web Collections only
- Photograph clips

4. Insert a fireworks clip with a black background and a couple of explosions. (The clip is taller than it is wide.)

5. Convert the clip to a watermark with the necessary wrapping option, centered. Set a 9.9″ height and 7.7″ width; deselect the *Lock <u>a</u>spect ratio* option in order to change both the height and width.

6. Save, print, and close the document.

3. Enhancing a Halloween Invitation

You created a Halloween invitation. You want to search the Microsoft Clip Gallery Live to find an appropriate image. In addition, you want to create a title using WordArt.

1. Open *ew1-0805*, and save it as `Halloween Party-WB8CH3`.

2. At the top of the document, create a WordArt image using the third style on the fourth row in the Gallery. Enter `Halloween Party!` as the text in 44-point Comic Sans MS. Select the text-wrapping option that does not allow text on the left and right sides of the image, and then center-align the WordArt.

3. Apply 24-point Comic Sans MS, bold, Orange font color to the last line in the document. With the text still selected, create a 3-point Orange paragraph border with Tan shading.

4. In the blank space below *Let the Good Times Roll*, insert a clip art image from Microsoft's Web site. Access Microsoft's Web site from within the Clip Organizer. Search for clips by using the keyword `jack-o-lantern`. Search through the images to find an image with contains a jack-o-lantern, a ghost, and a tombstone. Download it to your Clip Organizer and then insert it into your invitation. Adjust the size, wrap style, and alignment of the image as needed. Make sure you have a little space above and below the image.

5. Apply a page border using the pumpkin art border. Change the color of the art border to orange.

6. Choose the option to vertically center the page.

7. Save, print, and close the document.

4. Creating an Airline Information Sheet

You work for a small airline service that provides transportation from Oklahoma City to special-attraction vacation spots, such as Las Vegas, Denver, and Salt Lake City. You want to design an attractive information sheet about safety instructions for the passengers.

1. Open *ew1-0806*, and save it as `Airline Information-WB8CH4`.

2. If the current font is unreadable, change the text to Comic Sans MS or Bookman Old Style font.

3. Select the list of rules at the bottom of the document. Use the Bullets and Numbering dialog box to create a customized bulleted list using the Wingdings symbol of an airplane. *Note:* The airplane symbol is on the fourth row of symbols. Change the symbol font color to Blue, but make sure the text remains in Black.

4. Apply a Blue paragraph border around the selected bulleted list. Select Light Yellow shading.

5. Position the insertion point at the beginning of the document, and access the Microsoft Design Gallery Live from within the Clip Organizer.

6. Search for airplane photographs in the Transportation category.

7. Preview the clip of the plane with the sun in the background; then download it.

8. Insert the clip at the beginning of the first paragraph. Move it to the right side of the paragraph. Set a 2″ height, Behind Text wrapping style in the Layout section, and a 58% picture Brightness.

9. Create a WordArt banner using the third style in the first column of the Gallery. Type Sunset Airlines for the text. Move the WordArt above the first paragraph, apply a Top and Bottom wrap, and center it between the left and right margins.

10. Select Center vertical alignment in the Page Setup dialog box.

11. Save, print, and close the document.

Discovery Zone exercises help you gain advanced knowledge of project topics and/or application of skills. These exercises focus on enhancing your problem-solving skills. Numbered steps are not provided, but you are given hints, reminders, screen shots, and/or references to help you reach your goal for each exercise.

1. Creating a Watermark in a Header

The top administrators at Seatek-Parkway Enterprises paragraph are pleased with your work on the annual report. They have one more request before finalizing the report: They want you to insert a watermark that appears on all pages. Use Help to learn how to use a watermark within a header.

Open *ew1-0807*, and save it as **Annual Report-WB8DZ1**. From the Insert Clip Art task pane, search the Web Collections to find clip art images of **profits**. After you find a bar chart that depicts increasing profits, select it, and insert it. Convert the image to a watermark, and apply all necessary image formats to make the watermark look correct, including an approximate 1.15″ absolute vertical position and 90% contrast. Make sure that the watermark appears on all document pages.

Create a footer that displays the page number in the center.

Save, print, and close the document.

2. Inserting Scanned Images in a Flier

You were assigned to create a flier for a Hawaiian Touring Agency. The company has sent you three scanned photographs from the island of Kauai for you to include in the flier. Open *ew1—0808*, and save it as **Hawaiian Paradise-WB8DZ2**.

Insert a WordArt image that displays the text **Escape to Paradise: Island of Kauai**, using the fifth row in the fifth column of the gallery. Display the Drawing toolbar, and use Help to learn how to remove the 3-D style. Center the WordArt above the first paragraph, and set a 0.44″ WordArt height.

Insert Hawaii1.jpg, Hawaii2.jpg, and Hawaii3.jpg from the location of your data files for this project. Apply a Square wrap for the three images. Use Help to learn how to overlap the images with the Order option. Use the Click and Type method to insert the descriptions of the photos.

Apply paragraph formatting and WordArt formatting—use WordArt help if needed for the last two— as indicated in Figure 8.25.

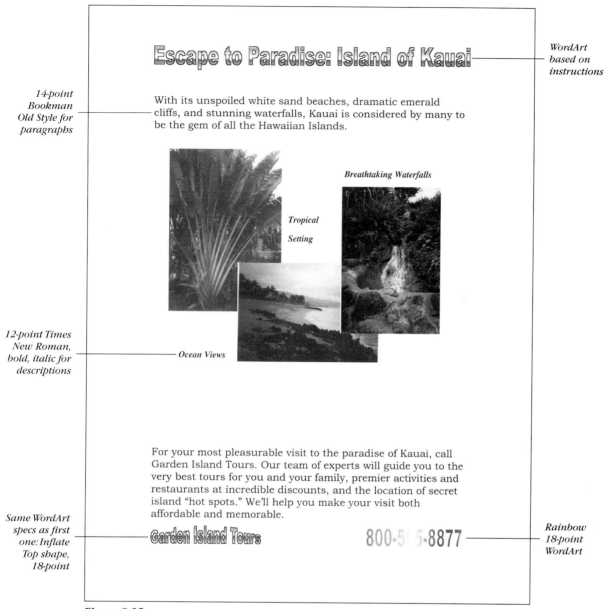

14-point Bookman Old Style for paragraphs

12-point Times New Roman, bold, italic for descriptions

Same WordArt specs as first one: Inflate Top shape, 18-point

WordArt based on instructions

Rainbow 18-point WordArt

Figure 8.25

The phone number in the WordArt is 800-555-8877, and the other WordArt is Garden Island Tours. Save, print, and close the document.

Excel

MARIANNE FOX
LAWRENCE C. METZELAAR

P
A
R
T

II

Getting Started with Excel

Objectives

In this project, you learn how to

- ✔ Explore the Excel Workspace
- ✔ Enter Text and Numbers
- ✔ Save a Workbook
- ✔ Get Help
- ✔ Enter a Formula
- ✔ Prepare a Worksheet for Printing
- ✔ Print a Worksheet
- ✔ Close a File and Exit Excel

Key terms in this project include

- ❑ arithmetic operator
- ❑ AutoComplete
- ❑ cell
- ❑ cell address
- ❑ column letter
- ❑ constants
- ❑ current (or active) cell
- ❑ default
- ❑ Formatting toolbar
- ❑ formula
- ❑ formula bar
- ❑ landscape orientation
- ❑ long label
- ❑ menu bar
- ❑ mouse pointer
- ❑ name box
- ❑ Office Assistant
- ❑ portrait orientation
- ❑ row number
- ❑ scrollbars
- ❑ sheet tab
- ❑ spreadsheet
- ❑ Standard toolbar
- ❑ status bar
- ❑ task pane
- ❑ title bar
- ❑ toolbars
- ❑ workbook
- ❑ worksheet
- ❑ worksheet frame
- ❑ worksheet window

Why Would I Do This?

Electronic spreadsheets, such as Microsoft Excel, are versatile tools for both personal and business use. They are designed primarily for organizing and analyzing numeric data.

This project shows you how spreadsheets work and what you can do with them. After you start the program, you explore the Excel workspace, enter data, and learn how to access onscreen Help. You also save and print a partially completed worksheet, close a file, and exit Excel.

Visual Summary

A **spreadsheet**—called a **worksheet** in Excel—is comprised of rows and columns. Each intersection of a row and column forms a **cell**. You can enter text, a number, or a formula in a cell.

In this project, you create the partially completed worksheet shown in Figure 1.1. You begin by exploring the Excel workspace.

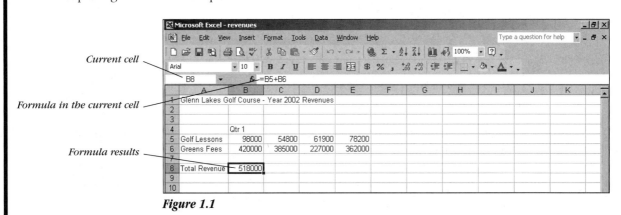

Current cell

Formula in the current cell

Formula results

Figure 1.1

Lesson 1: Exploring the Excel Workspace

An Excel screen consists of a **title bar** and six additional sections: the **menu bar,** one or more **toolbars**, the **name box**, the **formula bar**, the **worksheet window**, and the **status bar**. The additional sections form the Excel workspace (see Figure 1.2).

In the sample workspace, the **Formatting toolbar** displays below the **Standard toolbar** (refer to Figure 1.2). You may prefer to show only the most commonly used Standard and Formatting buttons on a single toolbar. You control this view by checking on or off an option titled *Show Standard and Formatting toolbars on two rows*. This option appears on the Options tab of the Customize dialog box (choose the menu sequence Tools, Customize to display the dialog box). The figures in this book show separate toolbars.

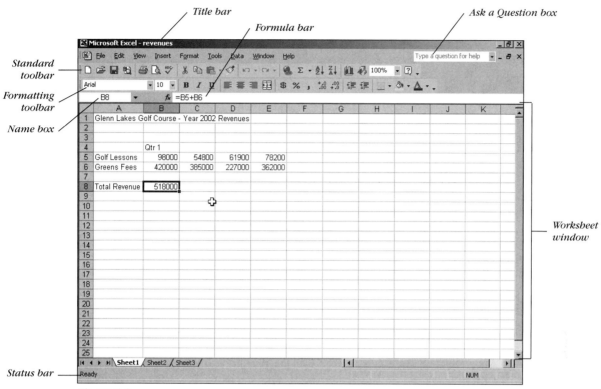

Figure 1.2

Excel features easy access to onscreen Help. For example, you can type a word or phrase in the Ask a Question text box and then press ⏎Enter). You can also display the ***Office Assistant***, a component of onscreen Help. It appears when Help is activated and hides itself when Help is completed. You learn how to access Help, and how to show or hide the Office Assistant, in Lesson 4, "Getting Help." Figures in projects do not display the Office Assistant unless its use is part of a lesson.

Explanations of Excel's screen elements are provided in a table at the end of this lesson. For now, launch Excel and explore the workspace.

To Start Excel and Explore the Excel Workspace

❶ **Move the mouse pointer to the Start button at the left edge of the Windows taskbar; then click the left mouse button.**
The Start button's popup menu displays.

❷ **Move the mouse pointer to the <u>P</u>rograms menu item.**
You see a listing of available programs on your system.

❸ **Move the mouse pointer to Microsoft Excel; then click the left mouse button.**

(Continues)

To Start Excel and Explore the Excel Workspace (Continued)

If you have problems...

If you don't see Microsoft Excel on the Programs submenu, move the mouse pointer over the Microsoft Office folder. Then, click the Microsoft Excel icon from the Microsoft Office submenu.

If a shortcut icon for Excel is displayed on your Windows desktop, you can also start Excel by double-clicking the icon. (If Windows was configured to use the Active Desktop, you can single-click the shortcut icon.)

Many systems are also set up to automatically display the Microsoft Office Shortcut Bar on the Windows desktop. This bar contains buttons you can use to launch Microsoft Office programs, including Excel.

Excel is loaded into the computer's memory, and a blank worksheet displays (see Figure 1.3). The default view includes a task pane at the right side of the screen. In this context, **default** refers to a setting that a program uses unless you specify another setting. A **task pane** provides a quick means to execute commands. The task pane that displays when you start Excel enables you to create new workbooks or to select a workbook to open from a list of files used in recent work sessions.

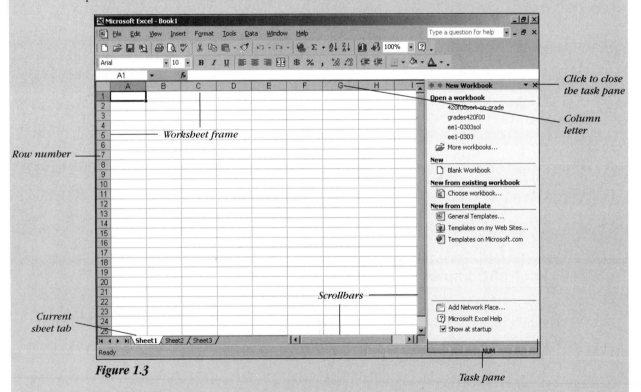

Figure 1.3

Now, enlarge the worksheet area by closing the task pane.

❹ Click the Close button for the task pane (refer to Figure 1.3).

❺ Move the mouse pointer to cell C6 in the worksheet and then click the left mouse button.
Clicking a cell selects it. An outline appears around the cell to indicate that it is the **current cell** (also called the **active cell**). The cell address C6 appears in the name box to let you know which cell is selected (see Figure 1.4). The **cell address** refers to the

To Start Excel and Explore the Excel Workspace

column and row that intersect to form the cell—in this case, column C and row 6. Typing data or executing a new action takes place at the current cell address.

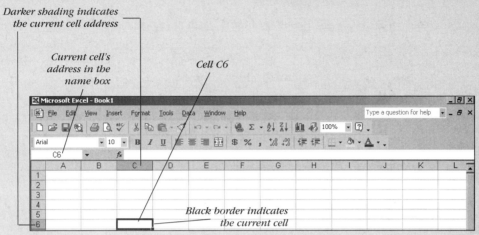

Figure 1.4

6 Press ⬇; then press ➡.
Pressing an arrow key shifts the active cell by one cell in the direction indicated on the key.

7 Press End and then press ⬇.
The active cell is in row 65536, the last row in the worksheet.

8 Press End and then press ➡.
The active cell is IV65536, the lower-right corner of the worksheet.

9 Press F5.
The Go To dialog box opens. A flashing cursor appears in the Reference text box.

10 Type aa300 in the Reference text box, and press ⬅Enter or click OK.
Cell AA300 is the current cell.

11 Press the two-key combination Ctrl+Home.
Pressing Home while holding down Ctrl makes cell A1 the current cell. Leave the blank worksheet open for the next lesson, in which you enter data.

In this lesson, you were introduced to a number of spreadsheet basics. Table 1.1 lists and describes the screen elements illustrated in this lesson.

TABLE 1.1	Parts of the Microsoft Excel Screen
Element	**Description**
Ask a Question text box	Part of the Excel onscreen Help system that appears near the right side of the menu bar. Allows you to specify a new Help topic or redisplay a previous Help topic without using the Office Assistant.
Cell	The intersection of a column and a row.
Cell address	Describes which column and row intersect to form the cell; for example, A1 is the cell address for the first cell in the first column (column A) and the first row (row 1).

(Continues)

TABLE 1.1	**Parts of the Microsoft Excel Screen (Continued)**
Element	**Description**
Column letter	Lettered *A* through *Z, AA* through *AZ,* and so on through *IV,* up to 256 columns.
Current (or active) cell	The cell surrounded with a thick black border. The next action you take, such as typing or formatting, affects this cell.
Formatting toolbar	Provides—in button form—shortcuts to frequently used commands for changing the appearance of data.
Formula bar	Displays the contents of the current or active cell.
Menu bar	Contains common menu names that, when activated, display a list of related commands; the File menu, for example, contains such commands as Open, Close, Save, and Print.
Mouse pointer	Selects items, and positions the insertion point (cursor).
Name box	Displays the cell address of the current cell or the name of a range of cells.
Office Assistant	A component of onscreen Help in the form of an animated graphics image that can be turned on or off; brings up a list of subjects related to a question you type.
Row number	Numbered 1 through 65,536.
Scrollbars	Allow you to move the worksheet window vertically and horizontally to see other parts of the worksheet.
Sheet tab	A means to access each sheet in a workbook. Click a sheet tab to quickly move to that sheet.
Standard toolbar	Provides—in button form—shortcuts to frequently used commands including Save, Print, Cut (move), Copy, and Paste.
Status bar	Provides information about the current operation or workspace, such as displaying *CAPS* if you set Caps Lock on.
Task pane	A window providing quick access to execute commands. For example, the task pane that displays when you open Excel enables you to create or open files. To display a task pane, select View in the menu bar and click Task Pane.
Title bar	Displays the name of the software and the name of the active workbook—either a default name, such as Book1, or a saved file.
Workbook	An Excel file that contains one or more worksheets.
Worksheet frame	The row and column headings that appear along the top and left edge of the worksheet window.
Worksheet window	Contains the current worksheet—the work area.

Lesson 2: Entering Text and Numbers

Now that you know the parts of the Excel workspace and how to move around a worksheet, it's time to enter data. Excel accepts two broad types of cell entries: constants and formulas. **Constants** can be text values (also called labels), numeric values (numbers), or date and time values. Constants do not change unless you edit them.

A **formula** produces a calculated result, usually based on a reference to one or more cells in the worksheet. The results of a formula change if you change the contents of a cell referenced in the formula.

In this lesson, you begin creating the worksheet shown in Figure 1.1. As you type, you may notice that sometimes Excel seems to anticipate what you will enter into a cell. For example, you may start typing text, and Excel automatically completes the word or phrase you have begun. This is a feature called **AutoComplete**, which compares text you are typing into a cell with text already entered in the same column. For example, if text in a cell begins with *Golf* and you start typing **G** into another cell in the same column, Excel assumes that you are entering `Golf` again. If Excel is correct, this saves you some typing. If not, just keep typing.

To Enter Text and Numbers

① If necessary, start Excel and display a blank worksheet.

② Click cell A1.

A thick black border surrounds cell A1, indicating that it is the current cell. Now enter the worksheet title.

③ Type `Glenn Lakes Golf Course-Year 2002 Revenues` **and press** ⏎Enter.

If you have problems...

If you make a mistake as you enter the text, you can make corrections the same way you do in a word processing program. Just press Del or ←Backspace to delete the error; then continue typing. Use Del to erase text to the right of the cursor, and press ←Backspace to erase text to the left of the cursor.

If you discover a mistake after you move to another cell, click the mouse or use the arrow keys to select the cell that contains the mistake, double-click the cell to change to edit mode, and then use ←Backspace or Del to correct the mistake. If you want to replace the entire contents of the cell, click the cell and then begin typing; the new data you enter replaces the cell's previous contents.

Excel enters the text you typed into cell A1, and cell A2 becomes the current cell. The text appears to be in cells A1 through E1 of the worksheet.

④ Click cell A1, and look in the formula bar (see Figure 1.5).

Current cell ————————   *A long label*
                                                                                                          in cell A1

Figure 1.5

The formula bar indicates that the entire worksheet title is stored in cell A1. Text that exceeds the width of its cell is sometimes referred to as a **long label**. Overflow text displays if the adjacent cells are blank.

(Continues)

To Enter Text and Numbers (Continued)

⑤ Click cell B4, type `Qtr 1`**, and press** `↵Enter`**.**
Qtr 1 appears left-aligned in cell B4, and cell B5 becomes the current cell.

⑥ Enter the following text in the cells indicated:

Cell A5	Golf Lessons
Cell A6	Greens Fees
Cell A8	Total Revenue

⑦ Click cell B5, type `98000`**, and press** `↵Enter`**.**
The number *98000* displays right-aligned in cell B5. The last two letters of the *Golf Lessons* label that extended into cell B5 no longer display (see Figure 1.6). Column A needs to be widened to accommodate the labels in rows 5 through 8.

Because the adjacent cell is not blank, the text display is limited to the width of cell A5

Figure 1.6

⑧ Position the mouse pointer between column letters A and B in the worksheet frame; click and hold down the left mouse button (see Figure 1.7).

Bidirectional arrow

Current width

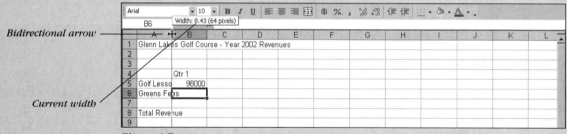

Figure 1.7

The pointer changes to a bidirectional arrow. Drag right to increase the width of column A; drag left to reduce the width of column A.

⑨ Drag the pointer to the right until the column is wide enough to display the *Total Revenue* label in cell A8 (continue to hold down the mouse button while you check your work against Figure 1.8).
The thin vertical dotted line extending from the pointer to the bottom of the worksheet makes it easy to see the distance you must drag to expand the column to the desired width.

To Enter Text and Numbers

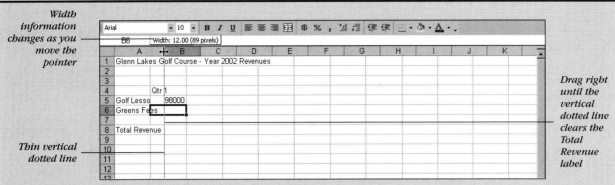

Width information changes as you move the pointer

Drag right until the vertical dotted line clears the Total Revenue label

Thin vertical dotted line

Figure 1.8

⑩ Release the mouse button.

Column A widens to display *Total Revenue* within the boundaries of cell A8.

If you have problems...

You can use Excel's <u>U</u>ndo command on the <u>E</u>dit menu to quickly reverse an action. If you change the width of the wrong column, for example, you can use the <u>U</u>ndo command to restore the original column width.

⑪ Enter the following numbers in rows 5 and 6 in the cells indicated (pressing ⊡ enters the number and moves the cell pointer to the next cell in a row):

Cell C5	54800
Cell D5	61900
Cell E5	78200
Cell B6	420000
Cell C6	385000
Cell D6	227000
Cell E6	362000

⑫ Check that your entries match those shown in Figure 1.9, and make changes as necessary.

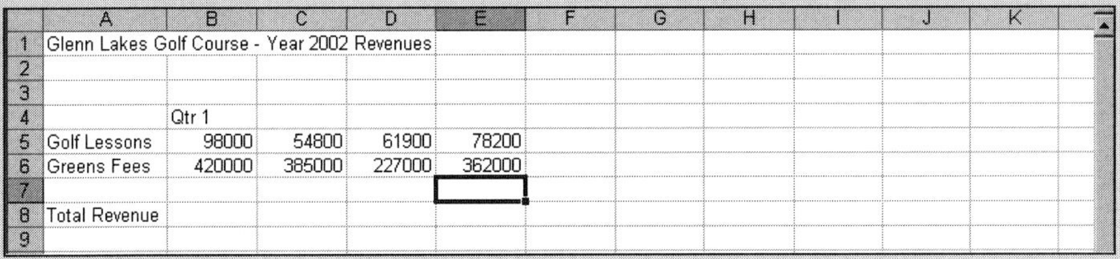

	A	B	C	D	E	F
1	Glenn Lakes Golf Course - Year 2002 Revenues					
2						
3						
4		Qtr 1				
5	Golf Lessons	98000	54800	61900	78200	
6	Greens Fees	420000	385000	227000	362000	
7						
8	Total Revenue					
9						

Figure 1.9

The text entries in column A describe the content of rows 5, 6, and 8. Cells B5 through E6 contain numbers.

Leave the partially completed worksheet open and continue to the next lesson, in which you save your work.

To extend your knowledge...

Changing Column Width and Row Height

Clicking the mouse pointer between two columns in the worksheet frame and then dragging left or right provides a quick and easy way to change the width of the leftmost column. Clicking the mouse pointer between two rows in the worksheet frame and then dragging up or down provides a quick and easy way to change the width of the topmost row. You can also choose Column, Width or Row, Height from the Format menu to change the widths of selected columns or the heights of selected rows. You learn to choose menu commands in the next lesson.

Lesson 3: Saving a Workbook

Up to this point, none of the data that you entered has been safely stored for future use. At the moment, your worksheet and the workbook that contains it are stored in the computer's random-access memory (RAM). If your computer were to crash or shut down for any reason, you would have to re-create the workbook. For this reason, it is important to save your work frequently. When you save a workbook or file, you assign the file a name and location on a disk.

You can type any name you want using Windows' file-naming rules. You can include spaces as well as upper- and lowercase letters. Excel automatically stores the file in the default Excel file format, adding the XLS (Excel spreadsheet) file extension.

You save a file by executing a File, Save command or a File, Save As command. As in other Windows programs, you can execute a command by clicking a command on the menu bar and then clicking the command you want from the submenu.

When you choose an option on the menu bar, Excel gives you the opportunity to use either short or full menus. The short menu displays an abbreviated list of commonly used commands (see Figure 1.10). The full menu includes all available commands (see Figure 1.11). By default, the short menu displays first; after a momentary delay, the full menu displays.

Use the menu bar now to save your partially completed worksheet in a workbook named *revenues*.

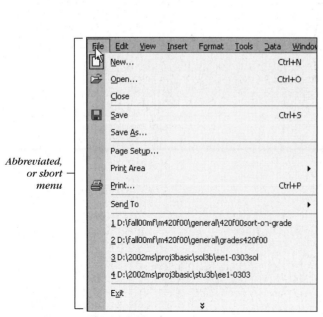

Abbreviated, or short menu

Figure 1.10

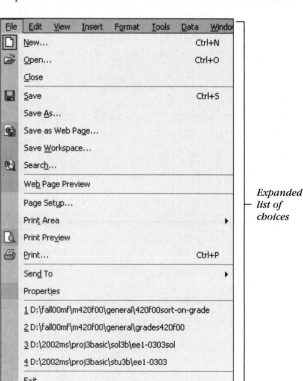

Expanded list of choices

Figure 1.11

To Save the Current Workbook

❶ Click File in the menu bar.

The short File menu appears first, followed by the full File menu after a momentary delay (refer to Figures 1.10 and 1.11).

❷ In the File submenu, click Save As.

The Save As dialog box appears (see Figure 1.12). You specify the filename and select the file type near the bottom of the dialog box. You specify the storage location in the Save in box near the top of the dialog box. Notice that *Book1* appears as the filename (you may see *Book1.xls* instead of *Book1* if your Windows environment is set to display file extensions). This is the temporary filename that Excel assigns to your workbook.

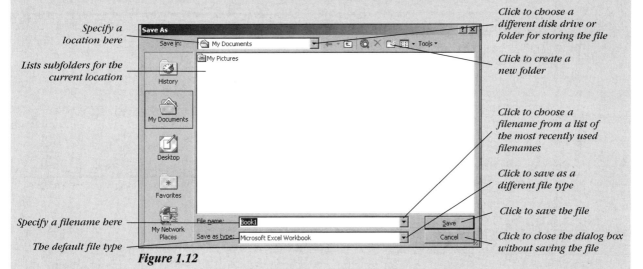

Figure 1.12

❸ Change *Book1* to `revenues` in the File name box.

The name you type replaces the temporary name assigned by Excel.

❹ Click the down arrow at the right end of the Save in box.

The display in the Save in drop-down list reflects the drives, folders, and files on your system. In the Save As dialog box, Excel automatically proposes to save the workbook on the current drive and in the default folder.

❺ Select the drive and folder where you want to save your current workbook.

Figure 1.13 shows the settings for saving a file named *revenues* as a Microsoft Excel workbook on a disk in drive A. You may prefer to store your work on a hard disk, a Zip disk,

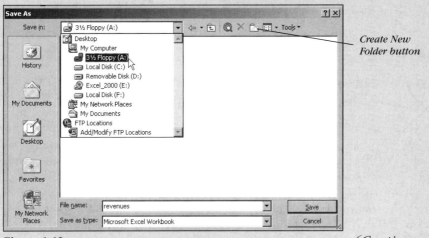

Figure 1.13

(Continues)

To Save the Current Workbook (Continued)

or a network drive, depending on the drives supported by your system. If you want to save the file in a different folder, select the folder from the Save in list, or click the Create New Folder button to create and name a new folder. Ask your instructor if you are not sure about the location for saving the files you create.

6 **After checking your settings for location, filename, and file type, click the Save button in the lower-right corner of the dialog box.**
Leave the *revenues* workbook open for the next lesson, in which you learn to use onscreen Help.

To extend your knowledge...

Comparing Save and Save As

If you have not yet saved a new workbook, you can click the Save button on the Standard toolbar to display the Save As dialog box. However, if you have already saved a workbook, clicking the Save button immediately resaves the current file under its current name without displaying a dialog box.

If you haven't yet saved a new workbook and you choose Save instead of Save As from the File menu, Excel automatically displays the Save As dialog box.

Lesson 4: Getting Help

You have entered text and numbers in Sheet1 of your *revenues* workbook. Now, you want to enter a formula, but you need more information about formulas in general and how to enter them.

Excel provides a number of onscreen Help options. Each Excel worksheet includes an Ask a Question box near the right end of the menu bar. To use this feature, type the word or phrase about which you seek help, and press **Enter** (see Figure 1.14). You can also activate the Office Assistant to help you find the answer to a specific question.

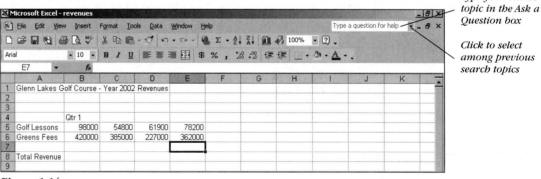

Type your search topic in the Ask a Question box

Click to select among previous search topics

Figure 1.14

Another method of accessing Help information is to use the Contents tab in the Microsoft Excel Help window to scroll through general topics and related subtopics. The Help window also includes an Index tab that enables you to search on a keyword. You can also use the What's This? pointer to display a description of any feature on the screen.

In this lesson, you use the Ask a Question box and the Contents tab in the Help window to learn about formulas. Tips on other ways to use onscreen Help are provided in the "To extend your knowledge" section at the end of this lesson.

To Get Help

❶ Display Sheet1 in the *revenues* workbook.

**❷ Type `math operators` in the Ask a Question box at the right end of the menu
bar (refer to Figure 1.14) and then press ⏎Enter.**
Three choices display in a popup box (see Figure 1.15).

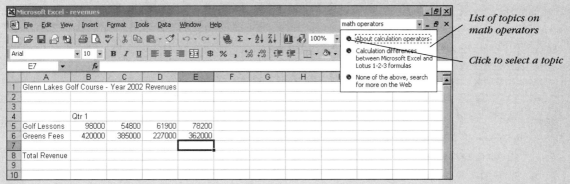

*List of topics on
math operators*

Click to select a topic

Figure 1.15

❸ Select the first option: *About calculation operators.*
The Microsoft Excel Help window opens and displays general information about calculation operators (see Figure 1.16). You can enlarge or reduce the width of the Help window by dragging its left edge to the left or right.

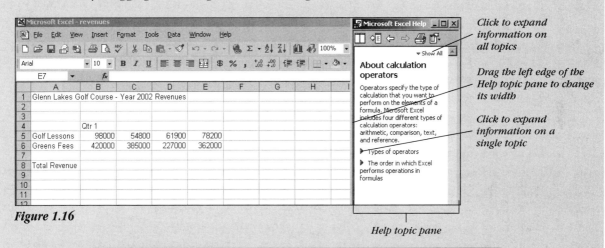

*Click to expand
information on
all topics*

*Drag the left edge of the
Help topic pane to change
its width*

*Click to expand
information on a
single topic*

Figure 1.16

Help topic pane

If you have problems...

Your Help display may vary from that shown in Figure 1.16. The Help topic
pane may be larger. The display might include a navigation pane with Contents, Answer Wizard, and Index tabs. These differences are possible
because Excel retains the settings specified during the most recent use of
onscreen Help. You can omit Step 4 if you do not want to increase the
width of the Help pane. You can omit Step 6 if the Contents, Wizard, and
Index tabs display in a pane to the left of the Help topic pane.

Clicking a small arrowhead in front of a topic, such as the one pointing to the phrase *Types
of operators*, expands the display to include information on the specific topic. Clicking the
small arrowhead in front of *Show All* near the top of the Help window displays all related
topics.

(Continues)

To Get Help (Continued)

4 **Drag the left edge of the Help topic pane to the left, until it fills approximately half of the screen.**

5 **Click *Show All* near the top of the Help window.**
Additional information displays in the enlarged Help window (see Figure 1.17).

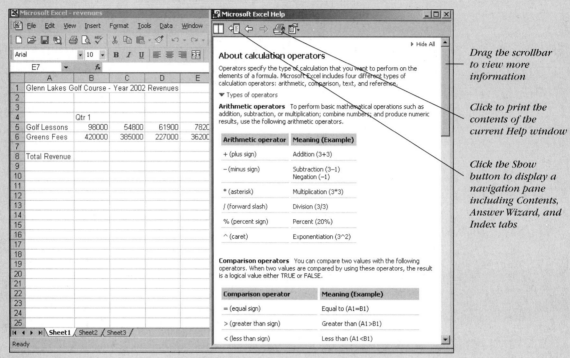

Drag the scrollbar to view more information

Click to print the contents of the current Help window

Click the Show button to display a navigation pane including Contents, Answer Wizard, and Index tabs

Figure 1.17

6 **Click the Show button near the upper-left corner of the Help window.**
Clicking the Show button displays a navigation pane to the left of the current Help topic pane. The navigation pane includes Contents, Answer Wizard, and Index tabs.

7 **Click the Contents tab in the navigation pane.**
Excel displays a list of topics (see Figure 1.18).

To Get Help

Click the Hide button to remove the navigation pane from view

Click Contents to select among general Help topics

Click Answer Wizard to type your request for help

Click Index to search by keyword

Navigation pane

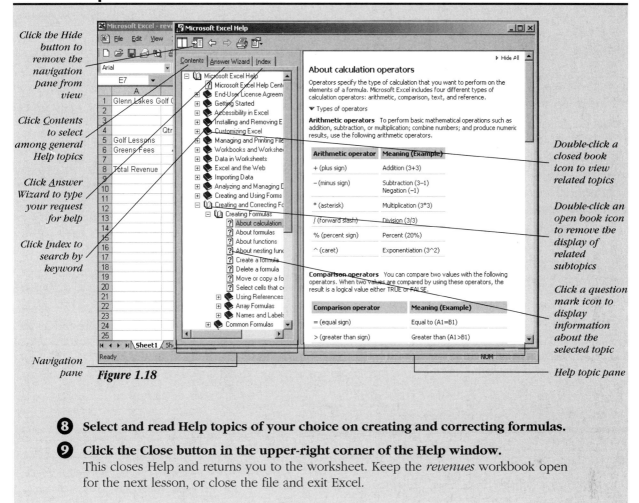

Figure 1.18

Double-click a closed book icon to view related topics

Double-click an open book icon to remove the display of related subtopics

Click a question mark icon to display information about the selected topic

Help topic pane

❽ Select and read Help topics of your choice on creating and correcting formulas.

❾ Click the Close button in the upper-right corner of the Help window.
This closes Help and returns you to the worksheet. Keep the *revenues* workbook open for the next lesson, or close the file and exit Excel.

 ## To extend your knowledge...

Displaying and Using the Office Assistant

You can use the Office Assistant instead of the Ask a Question box to display help on a specified topic. If the Office Assistant image is onscreen, simply click it to open a balloon, in which you can type a question. To quickly open the Office Assistant, press F1 at any time, or click the Microsoft Excel Help button on the Standard toolbar. If the Office Assistant has been turned off, you can choose Help, Show the Office Assistant to display it.

If the Office Assistant can't find topics related to the question you type, a balloon appears, telling you so. Check to be sure you typed the question correctly, or try to be more specific; then click Search again.

To hide the Office Assistant, select the menu sequence Help, Hide the Office Assistant, or right-click the Office Assistant image and click Hide.

Other Tips on Using Help

The Index tab in the Help window includes an alphabetical listing of topics (or keywords) that you can use to find related topics. For example, if you enter the keyword Print, Excel finds dozens of

(Continues)

topics related to the word, and displays them in the Help window. You can click a topic to select it and display its associated Help screen.

To print the contents of a Help Topics window, click the Print button at the top of the window.

To use the What's This? pointer to display a ScreenTip about an item onscreen, choose <u>H</u>elp, What's <u>T</u>his, or press ◆Shift+F1. When the pointer resembles a question mark with an arrow, click the item for which you need information.

If you can't find the information you need within Excel, you can access resources available on the World Wide Web. Assuming that you have Internet access, you can choose <u>H</u>elp, Office on the <u>W</u>eb to view information on Microsoft's Web site for Excel.

To display the version number of the Excel software you are using, choose <u>H</u>elp, <u>A</u>bout Microsoft Excel.

Lesson 5: Entering a Formula

The true power of a spreadsheet program resides in formulas. In Excel, starting an entry with an equal sign (=) identifies it as a formula rather than data to be entered in the cell.

Generally, a formula consists of arithmetic operators and references to cells. You can also include numeric values. ***Arithmetic operators*** include +, −, *, and / (to add, subtract, multiply, and divide, respectively). The order of the elements in a formula determines the final result of the calculation. Excel evaluates a formula from left to right, according to the order of operator precedence. For example, multiplication and division take place before addition and subtraction.

In this lesson, you type a simple formula to add the contents of two cells.

To Enter a Formula

1 **Click cell B8 in Sheet1 of the *revenues* workbook.**

2 **Type =B5+B6, and press ↵Enter.**
You entered a formula to add the contents of cell B6 to the contents of cell B5, and display the result in cell B8.

3 **Click cell B8, and look in the formula bar.**
The formula displays in the formula bar, and the results of the formula display in cell B8 (see Figure 1.19).

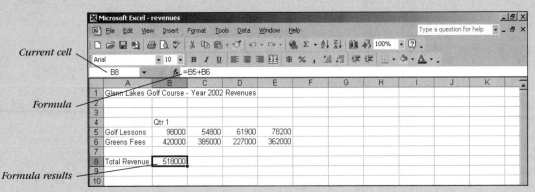

Figure 1.19

4 **Click the Save button on the Standard toolbar.**
This saves your latest change to the *revenues* workbook. Keep the workbook open for the next lesson, which focuses on printing your work.

Lesson 6: Preparing a Worksheet for Printing

With Excel, you can quickly print a worksheet using the default page setup: portrait orientation, 100% of normal size, 8½-by-11-inch paper, one-inch top and bottom margins, and 0.75-inch left and right margins. ***Portrait orientation*** produces a printed page that is longer than it is wide.

You can also change settings to meet your requirements for printed output. For example, you can add a header or footer to help identify the contents of the printed page, adjust the page margins, or turn on printing of gridlines and row and column headings. You can also switch to ***landscape orientation***, which produces a printed page that is wider than it is long. When you save a file, Excel also saves the current page setup specifications.

Now, use Excel's Page Setup feature to review current settings, and to turn on the display of gridlines and row and column headings.

To Prepare a Worksheet for Printing

❶ **Select Sheet1 in the *revenues* workbook; then open the File menu, and choose Page Setup.**
The Page Setup dialog box with four tabs appears. Use this dialog box to adjust the page setup before you print your worksheet.

❷ **Click the Page tab, if necessary (see Figure 1.20).**

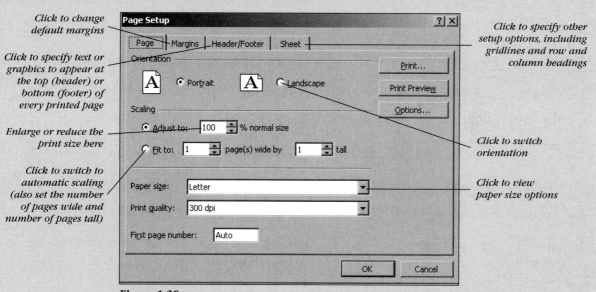

Figure 1.20

❸ **Click the Margins tab in the Page Setup dialog box.**
This displays the Margins options. The default top and bottom margins are one inch. The default left and right margins are 0.75 inch. If you want to center the printed output, click the Horizontally check box to center printed output from left to right and/or click the Vertically check box to center the printed output from top to bottom.

❹ **Click the Header/Footer tab in the Page Setup dialog box, and click the Custom Footer button in the middle of the dialog box.**
This displays the Footer dialog box (see Figure 1.21). Directions to enter the contents of the footer appear in the upper-left corner of the dialog box. You can type the text of your

(Continues)

To Prepare a Worksheet for Printing (Continued)

choice, such as your name, in the <u>C</u>enter section. You can also use buttons to insert pre-defined contents, such as the current date in the <u>L</u>eft section and the filename in the <u>R</u>ight section.

5 **Click within the <u>L</u>eft section of the Footer dialog box; then click the Date button (refer to Figure 1.21).**

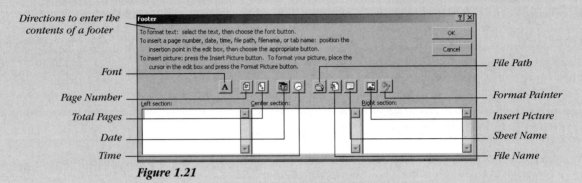

Figure 1.21

This enters the code &[Date] left-aligned in the <u>L</u>eft section.

6 **Click within the <u>C</u>enter section of the Footer dialog box; then type your first and last names.**
This centers your full name in the <u>C</u>enter section. Entering your name in a header or footer makes it easy to identify your work if you share a printer with others.

7 **Click within the <u>R</u>ight section of the Footer dialog box; then click the File Name button (refer to Figure 1.21).**
This enters &[File] right-aligned in the <u>R</u>ight section.

8 **Click OK.**
This accepts your settings and closes the Footer dialog box. The settings you specified appear in the Footer window on the Header/Footer tab.

9 **Click the Sheet tab in the Page Setup dialog box; then click the check box in front of <u>G</u>ridlines.**
A check mark appears in the <u>G</u>ridlines box, indicating that the feature is turned on (see Figure 1.22). This setting prints the lines that border cells.

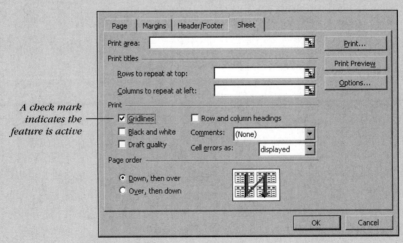

Figure 1.22

To Prepare a Worksheet for Printing

⑩ Click the check box in front of Row and column headings.
A check mark appears in the Row and column headings box, indicating that the feature is turned on. This setting prints the worksheet frame.

⑪ Click OK.
This closes the Page Setup dialog box. You have now finished setting up the worksheet page for printing.

⑫ Click the Save button on the Standard toolbar.
This saves the changes you made to the *revenues* workbook. Leave the workbook open for the next lesson, in which you learn how to preview and print the current worksheet.

To extend your knowledge...

Other Page Setup Options on the Page Tab

Use the Page tab (refer to Figure 1.20) to specify orientation (portrait or landscape), scaling, paper size, print quality in terms of dpi (density per inch), and the starting page number. Excel provides two scaling options: Adjust to (a user-specified higher or lower percentage of original size) or Fit to (a user-specified number of pages wide by number of pages tall).

Other Page Setup Options on the Sheet Tab

The Sheet tab includes four sections (refer to Figure 1.22): Print area, Print titles, Print, and Page order. You can specify a range to print by entering the upper-left and lower-right cells in the range separated by a colon (for example, B5:H25) in the Print area box. It is helpful to set a print area when there is a specific portion of a large worksheet that you print frequently.

Set a print title to specify worksheet rows and/or columns to repeat on each page of a multi-page printout. You can specify one or more rows (for example, $1:$3 for rows one through three) in the *Rows to repeat at top* box. You can also specify one or more columns (for example, $A:$A for column A) in the *Columns to repeat at left* box.

Lesson 7: Printing a Worksheet

Now that you adjusted the page setup and saved your changes, you can print a copy of your worksheet for your files or to review while you are away from the computer.

It's a good idea to save documents immediately before printing them, as you did in Lesson 6. It's also a good idea to preview onscreen the way the worksheet will look when it is printed. That way, you can make adjustments to the page setup before you print, and also save paper. Now, preview and print the first sheet in your *revenues* workbook.

To Print a Worksheet

❶ Make sure that the printer is turned on, has paper, and is online.
You can't print if the printer is not turned on, if the printer is out of paper, or if the printer is not online. Printers often have a light that shows whether the printer is online or receiving commands from the computer. If the printer is not online, Excel displays an error message when you attempt to print.

(Continues)

To Print a Worksheet (Continued)

2 Select Sheet1 in the *revenues* workbook; then choose File, Print from the menu.

The Print dialog box appears, as shown in Figure 1.23.

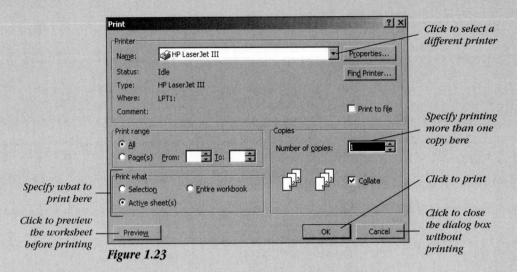

Click to select a different printer

Specify printing more than one copy here

Specify what to print here

Click to print

Click to preview the worksheet before printing

Click to close the dialog box without printing

Figure 1.23

3 Click the Preview button in the Print dialog box.

The worksheet now appears in the Print Preview window, which enables you to see how the entire worksheet will look when printed (see Figure 1.24). In Print Preview, you can see the effects of the changes you made to the page setup, including the footer, gridlines, and worksheet frame.

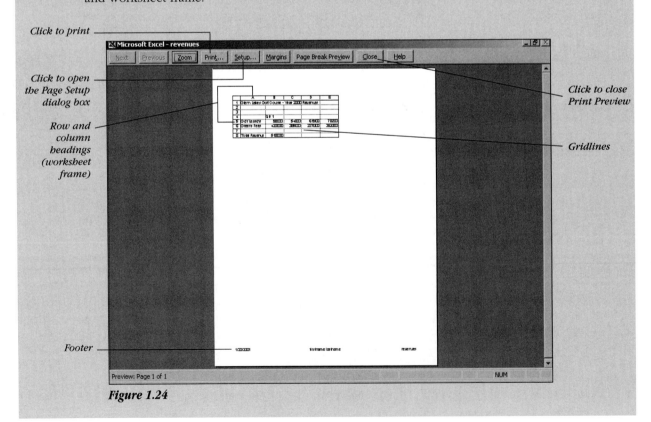

Click to print

Click to open the Page Setup dialog box

Click to close Print Preview

Row and column headings (worksheet frame)

Gridlines

Footer

Figure 1.24

To Print a Worksheet

④ Click anywhere in the worksheet.
Your view of the worksheet becomes enlarged so that you can more easily read it, but you can't see the entire page.

⑤ Click the worksheet again.
This restores the view of the whole page. If you decide you want to make a change in the worksheet data or print settings before you print it, click the Close button to close the view and return to the worksheet in Excel, or click the Setup button to open the Page Setup dialog box.

⑥ Click the Print button to begin printing the worksheet (or click Close to exit Print Preview without printing).
If you clicked the Print button, Excel sent a copy of your worksheet to the printer and closed the Preview window. In the next lesson, you learn how to close the *revenues* workbook and exit the program.

To extend your knowledge...

Using Toolbar Buttons to Preview and Print

To change to Print Preview without opening the Print dialog box, click the Print Preview button on the Standard toolbar, or choose File, Print Preview from the menu.

To quickly print the current worksheet without opening the Print dialog box, click the Print button on the Standard toolbar.

Lesson 8: Closing a File and Exiting Excel

Before you turn off your computer, you should first close the file you created and then exit Excel so that you don't lose any of your work. Complete this project by closing your file and exiting the Excel software.

To Close a File and Exit Excel

① Choose File, Close.
If you haven't saved your work, Excel displays a dialog box—or a balloon if the Office Assistant is active—that asks if you want to save your work. Choosing Yes saves the workbook and then closes it. Choosing No closes the workbook and erases any work you have done since the last time you saved. Choosing Cancel stops the save operation and keeps the workbook open.

② Choose File, Exit.
Excel closes. If there are any files left open, Excel displays a dialog box that asks if you want to save your work. Choosing Yes saves all open files and then closes the program. Choosing No closes the program without saving the files; any work you have done since the last time you saved is erased. After you close Excel, the Windows desktop appears if no other software applications are running.

This concludes Project 1. You can reinforce and extend the learning experience by working through the end-of-project activities that follow.

Summary

This project began with an introduction to the components of the Excel workspace, accompanied by explanations of a variety of terms. Once you knew the language of spreadsheets, you began to develop a small worksheet to sum two sources of revenue. After entering text and numbers in cells, you put the extensive onscreen Help system to work, so that you could understand how formulas calculate and how to construct them. Saving and printing your work, followed by closing the file and exiting Excel, completed the Project 1 learning experience.

Once you know the basics, you can quickly expand your skills through a read-and-do approach. You read when you make the use of onscreen Help, an integral part of your learning strategy. You convert knowledge to a skill when you apply what you have learned in the worksheets you create.

Checking Concepts and Terms

Multiple Choice

Circle the letter of the correct answer for each of the following.

1. Which of the following describes an Excel feature that automatically completes the word or phrase as you type a cell entry? [L2]

   a. AutoFinish

   b. AutoComplete

   c. Repeat button on a toolbar

   d. None of the above; not an Excel feature.

2. Which of the following is a valid cell address? [L1]

   a. b-12

   b. B:12

   c. B12

   d. B/12

3. Assume that the following data are entered in cells A1 through A3. The result of entering the formula =A1–A2*A3 in cell B1 would be the following: [L5]

```
Cell A1  15
Cell A2   3
Cell A3   2
```

   a. 9

   b. 20

   c. 24

   d. Some other result

4. Which of the following is an example of an Excel formula? [L5]

   a. =B2+B3+B4

   b. $240

   c. C1+C2

   d. Both a and c

5. In Excel, the arithmetic operator for multiplication is [L5]

   a. x

   b. @

   c. %

   d. None of the above

Screen ID

Label each element of the Excel screen shown in Figure 1.25. [L1]

A. worksheet frame
B. Ask a Question text box
C. name box
D. title bar
E. Standard toolbar
F. active (current) sheet
G. formula bar
H. Formatting toolbar
I. mouse pointer
J. menu bar
K. status bar
L. active (current) cell

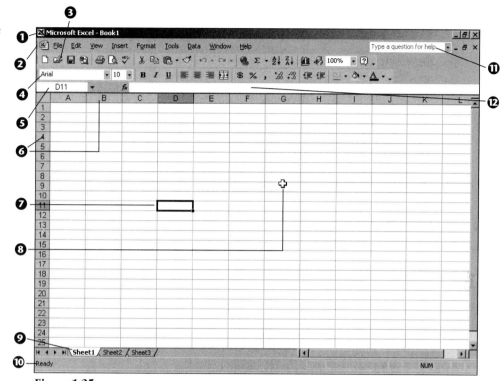

Figure 1.25

1. _____   7. _____

2. _____   8. _____

3. _____   9. _____

4. _____   10. _____

5. _____   11. _____

6. _____   12. _____

Discussion

1. Excel accepts two broad types of cell entries: constants and formulas. What is a formula? What types of constants can be entered in an Excel worksheet? Think about the entries you would make in a personal budget worksheet, and give examples of formulas and constants it might contain. (Hint: A personal budget shows sources of income and categories of expenses.) [L2 and L5]

2. Excel provides extensive onscreen Help. Describe at least four ways to get information using Help, and provide specific examples of using each method. [L4]

3. Save and Save As are two commands associated with storing a workbook for future retrieval and edit. Explain the similarities and differences between the two commands. [L3]

Skill Drill

Skill Drill exercises reinforce project skills. Each skill reinforced is the same, or nearly the same, as a skill presented in the project. Detailed instructions are provided in a step-by-step format.

Several exercises in this project direct you to access a new blank workbook. Starting Excel displays a new blank workbook. If you are working in another file, you can display a new workbook by clicking the New button at the left end of the Standard toolbar.

Each exercise is independent of the others, so you can do the exercises in any order. If you need a paper copy of a completed exercise, enter your name centered in a header before printing.

1. Changing Column Widths

You are compiling a list of selected state names and postal codes, and you want to adjust the default column widths.

To enter data and change column widths, follow these steps:

1. Start Excel and access a new blank workbook.

2. Click cell A1, type `Selected State Codes`, and press ↵Enter.

3. Click cell A3, type `Indiana`, and press ↵Enter.

4. Enter the remaining text, as shown in Figure 1.26 (do not change the width of a column yet).

	A	B	C	D	E	F	G	H	I	J	K	L
1	Selected State Codes											
2												
3	Indiana	IN										
4	California	CA										
5	New Mexico	NM										
6	New Hampshire	NH										
7												
8												
9												

Figure 1.26

5. Position the mouse pointer between column letters A and B in the worksheet frame; click and hold down the left mouse button.

6. Drag the pointer to the right a short distance until there is some white space between the word *Hampshire* and the right edge of cell A6 (refer to Figure 1.26); then release the mouse button.

7. Position the mouse pointer between column letters B and C in the worksheet frame; click and hold down the left mouse button.

8. Drag the pointer to the left to decrease the width of column B (refer to Figure 1.26); then release the mouse button.

9. Choose File, Save As.

10. Enter `states` in the File name box.

11. Select the drive and folder where you want to save the workbook from the Save in list; then click the Save button in the lower-right corner of the dialog box.

12. Choose File, Close (or choose File, Exit to quit Excel in addition to closing the workbook).

2. Using the Subtraction Operator in a Formula

Your supervisor asked you to prepare a report summarizing sales and sales returns for the year. You decide to include a calculation of the net sales as well.

To use the subtraction operator in a formula, follow these steps:

1. Start Excel and access a new blank workbook.

2. Click cell A1, type **Year 2002 Summary**, and press ⏎Enter.

3. Enter the remaining text and numbers, as shown in Figure 1.27 (text in cells A3, A4, and A5; numbers in cells B3 and B4).

	A	B	C	D	E	F	G	H	I	J	K	L
1	Year 2002 Summary											
2												
3	Sales	10000										
4	Returns	200										
5	Net Sales	??										
6												
7												
8												
9												

Figure 1.27

4. Click cell B5, type **=B3-B4**, and press ⏎Enter.

Check that *9800* appears in cell B5—the result of subtracting the contents of cell B4 (*200*) from the contents of cell B3 (*10000*).

5. Choose <u>F</u>ile, Save <u>A</u>s.

6. Enter **sales** in the File <u>n</u>ame box.

7. Select the drive and folder where you want to save the workbook from the Save <u>i</u>n list; then click the <u>S</u>ave button in the lower-right corner of the dialog box.

8. Choose <u>F</u>ile, <u>C</u>lose (or choose <u>F</u>ile, E<u>x</u>it to quit Excel in addition to closing the workbook).

3. Using the Multiplication Operator in a Formula

You want to calculate the sales tax due on an item. You plan to put the tax rate in a separate cell and label it so that a user can see the current rate and easily modify it, if necessary.

To use the multiplication operator in a formula, follow these steps:

1. Start Excel and access a new blank workbook.

2. Click cell A1, type **Calculating Sales Tax**, and press ⏎Enter.

3. Click cell A3, type **Tax Rate**, and press →.

4. Type **5%** in cell B3, and press ⏎Enter.

5. Enter the remaining text and numbers, as shown in Figure 1.28 (text in cells B5, C5, and A6; a number in cell B6).

	A	B	C	D	E	F	G	H	I	J	K	L
1	Calculating Sales Tax											
2												
3	Tax Rate	5%										
4												
5		Price	Sales Tax									
6	Item #1	160	??									
7												
8												
9												

Figure 1.28

6. Click cell C6, type **=B6*B3**, and press ⏎Enter.

Check that *8* appears in cell C6—the result of multiplying the contents of cell B6 (*160*) by the contents of cell B3 (*5%*).

7. Choose <u>F</u>ile, Save <u>A</u>s.

8. Enter **salestax** in the File <u>n</u>ame box.

9. Select the drive and folder where you want to save the workbook from the Save <u>i</u>n list; then click the <u>S</u>ave button in the lower-right corner of the dialog box.

10. Choose <u>F</u>ile, <u>C</u>lose (or choose <u>F</u>ile, E<u>x</u>it to quit Excel in addition to closing the workbook).

4. Using the Division Operator in a Formula

You want to compute your share of a rental fee, assuming that the cost is shared equally. You plan to enter the number of people in a separate cell and label it so that the calculation will work for any fee and any number of people sharing the cost.

To use the division operator in a formula, follow these steps:

1. Start Excel, and access a new blank workbook.
2. Click cell A1, type `Calculating Cost per Person`, and press `Enter`.
3. Enter the remaining text and numbers, as shown in Figure 1.29 (numbers in cells A3 and A4; text in cells B3, B4, and B5).

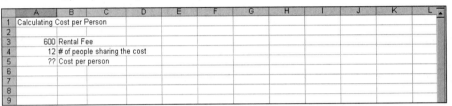

Figure 1.29

4. Click cell A5, type `=A3/A4`, and press `Enter`.
5. Check that *50* appears in cell A5—the result of dividing the contents of cell A3 (*600*) by the contents of cell A4 (*12*).
6. Choose File, Save As.
7. Enter `share` in the File name box.
8. Select the drive and folder where you want to save the workbook from the Save in list; then click the Save button in the lower-right corner of the dialog box.
9. Choose File, Close (or choose File, Exit to quit Excel in addition to closing the workbook).

5. Exploring Ways to Get Assistance While You Work

You want to learn more about onscreen Help features in general.

To get help using the Ask a Question text box, follow these steps:

1. Start Excel, and access a new blank workbook.
2. Type `learn about help` in the Ask a Question text box near the right end of the menu bar, and press `Enter`.
3. Select the topic *About getting help while you work* from the list of topics.
   The Microsoft Excel Help window opens. Five resources are listed, and each is preceded by an arrowhead that points toward the name of the resource. The types of help are *Ask a Question box, The Office Assistant, Help, ScreenTips,* and *Help on the World Wide Web.*
4. Click the topic *ScreenTips.*
   The arrowhead preceding *ScreenTips* points down instead of to the right, and Excel displays information about the selected resource.
5. After using the scrollbars to view the remaining information in this section (if necessary), click the arrowhead preceding *ScreenTips.*
   The view collapses to the original list of five resources.
6. Select the topic *Help on the World Wide Web,* and read the information displayed.
7. Read about other resources of your choice; then click the Close button in the upper-right corner of the Help window.
8. Continue working in Excel, or choose File, Exit.

6. Using the What's This? Feature of Onscreen Help

You know that Excel provides a "What's This?" feature as part of onscreen Help.

To use the What's This? feature to learn about buttons in the Footer dialog box, follow these steps:

1. Start Excel, and access a new blank workbook.

2. Choose File, Page Setup.

3. Click the Header/Footer tab in the Page Setup dialog box; then click the Custom Footer button.

4. Click the Help button in the upper-right corner of the Footer dialog box (a question mark symbol just above the OK button).

A large question mark symbol displays to the right of the mouse pointer.

5. Drag the mouse pointer toward the left side of the Footer dialog box.

The large question mark moves with the pointer, indicating that the What's This? Help feature is active.

6. Click the button displaying an uppercase A (the leftmost of 10 buttons in a row across the middle of the Footer dialog box).

The name and purpose of the selected button displays—in this case, the Font button.

7. Click a blank area within the dialog box.

The explanation of the selected button disappears, and What's This? Help is no longer active.

8. View explanations of the other buttons, as desired.

9. Click Cancel to close the Footer dialog box; then click Cancel to close the Page Setup dialog box.

10. Continue working in Excel, or choose File, Exit.

Challenge

Challenge exercises expand on or are somewhat related to skills presented in the lessons. Each exercise provides a brief narrative introduction, followed by instructions in a numbered-step format that are not as detailed as those in the Skill Drill section.

Each exercise is independent of the others, so you may complete the exercises in any order. If you need a paper copy of the completed exercise, enter your name centered in a header before printing.

1. Calculating a Monthly Rental Fee

You rent a copy machine, for which the rental company charges a fixed amount for the month plus an amount for each copy. Create a worksheet to calculate the amount due for any month. Test your results by changing one or more variables: the rental fee per month, the charge per copy, or the number of copies made in a month.

To calculate a monthly rental fee for a copy machine, follow these steps:

1. Start Excel, and access a new blank workbook.

2. Change the width of column A, and enter text and numbers, as shown in Figure 1.30.

	A	B	C	D	E	F	G	H	I	
1	Calculating the Monthly Charge for a Copy Machine									
2										
3	Rental fee per month	200								
4	Charge per copy	0.05								
5	# of copies made during the month	1000								
6										
7	Total rental fee	??								
8										
9										

Figure 1.30

3. In cell B7, enter the formula to calculate *Total rental fee*. (Hint: Multiply the # of copies by the charge per copy, and add the result to the rental fee per month; use cell references instead of numbers in the formula.)

Ensure that *250* displays as the total rental fee in cell B7.

4. In cell B5, change the number of copies to **2000**.

Make sure that *300* displays as the total rental fee in cell B7. Doubling the number of copies increased the total rental fee by 50 dollars. Now, find out how much you would pay if you could negotiate a charge of four cents per copy.

5. In cell B4, change the charge per copy to **0.04**.

Ensure that *280* displays as the total rental fee in cell B7. You save 20 dollars if you pay one cent less on each of 2000 copies.

6. In the drive and folder of your choice, save the workbook as **rental**.

7. Close the workbook (also exit Excel if you want to end your work session).

2. Calculating Your New Rate of Pay per Hour

You put in a request for a raise. Create a worksheet to calculate the new wage rate per hour. Test your results by changing one or both variables—the original wage rate per hour and the % increase.

To calculate a new rate of pay per hour, follow these steps:

1. Start Excel, and access a new blank workbook.

2. Enter the text and numbers shown in Figure 1.31.

	A	B	C	D	E	F	G	H	I	
1	Calculating Your New Rate of Pay per Hour									
2										
3	Original wage rate per hour	8								
4	% increase	5%								
5	New wage rate per hour	??								
6										
7										
8										
9										

Figure 1.31

3. In cell B5, enter the formula to calculate *New wage rate per hour*. (Hint: Multiply the original wage rate by the % increase, and add the result to the original wage rate; use cell references instead of numbers in the formula).

Make sure that *8.4* displays as the new wage rate per hour in cell B5 (you learn to change the display to **$8.40** in Project 3).

4. In cell B3, change the wage rate per hour to **10**.

Ensure that *10.5* displays as the new wage rate in cell B5.

5. In cell B4, change the % increase to **10%**.

Make sure that *11* displays as the new wage rate in cell B5.

6. In the drive and folder of your choice, save the workbook as **raise**.

7. Close the workbook (also exit Excel if you want to end your work session).

3. Preparing to Print a Worksheet

You know that you'll be creating a worksheet slightly larger than can fit on one page, printed with one-inch margins in landscape orientation. You want to print the worksheet periodically by clicking the Print button on the toolbar.

Follow these steps to set up and save the desired print specifications:

1. Start Excel, and access a new blank workbook.

2. Access the <u>F</u>ile menu, and display the Page Setup dialog box.

3. Select the Page tab, and specify <u>L</u>andscape orientation.

4. Set scaling to fit to one page wide by one page tall.

5. Select the Margins tab, and set all margins to one inch.

6. Close the Page Setup dialog box and save your workbook as **print**.

7. Close the workbook (also exit Excel if you want to end your work session).

4. Printing a Help Topic

You want to find and print information about editing cell contents.

Follow these steps to produce the desired output:

1. Access a new blank Excel workbook and enter `edit cell contents` in the Ask a Question box.
2. From the list of related topics, select *Edit cell contents*.
   The Microsoft Excel Help window displays a bulleted item named *Tips* below three steps to edit cell contents.
3. Display the tips.
   The tips explain how to turn in-cell editing on or off, and how to position the cursor at the end of cell contents.
4. Use the Print button in the Help window to print the selected subtopic (or proceed to Step 5 if you do not want to print at this time).
5. Exit onscreen Help.
6. Close the workbook (also exit Excel if you want to end your work session).

Discovery Zone exercises require advanced knowledge of topics presented in *Essentials* lessons, application of skills from multiple lessons, or self-directed learning of new skills. Each exercise is independent of the others, so you may complete the exercises in any order.

1. Using Help to Learn How to Disable AutoComplete

You have heard that many features in Excel can be turned on or off to suit your work preferences. Use one or more of Excel's Help options to find out how to turn off AutoComplete. For example, you can type your search topic in the Ask a Question text box or in the message balloon provided by the Office Assistant. You can also display Help's Index and specify your search topic as a keyword.

2. Using Help to Answer Questions About a Custom Footer

You want to know if you can have more than one custom footer in a worksheet, and if you can enter more than one line of text in a footer. Use Excel's onscreen Help to find the answers to your questions. For example, you might look in Contents for subtopics related to printing.

Modifying a Worksheet

Objectives

In this project, you learn how to

- ✔ Open an Existing Workbook
- ✔ Select Worksheet Items
- ✔ Use AutoFill
- ✔ Insert and Delete Rows and Columns
- ✔ Copy and Move Cell Contents
- ✔ Use AutoSum
- ✔ Copy a Formula with Relative References
- ✔ Spell-check a Worksheet

Key terms in this project include

- ❑ absolute cell reference
- ❑ AutoCorrect
- ❑ AutoFill
- ❑ AutoSum
- ❑ Clipboard
- ❑ fill handle
- ❑ function
- ❑ range
- ❑ relative cell reference
- ❑ select
- ❑ shortcut menu
- ❑ spelling checker

Why Would I Do This?

Now that you are familiar with the Excel screen and the basics of entering data and saving files, it's time to work with some of Excel's more powerful editing tools. In this project, you expand a worksheet with revenue data for one quarter by adding data for three more quarters. For each revenue source—Greens Fees, Golf Lessons, and Pro Shop Sales—you also calculate total revenue for each quarter and for the year.

Visual Summary

Figure 2.1 shows the entries to be made in the first sheet of the workbook.

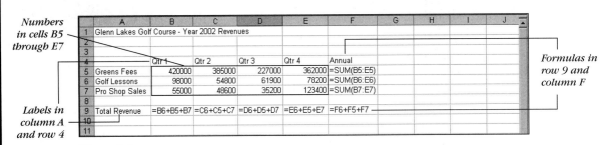

Figure 2.1

The results of entering those numbers and formulas are shown in Figure 2.2.

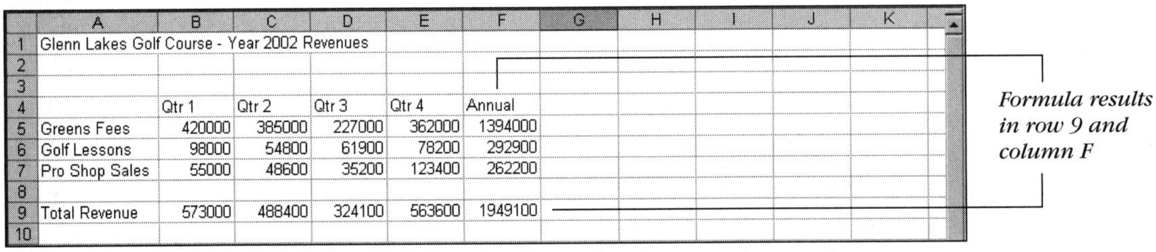

Figure 2.2

Lesson 1: Opening an Existing Workbook

After you create and save a workbook, you can reopen the workbook and resume working with its data. In this lesson, you open a student data file containing revenue data for four quarters.

To Open an Existing Workbook

❶ Start Excel if it is not already open; then choose File in the menu bar.

The File menu opens to display a number of commands.

❷ Choose the Open command.

The Open dialog box appears. You can also display the Open dialog box by clicking the Open button on the Standard toolbar.

❸ Click the down arrow at the right end of the Look in box (see Figure 2.3).

Open dialog box →

Five buttons provide quick access to common storage locations →

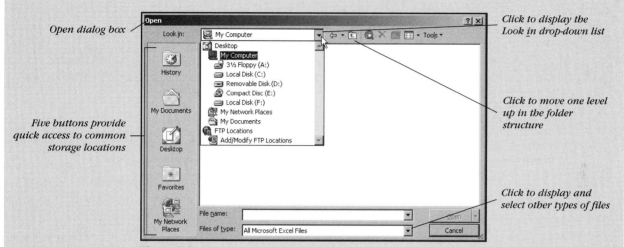

Click to display the Look in drop-down list

Click to move one level up in the folder structure

Click to display and select other types of files

Figure 2.3

The Look in drop-down list shown in Figure 2.3 reflects the drives, folders, or files on a specific computer. The drives, folders, and files on your system may be different, depending on what software and hardware you have installed.

❹ Select the drive and folder containing the student files for this book, and click the *ee1-0201* file icon to select the file.

If you don't see *ee1-0201* in the list, try opening another folder from the Look in drop-down list, or try looking on another drive. The file may be stored in a different location on your system. If you can't find the file on your computer, ask your instructor for the location of the data files you will use with this book.

If you have problems...

If a border surrounds the selected filename and a flashing cursor displays at the end of the highlighted filename, it means you changed to Rename mode. In Rename mode, you can change the name of an existing file or folder. To select a file, make sure you click its icon.

❺ Click the Open button in the lower-right corner of the Open dialog box.

The partially completed worksheet shown in Figure 2.4 appears onscreen. The worksheet is a duplicate of the worksheet created in Project 1. Now, use the Save As command to save a copy of this file under a more descriptive filename. The original data file will be stored intact.

(Continues)

To Open an Existing Workbook (Continued)

Name of the currently active file

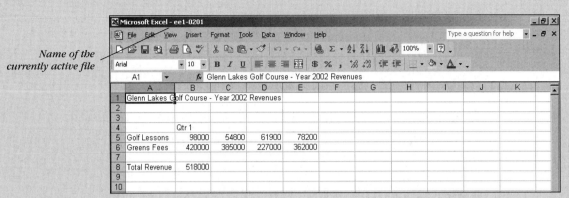

Figure 2.4

6 **Choose the <u>F</u>ile menu again; then choose the Save <u>A</u>s command.**
The Save As dialog box appears.

7 **In the File <u>n</u>ame text box, type** revenues2002 **to replace** *ee1-0201.*

8 **From the Save <u>i</u>n drop-down list, select the appropriate drive and folder for saving the new file.**
If necessary, ask your instructor where you should save the new workbook file.

9 **Click the <u>S</u>ave button in the dialog box.**
Excel saves the workbook as *revenues2002* and adds the extension .xls to the filename. The name of the file changes to *revenues2002* in the title bar at the top of the screen. There are now two identical files—the original student data file named *ee1-0201.xls* and a copy named *revenues2002.xls*. Throughout this book, you modify copies of student data files. Each original file remains intact in case you want to rework a project. Keep the workbook open for the next lesson, or close the workbook and exit Excel.

To extend your knowledge...

Opening a File

To open a file quickly from the Open dialog box, double-click the file's icon in the list of files. If you double-click the filename instead of the file icon, however, you may end up in Rename mode.

Lesson 2: Selecting Worksheet Items

In order to build a worksheet, you must learn how to select items in the worksheet. When you *select* an item, you highlight that item so you can make changes to it. You select a cell, for example, so you can enter data in the cell or copy the cell's content into another cell. You select a column so that you can change the column's width or delete the column.

In this lesson, you learn how to select items in the *revenues2002* workbook.

To Select Worksheet Items

1 **Open the *revenues2002* workbook, if necessary, and click cell A5 in Sheet1.**

You have selected cell A5 by clicking it. Once you select a cell, the cell's border is highlighted in bold, the cell's address appears in the name box of the formula bar, and the cell's content appears in the formula bar. In addition, the background of the letter heading of the column and the number heading of the row in which the cell is located appear in a darker color.

2 **Click cell A5, press and hold down the left mouse button, and drag the mouse pointer to cell E5. Release the left mouse button when the mouse pointer is in cell E5.**

Several adjacent cells—called a range—are now selected (refer to Figure 2.5). In Excel, a ***range*** can be a cell or a rectangular group of adjacent cells. As you drag the mouse, the name box on the formula bar shows you how many rows and columns you are selecting; in this case, 1R x 5C. After you finish selecting the range, the entire range of selected cells is highlighted.

Select All button

The range A5:E5 is selected

	A	B	C	D	E	F	G	H	I	J	K
1	Glenn Lakes Golf Course - Year 2002 Revenues										
2											
3											
4		Qtr 1									
5	Golf Lessons	98000	54800	61900	78200						
6	Greens Fees	420000	385000	227000	362000						
7											
8	Total Revenue	518000									
9											
10											

Figure 2.5

3 **Click column heading B in the worksheet frame.**

This deselects the range A5 through E5 and selects (highlights) the entire column B.

4 **Click row heading 8 in the worksheet frame.**

This deselects column B and selects row 8.

5 **Click the Select All button, the rectangle in the top-left corner of the worksheet frame (refer to Figure 2.5).**

This selects the entire worksheet.

6 **Click any cell to deselect the worksheet.**

Keep the workbook open for the next lesson, or close the workbook and exit Excel.

To extend your knowledge...

Selecting Cells and Cell Contents

In Excel, the standard notation for identifying ranges is to list the first cell in the range, then a colon, and then the last cell in the range. For example, *A5:E5* refers to the range of cells in row 5 from column A through column E.

You can select a range of adjacent cells by clicking the first cell and then by pressing and holding down ⬆Shift while you click the last cell. For example, to select all cells in column A from row 3 through row 50, you can click cell A3, press and hold down ⬆Shift, click cell A50, and release ⬆Shift. Excel highlights all cells in the range A3:A50.

(Continues)

To select nonadjacent cells, click the first cell; then press and hold Ctrl, and click additional cells. The last cell that you click is the active cell, but the others remain selected.

To select just the content or part of the content of a cell, you can double-click in the active cell to display the I-beam mouse pointer; then drag the I-beam across any part of the text or data in the cell or the formula bar to select it. For example, you might want to boldface only a selected portion of the text in a long label.

Lesson 3: Using AutoFill

Currently, Sheet1 in the *revenues2002* workbook has values for two sources of revenue over four quarters. Before the worksheet is complete, however, a few items need to be changed. For example, row 4 should have column headings for each quarter of revenues you track. Using Excel's **AutoFill** feature, you can easily fill in a series of numbers, dates, or other items in a specified range.

In this case, by selecting the cell containing the label *Qtr 1* and then selecting a range of cells, you can automatically add a sequence of quarter labels (Qtr 2, Qtr 3, and Qtr 4) to the range you select.

To Use AutoFill

❶ Open the *revenues2002* workbook, if necessary, and click cell B4 in Sheet1.
The *fill handle*, a small black square, displays in the lower-right corner of cell B4. Dragging the fill handle to adjacent cells produces a data series based on the contents of the current cell or selected range. Now, drag the fill handle to create a series of consecutive quarter labels.

❷ Move the mouse pointer to the lower-right corner of cell B4 until the pointer changes to a thin black cross.
When the mouse pointer changes to a black cross, Excel is ready to select a range of cells to be filled (refer to Figure 2.6).

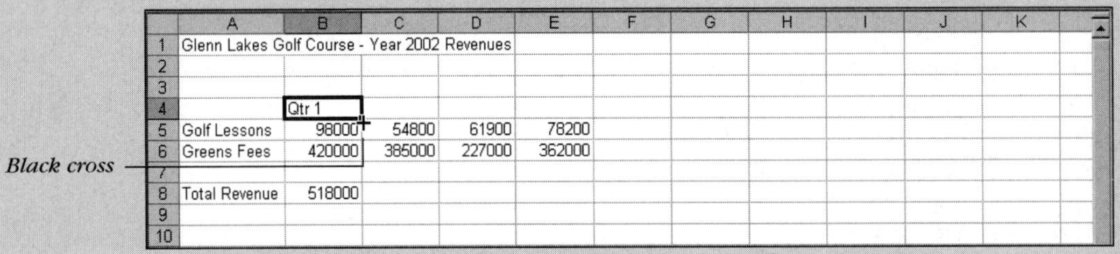

Black cross ——

Figure 2.6

❸ Press the left mouse button, drag right to cell E4, and release the mouse button.
The range B4 through E4 is selected. When you release the mouse button, Excel fills the range with quarter labels (starting with *Qtr 2* and increasing by one quarter for each cell in the range), and displays the Auto Fill Options button, as shown in Figure 2.7.

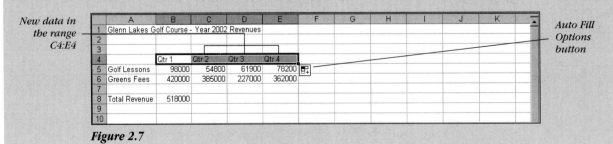

New data in the range C4:E4

Auto Fill Options button

Figure 2.7

To Use AutoFill

If you have problems...

When using AutoFill, if you select cells that already contain data, Excel overwrites the data in the cells. If the results of an AutoFill are not what you want, you can reverse the fill action and restore the original data by choosing Edit, Undo.

4 **Position the mouse pointer on the Auto Fill Options button and click its down arrowhead.**

A drop-down list of four fill options displays (see Figure 2.8). The options in the drop-down list vary with the type of data being copied. In this case, the default option, Fill Series, produced the incremental change in numbers in each successive quarter label. You can modify fill results by selecting one of the other options. Now, view the effect of selecting the Copy Cells option (you learn about formatting features in Project 3 "Improving the Appearance of a Worksheet").

	A	B	C	D	E	F	G	H	I	J	K
1	Glenn Lakes Golf Course - Year 2002 Revenues										
2											
3											
4		Qtr 1	Qtr 2	Qtr 3	Qtr 4						
5	Golf Lessons	98000	54800	61900	78200						
6	Greens Fees	420000	385000	227000	362000						
7						○ Copy Cells					
8	Total Revenue	518000				◉ Fill Series					
9						○ Fill Formatting Only					
10						○ Fill Without Formatting					
11											
12											

Figure 2.8

5 **Click the Copy Cells option button in the Auto Fill Options drop-down list.**

Qtr 1 displays in cells C4 through E4 instead of Qtr 2, Qtr 3, and Qtr 4. Excel copied the contents of cell B4 instead of creating a series patterned on the contents of cell B4.

6 **Display the Auto Fill Options drop-down list and select Fill Series.**

Excel restores the display of a series of labels: *Qtr 2, Qtr 3,* and *Qtr 4.*

7 **Click any cell.**

This deselects the range. Now, you can take the next step to build your worksheet—inserting and deleting columns and rows.

8 **Click the Save button in the Standard toolbar.**

Keep the *revenues2002* workbook open for the next lesson, or close the workbook and exit Excel.

To extend your knowledge...

Creating Fill Effects

You can fill data in columns as well as rows. To fill in ascending order, drag down or to the right. To fill in descending order, drag up or to the left.

If you want to create a sequence of consecutive entries, you can provide an example in one or two cells, select the cell(s) containing the example, and then drag the lower-right corner of the selection. The sequences can be text, numbers, or a combination of text and numbers, such as

(Continues)

Qtr 1. For example, if you enter `Jan` in a cell and then use the fill handle to drag right or down eleven more cells, Excel automatically enters *Jan, Feb,...* through *Dec* in the sequence of twelve cells. If you enter `January` in a cell as the example to start a sequence, Excel enters *January, February, March,...* through *December.*

If a fill sequence is to be a set of numbers incrementing by the same amount, provide a pattern in two adjacent cells, such as the number `10` in one cell and the number `20` in the next. If you select both cells and drag right or down, Excel fills the copy range with numbers incrementing by 10 (*10, 20, 30, 40,* and so on).

You can also use the AutoFill feature to enter a series of dates. If you fill a range of dates based on the contents of one cell, each additional date increments by one. For example, applying AutoFill to a cell containing *1/1/2002* produces the series of dates *1/1/2002, 1/2/2002, 1/3/2002,* and so forth. If you desire a different sequence, such as the last day of each month, provide a pattern in two cells. For example, if you enter `1/31/2002` in one cell and `2/28/2002` in the next cell, and then select and drag those cells, Excel continues the sequence with *3/31/2002, 4/30/2002,* and so forth.

If you specify a start value in one cell and then click and drag the fill handle with the right mouse button instead of the left, a shortcut menu displays with predefined increments including days, weekdays, months, and years if the start value is a date. A **shortcut menu** is a menu that pops up in the worksheet area and displays common commands.

Excel also provides a Series dialog box that you can access by choosing Edit, Fill, Series. A variety of options are available that vary with the type of data set up as the start value.

Lesson 4: Inserting and Deleting Rows and Columns

If you decide to add more data within an existing worksheet, you can insert rows and columns. Inserting a row is a two-step process: Select any cell in a row and then choose Insert, Rows. Inserting a column involves a similar process: Select any cell in a column and then choose Insert, Columns. Excel always inserts a new row above the row you select, and inserts a new column to the left of the column you select.

Sometimes, you no longer want to include an entire row or column of data. Deleting a row or column can be done in two steps: Select a row heading or a column heading in the worksheet frame and then choose Edit, Delete.

In this lesson, you insert a row in the first sheet of the *revenues2002* workbook and enter another revenue category called *Pro Shop Sales.*

To Insert a Row

① Open the *revenues2002* workbook, if necessary, and click any cell in row 6 of Sheet1.

② Choose Insert, Rows.
The contents of row 6 and all rows below it move down one row. A new blank row is inserted as the new row 6 (see Figure 2.9). Excel automatically renumbers the rows beneath the new row 6.

To Insert a Row

Inserted row

Contents move
down

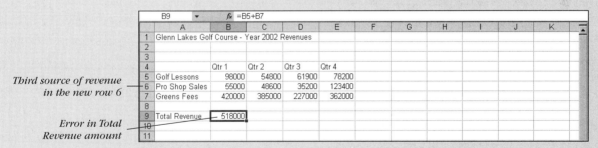

Figure 2.9

If you have problems...

If you inserted the row in the wrong position, you can reverse the action by choosing Edit, Undo Insert Rows.

❸ Click cell A6, type `Pro Shop Sales`, and then press ➡.
You have labeled a new row for *Pro Shop Sales* and moved the cell pointer one cell to the right. Now, enter sales data for quarters one through four.

❹ In cell B6, type 55000 and then press ➡.

❺ In cell C6, type 48600 and then press ➡.

❻ In cell D6, type 35200 and then press ➡.

❼ In cell E6, type 123400 and then press ⏎Enter.

❽ Widen column A to display the *Pro Shop Sales* label; then click cell B9.
Your worksheet should now look similar to Figure 2.10. The *Total Revenue* amount is not correct. The current formula *=B5+B7* must be edited to include the third source of revenue. You will correct this error in the next lesson, after moving cell contents.

*Third source of revenue
in the new row 6*

*Error in Total
Revenue amount*

Figure 2.10

❾ Make changes to the *revenues2002* workbook as necessary, and click the Save button in the Standard toolbar.
Keep the *revenues2002* workbook open for the next lesson, or close the workbook and exit Excel.

To extend your knowledge...

Inserting or Deleting Rows and Columns

If you want to insert more than one row or column at a time, select as many adjacent rows or columns as you need blank rows or columns, and choose Insert, Rows or Insert, Columns. For example, if you want to insert five new rows beginning at row 4, select rows 4 through 8 and choose Insert, Rows.

If an inserted row is bordered by formatted cells, a Format Painter button displays (Figure 2.11). You can clear all formatting from the new row, or you can format the new row the same as the row above or the row below.

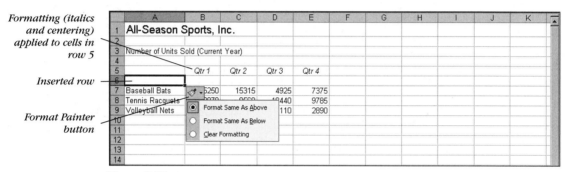

Figure 2.11

If you want to delete more than one row or column at a time, select the row or column headings in the worksheet frame, and choose Edit, Delete.

If you select a row heading or a column heading in the worksheet frame and then choose Edit, Delete, Excel immediately removes the selected row or column. Additional options are available if you click any cell in a row or column instead of the worksheet frame, and choose Edit, Delete. Excel displays the Delete dialog box with four options: Shift cells left, Shift cells up, Entire row, and Entire column. Use the first two options to delete a cell's contents and shift adjacent data to fill the blank cell.

You can use a shortcut menu to insert or delete columns, rows, and cell contents. Follow these steps: Select the column, row, or cell(s); move the mouse pointer to the selected area; right-click the mouse to display the shortcut menu; and choose the appropriate command.

Lesson 5: Copying and Moving Cell Contents

By inserting a row, you made an important change to Sheet1 of your *revenues2002* workbook. As you look at the three sources of revenue, however, you decide to change the order by listing the primary revenue source first. You could insert a new row 5 and retype the *Greens Fees* label and associated amounts. However, copying or moving data is generally much quicker than typing it a second time.

You can copy or move text, numbers, and formulas from one cell (or range) to another; from one worksheet to another; and from one file to another. After a copy operation, the selected cell contents appear in two places—the original location and the new location. After a move (cut) operation, the selected cell contents appear in only the new location.

Both operations involve a four-step process: Select the cell(s) containing the data you want to copy or move; choose either Copy or Cut from the Edit menu; position the cell pointer on the upper-left cell of the target range; and choose Edit, Paste.

In this lesson, you insert a blank row, move selected cell contents to the new row, and delete the blank row that formerly held the moved data.

To Move Cell Contents

❶ Open the *revenues2002* workbook, if necessary, and then click any cell in row 5 of Sheet1.

❷ Choose Insert, Rows.
A new blank row appears above the renumbered row 6 containing *Golf Lessons* data.

❸ Select the *Greens Fees* label and data (the range A8:E8).
The range A8:E8 appears highlighted.

❹ Click the Cut button in the Standard toolbar (or choose the menu sequence Edit, Cut).
A copy of the selected cells' contents is placed in the Windows Clipboard. The **Clipboard** stores data that you want to copy or move to another location. A flashing dotted line appears around the selected cells.

❺ Click cell A5, the first cell in the new blank row.
The location where you want the cut cell contents to appear is selected. You do not have to select a range that is the same size as the range you are moving. Excel automatically fills in the data, starting with the cell you select.

❻ Click the Paste button in the Standard toolbar (or choose the menu sequence Edit, Paste).
The contents of selected cells disappear from the range A8:E8 and appear in cells A5 through E5, as shown in Figure 2.12. As indicated by the commands you chose, this move process (called cutting and pasting) is a very common procedure in Windows applications.

Pasted data in the range A5:E5

	A	B	C	D	E	F	G	H	I	J	K
1	Glenn Lakes Golf Course - Year 2002 Revenues										
2											
3											
4		Qtr 1	Qtr 2	Qtr 3	Qtr 4						
5	Greens Fees	420000	385000	227000	362000						
6	Golf Lessons	98000	54800	61900	78200						
7	Pro Shop Sales	55000	48600	35200	123400						
8											
9											
10	Total Revenue	518000									
11											
12											

Figure 2.12

❼ Click the row heading for row 8.
The blank row 8 is selected (highlighted).

❽ Choose Edit, Delete.
This removes the extra blank row before the *Total Revenue row*.

If you have problems...
If you deleted the wrong row, you can reverse the action by choosing Edit, Undo Delete or clicking the Undo button on the toolbar.

❾ Click cell B9.
The formula in the formula bar references only cells B5 and B6. You must edit the formula to include the third source of revenue in cell B7.

(Continues)

To Move Cell Contents (Continued)

⑩ Click in the formula bar at the end of the current formula; then type +B7 and press ↵Enter.

⑪ Click cell B9 again.

The corrected formula displays in the formula bar, and the result of the calculation appears in cell B9 (see Figure 2.13).

Formula stored in cell B9

Correct total for three sources of revenue

	A	B	C	D	E	F	G	H	I	J	K
	B9	▼	ƒx =B6+B5+B7								
1	Glenn Lakes Golf Course - Year 2002 Revenues										
2											
3											
4		Qtr 1	Qtr 2	Qtr 3	Qtr 4						
5	Greens Fees	420000	385000	227000	362000						
6	Golf Lessons	98000	54800	61900	78200						
7	Pro Shop Sales	55000	48600	35200	123400						
8											
9	Total Revenue	573000									
10											
11											

Figure 2.13

⑫ Save your changes to the current worksheet.

Keep the *revenues2002* workbook open for the next lesson, or close the workbook and exit Excel.

To extend your knowledge...

Copy and Paste

Executing a copy-and-paste operation differs from a cut-and-paste operation in only the second step of the four-step process. After selecting the cells to copy, click the Copy button on the Standard toolbar instead of the Cut button (or select the menu sequence Edit, Copy instead of Edit, Cut).

Shortcut Menus and Drag and Drop

You can use Excel's shortcut menus to perform many common commands, including cut, copy, and paste. To open a shortcut menu, move the mouse pointer to the cell or area you want to affect, and right-click.

A handy way to move one or more cells of data quickly is to select the cells, and position the mouse pointer on any border of the cells so the mouse pointer changes to a white arrow with a four-headed black arrow attached. Click and drag the mouse pointer to the new location. An outline of the cells that you are moving appears as you drag, and a ScreenTip shows you the current active cell (or range) where the data will appear if you release the mouse button. When you release the mouse button, the cells' contents appear in the new location. If the new location already contains data, a dialog box appears, asking whether you want to replace the contents of the destination cells.

Paste Button Options

The Paste button drop-down list (see Figure 2.14) provides quick access to a variety of paste options. For example, you can select Transpose to paste a selected range across a row that was originally entered down a column. Onscreen Help provides detailed information about all paste options.

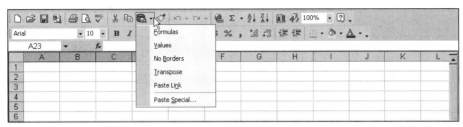

Figure 2.14

Lesson 6: Using AutoSum

You entered all labels and numbers in Sheet1 of the *revenues2002* workbook. Now, you want to enter formulas to total revenues for the year by type of revenue and for each quarter. Excel provides an ***AutoSum*** feature that you can use to insert a formula to sum a range of cells automatically. Excel suggests a formula, which you can accept or edit.

The suggested formula is a SUM function that includes Excel's suggestion for a range of cells to sum. A ***function*** is a predefined formula in Excel (Project 5, "Working with Functions," provides in-depth coverage of functions).

Now, use the AutoSum feature to calculate the total Greens Fees in the *revenues2002 workbook*.

To Calculate Using AutoSum

❶ Open the *revenues2002* workbook, if necessary, and click cell F4 in Sheet1.
The current cell is just to the right of the label *Qtr 4*. Now, enter a label to describe new entries in column F.

❷ Type Annual, and press ↵Enter.
The word *Annual* displays left-aligned in cell F4. The current cell is F5.

❸ Click the AutoSum button in the toolbar.
AutoSum evaluates cells above and to the left of the current cell. Upon finding an adjacent set of consecutive cells containing values, AutoSum automatically displays the suggested range to sum (see Figure 2.15).

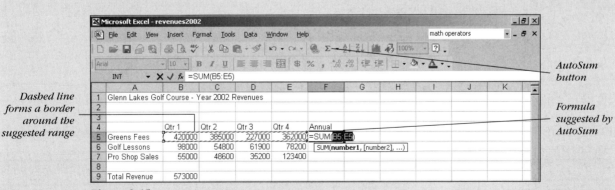

Dashed line forms a border around the suggested range

AutoSum button

Formula suggested by AutoSum

Figure 2.15

(Continues)

To Calculate Using AutoSum (Continued)

4 **Press ⏎Enter to accept the suggested function.**
Excel enters the function *=SUM(B5:E5)* in cell F5, and displays *1394000* as the calculated result.

5 **Save your changes to the current worksheet.**
Keep the *revenues2002* workbook open for the next lesson, or close the workbook and exit Excel.

To extend your knowledge...

AutoSum Button Options

Clicking the AutoSum button automatically starts the entry of the SUM function in the current cell. You can, however, display the AutoSum button drop-down list (see Figure 2.16) for quick access to a variety of other functions.

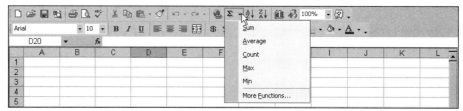

Figure 2.16

Lesson 7: Copying a Formula with Relative References

The Year 2002 Revenues worksheet is nearly complete. All that remains is to copy two formulas to adjacent cells (refer to Figure 2.1). Each formula in row 9 performs the same calculation—adding the contents of cells in rows 5, 6, and 7. Only the column designation changes from one formula to the next. Figure 2.1 also shows that the remaining formulas in column F perform the same calculation—adding the contents of cells in columns B through E. Only the row designation changes from one formula to the next.

When row and/or column cell references change as a formula is copied, each reference to a cell in the formula is a ***relative cell reference***. If you don't want Excel to adjust a reference to a cell when you copy a formula, use an ***absolute cell reference***. You can create an absolute reference by placing a dollar sign ($) in front of the part(s) of the cell reference you do not want to change during the copy operation.

Now, copy the two formulas in Sheet1 of the *revenues2002 workbook*.

To Copy a Formula with Relative References

1 **Open the *revenues2002* workbook, if necessary, and click cell F5 in Sheet1.**

2 **Position the mouse pointer in the lower-right corner of cell F5.**
The cursor changes to a thin black cross (see Figure 2.17).

To Copy a Formula with Relative References

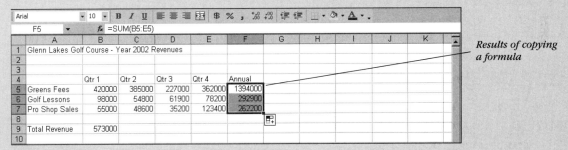

Formula with relative cell references

Figure 2.17

❸ **Press the left mouse button, drag down to cell F7, and release the mouse button.**

The formula in cell F5 is copied to cells F6 and F7 (see Figure 2.18). The copied formula did not contain any absolute cell references, so the formulas in cells F6 and F7 adjust to the appropriate row reference: row 6 for the formula in cell F6 and row 7 for the formula in cell F7.

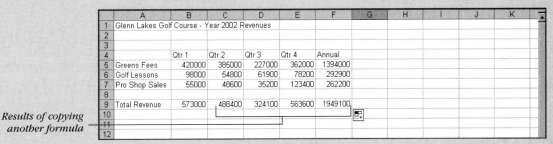

Results of copying a formula

Figure 2.18

❹ **Click cell B9 and position the mouse pointer in the lower-right corner of the cell.**

❺ **Press the left mouse button, drag right to cell F9, and release the mouse button.**

The formula in cell B9 is copied to cells C9 through F9. The copied formula did not contain any absolute cell references, so the formulas in cells C9 through F9 adjust to the appropriate column reference.

❻ **Click any cell—such as cell A1—to deselect the highlighted range.**

❼ **Make sure that your formula results match those in Figure 2.19, and edit data or formulas as necessary.**

Results of copying another formula

Figure 2.19

❽ **Save your changes to the *revenues2002* workbook.**

Keep the *revenues2002* workbook open for the last lesson, or close the workbook and exit Excel.

To extend your knowledge...

Moving Formulas Containing Relative Cell References

When you move a formula containing relative cell references, the cell references do not adjust to the new row or column position. For example, if you move the formula =SUM(A3:A9) from cell A10 to cell C12, the result in cell C12 is still =SUM(A3:A9).

Lesson 8: Spell-Checking a Worksheet

Microsoft Excel includes an **AutoCorrect** feature that can correct common errors as you type, such as changing *adn* to *and*. The program also includes a **spelling checker** that highlights words that are not in its dictionary. You have the option to change or ignore any highlighted word. If a highlighted word, such as a person's name or a technical term, is spelled correctly and you use the word frequently, you can add it to a custom dictionary file.

The spelling checker doesn't catch all errors. You should still read text entries carefully to see if words are missing or used incorrectly, such as using "affect" when you mean "effect."

In the following steps, you enter a misspelled word and correct it using the spelling checker.

To Check Spelling in a Worksheet

1 Open the *revenues2002* workbook, if necessary, and click cell A2 in Sheet1.

2 Type Prepaired by: and press ⏎Enter (make sure you type the entry as shown, including the spelling error).

3 Click cell A1.
The spell-check is set to begin at the top of the worksheet.

4 Click the Spelling button on the Standard toolbar.
The Spelling dialog box opens. The spelling checker highlights the first occurrence of a word not found in its dictionary (see Figure 2.20)

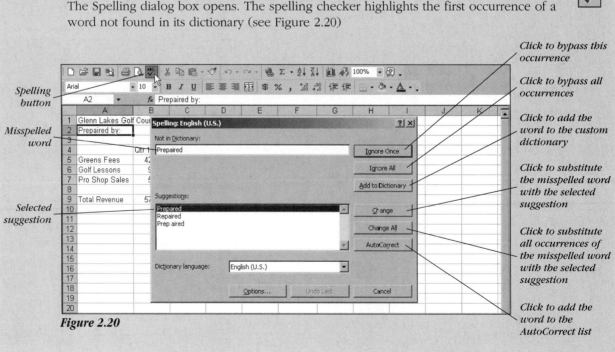

Figure 2.20

To Check Spelling in a Worksheet

⑤ Click Change, and click OK.
The Spelling dialog box closes, and the corrected spelling *Prepared by:* displays in cell A2.

⑥ Enter your full name in cell B2, and save your changes.
This concludes Project 2. Close the workbook; then either continue with the end-of-project activities or exit Excel.

To extend your knowledge...

Tips on Using the Spelling Checker

A check of spelling begins at the current worksheet cell and continues to the end of the worksheet. If you do not start the spelling checker at the beginning of the worksheet, Excel asks if you want to continue checking from the beginning. Choose *Yes* to continue a check of the entire worksheet, or choose *No* to close the spelling checker.

You can select a different language for the spell-check by clicking the Cptions button at the bottom of the Spelling dialog box (refer to Figure 2.20). For example, you can specify one of four English languages (Australia, Canada, U.K., and U.S) or one of two French languages (Canada and France).

Summary

In this project, you learned several essential tasks for developing a worksheet with a minimum of effort. Your experiences included using AutoFill to enter a sequence of labels, using AutoSum to enter a function that adds the contents of adjacent cells, and entering a formula once and copying it to other cells. You also learned basic editing techniques: selecting worksheet items, inserting or deleting rows and columns, executing a four-step process to move or copy cell contents, and spell-checking a worksheet.

You can extend your learning by practicing variations of techniques presented in the lessons. For example, in Lesson 3, you used AutoFill to enter a series of quarter labels. In a blank worksheet, try using AutoFill to enter the months of the year, the days of the week, and a series of numbers incrementing by a set amount (for example, 1, 2, 3... or 10, 20, 30...). Reinforce the skills presented in Lesson 5 by moving and copying the ranges you created by using AutoFill. You inserted a row in Lesson 4. On your own, try to insert a column and delete a column or row. Be sure to browse the extensive onscreen Help for related topics.

Checking Concepts and Terms

Multiple Choice

Circle the letter of the correct answer for each of the following.

1. What function is used to add the values in a range of cells? [L6]

   a. TOTAL
   b. SUM
   c. PLUS
   d. ADD

2. Which of the following is a true statement? [L2]

   a. In Excel, a range can be a single cell.
   b. In Excel, a range can be a rectangular group of adjacent cells.
   c. Both a and b are true statements.
   d. Neither a or b is a true statement.

3. Which of the following statements is false? [L5]

   a. The move process is called cutting and pasting, which is a common procedure in Windows applications.
   b. Using Excel, you can copy or move text, numbers, and formulas from one worksheet to another.
   c. After a cut operation, the selected cell contents appear in two places—the original location and the new location.
   d. You can use buttons on a toolbar or choose menu options to copy or move worksheet contents.

4. When row and/or column cell references change as a formula is copied, each reference to a cell in the formula is a(n) _____. [L7]

   a. relative cell reference
   b. absolute cell reference
   c. static cell reference
   d. None of the above.

5. Excel uses different cursors to indicate the current operation. A thin black cross indicates that you can _____. [L5]

   a. move cell contents by dragging
   b. copy cell contents by dragging
   c. insert one or more rows
   d. None of the above.

Discussion

1. Excel provides a number of shortcut menus. What is a shortcut menu, and how do you activate one? Provide at least three examples of operations in this project that you can start by activating a shortcut menu. [L4]

2. You worked with AutoFill and AutoSum features in this project. What is the purpose of each? Provide your own examples of how you might use each feature. For each example, briefly describe the steps you would take to produce the result you want. [L3 and L6]

3. Assume that you are creating the worksheet shown in Figure 2.21. Provide the formulas or functions needed to calculate Annual Sales, as well as the Gross Profit, Total Operating Expenses, and Net Income for Qtr 1. Could you copy these formulas to complete the worksheet? Include an explanation of relative cell addresses in your answer. [L7]

	A	B	C	D	E	F	G	H	I	J
1	Software Sharing, Inc									
2	Quarterly Budget, 2002									
3										
4										
5		Qtr 1	Qtr 2	Qtr 3	Qtr 4	Annual				
6	Sales	33000	46000	8000	75000					
7	less Cost of Goods Sold	9000	11000	14500	21700					
8	Gross Profit									
9										
10	less Operating Expenses:									
11	Selling	4000	6000	7000	10000					
12	Administrative	6000	8000	10000	11000					
13	Total Operating Expenses									
14										
15	Net Income									
16										

Figure 2.21

Skill Drill

Skill Drill exercises reinforce project skills. Each skill reinforced is the same, or nearly the same, as a skill presented in the project. Detailed instructions are provided in a step-by-step format.

Before beginning your Project 2 Skill Drill exercises, complete the following steps:

1. Open the file named *ee1-0202*, and immediately save it as `ee1-p2drill`.
   The workbook contains seven sheets: an overview and six exercise sheets labeled #1-InsertRow, #2-DeleteCol, #3-Copy, #4-Move, #5-AutoFill, and #6-AutoSum.
2. Click the Overview sheet to view the organization and content of the Project 2 Skill Drill Exercises workbook.

Each exercise is independent of the others, so you may complete the exercises in any order. Be sure to save the workbook after completing each exercise. If you need a paper copy of one or more completed exercises, enter your name, centered in a header, before printing. Other print options have already been set to print compressed to one page and to display the filename, sheet name, and current date in a footer.

Be sure to save your changes and close the workbook if you need more than one work session to complete the desired exercises. Then, continue working on *ee1-p2drill* instead of starting all over again in the original *ee1-0202* file.

1. Inserting a Row

You are modifying a worksheet to summarize volunteer hours, and you want to insert a row for another organization.

To insert a row, follow these steps:

1. If necessary, open the *ee1-p2drill* workbook; then click the #1-InsertRow sheet tab.
2. Click any cell in row 9, such as cell A9.
3. Choose Insert, Rows.
   A blank row 9 appears. The *Big Brothers-Big Sisters* row is now row 10.
4. Click cell A9, and type `Literacy League`.
5. Click cell B9, and type `670` for Qtr 1 hours.
6. Click cell C9, and type `840` for Qtr 2 hours.
7. Click cell D9, and type `1130` for Qtr 3 hours.
8. Click cell E9, and type `935` for Qtr 4 hours.
9. Save your changes to the *ee1-p2drill* workbook.

2. Deleting a Column

Your initial design for summarizing volunteer hours included a column for summing hours after the first and second quarters. Now, you want to present only the annual totals for each organization.

To delete a column, follow these steps:

1. If necessary, open the *ee1-p2drill* workbook; then click the #2-DeleteCol sheet tab.
2. Click any cell in column D, such as D7, which holds the label *1/2 Year*.
3. Choose Edit, Delete to display the Delete dialog box.
4. Click Entire column, and click OK.
5. Save your changes to the *ee1-p2drill* workbook.

3. Copying Cell Contents

As you create a worksheet to summarize volunteer hours, you decide to display data for two years. After setting up worksheet labels for the first year, you can copy those labels to another part of the worksheet and avoid retyping them.

To copy cell contents, follow these steps:

1. If necessary, open the *ee1-p2drill* workbook; then click the #3-Copy sheet tab.
2. Select the range A6:F9.
3. Click the Copy button in the Standard toolbar (or choose Edit, Copy).
4. Click cell A12 to select the first cell in the destination range.
5. Click the Paste button in the Standard toolbar (or choose Edit, Paste).
6. Press Esc to deselect the copied range.
7. Click cell A12, and type **2002** to replace *2001*.
8. Save your changes to the *ee1-p2drill* workbook.

4. Moving Cell Contents

You decide to change the original location of a title and subtitle on a worksheet that summarizes volunteer hours.

To move cell contents, follow these steps:

1. If necessary, open the *ee1-p2drill* workbook; then click the #4-Move sheet tab.
2. Select the range E1:E2.
   This selects the worksheet's title and subtitle. These titles display across several columns, but are stored in the two cells in column E.
3. Click the Cut button in the Standard toolbar (or choose Edit, Cut).
4. Click cell A3 to select the first cell in the destination range.
5. Click the Paste button in the Standard toolbar (or choose Edit, Paste).
6. Save your changes to the *ee1-p2drill* workbook.

5. Using AutoFill to Enter Names of Months

You begin to set up a worksheet to show volunteer hours each month. You know that Excel has an AutoFill feature to automate entry of selected labels.

To use the AutoFill feature to enter the names of months, follow these steps:

1. If necessary, open the *ee1-p2drill* workbook; then click the #5-AutoFill sheet tab.
2. Type **Jan** in cell B6.
3. Click cell B6, and position the cell pointer on the fill handle at the lower-right corner.
4. Click and drag to cell M6, and release the mouse button.
   The labels *Jan, Feb, Mar,* and so on appear in the range B6:M6.
5. Save your changes to the *ee1-p2drill* workbook.

6. Using AutoSum and Copy with Relative Cell References

You entered labels and numbers in a worksheet to keep track of volunteer hours. Now, use AutoSum to enter a function summing hours for the first organization and copy the formula to compute total hours for other organizations.

To use AutoSum and then copy the formula suggested by AutoSum, follow these steps:

1. If necessary, open the *ee1-p2drill* workbook; then click the #6-AutoSum sheet tab.

2. Click cell F7, the first cell under the *Annual* label.

3. Click the AutoSum button in the Standard toolbar.

4. Press ⏎Enter to accept the suggested function =SUM(B7:E7).

5. Click cell F7, and position the cell pointer on the fill handle at the lower-right corner.

6. Click and drag to cell F9, and release the mouse button.

7. Save your changes to the *ee1-p2drill* workbook.

Challenge exercises expand on or are somewhat related to skills presented in the lessons. Each exercise provides a brief narrative introduction, followed by instructions in a numbered-step format that are not as detailed as those in the Skill Drill section.

Before beginning your first Project 2 Challenge exercise, complete the following steps:

1. Open the file named *ee1-0203*, and immediately save it as **ee1-p2challenge**.
The workbook contains five sheets: an overview and exercise sheets named #1-Flowers, #2-Flowers, #3-% Change and #4-Fill.

2. Click the overview sheet to view the organization of the Project 2 Challenge Exercises workbook.

Each exercise is independent of the others, so you may complete the exercises in any order. Be sure to save the workbook after completing each exercise. If you need a paper copy of the completed exercise, enter your name, centered in a header, before printing. Other print options have already been set to print compressed to one page and to display the filename, sheet name, and current date in a footer.

Be sure to save your changes and close the workbook if you need more than one work session to complete the desired exercises. Then, continue working on *ee1-p2challenge* instead of starting all over again in the original *ee1-0203* file.

1. Adding Labels and Formulas to a Sales Data Worksheet

Among your responsibilities as the sales manager of Flowers Your Way is the preparation of a five-year analysis of sales. You have already entered data for sales by type: in-store sales, phone/fax orders, and Web sales. Within each type, you show sales to corporations separately from sales to individuals. Now, you want to complete the worksheet by adding labels and formulas.

To add labels using AutoFill, add a formula using AutoSum, and copy formulas:

1. If necessary, open your *ee1-p2challenge* workbook; then click the #1-Flowers sheet tab.

2. Use AutoFill to enter the years 1998 through 2002 in the range B6:F6.

3. Click cell B10, and use AutoSum to enter the function =SUM(B8:B9).

4. Copy the formula in cell B10 to the range C10:F10.

You copied a formula with relative cell addresses to a range of adjacent cells. Now, copy a formula to nonadjacent cells.

5. Click cell B10 again, and click the Copy button on the Standard toolbar.
6. Select the range B15:F15, hold down Ctrl, and select the range B20:F20.
7. Click the Paste button on the Standard toolbar.
   In each of the highlighted cells in B15:F15 and B20:F20, Excel enters a formula to sum the contents of the two cells above the formula.
8. Select cell B22, and enter a formula to add cells B10, B15, and B20.
9. Copy the formula in B22 to the range C22:F22.
10. Save your changes to the *ee1-p2challenge* workbook.

2. Changing the Order of Data Using Insert, Move, and Delete

Among your responsibilities as the sales manager of Flowers Your Way is the preparation of a five-year analysis of sales. You have categorized sales by type: in-store sales, phone/fax orders, and Web sales. Now, you decide to list Web sales first rather than last. You can make the switch by inserting rows, moving the Web sales data, and then deleting extra blank rows.

To move cell contents, including formulas, follow these steps:

1. If necessary, open your *ee1-p2challenge* workbook; then click the #2-Flowers sheet.
2. Select the range A7:A11, and choose Insert, Rows.
   Blank rows 7 through 11 appear above the label *In-Store Sales*.
3. Select the Web sales data in the range A22:F25, and click the Cut button on the Standard toolbar.
4. Click cell A7, and click the Paste button on the Standard toolbar.
   Web sales data are moved to the blank rows 7 through 10.
5. Select the range A22:A26, and then choose Edit, Delete.
6. Select Entire row in the Delete dialog box, and click OK.
7. Save your changes to the *ee1-p2challenge* workbook.

3. Calculating the % Change From One Year to the Next

You are one of the managers in a small firm and you are responsible for monitoring the following assets: Cash, Accounts Receivable, Inventory, and Supplies. At the moment, you are interested in finding out how the amounts in these accounts at the end of the year compare to the amounts in these accounts at the beginning of the year. You want to show the percentage increase or decrease in each account.

To enter and copy a formula, follow these steps:

1. If necessary, open your *ee1-p2challenge* workbook; then click the #3-% Change sheet tab.
2. Select cell D6, and enter a formula to compute the percentage change in Cash.
3. Check that the formula produces the correct % change results.
   The drop in Cash from $10,000 at 1/1/02 to $8,000 at 12/31/02 is a 20% decrease (a minus sign displays in front of 20.0% in cell D6).

If you have problems...

You want to know how the end-of-year $8,000 compares to having $10,000 in cash at the beginning of the year. The % change is calculated by finding the difference between the two amounts and dividing the result by the amount at the beginning of the year. Excel performs calculations within parentheses first. You need to be sure you find the difference between the two amounts before the division takes place. Use onscreen Help if you do not remember which math operator indicates division.

4. Correct the formula if necessary, and copy the formula down to compute the % change in the other three accounts.

5. Check that the copied formulas produce the correct % change results.

Accounts Receivable, for example, increased by 12.5%.

6. Save your changes to the *ee1-p2challenge* workbook.

4. Using the Auto Fill Options Button

You want to know more about Excel's AutoFill feature, including use of the Auto Fill Options button. Complete the following steps to enter dates in a variety of sequences:

1. If necessary, open your *ee1-p2challenge* workbook; then click the #4-Fill sheet tab.

2. Click cell A6, drag its fill handle down to cell A36, and release the mouse button.

Excel fills the range A7:A36 with dates that increment by one (from 1/1/2002 through 1/31/2002).

3. Click cell B6, drag its fill handle down to B28, and release the mouse button.

The Auto Fill Options button displays next to the fill handle of cell B28.

4. Display the Auto Fill Options drop-down list, and select Fill <u>W</u>eekdays.

The range B6:B28 is filled with dates representing weekdays only. For example, 1/4/2002 (a Friday) displays in cell B9 and 1/7/2002 (a Monday) displays in the next cell, B10.

5. Click cell C6, drag its fill handle down to C29, and use the appropriate Auto Fill Options button to enter a series of dates that increment by one month.

Check that each date in the series is the first day of a month. The series includes monthly dates for the years 2001 and 2002.

6. Repeat the process described in Step 5, and enter a series of dates in the range D6:D29, in which each date is the last day of a month.

7. Click cell E6, drag its fill handle down to E29, and use the appropriate Auto Fill Options button to enter a series of dates that increment by one year.

8. Check that each date in the series is the first day of a year. The series includes yearly dates for the years 2001 through 2024.

9. Repeat the process described in Step 7 and enter a series of dates in the range F6:F29, in which each date is the last day of a year.

10. Save your changes to the *ee1-p2challenge* workbook.

iscovery Zone

Discovery Zone exercises require advanced knowledge of topics presented in *Essentials* lessons, application of skills from multiple lessons, or self-directed learning of new skills.

Before beginning your first Project 2 Discovery Zone exercise, complete the following steps:

1. Open the file named *ee1-0204*, and immediately save it as `ee1-p2discovery`.

The workbook contains three sheets: an overview and two exercise sheets named #1-Signup and #2-Expenses.

2. Click the overview sheet to view the organization of the Project 2 Discovery Zone Exercises workbook.

Each exercise is independent of the others, so you may complete the exercises in any order. Be sure to save the workbook after completing each exercise. If you need a paper copy of the completed exercise, enter your name, centered in a header, before printing. Other print options have already been set to print compressed to one page and to display the filename, sheet name, and current date in a footer.

Be sure to save your changes and close the workbook if you need more than one work session to complete the desired exercises. Continue working on *ee1-p2discovery* instead of starting all over again in the original *ee1-0204* file.

1. Creating a Signup Sheet Using AutoFill to Enter Dates

Your organization seeks volunteers to work on Sundays during the year 2002—one person each week. You agreed to make a signup sheet to circulate at the next meeting. Initially, you thought you would make the sheet using a word-processing program, but then you remembered that Excel includes a feature to automatically fill a range with dates. Use this AutoFill feature to complete the #1-Signup sheet in your *ee1-p2discovery* workbook.

Suggestions: The signup sheet can fit on one page if you divide the dates into two columns—January through June dates in one column and July through December dates in the other. (There are 52 Sundays in the year 2002.) First, use AutoFill to fill down column A with Sunday dates for the entire year (before dragging the fill handle, give Excel a pattern to follow by highlighting the first two dates already provided). Then, move the July–December dates to column C, starting in row 5. Set the following print specifications: portrait orientation, 100% of normal size, and gridlines. Also, turn row and column headings off.

2. Modifying an Office Expenses Worksheet

It's July, and your supervisor has asked you to look into ways to reduce the expenses of running the office. Before you make any suggestions, you want a clear idea of what those office-related expenses were during the first six months of the year. You already started to develop an Excel worksheet to show individual expenses and totals for each month.

At this point, the worksheet contains only a few expense names (see the #2-Expenses sheet in your *ee1-p2discovery* workbook). Modify the worksheet in the following ways: Use AutoFill to enter the names of the months Jan through Jun across row 4. Change the order of expenses by putting those related to utilities (electricity, water, and phone) in adjacent cells in column A. Add at least three other expenses related to maintaining an office (insurance, cleaning, and so on). Insert a column between March and April, and enter a Qtr 1 label. Set up a column for Qtr 2 data to the right of the June data. Enter and copy formulas, as necessary, to complete the worksheet. Add sample data to test formula results.

Improving the Appearance of a Worksheet

Objectives

In this project, you learn how to

- ✔ Format Numbers
- ✔ Align Cell Contents
- ✔ Change Font and Font Size
- ✔ Apply Bold, Italic, and Underline
- ✔ Add Color
- ✔ Add Borders
- ✔ Use Format Painter
- ✔ Remove Formatting

Key terms in this project include

- ❑ border
- ❑ font
- ❑ format
- ❑ pattern
- ❑ point
- ❑ typeface

Why Would I Do This?

After you create a worksheet, you may want to format it so that it is more readable and attractive. When you **format** a worksheet, you apply attributes to cells that alter the display of cell contents. For example, you can format a worksheet by italicizing text and displaying a border around a cell or group of cells.

Visual Summary

Figure 3.1 shows the unformatted worksheet you will open for the first lesson.

	A	B	C	D	E	F	G	H	I	J	K
1	Glenn Lakes Golf Course										
2	Year 2002 Revenues										
3											
4		Qtr 1	Qtr 2	Qtr 3	Qtr 4	Annual					
5	Greens Fees	420000	385000	227000	362000	1394000					
6	Golf Lessons	98000	54800	61900	78200	292900					
7	Pro Shop Sales	55000	48600	35200	123400	262200					
8											
9	Total Revenue	573000	488400	324100	563600	1949100					
10											

Figure 3.1

The results of applying selected formatting options throughout the project are shown in Figure 3.2.

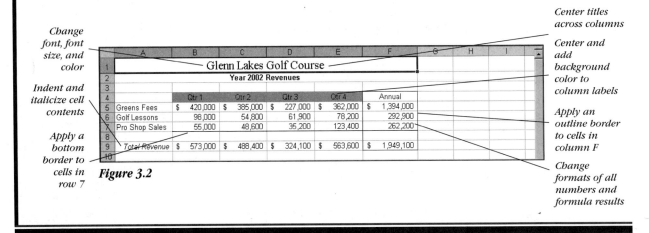

Change font, font size, and color

Indent and italicize cell contents

Apply a bottom border to cells in row 7

Center titles across columns

Center and add background color to column labels

Apply an outline border to cells in column F

Change formats of all numbers and formula results

Figure 3.2

Lesson 1: Formatting Numbers

When you enter a number or a formula into a cell, the entry may not appear as you hoped it would. You might type *5*, for example, but want it to look like *$5.00*. You could type the dollar sign, decimal point, and zeros; or you can have Excel automatically format the number for you. When you want to apply a standard format to a number, you format the cell in which the number is displayed.

In Excel, you can format numbers in many ways using the Number tab of the Format Cells dialog box (see Figure 3.3). You will usually format numbers as currency, percentages, or dates.

Excel provides toolbar buttons for three common number formats: Currency Style, Percent Style, and Comma Style. In this lesson, you use the Currency Style and Comma Style buttons on the toolbar to format the display of values in the *format* workbook. You also use a toolbar button to change the number of decimal places.

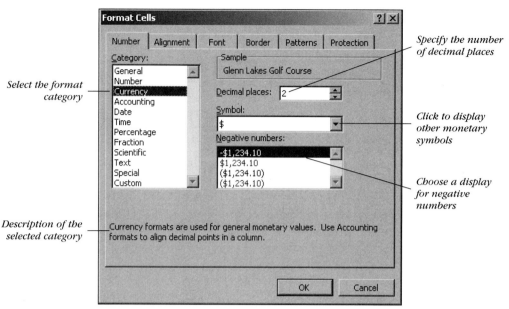

Select the format category

Specify the number of decimal places

Click to display other monetary symbols

Choose a display for negative numbers

Description of the selected category

Figure 3.3

To Format Numbers

❶ Open the file *ee1-0301* and save it as format.

❷ Select cells B5 through F5 in Sheet1.
You want to format the first row of numbers to display in a currency format.

❸ Click the Currency Style button on the Formatting toolbar.
The selected cells display the default currency format, as shown in Figure 3.4.

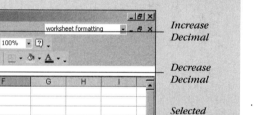

Currency Style

Percent Style

Comma Style

Increase Decimal

Decrease Decimal

Selected numbers formatted in currency style

Figure 3.4

❹ With cells B5:F5 still selected, click the Decrease Decimal button twice.
Each time you click the Decrease Decimal button, Excel removes one decimal place. Clicking the button twice causes the amounts in row 5 to appear with zero decimal places.

❺ Select cells B6:F7; then click the Comma Style button.

❻ Click the Decrease Decimal button twice.
The amounts for Golf Lessons and Pro Shop Sales in rows 6 and 7 display with commas to indicate thousands and zero decimal places.

(Continues)

To Format Numbers (Continued)

7 **Select cells B9:F9, click the Currency Style button, and click the Decrease Decimal button twice.**

The amounts for Total Revenue in row 9 display the Currency format with zero decimal places (see Figure 3.5, which shows the results of all changes in number formatting).

	A	B	C	D	E	F	G	H	I
1	Glenn Lakes Golf Course								
2	Year 2002 Revenues								
3									
4		Qtr 1	Qtr 2	Qtr 3	Qtr 4	Annual			
5	Greens Fees	$ 420,000	$ 385,000	$ 227,000	$ 362,000	$ 1,394,000			
6	Golf Lessons	98,000	54,800	61,900	78,200	292,900			
7	Pro Shop Sales	55,000	48,600	35,200	123,400	262,200			
8									
9	Total Revenue	$ 573,000	$ 488,400	$ 324,100	$ 563,600	$ 1,949,100			
10									

Figure 3.5

8 **Click the Save button in the toolbar.**
Excel saves your changes to the workbook named *format*. Keep the workbook open for the next lesson, or close the workbook and exit Excel.

To extend your knowledge...

Applying Number Formats

Excel rounds the display of values to fit the specified number of decimal places. For example, if you enter **235.75** in a cell that is set to display zero decimal places, the number *236* displays. However, the actual value stored in the cell—in this case, *235.75*—is used in any calculations.

When you apply any kind of formatting, you apply it to the worksheet cell, not to specific cell contents. This means that if you change the content of a cell, the formatting still applies. You can even format empty cells so that when data are entered, the data automatically appear with the correct format.

You can apply a Percent Style format as you enter the data. Simply type the number followed by a percent sign. For example, if you enter **12.5%** in an unformatted cell, Excel displays *12.50%*. If you'd rather use the Percent Style button on the toolbar, first enter the data as a decimal. For example, if you enter **.125** in an unformatted celll and click the Percent Style button, Excel displays *13%*. Use the Increase Decimal and Decrease Decimal buttons on the Formatting toolbar to change the number of decimal places displayed.

You may enter a number or formula and then find that the display is not consistent with the data. For example, suppose that you enter a formula to subtract an order date of 6/15/01 from a date shipped of 6/24/01. You want the number 9 to appear as the result of the formula, indicating the number of days it took to ship the order. Instead, you are likely to see *1/9/1900* (for January 9, 1900—the date represented by the number 9). In this case, the formula is correct; the display is not. To fix the display problem, apply a nondate format such as General or Comma to the problem cell.

Lesson 2: Aligning Cell Contents

When you enter data into a cell, text aligns with the left side of the cell; and numbers, dates, and times automatically align with the right side of the cell. You can change the alignment of data at any time. For instance, you may want to fine-tune the appearance of column headings by centering all the information in the column.

In this lesson, you use the Merge and Center toolbar button to center the worksheet title and subtitle across six columns. You also use toolbar buttons to center column headings within cells and to indent text in a cell (see Figure 3.6).

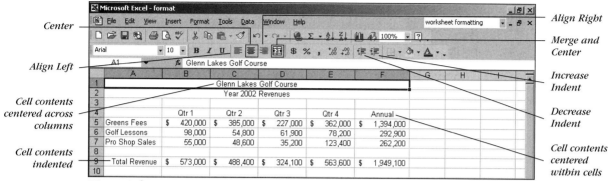

Figure 3.6

To Align Text

1 Open the workbook named *format*, if necessary, and select cells A1 through F1 in Sheet1.
You want the title in A1 centered across columns A through F.

2 Click the Merge and Center button on the toolbar.
Excel merges the selected cells into one cell, and centers the title *Glenn Lakes Golf Course* across worksheet data in columns A through F (refer to row 1 in Figure 3.6).

 If you have problems...
If you selected a range other than A1:F1, click the Merge and Center button again to separate the merged cells, and repeat Steps 1 and 2.

3 Select cells A2 through F2; then click the Merge and Center button.
Excel merges the selected cells into one cell, and centers the subtitle *Year 2002 Revenues* across columns A through F (refer to row 2 in Figure 3.6).

4 Select cells B4 through F4.
The range B4 through F4 contains the column headings you want to center.

5 Click the Center button on the toolbar.
Excel centers the *Qtr* and *Annual* labels (refer to row 4 in Figure 3.6).

6 Click cell A9.
The cell containing the label you want to indent is selected.

7 Click the Increase Indent button once.
Excel indents the *Total Revenue* label (refer to cell A9 in Figure 3.6).

8 Click the Save button in the toolbar.
Excel saves your changes to the workbook named *format*. Keep the workbook open for the next lesson, or close the workbook and exit Excel.

To extend your knowledge...

Other Alignment Options

Toolbar buttons are provided for only the six most common alignment options. You can access all alignment options by selecting F<u>o</u>rmat, C<u>e</u>lls and choosing the Alignment tab in the Format Cells dialog box (see Figure 3.7).

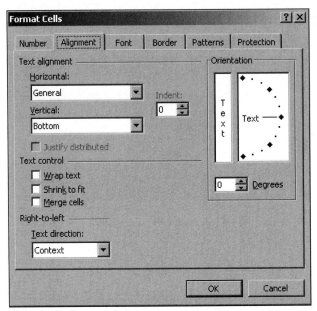

Figure 3.7

Several options in the *Text control* area of the Format Cells dialog box allow you to keep columns narrow and still display longer labels. Choose <u>*W*</u>*rap text* when you want to enter more than one line of text within a cell. As you type, the text automatically wraps to the next line in the cell. Choose *Shri<u>n</u>k to fit* if cell contents slightly exceed the current column width, and you want to display contents on one line without increasing column width.

Sometimes, a label describing data takes up more space than its associated data. For example, a column heading might be *Days to Ship*, and the data in cells below are comprised of no more than two characters (it assumes no more than 99 days to ship an order). To keep the column narrow, yet display the entire column heading, select settings in the *Orientation* section of the Format Cells dialog box. You can click an option to display each character below the previous one, drag a red marker to change the degrees of orientation, or enter the desired rotation in the <u>*D*</u>*egrees* text box.

Excel also supports aligning text vertically within a cell, such as at the top or centered rather than at the bottom.

Lesson 3: Changing Font and Font Size

You can dramatically improve the appearance of your worksheet by using different fonts. Used as a general term, ***font*** refers to the type style, type size, and type attributes that you apply to text and numbers. As a specific command in Excel, font refers to the ***typeface***—a style of print such as Arial, Courier, or Times New Roman. The default font in an Excel worksheet is Arial.

Type size is measured in points. A ***point*** is a unit of measurement used in printing and publishing to designate the height of type. There are roughly 72 points in an inch. The default type size in a worksheet is 10 points.

Toolbar buttons let you quickly apply a single formatting characteristic, such as a different font or font size. You can also change typeface, type size, and type attributes using the Font tab of the Format Cells dialog box, which enables you to preview and apply many formatting characteristics at one time.

In this lesson, you use toolbar buttons to change the font and font size of the worksheet title *Glenn Lakes Golf Course*, as shown in Figure 3.8.

Click to view available fonts

Selected font for the current cell

Selected font size for the current cell

Click to view available font sizes

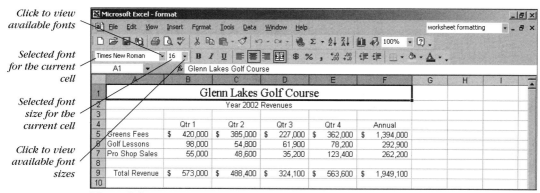

Figure 3.8

To Change Font and Font Size

① **Open the workbook named *format*, if necessary, and click cell A1 in Sheet1.**
The merged cells containing the title *Glenn Lakes Golf Course* are selected.

② **Click the down arrow to the right of the current font in the toolbar.**

③ **In the Font drop-down list, select Times New Roman.**
The typeface you want to apply to the active cell is selected. You might have to use the scroll arrows to scroll down through the list of fonts to get to Times New Roman.

④ **Click the down arrow to the right of the current font size in the toolbar.**

⑤ **In the Font Size drop-down list, select 16.**
The font size increases to 16 points. Notice that the row height automatically adjusts to accommodate the new font size.

⑥ **Check that the title in your worksheet reflects the changes in font and font size shown in Figure 3.8, and click the Save button in the toolbar.**
Excel saves your changes to the workbook named *format*. Keep the workbook open for the next lesson, or close the workbook and exit Excel.

To extend your knowledge...

Selecting Fonts

To quickly open the Format Cells dialog box, right-click the active cell and choose *Format Cells* from the shortcut menu. Click the Font tab to see additional font options. The fonts available in the Font list vary, depending on the software installed on your computer and the printer(s) you use.

To quickly scroll through the Font drop-down list, click the down arrow to the right of the current font style in the toolbar; then start typing the name of the font you want to apply. Excel locates the fonts alphabetically.

Lesson 4: Applying Bold, Italic, and Underline

You can use buttons on the toolbar to apply three common font attributes: **bold**, *italic*, and <u>underline</u>. To change attributes (called font styles in Excel), simply select the cells that you want to format and click the relevant button on the Formatting toolbar. To remove an attribute, click its button again.

In this lesson, you make bold the subtitle *Year 2002 Revenues*, and apply italic to the *Total Revenue* label, as shown in Figure 3.9.

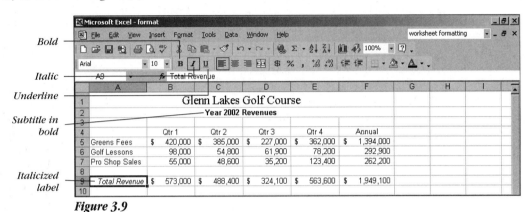

Figure 3.9

To Apply Bold and Italic

❶ **Open the workbook named *format*, if necessary, and click cell A2 in Sheet1.**
The merged cells containing the subtitle *Year 2002 Revenues* are selected.

❷ **Click the Bold button in the toolbar.**

❸ **Click cell A9.**
The cell containing the label *Total Revenue* is selected.

❹ **Click the Italic button in the toolbar.**

❺ **Check that the subtitle in cell A2 and the label in cell A9 reflect the changes in font style shown in Figure 3.9, and click the Save button in the Standard toolbar.**
Excel saves your changes to the workbook named *format*. Keep the workbook open for the next lesson, or close the workbook and exit Excel.

To extend your knowledge...

Applying Font Formats

The Font tab in the Format Cells dialog box includes a Bold Italic option. You can also apply color, and select among a variety of underline styles (Single, Double, Single Accounting, Double Accounting) and special effects (Strikethrough, Superscript, Subscript).

You can also apply font styles to individual characters within a cell, rather than the entire cell's contents. To do so, double-click the cell, drag to select the characters you want to format, apply the format, and press ⏎Enter).

Lesson 5: Adding Color

Selective use of color can enhance the appearance of a worksheet. You can apply color to cell contents, to the background of a cell, or to a border surrounding cells. In this lesson, you display the worksheet title in blue and apply a green background to the column headings for quarters by using the buttons shown in Figure 3.10.

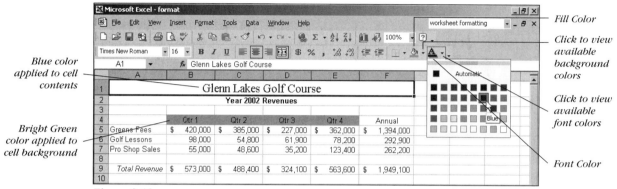

Figure 3.10

To Add Color

1 **Open the workbook named** *format*, **if necessary, and click cell A1 in Sheet1.**
The merged cells that contain the title *Glenn Lakes Golf Course* are selected.

2 **Click the down arrow to the right of the Font Color button in the toolbar.**
A palette of 40 colors appears. If you position the mouse pointer on a color square and pause, you see the name assigned to that color.

3 **Click the square named Blue in the Font Color palette (refer to Figure 3.10).**
The title *Glenn Lakes Golf Course* displays in blue.

[?] ## If you have problems...

If the background instead of the text displays in blue, you used Fill Color instead of Font Color. Click the Undo button in the toolbar to reverse the incorrect action and repeat steps 2 and 3.

---

4 **Select cells B4 through E4.**
The column headings for quarters 1 through 4 are selected.

5 **Click the down arrow to the right of the Fill Color button in the toolbar.**
A palette of 40 colors appears.

6 **Click the square named Bright Green in the Fill color palette.**
The backgrounds of cells B4 through E4 display in bright green (refer to Figure 3.10).

7 **Click the Save button in the toolbar.**
Excel saves your changes to the workbook named *format*. Keep the workbook open for the next lesson, or close the workbook and exit Excel.

To extend your knowledge...

Removing Color

You can remove color applied to text by selecting the text, clicking the down arrow next to the Font Color button, and selecting Automatic at the top of the color palette.

You can remove a color background by selecting the cell(s), clicking the down arrow next to the Fill Color button, and selecting No Fill at the top of the color palette.

Applying Patterns

You can draw attention to selected worksheet cells by shading them with a pattern. A ***pattern*** repeats an effect such as a horizontal, vertical, or diagonal stripe. To apply a pattern, select the Patterns tab in the Format Cells dialog box, and display the Pattern drop-down list. Choose one of 18 predefined settings that include crosshatch and stripe patterns, as well as various percentages of gray. The default pattern color is black, but you can select from a palette of colors.

Color Concerns in Printed Worksheets

You can apply more than one color setting to a cell, such as blue text, yellow background, and red border. However, overuse of color may be distracting. Also, color may be an effective enhancement when viewing a worksheet onscreen, but its use can produce printed output that is hard to read, especially if you are not printing on a color printer. For best results when printing, keep the choices of colors and patterns simple.

Lesson 6: Adding Borders

A ***border*** is a solid or dashed line applied to one or more sides of a cell or range of cells. You can use a border as a divider between cell entries. Selective use of borders can also help to focus a user's attention on a specific section of a worksheet.

You can use the Borders button on the toolbar to select among 12 common border styles, or you can draw a border. Additional options—including one to apply color to a border—are available through the Borders tab of the Format Cells dialog box.

In this lesson, you set up two borders (see Figure 3.11)—one using the toolbar and the other using the Format Cells dialog box.

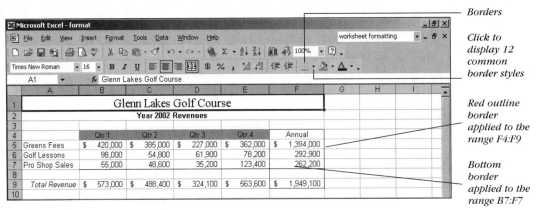

Figure 3.11

To Add a Border

① **Open the workbook named *format*, if necessary, and select the range B7:F7 in Sheet1.**
The cells containing numbers and a formula related to *Pro Shop Sales* are selected.

② **Click the down arrow to the right of the Borders button in the toolbar.**
A palette of 12 border styles appears. You can also select an option to draw a border.

③ **Position the mouse pointer on the second border style in the first row—the style named Bottom Border (see Figure 3.12).**

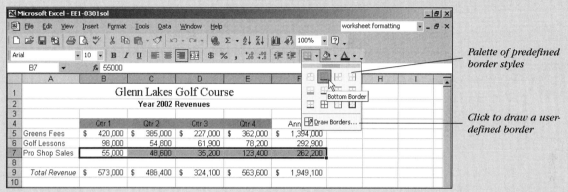

Figure 3.12

④ **Click the border style named Bottom Border.**
Excel applies a solid-black single-line border to the bottom edges of the selected cells (refer to row 7 in Figure 3.11).

⑤ **Select cells F4 through F9.**

⑥ **Choose Format, Cells.**
The Format Cells dialog box displays.

⑦ **Click the Border tab.**

⑧ **Click the down arrow to the right of the Color box, and choose Red.**
The selected color appears in the color window (see Figure 3.13).

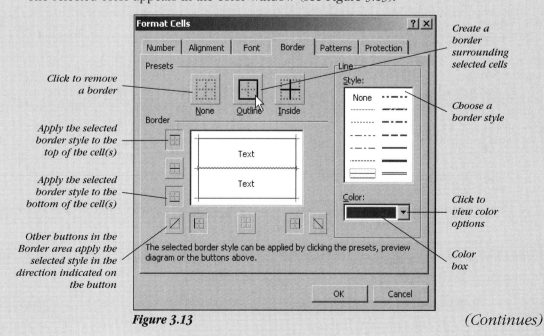

Figure 3.13

(Continues)

To Add a Border (Continued)

9 Click the <u>O</u>utline button in the Presets area (marked by the mouse pointer in Figure 3.13), and click OK.

10 Deselect the range and check that the borders applied to your worksheet match those shown in Figure 3.11.

11 Make changes, if necessary; then click the Save button in the toolbar.
Excel saves your changes to the workbook named *format*. Keep the workbook open for the next lesson, or close the workbook and exit Excel.

To extend your knowledge...

Avoiding Style and Color Problems with Borders

The order in which you select options from the Border tab in the Format Cells dialog box is important. If you select a border style and/or border color after selecting the border's position, Excel ignores the style and color settings.

Drawing and Erasing Borders Quickly

You can click the down arrow by the Borders button on the Formatting toolbar and select the <u>D</u>raw Borders option to draw a new border or erase an existing one. The pointer changes to a pencil, and the Borders toolbar displays with four buttons: Draw Border, Erase Border, Line Style, and Line Color.

To draw an outline border, follow these steps: select a different line style and/or a color on the Borders toolbar if desired, click in the worksheet where you want the upper-left corner of the border to appear, drag right and down to expand the border to include more cells as needed, and click the Close button on the Borders toolbar to turn off drawing. If you prefer a grid effect—showing borders around each cell in the drawn range—over an outline effect, click the down arrow by the Draw Border button, and select <u>D</u>raw Border Grid before you begin drawing.

To erase a border without using the Border tab in the Format Cells dialog box, click the down arrow by the Borders button on the Formatting toolbar, select the Draw Borders option, and click the Erase Border button (the pointer changes to an eraser). Drag the pointer over the borderlines you want to erase, and click the Close button on the Borders toolbar to turn off erasing.

Lesson 7: Using Format Painter

Excel provides a Format Painter button that you can use to copy formatting applied to worksheet cells. This feature makes it possible to apply existing formats without opening dialog boxes or making multiple selections from toolbars. Use this feature now to copy the color and alignment settings for the quarterly column headings to the row descriptions of revenue sources (see Figure 3.14).

Copied formats: center alignment and bright green fill color —

	A	B	C	D	E	F	G	H	I
1			Glenn Lakes Golf Course						
2			Year 2002 Revenues						
3									
4			Qtr 1	Qtr 2	Qtr 3	Qtr 4	Annual		
5	Greens Fees	$	420,000	$ 385,000	$ 227,000	$ 362,000	$ 1,394,000		
6	Golf Lessons		98,000	54,800	61,900	78,200	292,900		
7	Pro Shop Sales		55,000	48,600	35,200	123,400	262,200		
8									
9	Total Revenue	$	573,000	$ 488,400	$ 324,100	$ 563,600	$ 1,949,100		
10									

Figure 3.14

To Copy Formats Using Format Painter

❶ Open the *format* workbook, if necessary, and click cell B4 in Sheet1.
A cell containing the formats you want to copy is selected.

❷ Click the Format Painter button in the toolbar.
A flashing dotted line appears around the selected cell (see Figure 3.15).

Format Painter button

Format Painter is active

Figure 3.15

❸ Move the mouse pointer toward cell A5.
The pointer changes to a white block cross. A paintbrush displays to the right of the cross.

❹ Select cells A5 through A7, release the mouse button, and deselect the range.
Excel applies center alignment and a bright green fill color to the specified cells in column A.

❺ Save your changes to the *format* workbook.
Keep the workbook open for the last lesson in this project, or close the workbook and exit Excel.

To extend your knowledge...

Copying Formats to Multiple Locations

If you single-click the Format Painter button to start a copy operation, the feature automatically turns off as soon as you select the target cell or range. If you want to copy formatting to more than one location, double-click the Format Painter button to start the copy. The feature remains active until you click the Format Painter button again.

Copying Column Widths

You can use Format Painter to copy a column width. Select the heading of a column that is already set to the desired width, click the Format Painter button, and then click the heading of the column you want to change.

Lesson 8: Removing Formatting

The quickest way to remove all applied formats is to select the cell(s) and choose Edit, Clear, Formats. If you want to remove some, but not all, of the formats applied to a cell, you must remove the effects one at a time. In most cases, you start the process to apply the format and then select an option to restore the default setting (such as Automatic to remove color or None to remove a border). Some effects can be removed by choosing a related button on the toolbar, such as Left Align to remove centering, Decrease Indent to remove indenting, or one of the decimal buttons to adjust number of decimal places.

In this lesson, you remove one format (a border) and then remove multiple formats with a single command (centering and fill color).

To Remove Formatting

1 **Open the *format* workbook, if necessary, and select the range F4:F9 on Sheet1.**
The cells surrounded with a red border are selected.

2 **Choose F*o*rmat, C*e*lls; then select the Border tab.**

3 **Click None in the Presets area and then click OK.**
Excel removes the single-line red border surrounding the range F4:F9. Now, remove multiple formats with a single command.

4 **Select the range A5:A7; then choose E*d*it, Cle*a*r.**
Four options display on the Cle*a*r menu (see Figure 3.16). The first option removes both contents and formats. Choose the second option to remove only formats.

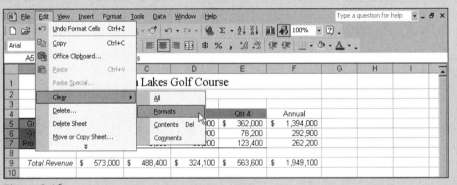

Figure 3.16

5 **Choose F*o*rmats, and click cell A1.**
Excel removes all current formats in the range A5:A7, but keeps the cell contents.

6 **Save your changes and close the *format* workbook.**
This concludes Project 3. Continue with end-of-project activities, or exit Excel.

Summary

In this project, you learned how to apply the most basic formatting options. Your experiences focused primarily on using toolbar buttons to apply effects to the selected cell(s) quickly. You formatted numbers in currency and comma styles, centered cell contents across columns and within cells, indented text, changed font style, increased font size, applied bold and italics, added color and borders, copied formats using Format Painter, and removed formats.

You can extend your learning by practicing variations of techniques presented in the lessons. Experiment with different number formats, including date and percent. Explore different options in the Format Cells dialog box, such as discovering the difference between Double underline and Double Accounting underline. Use onscreen Help to get information; then try out Excel's AutoFormat and Conditional Formatting features.

Checking Concepts and Terms

Multiple Choice

Circle the letter of the correct answer for each of the following.

1. Which of the following is a font style, as opposed to a typeface? [L3]

   a. Italic

   b. Times New Roman

   c. Arial

   d. Courier

2. Which of the following number formats cannot be applied using a toolbar button? [L1]

   a. currency

   b. percent

   c. date

   d. comma

3. Which of the following is not a way in which color can be used to enhance a worksheet? [L5]

   a. To display the contents of cells in color.

   b. To fill cells with background color.

   c. To apply a color to a border.

   d. All of the above describe possible color enhancements.

4. Which of the following best describes the effect(s) of increasing font size? [L3]

   a. Row height automatically adjusts, but column width does not.

   b. Column width automatically adjusts, but row height does not.

   c. Both row height and column width automatically adjust.

   d. Neither row height nor column width automatically adjusts.

5. Which of the following is/are true about formatting in Excel? [L1 and L3]

   a. When you apply formatting, it applies to the worksheet cell—not to the text, number, or formula entered in the cell.

   b. A 36-point font size produces characters that are approximately one-half inch high.

   c. Both a and b.

   d. Neither a nor b.

Discussion

1. You enter a number or formula into a cell, and the results do not display correctly. For example, you expect to see the number 5, but it displays as *500%*. What might have caused the unexpected results? How would you fix the display problem? [L1]

2. You can specify the size and style of font applied to cells in a worksheet. What is the approximate height, in inches, of an 18-, 36-, and 54-point font, respectively? Describe three reasons to apply a point-size change to selected cells in a worksheet. [L3]

3. Through the Number tab of the Format Cells dialog box, you can apply a variety of number formats that are not assigned to a toolbar button (refer to the Category list in Figure 3.3). Describe the options available when applying a Currency format through the Format Cells dialog box as opposed to an Accounting format. [L1]

Skill Drill

Skill Drills reinforce project skills. Each skill reinforced is the same, or nearly the same, as a skill presented in the lessons. Detailed instructions are provided in a step-by-step format.

Before beginning your first Project 3 Skill Drill exercise, complete the following steps:

1. Open the file named *ee1-0302* and immediately save it as `ee1-p3drill`.
   The Community Volunteer Corps (CVC) workbook contains eight sheets: an overview, and exercise sheets named #1-Format, #2-Alignment, #3-Fonts, #4-Font Style, #5-Color, #6-Border, and #7-Remove.
2. Click the Overview sheet to view the organization of the Project 3 Skill Drill Exercises workbook.

Each exercise is independent of the others, so you may complete the exercises in any order. Be sure to save the workbook after completing each exercise. If you need a paper copy of the completed exercise, enter your name, centered in a header, before printing. Other print options have already been set to print compressed to one page and to display the filename, sheet name, and current date in a footer.

If you need more than one work session to complete the desired exercises, continue working on *ee1-p3drill* instead of starting over again in the original *ee1-0302* file.

1. Formatting Numbers

Having completed a simple worksheet to summarize volunteer hours at the Community Volunteer Corps, you decide to add some enhancements to make the data more readable. You want to display volunteer hours without decimal places using the comma as a thousands separator. You also realize that the date in the worksheet doesn't display in a common date format. You want the date represented by the number to display in the form *mm/dd/yyyy* (for example, *12/25/2001*).

To make the desired formatting changes, follow these steps:

1. If necessary, open the *ee1-p3drill* workbook; then click the sheet tab named #1-Format.
2. Select the range B9:F12.
3. Click the Comma Style button on the toolbar.
4. Click the Decrease Decimal button twice.
5. Select cell F5.
6. Choose F̲ormat, C̲ells and click the Number tab.
7. Select the Date category.
8. Select the *mm/dd/yyyy* format (**3/14/2001**) near the bottom of the list of date formats, and click OK.
9. Save your changes to the *ee1-p3drill* workbook.

2. Aligning Cell Contents

Aligning the contents of cells can improve the readability of a worksheet. You decided to right-align the *Qtr* and *Annual* column headings in the Community Volunteer Corps worksheet so they line up with the numeric data below. You also want to indent the *Total Hours* label so it is easier to distinguish it from other row headings.

To make alignment changes to your worksheet, follow these steps:

1. If necessary, open the *ee1-p3drill* workbook; then click the sheet tab named #2-Alignment.
2. Select range B8:F8.

3. Click the Align Right button.

4. Select cell A12.

5. Click the Increase Indent button twice.

6. Save your changes to the *ee1-p3drill* workbook.

3. Changing Font and Font Size

To draw the reader's attention to the title of the worksheet, you plan to display the title in a CG Times 14pt font.

To change font and font size, follow these steps:

1. If necessary, open the *ee1-p3drill* workbook; then click the sheet tab named #3-Fonts.

2. Select cell A4.

3. Click the down arrow to the right of the current font displayed in the toolbar.

4. Scroll through the list of available fonts, and select *CG Times*.

   If your font options do not include CG Times, select another font of your choice.

5. Click the down arrow to the right of the current font size displayed in the toolbar, and select *14*.

6. Save your changes to the *ee1-p3drill* workbook.

4. Applying Bold and Italic

You know that you can emphasize important data such as totals by using Bold and Italic font styles. You decide to italicize all subtotals and make bold the annual total in your Community Volunteer Corps workbook.

To apply bold and italic font styles, follow these steps:

1. If necessary, open the *ee1-p3drill* workbook; then click the sheet tab named #4-Font Style.

2. Select cells B12:E12, hold down Ctrl, and select cells F9:F11.

3. Click the Italic button in the toolbar.

4. Select cell F12, and click the Bold button in the toolbar.

5. Save your changes to the *ee1-p3drill* workbook.

5. Adding Color

You decide to focus a viewer's attention by adding color to your Community Volunteer Corps workbook two ways. You plan to change the color of the title text, and add background color to column headings.

To apply color to the worksheet, follow these steps:

1. If necessary, open the *ee1-p3drill* workbook; then click the sheet tab named #5-Color.

2. Select cell A4.

3. Click the down arrow to the right of the Font Color button on the toolbar.

4. Click Red on the Font Color palette.

5. Select the range B8:F8.

6. Click the down arrow to the right of the Fill Color button on the toolbar.

7. Click Light Green on the Fill Color palette.

8. Save your changes to the *ee1-p3drill* workbook.

6. Adding Borders

To enhance the appearance of your worksheet by separating data from labels and totals, you decide to add a border around cells containing volunteer hours.

To add a gold, double-line border, follow these steps:

1. If necessary, open the *ee1-p3drill* workbook; then click the sheet tab named #6-Border.

2. Select the range B9:E11.

3. Choose Format, Cells and select the Border tab in the Format Cells dialog box.

4. Select the double-line style in the Style list.

5. Display the drop-down palette of colors, and select *Gold*.

6. Click Outline in the Presets area, and click OK.

7. Save your changes to the *ee1-p3drill* workbook.

7. Removing Formats

You have applied several formats to the Community Volunteer Corps worksheet, and now you want to remove one or more of them. You decide that you don't like the underline effect you applied to offset data from total hours. You also plan to remove all formatting applied to the names of volunteer organizations.

To remove formats, follow these steps:

1. If necessary, open the *ee1-p3drill* workbook; then click the sheet tab named #7-Remove.

2. Select the range B11:F11.

3. Choose Format, Cells and select the Font tab in the Format Cells dialog box.

4. Click the down arrow at the right end of the Underline window, select *None* from the list of Underline options, and click OK.

5. Select the range A9:A11, which contains 12-point right-aligned labels with a light green background.

6. Choose Edit, Clear, Formats.

7. Save your changes to the *ee1-p3drill workbook.*

Challenge

Challenge exercises expand on or are somewhat related to skills presented in the lessons. Each exercise provides a brief narrative introduction, followed by instructions in a numbered-step format that are not as detailed as those in the Skill Drill section.

Before beginning your first Project 3 Challenge exercise, complete the following steps:

1. Open the file named *ee1-0303* and immediately save it as `ee1-p3challenge`.

The Flowers Your Way (FYW) workbook contains five sheets: an overview and exercise sheets named #1-Format, #2-Indent, #3-Pattern, and #4-Compare.

2. Click the Overview sheet to view the organization of the Project 3 Challenge Exercises workbook.

Each exercise is independent of the others, so you may complete the exercises in any order. Be sure to save the workbook after completing each exercise. If you need a paper copy of the completed exercise, enter your name, centered in a header, before printing. Other print options have already been set to print compressed to one page and to display the filename, sheet name, and current date in a footer.

If you need more than one work session to complete the desired exercises, continue working on *ee1-p3challenge* instead of starting over again on the original *ee1-0303* file.

1. Formatting Numbers and Dates

You have received the five-year trend analysis for Flowers Your Way, and it is now your job to improve the appearance of the worksheet for the next meeting of the managers. You don't like the formatting someone else applied. You decide to correct the date format and remove other formatting (but not the data).

To remove formatting and change the date format, follow these steps:

1. If necessary, open your *ee1-p3challenge* workbook; then click the sheet tab named #1-Format.
2. Select the cell range A9:F24.
3. Choose an option on the <u>E</u>dit menu to remove all formatting in the selected range (don't remove contents).

If you have problems...

If you accidentally clear the contents of the range, use Undo to reverse the effects and try again.

4. Select cell E6, which contains a number that displays in a Comma format with two decimal places instead of as a date.
5. Apply the long date format (in the form **March 14, 2001**) to cell E6.
   Recall that dates are numbers, and when ####### appears in a cell, it means that cell contents are too long to display in the cell.
6. Display the full date by centering the contents of cell E6 across two cells, E6 and F6.
7. Apply the Comma Style (zero decimal places) to the *Total Sales* amounts in row 24.
8. Save your changes to the *ee1-p3challenge* workbook.

2. Indenting Cell Contents

As you look for ways to improve the readability of the Flowers Your Way worksheet, you decide to offset each occurrence of the labels *Corporate* and *Individual* a few characters from the left edge of their respective cells. You decide to indent even further the labels describing totals for each of the three sources of sales (*In-Store*, *Phone/Fax*, and the *Web*).

You want to apply these changes as quickly and efficiently as possible. Therefore, you plan to use a combination of selecting nonadjacent cells and clicking the Increase Indent button once or twice.

To apply indenting to multiple, nonadjacent cells, follow these steps:

1. If necessary, open your *ee1-p3challenge* workbook; then click the sheet tab named #2-Indent.
2. Hold down the Ctrl key, and select the following cell ranges: A10:A11, A15:A16, and A20:A21.
3. Click the Increase Indent toolbar button once.
4. Select the nonadjacent cells labeling the totals for the three sources of sales (cells A12, A17, and A22), and double-indent cell contents.
5. Save your changes to the *ee1-p3challenge* workbook.

3. Applying a Pattern Instead of a Color

You know how to apply a color background to a cell or range of cells using the Fill Color button on the toolbar. You also know that additional options for shading cells can be found on the Font tab of the Format Cells dialog box. Assume that you do not have access to a color printer, and experiment with applying a black and white pattern instead of color to enhance the appearance of printed output.

To apply a pattern, follow these steps:

1. If necessary, open your *ee1-p3challenge* workbook; then click the sheet tab named #3-Pattern.
2. Select the column headings and data for years *1998*, *2000*, and *2002* (the ranges B8:B24, D8:D24, and F8:F24).
3. Display the Patterns tab in the Format Cells dialog box.
4. Display the pattern options by clicking the arrow at the right end of the <u>P</u>attern box located in the lower-left corner of the dialog box.

5. Move the mouse pointer back and forth over the eighteen options at the top of the pattern drop-down list (the first three rows, six samples per row).

Resting the mouse pointer on a sample displays its description, such as 6.25% Gray for the upper-right sample.

6. Select 12.5% Gray; then click OK.

7. Deselect the cells to view the results; then look at the pattern effect using Print Preview.

8. Print the worksheet (optional).

You will probably find that the pattern effect is much clearer on printed output than it appeared to be onscreen.

9. Save your changes to the *ee1-p3challenge* workbook.

4. Comparing Number Formats

You know that you can apply currency, comma, and percentage formats using buttons on the Formatting toolbar. However, you plan to use a variety of other number formats in your worksheets. To practice applying other number formats, follow these steps:

1. If necessary, open your *ee1-p3challenge* workbook; then click the sheet tab named #4-Compare.

2. Read the format description in cell A4, and apply that format to cell B4 using the appropriate toolbar button.

3. Read the format description in cell A7, and apply that format to cell B7 using the appropriate toolbar buttons.

4. Use the Number tab on the Format Cells dialog box to apply all remaining formats described in column A.

The descriptive labels in blue (cells A3, A16, and A22) indicate the appropriate category. Display the $ sign drop-down list to view options other than the United States dollar sign.

5. Save your changes to the *ee1-p3challenge workbook*.

Discovery Zone

Discovery Zone exercises require advanced knowledge of topics presented in *Essentials* lessons, application of skills from multiple lessons, or self-directed learning of new skills.

Before beginning your first Project 3 Discovery Zone exercise, complete the following steps:

1. Open the file named *ee1-0304*, and immediately save it as **ee1-p3discovery**.

2. The *ee1-p3discovery* workbook contains four sheets: an overview and three exercise sheets named #1-AutoFormat, #2-Text Orientation, and #3-Borders.

3. Click the Overview sheet to view the organization of the Project 3 Discovery Zone Exercises workbook.

Each exercise is independent of the others, so you may complete the exercises in any order. Be sure to save the workbook after completing each exercise. If you need a paper copy of the completed exercise, enter your name, centered in a header, before printing. Other print options have already been set to print compressed to one page and to display the filename, sheet name, and current date in a footer.

If you need more than one work session to complete the desired exercises, continue working on *ee1-p3discovery* instead of starting over again on the original *ee1-0304* file.

1. Using AutoFormat to Improve the Appearance of a List

You are looking for ways to enhance the appearance of the Telemarketing Sales data for Flowers Your Way, Inc. You have heard about a feature called AutoFormat, which enables you to choose among a variety of predefined formats, and now you want to try it out.

Before you begin, use onscreen Help to learn how to apply an AutoFormat. When you are ready, select an AutoFormat for the data in the range A5:F16 on the sheet named #1-AutoFormat in your *ee1-p3discovery* workbook. Adjust column widths, as necessary. Undo the initial AutoFormat, and experiment with applying number formats before and after applying an AutoFormat. Why would it be best to apply a number format, such as Comma, before applying an AutoFormat? Before you save your final version, apply some of the other enhancements you learned in Project 3.

2. Changing Text Orientation of Column Headings

You have an idea in mind of how to align column headings, as shown in Figure 3.17.

	A	B	C	D	E	F
1	Project 3 Discovery Zone: Changing Text Orientation of Column Headings					
2						
3	Flowers Your Way					
4	5-year Trend Analysis of Sales (in thousands of U.S. dollars)					
5						
6				As of:	1/15/03	
7						
8		1998	1999	2000	2001	2002
9	In-Store Sales					
10	Corporate	108	111	96	81	58
11	Individual	321	371	305	330	319
12	Total In-Store	429	482	401	411	377
13						
14	Phone/Fax Sales					
15	Corporate	450	425	510	452	215
16	Individual	225	229	241	247	252
17	Total Phone/Fax	675	654	751	699	467
18						
19	Web Sales					
20	Corporate	57	65	89	271	502
21	Individual	11	14	17	48	112
22	Total Web	68	79	106	319	614
23						
24	Total Sales	1172	1215	1258	1429	1458

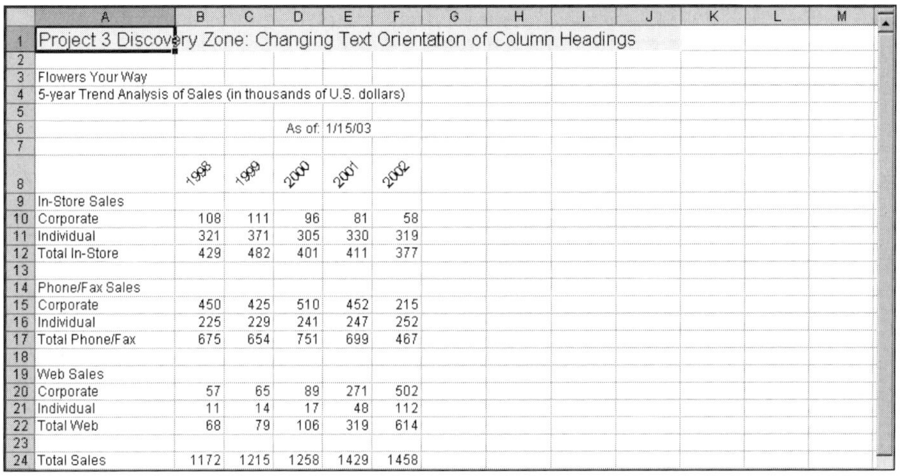

Figure 3.17

Learn all you can about changing the orientation of text using onscreen Help. Also, study the orientation options on the Alignment tab of the Format Cells dialog box. When you are ready, modify the worksheet named #2-Text Orientation in your *ee1-p3discovery* workbook to include the text orientation shown in row 8 in Figure 3.17. After making the orientation change, narrow columns B through F as much as possible while still displaying the year labels in row 8.

3. Creating and Erasing Borders Using the Borders Toolbar

You understand that buttons on the Borders toolbar allow you to create an outline or grid border and remove borders without opening the Format Cells dialog box. Use that toolbar now to modify the worksheet named #3-Borders in your *ee1-p3discovery* workbook.

Use the Erase Border button on the Borders toolbar to remove the dashed-line border surrounding the labels in rows 5 through 7. The mouse pointer changes to an eraser when the Erase Border button is active.

Use the Draw Border button to draw a blue double-line outline border surrounding the labels and data in the range B10:E15. The mouse pointer changes to a pencil when the Draw Border feature is active. Clicking either button activates the associated feature. Clicking it again turns the feature off.

You can display the Borders toolbar two ways: using menus or the Borders button on the toolbar. If you choose View, Toolbars and select Borders, the toolbar displays, but the draw and erase features are not active until you click the associated button. If you display the Borders button drop-down list and select Draw Borders, the toolbar displays and Draw Border is already turned on.

Entering Formulas in Well-Designed Worksheets

Objectives

In this project, you learn how to

✔ Work with Operators and Order of Precedence

✔ Use Type-and-Point to Enter Formulas

✔ Compare Absolute and Relative Cell References

✔ Create and Copy Formulas with Absolute or Relative Cell References

✔ Freeze and Split the Worksheet Display

✔ Hide and Unhide Rows and Columns

✔ Display Formulas Instead of Formula Results

✔ Use Save As to Change Filename, File Type, or Storage Location

Key terms in this project include

❑ comparison operator

❑ concatenation operator

❑ order of precedence

❑ reference operator

Why Would I Do This?

In previous projects, you created a simple worksheet containing one formula. By copying that formula, you were able to expand the worksheet quickly. Through those experiences, you acquired the basic skills needed to develop larger and more complex worksheets.

Multiple formulas add complexity to a worksheet. Larger worksheets exceed the viewing area on the screen and require multiple-page printouts. Excel provides a variety of ways to create and copy formulas, display formulas, and view more than one area of a worksheet at a time.

Visual Summary

You should plan the layout of each worksheet in a workbook before you begin to enter constants and formulas. Good worksheet design includes explanations about purpose and revisions, separate cells for data subject to change, and instructions to users.

In this project, you create the worksheet shown in Figure 4.1. The worksheet contains monthly and annual data.

Purpose of the worksheet

Formulas calculate the amounts in rows 7, 8, 10 and 13

A separate cell for data that is subject to change

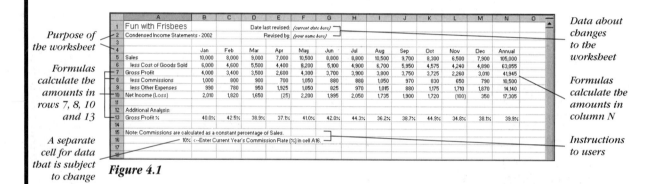

Data about changes to the worksheet

Formulas calculate the amounts in column N

Instructions to users

Figure 4.1

Lesson 1: Working with Operators and Order of Precedence

Let's review what you know about calculations from Projects 1 and 2. The terms *formula* and *arithmetic operator* were introduced in Project 1. You used the arithmetic operator (+) in a formula to add the contents of two cells.

The terms *AutoSum* and *function* were introduced in Project 2. In that project, you used AutoSum to enter the function =SUM(B5:E5). The colon (:) connected the first and last cells of the range to be summed. The colon is an example of a **reference operator**, which is used to combine cell references in calculations.

Excel provides two other types of operators: comparison and concatenation. A **comparison operator** is used to test the relationship between two items, such as finding out whether the items are equal, or if one is greater than the other. A **concatenation operator** joins one or more text entries to form a single entry.

This lesson provides an in-depth look at operators and the order in which Excel performs calculations—sometimes referred to as the ***order of precedence***. For example, you learn that multiplication and division take place before addition and subtraction. If you understand the order of precedence and how to modify that order by using parentheses, you have the minimum skills required to create and edit formulas and functions.

To Work with Operators and Order of Precedence

❶ Open the file *ee1-0401*, and save it as `frisbees`.

❷ Click the sheet tab named Operators.
The Operators worksheet displays four categories of operators in blue: arithmetic, comparison, text concatenation, and reference (see Figure 4.2). The symbol to type for each operator appears in red.

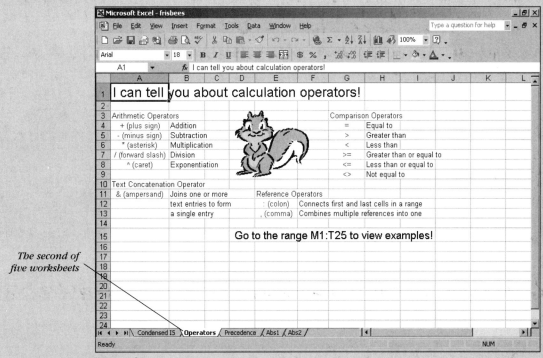

The second of five worksheets

Figure 4.2

❸ After studying the categories of operators, display columns M through T on the screen, starting with row 1.
This area of the worksheet contains one example for each operator category (see Figure 4.3). An arrow points to each cell that contains an operator in the formula.

(Continues)

To Work with Operators and Order of Precedence (Continued)

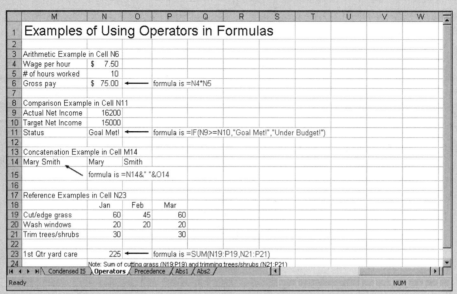

Figure 4.3

④ Click cell N6.

A formula that contains the arithmetic operator for multiplication (*) appears in the formula bar.

⑤ Click cell N11.

An IF function that contains the comparison operator for greater than or equal to (>=) appears in the formula bar. The operator tests whether the contents of cell N9 (*Actual Net Income*) are greater than or equal to the contents of cell N10 (*Target Net Income*); and displays one of two messages, depending on whether the comparison is true or false. You work with IF functions in Project 5, "Working with Functions."

⑥ Click cell M14.

A formula that contains the concatenate operator (&) appears in the formula bar. The formula joins the contents of cells N14 and O14, and adds a space between the first and last names. Quotation marks surround literal text in a formula. Literal text is text that does not change—in this case, the blank space.

⑦ Click cell N23.

A formula that contains the reference operators colon (:) and comma (,) appears in the formula bar. The colon marks the beginning and ending cells in a range; the comma separates the ranges in the formula.

⑧ Click the sheet tab named Precedence.

A text box, which contains the question *What is 5 plus 3 times 2?* appears near the top of the worksheet. How would you answer the question?

⑨ Click cell D8.

The formula =5+3*2 appears in the formula bar; the formula result displays in cell D8. Excel first multiplies 3*2 and then adds the result (6) to the number 5.

⑩ Click cell D12.

The formula =(5+3)*2 appears in the formula bar; the formula result displays in cell D12. Operations within parentheses take precedence over those not encased in parentheses. In this case, Excel first adds the numbers 5 and 3; then multiplies the result (8) by 2.

To Work with Operators and Order of Precedence

⑪ After studying the two examples, display columns M through R on the screen, starting with row 1.

This area of the worksheet lists the order of Excel operations in formulas (see Figure 4.4). Keep this order in mind as you construct your own formulas.

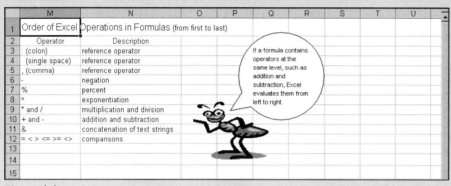

Figure 4.4

This concludes the overview of operators and order of calculations. Now that you have a better understanding of operators and order of calculations, you are ready to enter the five formulas needed to complete the condensed income statements for Fun with Frisbees. Keep the *frisbees* workbook open for the next lesson, or close the workbook and exit Excel.

Lesson 2: Using Type-and-Point to Enter Formulas

You can complete the design of the Condensed IS worksheet for Fun with Frisbees by entering five formulas and copying them to related cells. One of the formulas involves addition—computing annual sales as the sum of sales for each month. Calculations performed by the other formulas include subtraction, multiplication, and division.

You can easily create a basic formula by typing an equation into a cell, as you did in Project 1 to add the contents of two cells. You can also enter a cell or range of cells in a formula by clicking the cell or selecting the range of cells in the worksheet. This simplifies the process of creating a formula and also helps to ensure that you enter the correct cell addresses.

In this lesson, you use the type-and-point method to create a Gross Profit formula. This is the first of five formulas needed to complete the Condensed Income Statements for Fun with Frisbees.

To Use Type-and-Point to Enter Formulas

❶ Open the *frisbees* workbook, if necessary, and click the sheet tab named Condensed IS.

❷ Click cell B7, and type the equal sign (see Figure 4.5).

(Continues)

To Use Type-and-Point to Enter Formulas (Continued)

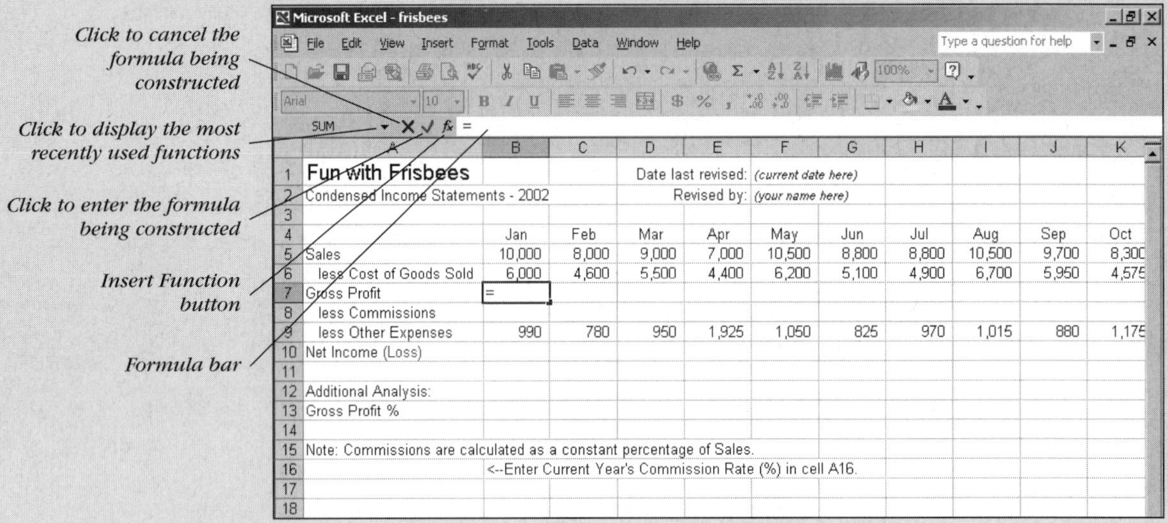

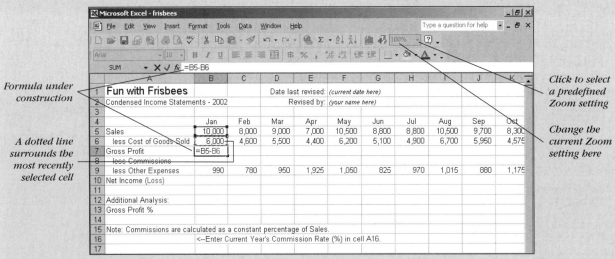

Figure 4.5

❸ Click cell B5.

=B5 appears in the formula bar and in cell B7.

❹ Type a minus sign, and click cell B6.

Excel enters *–B6* into the formula (see Figure 4.6). A flashing dotted line appears around cell B6 to remind you that it is the cell you most recently selected for the formula.

Figure 4.6

❺ Click the Enter button on the formula bar (a green check mark).

Excel enters the formula to calculate January's Gross Profit in cell B7, and cell B7 is the active cell. You could also press ↵Enter in place of Step 5. If you did, the active cell would be cell B8. Now, copy the formula to calculate Gross Profit for the other months. If your screen already displays all months—January through December—you can skip the next step that reduces the zoom percentage.

❻ Display the drop-down list of predefined Zoom percentages (refer to the toolbar in Figure 4.6), and select 75%.

All months—January through December—display.

To Use Type-and-Point to Enter Formulas

7 **Click cell B7, and position the mouse pointer on the lower-right corner of the cell.**

8 **Press the left mouse button, drag the fill handle right to cell M7, and release the mouse button.**

Excel fills the range C7:M7 with the formula, and displays the results of the formula in each cell (see Figure 4.7). The copied formulas are relative to their locations: *=C5-C6* in column C, *=D5-D6* in column D, *=E5-E6* in column E, and so forth.

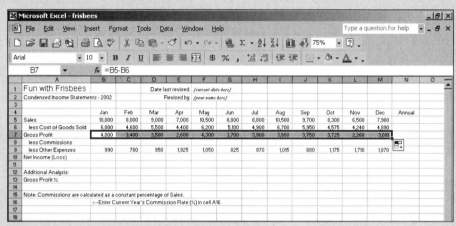

Figure 4.7

9 **Click any cell to deselect the highlighted range.**

10 **Save your changes to the *frisbees* workbook.**

You entered and copied the first of five formulas needed to complete the condensed income statements for Fun with Frisbees. The next formula requires an understanding of when to use absolute cell references and how to create them. Keep the *frisbees* workbook open for the next lesson, or close the workbook and exit Excel.

Lesson 3: Comparing Absolute and Relative Cell References

As explained briefly in Project 2, each reference to a cell in a formula is a relative reference if the row and/or column cell references change as a formula is copied. If you don't want Excel to adjust a reference to a cell when you copy a formula, use an absolute reference to that cell in the formula.

You may find it easier to understand the concept of relative and absolute cell references if you compare the effects of copying with and without absolute cell references. In this lesson, you view results of copying a formula that is similar to the one needed for the Fun with Frisbees workbook. In the first example, copying a formula with only relative cell references produces errors. In the second example, changing one cell reference to absolute—by placing a dollar sign ($) in front of both the column letter and row number—produces correct results.

To Compare Absolute and Relative Cell References

1 **Open the** *frisbees* **workbook, if necessary; select the sheet tab named Abs1 and click cell B9.**

Case 1 displays, showing errors after copying the Commissions formula *=B8*A4* from B9 to C9:E9.

2 **Click cell C9.**

#VALUE! displays in cell C9, indicating an error in the formula *=C8*B4*. The formula tells Excel to multiply Qtr 2 Sales by the contents of cell B4. Excel cannot multiply an amount by a label.

3 **Click cell D9.**

The number zero displays in cell D9, indicating an error in the formula *=D8*C4*. The formula tells Excel to multiply Qtr 3 Sales by the contents of cell C4, which is blank. Multiplying a value by zero produces zero as the result.

4 **Read the analysis provided in the Problem text box, select the sheet tab named Abs2, and click cell B9.**

Case 2 displays, showing the correct results after copying the Commissions formula *=B8*A\$4* from B9 to C9:E9 (see Figure 4.8).

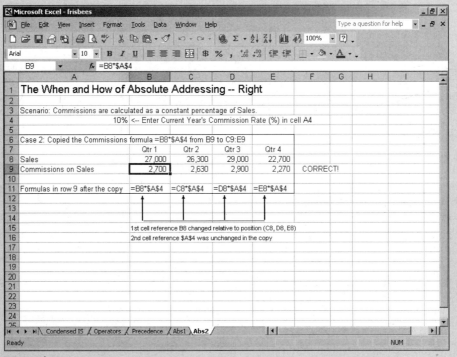

Figure 4.8

5 **Click cells C9, D9, and E9, one after the other. After selecting each cell, look at the associated formula in the formula bar.**

Formula results are consistent with the explanation provided in rows 11 through 16. Keep the workbook open for the next lesson, or close the workbook and exit Excel.

To extend your knowledge...

Using Mixed Cell References

You already know that you can mix relative and absolute cell references in a formula. For example, the previous Case 2 showed the effects of copying the formula =B8*$A$4. In that formula, the reference to cell B8 is relative and the reference to cell A4 is absolute. You can also mix relative and absolute settings within a single cell reference, if needed, to produce the desired copy results.

Using F4 to Make Cell References Absolute

Excel can enter the dollar sign(s) to make one or more parts of a cell reference absolute. While you create or edit a formula, click within a cell reference and press F4 until you get the desired result (such as =$B$8, =B$8, =$B8 or =B8).

Lesson 4: Creating and Copying Formulas with Absolute or Relative Cell References

Now that you have a better understanding of the effects on copying with absolute references in formulas, you can enter the remaining formulas in the Condensed IS worksheet of the *frisbees* workbook.

To Create and Copy Formulas with Absolute or Relative Cell References

1 Open the *frisbees* workbook, if necessary, and click cell A16 in the Condensed IS worksheet.
This selects the cell in which to enter the current year's commission rate.

2 Type 10% and press ↵Enter.

3 Click cell B8, and enter the formula =B5*$A$16.
The formula multiplies January Sales (B5) by the current commission rate (A16).

4 Drag the formula to fill the range C8:M8, and click any cell to deselect the range.
The copied formulas multiply February Sales through December Sales by the commission rate in A16 (see Figure 4.9).

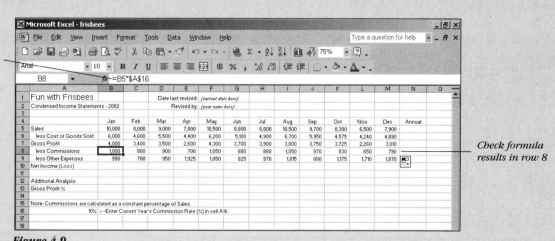

Figure 4.9

(Continues)

To Create and Copy Formulas with Absolute or Relative Cell References (Continued)

If you have problems...

If your calculated results in row 8 do not match those shown in Figure 4.9, you may have an incorrect or missing percentage in cell A16, there may be an error in the formula in cell B8, or you may have had trouble copying the formula. Check your work, correct any mistakes, and try the copy operation again.

5 **Click cell B10, and enter =B7-B8-B9 by typing the entire formula or by using the type-and-point technique.**

The formula **=B7-B8-B9** in cell B10 calculates the 2,010 January Net Income by subtracting the contents of cells B8 (Commissions) and B9 (Other Expenses) from the amount in cell B7 (Gross Profit).

6 **Copy the formula in cell B10 to the range C10:M10 (see Figure 4.10).**

Formula to copy

Check formula results in row 10

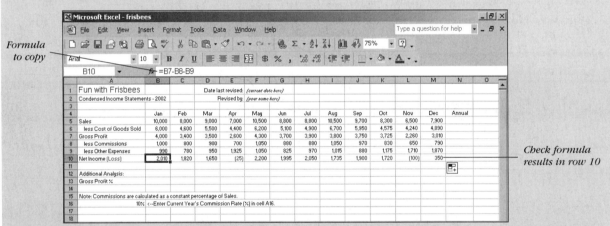

Figure 4.10

A negative amount indicates a Net Loss instead of Net Income (see cells E10 and L10). The cells in row 10 were previously formatted to display negative numbers in red within parentheses.

7 **Click cell N5, and click AutoSum in the toolbar.**

The formula **=SUM(B5:M5)** appears in the formula bar.

8 **Press ↵Enter to accept the suggested range of cells to sum.**

Excel adds the contents of cells B5 through M5, and displays *105,000* as Annual Sales.

9 **Copy the formula in cell N5 to the range N6:N10, and deselect the range.**

Annual totals for other line items in the condensed income statement display in column N (see Figure 4.11).

To Create and Copy Formulas with Absolute or Relative Cell References

Formula to copy

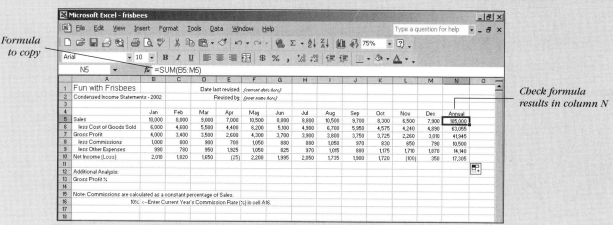

Figure 4.11

Check formula results in column N

⑩ **Click cell B13, and enter =B7/B5 by typing the entire formula or by using the type-and-point technique.**

The formula *=B7/B5* in cell B13 calculates the 40.0% January Gross Profit % by dividing the contents of cell B7 (Gross Profit) by the amount in cell B5 (Sales).

⑪ **Copy the formula in cell B13 to the range C13:N13, and deselect the range.**

Gross Profit percentages display in row 13 for each month and for the year (see Figure 4.12).

Formula to copy

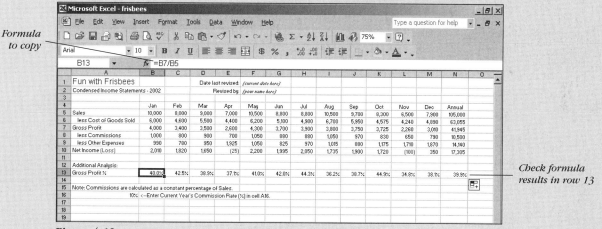

Figure 4.12

Check formula results in row 13

⑫ **Save your changes to the *frisbees* workbook.**

The Condensed IS worksheet is complete. Keep the workbook open for the next lesson, in which you learn techniques to view large worksheets, or close the workbook and exit Excel.

Lesson 5: Freezing and Splitting the Worksheet Display

The combination of screen size, screen resolution, font size, and zoom level determines the amount of a worksheet that you can view on one screen. Font size and zoom level settings are controlled within Excel. As a general guideline, do not alter font sizes just to view a larger area of a worksheet because changes in font size are also reflected on printed output. Changing the zoom level on the toolbar increases or decreases your view of one area of a worksheet without affecting your printed output.

If you want to view different sections of a worksheet at one time, Excel provides two features that you can use alone or in combination. You can split the worksheet window into two or four panes, and scroll to any area of the worksheet in any pane. You can also freeze selected rows and/or columns on the screen. Freezing enables you to keep row and column headings in view as you scroll right and left to view other columns or scroll up and down to view other rows.

In this lesson, you use both features to view different sections of the Condensed IS worksheet.

To Freeze and Split the Worksheet Display

❶ **Open the *frisbees* workbook, if necessary, and click the sheet tab named Condensed IS.**

❷ **Change the Zoom level to 100% if another setting is active.**

❸ **Click cell B5 to make it the current cell.**
The current cell determines which rows and columns are affected by a freeze command. Excel freezes rows above the current cell and columns to the left of the current cell.

❹ **Choose Window, Freeze Panes.**
Horizontal and vertical lines intersect at the upper-left corner of the current cell B5 (see Figure 4.13).

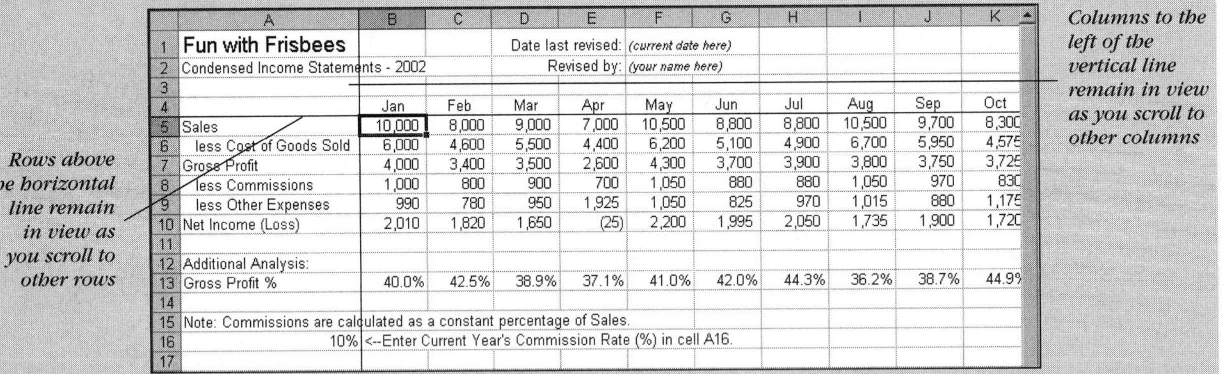

Rows above the horizontal line remain in view as you scroll to other rows

Columns to the left of the vertical line remain in view as you scroll to other columns

Figure 4.13

❺ **Scroll right until column G displays next to column A.**
Columns B through F disappear from view, but the row headings in Column A remain on the screen (see Figure 4.14).

To Freeze and Split the Worksheet Display

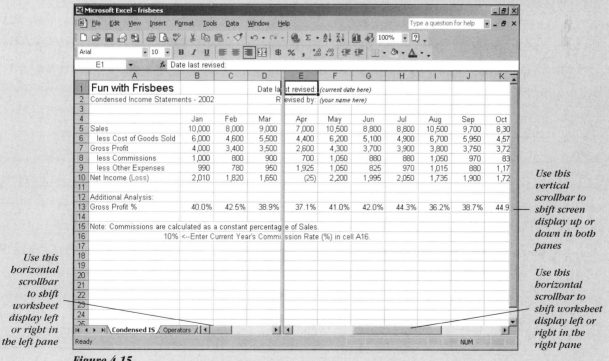

	A	G	H	I	J	K	L	M	N	O	P
1	Fun with Frisbees *(e here)*										
2	Condensed Income Statement *(here)*										
3											
4		Jun	Jul	Aug	Sep	Oct	Nov	Dec	Annual		
5	Sales	8,800	8,800	10,500	9,700	8,300	6,500	7,900	105,000		
6	less Cost of Goods Sold	5,100	4,900	6,700	5,950	4,575	4,240	4,890	63,055		
7	Gross Profit	3,700	3,900	3,800	3,750	3,725	2,260	3,010	41,945		
8	less Commissions	880	880	1,050	970	830	650	790	10,500		
9	less Other Expenses	825	970	1,015	880	1,175	1,710	1,870	14,140		
10	Net Income (Loss)	1,995	2,050	1,735	1,900	1,720	(100)	350	17,305		
11											
12	Additional Analysis:										
13	Gross Profit %	42.0%	44.3%	36.2%	38.7%	44.9%	34.8%	38.1%	39.9%		
14											
15	Note: Commissions are calc										
16	10%	l A16.									
17											

Figure 4.14

⑥ Choose Window, Unfreeze Panes.

The horizontal and vertical lines disappear, and columns B through F reappear. Panes are no longer frozen onscreen.

⑦ Display cell A1 in the upper-left corner of the worksheet window; then click cell E1.

This makes cell E1 the current cell. Excel splits a worksheet into panes above and to the left of the current cell.

⑧ Choose Window, Split.

Because the current cell is at the top of the worksheet, Excel can split the worksheet only into left and right panes (see Figure 4.15). You can scroll around the worksheet in either pane. You also can drag the gray bar left or right to change the width of the panes.

Figure 4.15

(Continues)

To Freeze and Split the Worksheet Display (Continued)

9 **Scroll the worksheet display in either pane as desired, and choose <u>W</u>indow, Remove <u>S</u>plit.**
The split view disappears. You also can drag the gray bar to the edge of the screen to quickly remove the split panes.

10 **Make cell A1 the current cell, and save your changes to the *frisbees* workbook.**
Keep the workbook open for the next lesson on hiding and unhiding rows and columns, or close the workbook and exit Excel.

To extend your knowledge...

Editing When Split Panes are Active

When a worksheet is split into panes, it's possible to see the same section of a worksheet in multiple panes. This effect relates only to screen display; the command does not create duplicate cells. Therefore, you can edit the contents of a cell in one pane, and the changes immediately appear in any other pane that displays the same cell.

Lesson 6: Hiding and Unhiding Rows and Columns

For privacy or other reasons, there may be rows or columns in a worksheet that you do not want to display at the moment. Perhaps you generally want to keep a column containing employees' salary data hidden, displaying it only when you want to edit an entry. Or you may want to temporarily hide 12 columns that store monthly data so you can concentrate on reviewing annual amounts.

When you hide rows or columns in a worksheet, the data in those hidden parts are removed from view but not deleted. If you print the worksheet, the hidden parts do not print.

In this lesson, you hide 12 columns and three rows, view the results in Print Preview, and then restore display of hidden columns and rows.

To Hide and Unhide Rows and Columns

1 **Open the *frisbees* workbook if necessary, click the sheet tab named Condensed IS, and set the Zoom level to 75%.**

2 **Click on the B column heading in the worksheet frame, and drag right until columns B through M are selected.**

3 **Choose F<u>o</u>rmat, <u>C</u>olumn, <u>H</u>ide.**
Excel hides columns B through M (see Figure 4.16). A thick border displays between columns A and N. The border disappears when you move the cell pointer.

To Hide and Unhide Rows and Columns

Columns between A and N are hidden

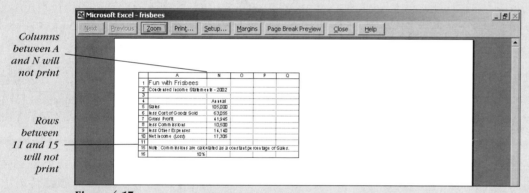

Figure 4.16

4 **Click on the row heading 12 in the worksheet frame, and drag down until rows 12 through 14 are selected.**

5 **Choose F̲ormat, R̲ow, H̲ide.**
Excel hides rows 12 through 14. A thick border displays between rows 11 and 15.

6 **Choose F̲ile, Print Pre̲view.**
The hidden columns and rows do not appear in Print Preview mode (see Figure 4.17). Now, close Print Preview and restore the display of the hidden columns and rows.

Columns between A and N will not print

Rows between 11 and 15 will not print

Figure 4.17

7 **Click the C̲lose button to exit Print Preview.**

8 **Click on the A column heading in the worksheet frame, and drag right until column N is also selected.**
By selecting at least one column heading or cell on each side of the hidden columns, you are also selecting the hidden columns.

9 **Choose F̲ormat, C̲olumn, U̲nhide.**
Excel restores the display of columns B through M.

10 **Click on row 11 in the worksheet frame, and drag down until row 15 is also selected.**
By selecting at least one row heading or cell on each side of the hidden rows, you are also selecting the hidden rows.

11 **Choose F̲ormat, R̲ow, U̲nhide.**
Excel restores the display of rows 12 through 14.

12 **Click cell A1 to deselect the restored range, and save the *frisbees* workbook.**
This concludes Lesson 6. You can continue with the next lesson or exit Excel.

To extend your knowledge...

Unhiding Column A or Row 1

If the first column or row in a worksheet is hidden, you can select it by choosing Edit, Go To and then specifying A1 in the Reference box. After clicking OK to exit the Go To dialog box, point to either Row or Column on the Format menu, and click Unhide.

Hiding Worksheets and Workbooks

You can also hide and unhide workbooks, and worksheets within workbooks. To hide the current worksheet, choose Format, Sheet, Hide. To hide a workbook, open it and then choose Window, Hide.

To unhide a worksheet, choose Format, Sheet, Unhide and select from a list of hidden sheets in the Unhide dialog box. To unhide a workbook, choose Window, Unhide and select from a list of hidden workbooks.

Lesson 7: Displaying Formulas Instead of Formula Results

As you create larger, more complex worksheets, you may find it useful to check your work by displaying formulas instead of formula results. Viewing or printing a worksheet in this display mode can help you understand the calculations performed by the worksheet. Printed copy can also be a valuable resource if disk versions are damaged or missing, and you have to reconstruct the worksheet.

In this lesson, you set the worksheet display to show the formulas in the Condensed IS worksheet and then you turn the setting off.

To Display Formulas Instead of Formula Results

❶ **Open the** *frisbees* **workbook, if necessary, and click the sheet tab named Condensed IS.**

❷ **Choose Tools, Options.**
The Options dialog box appears with 13 tabs: View, Calculation, Edit, General, Transition, Custom Lists, Chart, Color, International, Save, Error Checking, Spelling, and Security.

❸ **Click the View tab if it is not the active tab.**

❹ **In the Window options section, click the check box to the left of Formulas (see Figure 4.18).**

To Display Formulas Instead of Formula Results

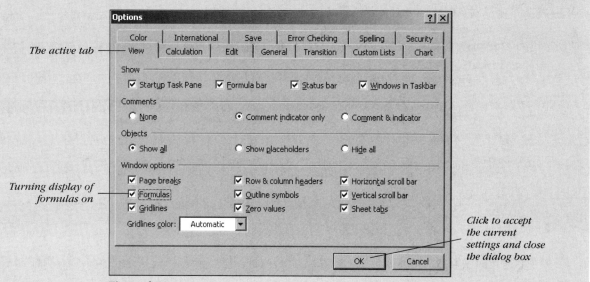

The active tab

Turning display of formulas on

Figure 4.18

Click to accept the current settings and close the dialog box

5 **Click OK.**

Excel displays the Formula Auditing toolbar, doubles the width of each column, and displays what is stored in each cell (see Figure 4.19).

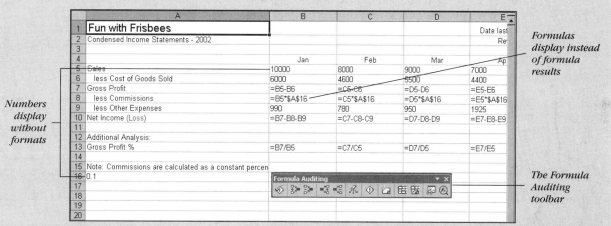

Numbers display without formats

Formulas display instead of formula results

The Formula Auditing toolbar

Figure 4.19

6 **Choose Tools, Options.**

7 **Click the View tab if it is not the active tab.**

8 **In the Window options section, click the check mark in the box to the left of Formulas.**

The check mark disappears, indicating that Formulas view is turned off.

9 **Click OK to close the Options dialog box, and close the *frisbees* workbook without saving your changes.**

This concludes Lesson 7. You can continue with the last lesson in this project or exit Excel.

To extend your knowledge...

Error Checking

Excel includes error-checking that uses certain rules to check for problems. For example, one rule checks to see if a formula evaluates to an error value such as *#REF!* or *#VALUE!*. Other rules check to see if a formula matches the pattern of other formulas near it, and if a number has been stored as text. A triangle appears in the top-left corner of a cell when a problem is found (see Figure 4.20).

A triangle in the upper-left corner of a cell indicates a problem according to the active rules for error-checking

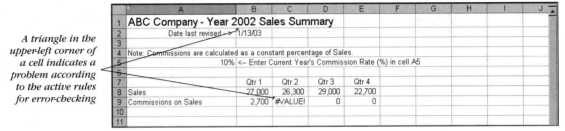

Figure 4.20

A problem can be corrected using options on a drop-down list that you can display after clicking a problem cell (see Figure 4.21).

Click to display a list of options for correcting a problem

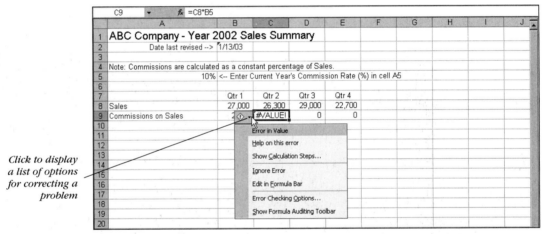

Figure 4.21

You can turn the error-checking rules on or off individually. Select <u>T</u>ools, <u>O</u>ptions and click the Error Checking tab in the Options dialog box. Uncheck each rule that you do not want to be active.

Lesson 8: Using Save As to Change the Filename, File Type, or Storage Location

Clicking the Save button on the toolbar immediately resaves the current workbook under its current name and in its current storage location. If you want to change the name or storage location, or save the workbook as another file type, use the Save <u>A</u>s option on the <u>F</u>ile menu to display the Save As dialog box (see Figure 4.22).

Always check that you have specified the desired settings in three areas of the dialog box—Save <u>i</u>n, File <u>n</u>ame, and Save as <u>t</u>ype—before clicking the <u>S</u>ave button.

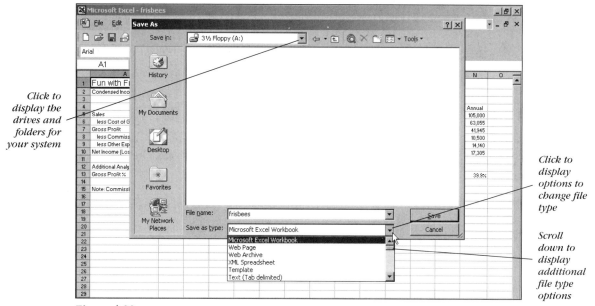

Click to display the drives and folders for your system

Click to display options to change file type

Scroll down to display additional file type options

Figure 4.22

There is a Save as type window at the bottom of the Save As dialog box. Clicking the arrow at the right end of the box displays predefined file types. For example, you can save as a Web page; save as a template; save as an earlier version of Excel, such as 5.0/95; and save as a (Lotus) 1-2-3, Quattro Pro, or dBASE IV file.

In this lesson, you change the name of a workbook as you save it, delete several worksheets in the workbook, and then resave.

To Change a Filename and Delete Sheets

❶ If necessary, open the *frisbees* workbook, and click the sheet tab named Condensed IS.

❷ Choose File, Save As.
The Save As dialog box displays, similar to that shown in Figure 4.22.

❸ Check that the entry in the Save in text box at the top of the dialog box is the desired location in which to save the file (for example, the A drive in Figure 4.22).

❹ Click within the File name text box and change the filename from *frisbees* to demoabsolute (see Figure 4.23).

(Continues)

To Change a Filename and Delete Sheets (Continued)

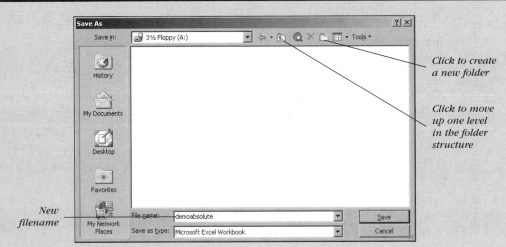

Figure 4.23

5 **Click the Save button in the dialog box.**
The dialog box closes, and the new name *demoabsolute* displays in the title bar at the top of the screen.

6 **Click the Condensed IS sheet, if necessary, and then display the Edit menu.**

7 **Choose Delete Sheet.**
A Microsoft Excel dialog box displays with a warning that the sheet selected for deletion may contain data.

8 **Click the Delete button to confirm the deletion.**
The Condensed IS worksheet is permanently deleted from the *demoabsolute* workbook. Now, try an alternative way to delete a sheet.

9 **Right-click the Operators sheet tab.**
A shortcut menu displays (see Figure 4.24).

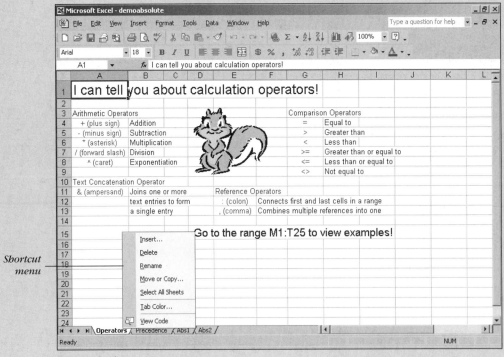

Figure 4.24

To Change a Filename and Delete Sheets

10 **Choose Delete from the shortcut menu, and click the Delete button.**
The Operators worksheet is permanently deleted from the *demoabsolute* workbook.

11 **Delete the Precedence worksheet from the *demoabsolute* workbook.**
The Precedence worksheet is permanently deleted from the *demoabsolute* workbook. The remaining two sheets demonstrate the "wrong" and "right" ways to use absolute cell addressing.

12 **Save your changes to the *demoabsolute* workbook, and close the workbook.**
This concludes Project 4. You can continue with end-of-project exercises, start another project, or exit Excel.

To extend your knowledge...

Recovering a Deleted Sheet

You cannot use Excel's Undo feature to restore a deleted sheet. As a precaution, save a workbook immediately before applying any action that cannot be undone. If the results are not what you want, such as deleting the wrong sheet, close the current workbook without saving the most recent change. You can then open the workbook, which includes the sheet deleted in error, and continue to edit.

Summary

This project included an introduction to basic worksheet design techniques, with emphasis on providing adequate documentation and using cell references instead of numbers in formulas. You learned how operators and order of precedence impact formulas. You also used the type-and-point method to enter formulas, and copied formulas containing relative and absolute cell references. As a natural extension of a focus on formulas, the remaining lessons presented features for viewing and saving your work—freezing panes or splitting the screen display into multiple windows, hiding and unhiding rows and columns, showing formulas instead of formula results, saving under different filenames or file types, and saving to another location.

You can extend your learning by viewing related Help topics. You'll find numerous subtopics under *Creating and Correcting Formulas* using Help's Contents tab. Take advantage also of the many opportunities to enter and copy formulas provided in the end-of-project exercises.

Checking Concepts and Terms

Multiple Choice

Circle the letter of the correct answer for each of the following.

1. Assume that numbers are entered in three cells, as follows: 50 in cell A1, 20 in cell B1, and 10 in cell C1. The formula =A1+B1/C1 is stored in cell D1. What result displays in cell D1? [L1]

   a. 7

   b. 52

   c. 0

   d. some other value

2. Which of the following is an arithmetic operator? [L1]

   a. $ (dollar sign)

   b. @ (at sign)

   c. ^ (caret)

   d. ? (question mark)

3. Which is not a valid relational operator? [L1]

   a. >

   b. <=

   c. *

   d. <>

4. Which window option would you apply to display two or four panes on the screen? [L5]

   a. Freeze Panes

   b. Arrange

   c. Split

   d. New Window

5. Which symbol(s) is/are used to change the order of operations in a formula? [L1]

   a. =

   b. ( )

   c. [ ]

   d. ^

Discussion

1. Explain the following statement: Good spreadsheet design techniques include using relative and/or absolute cell references in formulas to be copied. Include at least one specific example in your discussion that was not already presented in a project lesson. [L3]

2. The Formula Auditing toolbar includes a Show Watch Window button. Briefly explain the purpose of the Watch Window feature. (Hint: Onscreen Help provides the information you need.) [L7]

3. If you enter a formula, you may see an error value instead of the expected formula results. Six common error values are listed as follows. For each type of error, explain what the error value means, what might have caused the problem, and what might be done to fix the problem. (Hint: Onscreen Help provides the information you need.) [L7]

   #####
   #DIV/0!
   #NAME?
   #NULL!
   #REF!
   #VALUE!

S kill Drill

Skill Drill exercises reinforce project skills. Each skill reinforced is the same, or nearly the same, as a skill presented in the project. Detailed instructions are provided in a step-by-step format.

Before beginning your first Project 4 Skill Drill exercise, complete the following steps:

1. Open the file named *ee1-0402* and immediately save it as **ee1-p4drill**.
   The workbook contains seven sheets: an overview, and exercise sheets named #1-Document, #2-Point, #3-Absolute, #4-Formulas, #5-Split, and #6-Freeze.
2. Click the Overview sheet to view the organization of the Project 4 Skill Drill Exercises workbook.

Each exercise is independent of the others, so you may complete the exercises in any order. Be sure to save the workbook after completing each exercise. If you need a paper copy of the completed exercise, enter your name, centered in a header, before printing. Other print options have already been set to print compressed to one page and to display the filename, sheet name, and current date in a footer.

If you need more than one work session to complete the desired exercises, continue working on *ee1-p4drill* instead of starting all over on the original *ee1-0402* file.

1. Adding User Instructions and Other Documentation

Each year, your organization selects an item to sell as part of its fund-raising activities. This year, the item is a calendar, and the manufacturer's charge is 60% of the negotiated selling price of $2.50. You developed a model to calculate the profit generated by each participant, and tested the model with sample data for six people. Now, you want to add user instructions and other documentation to the worksheet so that anyone can enter data with little training.

To add user instructions and other documentation, follow these steps:

1. Open the *ee1-p4drill* workbook, and select the sheet tab named #1-Document.
2. Enter the following text in the cells indicated.

Cell	Cell Contents
A3	Community Volunteer Corps - Year 2002 Fundraiser
A4	Worksheet to Calculate Profit on Sales
A6	Calendar
A10	Note: Enter data in light yellow cells only. Formulas generate the other values.
B6	<— Enter the product sold in cell A6
B7	<— Enter the selling price per unit in cell A7
B8	<— Enter the manufacturer's percent in cell A8
E4	Designed by:

3. Select the range A6:A8, display the Fill Color drop-down list, and apply light yellow.
4. Repeat the process described in Step 3 to apply the light yellow fill color to the range B13:B18.
5. Select the range A12:E12, display the Font Color drop-down list, and apply blue.
6. Click cell A6, and click the Align Right button on the toolbar.
7. Enter your name in cell F4.
8. Save your changes to the *ee1-p4drill* workbook.

2. Using the Type-and-Point Method to Enter Formulas

You are developing a simple worksheet model to calculate sales tax due on one purchase. You designed the model to work with any specified sales tax rate. Now, you are ready to enter the two formulas—one to calculate the amount of tax; the other to add the tax to the original purchase amount. You know that you are less likely to make mistakes if you point to cell references instead of typing them.

To enter formulas using the type-and-point method, follow these steps:

1. Open the *ee1-p4drill* workbook, and select the sheet tab named #2-Point.
2. Click cell B8, and type an equal sign (=).
   This starts the formula to calculate sales tax.
3. Click cell B7 and then type an asterisk (*).
   The partially completed formula *=B7** appears in the formula bar.
4. Click cell B5 and then click the Enter button (a green check mark) in the formula bar.
   The formula *=B7*B5* appears in the formula bar. The formula result (Sales tax of *1.00*) appears in cell B8.
5. Click cell B9, and type an equal sign (=).
   This starts the formula to calculate total due on the purchase.
6. Click cell B7 and then type a plus sign (+).
7. Click cell B8, and click the Enter button in the formula bar or press ⏎Enter on the keyboard.
   The formula *=B7+B8* results in *20.95* as the total due on the purchase.
8. Test the model by entering other combinations of sales tax rate in cell B5 and purchase amount in cell B7.
9. Save your changes to the *ee1-p4drill* workbook.

3. Creating and Copying a Formula with an Absolute Cell Reference

You are in charge of putting price tags on 10 products, all of which are to be marked up by the same percentage on cost. You are nearly finished with a worksheet that will do the necessary calculations. The final step involves entering a formula to compute the selling price of the first item and copying it to calculate selling price for the other products. The formula must include an absolute reference to the cell containing the current markup on cost percentage.

To create and copy the formula, follow these steps:

1. Open the *ee1-p4drill* workbook, and select the worksheet named #3-Absolute.
2. Click cell C6, and type an equal sign (=).
   This starts the formula to calculate Selling Price for Product A.
3. Click cell B6; then type an asterisk (*).
4. Click cell D4.
   The partially completed formula *=B6*D4* appears in the formula bar. The flashing cursor displays at the end of *=B6*D4* in cell C6.
5. Press F4.
   The formula *=B6*$D$4* appears in the formula bar.
6. Type a plus sign (+), and click cell B6.
   The formula *=B6*$D$4+B6* appears in the formula bar.
7. Click the Enter button in the formula bar, or press ⏎Enter.
   The formula *=B6*$D$4+B6* results in *10* as the Selling Price (marked up 25% over its $8.00 cost). Excel performs the multiplication first—B6*$D$4 computes the increase of two dollars over cost—and then adds the increase to the cost.
8. Click cell C6, and drag its fill handle down to copy the formula to the other cells in the range C7:C15.
9. Test the model by entering other markup percentages in cell D4.
10. Save your changes to the *ee1-p4drill* workbook.

4. Displaying Formulas Instead of Formula Results

A friend of yours just gave you a copy of a worksheet on disk, which keeps track of workout time in hours. You plan to modify the worksheet to fit your own exercise plan. Before you begin, you want to turn on display of formulas to get a better understanding of what the current worksheet does.

To turn on display of formulas, follow these steps:

1. Open the *ee1-p4drill* workbook, and select the worksheet named #4-Formulas.
   The worksheet tracks hours spent jogging, working with weights, and doing aerobics during January, February, and March of the year 2002.
2. Choose Tools, Options.
3. Click the View tab if it is not the active tab.
4. In the Window options section, click the check box to the left of Formulas, and click OK.
   Excel doubles the width of each column, and displays formulas in rows 12 through 15.
5. Save your changes to the *ee1-p4drill* workbook.

5. Splitting the Screen into Top and Bottom Panes

You are under consideration for a promotion that would involve a move to another city. While you are waiting for a decision, you continue to collect information through the World Wide Web on homes available in selected areas. Now that the list is getting too long to fit on one screen, you want to split the screen into two panes of about equal size. Doing so enables you to view different parts of the worksheet on one screen.

To split the screen into top and bottom panes, follow these steps:

1. Open the *ee1-p4drill* workbook, and select the worksheet named #5-Split.
2. Select cell A13.
3. Choose Window, Split.
4. Click any cell in either pane, and use the scrollbar(s) to shift worksheet display.
5. Save your changes to the *ee1-p4drill* workbook.

6. Freezing Column Headings

You are under consideration for a promotion that would involve a move to another city. While you are waiting on a decision, you continue to collect information through the World Wide Web on homes available in selected areas. Now that the list is getting too long to fit on one screen, you want to set the screen display so that the rows describing the data stay in view as you scroll down your list.

To freeze column headings, follow these steps:

1. Open the *ee1-p4drill* workbook, and select the worksheet named #6-Freeze.
2. Select cell A6.
3. Choose Window, Freeze Panes.
4. Scroll to the bottom of the worksheet.
   Rows 1 through 5 remain onscreen.
5. Save your changes to the *ee1-p4drill* workbook.

Challenge exercises expand on or are somewhat related to skills presented in the lessons. Each exercise provides a brief narrative introduction, followed by instructions in a numbered-step format that are not as detailed as those in the Skill Drill section.

Before beginning your first Project 4 Challenge exercise, complete the following steps:

1. Open the file named *ee1-0403*, and immediately save it as `ee1-p4challenge`.

   The *ee1-p4challenge* workbook contains five sheets: an overview and four exercise sheets named #1-Sale Price, #2-Years, #3-Rental Fee, and #4-Overtime.

2. Click the Overview sheet to view the organization of the Project 4 Challenge Exercises workbook.

Each exercise is independent of the others, so you may complete the exercises in any order. Be sure to save the workbook after completing each exercise. If you need a paper copy of the completed exercise, enter your name, centered in a header, before printing. Other print options have already been set to print compressed to one page and to display the filename, sheet name, and current date in a footer.

If you need more than one work session to complete the desired exercises, continue working on *ee1-p4challenge* instead of starting over again on the original *ee1-0403* file.

1. Entering a Formula to Compute Adjusted Selling Price

Even if you have only been using Excel for a short time, you realize that its power lies in performing calculations. You are interested in developing your ability to set up formulas so that the worksheet can still be used if the data changes. You are currently developing a simple worksheet to calculate the amount due if an item is on sale at a reduced percent. For example, if an item with an original cost of $30.00 is now on sale at 25% off, the pre-tax sale price is $22.50.

The labels are already in place. To enter and test a formula to compute adjusted selling price, follow these steps:

1. Open your *ee1-p4challenge* workbook, and select the worksheet named #1-Sale Price.
2. Enter a sample original price, such as **30**, in cell B5.
3. Enter a sample % discount, such as **25%**, in cell B6.
4. Enter a formula in cell B7 to compute the pre-tax sale price.

   If the formula in cell B7 is correct, **22.5** is the pre-tax sale price that displays in cell B7.
5. Correct the formula, if necessary, and test the formula again by changing the sample numbers to **100** in cell B5 and **10%** in cell B6.

   If the formula in cell B7 is correct, **90** is the pre-tax sale price that displays in cell B7.
6. Make changes as necessary, and save the *ee1-p4challenge* workbook.

2. Entering a Formula to Compute Years of Service

You are a member of a committee that is planning an employee recognition program to be held next month, and you need to know the number of years each employee has worked for the company. You have already entered descriptive labels and data for four employees in a worksheet. Before you enter data for more than 100 other employees, you want to enter the formula to compute years of service and test the results on your small sample.

To enter and test a formula to compute years of service, follow these steps:

1. Open your *ee1-p4challenge* workbook, and select the worksheet named #2-Years.
2. Select cell C8, and think through the calculation needed in that cell.

   Assume that the current date is March 15, 2002. If you calculate the difference between that current date (in cell E8) and the date of hire for the first employee (in cell B8), you will know the number of *days* that John Byrd worked for the company. You also have to include a way to change days into years in the formula.
3. Enter a formula in cell C8 to calculate the years of service for the first employee (enter the formula so that it can be copied to compute years of service for the other three employees).

Check that the formula result is reasonable, and make changes as necessary. You can look at the dates in row 8 and see that John Byrd worked for the firm just slightly more than seven years.

4. Copy the formula to compute years of service for the other three employees.

5. Check that the formula results are reasonable, and make changes as necessary.

If you have problems...

If the initial formula produces correct results, but errors are evident in the copied formulas, check that the appropriate cell references are absolute in the first formula.

---

6. Save your changes to the *ee1-p4challenge* workbook.

3. Designing a Worksheet to Calculate Rental Fees

You must make a decision soon on buying or renting a copy machine. As part of the decision process, you are evaluating three pricing structures from firms that rent copy machines. All have a two-part rental plan—a monthly charge plus an amount per copy. You spent a few minutes yesterday setting up a worksheet to evaluate the rental options. Now, you need to finish the design and test the model with various assumptions about the numbers of copies made in a month.

To design a worksheet to calculate rental fees, follow these steps:

1. Open your *ee1-p4challenge* workbook, and select the worksheet named #3-Rental Fee.

2. Think about the elements that affect total rental fee—two are set by the rental companies (monthly fee and charge per copy,) and the other is related to actual usage (number of copies).

3. Enter appropriate labels in cells A8, A9, and A10 to describe each of the three elements of total rental fee.

4. For the rows described as monthly fee and charge per copy, enter the appropriate numbers in columns B, C, and D that are related to the three rental options:

    ```
    Option A    Monthly Fee $500, Charge per Copy $0.03
    Option B    Monthly Fee $200, Charge per Copy $0.04
    Option C    Monthly Fee $800, Charge per Copy $0.015
    ```

5. Click the cell containing the charge per copy for Option C, and format it to display to three decimal places.

6. Enter 10,000 as the initial number of copies for all three options.

7. Enter a formula in cell B12 to compute the total rental fee, and copy the formula to cells C12 and D12.

8. Check the accuracy of your results, and make changes in formulas as necessary.
   At the 10,000-copy level, the total rental fees are as follows: Option A: $800; Option B: $600; Option C: $950. Assuming that service arrangements are comparable, you would probably select Option B as the most attractive pricing structure.

9. Change the number of copies to 20,000.

10. Below row 12, type a note in the worksheet summarizing the best option if copies per month are likely to average 20,000.

11. Change the number of copies to 30,000.

12. Below your previous note, type another note that summarizes the best option if copies per month are likely to average 30,000.

13. Save your changes to the *ee1-p4challenge* workbook.

4. Designing a Worksheet to Calculate Gross Pay

You started a full-time job recently, and, for the first time, you work for a firm that pays overtime (the usual rate of 1.5 times your regular pay rate per hour, which is applied to every hour worked over

40 hours). You want to be sure that your pay is computed correctly each week, so you are designing a worksheet to calculate your weekly pay before any deductions for taxes and benefits.

To design a worksheet to calculate gross pay, follow these steps:

1. Open your *ee1-p4challenge* workbook, and select the worksheet named #4-Overtime.
2. To avoid using a number instead of a cell reference in a formula, enter the label `Overtime Premium Rate` in cell A8 and the number `1.5` in cell B8.
3. Select cell B15, and enter a formula to compute the total gross pay for the week.

    The formula you enter should reflect the fact that your pay has two components: regular hours at regular pay (a maximum of 40 hours) and overtime hours (those in excess of 40) at 1.5 times your regular pay. Remember to use cell references instead of numbers in your formula.

4. Test the formula by entering simple numbers in the input cells: `40` in B11, `1` in B12, and `10` in B13.

    If the formula in B15 is correct, the total gross pay for the week is **$415**—40 hours at $10 an hour (or $400), plus $15 for the one overtime hour.

5. Test that the formula computes correctly if there are no overtime hours: Enter `38` in B11, `0` in B12, and `12` in B13.

    If the formula in B15 is correct, total gross pay for the week is **$456**: 38 hours at $12 an hour.

6. Test the overtime calculation again, assuming that the total hours worked are **45** and pay per hour does not change.

    The total gross pay for the week is **$570**: 40 hours at $12 an hour, plus five hours at $18 an hour.

7. Save your changes to the *ee1-p4challenge* workbook.

iscovery Zone

Discovery Zone exercises require advanced knowledge of topics presented in *Essentials* lessons, application of skills from multiple lessons, or self-directed learning of new skills.

Before beginning your first Project 4 Discovery Zone exercise, complete the following steps:

1. Open the Excel file named *ee1-0404*, and immediately save it as `ee1-p4discovery`.

    The *ee1-p4discovery* workbook contains four sheets: an overview and three exercise sheets named #1-Improve Design, #2-Find and Fix, and #3-Join.

2. Click the Overview sheet to view the organization of the Project 4 Discovery Zone Exercises workbook.

Each exercise is independent of the others, so you may complete the exercises in any order. Be sure to save the workbook after completing each exercise. If you need a paper copy of the completed exercise, enter your name, centered in a header, before printing. Other print options have already been set to print compressed to one page and to display the filename, sheet name, and current date in a footer.

If you need more than one work session to complete the desired exercises, continue working on *ee1-p4discovery* instead of starting over again on the original *ee1-0404* file.

1. Improving Worksheet Design and Documentation

You are the owner and manager of a small firm with 10 employees. In a few weeks, you will announce an increase in wages per hour for all employees. This year, everyone has been working hard, and you plan to give the same percentage increase to all employees.

Open the *ee1-p4discovery* workbook, and select the worksheet named #1-Improve Design. The worksheet reflects your initial attempt to have Excel calculate each employee's proposed new rate. Now, you want to modify the worksheet to incorporate good design techniques, including sufficient documentation. One improvement you have in mind is to put the percent in a separate cell, so that you can easily change just that one cell and immediately see the results of using a different percentage in the calculation of each employee's proposed pay per hour.

2. Finding and Fixing Errors in Calculations

A coworker asked you to review a worksheet designed to report monthly and annual income. You already verified that the data are correct—the current commission rate and amounts reported for Sales, Cost of Goods Sold, and Other Expenses. Now, you need to check the accuracy of the calculations.

Open the *ee1-p4discovery* workbook, and select the worksheet named #2-Find and Fix. Find any errors that affect calculations, and type a brief description of each error below the Net Income row. Make the corrections needed to produce accurate results.

Remember that Excel displays a small green triangle in the upper-left corner of a cell to indicate a problem according to the active rules for error-checking. However, do not assume that built-in features catch all the errors in a worksheet.

You do not have to work with the actual data when you test the accuracy of a worksheet. For example, in the #2-Find and Fix worksheet, enter a percent commission rate that is easy to verify visually, such as 1%.

Sometimes, it is easier to spot an error if formulas display instead of formula results. You might find an inconsistency in a range used in a formula or notice a number that should have been entered as a formula.

3. Using the Concatenate Operator to Join Text Entries

You entered names in a worksheet by using two columns: one for last name and the other for first name. This design made it easy to sort the data alphabetically by last name. You will introduce the individuals named in the worksheet at a meeting this evening. You want to have a list of full names in another column—first name and then last name (Steve Bachman, Barbara Chan, and so forth)—but you don't want to type the data again.

Open the *ee1-p4discovery* workbook and select the worksheet named #3-Join. Create the full-name data in the third column by using concatenate (join) operators and references to cells in the first and second columns.

The Operators worksheet in the *ee1-0401* workbook provides general information about and an example of the concatenate operator. Don't forget to use onscreen Help as an alternate resource.

Working with Functions

Objectives

In this project, you learn how to

- ✔ Analyze Data with AVERAGE, MAX, and MIN
- ✔ Calculate a Loan Payment with PMT
- ✔ Create a Loan Payment Table
- ✔ Evaluate Investment Plans with FV
- ✔ Use IF to Display Messages
- ✔ Use IF to Calculate
- ✔ Use NOW to Display the Current Date
- ✔ Use Dates in Calculations

Key terms in this project include

- ❏ annuity
- ❏ argument
- ❏ AVERAGE function
- ❏ FV function
- ❏ IF function
- ❏ MAX function
- ❏ MIN function
- ❏ NOW function
- ❏ PMT function
- ❏ variable data
- ❏ worksheet model

Why Would I Do This?

Excel provides hundreds of functions to help you with tasks, such as adding a list of values and determining loan payments. Functions are presented in nine categories: Financial, Date & Time, Math & Trig, Statistical, Lookup & Reference, Database, Text, Logical, and Information. In this project, you glimpse the power of functions by working with one or more functions from four categories: Statistical, Financial, Logical, and Date & Time.

Visual Summary

You start this project by using the statistical functions AVERAGE, MAX, and MIN to find the average, highest, and lowest monthly sales, respectively (see Figure 5.1).

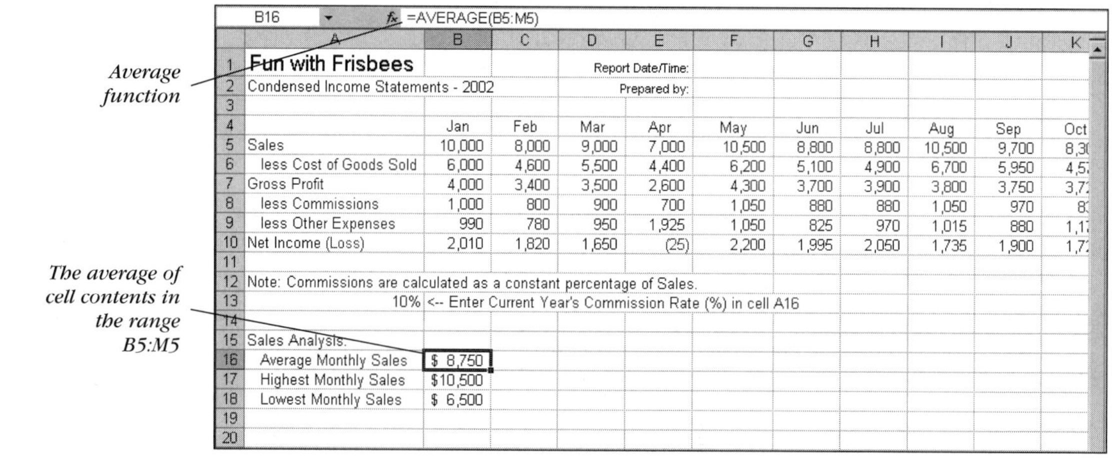

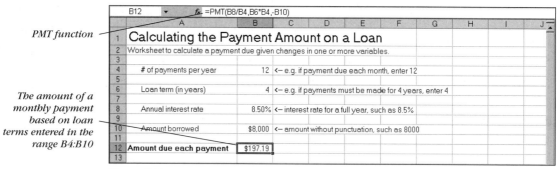

Average function

The average of cell contents in the range B5:M5

Figure 5.1

In Lesson 2, you use the financial function PMT to determine a monthly loan payment (see Figure 5.2).

PMT function

The amount of a monthly payment based on loan terms entered in the range B4:B10

Figure 5.2

After you create a table of PMT functions in Lesson 3, you use the financial function FV to evaluate investment plans. Two of the remaining lessons focus on using the logical function IF to display messages and perform calculations that vary, according to whether or not a test condition is met. To complete the project, you use the date-and-time function NOW in two ways: as the only entry in a cell and as part of a formula that calculates based on dates.

Lesson 1: Analyzing Data with AVERAGE, MAX, and MIN

A function is a predefined formula that calculates by using arguments in a specific order. An ***argument*** is a specific value in a function, such as a range of cells. For example, the function =AVERAGE(B5:M5) has one argument—the range of cells from B5 through M5.

You can enter functions in more than one way. If you know the name and structure of the function you want to use, you can type it into the cell in which you want the results to appear or you can type it into the formula bar. You can also use the Insert Function dialog box to select from a list of functions.

Excel provides a substantial number of statistical functions, including AVERAGE, MAX, and MIN. The ***AVERAGE function*** calculates the average of specified values. Use the ***MAX function*** to display the largest value among specified values. The ***MIN function*** calculates the smallest value among specified values.

In this lesson, you use the three statistical functions AVERAGE, MAX, and MIN to analyze sales. Each function has the same structure—equal sign, function name, and a range of cells within parentheses.

To Analyze Data with AVERAGE, MAX, and MIN

1 **Open the *ee1-0501* workbook, and save the file as** functions1.
The workbook contains one sheet named Condensed IS.

2 **Click cell B16, and type** =AVERAGE(B5:M5.
The nearly complete function appears in the formula bar and in cell B16 (see Figure 5.3).

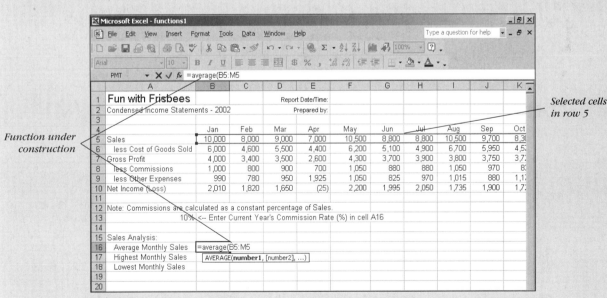

Figure 5.3

3 **Click the green check mark in the formula bar.**
Excel automatically adds the closing parenthesis. The function =AVERAGE(B5:M5) appears in the formula bar. The function result *$8,750* displays in cell B16.

(Continues)

To Analyze Data with AVERAGE, MAX, and MIN (Continued)

If you have problems...

If you press ⏎Enter instead of the green check mark in the formula bar, the cell below cell B16 is the current cell. Click cell B16 to see the AVERAGE function in the formula bar.

④ **Enter** =MAX(B5:M5) **in cell B17, and make cell B17 the current cell.**
The function =MAX(B5:M5) appears in the formula bar. The function result $10,500 displays in cell B17.

⑤ **Enter** =MIN(B5:M5) **in cell B18, and make cell B18 the current cell.**
The function =MIN(B5:M5) appears in the formula bar. The function result $6,500 displays in cell B18.

⑥ **Close the** *functions1* **workbook, saving your changes.**
This concludes Lesson 1. Continue with the next lesson or exit Excel.

To extend your knowledge...

Other Functions to Analyze a Set of Values

Other statistical functions to analyze a set of values include MODE, MEDIAN, COUNT, COUNTA, and COUNTBLANK. The MODE function returns the value that appears most frequently in a specified set of values. If there are no duplicate data points, the error value *#N/A* displays. The MEDIAN function displays the middle value in the data set.

Use one of the COUNT functions to count selected cells within a specified range. The COUNT function returns a count of the cells that contain numbers or the results of formulas. The COUNTA function—think of the "A" as meaning "All"—counts all cells in the specified range that are not blank. The COUNTBLANK function counts all cells in the specified range that are blank.

Lesson 2: Calculating a Loan Payment with PMT

The **PMT function** calculates the payment due on a loan, assuming equal payments and a fixed interest rate. In this lesson, you use the Insert Function dialog box to enter a PMT function that calculates the monthly payment on a loan. You set the worksheet up as a model. A **worksheet model** generally contains labels and formulas, but the cells that hold variable data are left blank. **Variable data** are amounts that are subject to change, such as the interest rate or the amount borrowed in a loan situation.

The PMT function requires that you specify three arguments in order: the annual interest rate adjusted for the number of payments within a year, the total number of payments, and the amount borrowed.

If a minus sign (–) precedes the amount borrowed, the function result is a positive number. If a minus sign does not precede the amount borrowed, the function result is a negative number. You determine the display you want; either way, the dollar amount is the same.

In this lesson, you work with the first three worksheets in a four-sheet workbook. On the first worksheet, you look at the questions that can be answered by using a PMT function. On the second worksheet, you vary the results of an existing PMT function by changing data in cells that are referenced by the function. In the third worksheet, you enter and test a PMT function.

To Calculate a Loan Payment with PMT

1 **Open the *ee1-0502* workbook, and save it as** `functions2`.
The workbook includes four worksheets: Intro PMT, Single PMT, Create PMT, and Multiple PMT.

2 **Click the sheet tab named Intro PMT, and read its contents to learn about uses for the PMT function.**

3 **Select the Single PMT worksheet, and click cell B10.**
The function *=PMT(B6/B7,B8,-B5)* appears in the formula bar. The function result displays in cell B10 (see Figure 5.4). The monthly payment on an 8.5%, 4-year, $8,000 loan is *$197.19*.

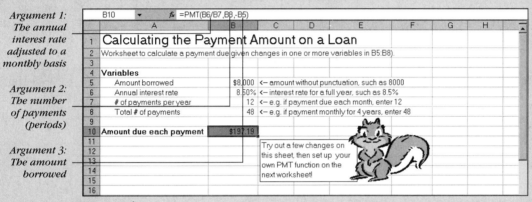

Argument 1:
The annual interest rate adjusted to a monthly basis

Argument 2:
The number of payments (periods)

Argument 3:
The amount borrowed

Figure 5.4

4 **Press** `PgDn`, **review the syntax explanation in the range A31:F44, and press** `PgUp`.

5 **Click cell B8, and enter 36 instead of *48* as the total number of payments.**
The function recalculates by using the revised number of payments. Reducing the loan term to 36 months raises the monthly payment on an 8.5%, $8,000 loan to *$252.54*. You now enter a PMT function by using the Function Arguments dialog box.

6 **Select the Create PMT worksheet.**
A worksheet similar to the Single PMT worksheet displays. Because the worksheet is set up to be a model for any combination of loan terms, a note about an error message has been set up in a text box.

7 **Click cell B12, and click the Insert Function button in the formula bar.**
The Insert Function dialog box displays (see Figure 5.5). The most recently used function category appears selected. (This may vary from the selection on your screen.)

(Continues)

To Calculate a Loan Payment with PMT (Continued)

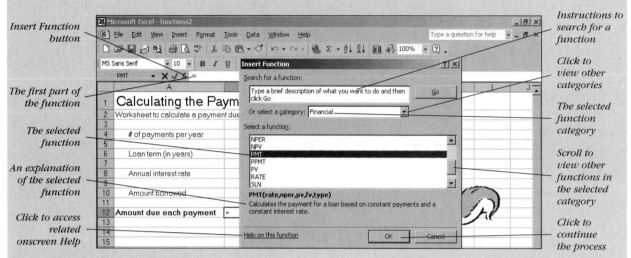

Figure 5.5

8 **Select the Financial function category and the PMT function, as shown in Figure 5.5, and click OK.**

The Function Arguments dialog box for PMT displays. If the dialog box covers the cells in column B, click the title bar of the dialog box and drag it to the right. The dialog box includes text boxes to define up to five arguments. If equal payments are made at the end of each time period, as opposed to the beginning, you specify only the first three arguments.

9 **Click in the Rate text box, and click cell B8.**

Excel displays *B8* in the Rate text box, and displays *=PMT(B8)* in cell B12 and the formula bar.

10 **Type / (the symbol for division), and click cell B4.**

The specification of the first argument, the annual interest rate adjusted to a monthly basis, is complete. Excel displays *B8/B4* as the first argument in the dialog box, and displays *=PMT(B8/B4)* in cell B12 and the formula bar (see Figure 5.6).

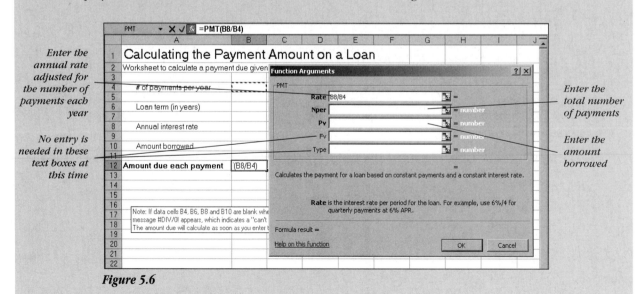

Figure 5.6

To Calculate a Loan Payment with PMT

⑪ Click in the Nper (number of periods) text box of the Function Arguments dialog box.

⑫ Click cell B6, type an asterisk (*), and click cell B4.

The specification of the second argument, the number of payments, is complete. This argument calculates the total payments as the number of years for the loan multiplied by the number of payments each year. Excel displays *B6*B4* in the dialog box, and displays *=PMT(B8/B4,B6*B4)* in cell B12 and the formula bar.

⑬ Click in the Pv (Present value) text box of the Function Arguments dialog box, and click cell B10.

The specification of the third argument, the amount borrowed, is complete. Make sure that the display in your formula bar matches that shown in Figure 5.7, and make changes in the PMT Function Arguments dialog box as necessary.

Arguments are enclosed in parentheses

Within the parentheses, arguments are separated by commas

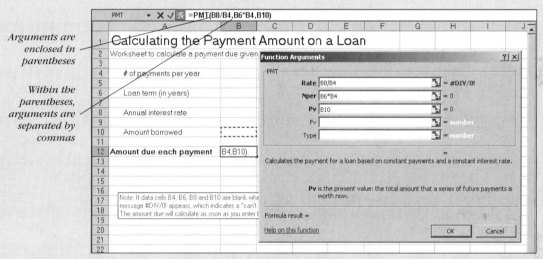

Figure 5.7

⑭ Click OK, and save your changes to the *functions2* workbook.

Excel enters the function, closes the Function Arguments dialog box, and saves the worksheet shown in Figure 5.8. You can now use this worksheet to calculate the monthly payment due for any combination of loan terms and amount borrowed.

Message that appears until values are entered in cells B4, B6, B8, and B10

Note explaining the error message in cell B12

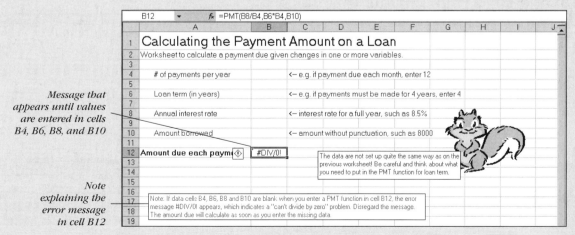

Figure 5.8

(Continues)

To Calculate a Loan Payment with PMT (Continued)

15 **Use the model by entering the data to compute the loan payment on a 4-year, 8.5%, $8,000 loan assuming monthly payments—12 in cell B4, 4 in cell B6, 8.5% in cell B8, and 8000 in cell B10.**

The payment amount *($197.19)* displays in cell B12. The parentheses indicate a negative number. If you prefer that the result be expressed as a positive number, precede the third argument in the PMT function with a minus sign.

16 **Try other combinations of the four variables, and close the workbook without saving your changes to the data.**

You saved the labels and the PMT function in Step 13. By closing without saving your changes to cells containing loan-specific data, the model is ready to use with another set of loan terms. You can now exit Excel or continue with the next lesson.

To extend your knowledge...

Other Financial Functions

Excel provides a variety of financial functions for business and personal use. Some relate to the time value of money, such as FV (future value) and NPV (net present value). Others provide investment information such as IRR (internal rate of return). There are even functions to calculate depreciation under a variety of methods, including SLN (straight line), DDB (double-declining balance), and SYD (Sum-of-the-Years Digits).

Lesson 3: Creating a Loan Payment Table

Calculating loan payment due, based on one set of loan terms, has limited use. You understand how to set up and copy formulas containing absolute and relative cell references, so you decide to create a table of payments at varying interest rates, loan terms, or amounts borrowed.

In this lesson, you create a table that shows payments due on loans of varying length. You also set up two additional columns for summary information over the life of the loan—one for total payments and the other for total interest.

To Create a Loan Payment Table

1 **Open the *functions2* workbook, and select the worksheet named Multiple PMT.**
The partially completed Multiple PMT worksheet is designed to provide three items of information over multiple loan terms: the amount of a payment on a loan (column C), the total payments on a loan (column D), and the total interest on a loan (column E). Loan terms in half-year increments are listed in column A, and formulas in column B calculate the corresponding number of months. Once the appropriate formulas are entered in columns C through E, you can quickly generate information by varying the interest rate in cell B7 or the amount borrowed in cell D7.

2 **Click cell C11, and click the Insert Function button in the formula bar.**
This action starts the process of entering a PMT function in the first cell below the *Amount of Each Payment* column heading.

To Create a Loan Payment Table

❸ Select the Financial function category, select the PMT function, and click OK.

The PMT Function Arguments dialog box displays. If the dialog box covers row 7 or cell C11, drag the dialog box to the right.

❹ Enter the three arguments shown in Figure 5.9.

Enter both cells as absolute cell references

Enter as a relative cell reference

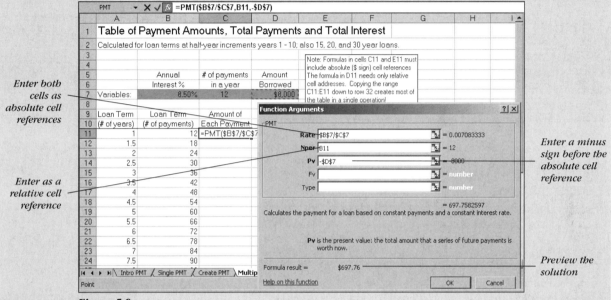

Enter a minus sign before the absolute cell reference

Preview the solution

Figure 5.9

You can type each argument in its text box: **$B$7/$C$7** in the Rate text box, **B11** in the Nper text box, and **-$D$7** in the Pv text box. You can also use a combination of typing the arithmetic operators and pointing to (clicking) the cell references, followed by changing all but one cell reference to an absolute reference. To convert a relative cell reference to absolute, click it in the PMT dialog box, and press F4.

❺ Click OK.

The function *=PMT($B$7/$C$7,B11,-$D$7)* appears in the formula bar. The function result *$697.76* displays in cell C11. Now, enter formulas to calculate total payments and total interest for the first loan term of 12 months.

❻ Click cell D11, and enter the formula =B11*C11.

This formula calculates the total payments as the number of payments multiplied by the amount of each payment. If you copy the function down the column, Excel correctly calculates total payments for other loan terms because both cell references are relative.

❼ Click cell E11, and enter the formula =D11 - $D$7 (see Figure 5.10).

	E11	▼	ƒₓ =D11-$D$7				
	A	B	C	D	E	F	G	H
1	Table of Payment Amounts, Total Payments and Total Interest						
2	Calculated for loan terms at half-year increments years 1 - 10; also 15, 20, and 30 year loans.						
3							
4					Note: Formulas in cells C11 and E11 must		
5		Annual	# of payments	Amount	include absolute ($ sign) cell references.		
6		Interest %	in a year	Borrowed	The formula in D11 needs only relative cell addresses. Copying the range		
7	Variables:	8.50%	12	$8,000	C11:E11 down to row 32 creates most of the table in a single operation!		
8							
9	Loan Term	Loan Term	Amount of	Total	Total Interest		
10	(# of years)	(# of payments)	Each Payment	Payments	on the Loan		
11	1	12	$697.76	$8,373.10	$373.10		
12	1.5	18					
13	2	24					
14	2.5	30					

Figure 5.10

(Continues)

To Create a Loan Payment Table (Continued)

This formula calculates the total interest on the loan as the total of the payments minus the original amount borrowed. If you copy the function down the column, Excel correctly calculates total interest for other loan terms because the reference to the amount borrowed is absolute. Now, create the rest of the table with a single copy operation.

8 **Select the range C11:E11, and position the mouse pointer on the lower-right corner of cell E11.**

9 **Press and hold down the left mouse button, drag the fill handle down to include row 32, release the mouse button, and click any cell to deselect the highlighted range.**

Excel fills the range C12:E32 with the formula heading each column, and displays the results of the formulas in each cell. You can scroll down to view the end of the table, if necessary (see Figure 5.11).

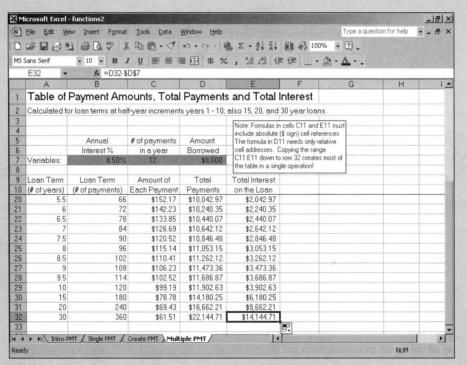

Figure 5.11

10 **Save your changes to the *functions2* workbook.**

Now, you can use the Multiple PMT worksheet to perform a what-if analysis, such as calculating the monthly payment for a home mortgage.

11 **Change the amount borrowed to 150000 in cell D7.**

The monthly payment on a $150,000, 8.5% loan for 30 years is approximately $1,153 (see the formula results in row 32). Over the life of the loan, you would pay $415,213 to retire a $150,000 loan. The monthly payment on a $150,000, 8.5% loan for 15 years is approximately $1,477 (see the formula results in row 30). Over the life of the loan, you would pay about $265,880 to retire a $150,000 loan—approximately $149,334 less than for the 30-year loan.

12 **Try other combinations of interest rates and amounts borrowed, as desired.**

13 **Close the *functions2* workbook without saving your changes to the loan terms in Steps 11 and 12.**

This concludes Lesson 3. Continue with the next lesson, or exit Excel.

Lesson 4: Evaluating Investment Plans with FV

The **FV function** calculates the future value of an investment based on fixed payments (deposits) that earn a fixed rate of interest across equal time periods. Excel refers to such fixed payments at equal intervals as an **annuity**, a term used in explanations of the function's arguments.

The FV function requires that you specify three arguments in order: the annual interest rate adjusted for the number of payments within a year, the total number of payments, and the amount of each periodic payment. If a minus sign (–) precedes the amount of the periodic payment, the function result is a positive number.

In this lesson, you enter and copy a FV function that calculates future value based on a variety of interest rates. Let's begin with an introduction to future value.

To Evaluate Investment Plans with FV

1 Open the *ee1-0503* workbook, and save it as `functions3`. Select the Intro FV worksheet.

The Intro FV worksheet shows two ways to calculate the future value of a 10-year investment plan: computing interest earned each year (the range A9:E19) and a FV function (cell G8).

2 Click a variety of cells within the range B10:E19 to learn how formulas in that area calculate future value (principal plus interest), one year at a time.

3 Click cell G8.

The function *=FV(D4,D5,-D6)* appears in the formula bar. The function result displays in cell G8 (see Figure 5.12). The future value of a series of equal deposits earning 8% interest is *$14,486.56* at year's end.

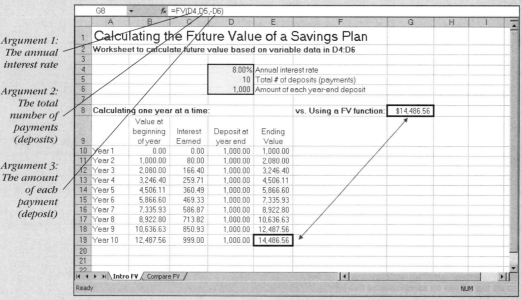

Figure 5.12

(Continues)

To Evaluate Investment Plans with FV (Continued)

4 **Click cell D4, and enter 9% instead of 8% as the annual interest rate.**
The function recalculates by using the revised interest rate. An increase of 1% in the interest rate increases the future value to *$15,192.93*. Now, it's your turn to enter a FV function.

5 **Select the Compare FV worksheet.**
This worksheet is designed to calculate future value at various levels of interest rates. If you use the correct combination of absolute and relative addressing when you enter a FV function in cell B9, you can compute future value at other interest rates by copying the function across row 9.

6 **Click cell B9, click the Insert Function button in the formula bar, and select the FV function in the Financial category.**
The FV Function Arguments dialog box displays. If the dialog box covers the cells in column B, drag the dialog box to the right.

7 **Enter the FV arguments shown in Figure 5.13 (B8 in the Rate text box, $B$6 in the Nper text box, and –$B$5 in the Pmt text box).**

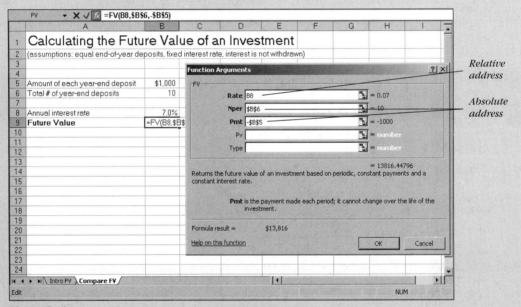

Figure 5.13

8 **Click OK.**
The function *=FV(B8,$B$6,-$B$5)* appears in the formula bar. The function result displays in cell B9. The future value of end-of-year deposits of $1,000 for ten years, using a 7% interest rate, is *$13,816*.

9 **Copy the function to the range C9:G9, and click cell G9.**
Excel calculates future values at other interest rates (see Figure 5.14).

To Evaluate Investment Plans with FV

G9	▼	*fx* =FV(G8,$B$6,-$B$5)							
	A	B	C	D	E	F	G	H	I
1	Calculating the Future Value of an Investment								
2	(assumptions: equal end-of-year deposits, fixed interest rate, interest is not withdrawn)								
3									
4									
5	Amount of each year-end deposit	$1,000							
6	Total # of year-end deposits	10							
7									
8	Annual interest rate	7.0%	7.5%	8.0%	8.5%	9.0%	9.5%		
9	Future Value	$13,816	$14,147	$14,487	$14,835	$15,193	$15,560		
10									
11									
12									

Figure 5.14

⑩ Enter 2000 in cell B5.
Values in row 9 reflect doubling the deposit amount. For example, the future value of investing $2,000, earning 9%, at the end of each year for 10 years is *$30,386*.

⑪ Close the *functions3* workbook, and save your changes.
This concludes Lesson 4. Continue with the next lesson, or exit Excel.

Lesson 5: Using IF to Display Messages

You have heard that you can use a logical function named IF to implement different actions, depending on whether a condition is true or false. If the condition is true, Excel displays one result; if the condition is false, Excel displays a different result. The ***IF function*** requires that you specify three arguments in order: the logical test, the value if true, and the value if false.

In this lesson, you use this feature to display a *Met Goal!* message if an individual's sales for the month meet or exceed the target sales. Otherwise, you don't want any message to display.

To Use IF to Display a Message

❶ Open the *ee1-0504* workbook, and save the file as functions4. **Select the IF-duo worksheet.**
The IF-duo worksheet displays a partially completed Sales Force Monthly Earnings Report for Fun with Frisbees.

❷ Click cell C11, and click the Insert Function button in the formula bar.

❸ Select the Logical function category in the Insert Function dialog box, and select the IF function (see Figure 5.15).

(Continues)

To Use IF to Display a Message (Continued)

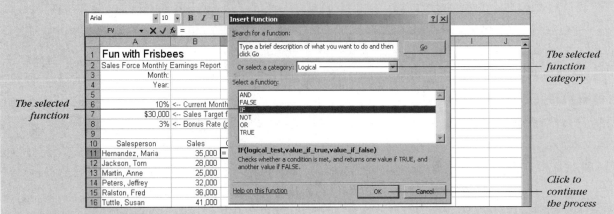

Figure 5.15

❹ **Click OK.**

The Function Arguments dialog box for the IF function displays. If columns A through C are not visible, drag the dialog box to the right.

❺ **Click in the Logical_test text box, click cell B11, and type >= (a greater-than symbol followed by an equal sign).**

❻ **Click cell A7, and press F4 to make the reference absolute.**

The first argument in the IF function, which tests whether sales for the first salesperson are greater than or equal to the sales target for the month, is entered (see Figure 5.16). Excel displays *B11>=$A$7* in the Function Arguments dialog box and displays *=IF(B11>=$A$7)* in cell C11 and the formula bar.

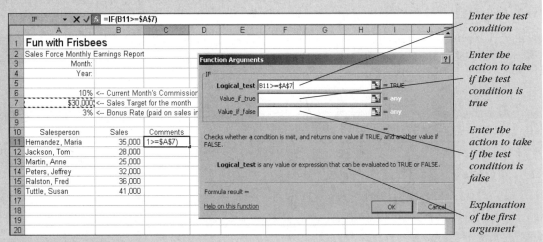

Figure 5.16

❼ **Click in the Value_if_true text box, type Met Goal!, and click in the Value_if_false text box.**

Excel automatically adds quotations around the text you entered in the Value_if_true text box.

❽ **Type " " in the Value_if_false text box (that is, type a quotation mark, press Spacebar, and type another quotation mark).**

Make sure that your specifications for the three arguments match those shown in Figure 5.17. If you do not enter a second argument, Excel displays the word *TRUE* if the test

To Use IF to Display a Message

condition is met. If you do not enter a third argument—in this case, a space between quotation marks that makes a cell appear blank—Excel displays the word *FALSE* if the test condition is not met.

Current function based on entries in the Function Arguments dialog box

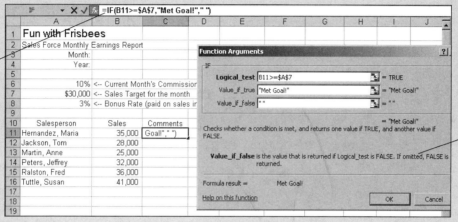

Explanation of the third argument

Figure 5.17

9 **Click OK.**

The phrase *Met Goal!* displays in cell C11. The sales amount in cell B11 (*35,000*) exceeds the target sales amount in cell A7 (*$30,000*).

10 **Click cell C11, and drag the cell's fill handle down to copy the IF function to the range C12:C16.**

The phrase *Met Goal!* displays in three more cells: C14, C15, and C16. No message appears in cells C12 and C13 because the corresponding sales amounts in column B are less than the target sales in cell A7.

11 **Deselect the highlighted range, and save your changes to the** *functions4* **workbook.**

Now that you know how to display text based on whether or not a condition is met, you can work with more complex IF functions that perform calculations. Keep the workbook open for the next lesson, or close the workbook and exit Excel.

Lesson 6: Using IF to Calculate

As you continue to develop the Sales Force Monthly Earnings Report for Fun with Frisbees, you realize that you can use an IF function to calculate bonuses. Only those members of the sales staff whose sales exceed the sales target for the month earn a bonus, currently calculated as 3% of sales in excess of target sales. If sales are equal to or below the target sales, the bonus is zero.

In this lesson, you enter and copy two formulas and one logical function. The first formula calculates each salesperson's commission on sales at the current rate of 10%. The IF function calculates a bonus, if applicable. The second formula computes total earnings by adding commission and bonus.

To Use IF to Calculate

1 Open the *functions4* workbook, if necessary, and click cell E11 in the sheet named IF-duo.

2 Type =B11*$A$6, press Enter, and click cell E11.

The formula *=B11*$A$6* displays in the formula bar, and *3,500* displays as the commission amount in cell E11.

3 Drag the fill handle for cell E11 down to copy the formula to the range E12:E16.

Ensure that the commissions for the other members of the sales force compute correctly at 10% of sales. For example, Tom Jackson's commission is *2,800*; Susan Tuttle's commission is *4,100*.

If you have problems...

If your results are not consistent with the previous examples, make sure that the reference to cell A6 is absolute in the commission formula (a dollar sign should precede both the column letter A and the row number 6).

4 Click cell F11, and click the Insert Function button in the formula bar.

5 Select the Logical function category, select the IF function, and click OK.

The Function Arguments dialog box for the IF function displays. If cell contents in rows 1 through 11 are not visible, drag the dialog box below row 11.

6 Click in the Logical_test text box, click cell B11, and type > (a greater-than symbol).

7 Click cell A7, and press F4 to make the reference absolute.

The first argument in the IF function, which tests whether sales for the first salesperson are greater than the sales target for the month, is entered.

8 In the Value_if_true text box, enter (B11-$A$7)*$A$8.

The second argument in the IF function, which subtracts target sales from actual sales and then multiplies the difference by the current bonus percentage, is entered.

9 In the Value_if_false text box, enter 0 (zero).

The third argument in the IF function is entered. In this case, you decide to enter a zero if no bonus is earned, instead of leaving the cell blank. Make sure that your specifications for the three arguments match those shown in Figure 5.18.

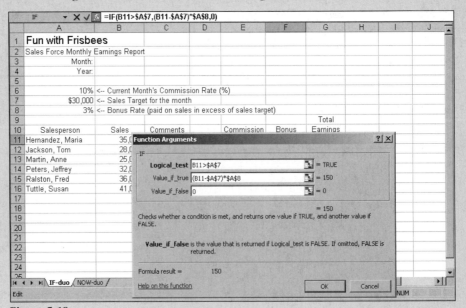

Figure 5.18

To Use IF to Calculate

10 **Click OK, copy the function in cell F11 down to the range F12:F16, and deselect the highlighted range.**

Four members of the sales force earn bonuses and two do not (see Figure 5.19).

IF function

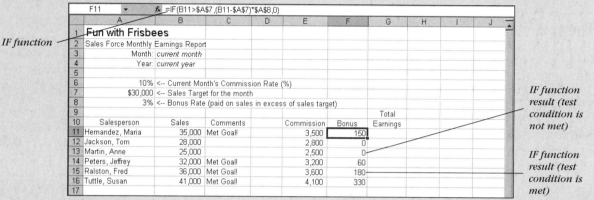

IF function result (test condition is not met)

IF function result (test condition is met)

Figure 5.19

11 **Click cell G11, and enter the formula =E11+F11.**

12 **Copy the formula in cell G11 to the range G12:G16.**

13 **Enter the current month and year in cells B3 and B4, respectively; and save your changes to the *functions4* workbook.**

This concludes Lesson 6. Keep the workbook open for the next lesson, or close the workbook and exit Excel.

To extend your knowledge...

Nested IF Functions

You can, in effect, set up more than one test condition in an IF function by including additional IF functions as Value_if_true and Value_if_false arguments. Up to seven IF functions can be nested in one IF statement. For example, you can create a nested IF to display Overbooked if reservations exceed capacity, Full if reservations match capacity, and Available if reservations are less than capacity. A more complex nested IF can assign an A, B, C, D, or F grade after comparing the earned score to the associated grade levels of >=90, >=80, and so forth. You can use onscreen Help to learn more about nesting functions within functions.

Lesson 7: Using NOW to Display the Current Date

Excel stores dates as sequential (also called serial) numbers. For example, a 1900 date system assigns the number 1 to January 1, 1900 and the number 2 to January 2, 1900. For each succeeding day, the assigned number increments by one. Under this system, the numbers 36892 and 37257 are assigned to January 1, 2001 and January 1, 2002, respectively.

A variety of Date & Time functions are available, including DATE, NOW, and TODAY. For example, the ***NOW function*** enters the serial number of the current date and time—numbers to the left of a decimal point represent the date, and numbers to the right of the decimal point represent the time. Before or after you enter a NOW function, you can apply a variety of date and/or time formats to the cell.

In this lesson, you enter a NOW function and change its format to display only the current date.

To Use NOW to Display the Current Date

1 Open the *functions4* workbook, if necessary; select the NOW-duo worksheet, and click cell D1.

2 Type =NOW(), and press ⏎Enter.
The current date and time displays in cell D1. Now, change the format of cell D1 to display only the date.

3 Click cell D1, and choose Fo̲rmat, C̲ells.
The Format Cells dialog box displays.

4 Choose the Number tab, select Date in the C̲ategory window, and select the setting in the T̲ype window that displays only a date in the form 03/14/01.
Check that your selections match those displayed in Figure 5.20, and make changes as necessary.

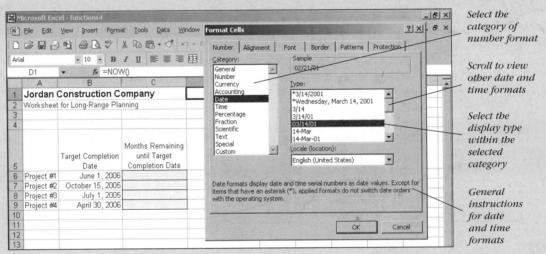

Figure 5.20

5 Click OK.
The current date displays in cell D1 in the form *mm/dd/yy*.

6 Save your changes to the *functions4* workbook.
Keep the workbook open for the last lesson, or close the workbook and exit Excel.

To extend your knowledge...

Entering a Date that Doesn't Change

If you do not want the date to update each time you open a workbook, just type the date without using a function. If you type the date in a common format, such as **12/31/01**, you can still use the Format Cells dialog box to apply a different date style.

Lesson 8: Using Dates in Calculations

There are many uses for calculations involving date and time data. For example, you can calculate the time it takes to complete a job by finding the difference between the start and end times. You can also find the days, weeks, months, or years until some future event.

In this lesson, you enter and copy a formula that calculates the months remaining until the target completion date for a long-term construction project. The formula includes a reference to a cell containing a NOW function, so that the months remaining update each day.

To Use Dates in Calculations

1 **Open the *functions4* workbook, if necessary; and select the NOW-duo worksheet.**

2 **Enter** `# of days in a month` **in cell E3.**

3 **Enter 30 in cell D3.**
You use the contents of cell D3 to convert days to months. Using 30 as the average days in a month is an accepted business practice. Putting the number 30 in a separate cell instead of entering the number 30 in a formula makes it easy to view and change the basis for the days-to-months conversion.

4 **Click cell C6, and type** `=(B6-$D$1)/$D$3` **(do not press** ↵Enter **yet).**
The formula under construction displays in cell C6 and the formula bar (see Figure 5.21). The formula subtracts the current date (produced by the NOW function in cell D1) from the first target completion date (cell B6), and divides the result by the number of days in a month (cell D3).

	A	B	C	D	E	F	G	H	I	
IF	▼ X ✓ ƒ	=(B6-$D$1)/$D$3								
1	Jordan Construction Company			02/21/01	<-- Current Date					
2	Worksheet for Long-Range Planning									
3				30	# of days in a month					
4										
5		Target Completion Date	Months Remaining until Target Completion Date							
6	Project #1	June 1, 2006	=(B6-$D$1)/$D$3							
7	Project #2	October 15, 2005								
8	Project #3	July 1, 2005								
9	Project #4	April 30, 2006								
10										

Figure 5.21

5 **Press** ↵Enter**.**
The number of months remaining until the first project completion date displays in cell C6. A different result displays each day because the current date changes daily. Check that your answer is reasonable. For example, if the difference between the first target completion date and the current date is just over two years, the result should be 24+ months.

6 **Format the range C6:C9 to Comma, one decimal place.**

7 **Copy the formula in cell C6 to the range C7:C9, save your changes to the *functions4* workbook, and close the workbook.**
This concludes Project 5. You can continue with end-of-project activities or exit Excel.

Summary

This project presented a small sample of the hundreds of predefined formulas that Excel provides. By working with AVERAGE, MAX, and MIN, you added to your knowledge of statistical functions (SUM was presented in Project 2). You had a rather in-depth experience with one financial function—first by using PMT to calculate a single monthly payment and then by constructing a table of monthly payments and other data. The FV scenario provided you with the opportunity to see the effects of varied interest rates on the future value of a savings plan.

You glimpsed the power of an electronic worksheet over a calculator when you used the logical IF function to vary results, depending on whether a test condition was met or not. After you learned how Excel stores dates, you used the date and time function NOW to enter a date that automatically updates to the current system date. The project ended with a calculation that used the results of a NOW function.

You can extend your learning by viewing related Help topics. If you enter *functions* in the Ask a Question box, the list of topics includes *Worksheet functions listed by category* and *About functions*.

Checking Concepts and Terms

Multiple Choice

Circle the letter of the correct answer for each of the following.

1. Which of the following is a function that returns different results, depending on whether a specified condition is true or false? [L5]

 a. OR
 b. IF
 c. EITHER
 d. None of the above

2. Which of the following characters separates the arguments in a function? [L2]

 a. $ (dollar sign)
 b. : (colon)
 c. / (forward slash)
 d. None of the above

3. Which of the following is a valid function, assuming that the range B5:B15 includes numbers? [L1]

 a. =AVG(B5:B15)
 b. =SUM(B5:B15)
 c. Both a and b are valid functions
 d. Neither a nor b is a valid function

4. Assume that you plan to use an IF function to display the message *Over Budget* if actual costs in cell A3 exceed budgeted costs in cell B3, and the message *Within Budget* if actual costs are equal to or less than budgeted costs. Which of the following would be a valid test condition in the IF function? [L5]

 a. A3<B3
 b. A3<=B3
 c. A3>B3
 d. b or c could be used as the test condition

5. Which of the following is a valid function? [L7]

 a. =NOW
 b. =NOW()
 c. =NOW[]
 d. None of the above

Discussion

1. In this project, you completed a worksheet model to calculate the payment due on a loan. It is worth the effort to set up and test a worksheet model if you need the same or similar information repeatedly. Identify a personal, school-related, or business information need that could be met by creating a worksheet model. Self-assess your understanding of the worksheet model concept by sketching the layout of the worksheet you have in mind. Identify which cell(s) would hold variable data (data likely to change as you use the model).

2. You have been assigned—or you can select—one of the nine categories of Excel functions: Financial, Date & Time, Math & Trig, Statistical, Lookup & Reference, Database, Text, Logical, and

Information. Use onscreen Help to learn about five functions in your category that were not already presented in this project. For each of the five functions, describe its purpose, explain its syntax or structure, and provide a specific example of a worksheet in which the function might be used.

3. Assume that you have a summer job, participate in a team sport, or volunteer on a regular basis. Think of an information need in your area of interest that could be met using an IF function in an electronic worksheet. Describe the test condition, the action(s) to be performed if the condition is met (Value_if_true), and the action(s) to be performed if the condition is not met (Value_if_false). [L5 and L6]

Skill Drill exercises reinforce project skills. Each skill reinforced is the same, or nearly the same, as a skill presented in the project. Detailed instructions are provided in a step-by-step format.

Before beginning your first Project 5 Skill Drill exercise, complete the following steps:

> **1.** Open the file named *ee1-0505*, and immediately save it as `ee1-p5drill`.
>   The workbook contains seven sheets: an overview, and exercise sheets named #1-Stats, #2-MoreStats, #3-Text-IF, #4-Calc-IF, #5-NOW, and #6-COUNT.
> **2.** Click the Overview sheet to view the organization of the Project 5 Skill Drill Exercises workbook.

Each exercise is independent of the others, so you may complete the exercises in any order. Be sure to save the workbook after completing each exercise. If you need a paper copy of the completed exercise, enter your name, centered in a header, before printing. Other print options have already been set to print compressed to one page and to display the filename, sheet name, and current date in a footer.

If you need more than one work session to complete the desired exercises, continue working on *ee1-p5drill* instead of starting over again on the original *ee1-0505* file.

1. Analyzing Data with SUM, AVERAGE, MAX, and MIN

You manage a sales force of 10, and it's time to analyze last month's data on commissions earned. To perform simple statistical analyses, follow these steps:

> **1.** Open the *ee1-p5drill* workbook, and select the sheet tab named #1-Stats.
> **2.** Click cell E11 and enter the function =SUM(C11:C20).
> **3.** Click cell E12 and enter the function =AVERAGE(C11:C20).
> **4.** Click cell E13 and enter the function =MAX(C11:C20).
> **5.** Click cell E14 and enter the function =MIN(C11:C20).
> **6.** Save your changes to the *ee1-p5drill* workbook.

2. Analyzing Data with AVERAGE, MEDIAN, and MODE

You understand the differences between AVERAGE, MEDIAN, and MODE results, as explained in the "To extend your knowledge..." section at the end of Lesson 1. Now, you want to analyze data on the number of employees' children.

To perform simple statistical analysis using these functions, follow these steps:

1. Open the *ee1-p5drill* workbook, and select the sheet tab named #2-MoreStats.
2. Click cell B4 and enter the function =AVERAGE(B9:B18).
3. Click cell B5 and enter the function =MEDIAN(B9:B18).
4. Click cell B6 and enter the function =MODE(B9:B18).
5. Save your changes to the *ee1-p5drill* workbook.

3. Using IF to Display a Message

Your firm's monthly sales meeting is next month, and you are in charge of identifying those members of the sales force who will receive the Super Star Award. You already have a worksheet that lists names alphabetically, along with the amount of sales and commissions earned. Now, you want to add a column in which the phrase *Super Star* appears for those whose sales meet or exceed the minimum sales for the award. You also decide to display the phrase *Keep Trying* for those who did not reach the award minimum.

To use an IF function to produce the desired results, follow these steps:

1. Open the *ee1-p5drill* workbook, and select the sheet tab named #3-Text-IF.
2. Click cell D10, and click the Insert Function button in the formula bar.
3. Select the IF function in the Logical category, and click OK.
   The Function Arguments dialog box for the IF function displays. If the cells in rows 1 through 10 are not visible, drag the dialog box below row 10.
4. Click within the Logical_test text box, click cell B10, and type >= (a greater-than symbol followed by an equal sign).
5. Click cell D5, and press F4.
   The first argument in the IF function, which tests whether sales for the first salesperson are greater than or equal to the sales needed for the award, is entered.
6. Click within the Value_if_true text box, and type Super Star.
7. Click within the Value_if_false text box, and type Keep Trying.
8. Click OK, and check that the phrase *Keep Trying* displays in cell D10.
9. Click cell D10, and drag the cell's fill handle down to copy the IF function to the range D11:D19.
   The phrase *Super Star* displays for Jessica Keller, Shea Lewis, and Sarah Tyler if the function has been entered and copied correctly.
10. Save your changes to the *ee1-p5drill* workbook.

4. Using IF to Calculate a Bonus

Recently, your company set up a bonus program as part of its marketing plan to attract new customers. Currently, the bonus is $100 for each new customer over 50 during the quarter, but either amount is subject to change. To calculate the bonus using an IF function, follow these steps:

1. Open the *ee1-p5drill* workbook, and select the worksheet named #4-Calc-IF.
2. Click cell C9, and click the Insert Function button in the formula bar.
3. Select the IF function in the Logical category, and click OK.
   The Function Arguments dialog box for the IF function displays. If the cell contents in rows 1 through 9 are not visible, drag the dialog box below row 9.
4. Click within the Logical_test text box, click cell B9, and type > (greater-than symbol).
5. Click cell A3, and press F4.

The first argument in the IF function, which tests whether the number of new customers for the first salesperson is greater than the quarterly quota for new customers, is entered.

6. Enter `(B9-$A$3)*$A$4` in the Value_if_true text box.

The second argument in the IF function, which subtracts the quarterly quota for new customers from the actual number of new customers and then multiplies the difference by the current bonus, is entered.

7. Click in the Value_if_false text box, type a quotation mark, press Spacebar, and type another quotation mark.

8. Click OK, and copy the function in cell C9 to the range C10:C18.

Jordan Fields and Jessica Keller earn bonuses if the function has been entered and copied correctly. The cells in column C appear blank for the other names.

9. Save your changes to the *ee1-p5drill* workbook.

5. Using NOW to Determine the Number of Years as an Employee

You created a worksheet to calculate the number of years of service of the employees under your supervision. All that remains to complete the worksheet is to calculate the difference between the current date and the date of hire. To set up the calculation so that it always displays results as of the current system date, follow these steps:

1. Open the *ee1-p5drill* workbook, and select the worksheet named #5-NOW.

2. Enter the function `=NOW()` in cell A3, and enter the number **365** in cell A4.

The formula to calculate number of years of service must contain absolute references to cells A3 and A4.

3. In cell C8, enter the formula `=($A$3-B8)/$A$4`.

Subtracting the date of hire (B8 for the first salesperson) from the current date (A3) calculates the number of *days* of service. Dividing by the contents of cell A4 converts days to years.

4. Copy the formula in cell C8 to the range C9:C17.

5. Save your changes to the *ee1-p5drill* workbook.

6. Analyzing Data with COUNT and COUNTIF

You already know how to use the SUM, AVERAGE, MAX, and MIN functions in data analysis. Now, you want to see whether there are functions that count—such as counting all cells containing sales numbers, and counting only those cells that contain sales greater than a specified amount. The functions include COUNT (cells that contain numbers), COUNTA (all cells), COUNTBLANK (blank cells), and COUNTIF (cells that meet specified criteria). You decide to use two of the four functions to analyze sales.

To analyze data using COUNT and COUNTIF, follow these steps:

1. Open the *ee1-p5drill* workbook, and select the worksheet named #6-COUNT.

2. Click cell A4, and enter the function `=COUNT(B13:B22)`.

Excel displays *10* as the count of cells containing numbers in the range B13:B22.

3. Click cell A8, and enter **25000** as the Target Sales.

4. Click cell A6, and click the Insert Function button in the formula bar.

5. Select the COUNTIF function in the Statistical category, and click OK.

The Function Arguments dialog box for the COUNTIF function displays. If cell contents in columns A and B are not visible, drag the dialog box to the right of column B.

6. Click within the Range text box, and select the range B13:B22.

7. Click within the Criteria text box, type > (greater-than symbol), and click cell A8.

8. Click OK to close the Function Arguments dialog box.

The results are not correct. Cell A6 displays a count of 0 (zero). The problem relates to the >A8 portion of the COUNTIF function. Excel encases the stated criteria >A8 in quotation marks (see the formula bar), which keeps the contents of cell A8 from being treated as number data.

9. Click cell A8, and edit the entry to read **>25000** instead of *25000*.
10. Click cell A6, and edit the function to delete the greater-than sign (>) and the quotation marks. The results are now correct. The function *=COUNTIF(B13:B22,A8)* returns a count of 7 in cell A6.
11. Save your changes to the *ee1-p5drill* workbook.

Challenge exercises expand on or are somewhat related to skills presented in the lessons. Each exercise provides a brief narrative introduction, followed by instructions in a numbered-step format that are not as detailed as those in the Skill Drill section.

Before beginning your first Project 5 Challenge exercise, complete the following steps:

1. Open the file named *ee1-0506*, and immediately save it as **ee1-p5challenge**.
   The *ee1-p5challenge* workbook contains five sheets: an overview and four exercise sheets named #1-NewData, #2-Overtime, #3-Status, and #4-Rate Table.
2. Click the Overview sheet to view the organization of the Project 5 Challenge Exercises workbook.

Each exercise is independent of the others, so you may complete the exercises in any order. Be sure to save the workbook after completing each exercise. If you need a paper copy of the completed exercise, enter your name, centered in a header, before printing. Other print options have already been set to print compressed to one page and to display the filename, sheet name, and current date in a footer.

If you need more than one work session to complete the desired exercises, continue working on *ee1-p5challenge* instead of starting over again on the original *ee1-0506* file.

1. Using Functions to Create New Data

You enjoy tracking daily average temperatures each month. For the current month, you want to calculate the average temperature for the month, and to find the highest and lowest temperatures in the month. You also want to display the message *Below Freezing* each day that the average temperature was less than 32 degrees Fahrenheit.

To use functions to create the new data, follow these steps:

1. Open your *ee1-p5challenge* workbook, and select the worksheet named #1-NewData.
2. In cell F9, enter a function to display the highest temperature stored in column B.
3. In cell F10, enter a function to display the lowest temperature stored in column B.
4. In cell F11, enter a function to calculate the average of the temperatures stored in column B.
5. In cell C6, enter a function to display the message *Below Freezing* if the average temperature for the first day of the month is less than the freezing temperature stored in cell E5. Cell C6 should appear blank if the average temperature for Day 1 is above the freezing temperature. Use good worksheet design techniques. Do not use raw numbers in formulas!
6. Copy the function down column C to all cells adjacent to the temperatures for days 1 through 31.
7. Ensure that the results are accurate, and make changes as necessary.
8. Save your changes to the *ee1-p5challenge* workbook.

2. Using IF to Calculate Gross Pay Including Overtime

You want to calculate gross pay, including overtime, by using the minimum number of columns for data and formulas. At the present time, your firm follows a common policy of paying one-and-a-half times the base wage rate for each hour worked over 40. The overtime premium and number of hours to work are subject to change, and you want to set up a worksheet model that still works if there are changes in policy. Your worksheet model to calculate weekly gross pay is almost finished.

To use an IF function to calculate weekly gross pay, follow these steps:

1. Open your *ee1-p5challenge* workbook, and select the worksheet named #2-Overtime.
2. Select cell D10, click the Insert Function button in the formula bar, and display the Function Arguments dialog box for the IF function.
3. Enter appropriate arguments in the Function Arguments dialog box for the IF function. Remember to use cell references, not numbers, in formulas; and check whether a cell reference needs to be absolute before copying.
4. Make sure that the function in cell D10 correctly computes the $550 weekly gross pay for Jordan Fields, and make corrections to the function, as needed.
5. Copy the function to compute weekly gross pay for the other employees.
6. Format the range D10:D19 to Comma, 2 decimal places; and save your changes to the *ee1-p5challenge* workbook.

3. Using a Nested IF to Monitor Capacity

Your job responsibilities include monitoring seat availability on airplane flights. For each scheduled flight, you want to compare the plane's capacity to the number of seats sold; and to display one of three messages: *overbooked*, *full*, or *available*.

To produce the desired results using a nested IF statement, follow these steps:

1. Open your *ee1-p5challenge* workbook, and select the worksheet named #3-Status.
2. Click cell D5, click the Insert Function button on the formula bar, and display the Function Arguments dialog box for the IF function.
3. Specify C5>B5 in the Logical_test text box.
4. Click within the Value_if_true text box, and type overbooked.
5. Click within the Value_if_false text box, and click the large IF button at the left end of the formula bar.

   A new Function Arguments dialog box for the IF function opens. Now, begin to enter the specifications for a nested IF.
6. Type C5<B5 in the new Logical_test text box.
7. Type available in the new Value_if_true text box.
8. Type full in the new Value_if_false text box.
9. Click OK to accept the current specifications for the nested IF function.

   If the nested IF was entered correctly, the message overbooked displays in cell D5, and the function =IF(C5>B5,"overbooked",IF(C5<B5,"available","full")) displays in the formula bar.
10. Correct the function, if necessary, and copy it to the range D6:D9.

    The message *overbooked* displays in cells D5 and D7 because the number of seats sold exceeded the capacity. The message *available* displays in cells D8 and D9 because the number of seats sold is less than the capacity. The message *full* displays in cell D6 because the number of seats sold was neither more than nor less than the capacity. Therefore, seats sold must be equal to capacity.
11. Save your changes to the *ee1-p5challenge* workbook.

4. Creating a PMT Table with Multiple Interest Rates

You have a PMT table that displays loan payments at varying loan terms. Now, you want to have a PMT table that displays loan payments at varying interest rates. Rather than create the entire table from a blank worksheet, you decide to make a copy of the existing one and modify the copy.

Follow these steps to produce the desired results:

1. Open your *ee1-p5challenge* workbook, and select the worksheet named #4-Rate Table.
2. Choose Edit, Move or Copy Sheet.
   The Move or Copy dialog box displays.
3. Click the Create a copy check box near the lower-left corner of the dialog box, specify that you want the copy to be moved to the end in the current workbook, and click OK.
4. Change the name of the original #4-Rate Table sheet to #4-TermPMT, and change the name of the worksheet copy to #5-RatePMT.
   You can display a shortcut menu containing a Rename option by right-clicking a sheet name.
5. Think about how to rearrange the data, and what changes need to be made in titles and formulas in the worksheet copy.
   For example, you can keep the area for variables in rows 5 through 7, but interest % should be replaced with loan terms in that area. You like the idea of a schedule filling rows 11 through 32, but interest rates should display in column A instead of loan terms. The data in column B on the # of payments are not needed.
6. Make sure that #5-RatePMT is the current sheet, and use Excel's AutoFill feature to enter interest rates in column A—starting with 5% in cell A11 and incrementing by one-half percent (5%, 5.5%, 6% 6.5%, and so forth).
7. Select the range B9:B32, and choose Edit, Delete. Select Shift cells left in the Delete dialog box.
8. Complete other editing of labels, and revise the PMT function now in cell B11.
9. Revise the formulas in cells C11 and D11 to reflect the new organization of the worksheet.
10. Use a single drag process to copy the formulas in cells B11 through D11 down their respective columns.
11. Check your results, and make changes as necessary.
12. Save your changes to the *ee1-p5challenge* workbook.

Discovery Zone

Discovery Zone exercises require advanced knowledge of topics presented in *Essentials* lessons, application of skills from multiple lessons, or self-directed learning of new skills.

Before beginning your first Project 5 Discovery Zone exercise, complete the following steps:

1. Open the Excel file named *ee1-0507*, and immediately save it as **ee1-p5discovery**.
   The *ee1-p5discovery* workbook contains four sheets: an overview and three exercise sheets named #1-Design-IF, #2-FixError, and #3-Compare.
2. Click the Overview sheet to view the organization of the Project 5 Discovery Zone Exercises workbook.

Each exercise is independent of the others, so you may complete the exercises in any order. Be sure to save the workbook after completing each exercise. If you need a paper copy of the completed exercise, enter your name, centered in a header, before printing. Other print options have already been set to print compressed to one page and to display the filename, sheet name, and current date in a footer.

If you need more than one work session to complete the desired exercises, continue working on *ee1-p5discovery* instead of starting over again on the original *ee1-0507* file.

1. Using IF to Calculate Customer Discounts

Your firm recently implemented a program to allow customers a 2% discount on the amount due if the payment is received within 10 days of the billing date. Both the % discount and the restriction on the number of days are subject to change. You are in the process of creating a worksheet that calculates the correct discount after checking to see whether the payment was made within the required time period.

Open the *ee1-p5discovery* workbook, and select the worksheet named #1-Design-IF. You already entered data on eight sample customers. Now, you are ready to set up the necessary calculations and enter sufficient documentation so that others can easily use the model. You plan to incorporate good worksheet-design techniques, which include not using raw numbers in formulas.

2. Using ROUNDDOWN or INT to Solve a Problem

You are the production supervisor for a small manufacturing firm, and you are designing a worksheet to monitor the maximum production possible, given the raw materials on hand. At the moment, you are working with only one finished product that comes in three models: Standard, Super, and Deluxe. The wheel type changes from model to model, but each model requires four wheels.

You want to display the maximum production possible in units, but you have encountered a problem. Open the *ee1-p5discovery* workbook, and select the worksheet named #2-FixError. The problem is described on the worksheet. Merely changing the number of decimal places displayed will not correct the problem.

Use onscreen Help to learn about how to use and enter ROUNDDOWN and INT functions. Use one or the other, as appropriate, to make the necessary changes to the worksheet. If both produce correct results, show both solutions.

3. Comparing COUNT, COUNTA, and COUNTBLANK

The "To extend your knowledge..." section at the end of Lesson 1 provided a brief description of the COUNT, COUNTA, and COUNTBLANK functions. Use onscreen Help to view explanations and examples of the three functions. Open the *ee1-p5discovery* workbook, and select the #3-Compare worksheet. Set up and label a comparison of the three functions. The argument for each function should be the range B4:B18.

Sorting, Filtering, and Editing Lists

PROJECT

6

Objectives

In this project, you learn how to

- ✔ Use an Excel List as a Database
- ✔ Sort Records on the Contents of One Field
- ✔ Sort Records on the Contents of Two or More Fields
- ✔ Use AutoFilter with One Search Condition
- ✔ Use Custom AutoFilter with OR Search Criteria
- ✔ Use Custom AutoFilter with AND Search Criteria
- ✔ Add and Delete Records Using a Form
- ✔ Edit Records Using a Form

Key terms in this project include

- ❑ Advanced Filter
- ❑ AND search criteria
- ❑ ascending order
- ❑ AutoFilter
- ❑ data
- ❑ database
- ❑ data form
- ❑ descending order
- ❑ field
- ❑ filter
- ❑ information
- ❑ list
- ❑ OR search criteria
- ❑ record
- ❑ sort
- ❑ sort field
- ❑ sort key

Why Would I Do This?

In general terms, you can think of a ***database*** as an organized collection of related data. Many database programs use a table to organize the data contained in a database file. In Excel, this concept is referred to as a ***list***, which is simply a worksheet of columns and rows.

The purpose of creating a list is to store data so that it can be viewed in a variety of useful ways. ***Data*** are unprocessed raw facts or assumptions that are stored in a database. Data are transformed into a useful form called ***information*** when users select the data they need, organize the data in a meaningful order, format the data into a useful layout, and display the results—usually to the screen or a printer.

Visual Summary

In this project, you learn to sort, filter, and maintain a sample database of residential real estate listings. You start by using onscreen Help to learn about creating a database in a worksheet. In the next two lessons, you sort records in a residential real estate list, including a sort first by area and then by price (see Figure 6.1). The list includes nine fields (columns A through I), a header row (row 3), and 35 records (rows 4 through 38).

	A	B	C	D	E	F	G	H	I
3	Listed	Price	Area	Address	Bed	Bath	Heat	Built	Pool
4	23-Jan	98,200	Autumn Woods	6370 Elm Street	3	1.5	Gas	1994	N
5	12-Mar	85,500	Autumn Woods	6415 Elm Street	2	1.5	Gas	1995	N
6	6-Feb	79,600	Autumn Woods	3212 Popler Circle Drive	2	2	Gas	1995	N
7	1-Mar	74,500	Autumn Woods	6250 Maple Street	2	1.5	Gas	1995	N
8	15-Feb	98,500	Cape Cod Village	9374 Cape Cod Court	3	2	Elec	1989	N
9	17-Feb	91,600	Cape Cod Village	8247 Cape Cod Drive	3	2	Solar	1988	N
10	6-Feb	87,300	Cape Cod Village	2394 Gerking Court	2	2	Solar	1988	N
11	9-Jan	86,300	Cape Cod Village	9122 Barnes Drive	2	2	Solar	1988	N
12	13-Mar	85,600	Cape Cod Village	7421 Crook Drive	2	2	Solar	1988	N
13	6-Feb	156,400	Champions Village	2398 Sulky Court	4	2	Gas	1990	N
14	12-Feb	152,900	Champions Village	5429 Bridle Avenue	4	2.5	Elec	1990	N
15	12-Mar	127,500	Champions Village	3456 Silk Lane	3	1.5	Elec	1991	N
16	6-Jan	120,700	Champions Village	8882 Derby Lane	3	1.5	Elec	1990	N
17	25-Mar	115,500	Champions Village	3654 Silk Lane	3	1.5	Gas	1991	N
18	28-Feb	102,900	Champions Village	9341 Champions Drive	3	2	Elec	1989	N
19	3-Jan	180,500	Glenn Lakes	6873 Wellington Drive	4	2	Elec	1997	Y
20	5-Feb	174,600	Glenn Lakes	4874 Manatee Avenue	3	2	Elec	1995	Y
21	23-Jan	172,900	Glenn Lakes	3452 Cortex Street	3	2	Elec	1996	Y
22	5-Jan	170,000	Glenn Lakes	1025 Wellington Circle	3	2	Elec	1998	Y
23	3-Mar	169,700	Glenn Lakes	2984 44th Street West	3	2	Elec	1997	Y
24	3-Mar	167,200	Glenn Lakes	5778 Wellington Drive	3	2	Elec	1997	Y

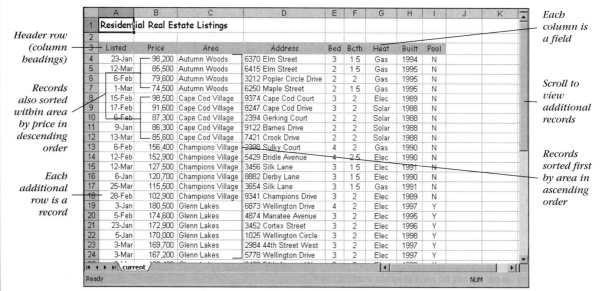

Figure 6.1

In Lessons 4 through 6, you limit the display of records to those that meet one or more conditions. For example, you limit display to homes in the Glenn Lakes area that have four bedrooms (see Figure 6.2). In Lessons 7 and 8, you use a form to add, delete, and edit records.

	A	B	C	D	E	F	G	H	I
3	Listed	Price	Area	Address	Be	Ba	Hea	Bui	Poo
22	3-Jan	180,500	Glenn Lakes	6873 Wellington Drive	4	2	Elec	1997	Y
36	15-Jan	121,500	Glenn Lakes	5562 Kensington Drive	4	2.5	Elec	1998	N

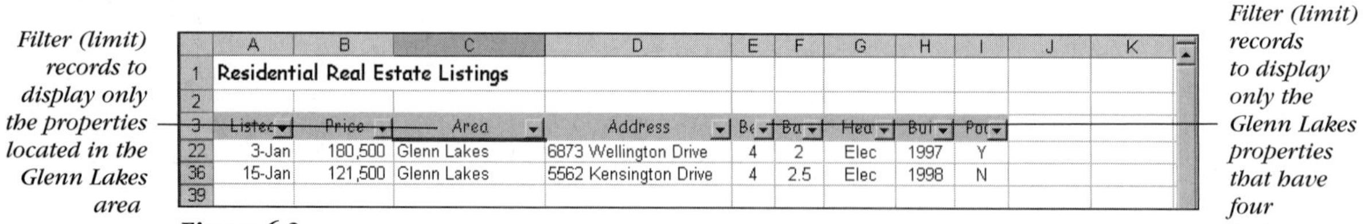

Figure 6.2

Lesson 1: Using an Excel List as a Database

Each collection of related data in a database is called a ***record***. In the Residential Real Estate Listings database, the first record relates to property at *7421 Crook Drive* in *Cape Cod Village* (row 4), and the second record relates to property at *4191 Glenn Avenue* in *Hunter's Run* (row 5).

Each record in a database contains several parts, or ***fields***. The first four fields in the Residential Real Estate Listings database are the date listed (column A), the asking price (column B), the area (column C), and the address (column D).

Before you begin to work with the Listings database, use Excel's onscreen Help to learn about the guidelines for creating a list on a worksheet.

To Get Help on Using an Excel List as a Database

① **Open the file *ee1-0601*, and save it as** sort**.**

② **Type** use a list **in the Ask a Question box near the right end of the menu bar, and press** ⏎Enter**.**

③ **Select the topic *Guidelines for creating a list on a worksheet*.**
   The associated Microsoft Excel Help window opens.

④ **Click *Show All* near the upper-right corner of the Help window.**
   Excel displays detailed information about the selected topic (see Figure 6.3).

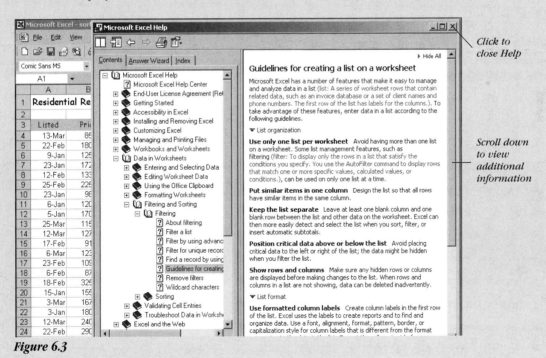

Figure 6.3

⑤ **Close the Help window.**
   Keep the *sort* workbook open for the next lesson, or close the workbook and exit Excel.

To extend your knowledge...

Entering Data in a List

Every record must have the same fields, but you don't have to enter data into all the fields for every record. If data are not available, one or more cells in the record will be blank.

Lesson 2: Sorting Records on the Contents of One Field

Now that you have a better understanding of the way an Excel database (list) is organized, you can focus on retrieving data in a useful form. Some information needs can be met by sorting a list. To *sort* a list means to rearrange the records in the list, based on the contents of one or more fields. In the Listings database, for example, you might sort records according to price, from lowest to highest. Or you might sort by the date listed—the most recent first.

Executing a sort involves two selections. First, you must specify the column you want Excel to use in sorting, known as the *sort field* (sometimes called a *sort key*). You can also choose the order you want Excel to follow when sorting records: *ascending order* (A to Z, lowest to highest value, earliest to most recent date, and so on) or *descending order* (Z to A, highest to lowest value, most recent to earliest date, and so on).

In this lesson, you sort the residential real estate records on a single sort field by using the Sort Ascending and Sort Descending buttons on the Standard toolbar.

To Sort Records on the Contents of One Field

❶ **Open the *sort* workbook, if necessary.**

❷ **Click any cell within column B between row 3 (the field name row) and row 38 (the last record in the list).**
Clicking a cell in column B within the top and bottom boundaries of the list tells Excel that you want to sort on the contents of the Price field.

❸ **Click the Sort Ascending button in the Standard toolbar.**
Records appear in order of price, from lowest to highest (see Figure 6.4). Because there are no blank columns or rows in the database area A3:I38, Excel automatically treats the area as a list, and sorts entire records instead of sorting only the contents in column B.

To Sort Records on the Contents of One Field

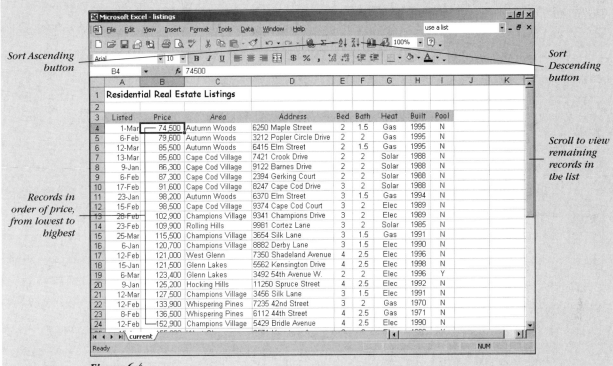

Sort Ascending button

Sort Descending button

Records in order of price, from lowest to highest

Scroll to view remaining records in the list

Figure 6.4

④ Choose Edit, Undo Sort.

Excel restores the original order of records. The list remains selected (see Figure 6.5).

Field name row is not selected

All records in the list are selected

Figure 6.5

⑤ Click any cell within column E, between row 3 and row 38.

Clicking a cell in column E within the top and bottom boundaries of the list tells Excel that you want to sort on the contents of the Bed (number of bedrooms) field.

(Continues)

To Sort Records on the Contents of One Field (Continued)

6 **Click the Sort Descending button in the Standard toolbar.**
Records appear in order according to the number of bedrooms, starting with one six-bedroom listing in *Sago Estates* and followed by two five-bedroom listings—one in *Hunter's Run* and the other in *Sago Estates*.

7 **Save your changes to the *sort* workbook.**
Continue with the next lesson, in which you sort on two fields, or close the workbook and exit Excel.

To extend your knowledge...

Restoring the Original Order of Sorted Records

Usually, there is no need to restore records to their original order. You can quickly rearrange records in any order you choose, and view or print the results.

If you do want the ability to display records in their original order after one or more sorts, design the layout of the list to include an initial column of sequential numbers. For example, specify a column heading of Rec# (for record number), and fill subsequent rows in the column with numbers incrementing by one—1, 2, 3, 4, and so forth. After sorting on one or more other columns, you can then restore the original order through an ascending sort on the Rec# column.

Lesson 3: Sorting Records on the Contents of Two or More Fields

You can carry out a meaningful sort on two or more fields in a list if there is a relationship or order of importance between the fields. In the Listings database, for example, you can organize records first by area and then by price within area. Sorting the records in this way enables you to see the price range of homes in various areas quickly.

Now, sort on the contents of two fields by using Excel's Sort dialog box.

To Sort Records on the Contents of Two or More Fields

1 **Open the *sort* workbook, if necessary, and click any cell within the list range A3:I38.**

2 **Choose Data, Sort.**
The Sort dialog box appears, with settings from the most recent sort (see Figure 6.6).

To Sort Records on the Contents of Two or More Fields

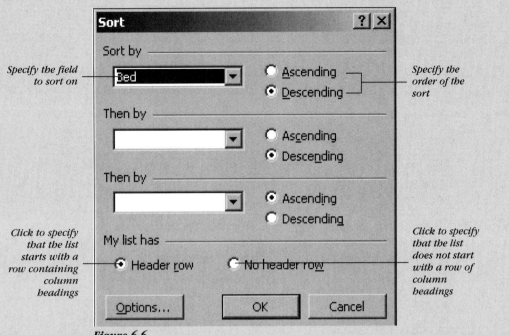

Specify the field to sort on

Specify the order of the sort

Click to specify that the list starts with a row containing column headings

Click to specify that the list does not start with a row of column headings

Figure 6.6

❸ Click the drop-down arrow at the right end of the *Sort by* text box.

A scrollable drop-down list appears that includes all field names in the list (see Figure 6.7).

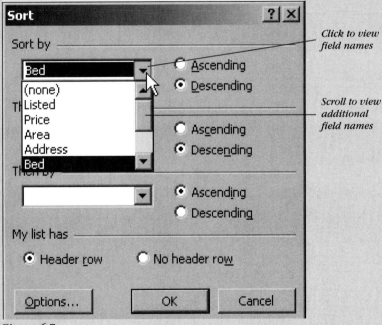

Click to view field names

Scroll to view additional field names

Figure 6.7

❹ Click *Area* in the drop-down list, and select *Ascending*.

You have specified that Excel should initially sort records in ascending order, based on the contents of the Area column.

(Continues)

To Sort Records on the Contents of Two or More Fields (Continued)

5 Click the drop-down arrow at the right end of the first *Then by* text box, and select *Price*.

6 Select *Descending* as the sort order.

You have specified that Excel should execute a second sort after sorting on Area—within each area, records are sorted in descending order on the contents of the Price field (see Figure 6.8).

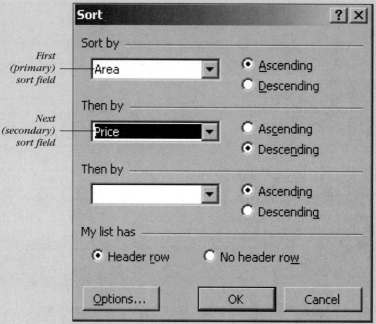

First (primary) sort field

Next (secondary) sort field

Figure 6.8

7 Click OK.

Excel closes the Sort dialog box and sorts the records (see Figure 6.9). Within each group of homes in the same area, the records are arranged by price in descending order.

Within Autumn Woods, sorted descending on price

Within Cape Cod Village, sorted descending on price

	A	B	C	D	E	F	G	H	I	J	K
1	Residential Real Estate Listings										
2											
3	Listed	Price	Area	Address	Bed	Bath	Heat	Built	Pool		
4	23-Jan	98,200	Autumn Woods	6370 Elm Street	3	1.5	Gas	1994	N		
5	12-Mar	85,500	Autumn Woods	6415 Elm Street	2	1.5	Gas	1995	N		
6	6-Feb	79,600	Autumn Woods	3212 Popler Circle Drive	2	2	Gas	1995	N		
7	1-Mar	74,500	Autumn Woods	6250 Maple Street	2	1.5	Gas	1995	N		
8	15-Feb	98,500	Cape Cod Village	9374 Cape Cod Court	3	2	Elec	1989	N		
9	17-Feb	91,600	Cape Cod Village	8247 Cape Cod Drive	3	2	Solar	1988	N		
10	6-Feb	87,300	Cape Cod Village	2394 Gerking Court	2	2	Solar	1988	N		
11	9-Jan	86,300	Cape Cod Village	9122 Barnes Drive	2	2	Solar	1988	N		
12	13-Mar	85,600	Cape Cod Village	7421 Crook Drive	2	2	Solar	1988	N		
13	6-Feb	156,400	Champions Village	2398 Sulky Court	4	2	Gas	1990	N		
14	12-Feb	152,900	Champions Village	5429 Bridle Avenue	4	2.5	Elec	1990	N		
15	12-Mar	127,500	Champions Village	3456 Silk Lane	3	1.5	Elec	1991	N		
16	6-Jan	120,700	Champions Village	8882 Derby Lane	3	1.5	Elec	1990	N		
17	25-Mar	115,500	Champions Village	3654 Silk Lane	3	1.5	Gas	1991	N		
18	28-Feb	102,900	Champions Village	9341 Champions Drive	3	2	Gas	1989	N		
19	3-Jan	180,500	Glenn Lakes	6873 Wellington Drive	4	2	Elec	1997	Y		
20	5-Feb	174,600	Glenn Lakes	4874 Manatee Avenue	3	2	Elec	1995	Y		
21	23-Jan	172,900	Glenn Lakes	3452 Cortex Street	3	2	Elec	1996	Y		
22	5-Jan	170,000	Glenn Lakes	1025 Wellington Circle	3	2	Elec	1998	Y		
23	3-Mar	169,700	Glenn Lakes	2984 44th Street West	3	2	Elec	1997	Y		
24	3-Mar	167,200	Glenn Lakes	5778 Wellington Drive	3	2	Elec	1997	Y		

Figure 6.9

To Sort Records on the Contents of Two or More Fields

8 *Save your changes, and close the* ***sort*** *workbook.*
You can continue to the next lesson now, or exit Excel.

To extend your knowledge...

Sorting On Multiple Fields Using Toolbar Buttons

You can also sort on more than one field by using the Sort Ascending and Sort Descending toolbar buttons. If you choose this method, you are not limited to sorting on three fields. However, you must perform successive sorts, starting with a sort on the least important field first—which is the opposite of the order in which you specify sort fields in the Sort dialog box.

For example, to sort records first by area and then by price within area by using sort buttons, you execute two sorts. The first sort arranges records in descending order on the contents of the Price field. The second sort then arranges the records in ascending order on the content of the Area field.

Lesson 4: Using AutoFilter with One Search Condition

Users of large databases with hundreds or thousands of records generally do not want to view all of the records. It's more likely that their information needs focus primarily on finding records that meet one or more conditions.

Filtering data enables you to work with a more manageable set of records. To ***filter*** a list means to hide all the rows except those that meet specified criteria. This is a temporary view of your list. Canceling the filter operation redisplays all the records.

Excel provides two filtering commands: AutoFilter and Advanced Filter. You can use ***AutoFilter*** to limit the display based on simple search conditions. ***Advanced Filter*** enables you to specify more complex criteria and to copy filtered records to another location.

The Residential Real Estate Listings database is small and simple for practical reasons—so that you can see the results of your work while you learn Excel. In this lesson, you use AutoFilter to display only those records that match a single search condition. You begin by opening the original student data file and saving it as *filter*. Working with a copy of the original database ensures that your filters display records in the same order as those shown in figures.

To Use AutoFilter with One Search Condition

1 *Open the* ***ee1-0601*** *workbook, and save it as* `filter`.

2 *Click any cell in the list range A3:I38.*

3 *Choose* **Data***, point to* **Filter***, and click Auto***Filter***.*
Filter arrows appear next to each of the field names in the list (see Figure 6.10). A black filter arrow indicates that AutoFilter is active, but no filter is established.

(Continues)

To Use AutoFilter with One Search Condition (Continued)

Arrows indicate that AutoFilter is active

	A	B	C	D	E	F	G	H	I	J	K
1	Residential Real Estate Listings										
2											
3	Listec ▾	Price ▾	Area ▾	Address ▾	Be ▾	Ba ▾	Hea ▾	Bui ▾	Po ▾		
4	13-Mar	85,600	Cape Cod Village	7421 Crook Drive	2	2	Solar	1988	N		
5	22-Feb	180,000	Hunter's Run	4191 Glenn Avenue	4	2.5	Solar	1995	N		
6	9-Jan	125,200	Hocking Hills	11250 Spruce Street	4	2.5	Elec	1992	N		
7	23-Jan	172,900	Glenn Lakes	3452 Cortex Street	3	2	Elec	1996	Y		
8	12-Feb	133,900	Whispering Pines	7235 42nd Street	3	2	Gas	1970	N		
9	25-Feb	225,000	Hunter's Run	3360 Glade Avenue	5	3	Elec	1995	Y		
10	23-Jan	98,200	Autumn Woods	6370 Elm Street	3	1.5	Gas	1994	N		
11	6-Jan	120,700	Champions Village	8882 Derby Lane	3	1.5	Elec	1990	N		
12	5-Jan	170,000	Glenn Lakes	1025 Wellington Circle	3	2	Elec	1998	Y		
13	25-Mar	115,500	Champions Village	3654 Silk Lane	3	1.5	Gas	1991	N		
14	12-Mar	127,500	Champions Village	3456 Silk Lane	3	1.5	Elec	1991	N		
15	17-Feb	91,600	Cape Cod Village	8247 Cape Cod Drive	3	2	Solar	1988	N		
16	6-Mar	123,400	Glenn Lakes	3492 54th Avenue W.	2	2	Elec	1996	Y		
17	23-Feb	109,900	Rolling Hills	9981 Cortez Lane	3	2	Solar	1985	N		
18	6-Feb	87,300	Cape Cod Village	2394 Gerking Court	2	2	Solar	1988	N		
19	18-Feb	325,000	Sago Estates	12990 Augusta Lane	6	3.5	Elec	1994	N		
20	15-Jan	155,900	West Glenn	6571 Keystone Avenue	3	2	Elec	1996	Y		
21	3-Mar	167,200	Glenn Lakes	5778 Wellington Drive	3	2	Elec	1997	Y		
22	3-Jan	180,500	Glenn Lakes	6873 Wellington Drive	4	2	Elec	1997	Y		
23	12-Mar	240,000	Sago Estates	12983 Augustine Court	4	3	Elec	1993	Y		
24	22-Feb	290,000	Sago Estates	12543 Augusta Lane	4	3	Solar	1993	Y		

current

Ready   NUM

Figure 6.10

4 **Click the filter arrow for the Area field located in cell C3.**
A drop-down list of filtering criteria appears (see Figure 6.11).

Choose (Top 10) to filter based on the highest (or lowest) values

Choose (Custom) to specify two filters and/or comparisons other than an exact match

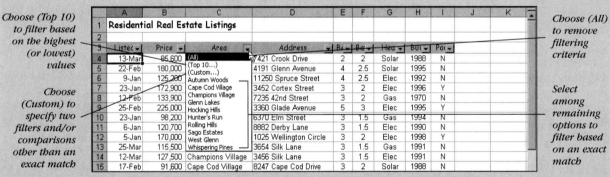

Choose (All) to remove filtering criteria

Select among remaining options to filter based on an exact match

Figure 6.11

5 **Click *Glenn Lakes* in the AutoFilter options list.**
Excel temporarily hides all but the eight records containing *Glenn Lakes* in the Area field (see Figure 6.12). The filter arrow next to Area is blue instead of black, indicating that there is an active filter on the field.

To Use AutoFilter with One Search Condition

	A	B	C	D	E	F	G	H	I	J	K
1	Residential Real Estate Listings										
2											
3	Listed	Price	Area	Address	Be	Ba	Hea	Bui	Po		
7	23-Jan	172,900	Glenn Lakes	3452 Cortex Street	3	2	Elec	1996	Y		
12	5-Jan	170,000	Glenn Lakes	1025 Wellington Circle	3	2	Elec	1998	Y		
16	6-Mar	123,400	Glenn Lakes	3492 54th Avenue W.	2	2	Elec	1996	Y		
21	3-Mar	167,200	Glenn Lakes	5778 Wellington Drive	3	2	Elec	1997	Y		
22	3-Jan	180,500	Glenn Lakes	6873 Wellington Drive	4	2	Elec	1997	Y		
27	3-Mar	169,700	Glenn Lakes	2984 44th Street West	3	2	Elec	1997	Y		
36	15-Jan	121,500	Glenn Lakes	5562 Kensington Drive	4	2.5	Elec	1998	N		
37	5-Feb	174,600	Glenn Lakes	4874 Manatee Avenue	3	2	Elec	1995	Y		

Row numbers of selected records

Blue arrow indicates that a filter is active

Status report

8 of 35 records found   NUM

Figure 6.12

6 **Click the filter arrow for the Bed field located in cell E3.**
The drop-down list for the Bed field appears.

7 **Click 4 in the AutoFilter options list.**
There are now one-condition filters attached to two fields. Fewer records (two) appear because the display is limited to records that meet both conditions: Glenn Lakes area and four bedrooms.

8 **Choose Data, point to Filter, and click Show All.**
The two filters are removed, and all records display. AutoFilter remains active.

9 **Choose Data, point to Filter, and click AutoFilter.**
The arrow at the end of each field name disappears, which indicates that AutoFilter is no longer active. You can close the *filter* workbook now, or leave it open and continue to the next lesson. It is not necessary to save the workbook because no changes have been made.

Lesson 5: Using Custom AutoFilter with OR Search Criteria

Retrieving the information you need from a database quite often requires filtering records based on multiple criteria. In the previous lesson, for example, you set two filters to display only records of four-bedroom homes in the Glenn Lakes area. Each filter required an exact match to data in one field—Glenn Lakes in the Area field and 4 in the Bed field. Both conditions had to be met for a record to display.

Using the Custom filter option within AutoFilter, you can specify two search conditions based on the contents of one field. If you specify that *either* condition must be met, you are using **OR search criteria**. For example, to display only the records of homes for sale in Glenn Lakes or West Glenn, filter for Area equal to Glenn Lakes *or* Area equal to West Glenn. You tell AutoFilter to examine the Area field of each record, and display the record if it contains either Glenn Lakes or West Glenn.

In this lesson, you filter using OR search criteria. Now, set a filter in the *filter* database to find homes for sale in the Glenn Lakes area or the West Glenn area.

To Use Custom AutoFilter with OR Search Criteria

❶ Open the *filter* workbook, if necessary, and click any cell in the list range A3:I38.

❷ Choose Data, point to Filter, and click AutoFilter.

❸ Click the filter arrow for the Area field in cell C3, and select *(Custom)*.
The Custom AutoFilter dialog box appears (see Figure 6.13). You use the default comparison option for the first search condition (*equals*) in the current filter operation.

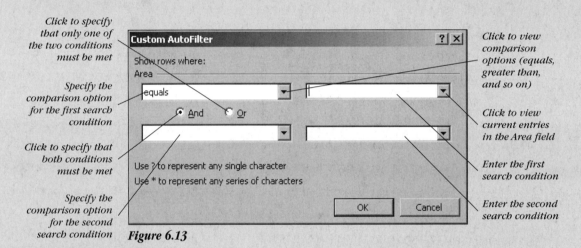

Click to specify that only one of the two conditions must be met

Specify the comparison option for the first search condition

Click to specify that both conditions must be met

Specify the comparison option for the second search condition

Click to view comparison options (equals, greater than, and so on)

Click to view current entries in the Area field

Enter the first search condition

Enter the second search condition

Figure 6.13

❹ In the upper-right section of the dialog box, click the arrow to view current entries in the Area field and select *Glenn Lakes*.
The search condition *Glenn Lakes* appears in the dialog box (see Figure 6.14).

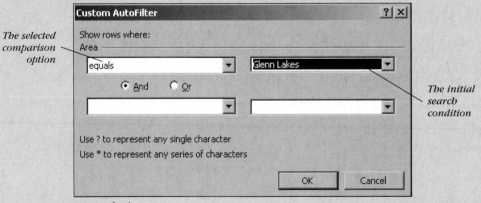

The selected comparison option

The initial search condition

Figure 6.14

❺ Select *Or* instead of *And* in the Custom AutoFilter dialog box.

To Use Custom AutoFilter with OR Search Criteria

6 **Click the arrow for viewing comparison options in the middle-left section of the dialog box.**

Comparison options display in a scrollable drop-down list (see Figure 6.15).

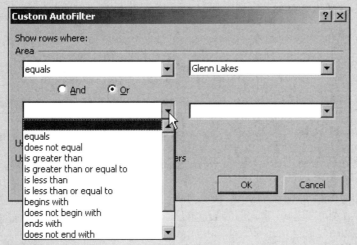

Figure 6.15

7 **Select *equals* from the drop-down list.**

8 **In the middle-right section of the dialog box, click the arrow to view current entries in the Area field; scroll down, and select *West Glenn*.**

Specifications are complete for limiting the display of records to those meeting either one of two conditions, both of which apply to the same field. Check that your criteria match those shown in Figure 6.16, and edit the dialog box as necessary.

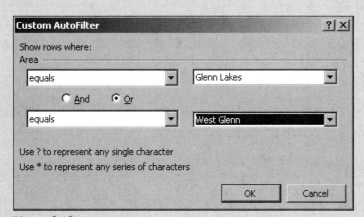

Figure 6.16

9 **Click OK in the Custom AutoFilter dialog box.**

The current filter limits the display to homes in either Glenn Lakes or West Glenn (see Figure 6.17).

(Continues)

To Use Custom AutoFilter with OR Search Criteria (Continued)

	A	B	C	D	E	F	G	H	I	J	K
1	Residential Real Estate Listings										
2											
3	Listec ▾	Price ▾	Area ▾	Address ▾	Be ▾	Ba ▾	Hea ▾	Bui ▾	Poi ▾		
7	23-Jan	172,900	Glenn Lakes	3452 Cortex Street	3	2	Elec	1996	Y		
12	5-Jan	170,000	Glenn Lakes	1025 Wellington Circle	3	2	Elec	1998	Y		
16	6-Mar	123,400	Glenn Lakes	3492 54th Avenue W.	2	2	Elec	1996	Y		
20	15-Jan	155,900	West Glenn	6571 Keystone Avenue	3	2	Elec	1996	Y		
21	3-Mar	167,200	Glenn Lakes	5778 Wellington Drive	3	2	Elec	1997	Y		
22	3-Jan	180,500	Glenn Lakes	6873 Wellington Drive	4	2	Elec	1997	Y		
27	3-Mar	169,700	Glenn Lakes	2984 44th Street West	3	2	Elec	1997	Y		
33	12-Feb	121,000	West Glenn	7350 Shadeland Avenue	4	2.5	Elec	1996	N		
36	15-Jan	121,500	Glenn Lakes	5562 Kensington Drive	4	2.5	Elec	1998	N		
37	5-Feb	174,600	Glenn Lakes	4874 Manatee Avenue	3	2	Elec	1995	Y		
39											

Figure 6.17

If you have problems...

It is important to verify that your results are correct. Ensure that all displayed records meet your criteria and that records are not missing that you know are stored in the database. If there is a problem, be sure that you selected the Or logical operator in the Custom AutoFilter dialog box. Also, make sure that you selected the *equals* comparison option for both criteria.

⑩ Choose Data, point to Filter, and click AutoFilter.

All records display, and the arrow at the end of each field name disappears; this indicates that AutoFilter is no longer active. Close the *filter* workbook now, or leave it open and continue to the next lesson. It is not necessary to save the workbook because no changes have been made.

To extend your knowledge...

Using Wildcards in Search Criteria

You can use two kinds of wildcards in the Custom AutoFilter dialog box: the asterisk character (*) in place of any sequence of characters and the question-mark character (?) in place of any one character (refer to the lower-left corner of the dialog box in Figure 6.16). For example, a filter for the single search condition *Glenn* in the Area field of the Listings database finds records of homes in Glenn Lakes or West Glenn. The first asterisk indicates that any sequence of characters can precede the word *Glenn*—for example, West Glenn. The second asterisk indicates that any sequence of characters can follow the word Glenn—for example, Glenn Lakes.

Lesson 6: Using Custom AutoFilter with AND Search Criteria

If you specify two search conditions in a filter, and both conditions must be met, you are using ***AND search criteria***. When you use Custom AutoFilter to apply AND search criteria to a single field, Excel displays records that fall within a range. For example, to display the records of homes selling only in the $150,000 to $175,000 range, filter for entries in the Price field that are less than or equal to $175,000 *and* greater than or equal to $150,000. To display the records of homes listed only in January 2002, filter for entries in the Listed field that are greater than 12/31/2001 *and* less than 2/1/2002.

In this lesson, you filter using AND search criteria applied to a single field. Now, set a filter in the *filter* workbook to find homes for sale in the $150,000 to $175,000 range.

To Use Custom AutoFilter with AND Search Criteria

1 Open the *filter* workbook, if necessary, and click any cell within the list range A3:I38.

2 Choose <u>D</u>ata, point to <u>F</u>ilter, and click Auto<u>F</u>ilter.

3 Click the filter arrow for the Price field, and select *(Custom)* from the drop-down list.

4 Specify the five settings shown in Figure 6.18 (select the two comparison options from drop-down lists, click <u>A</u>nd, and type the numbers 150000 and 175000).

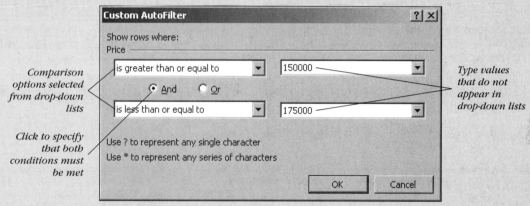

Comparison options selected from drop-down lists

Click to specify that both conditions must be met

Type values that do not appear in drop-down lists

Figure 6.18

5 Click OK to close the Custom AutoFilter dialog box and execute the filter.

The current filter limits the display to the eight homes priced between $150,000 and $175,000 (see Figure 6.19).

	A	B	C	D	E	F	G	H	I	J	K
1	Residential Real Estate Listings										
2											
3	Listec	Price	Area	Address	Be	Ba	Hea	Bui	Po		
7	23-Jan	172,900	Glenn Lakes	3452 Cortex Street	3	2	Elec	1996	Y		
12	5-Jan	170,000	Glenn Lakes	1025 Wellington Circle	3	2	Elec	1998	Y		
20	15-Jan	155,900	West Glenn	6571 Keystone Avenue	3	2	Elec	1996	Y		
21	3-Mar	167,200	Glenn Lakes	5778 Wellington Drive	3	2	Elec	1997	Y		
27	3-Mar	169,700	Glenn Lakes	2984 44th Street West	3	2	Elec	1997	Y		
32	12-Feb	152,900	Champions Village	5429 Bridle Avenue	4	2.5	Elec	1990	N		
34	6-Feb	156,400	Champions Village	2398 Sulky Court	4	2	Gas	1990	N		
37	5-Feb	174,600	Glenn Lakes	4874 Manatee Avenue	3	2	Elec	1995	Y		
39											
40											

Figure 6.19

If you have problems...

It is important to verify that your results are correct. Check that all displayed records meet your criteria. If there is a problem, be sure you selected the <u>A</u>nd button in the Custom AutoFilter dialog box. Also ensure that you selected the appropriate comparison options, and typed the upper and lower values correctly.

6 Choose <u>D</u>ata, point to <u>F</u>ilter, and click Auto<u>F</u>ilter.

All records display, and the arrow at the end of each field name disappears; this indicates that AutoFilter is no longer active.

(Continues)

To Use Custom AutoFilter with AND Search Criteria (Continued)

7 **Close the *filter* workbook.**
It is not necessary to save the workbook because no changes have been made. You can continue to the next lesson, or exit Excel.

Lesson 7: Adding and Deleting Records Using a Form

Keeping data current is an essential part of using any database. To add a record to a list, move to the first blank row below the list and type data in each field. To delete a record, find its row and delete the row.

If you work with a large list, you may prefer to add and delete records by using a form that shows all the fields in one record. Excel's ***data form*** is a dialog box that displays a list one record at a time.

In this lesson, you use a form to add a new listing. You also use a form to find and delete a record.

To Add and Delete Records Using a Form

1 **Open the *ee1-0601* workbook, save it as** dataform, **and click any cell in the list range A3:I38.**

2 **Choose Data, Form.**
A dialog box named *current* opens, and displays each field name to the left of the corresponding data in the first record (see Figure 6.20). The name of the dialog box is the name of the worksheet.

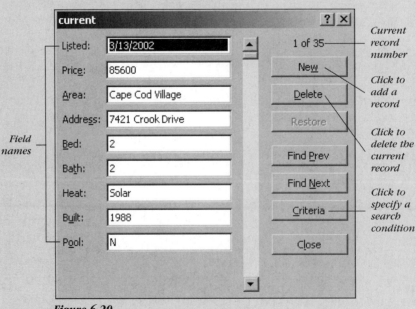

Figure 6.20

To Add and Delete Records Using a Form

3 **Click the New button in the dialog box.**
Excel displays a blank data form.

4 **Type 3/29/2002 in the Listed field text box, and press Tab⇄.**
Data is entered into the Listed field of the new record. Pressing Tab⇄ moves the insertion point to the next field text box. You can press ⬆Shift+Tab⇄ to move backward to the previous field. You can also move to any field by clicking that field.

If you have problems...
If you make a mistake while typing, use ⬅Backspace or Del to remove unwanted characters, and type the correct data. If you press ↵Enter or ↓ instead of Tab⇄ to move to the next field, Excel adds the new record to the list and displays a new blank data form. If you did not complete filling out the data form, click the Find Prev button to restore display of the previous record.

5 **Add the remaining data in the new record, as shown in Figure 6.21.**

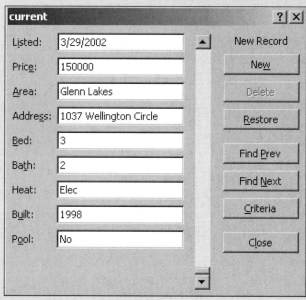

Figure 6.21

6 **Click the Close button to add the new record to the list.**
Excel adds the new record to the bottom of the list and closes the data form. Now, find and delete the record for a listed property that has been sold.

7 **Choose Data, Form, and click the Criteria button.**
Excel displays a blank data form. The word *Criteria* appears in the upper-right corner of the dialog box, instead of the record number.

8 **Click in the Address field, type *Sulky, and click the Find Next button.**
The asterisk preceding the word *Sulky* tells Excel to find records containing *Sulky*, no matter which characters precede the word. Excel finds the record containing *2398 Sulky Court* in the Address field, and displays its contents in the current data form (see Figure 6.22).

(Continues)

To Add and Delete Records Using a Form (Continued)

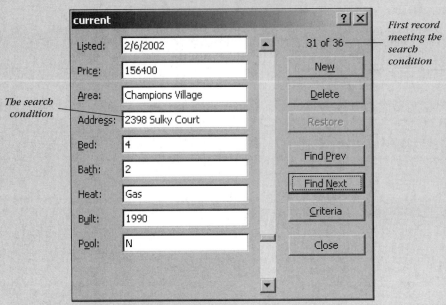

The search condition

First record meeting the search condition

Figure 6.22

9 **Click the Delete button.**
A dialog box opens with the message *Displayed record will be permanently deleted.*

10 **Click OK, click the Close button, and save your changes to the *dataform* workbook.**
You can close the *dataform* workbook now, or leave it open and continue with the final lesson in this project.

Lesson 8: Editing Records Using a Form

Keeping data current requires more than adding and deleting records. You must be able to revise data in one or more fields of an existing record. If there are many records in a list, you can specify a search condition on a data form to find a record you want to change.

In this lesson, you make two changes to the residential real estate data: reducing the price for one home and correcting the spelling of a street name for another. You use a data form to locate each record.

To Edit Records Using a Form

1 **Open the *dataform* workbook, if necessary, and click any cell in the list range A3:I38.**

2 **Choose Data, Form, and click the Criteria button.**

3 **Type 3360 Glade in the Address field, and click the Find Next button.**
Excel displays the record containing *3360 Glade Avenue* in the Address field.

4 **Click in the Price field, change *225000* to 215000, and click the Close button.**
The price of the property at 3360 Glade Avenue is reduced to 215,000.

To Edit Records Using a Form

5 Choose **D**ata, F**o**rm, and click the **C**riteria button.

6 Type 3452 Cortex in the Addre**ss** field, and click the Find **N**ext button.
Excel displays the record containing *3452 Cortex Street* in the Address field.

7 Click in the Addre**ss** field, and change *Cortex* to Cortez.

8 Click the Cl**o**se button.
The data form closes. The records in rows 7 and 9 reflect the changes you made (see cells D7 and B9 in Figure 6.23).

	A	B	C	D	E	F	G	H	I	J	K
1	Residential Real Estate Listings										
2											
3	Listed	Price	Area	Address	Bed	Bath	Heat	Built	Pool		
4	13-Mar	85,600	Cape Cod Village	7421 Crook Drive	2	2	Solar	1988	N		
5	22-Feb	180,000	Hunter's Run	4191 Glenn Avenue	4	2.5	Solar	1995	N		
6	9-Jan	125,200	Hocking Hills	11250 Spruce Street	4	2.5	Elec	1992	N		
7	23-Jan	172,900	Glenn Lakes	3452 Cortez Street	3	2	Elec	1996	Y		
8	12-Feb	133,900	Whispering Pines	7235 42nd Street	3	2	Gas	1970	N		
9	25-Feb	215,000	Hunter's Run	3360 Glade Avenue	5	3	Elec	1995	Y		
10	23-Jan	98,200	Autumn Woods	6370 Elm Street	3	1.5	Gas	1994	N		
11	6-Jan	120,700	Champions Village	8882 Derby Lane	3	1.5	Elec	1990	N		
12	5-Jan	170,000	Glenn Lakes	1025 Wellington Circle	3	2	Elec	1998	Y		

Changed Cortex to Cortez

Changed 225,000 to 215,000

Figure 6.23

9 Save your changes to the *dataform* workbook, and close it.
This concludes Project 6. Continue with end-of-project activities, or exit Excel.

Summary

You began this project by viewing onscreen Help about guidelines for creating a list. You learned to convert data into useful information by sorting and filtering the contents of the sample database of residential real estate listings. You also practiced basic database maintenance tasks by adding, deleting, and editing records.

You can reinforce your learning if you create your own list; and try sorting, filtering, and editing at the simple level demonstrated in the project. You can also use onscreen Help to learn about more advanced sorting and filtering techniques, and apply the more complex techniques to the database of your choice.

Checking Concepts and Terms

Multiple Choice

Circle the letter of the correct answer for each of the following.

1. Each collection of related data in a database is called a _____. [L1]

   a. list
   b. record
   c. field
   d. None of the above.

2. Which of the following search conditions would find the name Bellingham? [L5]

   a. Bell*
   b. Bell?
   c. Bell&
   d. None of the above.

3. Which of the following would not be a meaningful sort in a student list? [L3]

   a. Sort by student I.D. number and then by year in school.
   b. Sort by major and then by grade point average.
   c. Sort by last name and then by first name.
   d. All of the above.

4. Which of the following criteria displays records of males old enough to vote (assume that the voting age is 18)? [L5 or L6]

   a. Gender equals male and age greater than 18.
   b. Gender equals male or age greater than 18.
   c. Gender equals male or age greater than or equal to 18.
   d. None of the above.

5. Assume that a list contains a field for birth date named Birthday. Data are entered in the form mm/dd/yyyy, where m=month, d=day, and y=year. Which of the following criteria limits record display to individuals born in 1980? [L5 or L6]

   a. Birthday greater than or equal to 1/1/1980, and less than or equal to 1/1/1981
   b. Birthday greater than 12/31/1979, and less than 1/1/1981
   c. Birthday equal to 1980
   d. None of the above

Discussion

1. Describe an Excel list that you could create for your own use, including its purpose and the data fields it would contain. Describe two sorts and two filters that you could apply to the data, and explain the value of the results. [L2 through L6]

2. Refer to the Residential Real Estate Listings database, and explain the importance of adding, deleting, and editing records in a timely manner.

Include in your discussion at least three consequences of not updating the list. [L7 and L8]

3. Discuss the consequences of not having valid data in the FBI's National Crime Information Computer (NCIC), a credit bureau database such as TRW, or an inventory database that is used by General Motors to manage the materials used on automobile assembly lines.

Skill Drill

Skill Drill exercises reinforce project skills. Each skill reinforced is the same, or nearly the same, as a skill presented in the project. Detailed instructions are provided in a step-by-step format.

Before beginning your first Project 6 Skill Drill exercise, complete the following steps:

1. Open the file named *ee1-0602*, and immediately save it as `ee1-p6drill`.
   The workbook contains eight sheets: an overview, and exercise sheets named #1-Sort1, #2-Sort2, #3-Filter1, #4-FilterOR, #5-FilterAND, #6-Add, and #7-Edit.
2. Click the Overview sheet to view the organization of the Project 6 Skill Drill Exercises workbook.

Each exercise is independent of the others, so you may complete the exercises in any order. Be sure to save the workbook after completing each exercise. If you need a paper copy of the completed exercise, enter your name, centered in a header, before printing. Other print options have already been set to print compressed to one page and to display the filename, sheet name, and current date in a footer.

If you need more than one work session to complete the skill drill exercises, continue working on *ee1-p6drill* instead of starting all over on the original *ee1-0602* file.

1. Sorting a List Using One Field

You want to arrange the two-minute survey records alphabetically by the single field *Type Use*. For a simple sort, use the Sort Ascending or Sort Descending button on the toolbar.

To sort ascending on one field, follow these steps:

1. Open the *ee1-p6drill* workbook, if necessary, and select the worksheet named #1-Sort1.
2. Click any cell containing data in the Type Use column.
3. Click the Sort Ascending button on the toolbar.
   Check that *Bus* (business) records display before *Per* (personal) records.
4. Save your changes to the *ee1-p6drill* workbook.

2. Sorting a List Using Two Fields

You are interested in arranging the data into groups by car size. Within each group, you want to see the data arranged in descending order of the number of days the vehicle was rented.

To sort the data by using two fields of data, follow these steps:

1. Open the *ee1-p6drill* workbook, if necessary, and select the worksheet named #2-Sort2.
2. Click any cell in the list range A6:L36.
3. Choose Data, Sort.
4. Display the drop-down list for Sort by, and select the Car Size field.
5. Ensure that Ascending is the selected order for the Car Size field.
6. Display the drop-down list for *Then by*, and select the *Days Rented* field.
7. Specify Descending as the sort order.
8. Click OK.
   Make sure that records are organized first within groups (Compact, Full Size, and so on, and then within each group by days rented (highest to lowest).
9. Save your changes to the *ee1-p6drill* workbook.

3. Filtering with One Criterion

As you begin to analyze the data in your Indy 500 Motor Works list, you want to focus on selected data. For example, you want to limit the display to records of compact car rentals.

To filter data using one criterion, follow these steps:

1. Open the *ee1-p6drill* workbook, if necessary, and select the worksheet named #3-Filter1.
2. Click any cell within the list range A6:L36.
3. Choose Data, Filter, AutoFilter.
4. Click the arrow for the Car Size field.
5. Select *Compact* from the drop-down list.
   Make sure that the display is limited to records of compact car rentals.
6. Save your changes to the *ee1-p6drill* workbook.

4. Filtering with OR Search Criteria

As you review the car rental data, you decide to analyze the records for customer ratings 1 and 5—the lowest and highest customer ratings.

To filter with two search conditions on one field, limiting the display to records with Customer Rating 1 or Customer Rating 5, follow these steps:

1. Open the *ee1-p6drill* workbook, if necessary, and select the worksheet named #4-FilterOR.
2. Click any cell within the list, and choose Data, Filter, AutoFilter.
3. Click the filter arrow for the field Customer Rating.
4. Select *(Custom)* from the drop-down list.
5. Click the upper-right text box and type 1 (or select *1* from the drop-down list).
6. Click the Or option (as opposed to *And*) in the Custom AutoFilter dialog box.
7. Click the filter arrow for the lower-left text box and select *equals*.
8. Click the lower-right text box and type 5.
9. Click OK.
   Ensure that the record display is limited to those with a Customer Rating of 1 or 5.
10. Save your changes to the *ee1-p6drill* workbook.

5. Filtering with AND Search Criteria

As you look at your list, you decide to focus on records of cars rented for periods of between six and 10 days, inclusive (that is, including 6 and 10 within the range).

To filter for records within a range—days rented more than five and fewer than 11—follow these steps:

1. Open the *ee1-p6drill* workbook, if necessary, and select the worksheet named #5-FilterAND.
2. Click within any cell in the list, and choose Data, Filter, AutoFilter.
3. Click the filter arrow next to the field name *Days Rented*.
4. From the drop-down list, select *(Custom)*.
5. Click the drop-down arrow next to the upper-left text box, and select *is greater than*.
6. Click the upper-right text box and type 5.
7. Click the And option (as opposed to *Or*) in the Custom AutoFilter dialog box.
8. Click the drop-down arrow next to the lower-left text box, and select *is less than*.
9. Click the lower-right text box, and type 11.
10. Click OK.
    Be sure that the display of records is limited to those showing days rented between 6 and 10.
11. Save your changes to the *ee1-p6drill* workbook.

6. Adding a Record Using a Data Form

You have found a survey document that has not been entered in the list.

To add a record, follow these steps:

1. Open the *ee1-p6drill* workbook, if necessary, and select the worksheet named #6-Add.
2. Click any cell within the list, and choose Data, Form.
3. Click the New button.
4. Type 31 in the ID field text box.
5. Enter the remaining data as follows (remember to press Tab↹ to move from field to field):
   Type Use: Bus
   Type Pmt: cc
   Car Size: Mid Size
   Date Rented: 02/01/2002
   Date Returned: 02/15/2002
   Daily Rate: 11.50
   Customer Rating: 5
   Favorite Sport: tennis
   Favorite Magazine: WSJ
6. Select Close to add the record and close the data form.
7. Save your changes to the *ee1-p6drill* workbook.

7. Editing a Record Using a Data Form

You noticed an error in record number 8 in the list. The Car Size should read *Luxury*, not Mid Size.

To edit a record, follow these steps:

1. Open the *ee1-p6drill* workbook, if necessary, and select the worksheet named #7-Edit.
2. Click any cell within the list, and choose Data, Form.
3. Click the Criteria button, type 8 in the ID text box, and click Find Next.
4. Click in the Car Size text box of record 8.
5. Type Luxury in place of Mid Size, and click the Close button.
6. Save your changes to the *ee1-p6drill* workbook.

8. Learning More About Filters

You want to expand your knowledge of using filters. Onscreen Help provides a lot of information on the topic.

To view onscreen Help on using filters, follow these steps:

1. Display an existing or new workbook, type advanced filter in the Ask a Question box near the right end of the menu bar, and press ↵Enter.
   Excel displays Help topics related to advanced filter.
2. Click the topic *Filter by using advanced criteria*.
   The requested Microsoft Excel Help window opens.
3. Click Show All in the upper-right corner of the Help window, and scroll down to read the extensive information on the selected topic.
   If you want to print a Help topic, click the Print button near the upper-left corner of the Help window, and follow the instructions.
4. Select other topics on filtering, as desired, from the Contents tab on the left side of the Help window.
5. Close the Help window.

Challenge exercises expand on or are somewhat related to skills presented in the lessons. Each exercise provides a brief narrative introduction, followed by instructions in a numbered-step format that are not as detailed as those in the Skill Drill section.

Before beginning your first Project 6 Challenge exercise, complete the following steps:

1. Open the file named *ee1-0603*, and immediately save it as **ee1-p6challenge**.

   The workbook contains five sheets: an overview, and exercises named #1-Sort3, #2-Filter-High5, #3-FilterTop10, and #4-EditSeries.

2. Click the Overview sheet to view the organization of the Project 6 Challenge Exercises workbook.

Each exercise is independent of the others, so you may complete the exercises in any order. Be sure to save the workbook after completing each exercise. If you need a paper copy of the completed exercise, enter your name, centered in a header, before printing. Other print options have already been set to print landscape compressed to one page and to display the filename, sheet name, and current date in a footer.

If you need more than one work session to complete the desired exercises, continue working on *ee1-p6challenge* instead of starting all over on the original *ee1-0603* file.

1. Executing a Sort on Three Fields

You identified three fields on which you want to sort. First, you want to display records in two groups by Type Use: business and then personal. Within each type, you next want to sort records by Car Size (ascending order). Finally, within Car Size, you want to organize records by Customer Rating in descending order.

To sort your list by three criteria, follow these steps:

1. Open the *ee1-p6challenge* workbook, if necessary, and select the worksheet named #1-Sort3.
2. Display the Sort dialog box.
3. For each text box—*Sort by*, *Then by*, and *Then by*—select the appropriate fields and sort orders.
4. Execute the sort, and verify that records appear in the desired order.
5. Save your changes to the *ee1-p6challenge* workbook.

2. Filtering for the Highest Five Items

You notice a Top 10 option using AutoFilter, but you want to find the five highest values in the Rental Cost field. You can modify any of three initial settings in the Top 10 AutoFilter dialog box. Instead of *Top*, you can specify *Bottom*. Instead of *10*, you can specify the number of your choice. You can also select *Percent* instead of *Items*.

To filter your list using the Top 10 AutoFilter option, follow these steps:

1. Open the *ee1-p6challenge* workbook, if necessary, and select the worksheet named #2-FilterHigh5.
2. Turn on AutoFilter.
3. Select the *(Top 10)* option from the drop-down list for the Rental Cost field.
4. Change the number of items from 10 to **5**, and click OK to activate the filter.
5. Make sure that the display is limited to records with the top five values in the Rental Cost field. In this case, six records display because two records have the same $182 value.
6. Save your changes to the *ee1-p6challenge* workbook.

3. Filtering for the Top Ten Percent

You know that you can use AutoFilter's Top 10 option to display a user-specified number of top or bottom items, but now you want to limit display to the top 10 percent based on values in the Rental Cost field.

To set the desired filter, follow these steps:

1. Open the *ee1-p6challenge* workbook, if necessary, and select the worksheet named #3-FilterTop10.
2. Turn on AutoFilter.
3. Select the *(Top 10)* option from the drop-down list for the Rental Cost field.
4. Change settings in the Top 10 AutoFilter dialog box, as necessary, to filter for the top 10 percent.
5. Click OK to activate the filter and verify that only 10 percent (three of 30) of the records display. Make sure that the records displayed are those with the highest values in the Rental Cost field.
6. Save your changes to the *ee1-p6challenge* workbook.

4. Editing a Series of Records

You know how to use a data form to locate and edit a single record. Now, you want to locate a number of records based on the same search condition, and edit each one. You plan to enter the word *Discount* in the Special Action field for every record that indicates business use and a customer rating of 1 or 2.

To edit a series of records, follow these steps:

1. Open the *ee1-p6challenge* workbook, if necessary, and select the worksheet named #4-EditSeries.
2. Display a data form.
3. Select the Criteria option, and type =Bus in the Type Use field.
4. Type <=2 in the Customer Rating field.
5. Click Find Next, and type Discount in the Special Action field.
6. Press ↵Enter to update the Special Action field.
7. Repeat Steps 5 and 6 until all records meeting your criteria are changed.
8. Close the data form.
9. Save your changes to the *ee1-p6challenge* workbook.

Discovery Zone

Discovery Zone exercises require advanced knowledge of topics presented in *Essentials* lessons, application of skills from multiple lessons, or self-directed learning of new skills.

Before beginning your first Project 6 Discovery Zone exercise, complete the following steps:

1. Open the file named *ee1-0604*, and save it as ee1-p6discovery.
   The workbook contains four sheets: an overview, and exercise sheets named #1-Wildcard, #2-Filter3on1, and #3-Filter3on3.
2. Click the Overview sheet to view the organization of the Project 6 Discovery Zone Exercises workbook.

Each exercise is independent of the others, so you may complete the exercises in any order. Be sure to save the workbook after completing each exercise. If you need a paper copy of the completed exercise, enter your name, centered in a header, before printing. Other print options have already been set to print compressed to one page and to display the filename, sheet name, and current date in a footer.

If you need more than one work session to complete the desired exercises, continue working on *ee1-p6discovery* instead of starting over again on the original *ee1-0604* file.

1. Using Wildcards to Find Data

From past experience, you know that a variety of software programs support using wildcard characters to locate data or filenames. Open your *ee1-p6discovery* workbook, and select the #1-Wildcard sheet. Find information about the word *wildcard* using the Ask a Question box. Apply what you learn by setting a filter to display only those records containing the letters **news** in the Favorite Magazine field. Inspect the results to see that they meet the criteria you specified. Decide how you might use a wildcard to filter records in at least two other fields. Execute those filters and verify the results.

2. Filtering on Three Criteria (One Field)

You want to display only those records in which the car type is Mid Size, Full Size, or Luxury; but you realize there is a two-condition limit when using AutoFilter's Custom option. You notice that an Advanced Filter option appears when you choose Data, Filter.

Select the #2-Filter3on1 worksheet in the *ee1-p6discovery* workbook, and use onscreen Help to learn about the Advanced Filter option. Focus on examples that use a separate Criteria range. Now, set up the desired filter. The worksheet has already been modified to include the field names for a Criteria range in row 6. All fields are included, but you enter criteria below only the Car Size field. Execute the filter, and make sure that the results are limited to rental records of only Mid Size, Full Size, and Luxury cars. Execute another three-condition, one-field filter of your choice (be sure to delete the previous search conditions in the Criteria range), and verify the results.

3. Filtering on Three Criteria (Three Fields)

You are excited about the capabilities that the Advanced Filter option provides for viewing data. Now, you want to view only the records of luxury car rentals for business use with a rental period exceeding five days.

Select the #3-Filter3on3 worksheet in the *ee1-p6discovery* workbook, and use onscreen Help to learn about the Advanced Filter option. Focus on examples that use a separate Criteria range. Now, set up the desired filter. The worksheet is already modified to include the field names for a Criteria range in row 6. All fields are included, but you will enter criteria below only the Type Use, Car Size, and Days Rented fields. Execute the filter, and make sure that the results are limited to rental records for business use of Luxury cars for more than five days. Execute another three-condition, three-field filter of your choice (be sure to delete the previous search conditions in the Criteria range), and verify the results.

Working with Charts

Objectives

In this project, you learn how to

- ✔ Identify Common Chart Types and Features
- ✔ Use Chart Wizard to Create an Embedded Pie Chart
- ✔ Use Chart Wizard to Create an Embedded Column Chart
- ✔ Change the Chart Type
- ✔ Chart Non-Adjacent Data Series
- ✔ Modify Chart Formats
- ✔ Add, Reorder, and Delete a Data Series
- ✔ Create and Print a Combination Chart

Key terms in this project include

- ❑ chart
- ❑ clustered column chart
- ❑ column chart
- ❑ combination chart
- ❑ data series
- ❑ embedded chart
- ❑ legend
- ❑ line chart
- ❑ pie chart
- ❑ sizing handles
- ❑ stacked column chart
- ❑ X-axis
- ❑ Y-axis

Why Would I Do This?

After you create a worksheet, you may want to show the information to someone else. You can print the worksheet if you need only numerical detail. You can also transform data in the worksheet into a ***chart***, a graphical representation of data that makes it easy for users to see trends and make comparisons.

Visual Summary

This project shows you how to create an ***embedded chart***, a graphical representation of data created within the worksheet instead of as a separate worksheet. You create several charts based on sample data, including the one shown in Figure 7.1. You also learn how to enhance various types of charts and modify chart features.

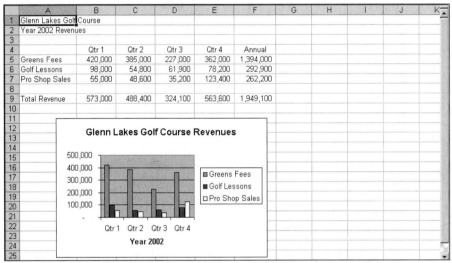

Figure 7.1

Lesson 1: Identifying Common Chart Types and Features

You can create a variety of chart types by using Excel. Chart features include titles and labels that explain the graphed data; and enhancements, such as gridlines and color, which improve readability or add visual appeal.

In this lesson, you view examples of common chart types and features. You apply this knowledge in the remaining lessons as you create and modify charts similar to those shown in the examples.

To Identify Common Chart Types and Features

❶ Open the file *ee1-0701* and save it as sample charts.
   The workbook includes seven sheets, the first of which is named Charts. The remaining sheets illustrate three common types of charts: pie (sheets Pie1 and Pie2), line (sheets Line1 and Line2), and column (sheets Column1 and Column2).

To Identify Common Chart Types and Features

②   Select the worksheet named Pie1.

The sample embedded pie chart shown in Figure 7.2 appears. A ***pie chart*** is a circular chart, in which each piece (wedge) shows a data segment and its relationship to the whole. A pie chart is limited to one ***data series***, which is a set of related values that is entered in a row or column of the worksheet. The chart shown in Figure 7.2 displays the percentage of Greens Fees earned in each quarter, based on the amounts in row 5. The corresponding text entries in row 4 (*Qtr 1, Qtr 2,* and so on) appear as data labels for the pie slices.

Fill color illustrates the range used to define the data series and data labels

One or more slices in a pie chart can be exploded, as shown for Qtr 3

Current sheet

Chart title

Data labels (label and %)

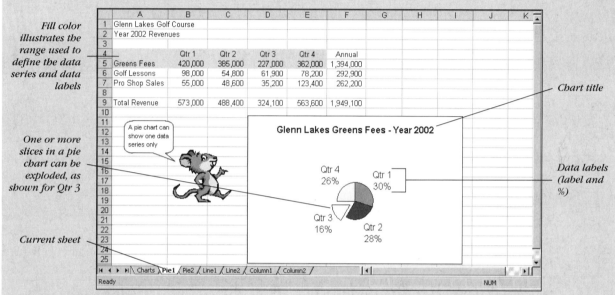

Figure 7.2

③   Click the sheet tab named Pie2.

The chart embedded in the Pie2 worksheet displays the percentage contribution that each revenue source made toward the total revenues for the year. The data series for this chart is a set of values entered in a column instead of a row. In this sample pie chart, a legend appears to the right of the pie. (A ***legend*** displays the colors, patterns, or symbols that identify data categories.)

④   Click the sheet tab named Line1.

A ***line chart*** plots one or more data series as connected points along an axis, as shown in Figure 7.3. The chart illustrates total revenue for each quarter in the year 2002. Data points for each quarter are arranged above the ***X-axis***, the horizontal axis of a chart that generally appears at the bottom edge. Each quarterly amount is reflected in the height of its data point in relation to the scale shown on the ***Y-axis***, a vertical axis of a chart that usually appears at the left edge.

(Continues)

To Identify Common Chart Types and Features (Continued)

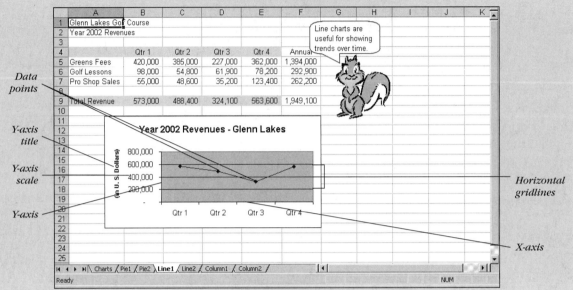

Figure 7.3

5 **Click the sheet tab named Line2.**

The sample line chart that is embedded in sheet Line2 includes three data series: Greens Fees, Golf Lessons, and Pro Shop Sales. A unique symbol marks each data point in a series, such as the diamond shape assigned to Greens Fees. The legend displays the symbols that identify each data series.

6 **Click the sheet tab named Column1.**

The sample embedded column chart shown in Figure 7.4 appears. In a *column chart*, each data point is reflected in the height of its column in relation to the scale shown on the Y-axis. In this chart, columns are grouped along the X-axis by quarter—a result achieved by specifying that data series are organized in rows.

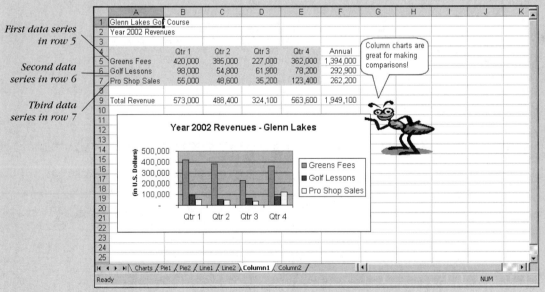

Figure 7.4

To Identify Common Chart Types and Features

7 **Click the sheet tab named Column2.**
Yellow highlighting indicates the range used to define the column chart, which is the same range used to produce the chart in the Column1 sheet. In this chart, however, columns are grouped along the X-axis by type of revenue—a result achieved by specifying that data series are organized in columns.

8 **Close the *sample charts* file.**
Now that you know the common chart types and the components of a chart, you can create your own charts. Continue to the next lesson, or exit Excel.

To extend your knowledge...

Printing a Chart

The steps to print a worksheet and its embedded chart(s) are the same as those for printing a worksheet without charts; that is, specify the desired settings in the Page Setup and Print dialog boxes. To print just a chart in Excel without printing the entire worksheet, select the chart by clicking any blank area inside the chart; then choose File, Print to open the Print dialog box. Make sure that the *Selected Chart* option is selected in the *Print what* area, and click OK.

There are advantages to printing a chart instead of viewing it onscreen. Printing lets you view the worksheets you create, even when you are away from your computer. A printed copy of a chart, combined with the worksheet data, makes a very effective presentation.

Lesson 2: Using Chart Wizard to Create an Embedded Pie Chart

To create a chart, you select the data you want to use in the chart; then choose Insert, Chart or click the Chart Wizard button on the Standard toolbar. The Chart Wizard provides step-by-step assistance, through a series of dialog boxes, for choosing a chart type and specifying chart options. It automatically creates the chart from the selected data and places it in a box (frame). You can then move, size, change, or enhance the chart. Now, try creating an embedded pie chart that shows the percentage of Year 2002 Greens Fees earned in each quarter.

To Create an Embedded Pie Chart

1 **Open the file *ee1-0702* and save it as** `mycharts`.
A workbook opens with seven sheets, the first of which is named Pie.

2 **Select the range A4:E5 in the Pie worksheet, and click the Chart Wizard button in the toolbar.**
The Chart Type dialog box opens (Chart Wizard – Step 1 of 4), as shown in Figure 7.5.

(Continued)

To Create an Embedded Pie Chart (Continued)

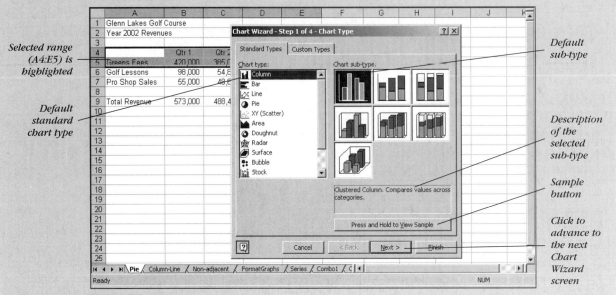

Figure 7.5

❸ In the **C**hart Type list, click Pie.

❹ Make sure that the selected Chart sub-**t**ype is Pie, the picture in the upper-left corner.

❺ Click the **N**ext button at the bottom of the dialog box.
    The Chart Source Data dialog box opens (Chart Wizard – Step 2 of 4), as shown in Figure 7.6.

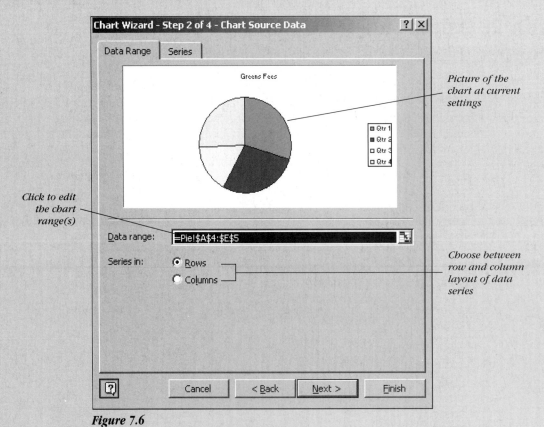

Figure 7.6

To Create an Embedded Pie Chart

6 **Make sure that the direction of the data series is Rows, and click Next.**
The Chart Options dialog box opens (Chart Wizard – Step 3 of 4). When the chart type is Pie, the dialog box displays three tabs: Titles, Legend, and Data Labels.

7 **Click the Titles tab, if necessary, to display the dialog box shown in Figure 7.7.**

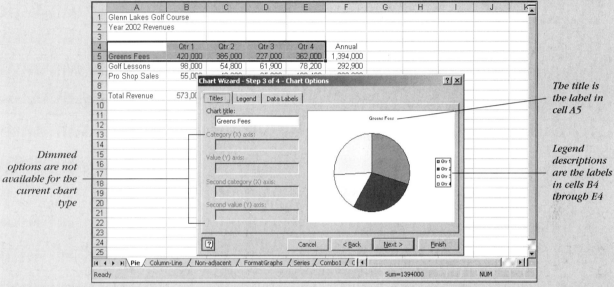

Dimmed options are not available for the current chart type

The title is the label in cell A5

Legend descriptions are the labels in cells B4 through E4

Figure 7.7

8 **Click within the Chart title text box, and edit the title to read** `Year 2002 – Greens Fees.`
After a short delay, the revised title automatically appears in the sample chart that fills the right half of the Chart Options dialog box.

If you have problems...

If you press ⏎Enter after editing the title, the Chart Location dialog box appears (Chart Wizard – Step 4 of 4). Click the Back button to return to the Chart Options dialog box.

9 **Click the Legend tab in the Chart Options dialog box, and click the Show legend text box to remove the check mark.**
The legend no longer appears on the pie chart.

10 **Click the Data Labels tab in the Chart Options dialog box, and click the Category name and Percentage options (see Figure 7.8).**

(Continues)

To Create an Embedded Pie Chart (Continued)

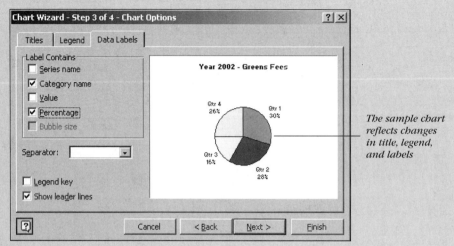

The sample chart reflects changes in title, legend, and labels

Figure 7.8

Quarter labels and associated percents appear by their respective pie slices.

⓫ Click Next.
The Chart Location dialog box appears (Chart Wizard – Step 4 of 4). Select the default option, *As object in*, if you want to see the chart displayed next to its source data. Select the option *As new sheet* if you prefer to work with the chart separately on its own sheet.

⓬ Make sure that the current setting is to place the chart as an object in Pie, and click Finish.
Excel creates the chart and displays it with eight black squares called ***sizing handles*** at the corners and midpoints of the border surrounding the chart box. The handles indicate that the chart is an object that can be moved and sized. To move a selected object, click within the object and drag it to its new location. To size a selected object, click a handle and drag it in the desired direction.

If you have problems...

Your screen may display a floating Chart toolbar after you click Finish to exit the Chart Wizard. If there is a floating toolbar and it displays on the chart you are about to move, click its Close button (the X in the upper-right corner of the toolbar).

⓭ Click inside the chart area (in any blank area), and drag the chart so that the upper-left corner is positioned near the middle of cell A11.
As you drag the chart, the pointer changes to a four-headed arrow.

⓮ Click outside the chart to deselect it.
The content and layout of the pie chart in your worksheet should resemble the one shown in Figure 7.9. If there are slight differences in chart height, width, or location, you can size or move the chart as desired.

To Create an Embedded Pie Chart

	A	B	C	D	E	F	G	H	I	J	K
1	Glenn Lakes Golf Course										
2	Year 2002 Revenues										
3											
4		Qtr 1	Qtr 2	Qtr 3	Qtr 4	Annual					
5	Greens Fees	420,000	385,000	227,000	362,000	1,394,000					
6	Golf Lessons	98,000	54,800	61,900	78,200	292,900					
7	Pro Shop Sales	55,000	48,600	35,200	123,400	262,200					
8											
9	Total Revenue	573,000	488,400	324,100	563,600	1,949,100					
10											
11											
12											
13											
14											
15											
16											
17											
18											
19											
20											
21											
22											
23											
24											
25											

Year 2002 - Greens Fees

Qtr 4 26%   Qtr 1 30%   Qtr 3 16%   Qtr 2 28%

Pie / Column-Line / Non-adjacent / FormatGraphs / Series / Combo1 / C

Ready   NUM

Figure 7.9

 Save your changes to the *mycharts* workbook.

The embedded pie chart is saved in the Pie worksheet, which is the first sheet within the *mycharts* workbook. Keep the workbook open for the next lesson, or close the workbook and exit Excel.

To extend your knowledge...

Deleting and Resizing Charts

If you want to delete a chart, simply select the chart and press Del.

When you resize a chart by dragging a handle on the middle of one side of the box, you change the size horizontally or vertically. When you drag a corner handle, you change the vertical and horizontal dimensions at the same time. If you hold down ⬆Shift while dragging a corner handle, you maintain the original proportions of the chart.

Lesson 3: Using Chart Wizard to Create an Embedded Column Chart

A pie chart is limited to one data series, and the data charted must be components of a whole. Excel provides a variety of other types, including a column chart, suitable for charting multiple data series. You can use the Chart Wizard to construct all chart types. Now, try creating an embedded column chart that compares Year 2002 quarterly revenues from three sources: Greens Fees, Golf Lessons, and Pro Shop Sales.

To Create an Embedded Column Chart

❶ Open the *mycharts* file, if necessary, and select the worksheet named Column-Line.

The Column-Line sheet, like the previous sheet named Pie, contains the Year 2002 revenue data for Glenn Lakes Golf Course.

❷ Select the range A4:E7, and click the Chart Wizard button in the Standard toolbar.

The Chart Type dialog box appears (Chart Wizard – Step 1 of 4).

❸ Click *Column* in the Chart type list, if it isn't already selected.

❹ Make sure that the Clustered Column sub-type from the Chart sub-type list is selected.

❺ Point to the *Press and Hold to View Sample* button, and click and hold down the left mouse button.

A sample of the chart is displayed in the Sample box, as shown in Figure 7.10.

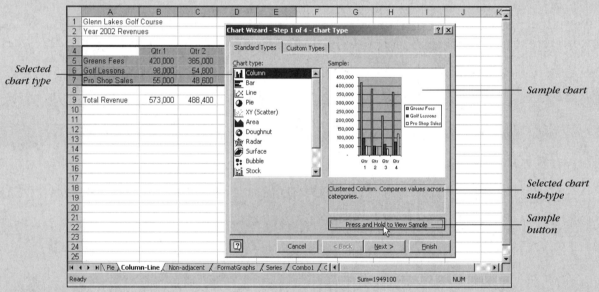

Figure 7.10

❻ Release the mouse button, and click Next.

The Chart Source Data dialog box appears (Chart Wizard – Step 2 of 4).

❼ Make sure that the data range is $A$4:$E$7 in the Column-Line worksheet and the data series is in Rows, and click Next.

The Chart Options dialog box appears (Chart Wizard – Step 3 of 4). When the chart type is Column, the dialog box displays six tabs: Titles, Axes, Gridlines, Legend, Data Labels, and Data Table.

❽ Click the Titles tab, if necessary, and enter the chart title and X-axis title shown in Figure 7.11.

To Create an Embedded Column Chart

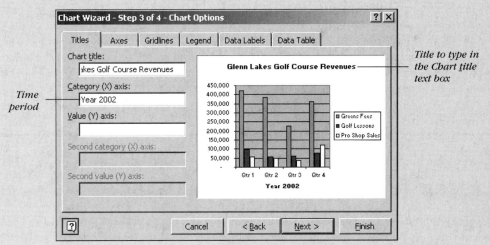

Figure 7.11

⑨ **Click Finish, move the embedded column chart below the worksheet data, as shown in Figure 7.12, and click outside the chart to deselect it.**

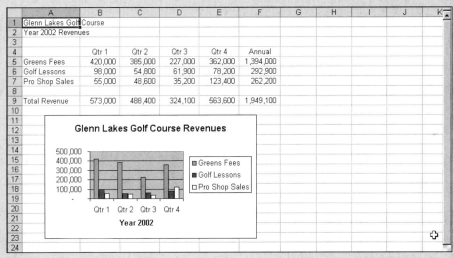

Figure 7.12

Clicking Finish now bypasses the Chart Location dialog box (Chart Wizard – Step 4 of 4). Excel automatically creates an embedded chart, as opposed to a chart on a separate sheet, unless you specify otherwise.

⑩ **Save your changes to the *mycharts* workbook.**

The embedded column chart is saved in the Column-Line worksheet, which is the second sheet in the *mycharts* workbook. Keep the workbook open for the next lesson, or close the workbook and exit Excel.

To extend your knowledge...

Comparing Clustered and Stacked Column Charts

A **clustered column chart** sub-type presents multiple data series as side-by-side columns (refer to Figure 7.12). If you select the **stacked column chart** sub-type, multiple data series appear as stacked components of a single column instead of as side-by-side columns. The stacked column sub-type is appropriate if the multiple data series total to a meaningful number. For example, stacking three revenue amounts—greens fees, golf lessons, and pro shop sales—in a single column for each quarter is meaningful because it shows the contribution of each revenue source to the total revenue for the quarter.

Lesson 4: Changing the Chart Type

It is important to select a chart type that can help you display the data in the most dramatic, appropriate, and meaningful manner possible. For example, you can usually spot trends more easily with a line chart, whereas a pie chart is best for showing parts of a whole.

After you create a chart, you may decide that you do not like the type of chart that you selected, or you may want to compare different chart types using the same data series. Excel enables you to change the chart type without re-creating the entire chart.

Now, make a copy of the embedded column chart and change the type of the copied chart to Line.

To Change the Chart Type

❶ Open the *mycharts* file, if necessary, and select the worksheet named Column-Line.
The Column-Line sheet includes the embedded column chart that you created in the previous lesson.

❷ Click inside the chart area (in any blank area) to select the entire chart, and click the Copy button.
A moving dashed line appears just inside the chart border. The chart is copied to the Windows Clipboard.

❸ Select a cell below the lower-left corner of the original column chart, and click the Paste button.
Two identical column charts appear in the Column-Line worksheet, one below the other.

❹ Scroll down to display the second chart, and right-click in any blank area of the second column chart.
A shortcut menu with chart options appears, as shown in Figure 7.13

To Change the Chart Type

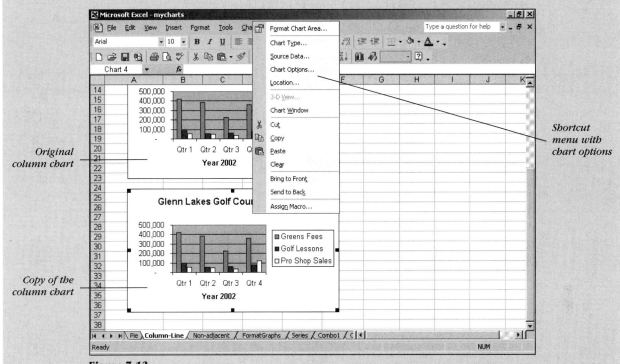

Figure 7.13

5 **Choose Chart Type on the shortcut menu, and choose Line in the Chart type list.**

The default Line chart is *Line with markers displayed at each data value*, as shown in Figure 7.14.

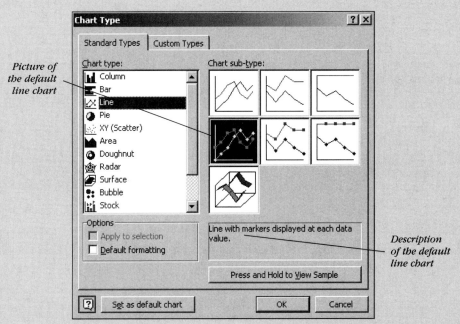

Figure 7.14

(Continues)

To Change the Chart Type (Continued)

6 **Click the OK button in the Chart Type dialog box, and click outside the line chart to deselect it.**
Data series are presented in lines instead of columns, as shown in Figure 7.15.

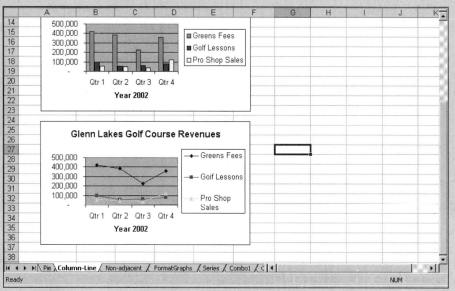

Figure 7.15

7 **Save your changes to the *mycharts* workbook.**
The embedded column and line charts are saved in the Column-Line worksheet, the second sheet within the *mycharts* workbook. Keep the workbook open for the next lesson, or close the workbook and exit Excel.

 ## To extend your knowledge...

Choosing an Appropriate Chart Type

In this lesson, you learned the steps to change the chart type. You need to know which chart type(s) to select, given the nature of the data. Onscreen Help provides examples of a variety of chart types. The standard built-in charts are Column, Bar, Line, Pie, XY (Scatter), Area, Doughnut, Radar, Surface, Bubble, Stock, Cylinder, Cone, and Pyramid. You can also select among built-in custom chart types—Area Blocks, Column – Area, Columns with Depth, Cones, Floating Bars, Line – Column on 2 Axes, and so forth—or create user-defined chart types.

Other Ways to Change the Chart Type

There are other ways to display a Chart Type dialog box after you select the chart you want to change. You can choose Chart, Chart Type, or click the Chart Wizard button.

You can also change a chart to one of 18 predefined types using the Chart toolbar. If this toolbar does not automatically appear when you select a chart, choose View, Toolbars, and select Chart. The drop-down list for the Chart Type button on this toolbar is a 3x6 display of chart icons. Click the icon that depicts the type of chart you want.

Lesson 5: Charting Non-Adjacent Data Series

You can select non-adjacent sets of numbers to be charted by holding down Ctrl while dragging over cells in the various areas of the worksheet. Make sure that the sets of numbers selected represent the same data series.

Now, try creating an embedded column chart that compares Year 2002 Greens Fees (the data series in row 5) to Total Revenue (the data series in row 9).

To Chart Non-Adjacent Data Series

1 **Open the *mycharts* file, if necessary, and select the worksheet named Non-adjacent.**
The Non-adjacent worksheet contains a copy of the data used in the previous sheets named Pie and Column-Line.

2 **Select the range A4:E5, and press and hold down Ctrl.**

3 **Select the range A9:E9, and release Ctrl.**
Only the ranges A4:E5 and A9:E9 are highlighted.

If you have problems...

Only the first five cells in rows 4, 5, and 9 should be highlighted. If any other cells are selected, click outside the selected areas to deselect them, and repeat Steps 2 and 3.

4 **Click the Chart Wizard button, and make sure that the Standard Types tab is selected in the Chart Type dialog box.**

5 **Select Column as the chart type and Clustered Column as the chart sub-type, and click Next.**
The Chart Source Data dialog box (Chart Wizard – Step 2 of 4) appears, as shown in Figure 7.16.

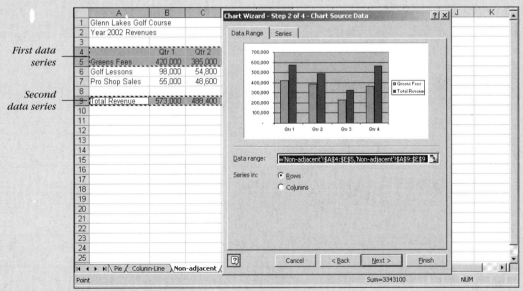

Figure 7.16

(Continues)

To Chart Non-Adjacent Data Series (Continued)

6 **Make sure that the *Series in* setting is <u>R</u>ows, and click <u>N</u>ext.**
The Chart Options dialog box appears (Chart Wizard – Step 3 of 4).

7 **On the Titles tab, type** Impact of Greens Fees on Revenue **in the Chart <u>t</u>itle text box.**

8 **Type** Glenn Lakes Golf Course - Year 2002 **in the <u>C</u>ategory (X) axis text box, and click <u>F</u>inish.**

9 **Move the newly created chart below its associated worksheet data, and deselect it.**
The embedded column chart compares revenue from Greens Fees to Total Revenue for each of four quarters, as shown in Figure 7.17.

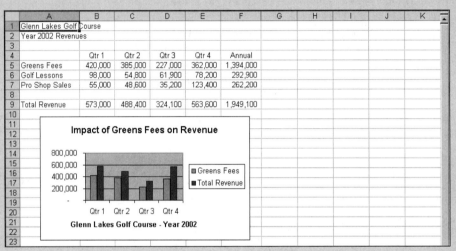

Figure 7.17

10 **Save your changes to the *mycharts* workbook.**
The embedded column chart is saved in the Non-adjacent worksheet, which is the third sheet in the *mycharts* workbook. Keep the workbook open for the next lesson, or close the workbook and exit Excel.

Lesson 6: Modifying Chart Formats

After you create a chart, you can make changes that improve readability or enhance visual appeal. For example, you can display dollar signs in front of the numbers in a Y-axis scale, italicize a title, add a textured background, and change the color of a data series. The chart in Figure 7.18 reflects these enhancements. You can make these changes yourself now.

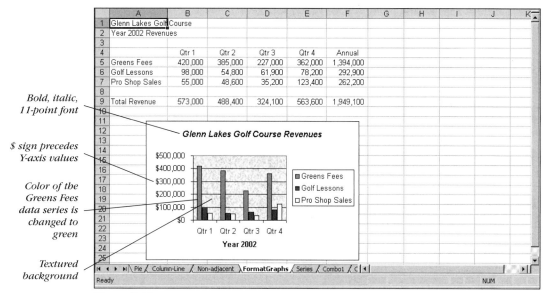

Bold, italic,
11-point font

$ sign precedes
Y-axis values

Color of the
Greens Fees
data series is
changed to
green

Textured
background

Figure 7.18

To Modify Chart Formats

1 **Open the *mycharts* file, if necessary, and select the worksheet named FormatGraphs.**

The FormatGraphs worksheet contains an embedded column chart below the worksheet data.

2 **Position the pointer on any value in the Y-axis scale, and right-click.**

A popup menu appears with two options: Format Axis and Clear. Two small square sizing handles at the top and bottom of the Y-axis indicate that the Y-axis is selected.

3 **Choose Format Axis.**

The Format Axis dialog box opens.

4 **Click the Number tab, and click Currency in the Category list (see Figure 7.19).**

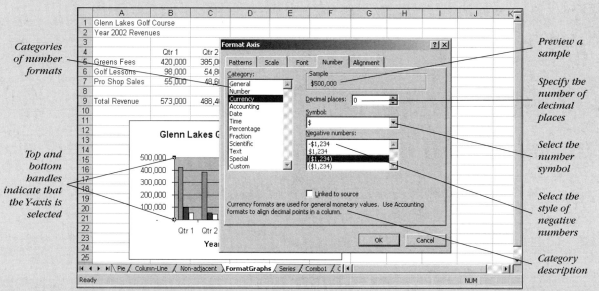

Categories
of number
formats

Top and
bottom
handles
indicate that
the Y-axis is
selected

Preview a
sample

Specify the
number of
decimal
places

Select the
number
symbol

Select the
style of
negative
numbers

Category
description

Figure 7.19

(Continues)

To Modify Chart Formats (Continued)

⑤ Specify the settings for Decimal places, Symbol, and Negative numbers that display in Figure 7.19, and click OK.

The Format Axis dialog box closes, and dollar signs appear in front of the Y-axis numbers. The Y-axis remains selected.

⑥ Position the pointer anywhere on the chart title, and right-click.

A shortcut menu appears with two options: Format Chart Title and Clear. Sizing handles at the corners and midpoints of the border surrounding the title indicate that the title is selected. The sizing handles on the Y-axis disappear, indicating that a selected area of a chart is deselected as soon as another area is selected.

⑦ Choose Format Chart Title, and click the Font tab in the Format Chart Title dialog box.

⑧ Select Bold Italic in the Font style list, select 11 in the Size list, and click OK.

The Format Chart Title dialog box closes, and the 11-point chart title displays in boldface and italic. The title remains selected.

⑨ Position the pointer on a blank area between gridlines in the chart, and right-click.

A shortcut menu appears with multiple options, the first and last of which are Format Plot Area and Clear. Sizing handles at the corners and midpoints of the gray shaded area indicate the plot area is selected.

⑩ Choose Format Plot Area.

The Format Plot Area dialog box opens.

⑪ Click the Fill Effects button, and click the Texture tab in the Fill Effects dialog box (see Figure 7.20).

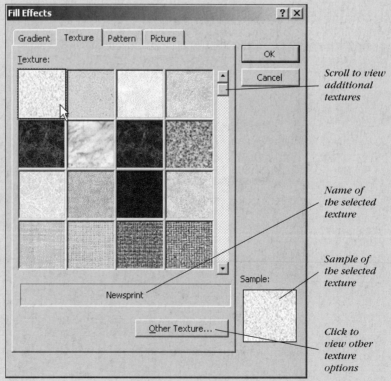

Figure 7.20

To Modify Chart Formats

12 **Click the first style in the upper-left corner of the display to select the texture named Newsprint, and click OK twice to close, in sequence, the Fill Effects and Format Plot Area dialog boxes.**

A textured background (fill) replaces the solid gray background. The plot area remains selected.

13 **Position the pointer on any of the blue columns that represent quarterly Greens Fees, and right-click.**

A shortcut menu appears with the options shown in Figure 7.21. The small black square in each blue column indicates that the Greens Fees data series is selected.

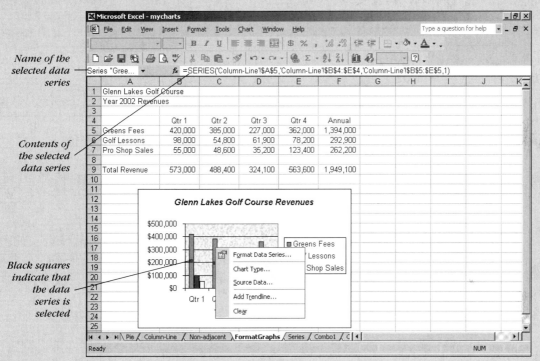

Figure 7.21

14 **Choose Format Data Series, and click the Patterns tab in the Format Data Series dialog box.**

The Patterns tab includes three sections: Border and Sample on the left, and Area on the right.

15 **Click the bright green-colored square (the fourth color square in the fourth row) in the Area section, and click OK.**

The color of the Greens Fees data series changes from blue to bright green. The data series remains selected.

16 **Click outside the chart to deselect the data series, and save your changes to the *mycharts* workbook.**

The modified column chart is saved in the FormatGraphs worksheet, which is the fourth sheet within the *mycharts* workbook. Keep the workbook open for the next lesson, or close the workbook and exit Excel.

To extend your knowledge...

Changing Other Chart Elements

In this lesson, you made changes to four areas in a chart: Y-axis, chart title, background, and a data series. You started the change process by positioning the pointer on the area and right-clicking. You can use the same steps to initiate changes in any other area of a chart, such as the legend or X-axis.

Alternatives to Shortcut Menus

Right-clicking a chart area displays a context-sensitive shortcut menu that allows you to clear or modify the selected area. You can access chart dialog boxes and modify settings in other ways as well. Double-clicking a chart area opens the dialog box for formatting that area. You can also access Chart options from the menu bar after you select a chart area or the entire chart.

Ways to View a Chart

Instead of scrolling through the worksheet to view an embedded chart, you can view the chart in its own window. Select the chart, and choose View, Chart Window. You can edit the chart while it is open in the window.

If you select an embedded chart before clicking the Print Preview button, Excel displays only the chart instead of the worksheet data and the chart. You can view but not change a chart displayed in the Print Preview mode.

Lesson 7: Adding, Reordering, and Deleting a Data Series

Even a relatively small set of data can be charted in a variety of ways. Look at the range A4:E7 in Figure 7.22. In that example, a data series can be a column of data, such as the sales for each year from 1999 through 2002. A data series can also be a row of data, such as the four-year sales pattern for each city.

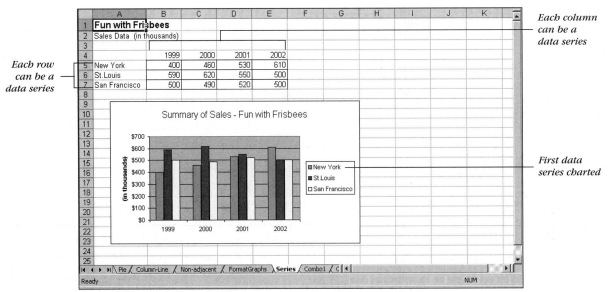

Each column can be a data series

Each row can be a data series

First data series charted

Figure 7.22

You can vary the data presented in a chart by adding a data series, rearranging the order of data series, and deleting a data series. In this lesson, you learn to use all three methods to manipulate data series on an existing chart.

To Add, Reorder, and Delete a Data Series

1 **Open the *mycharts* file, if necessary, and select the worksheet named Series.**
This worksheet contains a column chart showing sales for the New York office of Fun with Frisbees over a period of four years. Dollar amounts are displayed along the vertical axis to the left of the plot area, and a legend to the right of the plot area displays the color assigned to the single data series.

2 **Position the mouse pointer on one of the four columns in the chart.**
A text box shows the data series (New York), the year, and the value (in thousands) for that year. Next, add the data for St. Louis and San Francisco to the chart. Although there is more than one way to accomplish this, the easiest way is by using the drag-and-drop method.

3 **Select cells A6:E7, click on the border of the selected cells and drag them within the chart, release the mouse button, and deselect the chart.**
The chart displays data for all three cities, as shown in Figure 7.22. Next, exchange the positions of St. Louis and San Francisco so the cities will be in alphabetical order.

4 **Right-click any column in the chart, and select F̲ormat Data Series.**

5 **Select the Series Order tab in the Format Data Series dialog box, and select San Francisco in the S̲eries order list box (see Figure 7.23).**

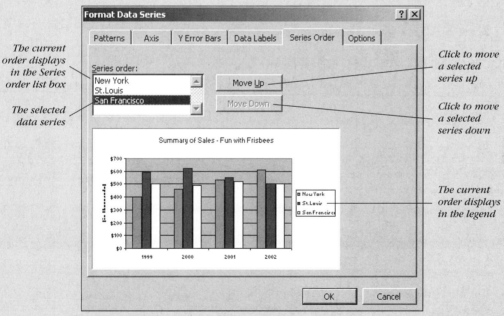

The current order displays in the Series order list box

The selected data series

Click to move a selected series up

Click to move a selected series down

The current order displays in the legend

Figure 7.23

6 **Click the Move U̲p button, and click OK.**
The order of the data series changes in both the legend and the plot area. Within the set of columns for each year, San Francisco is now the middle column. The reordering does not affect the order of the source data in the worksheet. Now, remove the St. Louis data from the chart.

7 **Click any column that represents St. Louis data, and press** Del.
Any reference to St. Louis data disappears from the plot area and the legend.

(Continues)

To Add, Reorder, and Delete a Data Series (Continued)

8 **Click outside the chart to deselect it, and save your changes to the *mycharts* workbook.**
The modified column chart is saved in the Series worksheet, which is the fifth sheet within the *mycharts* workbook. You can close the *mycharts* workbook now, or leave it open and continue to the last lesson.

To extend your knowledge...

Alternative Ways to Add or Delete Data Series

The methods used to add and delete data series illustrated in this lesson are the simplest ways to make those changes to an existing chart. Add by dragging a selected series and dropping it into the chart; remove by selecting the charted data series and pressing Del. You can also make both changes from the Series tab of the Source Data dialog box. Select the chart; choose Chart, Source Data; and select the Series tab. To add a data series, click the Add button and specify the location of the series. To delete a data series, select its name in the Series list, and click the Remove button.

Lesson 8: Creating and Printing a Combination Chart

A **combination chart** includes two or more chart types, such as showing one data series as a column and another as a line. Create a combination chart if the values in the data series vary widely or if you want to emphasize differences in the data.

The reasons for creating a combination chart do not apply to the Glenn Lakes Golf Course data charted in previous lessons. In this lesson, you chart two data series with widely varying values: the total miles walked and the average miles per walk.

To Create and Print a Combination Chart

1 **Open the *mycharts* file, if necessary, and select the worksheet named Combo1.**
The Combo1 sheet illustrates the problem encountered when you chart data series with values that vary widely.

2 **Read the Problem and Solution text, and click the Combo2 sheet tab.**
The sheet contains only the Year 2002 summary of walking data.

3 **Select the range A3:E5, and click the Chart Wizard button in the Standard toolbar.**

4 **Click the Custom Types tab in the Chart Type dialog box, scroll down the Chart type list, and click Line – Column on 2 Axes (see Figure 7.24).**

To Create and Print a Combination Chart

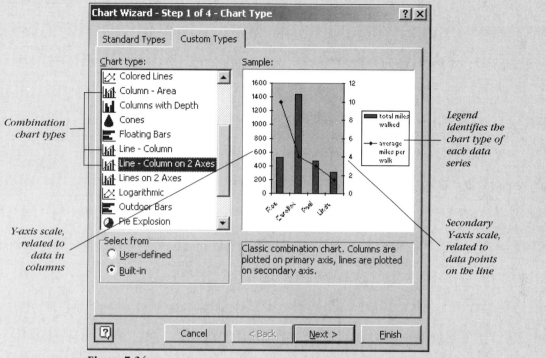

Figure 7.24

⑤ Click <u>N</u>ext two times to advance to the Chart Options dialog box (Chart Wizard – Step 3 of 4), and click the Titles tab.

⑥ Enter the titles for the chart, as shown in Figure 7.25.

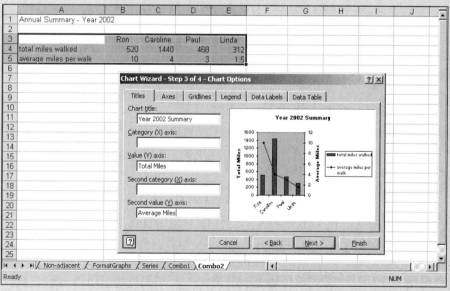

Figure 7.25

⑦ Click <u>F</u>inish, drag the embedded combination chart below the associated data (see Figure 7.26), and click outside the chart to deselect it.

(Continues)

To Create and Print a Combination Chart (Continued)

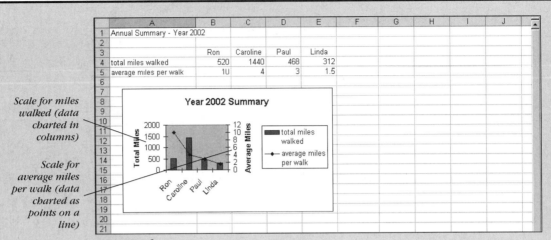

Scale for miles walked (data charted in columns)

Scale for average miles per walk (data charted as points on a line)

Figure 7.26

8 **Save your changes to the *mycharts* workbook.**
The embedded combination chart is saved in the Combo2 worksheet, which is the seventh sheet in the *mycharts* workbook. Get in the habit of saving changes before you print to protect against data loss if your system freezes and requires a reboot.

9 **Click any blank area inside the chart to select it, and choose File, Print.**

10 **Make sure that the Selected Chart option is selected in the *Print what* area (see Figure 7.27).**

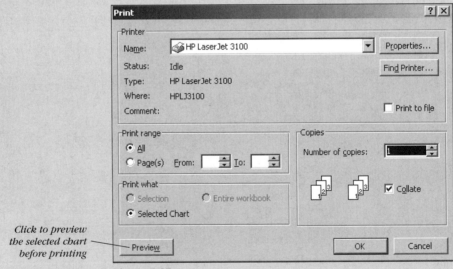

Click to preview the selected chart before printing

Figure 7.27

11 **Click OK (or click Cancel if you do not wish to print at this time).**
This concludes Project 7. Close the workbook, and either continue with the end-of-project activities or exit Excel.

Summary

In this project, you learned the tasks essential to creating, editing, saving, and printing embedded charts. You used the Chart Wizard to create embedded pie, column, line, and combination charts. You also modified some of the individual elements in a chart: the number format of Y-axis values, font style and size in the chart title, fill effect applied to the plot area, color assigned to a data series, the number of data series, and the order of data series.

You can extend your learning by experimenting with changes to other elements in a chart. For example, remove gridlines, or expand your ability to document a chart by learning how to insert a text box. Change a two-dimensional chart into a 3-D (three-dimensional) one to see if you like the effect. Be sure to browse the extensive coverage of charts available through onscreen Help.

Checking Concepts and Terms

Multiple Choice

Circle the letter of the correct answer for each of the following.

1. Which type of chart is limited to a single data series? [L1]

   a. column
   b. combination
   c. line
   d. pie

2. What is the element of a chart that identifies color, patterns, or symbols assigned to chart data series or categories? [L1]

   a. legend
   b. data-labels
   c. X-axis labels
   d. chart title

3. The horizontal axis of a chart is the [L1]

   a. Y-axis, which generally appears at the bottom edge of the chart.
   b. X-axis, which generally appears at the bottom edge of the chart.
   c. Y-axis, which generally appears at the left edge of the chart.
   d. X-axis, which generally appears at the left edge of the chart.

4. Which Excel feature provides step-by-step assistance to create a line chart? [L2]

   a. Drawing Wizard
   b. Line Chart Wizard
   c. Graph Wizard
   d. Chart Wizard

5. Which of the following is a reason for using a combination chart? [L8]

   a. A combination chart is more colorful.
   b. The values in the data series vary widely.
   c. Differences in the data can be emphasized.
   d. Both b and c.

Discussion

1. Data in the following worksheet (see Figure 7.28) can be charted in many ways. Describe a minimum of five data series or combinations of data series that would be meaningful to chart. Do not discuss the type of chart at this point. Focus instead on identifying the analysis you have in mind. For example, charting the non-adjacent ranges A4:F4 and A8:F8 allows you to compare the single data series Total In-Store Sales across five years. Review the analysis opportunities that you identified, and discuss which chart types and sub-types are appropriate to use for each analysis.

	A	B	C	D	E	F	G	H	I	J
1	Flowers Your Way									
2	5-year Trend Analysis of Sales (in thousands of U.S. dollars)									
3										
4		1998	1999	2000	2001	2002				
5	In-Store Sales									
6	Corporate	108	111	96	81	58				
7	Individual	321	371	305	330	319				
8	Total In-Store	429	482	401	411	377				
9										
10	Phone/Fax Sales									
11	Corporate	450	425	510	452	215				
12	Individual	225	229	241	247	252				
13	Total Phone/Fax	675	654	751	699	467				
14										
15	Web Sales									
16	Corporate	57	65	89	271	502				
17	Individual	11	14	17	48	112				
18	Total Web	68	79	106	319	614				
19										
20	Total Sales	1172	1215	1258	1429	1458				
21										

Figure 7.28

2. An end user looking at the following chart (see Figure 7.29) would not have sufficient information to interpret the results. Be specific when describing what should be done to improve the documentation on the chart. [L1]

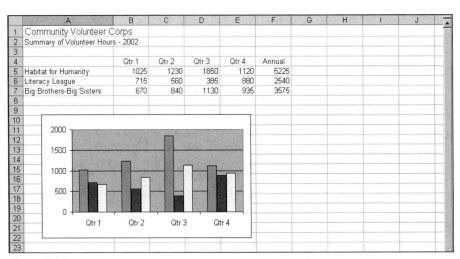

Figure 7.29

3. Find two examples of charts from newspapers, magazines, or Web sites that were published within the last six months. For each example, identify the chart type and the enhancements applied to the chart (color, number formatting, gridlines, and so on). Also, describe the components that are used to explain what each chart illustrates (Y-axis scale, titles, legend, and so on). Identify and discuss possible changes in enhancements or documentation that you think might improve either chart.

Skill Drill

Skill Drill exercises reinforce project skills. Each skill reinforced is the same, or nearly the same, as a skill presented in the project. Detailed instructions are provided in a step-by-step format.

Before beginning your first Project 7 Skill Drill exercise, complete the following steps:

1. Open the file named *ee1-0703*, and immediately save it as `ee1-p7drill`.
   The *ee1-p7drill* workbook contains seven sheets: an overview, and exercise sheets named #1-Pie, #2-Column, #3-Line, #4-Font, #5-Number, and #6-Add Series.
2. Click the Overview sheet to view the organization of the Project 7 Skill Drill Exercises workbook.

Each exercise is independent of the others, so you may complete the exercises in any order. Be sure to save the workbook after completing each exercise. If you need a paper copy of the completed exercise, enter your name, centered in a header, before printing. Other print options have already been set to print compressed to one page and to display the filename, sheet name, and current date in a footer.

If you need more than one work session to complete the desired exercises, continue working on *ee1-p7drill* instead of starting over again on the original *ee1-0703* file.

1. Creating an Embedded 3-D Pie Chart

You have used Excel to create a number of pie charts in the past. For the upcoming Community Volunteer Corps event, however, you want to present data in a three-dimensional pie chart.

To create an embedded 3-D pie chart, follow these steps:

1. Open the *ee1-p7drill* workbook, if necessary, and select the worksheet named #1-Pie.
   You plan to create a pie chart based on the labels and data shown in blue (the label range A6:A9 and the data range F6:F9 are non-adjacent).
2. Select the range A6:A9.
3. Press and hold down Ctrl.
4. Select the range F6:F9, and release Ctrl.
5. Click the Chart Wizard button to display the Chart Type dialog box.
6. Select Pie as the chart type, and select *Pie with a 3-D Visual Effect* as the chart sub-type.
7. Click Next to display the Chart Source Data dialog box, and ensure that the series is in Columns.
8. Click Next to display the Chart Options dialog box.
9. Type `Allocation of 11,340 Volunteer Hours` in the Chart title text box on the Titles tab.
10. Deselect Show legend on the Legend tab, and select the Category name and Percentage options on the Data Labels tab.
11. Click Finish to accept the default embedded chart, and exit Chart Wizard.
12. Move the chart below the data, size as appropriate, and click outside the chart to deselect it.
13. Save your changes to the *ee1-p7drill* workbook.

2. Creating an Embedded Stacked Column Chart

You are looking for a variety of ways to present data on volunteer hours at the upcoming Community Volunteer Corps event. As you look through the sub-types of a column chart, you discover that a stacked column chart compares the contribution of each value to a total across all categories. You decide to illustrate the proportion of volunteer hours associated with each volunteer organization in a stacked-column format.

To create a stacked column chart, follow these steps:

1. Open the *ee1-p7drill* workbook, if necessary, and select the worksheet named #2-Column. You plan to create a stacked column chart based on the labels and data shown in blue (the range A6:E9).
2. Select the range A6:E9, and click the Chart Wizard button.
3. In the Chart Type dialog box, select Column as the chart type, and select Stacked Column as the sub-type. Click <u>N</u>ext.
4. In the Chart Source Data dialog box, make sure that Series is in <u>R</u>ows. Click <u>N</u>ext.
5. In the Chart Options dialog box, specify the following titles, and then click <u>F</u>inish: `Community Volunteer Corps` (chart title), `Year Just Ended` (X-axis title), and `Volunteer Hours` (Y-axis title).
6. Move the chart below the data, size as appropriate, and deselect the chart.
7. Save your changes to the *ee1-p7drill* workbook.

3. Changing the Chart Type

As you explore creating a variety of charts for presenting volunteer data, you create a line chart by modifying the chart type of an existing column chart.

To change the chart type, follow these steps:

1. Open the *ee1-p7drill* workbook, if necessary, and select the worksheet named #3-Line. The sheet contains a column chart based on the labels and data shown in blue (the range A6:E9).
2. Right-click in a blank area of the chart, and select Chart T<u>y</u>pe from the shortcut menu.
3. Select Line as the chart type, and select *Line with markers displayed at each data value* as the sub-type.
4. Click OK, and click outside the line chart to deselect it.
5. Save your changes to the *ee1-p7drill* workbook.

4. Changing the Font Style and Size

Knowing that changes in the font can enhance the appearance of a chart, you decide to change the font style and size in the title of a chart illustrating volunteer data.

To apply italics and change the font size, follow these steps:

1. Open the *ee1-p7drill* workbook, if necessary, and select the worksheet named #4-Font. The sheet contains a column chart based on the labels and data in the range A6:E9.
2. Click once within the chart title, and select (highlight) all the text in the title.
3. Click the Italic button in the Formatting toolbar.
4. Click the Font Size down arrow in the Formatting toolbar, and select 14 as the point size.
5. Click outside the chart, and save your changes to the *ee1-p7drill* workbook.

5. Changing the Number Format on the Value (Y) Axis

As you finalize charts that illustrate volunteer data, you decide to display commas as the thousands separator in numbers on the Y-axis scale of each chart.

To apply the new number format in one chart, follow these steps:

1. Open the *ee1-p7drill* workbook, if necessary, and select the worksheet named #5-Number. The sheet contains a column chart based on the labels and data in the range A6:E9.
2. Position the mouse pointer on any number in the Y-axis scale to the left of the chart's plot area.

3. Right-click, and select F̲ormat Axis on the shortcut menu.

4. Click the Number tab in the Format Axis dialog box, and click Number in the C̲ategory window.

5. Change the number of decimal places to zero, and click the *Use 1000 Separator (,)* option.

6. Click OK to apply your changes and close the dialog box.

7. Click outside the chart, and save your changes to the *ee1-p7drill* workbook.

6. Adding a Data Series and Reordering Data Series

You charted two data series in a column chart. Now, you want to add a third series (Literacy League), and change the position of the first series (Habitat for Humanity).

To add a data series and reorder the data series, follow these steps:

1. Open the *ee1-p7drill* workbook, if necessary, and select the #6-AddSeries worksheet.

2. Select the *Literacy League* label and data in the range A8:E8.

3. Click on the border of the selected cells, drag them within the chart, release the mouse button, and deselect the chart.

Excel adds the Literacy League data to the chart and updates the legend to include a third data series.

4. Right-click any column in the chart, choose F̲ormat Data Series, and select the Series Order tab.

5. Make sure that Habitat for Humanity is the selected series in the S̲eries order list, and click the Move D̲own button twice.

The sample chart in the Format Data Series dialog box shows that the Habitat for Humanity data series is now the third data series instead of the first data series.

6. Click OK, deselect the chart, and save your changes to the *ee1-p7drill* workbook.

Challenge

Challenge exercises expand on or are somewhat related to skills presented in the lessons. Each exercise provides a brief narrative introduction, followed by instructions in a numbered-step format that are not as detailed as those in the Skill Drill section.

Before beginning your first Project 7 Challenge exercise, complete the following steps:

1. Open the file named *ee1-0704*, and immediately save it as `ee1-p7challenge`.

The Community Volunteer Corps (CVC) workbook contains seven sheets: an overview, and exercise sheets named #1-Explode, #2-DeleteChart, #3-DeleteSeries, #4-MoveTitle, #5-MoveLegend, and #6-ChangeScale.

2. Click the Overview sheet to view the organization of the Project 7 Challenge Exercises workbook.

Each exercise is independent of the others, so you may complete the exercises in any order. Be sure to save the workbook after completing each exercise. If you need a paper copy of the completed exercise, enter your name, centered in a header, before printing. Other print options have already been set to print compressed to one page and to display the filename, sheet name, and current date in a footer.

If you need more than one work session to complete the desired exercises, continue working on *ee1-p7challenge* instead of starting over again on the original *ee1-0704* file.

1. Exploding (Cutting) a Pie Slice

You already created a suitable pie chart that shows the allocation of hours among the three volunteer groups comprising the Community Volunteer Corps. Now, you want to modify the chart to draw attention to the volunteer activity with the least number of hours (Literacy League). You can do this by pulling that pie slice away from the rest of the pie.

To explode (pull out) a piece of a pie, follow these steps:

1. Open the *ee1-p7challenge* workbook, if necessary, and select the worksheet named #1-Explode.
2. Select only the pie slice representing the Literacy League.

 If you have problems...

Clicking a pie slice the first time selects the entire pie; clicking it again enables you to select the pie slice.

Sizing handles appear at only the corners and midpoints of the Literacy League pie slice.
3. Drag the Literacy League pie slice out a short distance from the rest of the pie.
4. If necessary, increase the size of the chart to restore the display of all labels.
5. Click outside the chart, and save your changes to the *ee1-p7challenge* workbook.

2. Deleting a Chart

You created several charts based on volunteer data just to try out different chart types and options. Now, you need to delete one that doesn't provide meaningful information.

To delete a chart, follow these steps:

1. Open the *ee1-p7challenge* workbook, if necessary, and select the worksheet named #2-DeleteChart.

The chart in this worksheet is a bar chart in which data are depicted by horizontal columns.
2. Click a blank area within the bar chart to select the entire chart.

Sizing handles should appear at the midpoints and corners of the border around the chart.

 If you have problems...

If sizing handles display for a chart element instead of the entire chart, you clicked a blank area within the framing area of that element. Click another blank area to deselect the element and try again.

3. Press Del, and save your changes to the *ee1-p7challenge* workbook.

3. Deleting a Data Series

After creating a line chart that shows the volunteer hours contributed to three organizations, you decide to modify the chart by removing one of the three data series.

To delete a data series, follow these steps:

1. Open the *ee1-p7challenge* workbook, if necessary, and select the worksheet named #3-DeleteSeries.
2. Click any part of the line representing the Literacy League data.

A small box displays at each data point on the line, which indicates that the Literacy League data series is selected.

3. Press Del.

4. Click outside the chart, and save your changes to the *ee1-p7challenge* workbook.

4. Moving a Title

You know that each component of a chart can be moved and sized independently of the other components. You decide to change the Y-axis title on a chart to appear horizontally above the numbers in the Y-axis scale, instead of appearing vertically to the left of the scale numbers.

To move a title and change its orientation, follow these steps:

1. Open the *ee1-p7challenge* workbook, if necessary, and select the worksheet named #4-MoveTitle.

2. Double-click the Y-axis title, and select the Alignment tab on the Format Axis Title dialog box.

3. Drag Orientation to 0 degrees, and close the dialog box.

4. Drag the title to just above the top number on the Y-axis scale.

5. Click outside the chart, and save your changes to the *ee1-p7challenge* workbook.

5. Moving a Legend and Enlarging a Plot Area

Long text descriptions may result in a legend that is quite large in comparison with the plot area of its associated chart. This effect appears in many of the charts based on volunteer data. You decide to move the legend to the bottom of the chart, reduce the font size in the legend, and enlarge the plot area.

To reposition a legend and enlarge a plot area, follow these steps:

1. Open the *ee1-p7challenge* workbook, if necessary, and select the worksheet named #5-MoveLegend.

2. Double-click a blank area within the legend, click the Placement tab on the Format Legend dialog box, and click Bottom.

3. Click the Font tab on the Format Legend dialog box, click the smallest point size, and close the dialog box.

4. Click the gray background within the plot area, and increase the width and height of the plot area as much as possible to fit within the outside chart border (be sure that the changes in height are proportional to the changes in width).

5. Click outside the chart, and save your changes to the *ee1-p7challenge* workbook.

6. Changing the Scale Increment

You know that Excel automatically assigns an increment to the numbers displayed on the Y-axis scale. However, you want to change to a lower increment on one of the charts that shows volunteer hours.

To change the Y-axis scale to display in increments of 300 (0, 300, 600, and so on) instead of increments of 500 (0, 500, 1,000, and so on), follow these steps:

1. Open the *ee1-p7challenge* workbook, if necessary, and select the worksheet named #6-ChangeScale.

2. Double-click any number on the Y-axis scale, and click the Scale tab on the Format Axis dialog box.

3. Change the Major Unit to **300** instead of *500,* and close the dialog box.

4. Increase the width of the chart in proportion to its height, click outside the chart, and save your changes to the *ee1-p7challenge* workbook.

iscovery Zone

Discovery Zone exercises require advanced knowledge of topics presented in *Essentials* lessons, application of skills from multiple lessons, or self-directed learning of new skills.

Before beginning your first Project 7 Discovery Zone exercise, complete the following steps:

1. Open the file named *ee1-0705*, and immediately save it as `ee1-p7discovery`.
   The *ee1-p7discovery* workbook contains five sheets: an overview, and four exercise sheets named #1-Data, #2-Reorder, #3-RowCol and #4-Fill.
2. Click the Overview sheet to view the organization of the Project 7 Discovery Zone Exercises workbook.

Each exercise is independent of the others, so you may complete the exercises in any order. Be sure to save the workbook after completing each exercise. If you need a paper copy of the completed exercise, enter your name, centered in a header, before printing. Other print options have already been set to print compressed to one page and to display the filename, sheet name, and current date in a footer.

If you need more than one work session to complete the desired exercises, continue working on *ee1-p7discovery* instead of starting over again on the original *ee1-0705* file.

1. Comparing Data Labels and a Data Table

You want the exact sales figures for baseball bats to be visible in a chart that will be presented at the sales meeting next week. A coworker just told you that Excel supports using data labels or a data table to display the numbers on which a chart is based. However, you are not sure which of the two methods to use. To make up your mind, you created identical column charts that chart the sales of baseball bats. You plan to set up data labels on one and a data table on the other, and then compare results (make your changes on the sheet named #1-Data in your *ee1-p7discovery* workbook).

Before you begin, use onscreen Help to learn about showing values as labels and displaying a data table. In the chart on the left in the #1-Data sheet, show the exact number of baseball bats sold that quarter above each column. In the chart on the right, display the associated data table. Which enhancement do you prefer? Would your answer change if you charted all three product lines instead of only baseball bats?

2. Changing the Order of Data Series

You created a column chart that compares the sales of baseball bats to sales of tennis racquets. Before finalizing the chart for a presentation at next week's sales meeting, however, you wonder whether it makes a difference which data series appears first. Make a copy of the column chart in the #2-Reorder worksheet in your *ee1-p7discovery* workbook. Position the copy to the right of the original chart. Reverse the order of the two data series in the second chart. Which order do you prefer? Why?

3. Charting Data Series in Rows or Columns

You know from using the Chart Wizard that you can chart data series in rows or columns. However, you don't have a clear idea about what difference that would make in presenting information about sales of baseball bats, tennis racquets, and volleyball nets.

On the #3-RowCol sheet in your *ee1-p7discovery* workbook, first create a well-documented clustered column chart based on the range A5:E8 (the blue cells). Specify that data series are in rows. Position the chart below the data and size, as appropriate. Next, create a well-documented clustered column chart based on the same range, and specify that data series are in columns. Position this chart to the right of the first one. (Hint: You can quickly create the second chart by copying the first one and changing the source data to columns on the copied chart.) What is the focus of the first chart? What is the focus of the second chart?

4. Applying a Fill Effect to a Plot Area

Excel provides four categories of fill effects suitable for charts: Gradient, Texture, Pattern, and Picture. First, use onscreen Help to learn about the specific fill effects and how to apply them to plot areas. Next, experiment with using fills on the #4-Fill sheet in your *ee1-p7discovery* workbook. This sheet displays four identical charts that show the sales of baseball bats. Apply the Blue tissue paper texture to the plot area of chart #2. Apply a pale yellow Divot pattern to the plot area of chart #3. Set up a two-color gradient as the fill effect for chart #4 (your choice of colors and shading style). Compare the results. Which do you prefer? Would your answer change if you were limited to a black-and-white display for your presentation (overhead transparencies or printed handouts)?

Developing a Multiple-Sheet Workbook

PROJECT 8

Objectives

In this project, you learn how to

- ✔ Copy Data from Another Application
- ✔ Insert, Move, and Rename Worksheets
- ✔ Edit Multiple Worksheets Simultaneously
- ✔ Subtotal Data
- ✔ Link Worksheets
- ✔ Apply Conditional Formatting
- ✔ Set a Print Area
- ✔ Save a Worksheet with Chart as a Web Page

Key terms in this project include

- ❑ conditional formatting
- ❑ embed
- ❑ link
- ❑ smart tag

Why Would I Do This?

The Excel workbook structure lets you move easily among the different worksheets, insert and delete worksheets, move worksheets around, and name each worksheet to make it more identifiable. In addition, you can copy, link, or move cell contents between worksheets, between workbooks, and between applications. With all these tools at your disposal, you can easily manage a workbook of any size.

Visual Summary

In this project, you learn to manage workbooks by creating a simple two-sheet workbook. In the process, you rename the sheets and apply changes to both sheets at once. You also explore using Excel's powerful integration features when you copy data from a Word table to your Excel workbook, link cells between worksheets, set a print area, and save a worksheet in a format that can be viewed with a Web browser.

The first worksheet provides counts of those planning to attend an event (see Figure 8.1).

You can subtotal on the field of your choice

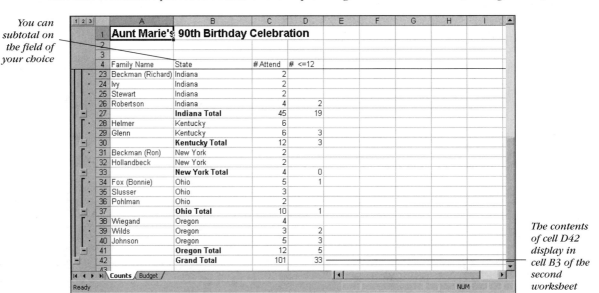

The contents of cell D42 display in cell B3 of the second worksheet

Figure 8.1

The second worksheet contains a budget for the event (see Figure 8.2).

A formula links this cell to cell D42 in the first worksheet

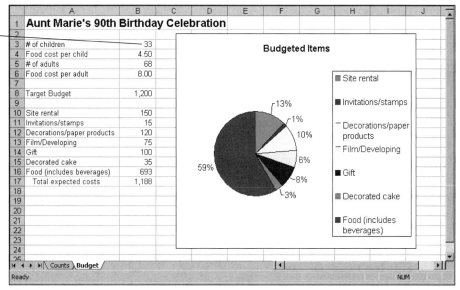

Figure 8.2

Lesson 1: Copying Data from Another Application

Assume that you are responsible for preparing a budget for your Aunt Marie's 90th birthday celebration at the annual family reunion. Your cousin prepared the invitations, tallied the responses, summarized selected data in a Word table, and e-mailed the information to you this morning. As you look through the table, you realize that you can copy it to a blank Excel workbook and calculate the counts you need to prepare a budget.

Copying from one application to another or copying within an application saves you from having to re-enter data that already exists. You can embed or link copied data, formulas, and objects. If you *link*, the copied item updates whenever that item changes in the source location. If you *embed*, the copied item does not update whenever that item changes in the source location.

In this lesson, you copy a Word table to an Excel worksheet as an embedded object. The source file relates to a one-time event and is not updated. You perform the copy by using the Windows Clipboard and task-switching capabilities.

To Copy Data from Another Application

❶ **Start Excel if it is not already running, and display a blank worksheet.**

❷ **Start Word if it is not already running, and open the Word document named** *ee1-0801.*
Three brief paragraphs and a table display.

❸ **Click any cell within the table.**

❹ **Choose T̲able, Sele̲ct, T̲able.**
The entire table appears highlighted.

❺ **Click the Copy button on the toolbar (or select E̲dit, C̲opy).**

❻ **Click the button labeled** *Microsoft Excel – Book1* **in the taskbar at the bottom of the screen.**
The display switches from Microsoft Word to Microsoft Excel.

(Continues)

To Copy Data from Another Application (Continued)

If you have problems...

If you have multiple applications and/or files open, you may not see the entire label. Pointing to a button in the taskbar displays a ScreenTip showing the full name of the button.

7 **Click cell A4, click the Paste button on the toolbar (or choose Edit, Paste), and click a blank cell to deselect the copied data.**

Excel copies the Word table to the blank worksheet. Data in each column of the table appears in its own column in the worksheet (see Figure 8.3).

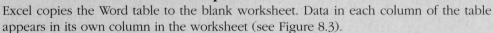

All columns at the default column width

	A	B	C	D	E	F	G	H	I	J	K	L
1												
2												
3												
4	Family Name	State	# Attend	# <=12								
5	Beckman (Marie)	Indiana	1									
6	Stetler	Florida	4	2								
7	Keller	Indiana	6	4								
8	Enloe	Indiana	2									
9	Beckman (Ron)	New York	2									
10	Wiegand	Oregon	4									
11	Fraley	Indiana	8	4								
12	Bennett	Indiana	4	2								
13	Fox (Bonnie)	Ohio	5	1								
14	Beckman (Jeffrey)	Florida	3	1								
15	Slusser	Ohio	3									

Current sheet — Sheet1 / Sheet2 / Sheet3 /

Ready — NUM

Figure 8.3

8 **Switch back to Microsoft Word, and exit Word without saving any changes.**

9 **In Excel, select the range A4:D34; choose Edit, Clear, Formats; and click a blank cell to deselect the cleared range.**

The unwanted formatting disappears (see Figure 8.4).

To Copy Data from Another Application

	A	B	C	D	E	F	G	H	I	J	K	L
1												
2												
3												
4	Family Nar	State	# Attend	# <=12								
5	Beckman i	Indiana	1									
6	Stetler	Florida	4	2								
7	Keller	Indiana	6	4								
8	Enloe	Indiana	2									
9	Beckman i	New York	2									
10	Wiegand	Oregon	4									
11	Fraley	Indiana	8	4								
12	Bennett	Indiana	4	2								
13	Fox (Bonn	Ohio	5	1								
14	Beckman i	Florida	3	1								
15	Slusser	Ohio	3									
16	Strauss	Florida	2									
17	Fields	Indiana	3	1								
18	Gray	Illinois	2									
19	Pickett	Indiana	1									
20	Pohlman	Ohio	2									
21	Fox (John)	Indiana	5	3								
22	Wilds	Oregon	3	2								
23	Kelsey	Florida	2									
24	Hollandbec	New York	2									
25	Russell	Indiana	5	3								

Sheet1 / Sheet2 / Sheet3 /

Ready   NUM

Figure 8.4

If you have problems...

If content as well as formatting disappears, you selected Edit, Clear, All instead of Edit, Clear Formats. Choose Edit, Undo Clear, and repeat Step 9.

You may see a smart tag indicator, a small purple triangle, in the lower-right corner of each cell containing state data in Column B. A **smart tag** recognizes and labels data as a particular type, and enables you to perform actions in Excel that you would usually open other programs to perform. The smart tags serve no purpose in this lesson, and may be ignored. Figures in this lesson do not show the smart tags.

10 **Widen column A to display long labels.**
Now, delete Sheet2 and Sheet3 to prepare the worksheet for the next lesson.

11 **Right-click the Sheet2 tab, and choose Delete from the shortcut menu.**
Sheet2 is permanently removed from the workbook.

12 **Right-click the Sheet3 tab, and choose Delete from the shortcut menu.**
Only the Sheet1 worksheet remains.

13 **Save the workbook as Marie90.**
Keep the workbook open for the next lesson, or close the workbook and exit Excel.

Lesson 2: Inserting, Moving, and Renaming Worksheets

You can insert, move, and rename worksheets as well as delete them. Excel positions an inserted worksheet to the left of the current worksheet. You can easily change its position by clicking its sheet name and dragging left or right. Changing the names of worksheets in a multiple-sheet workbook makes it easier to understand the purpose of each sheet.

In this lesson, you insert a sheet, move that sheet, and change the names of both worksheets in the *Marie90* workbook. You name one worksheet *Counts* and the other *Budget*.

To Insert, Move, and Rename Worksheets

① **Open the *Marie90* workbook, if necessary, and double-click the sheet tab named Sheet1.**
Sheet1 displays with a black background, indicating that rename mode is active. You can also begin a rename operation by right-clicking the Sheet1 tab and choosing <u>R</u>ename from the shortcut menu.

② **Type Counts and press ↵Enter).**
The sheet is renamed and the worksheet tab displays *Counts* instead of *Sheet1*.

③ **Choose <u>I</u>nsert, <u>W</u>orksheet.**
Excel inserts a worksheet to the left of the current worksheet (see Figure 8.5) and assigns the next available number for the sheet name. You can use navigation buttons to switch from one worksheet to another.

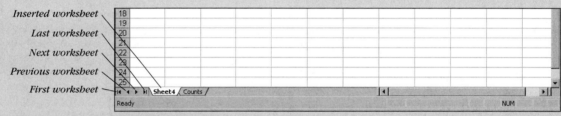

Figure 8.5

④ **Double-click the Sheet4 sheet tab.**

⑤ **Type Budget, and press ↵Enter).**
The names of the two sheets are Budget and Counts, respectively.

⑥ **Click and drag the Budget sheet to the right of the Counts sheet, and release the mouse button.**
The Counts worksheet is now the first sheet, and the blank Budget worksheet is the second sheet.

⑦ **Save your changes to the *Marie90* workbook.**
Keep the workbook open for the next lesson, or close the workbook and exit Excel.

To extend your knowledge...

Adding Color to Sheet Tabs

You can add color to a sheet tab. Right-click the sheet tab you want to color, select <u>T</u>ab Color, and click the color of your choice. If you add color to one or more sheet tabs in a multiple-sheet workbook, the active sheet displays a colored line below the sheet name. The other sheet tabs display with a color background.

Lesson 3: Editing Multiple Worksheets Simultaneously

Just as you can select multiple cells in Excel, you can select and work with more than one worksheet at a time. This is very helpful if you need to enter the same data or apply the same formatting to more than one sheet.

You can select consecutive sheets by clicking the first sheet, pressing ⬆Shift, and clicking the last sheet. Select nonadjacent sheets the same way you select nonadjacent cells—by holding down Ctrl and clicking the desired sheets. After selecting multiple worksheets, you can type data and specify settings in any one of the selected worksheets. Excel applies your changes to all the selected worksheets until you ungroup them.

In this lesson, you edit two worksheets simultaneously: the Counts and Budget worksheets of your birthday celebration workbook. After first selecting the worksheets, you enter a title and format the title to display 14-point and bold.

To Edit Multiple Worksheets Simultaneously

❶ Open the *Marie90* workbook, if necessary.

The workbook includes two worksheets: Counts and Budget.

❷ Click the Counts sheet tab, press and hold down Ctrl, and click the Budget sheet tab.

Both sheet tabs display with white backgrounds, and [Group] appears after the file-name in the title bar at the top of the screen (see Figure 8.6).

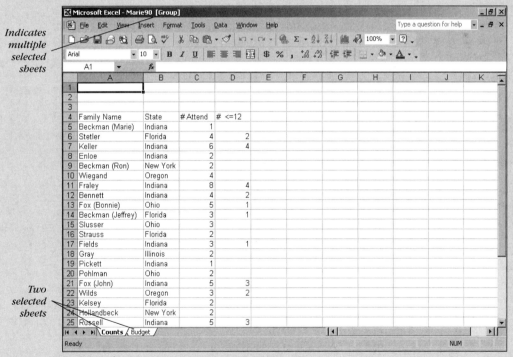

Figure 8.6

❸ In cell A1, enter the title Aunt Marie's 90th Birthday Celebration.

(Continues)

To Edit Multiple Worksheets Simultaneously (Continued)

④ Change the font size in cell A1 to 14pt, and click the Bold button on the toolbar.
The title is entered and formatted on both selected sheets. Now, turn off Group mode.

⑤ Right-click the Counts worksheet tab.
The shortcut menu for sheet operations displays (see Figure 8.7).

14-point, bold worksheet title —

Shortcut menu for sheet operations —

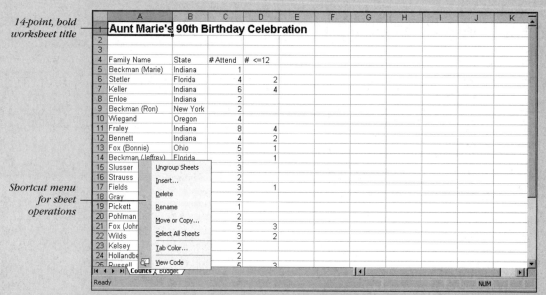

Figure 8.7

⑥ Choose <u>U</u>ngroup Sheets from the shortcut menu.
Only the current sheet displays with a white background, indicating that it is the current sheet.

⑦ Select the Budget worksheet to verify that the title you typed once is entered in both worksheets.

⑧ Select the Counts worksheet, and save your changes to the *Marie90* workbook.
Keep the workbook open for the next lesson, or close the workbook and exit Excel.

To extend your knowledge...

Use Group Mode with Caution

Exercise caution when changing the cell contents of grouped sheets. Any change to the active sheet results in the same change to all other selected sheets, which may result in unintended formatting or replacement of data.

Other Ways to Turn Group Mode On and Off

You can select all sheets in a workbook by right-clicking any sheet tab to display the related shortcut menu and then choosing <u>S</u>elect All Sheets.

If some but not all of the worksheets in a workbook are selected, you can turn Group mode off by clicking the sheet tab of any unselected worksheet.

Lesson 4: Subtotaling Data

If data is organized in a list and sorted, you can use Excel's automatic subtotaling tool to calculate sub-totals and a grand total. You realize that this feature is just one of several ways that Excel could provide the projected attendance totals that you need to prepare the birthday celebration budget. You decide to try this feature, instead of just clicking AutoSum or entering a Sum function, because you think subtotals by state might be of interest to those planning to attend.

In this lesson, you complete the two-step process to automatically subtotal and total data in a list: sort the list on the subtotal field (column), and apply the Data, Subtotals command.

To Subtotal Data

1 Open the *Marie90* workbook, if necessary, and select the worksheet named Counts.

2 Click any cell in the State column within the list, such as cell B5.

3 Click the Sort Ascending button on the toolbar.
The list of attendees sorts by state (see Figure 8.8).

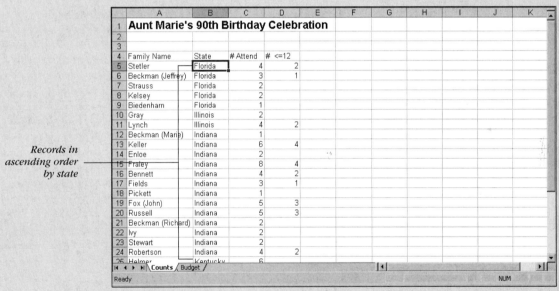

Records in ascending order by state

Figure 8.8

4 Click any cell in column A within the range A4:A34.
The column for the subtotal labels is specified.

5 Choose Data, Subtotals.

6 Select the settings in the Subtotal dialog box shown in Figure 8.9.

(Continues)

To Subtotal Data (Continued)

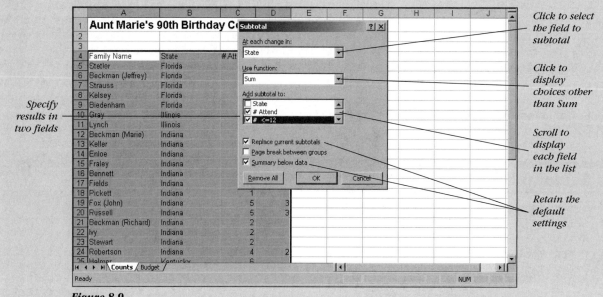

Figure 8.9

❼ Click OK, and widen column B to display the newly inserted subtotal labels.

❽ Scroll down to view the remaining subtotals by state and the grand totals in row 42 (see Figure 8.10).

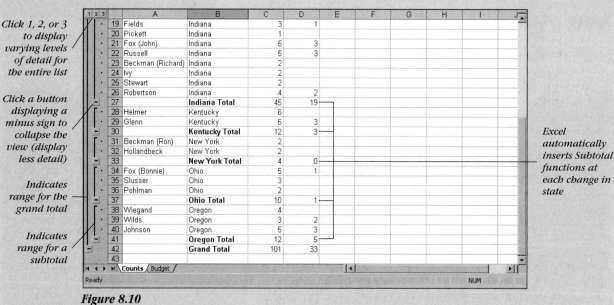

Figure 8.10

❾ Save your changes to the *Marie90* workbook, and close the workbook.

Continue with the next lesson, in which you use an expanded version of the *Marie90* workbook, or exit Excel.

To extend your knowledge...

Removing Subtotals

You can remove subtotals by using a two-step process. Select any cell within the subtotaled list; then choose <u>D</u>ata, Su<u>b</u>totals, and click the <u>R</u>emove All button.

Collapsing and Expanding Subtotaled Data

Excel outlines a subtotaled list by grouping detail rows with each related subtotal row, and by grouping subtotal rows with the grand total row. You can display the entire list at one of three levels of detail using small buttons labeled 1, 2, and 3 in the upper-left corner of the worksheet frame (refer to Figure 8.10). Clicking the 1 button displays only the grand total row. Clicking the 2 button displays the subtotal and grand total rows. Clicking the 3 button displays all rows.

You can also collapse or expand the display at the subtotal level by clicking minus (-) or plus (+) buttons, respectively. At the greatest level of detail, only minus (-) buttons display in the subtotal outline to the left of the row headings in the worksheet frame (refer to Figure 8.10).

Lesson 5: Linking Worksheets

You can link worksheets by creating a reference between cells on different worksheets (sometimes known as a *3-D reference*). The linked worksheets can be in the same workbook or in different workbooks.

In this lesson, you open an expanded version of a two-sheet workbook related to preparations for a 90th birthday party. The budget numbers are already entered in the Budget worksheet. To expand the Budget worksheet, you enter the number of children and adults expected to attend by creating links to data already entered in the Counts worksheet.

To Link Worksheets

① **Open the *ee1-0802* workbook, and save the file as** `Marie90budget`.
The workbook includes sheets named Counts and Budget.

② **Click cell D42 in the sheet named Counts.**
The cell containing the number of children 12 and under is selected.

③ **Click the Copy button in the toolbar (or choose <u>E</u>dit, <u>C</u>opy).**

④ **Click the sheet tab named Budget, and click cell B3.**
The screen display switches to the second worksheet. The destination for the copy is selected.

⑤ **Click the down arrow attached to the Paste button in the toolbar (see Figure 8.11).**

(Continues)

To Link Worksheets (Continued)

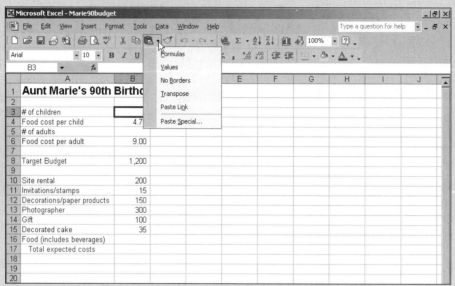

Figure 8.11

 Select Paste Link.

The formula *=Counts!$D$42* displays in the formula bar. The number *33* displays in cell B3 as the formula result. The *Counts!* portion of the formula is a reference to the sheet named Counts; the *$D$42* portion of the formula is an absolute reference to cell D42 in the Counts worksheet.

If you have problems...

If the number *33* instead of the formula *=Counts!$D$42* displays in the formula bar, you clicked the Paste button instead of selecting the Paste Link option on the Paste button's drop-down list. You can correct the problem in two ways. If a Paste button displays next to cell B3, position the mouse pointer on that button, click its down arrow to display the associated drop-down list, and select Link Cells. As an alternative, you can repeat Steps 4 through 6.

You can use the Paste Link option to link single cells or ranges of cells. Now, try a linking method that works for one cell only.

7 **Click cell B5 in the Budget sheet, and type an equal sign (=) to start a formula.**

8 **Click the sheet tab named Counts, and click cell C42.**

The formula under construction in the formula bar includes a reference to the cell containing the total number of people expected at the birthday celebration.

9 **Type a minus sign (-), click cell D42, and click the green check mark in the formula bar.**

The screen display switches back to the Budget worksheet. The number of adults expected to attend is calculated as the difference between the total expected and the number of children expected (see Figure 8.12).

To Link Worksheets

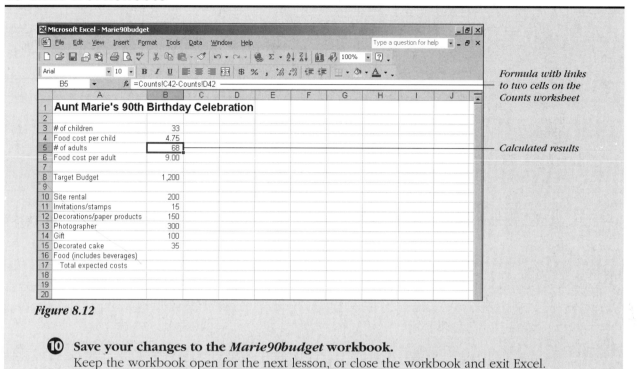

Formula with links to two cells on the Counts worksheet

Calculated results

Figure 8.12

⑩ Save your changes to the *Marie90budget* workbook.
Keep the workbook open for the next lesson, or close the workbook and exit Excel.

Lesson 6: Applying Conditional Formatting

Using formats to emphasize cells in a worksheet can call attention to specific data. When you format a cell, however, the formatting remains in effect, even if the data changes.

If you want to accent a cell, depending on the value of the cell, you can use ***conditional formatting***. Conditional formats return a result based on whether or not the value in the cell meets a specified condition. Formatting options include specifying font style, font color, shading, patterns, borders, bold, italic, and underline.

In this lesson, you enter two formulas: one to calculate projected food costs and the other to sum total budgeted costs for a birthday celebration. You also format the cell containing the second formula to display results in red and bold if the total costs exceed the target budget.

To Apply Conditional Formatting

❶ Open the *Marie90budget* workbook, if necessary, and click cell B16 in the Budget sheet.

❷ Enter the formula =B3*B4+B5*B6 in cell B16, and make cell B16 the active cell.
The formula *=B3*B4+B5*B6* displays in the formula bar, and the formula results (*769*) display in cell B16. This formula calculates the expected cost of food based on values in the range B3:B6.

(Continues)

To Apply Conditional Formatting (Continued)

3 **Click cell B17, enter the formula =SUM(B10:B16), and make cell B17 the active cell.**
The formula =*SUM(B10:B16)* displays in the formula bar, and the formula results (*1,569*) display in cell B17. This formula calculates budgeted total costs.

4 **Click cell B17, and choose Format, Conditional Formatting.**
The Conditional Formatting dialog box opens. Now, specify the condition shown in Figure 8.13.

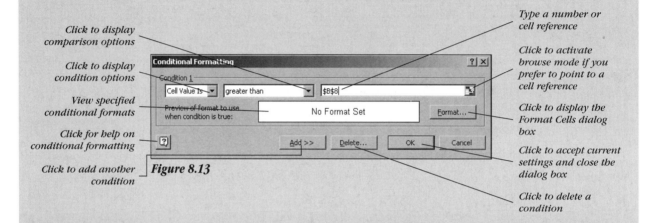

Click to display comparison options

Click to display condition options

View specified conditional formats

Click for help on conditional formatting

Click to add another condition

Type a number or cell reference

Click to activate browse mode if you prefer to point to a cell reference

Click to display the Format Cells dialog box

Click to accept current settings and close the dialog box

Click to delete a condition

Figure 8.13

5 **Display the comparison options drop-down list, and select *greater than* (refer to Figure 8.13).**

6 **In the text box to the right of the comparison option, type =$B$8 (refer to Figure 8.13).**
A condition for cell B17 is set with a cell value greater than the contents of cell B8. Now, specify the format of cell B17 if the condition is true—that is, if the total expected costs exceed the target budget.

7 **Click the Format button in the Conditional Formatting dialog box, and select the Font tab in the Format Cells dialog box.**

8 **Select Bold in the Font style list box.**

9 **Display the drop-down Color list, select red, and click OK.**
The Format Cells dialog box closes.

10 **Click OK.**
The Conditional Formatting dialog box closes. The amount in cell B17 displays in bold and red because it exceeds the target budget in cell B8.

11 **Save your changes to the *Marie90budget* workbook.**
Keep the workbook open for the next lesson, or close the workbook and exit Excel.

To extend your knowledge...

Removing Conditional Formatting

You can remove conditional formatting along with other formats by using an option on the Edit menu. Select the formatted cell, and choose Edit, Clear, Formats.

Specifying More than One Conditional Format

You can specify up to three conditions, with varying formats for each condition. In the previous exercise, for example, you could click the Add button in the Conditional Formatting dialog box and specify a second condition to display a blue border around the total expected costs cell if its contents were equal to or less than the target budget.

Lesson 7: Setting a Print Area

Excel provides more than one way to print part of a worksheet, instead of an entire worksheet. For a one-time printing of part of a worksheet, highlight the range of cells that you want to print, and click the Selection option in the *Print what* area of the Print dialog box.

If you want to print the same part(s) of a worksheet on a regular basis, set up a print area that includes one or more ranges of cells. The defined print area is saved when you save the file. If a worksheet includes a print area, only the print area is printed.

In this lesson, you first make changes in the Budget worksheet to bring total expected costs within the target budget. You are reluctant to change the target budget of $1,200 set by the planning committee several months ago. After looking over the list of expenses, you decide that the most likely areas for trimming costs are food and photographer. If additional reductions are needed, you plan to negotiate a lower site rental fee and spend less on decorations.

After you adjust the budget, you set up and save a print area that prints only the expected costs of the birthday celebration.

To Finalize a Budget and Set a Print Area

❶ Open the *Marie90budget* workbook, if necessary, and select the Budget sheet.
Now, enter reductions in food cost due to changes in the menu you arranged with the caterer.

❷ Select cell B4, and change the amount of the food cost per child to 4.50.

❸ Select cell B6, and change the amount of the food cost per adult to 8.00.
Total costs drop to just under $1,500. The amount *1,493* in cell B17 still appears in red and bold. Significant savings can be achieved only by eliminating the professional photographer.

❹ Select cell A13, and replace *Photographer* with Film/Developing.

❺ Select cell B13, and replace *300* with 75.
Total costs drop closer to the target budget of $1,200. The amount *1,268* in cell B17 still appears in red and bold. You negotiate a lower site rental fee in exchange for increased clean-up responsibilities and cut the amount allocated for decorations.

❻ Select cell B10, and change the amount of the site rental from *200* to 150.

❼ Select cell B12, and change the amount for decorations and paper products from *150* to 120.
The *1,188* total for expected costs no longer appears in red and bold because it is less than the $1,200 target budget (see Figure 8.14). Now, set a print area to print only the budget, and preview the results.

(Continues)

To Finalize a Budget and Set a Print Area (Continued)

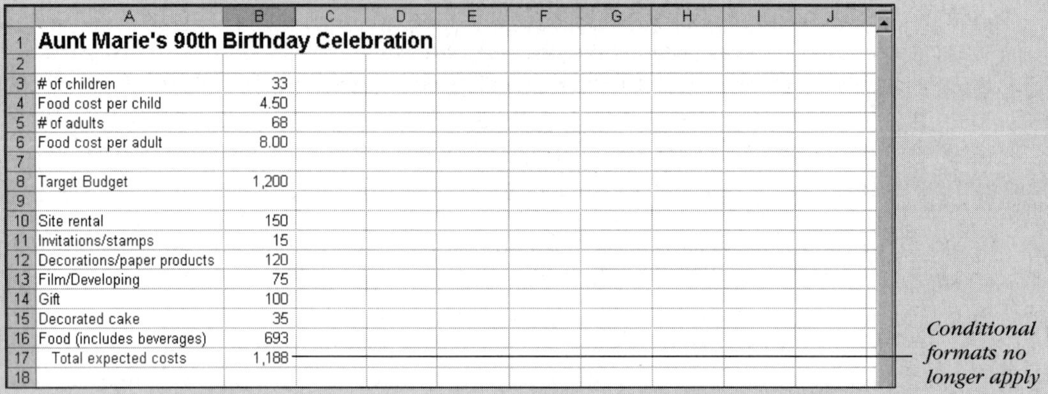

Figure 8.14

Conditional formats no longer apply

8 Select the range A10:B17.

9 Choose File, point to Print Area, and select Set Print Area.

10 Click cell A1 to deselect the highlighted range, click the Print Preview button in the toolbar, and click the Zoom button at the top of the print preview display.
Only the contents of the specified range are set to print (see Figure 8.15).

Figure 8.15

11 Close the print preview, and save your changes to the *Marie90budget* workbook.
Keep the workbook open for the next lesson, or close the workbook and exit Excel.

To extend your knowledge...

Removing a Print Area

The steps to clear a print area are similar to those for setting a print area. Choose File, point to Print Area, and select Clear Print Area.

Lesson 8: Saving a Worksheet with Chart as a Web Page

Now that you have created a workable budget for the birthday celebration, you want to distribute the information to members of the planning committee and anyone else with an interest in the event. You could attach the workbook to an e-mail message, but there is really no need for anyone to edit file contents. You decide instead to save the Budget worksheet as a Web page to be published later as part of a reunion Web site.

In this lesson, you first embed a pie chart in the Budget sheet to show the percentage of each cost in relation to total expected costs. You then save the worksheet as a Web page on your own computer system (sometimes referred to as a local system). Saving the worksheet to a local system enables you to view it prior to publishing it to a Web site by using a browser such as Netscape Navigator or Internet Explorer.

To Save a Worksheet with Chart as a Web Page

1 Open the *Marie90budget* workbook, if necessary, and select the sheet named Budget.

2 Select the range A10:B16, and click the Chart Wizard button on the toolbar.

3 Specify settings in the Chart Wizard dialog boxes to create a Pie chart titled *Budgeted Items* (show percentages, but do not place the chart on a separate sheet).

4 Move and size the chart, as shown in Figure 8.16.

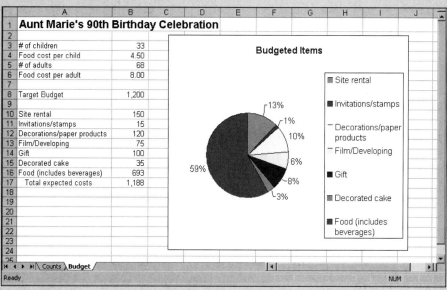

Figure 8.16

5 Click the Save button.
Excel saves the newly created pie chart in the Budget worksheet.

(Continues)

To Save a Worksheet with Chart as a Web Page (Continued)

6 **Choose File, Save as Web Page.**
The Save As dialog box opens, enabling you to select among Web-related options (see Figure 8.17).

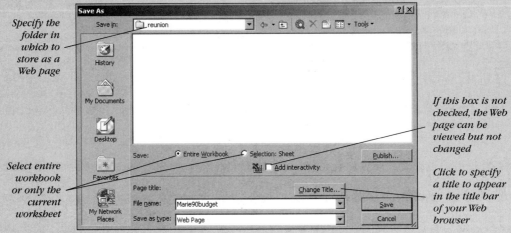

Specify the folder in which to store as a Web page

Select entire workbook or only the current worksheet

If this box is not checked, the Web page can be viewed but not changed

Click to specify a title to appear in the title bar of your Web browser

Figure 8.17

7 **Display the Save in drop-down list, and specify the folder where you want to store the current worksheet as a Web page.**
Unless you prefer another location, store the page in the same folder as the other files you have been saving.

8 **Click the Selection: Sheet option button to save the current sheet, as opposed to the entire workbook.**
Excel automatically assigns a filename that is the same as the sheet name, followed by the extension .htm, which indicates an HTML file.

9 **Click the Save button in the lower-right corner of the dialog box, and close the *Marie90budget* workbook.**
This completes the process to save a worksheet as a Web page. If you have access to a Web browser, you can use its File, Open feature to see how the worksheet data and chart would display on a Web page. Figure 8.18 shows the Budget sheet viewed through the Netscape Navigator browser.

This concludes Project 8. You can continue with end-of-project activities or exit Excel.

To Save a Worksheet with Chart as a Web Page

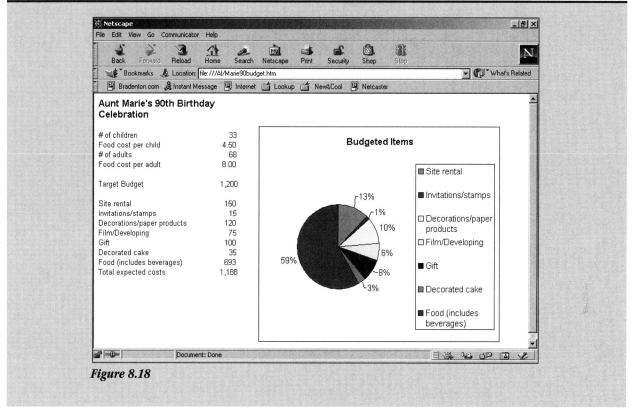

Figure 8.18

To extend your knowledge...

Changing Data on a Web Page

When you save or publish noninteractive data—as you did in Lesson 8—you can open the resulting HTML file in Excel, make changes, and save the file again as an HTML file. If you save or publish interactive data from Excel, you should not open the resulting HTML file in Excel to make changes. Instead, make your changes in the original workbook, and republish or save as a Web page.

Summary

This project provided opportunities to reinforce existing skills and learn new ones. You demonstrated basic skills by entering formulas, copying, widening a column, sorting a list, creating a pie chart, and varying data entry until you achieved the desired result. New skills included inserting, moving, and renaming sheets; editing multiple worksheets simultaneously; creating subtotals; linking worksheets; specifying conditional formatting; and saving a worksheet as a Web page.

You can extend your knowledge by experimenting with variations of skills. Select Count or Average instead of Sum to subtotal a list. You linked cells between worksheets; now try to link cells between workbooks. Specify conditional formatting with two conditions instead of one. Create a chart on a separate sheet in a workbook, and save the chart sheet as a Web page. Don't forget to take advantage of onscreen Help and the many opportunities to learn through the end-of-project activities.

Checking Concepts and Terms

Multiple Choice

Circle the letter of the correct answer for each of the following.

1. Which of the following is not a true statement about conditional formatting? [L6]

   a. A formatting change occurs when the value or formula in a cell meets a specified condition.

   b. Conditional formatting can be based on more than one condition.

   c. Conditional formatting can include borders.

   d. Choosing Edit, Clear, Formats does not clear conditional formats.

2. Which of the following is not a function you can select using the Data, Subtotals command? [L4]

   a. Max

   b. Average

   c. Count

   d. All of the above functions are available for selection when setting up a Data, Subtotals operation.

3. When you _____ data, you can make a change in the source, and the destination automatically updates. [L5]

   a. link

   b. embed

   c. copy

   d. paste

4. Assume that a workbook named *registration* includes sheets named Fees and Summary. Which of the following could be a valid formula in the Summary sheet, linking to one or more cells in the Fees sheet? [L5]

   a. =Registration:Fees!$B$5

   b. =Fees!$B$5-Fees!$B$7

   c. =Fees:$B$5-Fees:$B$7

   d. None of the above

5. Pressing which of the following keys allows you to select nonadjacent sheets in a workbook? [L3]

   a. (⬆Shift)

   b. (Ctrl)

   c. (Alt)

   d. None of the above

Discussion

1. Explain conditional formatting, and provide your own example of how you might use this feature. [L6]

2. In this project, you embedded a copy of a Word table in an Excel worksheet. Explain the difference between embedding and linking. How does the copy process change if you link a Word table instead of embedding it in an Excel worksheet? [L1 and onscreen Help]

3. In this project, you embedded a copy of a Word table in an Excel worksheet. Provide an example of an information need that can be met by copying all or part of an Excel worksheet and its accompanying chart to a Word document. Also, describe the copy process (assume that you want to embed, rather than link, the results of the copy). [L1]

Skill Drill

Skill Drill exercises reinforce project skills. Each skill reinforced is the same, or nearly the same, as a skill presented in the project. Detailed instructions are provided in a step-by-step format.

Before beginning your first Project 8 Skill Drill exercise, complete the following steps:

1. Open the file named *ee1-0803* and immediately save it as **ee1-p8drill**.
   The workbook contains seven sheets: an overview, and exercise sheets named #1-Rename, #2-Subtotal, #3-GroupLink1, #4-GroupLink2, #5-Conditional, and #6-CopyTo.
2. Click the Overview sheet to view the organization of the Project 8 Skill Drill Exercises workbook.

Each exercise is independent of the others, so you may complete the exercises in any order. Be sure to save the workbook after completing each exercise. If you need a paper copy of the completed exercise, enter your name, centered in a header, before printing. Other print options have already been set to print compressed to one page and to display the filename, sheet name, and current date in a footer.

If you need more than one work session to complete the desired exercises, continue working on *ee1-p8drill* instead of starting over again on the original *ee1-0803* file.

1. Renaming a Sheet

You use a multiple-sheet workbook to keep track of residential real estate listings and sales.

To change the name of a sheet to one that describes the contents of the worksheet, follow these steps:

1. Open the *ee1-p8drill* workbook, if necessary, and select the worksheet named #1-Rename.
2. Double-click the sheet tab name (or choose F_ormat, S_heet, R_ename).
   The current sheet name *#1-Rename* displays highlighted.
3. Type Listings, and press ↵Enter.
   The sheet name *Listings* replaces the sheet name #1-Rename.
4. Save your changes to the *ee1-p8drill* workbook.

2. Subtotaling Data

You use a multiple-sheet workbook to keep track of residential real estate listings and sales. You want a count of the homes available in each area.

To get the information you need by using Excel's Subtotal feature, follow these steps:

1. Open the *ee1-p8drill* workbook, if necessary, and select the worksheet named #2-Subtotal.
2. Click any cell within the Area column of the residential real estate list, such as cell C6.
3. Click the Sort Ascending button in the toolbar.
   The real estate listings sort by Area—homes in Autumn Woods first, Cape Cod Village second, and so forth.
4. Make sure that the current cell is within the residential real estate list, and choose D_ata, Su_btotals.
5. Specify Area as the _At each change in_ setting in the Subtotal dialog box.
6. Specify Count as the _Use function_ setting in the Subtotal dialog box.
7. Check only the Area box in the _Add subtotal to_ list in the Subtotal dialog box.

8. Click OK, and widen column B as necessary.

Excel subtotals at each change in Area, and provides a count of listings in that area.

9. Save your changes to the *ee1-p8drill* workbook.

3. Editing Multiple Worksheets Simultaneously

You are developing a multiple-sheet workbook to keep track of residential real estate listings and sales, and you want to make the same changes to two of the worksheets.

To make the desired changes to both sheets by editing only one of the sheets, follow these steps:

1. Open the *ee1-p8drill* workbook, if necessary, and select the worksheet named #3-GroupLink1.

2. Hold down Ctrl, and click the sheet tab named #4-GroupLink2.

Only the sheet names #3-GroupLink1 and #4-GroupLink2 are selected (that is, the sheet tabs display with a white background).

3. Select the quarter labels in the range A8:A11, and apply a bright blue font color to the text.

4. Narrow column A to be just wide enough to display the quarter labels.

5. Click cell A12, and click the Increase Indent button on the toolbar once.

You have now applied three formatting changes to column A.

6. Click any unselected sheet tab, such as #2-Subtotal.

The selected sheets ungroup. Sheets #3-GroupLink1 and #4-GroupLink2 no longer appear highlighted.

7. Check that the formatting changes to column A affect both the #3-GroupLink1 and #4-Group-Link2 worksheets.

8. Save your changes to the *ee1-p8drill* workbook.

4. Linking Worksheets

You are developing a multiple-sheet workbook to keep track of residential real estate listings and sales. You created a summary worksheet for annual sales and a detail worksheet for one real estate agent. You plan to link the individual's data to the summary sheet. Once you set the link and test that it works, you plan to add sheets for other agents.

To link worksheets, follow these steps:

1. Open the *ee1-p8drill* workbook, if necessary, and select the worksheet named #4-GroupLink2.

2. Select the range B8:B11.

The quarterly sales data for agent Jessica Blair are selected.

3. Click the Copy button in the toolbar (or choose Edit, Copy).

4. Click the sheet tab named #3-GroupLink1, and click cell B8.

The screen display switches from the individual worksheet to the summary worksheet. The first cell in the destination worksheet is selected.

5. Click the down arrow attached to the Paste button in the toolbar.

6. Select Paste Link.

Excel pastes links to the quarterly data for Jessica Blair. The number *249900* displays in cell B8 as the formula result. The formula *='#4-GroupLink2'!B8* displays in the formula bar.

7. Make sure that the formulas in cells B9 through B11 also link to cells on the worksheet named #4-GroupLink2.

8. Save your changes to the *ee1-p8drill* workbook.

5. Applying Conditional Formatting

You are developing a multiple-sheet workbook to keep track of residential real estate listings and sales. You want to use Excel's conditional formatting feature to display annual sales of one million or more with a blue border around the cell.

To set up the conditional formatting, follow these steps:

1. Open the *ee1-p8drill* workbook, if necessary, and select the worksheet named #5-Conditional.
2. Click cell B12.

   The cell containing annual sales for Jessica Blair is selected.
3. Choose Format, Conditional Formatting.

   The Conditional Formatting dialog box opens.
4. In the first of three boxes for condition 1, specify *Cell Value Is*.
5. In the second of three boxes for condition 1, specify *greater than or equal to*.
6. In the third of three boxes for condition 1, type **1000000**.
7. Click the Format button in the Conditional Formatting dialog box.
8. Select the Border tab in the Format Cells dialog box, and select a bright blue color from the Color drop-down list.
9. Choose the Outline preset, and click OK to close the Format Cells dialog box.
10. Click OK to close the Conditional Formatting dialog box, and click a cell other than cell B12. Cell B12 displays with a blue border because formula results are greater than or equal to one million dollars.
11. Save your changes to the *ee1-p8drill* workbook.

6. Copying from Another Application to Excel

You are developing a multiple-sheet workbook to keep track of residential real estate listings and sales. You decide to include a contact list of homes for sale by owners. You just received an attachment by e-mail from one of your friends, who agreed to check her neighborhood for signs. The attachment is a Word document that includes a table of data that you want to copy to your workbook.

To copy from another application, follow these steps:

1. Open the *ee1-p8drill* workbook, if necessary, and select the worksheet named #6-CopyTo.
2. Start Word if it is not already running, and open the Word document named *ee1-0804*.

   The document includes one brief paragraph and a table listing addresses of homes for sale by owners in Glenn Lakes.
3. Click any cell within the Word table.
4. Choose Table, point to Select, and click Table.
5. Click the Copy button in the toolbar (or select Edit, Copy).
6. Click *ee1-p8drill* in the taskbar at the bottom of the screen.
7. Click cell A4 in the #6-CopyTo sheet, and click the Paste button in the toolbar (or choose Edit, Paste).

   The four columns in the Word table copy to columns A through D of the Excel sheet named #6-CopyTo.
8. Switch to Microsoft Word, and exit Word without saving any changes.
9. In the #6-CopyTo worksheet, remove the copied formatting (borders and wrapped text), and widen columns A and C as necessary.
10. Save your changes to the *ee1-p8drill* workbook.

Challenge

Challenge exercises expand on or are somewhat related to skills presented in the lessons. Each exercise provides a brief narrative introduction, followed by instructions in a numbered-step format that are not as detailed as those in the Skill Drill section.

Before beginning your first Project 8 Challenge exercise, complete the following steps:

1. Open the file named *ee1-0805*, and immediately save it as **ee1-p8challenge**.

   The *ee1-p8challenge* workbook contains five sheets: an overview, and four exercise sheets named #1-AvgSubtotal, #2-TwoCondFormat, #3-InsertGroup, and #4-Chart.

2. Click the Overview sheet to view the organization of the Project 8 Challenge Exercises workbook.

Each exercise is independent of the others, so you may complete the exercises in any order. Be sure to save the workbook after completing each exercise. If you need a paper copy of the completed exercise, enter your name, centered in a header, before printing. Other print options have already been set to print compressed to one page and to display the filename, sheet name, and current date in a footer.

If you need more than one work session to complete the desired exercises, continue working on *ee1-p8challenge* instead of starting over again on the original *ee1-0805* file.

1. Subtotaling Data Using the Average Function

You use a multiple-sheet workbook to keep track of residential real estate listings and sales. You want to know the average listing price of the homes available in each area.

To get the information you need using Excel's Subtotal feature, follow these steps:

1. Open your *ee1-p8challenge* workbook, if necessary, and select the worksheet named #1-AvgSubtotal.
2. Sort the real estate listings in ascending order by Area.
3. Choose the option on the Data menu that displays the Subtotal dialog box.
4. Specify that Excel should use the Average function at each change in Area.
5. Specify placement of each subtotal only at the Price field, and include summary data at the bottom.
6. Close the dialog box in a way that executes the desired operation.
7. Make sure that the results are accurate.

   The average price of a home listed in Autumn Woods is *84,450*. The average price in Champions Village is *129,317*.
8. Save your changes to the *ee1-p8challenge* workbook.

2. Applying Two Conditional Formats to a Cell

You are developing a multiple-sheet workbook to keep track of residential real estate listings and sales. You want to use Excel's conditional-formatting feature to draw attention to quarterly sales greater than or equal to $250,000 or quarterly sales less than $150,000.

To set up the desired conditional formatting, follow these steps:

1. Open your *ee1-p8challenge* workbook, if necessary, and select the worksheet named #2-TwoCondFormat.
2. Select the range B10:E13 (do not include the totals in row 14), and choose Format, Conditional Formatting.
3. Specify condition 1 as cell value greater than or equal to 250000.
4. Click the Format button and specify gold shading (not gold text).
5. Restore display of the Conditional Formatting dialog box, and click the Add button.
6. Specify condition 2 as cell value less than 150000, and set up red text as the format.
7. Make sure that conditional formats display as intended, and make changes as necessary.

   Cells in the ranges D10:E10 and B12:E12 should display with gold backgrounds. Cell contents should display red in cells B11, B13, D11, and D13.
8. Save your changes to the *ee1-p8challenge* workbook.

3. Inserting Sheets and Editing the New Sheets Simultaneously

You are developing a residential real estate multiple-sheet workbook. The design that you have in mind includes a separate worksheet to track each agent's sales. Because you want identical layouts on these individual sheets, you decide to group new sheets and edit them simultaneously.

To create the desired worksheets, follow these steps:

1. Open your *ee1-p8challenge* workbook, if necessary, and select the worksheet named #3-InsertGroup.
2. Insert two blank worksheets and position them between the sheets named #3-InsertGroup and #4-Chart.
3. Rename the two new worksheets #3b and #3c, respectively.
4. Select the three sheets that have names beginning with #3.
5. Reproduce the cell content, alignment, and approximate column widths shown in Figure 8.19.

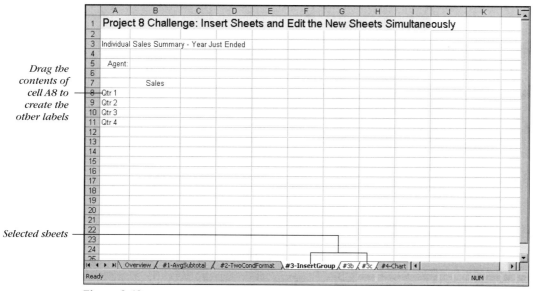

Figure 8.19

6. Ungroup the sheets, and make sure that the labels and column widths shown in Figure 8.19 are applied to the three sheets that have names beginning with #3.
7. Save your changes to the *ee1-p8challenge* workbook.

4. Creating a Chart Sheet and Saving It as a Web Page

You are developing a multiple-sheet workbook to track real estate listings and sales. You want to present summary data in chart form on your company's intranet. Before you make the chart available for general viewing, save it to your own computer system for viewing with a Web browser. You can edit it later, as necessary, and then publish it to the intranet.

Before you begin, use onscreen Help to learn how to save a chart as a Web page. To create and save the chart, follow these steps:

1. Open your *ee1-p8challenge* workbook, if necessary, and select the worksheet named #4-Chart.
2. Select the nonadjacent ranges A6:E6 and A11:E11.
3. Activate Chart Wizard, and create a pie chart showing values as data labels.
4. Specify the title `Individual Sales Summary - Year Just Ended`.
5. Save the pie chart as a new sheet.
6. Save only the new Chart1 sheet as a noninteractive Web page using the filename `sales-pie`.
7. Save your changes to the *ee1-p8challenge* workbook.

Discovery Zone exercises require advanced knowledge of topics presented in *Essentials* lessons, application of skills from multiple lessons, or self-directed learning of new skills.

Before beginning your first Project 8 Discovery Zone exercise, complete the following steps:

1. Open the Excel file named *ee1-0806*, and immediately save it as `ee1-p8discovery`. The *ee1-p8discovery* workbook contains seven worksheets: an overview; three exercise sheets named #1-FindCond, #2-CopyChart, and #3-LinkSheets; and three worksheets named Arrowhead, Ironwood, and Prestwick, which you use in the third exercise.
2. Click the Overview sheet to view the organization of the Project 8 Discovery Zone Exercises workbook.

Each exercise is independent of the others, so you may complete the exercises in any order. Be sure to save the workbook after completing each exercise. If you need a paper copy of the completed exercise, enter your name, centered in a header, before printing. Other print options have already been set to print compressed to one page and to display the filename, sheet name, and current date in a footer.

If you need more than one work session to complete the desired exercises, continue working on *ee1-p8discovery* instead of starting over again on the original *ee1-0806* file.

1. Finding Cells with Conditional Formats

Use onscreen Help to learn how to find cells with conditional formats. Open the *ee1-p8discovery* workbook, and apply what you have learned to find cells with conditional formatting in the sheet named #1-FindCond. Enter a note below the data, explaining which cells have conditional formatting and what condition(s) must be present for the formatting to display.

2. Copying from Excel to Another Program

Copying from Excel to another application requires a copy-and-paste operation similar to that for copying to Excel from another application. Start Word, open the document named *ee1-0807*, and save it as `democopy`. Switch to Excel, open the *ee1-p8discovery* workbook (if necessary), and select the sheet named #2-CopyChart. Select the pie chart, and copy it as an embedded chart to the appropriate place in the *democopy* Word document. Close the Word document, saving your changes.

3. Linking Worksheets

Open the *ee1-p8discovery* workbook, if necessary. On the worksheet named #3-LinkSheets, apply what you have learned about linking cells. Enter formulas in the range B8:B10 that reference the appropriate cells in the Arrowhead worksheet—that is, the cells that contain the annual total for each type of revenue. Enter similar formulas in C8:C10 and D8:D10 that reference the appropriate cells in the Ironwood and Prestwick worksheets, respectively. Enter SUM functions in Column E and Row 12 to calculate the subtotals described in cells E7 and A12, respectively. Complete the #3-LinkSheets worksheet by entering a formula or function to calculate total revenue in cell E14. Make sure that your formula results are accurate (check figures include *1,948* in cell B12; *3,822* in cell E8; and *5,143* in cell E14).

Access

DAWN PARRISH WOOD

P A R T III

Getting Started with Access

Objectives

In this project, you learn how to

- ✔ Create a New Database Using the Database Wizard
- ✔ Copy and Rename a Database File
- ✔ Open and Close a Database
- ✔ Open and Close a Database Table
- ✔ Identify Access Window Elements
- ✔ Get Help
- ✔ Exit Access and Windows

Key terms introduced in this project include

- ❑ database
- ❑ Database window
- ❑ field
- ❑ launch
- ❑ object
- ❑ Office Assistant
- ❑ properties
- ❑ read-only
- ❑ record
- ❑ ScreenTip
- ❑ switchboard
- ❑ table
- ❑ What's This?

Why Would I Do This?

Microsoft Access is a **database** program that enables you to store, retrieve, analyze, and print information. Companies use databases for many purposes: for managing customer files, tracking orders and inventories, and marketing purposes. An individual might set up a database to track household expenses or manage a list of family, friends, and business addresses. Teachers often set up a database to track student grades and other class information. A database allows the user to access and manage thousands, even millions of pieces of data in an organized, efficient, and accurate manner.

Tables are the foundation of the database, because they store the data and provide the structure by which it is organized. Each table stores a set of related data. Tables are made up of **records** that include related information about one object, person, event, or transaction. Records are displayed in rows. Each category of information in a record is known as a **field**. Fields are displayed in columns; the field name appears in the database table as a column heading. As such, a table organizes data within a predefined structure.

To make the best use of your time, you will use the numerous databases included with this book. In most instances, you will open and modify these sample files rather than create them from scratch. In this project, you learn how to create a new database using an existing structure by utilizing the Database Wizard. You also learn how to copy and rename a database file. You open a database and a database table in Access to get an idea of what databases look like. Finally, you learn how to get help and exit Access.

Visual Summary

When you have completed this project, you will have worked with a database that looks like Figure 1.1.

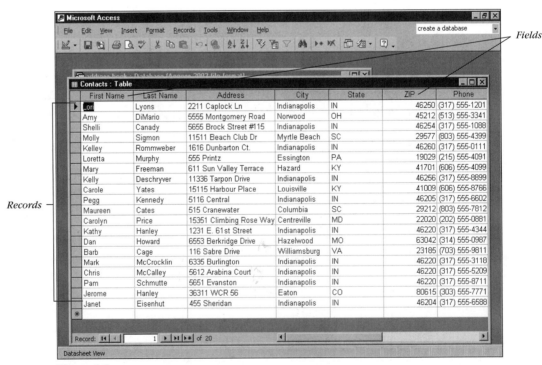

Figure 1.1

Lesson 1: Creating a New Database Using the Database Wizard

Databases are used for various purposes. However, there are certain types of database management that are used more frequently than others, such as contact management or records management. Access provides a few pre-designed database templates that can be used to set up a new database quickly and easily. The Database Wizard provides step-by-step help in choosing the tables and fields to be included in a database as well as a few design features.

In this lesson, you use the Database Wizard to create a new database to maintain your contact information.

To Create a New Database Using the Database Wizard

1 **Click the Start button on the Windows taskbar, and point to Programs on the Start menu.**
The Programs menu opens.

2 **Find Microsoft Access on the Programs menu, and left click it.**
This *launches* (starts) the Access program. The task pane appears on the right side of the window to let you choose the next step—start a new database, use a template, or open an existing database (see Figure 1.2).

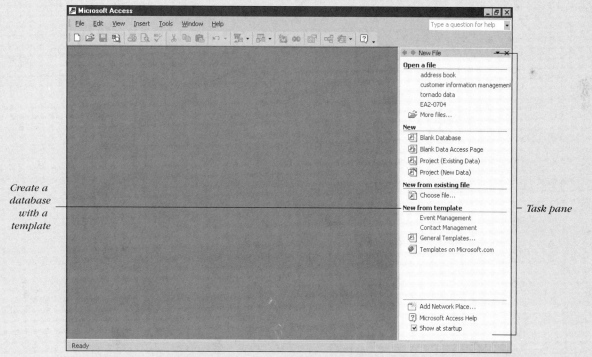

Create a database with a template

Task pane

Figure 1.2

3 **Click the General Templates option under the *New from template* category in the task pane.**
The Templates dialog box is displayed (see Figure 1.3).

(Continues)

To Create a New Database Using the Database Wizard (Continued)

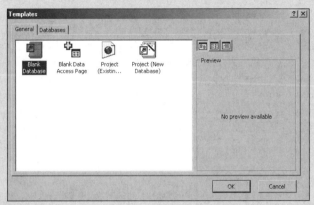

Figure 1.3

④ **Click the Databases tab. Select the Contact Management icon, and click OK.**
Before a database can be created, it must be named and saved.

⑤ **In the Save in drop-down list, select the drive and folder where you want to save the current file. Type** contacts **in the File name text box, and click Create.**
The Database Wizard is displayed, showing the type of information this database template stores (see Figure 1.4).

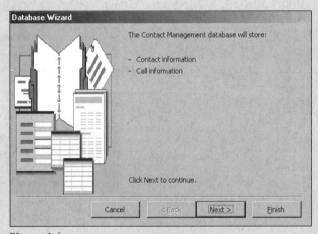

Figure 1.4

⑥ **Click Next.**
Three tables are created by default in this database template, as shown on the left side of the dialog box—Contact information, Call information, and Contact types. On the right side of the dialog box, a list of fields for the selected table is displayed. Fields to be included are checked (see Figure 1.5). You may choose to uncheck certain fields. Click another table on the left to see the list of fields displayed on the right.

To Create a New Database Using the Database Wizard

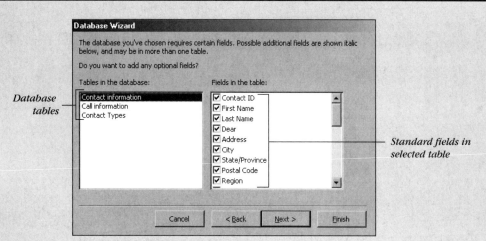

Database tables

Standard fields in selected table

Figure 1.5

7 **Click Next.**
The wizard prompts you to choose the screen display style you desire for the database. Each style adds a distinct characteristic to the database.

8 **Select *Stone*, and click Next.**
The report style is the next formatting option you must select. Select the style that conforms to the purpose for the reports in this database.

9 **Select *Corporate*, and click Next.**

10 **Leave the default title for the database. Click Next.**

11 **Select the *Yes, start the database* check box, if necessary, and click Finish.**
After a short delay, the Main Switchboard for the new database is displayed (see Figure 1.6). A *switchboard* makes access to the various components of a database easier for those persons who are less familiar with database structures. Switchboards are described in the *essentials* Access 2002 Level 3 book, Project 6.

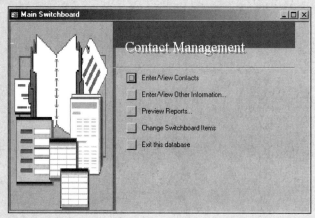

Figure 1.6

(Continues)

To Create a New Database Using the Database Wizard (Continued)

⑫ **Click the *Exit this database* button on the switchboard, or click the Close button in the upper-right corner of the switchboard. Then click the Close button on the menu bar.**
The database is saved automatically and closed.

To extend your knowledge...

Using the Switchboard

When the Database Wizard is used to create a database, a switchboard is automatically created and starts by default when the database is opened. A user who is new to databases may find the switchboard easier to use than the Access Database window. Click a switchboard option to view that component. When the component is closed, the switchboard is redisplayed.

Lesson 2: Copying and Renaming a Database File

During the learning process and even during the database creation process, it is a good idea to work from a copy of the database rather than the original. The original database is preserved and serves as a backup. To make the best use of your time, many databases are supplied for use with this book. By copying them, you keep the original files intact.

In this lesson, you use Access to copy a file from the location where the Project 1 data files are stored. The files may be located on a network or other drive, or you can download them from the Prentice Hall Web site as described in the Introduction to this book. You can then rename the file and remove the ***read-only*** property so you can make changes to the database using Access.

To Copy and Rename a Database File

❶ **Start Access, if necessary, and click the Open button on the Database toolbar.**
The Open dialog box is displayed.

If you have problems...

If you closed Access after the last lesson, click the Start button on the taskbar, point to Programs on the Start menu, and select Microsoft Access.

---

❷ **Click the list arrow next to the Look in drop-down list and select the drive and folder that contain the student data files supplied with this book.**
The files supplied with the book are on the Internet, or they may have been placed on a network drive if you are using this book in a classroom setting. If the files have not been made available to you, refer to the Introduction of this book for the Internet address.

❸ **Open the folder where the files for Project 1 are located.**
The databases used in Project 1 of this book are displayed.

❹ **Right-click the *ea1-0101* file.**
The filename may appear as *ea1-0101.mdb*.

To Copy and Rename a Database File

The *.mdb* extension shows only if the option to hide it has not been selected. To change this option, open Windows Explorer and choose View, Folder Options, View. Select the *Hide file extensions for known file types* check box. A check mark indicates you will not see the file extensions. Choose OK. These steps may vary depending on your version of Windows. If the extensions are showing, then the file extension (.mdb) must be included when renaming the file (later in this lesson).

A shortcut menu is displayed (see Figure 1.7).

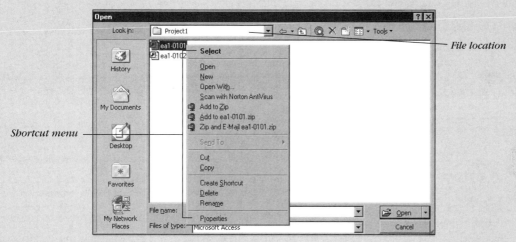

Figure 1.7

⑤ **Select Copy on the shortcut menu.**
The *ea1-0101* file is copied to the Windows Clipboard.

⑥ **Click the list arrow next to the Look in drop-down list and move to the folder in which you will store your files. Right-click in an open area of the Open dialog box. Select Paste on the shortcut menu.**
Right-clicking in an open area displays a shortcut menu for the folder, not for a particular file. Now your file is copied to the new location.

⑦ **Right-click *ea1-0101* and select Properties on the shortcut menu.**
Notice that the Attributes at the bottom of the Properties dialog box. **Properties** are the characteristics of the file. The files for this book have been distributed with the read-only property turned on. Files copied from a read-only storage medium such as a CD-ROM also have the read-only property set. You need to change this attribute to Archive before you can make changes to the database.

⑧ **Click the Archive check box to select it, and then click the Read-only check box to deselect it. Click OK.**

⑨ **Right-click *ea1-0101* and select Rename on the shortcut menu.**
The filename is highlighted.

⑩ **Type address book, then press ⏎Enter.**
The name of the file is changed (see Figure 1.8). Leave the Open dialog box displayed to continue with the next lesson.

(Continues)

To Copy and Rename a Database File (Continued)

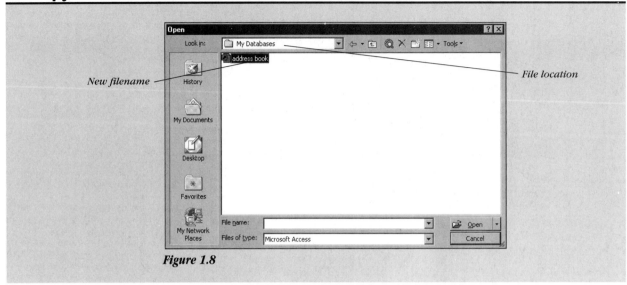

New filename *File location*

Figure 1.8

To extend your knowledge...

Another way to open files

You also can open a file by selecting Files (or More files) under the *Open a File* category in the task pane. If the task pane isn't showing, you can display it by right-clicking the Database toolbar and choosing task pane.

Differences Between Access and Other Office Applications

In other Microsoft applications, such as Word, Excel, or PowerPoint, you can make copies of files by opening them in the application and then choosing the File menu's Save As option. The Access program uses files differently than most other programs. The Save As menu option saves only what is selected—such as a report or a form—not the whole database.

Lesson 3: Opening and Closing a Database

Typically, the first thing you do when you launch Access is open an existing database. You can open any database you have created, any database that is included as part of this course, or any database that was included in the Access program.

In this lesson, you open a sample database called *address book* that contains the same kind of information you would include in a personal address book. Access can easily manage a database that lists contact information about family members, friends, and associates.

To Open and Close a Database

❶ If the Access program is not already running from the previous lesson, launch Access, click the Open button, click the list arrow next to the Look in text box, and find the disk drive and folder that contain the *address book* database.
If you left the program running at the end of the previous lesson, the *address book* database will already appear in the Open dialog box.

❷ Click *address book* to select it, then click the Open button to open the database.
The sample *address book* database appears onscreen (see Figure 1.9). The **Database window** lists all the tables in the database. The various database **objects**, such as tables,

To Open and Close a Database

forms, and reports, are displayed. Object buttons are displayed down the left side of the Database window. Action buttons (Open, Design, and New) are found in the Database Window toolbar. You can create or open tables from this window. You can also change the design of existing tables.

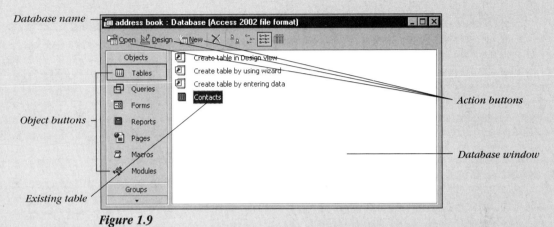

Figure 1.9

❸ Click the Queries object button.
The Queries object button is displayed on the left side of the window, along with the other object buttons. Clicking the button displays the only query in this database, named Indiana (see Figure 1.10). A query is used to sort, search, and limit the data to only those records that you need to examine.

Figure 1.10

❹ Close the database by clicking the Close button on the upper-right corner of the Database window.
Do not click the Close button on the right edge of the program title bar. The Database window closes, but the Access program is still running.

To extend your knowledge...

Shortcuts to Opening a Database

You can open a database with the commands used in the preceding steps, but two shortcut methods are also available. You can open a new database by clicking the New button on the Database toolbar, or by pressing Ctrl+N (holding down Ctrl and pressing the letter N). You can open an existing database by clicking the Open button on the Database toolbar, or by pressing Ctrl+O (holding down Ctrl and pressing the letter O). If you prefer to use the menu, you can select either New or Open from the File menu to create a new database or open an existing one.

Lesson 4: Opening and Closing a Database Table

Tables are the data storage areas of most databases. Access sets up tables as grids in which you can enter, edit, and view all the related information in your database. When you want to work with a table, you first open the database that contains the table, then open the table.

In this lesson, you open a table in the *address book* database that you opened and closed in Lesson 3.

To Open and Close a Database Table

① **Click the Open button on the toolbar.**
The Open dialog box is displayed. If necessary, change to the drive or folder containing the database files for this book.

② **Click *address book* to select it and then click Open.**
The *address book* database opens and displays the Database window. A database always opens to the object window that was in use when the program was closed; in this case, the Queries window.

③ **Click the Tables object button and then select the Contacts table, if necessary (see Figure 1.11).**

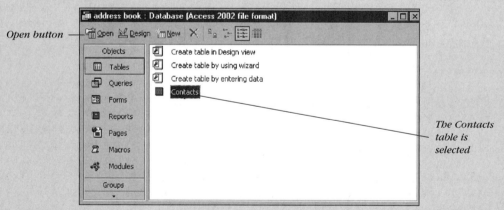

Figure 1.11

④ **Click the Open button on the toolbar in the Database window.**
The Contacts table displays onscreen. Tables contain a grid of information made up of records and fields. Remember: A record is a row of related data, whereas a field is a column of the same type of data.

Depending on the size of the table window, you may not be able to see all the information in the database table. To display other information, you can scroll the window using the horizontal and vertical scrollbars (see Figure 1.12).

To Open and Close a Database Table

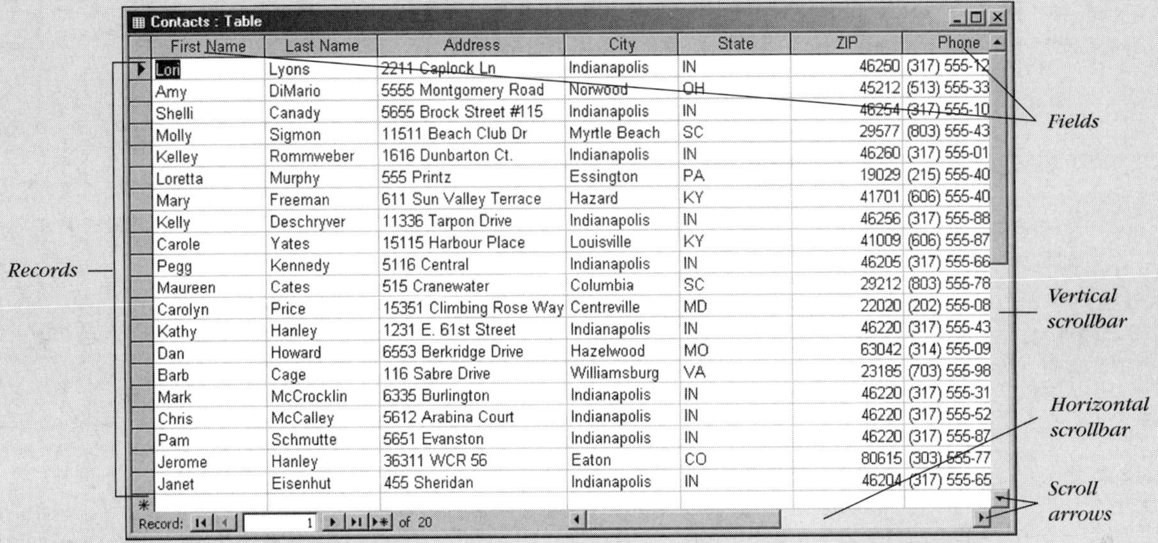

Contacts : Table

First Name	Last Name	Address	City	State	ZIP	Phone
Lori	Lyons	2211 Caplock Ln	Indianapolis	IN	46250	(317) 555-12
Amy	DiMario	5555 Montgomery Road	Norwood	OH	45212	(513) 555-33
Shelli	Canady	5655 Brock Street #115	Indianapolis	IN	46254	(317) 555-10
Molly	Sigmon	11511 Beach Club Dr	Myrtle Beach	SC	29577	(803) 555-43
Kelley	Rommweber	1616 Dunbarton Ct.	Indianapolis	IN	46260	(317) 555-01
Loretta	Murphy	555 Printz	Essington	PA	19029	(215) 555-40
Mary	Freeman	611 Sun Valley Terrace	Hazard	KY	41701	(606) 555-40
Kelly	Deschryver	11336 Tarpon Drive	Indianapolis	IN	46256	(317) 555-88
Carole	Yates	15115 Harbour Place	Louisville	KY	41009	(606) 555-87
Pegg	Kennedy	5116 Central	Indianapolis	IN	46205	(317) 555-66
Maureen	Cates	515 Cranewater	Columbia	SC	29212	(803) 555-78
Carolyn	Price	15351 Climbing Rose Way	Centreville	MD	22020	(202) 555-08
Kathy	Hanley	1231 E. 61st Street	Indianapolis	IN	46220	(317) 555-43
Dan	Howard	6553 Berkridge Drive	Hazelwood	MO	63042	(314) 555-09
Barb	Cage	116 Sabre Drive	Williamsburg	VA	23185	(703) 555-98
Mark	McCrocklin	6335 Burlington	Indianapolis	IN	46220	(317) 555-31
Chris	McCalley	5612 Arabina Court	Indianapolis	IN	46220	(317) 555-52
Pam	Schmutte	5651 Evanston	Indianapolis	IN	46220	(317) 555-87
Jerome	Hanley	36311 WCR 56	Eaton	CO	80615	(303) 555-77
Janet	Eisenhut	455 Sheridan	Indianapolis	IN	46204	(317) 555-65

Record: 1 of 20

Figure 1.12

5. **Click the right scroll arrow on the horizontal scrollbar until you scroll to the last field.**
   Access displays the information in the ZIP and Phone fields that you may not have been able to see.

6. **Click the left scroll arrow until you scroll back to the first field (First Name).**

7. **Click the Close button in the upper-right corner of the Contacts table.**
   The Database window is still open. Keep the *address book* database open to use in the next lesson.

Lesson 5: Learning About the Access Window

The look of the Access window changes, depending on what you are doing with the program. You may recognize many parts of the Access screen as familiar parts of every Windows program—elements such as the Minimize, Maximize/Restore, and Close buttons, as well as the scrollbars. Other parts of the Access screen offer features that can help you complete your work quickly and efficiently. For example, the menu bar and toolbar are convenient features that you will use in most of the projects in this book.

When you first launch Access, you see only a few items on the menu bar, and most of the buttons on the toolbar are dim (or grayed), which means that they are unavailable. When you open a database, additional menu items appear on the menu bar, and most of the toolbar buttons become available. As you open and work with individual objects within the database, you see that menu options and toolbar buttons change in relation to the type of object you selected. This lesson explains what you can expect to see in most Access windows.

To Learn About the Access Window

1 **Look at the elements that appear in the Access window when the *address book* database is open.**

The *address book* database window should be onscreen from the last lesson, and the Tables object button should be selected. Four key elements appear in the Access window: the title bar at the top of the window, the menu bar below the title bar, the toolbar under the menu bar, and the status bar at the bottom of the window (see Figure 1.13).

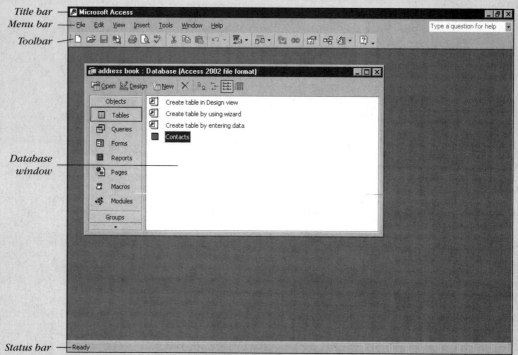

Figure 1.13

The title bar displays the program name. It also displays the database name and object type when the Database window is maximized. The other three elements display commands and tools that relate to the current database object shown in the Database window.

2 **Open the File menu.**

Notice that the commands on this menu deal with opening, closing, and working with databases. You can use Access menus the same way you use menus in all other Windows applications. If you choose a menu command followed by an ellipsis (…), Access leads you to a dialog box with additional options. Notice that shortcut keys are displayed to the right of some menu commands, such as Ctrl+O for Open. Also notice the buttons listed on the left side of the menu, which correspond to the buttons on the toolbars.

3 **Click an unused part of the screen outside the File menu.**

This step closes the menu. You can also close the menu by pressing Esc or clicking the File menu option again.

To Learn About the Access Window

4 **Move the mouse pointer over the button at the far left end of the toolbar.**
Access displays a ***ScreenTip***, telling you the name of the button—in this case, New (see Figure 1.14).

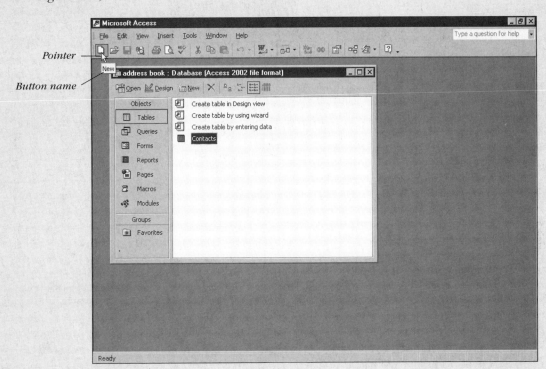

Figure 1.14

Now take a look at how these elements change when a table is open.

5 **Select the Contacts table in the Database window, if necessary. Click the <u>O</u>pen button.**
Access opens the table in Datasheet view. You could also double-click the table name to open it. The menu bar, toolbar, and status bar change to reflect the tasks you can perform with tables (see Figure 1.15).

(Continues)

To Learn About the Access Window (Continued)

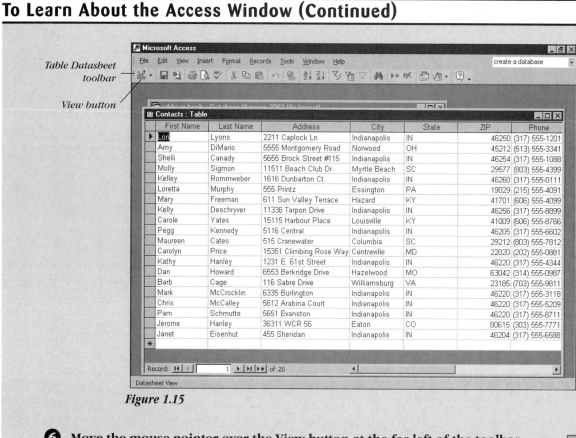

Table Datasheet toolbar

View button

Figure 1.15

6 **Move the mouse pointer over the View button at the far left of the toolbar.**
The View button can be used to display a list of available views for the table and to switch to another view of the table.

7 **Move the pointer over other buttons in the toolbar.**
As you move the pointer over other buttons, read the name that Access provides to get an idea of what each button does. Keep the Contacts table and the *address book* database open for now. At the end of this project, you learn how to close these files and exit Access. In the next lesson, you learn how to use the Access Help system.

Lesson 6: Getting Help

At some point, you may run into problems as you work with software such as Access. If you need a quick solution to a problem with Access, you can use the program's Help feature. The Help system makes it easy to search for information on particular topics. In Access Version 2002, you can use the ***Office Assistant***, an animated guide that helps you search for help, or the ***What's This?*** feature, which identifies the features of a single screen element. You can also use the Ask a Question box, located on the title bar, to ask a question without having the Office Assistant onscreen.

The Office Assistant is a flexible help feature included with all Microsoft Office applications. It enables you to ask questions, search for terms, or look at context-sensitive tips.

To Get Help Using the Office Assistant

1 **With the *address book* database and Contacts table still open from the preceding lesson, click Help on the menu bar to open the Help drop-down menu.**

Note that the first item in the Help menu uses the same icon as one of the buttons at the far right of the toolbar. Both of these options launch the Office Assistant. (You can also launch the Office Assistant by pressing F1 at any time.) If the Office Assistant already appears on your screen, all you have to do is click it once to open the Office Assistant window.

2 **Click the Microsoft Access Help command.**

Access opens the Office Assistant (see Figure 1.16).

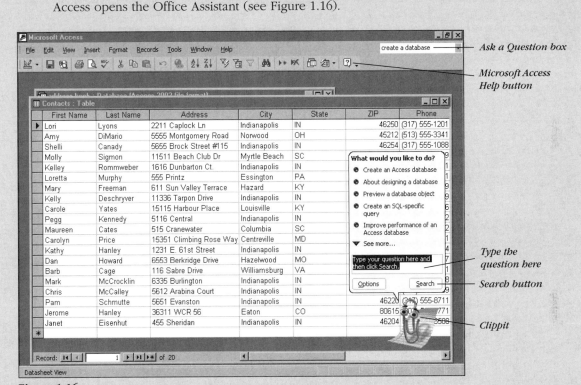

Figure 1.16

If you have problems...

If you get the Microsoft Access Help window instead of the Office Assistant, close the window and choose *Help, Show the Office Assistant* from the menu. Click the Office Assistant to activate his bubble.

The animated Office Assistant shown in the figure is called Clippit. You may see one of the other images available for the Office Assistant on your screen.

---

3 **Type** How do I get data from an Excel spreadsheet? **in the text box.**

4 **Click the Search button.**

(Continues)

To Get Help Using the Office Assistant (Continued)

The program searches through your sentence and looks for keywords. Topics related to your question are listed (see Figure 1.17). If there are too many topics to fit in the window, you may need to click the *See more* button.

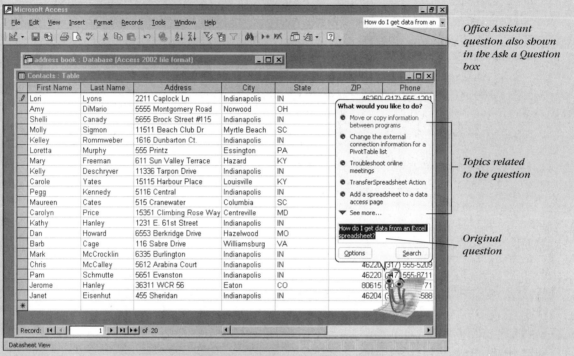

Figure 1.17

5 Select the topic *Move or copy information between programs.*
Access displays the Help window pertaining to this subject (see Figure 1.18).

To Get Help Using the Office Assistant

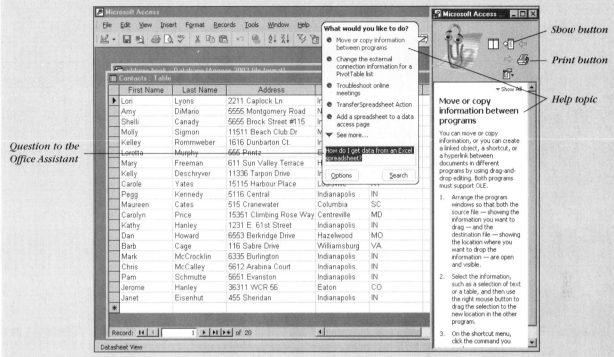

Figure 1.18

You can scroll down the Help window and read about moving and copying data between programs. You can click any of the words or phrases in blue (hypertext) to get more information.

At the top of the Help window are a couple of useful buttons. The first is the Print button, which enables you to print the contents of the Help window. The second is the Show button, which expands the Help window to enable you to search for help in a more organized way.

6 **Click the Show button at the top of the Help window, if necessary.**
Three tabs are available—Contents, Answer Wizard, and Index. You may have to drag the Office Assistant out of the way.

7 **Click the Index tab, if necessary. Type** spreadsheet **in the Type keywords text box, and click the Search button.**
Two boxes show a list of keywords and a list of topics (see Figure 1.19). Information about the highlighted topic is shown in the Help window.

(Continues)

To Get Help Using the Office Assistant (Continued)

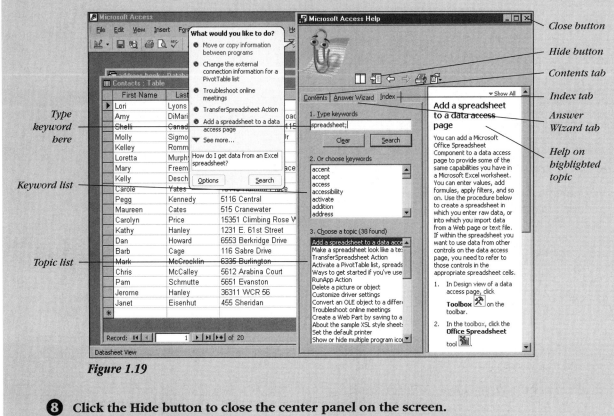

Figure 1.19

8 **Click the Hide button to close the center panel on the screen.**
The middle panel is closed.

9 **Click the Close button in the upper-right corner of the Help window.**
The Help window closes and the Access window expands to fill the screen. The Office Assistant remains on the screen.

10 **If the Office Assistant remains on the screen, right-click the Office Assistant, and select Hide from the shortcut menu.**
This closes the Office Assistant.

To extend your knowledge...

Using the Ask a Question Box

Office XP includes a new Ask a Question box to help users find help on desired topics. It appears in the top-right corner of each application's menu bar. To use it, simply click in the box, type a question, and press ↵Enter. Then click the topic you want to read.

You can get helpful descriptions of different buttons, menu items, or screen objects by using the *What's This?* option. In the following section, you learn how to use this feature.

To Use the What's This? Feature

1 **Click Help on the menu bar.**

2 **Click the *What's This?* option.**
The pointer changes to include a large question mark.

3 **Click the Find button on the toolbar.**
A window opens which describes this feature in greater detail (see Figure 1.20).

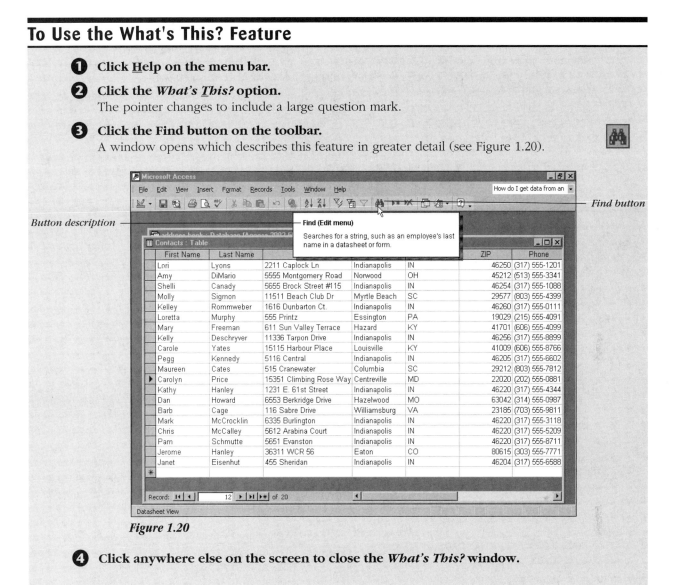

Figure 1.20

4 **Click anywhere else on the screen to close the *What's This?* window.**

Several other options that exist for getting help are available from the Help menu. When you clicked the Show button, you used the Index to search through the Help topics alphabetically by keyword. You can also search by topic using the list of topics in the Contents section, or use the Answer Wizard in much the same way as you use the Office Assistant.

Most of your questions about the basic operation of Access can be answered using one of these methods. If you do not find what you need in the Help topics supplied with the program, you can select Office on the Web to connect to Microsoft's support Web page on the Internet.

If you have problems...

To save space, some people delete Help files or don't install them in the first place. If you get a message stating that the Help file cannot be found, use your original CD-ROM and add the Help files. If you do not have the original CD-ROM, you may use the online help by choosing Help, Office on the Web.

Lesson 7: Exiting Access and Windows

When you have finished working with Access, you should close all open database objects and exit the program. If you turn off your computer without closing Access or if you lose power, you will probably be able to retrieve most of your data; however, some of the recent structural changes you have made may be lost. You should get in the habit of saving formatting changes and closing the database before you close Access. You should also exit Windows before you turn off your computer.

In this project, you close the *address book* database, exit Access, and shut down your computer.

To Exit Access and Windows

1 **Click the Close button on the Contacts Table window.**
This closes the Contacts table.

2 **Click the Close button on the *address book* Database window.**
This closes the Database window and leaves the main Access window open.

When you close a database object after having made structural changes, the program will automatically ask you if you want to save your work.

3 **Click the Close button to close Access.**
Access is closed and you are returned to the Windows desktop. Here you can launch another program or shut down Windows. If you want to work on the exercises at the end of the chapter at this time, do not exit Windows until you are done using the computer.

4 **To exit Windows and shut down the computer, click the Start button.**

5 **Click Shut Down on the menu, click the <u>S</u>hut down option button, and then click OK.**
Windows checks your programs and files to ensure that they are closed and saved properly, and then shuts down.

6 **When the message *It is now safe to turn off your computer* appears onscreen, turn off the power to the computer and monitor.**
Some computers with power management shut themselves down without this message appearing. If this is the case, you may have to turn off your monitor, but will not have to turn off the power to the computer.

If you are finished with your session at the computer, continue with the "Checking Concepts and Terms" section of this project.

Summary

In this project, you were introduced to some of the fundamental Access procedures and components. You created a new database using the Database Wizard. You learned how to copy a file and then how to rename the file. You opened and closed a database, and a table in a database. You identified some of the Access window elements and found out how to use various Help features to identify everything from buttons to concepts and procedures. Finally, you exited Access and closed Windows.

You can extend your grasp of Access by looking a little more closely at the Access Database window. Move the pointer over buttons and look at the ScreenTips that pop up. See if you can guess what each of the buttons might do. Use *What's This?* on those that you can't figure out. Don't worry if some of the terms are unfamiliar to you—you'll be adding many new terms to your Access repertoire throughout this book!

Checking Concepts and Terms

Multiple Choice

Circle the letter of the correct answer for each of the following questions.

1. Which of the following is not a type of object that you can display by clicking an object button in the database window? [L3]

  a. form

  b. table

  c. report

  d. spreadsheet

2. What does a table consist of? [L4]

  a. rows called records and columns called fields

  b. free-form information about each database item

  c. rows called fields and columns called records

  d. queries, reports, forms, and other database objects

3. When you pause the mouse pointer over a button, what does Access display? [L5]

  a. ScreenTip

  b. ButtonLabel

  c. TaskPointer

  d. ButtonTip

4. What does it mean when the mouse pointer has a question mark attached to it? [L6]

  a. Access has detected an error and is helping you find it.

  b. You have activated the What's This? feature.

  c. The database you've loaded is missing a major component.

  d. You have activated a query or a module.

5. What happens when you close a database object after having made structural changes? [L7]

  a. The program always asks you to save your changes.

  b. You lose your changes if you forgot to save them.

  c. The program automatically asks you if you want to save your work if you have made unsaved structural changes.

  d. Nothing.

Screen ID

Label each element of the Access screen shown in Figure 1.21.

A. Table name
B. Open button
C. Tables object button
D. New button
E. Microsoft Access Help
F. Filename
G. Action buttons
H. Close button
I. Title bar
J. Database window

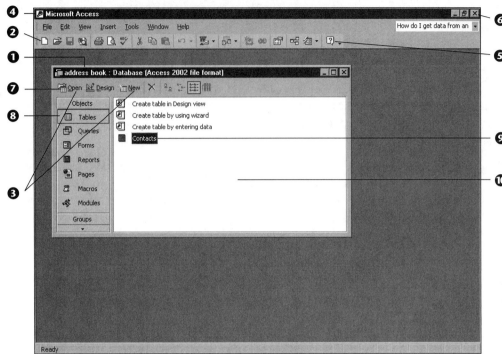

Figure 1.21

1. _____   6. _____

2. _____   7. _____

3. _____   8. _____

4. _____   9. _____

5. _____   10. _____

Discussion

1. Some databases have only one table; others have multiple tables that consist of data on the same general topic. For example, a small college might keep all of its student information in one database with several tables. What different but related tables might you find in that database? Can you think of other situations that might require the use of more than one table?

2. Most people who learn Access are already familiar with one or more Office programs, such as

Word, Excel, or PowerPoint. From what you've seen so far, what is similar between Access and the other programs? What is different? What similarities between the programs might help someone learn Access more quickly?

3. Think about your life, including school, work, and personal interests. How might a database be helpful in your activities? What types of databases could you create to assist you in your busy life?

Skill Drill

Skill Drill exercises reinforce project skills. Each skill reinforced is the same, or nearly the same, as a skill presented in the project. Each exercise includes a brief narrative introduction, followed by detailed instructions in a step-by-step format.

1. Opening a Database

You have been interested in a number of foreign places and want to visit them. One place that you have found particularly interesting is Alaska. Over the years, you have gathered pictures and data on geographic sites and area attractions in the state. You have finally decided to organize this data by using a database you were given that contains some geographic information. In this exercise, you open the database without copying it to another disk drive.

1. Launch Access.
2. From the Open dialog box, find the *ea1-0102* file.
3. Select *ea1-0102* and click the Open button. Notice that a dialog box appears, telling you that you can't make changes to this database because it is read-only.
4. Click OK to open the database in read-only mode.
5. Click the Close button in the Database window title bar to close the database. This will leave Access open for the next exercise.

2. Finding the Help Directions for Creating a Database

The Help features in Access can answer specific questions or can guide you in database processes and procedures.

1. Click the Microsoft Access Help button at the right end of the toolbar. (If you are not sure which one it is, point to any of the toolbar buttons and wait a moment. A ScreenTip appears that tells you the name of the button.)
2. Type the question `How do I copy a database?` and click Search. (*Hint*: You don't really need to add that question mark. The program assumes anything you type into the search box is a question!)
3. Find one of the options that enable you to make a duplicate copy of your database file and click that option.
4. Look over the instructions.
5. Close the Office Assistant.

3. Opening and Closing a Database Using the Menu

So far, you have opened your database files by using the task pane as well as by clicking the Open button on the toolbar. Some people prefer to use menus. Try using the menus occasionally throughout this book. You may find that you actually prefer this method.

1. Choose File, Open from the menu bar at the top of the screen. The Open dialog box is displayed.
2. Click the list arrow next to the Look in drop-down list and select the drive and folder that contain the *ea1-0102* database.
3. Make sure you have an empty diskette in drive A:. Right-click the *ea1-0102* file. Select Send To, and send the file to drive A:.
4. Move to drive A: and select *ea1-0102*.
5. Right-click the filename and select Properties from the shortcut menu. Deselect Read-only and select Archive from the Attributes area. Click OK.

6. Right-click the file and select Rename from the shortcut menu.

7. Change the name of the file to `Alaska information` and then click the Open button to open the database.

8. Choose File, Close from the menu.

4. Getting Help Using the Function Key

In Lesson 6, you learned how to use the Microsoft Access Help feature, how to use the What's This? option from the Help menu, and how to use the Ask a Question box. There is another way to get help and with this method you don't need to take your hand away from the keyboard to grab the mouse.

1. Open the *Alaska information* file you created in the previous exercise by whichever method you prefer.

2. Press the F1 key on the top row of your keyboard. Notice that the Office Assistant appears, ready for a search.

3. Ask the Office Assistant `How do I get online help?` and click the Search button in the Office Assistant window.

4. Change `online` to `on line`. Do the Help topics change, or is the Office Assistant "smart" enough to figure out what you mean either way?

5. Press the Esc key. Notice that the search box disappears but the Office Assistant remains on the screen.

6. Leave the *Alaska information* database open for the next exercise.

5. Determining What Elements Work with the What's This? Feature

In Lesson 6, you used the What's This? feature to get more details about a button. You found that you got more information from the What's This? feature than from a simple ScreenTip, which usually consists of only a word or two. Did you wonder what other screen elements work with the What's This? feature? The buttons mentioned in this exercise can be found in Figure 1.22. To find out what elements work with the What's This? feature:

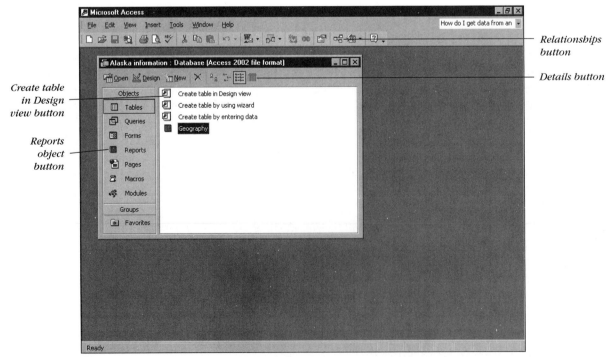

Figure 1.22

1. Choose <u>H</u>elp, <u>W</u>hat's This?. The question mark pointer is displayed.

2. Move the pointer over the buttons in the toolbar until you find the Relationships button. Notice that the ScreenTips work even when the What's This? pointer is on the screen.

3. Click the Relationships button and read the description. Did it help? (*Note*: You will use this feature in Project 7.) Click again to close the description.

4. Hold down ⬆Shift and press F1. Notice that this is a keyboard shortcut for activating the What's This? feature. Click the Reports object button on the left side of the Database window. Did you get a description of what this button does? Click anywhere to turn off the What's This? feature.

5. Hold down ⬆Shift and press F1 again. Click *Create table in Design view* above the Geography table name. Notice that the What's This? feature does not work with some screen elements.

6. Use the same procedure to click the Details button on the right edge of the toolbar in the Database window.

7. Close the Database window, but leave Access open if you are going to continue to the Challenge section. If not, click the Close button to close Access.

Challenge

Challenge exercises expand on or are related to skills practiced in the project. Each exercise provides a brief narrative introduction followed by instructions in a numbered step format that are not as detailed as those in the Skill Drill section.

1. Using the Ask a Question Box

If you have used earlier versions of Access, the following exercise will give you an idea of the improvements to this new version. If you have not used Access before, you will get an idea of some of the features of the database.

1. Click in the Ask a Question box in the upper-right corner of the Access window.

2. Type How do I create a database? in the Ask a Question box, and press ↵Enter.

3. Read the list of topics displayed. Select *See more…* at the bottom of the list of topics. Read the topics given.

4. Select *See previous* to return to the first few topics. Select *About designing a database* from the list. Read the information to learn how to effectively design a database.

5. Scroll to the bottom of the Help window to view steps for designing a database. Select *Determine the purpose of your database*. Read the topic.

6. When you are through, click the Close button to close the Help window.

2. Deciding What Fields to Use in a Home Inventory Table

As you review your personal insurance, you realize that you don't have a good idea of what you have bought over the years, or what you should insure and for how much.

Think about what categories would be included in a home inventory database and sketch out a table identifying each of the fields you would use. How detailed do you think you would need to be if you were trying to convince an insurance company that you really owned the items?

To get started, consider whether you would be better off with a field that contained the age of the items (e.g., 3 for a three-year-old end table), or with a field containing the year the item was purchased. Why would one be superior to the other?

3. Taking Control of the Office Assistant

Do you like Clippit? He's kind of cute, at least the first few times you see him. Some people, however, get tired of "cute" rather quickly, and would rather use the menu or Microsoft Access Help button to get help when needed than have a paper clip lurking on the edges of the screen. You have complete control over Clippit! (Remember: you can also use the Ask a Question box.)

1. Activate the Office Assistant, if necessary. Clippit should appear on the screen, although you might have another figure on your screen. Click Clippit if his bubble is not showing.
2. Click the Office Assistant Options button, and go to the Gallery tab in the Office Assistant dialog box. Scroll through the assistants using the Back and Next buttons to see if there is one you like better. If you find one, click OK to activate it. If there are no more assistants available, it means they were not installed.
3. Go back to the Office Assistant dialog box, and select the Options tab. Browse through your options. Notice the Use the Office Assistant check box at the top of the dialog box. If you turn off the check mark and click OK, Clippit will fade away, not to be seen again until you turn it back on using Help, Show the Office Assistant. Close the Office Assistant dialog box, if necessary.
4. Choose Help, Hide the Office Assistant. This is another way to close the Office Assistant.

4. Using the Index to Find Help

To get to the Index feature, you will need to open the Help window. If the Office Assistant is active, you will need to type a question, then choose an option to get to this window, even though the question may have nothing to do with what you want to look up. One way to get to the Index (and Contents) tab more quickly is to turn off the Office Assistant.

1. Click the Microsoft Access Help button on the toolbar, if necessary.
2. Click the Options button in the Office Assistant. Click the Use the Office Assistant check box to deselect it, then click OK.
3. Click the Microsoft Access Help button on the toolbar, and then click the Show button, if necessary.
4. Click the Index tab. Type `table` in the Type keywords text box.
5. Click the Search button. In the Choose a topic area, click *About tables*. Read the Help information.
6. Click *How data is organized in tables* to display the topic and read it.
7. When you are finished, click the Hide button. Leave the Help window open for the next exercise.

5. Using the Help Table of Contents to Read Help Like a Book

The Contents tab works like a table of contents in a book. You can glance down the list of general topics, choose one, and then open up help text or sub-chapters.

1. Click the Show button in the Help window, if necessary, then click the Contents tab.
2. Click the plus next to Microsoft Access Help, if necessary, and then click the plus next to *Tables* to see what topics are available.
3. Click the plus next to the *Primary Keys and Indexes* subtopic. Click the *About primary keys* topic. This information appears in the window on the right.
4. Click *Null* (in blue text). A definition displays. Click in the definition to close it.
5. Close Help, but leave Access open if you are going to continue to the Discovery Zone section. If not, click the Close button to close Access.

Discovery Zone exercises require advanced knowledge of topics presented in *essentials* lessons, application of skills from multiple lessons, or self-directed learning of new skills.

1. Sending a Database to the Desktop as a Shortcut

In many cases, the same database will be used repeatedly. For example, an inventory database for a small business might be opened many times every day. The same machine, however, might also be used for typing letters, doing budgets and payroll, and other office tasks. It is time-consuming to open Access and then search one or more hard disks or network drives for a database. It would be great if you could place an icon, or shortcut, on your desktop with the name of the database underneath it. That way you could simply double-click it to launch Access and load the database at the same time.

Goal: Figure out how to create a shortcut on your computer desktop.

Use the program's Help features to figure out how to place a shortcut to the *Alaska information* database on your desktop. Because this is your first Discovery Zone exercise, you'll get three hints:

Hint #1: The procedure involves a shortcut menu.

Hint #2: You have seen the procedure on the way to learning something else. If all else fails, review what you have done in this project that involves shortcut menus.

Hint #3: If you are working in a lab with security software, this may not work. It will depend on the level of security set by the lab administrator.

2. Examining Database Properties

As you will see as you go through this book, nearly every element on the Access screen has what are known as **properties**. Properties are the characteristics of a screen element. For example, a number has such properties as its number of decimal places, format, and font size. Databases also have properties. These include the date they were created, whether they are read-only, their size, and several others.

Goal: Find the properties of a database and change one of them.

Use the program's Help features to figure out how to display the properties of a database. Use the *Alaska information* database you worked on in this project to test your solution. When you get the Alaska information Properties dialog box open, change it to a read-only file.

3. Finding Online Help from Microsoft

Throughout this project, you have used several methods to get help. You have used the Office Assistant, the What's This? button, the Index tab, the Contents tab, and the Ask a Question box. These are all Help features included with the program. If you have access to the World Wide Web, you can get much more detailed help.

Goal: Explore Microsoft's online help.

Check with your instructor, and if possible, use the <u>H</u>elp menu to go to the online help available from Microsoft. Choose to look at Access help, and see what help is available on designing tables. Explore the various categories of help available there.

Creating a Database

PROJECT

Objectives

In this project, you learn how to

- ✔ Create a New Database
- ✔ Create a New Table Using the Table Design Wizard
- ✔ Add Fields
- ✔ Edit Fields
- ✔ Move Fields
- ✔ Delete Fields
- ✔ Create a New Primary Key

Key terms introduced in this project include

- ❏ data type
- ❏ Datasheet view
- ❏ Design view
- ❏ index
- ❏ normalize
- ❏ Object Linking and Embedding (OLE)
- ❏ primary key
- ❏ relational database
- ❏ relationship
- ❏ row selector

2

Why Would I Do This?

With Access, you can set up databases to perform a wide variety of tasks. For example, you may want a database (such as the one you create in this project) to keep track of staff training for your company. You can set up various databases to store different sets of related information, and you can create as many databases as you need.

Think of the database as the shell that holds together all related objects. Within the shell, you can create other objects. The fundamental type of object in an Access database is a table. You use tables to store data and organize the information into a usable structure. You can also create other objects, such as forms and queries. You learn about these other database objects later in other projects.

When you design a table, you need to determine what fields will be included. To answer this question, you should consider what kinds of information should be included in a printed report or what information you want to see if you look at a single record on the screen. Consider how you may want to sort or filter the records. For example, if you want to print a list of employee names that is sorted by employee seniority, you need to have a field that contains the date they were hired.

An Access database consists of parts that interact with each other, and it is hard to design one part until you know what the other parts can do. You will have a much better idea of what fields to include in a table once you have learned how to create queries, forms, and reports.

There are six fairly universal rules for designing tables that were originally proposed by Dr. Edgar F. Codd of IBM in the 1960s and which still hold true today. When you apply these rules to your tables, you are *normalizing* them. The rules are simplified and paraphrased as follows:

- **Rule 1**: Fields should be atomic; that is, each piece of data should be broken down as much as possible. For example, rather than creating a field called "Name," you would create two fields: one for the first name and the other for the last name.
- **Rules 2 and 3**: Each record should contain a unique identifier so that you have a way of safely identifying the record. A Social Security Number is ideal, because no two people have the same one. The unique identifier is called a *primary key*. You may select one of the fields in the table as the primary key if that field would never contain duplicate values for different records. If none of the fields is suitable, the program can add a counter field that will automatically assign a unique number to each record as it is entered.
- **Rule 4**: The primary key should be short, stable, and simple. Addresses and even last names may change several times during a person's life. This is why governments and companies assign permanent, unique identification numbers.
- **Rule 5**: Every other field in the record should supply additional information about the person or thing that is uniquely identified by the primary key. For example, a table that contains data about employees may include a field that indicates the employee's supervisor. It would be inappropriate to include a field that holds the supervisor's birth date.
- **Rule 6**: Information in the table should not appear in more than one place. For example, if you tried to create a table of the different committees in an organization and had fields with names such as Chairperson, Member1, Member2, and Member3; the same person could be the chairperson of one committee and Member1 in another. If that person changed his or her name, you would have to change it in more than one place. Avoid numbered field names such as those shown in this example.

To conform to these rules, you may need to create more than one table in a database and connect them together. Linking more than one table together is a feature of a *relational database* and is demonstrated throughout this project.

Fortunately, you do not need to understand all of this to get started, and the application of these rules will become evident as you use the example tables.

In this project, you learn how to create a database from scratch and a table using a wizard. You also learn how to edit the structure of the table.

Visual Summary

When you have completed this project, you will have created a table that looks like Figure 2.1.

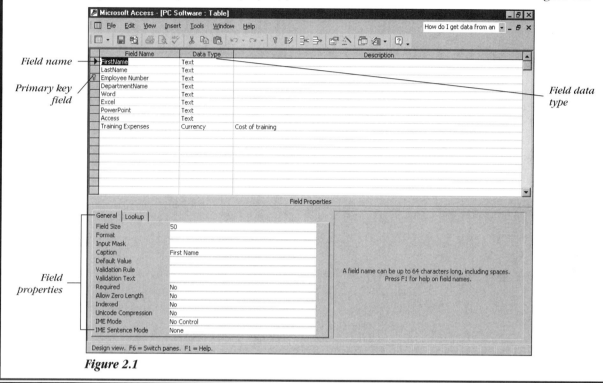

Figure 2.1

Lesson 1: Creating a New Database

Remember that the table is the object in which you actually store and define the structure for your data, and the database is the shell that houses all of the related tables and other objects. In this lesson, you create a new database to keep track of the personal computer software training received by your staff.

To Create a New Database

1 **Launch Access and click the Blank Database option in the task pane.**
Access displays the File New Database dialog box. Access suggests a default name (such as db1 or db2) for the new database; however, you can assign a more descriptive name here. You can also tell Access where you want to store the database.

2 **In the File name text box, type** `training`.
This is the name you want to use for the new database. After you name the database the first time, you won't have to do it again. As you add or edit records, Access updates the database automatically. As you add new objects or modify existing ones, however, you have to save each of them. When you add a table, for example, you must save it. Access then updates the database to incorporate this new database object.

3 **Click the list arrow next to the Save in text box, and select your drive or folder.**

(Continues)

To Create a New Database (Continued)

Access suggests a default drive and folder for saving the new database. Ask your instructor if you are unsure where to save your files (see Figure 2.2).

Select a drive and folder

Type a filename

Create button

Figure 2.2

❹ **Click the Create button.**

Access opens the database window for your new database (see Figure 2.3). The name of the database is displayed in the title bar of the Database window. Notice that there are no tables shown because you have not created any database objects. Three methods of creating new tables are displayed. Keep the *training* database open to use in the next lesson. In that lesson, you learn how to add a new table to the database.

Database name

Figure 2.3

To extend your knowledge...

Creating Smaller Databases

It's tempting to create one big database that includes multiple tables to meet many different needs, but it's a better idea to create smaller databases, each of which is dedicated to a particular function. Doing so makes managing and using each database much easier. You can relate these smaller databases to one another later, if necessary.

Other Ways to Create a New Database

There is usually more than one way to perform each function in Access. For example, to create a new database, you can press Ctrl+N, select New from the File menu, or click the New button on the toolbar.

Lesson 2: Creating a New Table Using the Table Design Wizard

After you create your database, you can add tables to it to store your information. A database is built on one or more tables, each of which holds a distinct set of information. The table defines the structure of the data—what pieces of data you enter and in what order. You should spend some time planning the structure of your database. How many fields do you need? What are their data types? Who will be using the database, and how will they be using the information? If necessary, you can add fields later if you need them, but it is very important to map out the fundamental structure of the table before you get started.

Building a database without a plan is like building a house without a blueprint. The more work you invest in the initial design, the less time you spend in patchwork repairs later. Design your table structures first so that you can immediately put the database to work with confidence.

In this lesson, you create a table containing fields for first names, last names, and department names.

To Create a New Table Using the Table Design Wizard

❶ With the Tables object button selected in the *training* database window, click the New button.

Access displays the New Table dialog box (see Figure 2.4). You can choose between two views of a blank database, or you can launch one of three wizards to create a new table. The wizards walk you through the process of setting up a table, bringing in a table from another source, or linking the database to another data source without actually moving the information into the database.

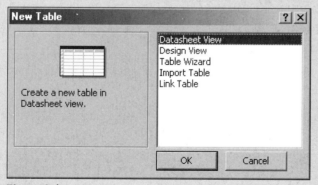

Figure 2.4

❷ Select Table Wizard, and click OK.

The first dialog box for the Table Wizard appears. The sample tables are divided into two categories: Business and Personal. Within these categories are a variety of tables with their own lists of fields. As the user, you control which tables and fields are included in the new database.

❸ Be sure the Business option is selected on the left side of the dialog box. Click *Employees* in the Sample Tables list box (see Figure 2.5).

(Continues)

To Create a New Table Using the Table Design Wizard (Continued)

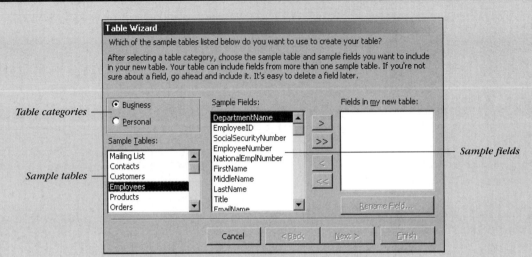

Figure 2.5

The Business option in the Table Wizard provides many tables based on common needs in a business environment, including contact management, event management, and resource management.

4 **In the Sample Fields box, select *FirstName* and then click the Select button (see Figure 2.6).**

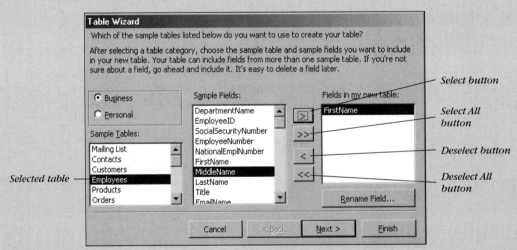

Figure 2.6

Once a table category is selected, sample tables are listed. As each table is selected, a different set of fields is displayed. The tables and fields are organized and related so that repetition of work is minimized. However, the user can decide which fields to use or not to use.

5 **Select *LastName*, and click the Select button.**
FirstName and LastName have been selected for the new table.

To Create a New Table Using the Table Design Wizard

6 At the top of the S**a**mple Fields list, choose *DepartmentName* and then click the Select button.

7 Click **N**ext.

8 Type PC Software in the *Wh**a**t do you want to name your table?* text box. Make sure *Yes, set primary key for me* is selected, and click **N**ext.

In addition to saving new tables, you should assign or create a primary key field for each table in your database. Each record's primary key field contains a value that uniquely identifies it; no two records can have the same value in their primary key field.

If you have a unique field in your table, such as an ID number, you can use that as the primary key field; or, you can have Access create a simple counter field. When using the Table Wizard, the primary key field can be added automatically, which creates an AutoNumber field.

If you have problems...

If other tables exist in the database, the Table Design Wizard prompts you next about the relationships between the tables.

9 Select *Enter data **d**irectly into the table*, if necessary. Click **F**inish.

The table is now displayed in *Datasheet view*, which is used for entering data into records. Keep the PC Software table and the *training* database open for the next lesson.

To extend your knowledge...

Using Design View to Create a Table

You can also create a table in Design view. To add fields to a table, you must first enter the field names, data types, and descriptions. The insertion point blinks in the first row of the Field Name column. Here, you type the first field name. Press `Tab↹` to move to the Data Type column. Press `Tab↹` again to move to the Description column. A description is optional when creating a field.

Rules for Field Names and Using Table Design View

You can create a field name using up to 64 characters. Try to use names that are short but meaningful (long names make the system work harder). You can use any combination of letters, numbers, spaces, and characters with a few exceptions: period (.), exclamation point (!), accent grave (`), single quotation marks ('), and brackets ([ ]) cannot appear anywhere in the name. Spaces are allowed, but not as the first character of the field name.

You can also use the `Tab↹` key in place of the `↵Enter` key when adding fields, accepting the displayed data type, and entering descriptions in the table Design view.

Lesson 3: Adding Fields

What happens if you decide you want to track more information than you included in your original PC Software table? You can add new fields to store this additional data. Keep in mind, however, that if you have already added records to the table, any new fields in those existing records will be empty until you type information into them. Other database objects such as queries, forms, or reports that are based on the table will not be automatically updated to include the new fields. Because you have not yet created any other database objects that use this table, this is a good time to make changes.

When you create a new table, you can add any fields you want. Remember that the table consists of records (one set of information such as the name, address, and phone number for one person) and fields. Fields are the individual pieces of information that together make up a record; for example, an address is a field. To add a field, you type a field name and then select a ***data type***, which defines the kind of information you can enter into that field. Table 2.1 explains the various data types you can use. You can also type a description for the field and set field properties. You learn how to set field properties in Project 7, "Customizing Fields and Tables." Field properties and data types are automatically set when the Table Design Wizard is used to create a table.

TABLE 2.1 Data Types and What They Mean

Data Type	Explanation
Text	The default data type. You can enter up to 255 numbers or letters.
Memo	This type of field is useful when you want to include sentences or paragraphs in the field—for example, a long product description. This type of field is not limited by size.
Number	You can enter only numbers.
Date/Time	You can enter only dates or times.
Currency	You can enter numbers. Access formats the entry as currency. If you type 12.5, for example, Access displays it as $12.50.
AutoNumber	Access enters a value that is incremented automatically with each new record added to a table.
Yes/No	A Yes/No field type limits your data to one of two conditions. You can enter only Yes or No, True or False, or On or Off. For example, you may have a Sent Christmas Card field in your address database that would work best as a Yes/No field.
OLE Object	You can insert ***Object Linking and Embedding*** (OLE) objects, which are things such as pictures or charts created in another application package.
Hyperlink	A field that enables you to enter active Web addresses.
Lookup Wizard	A field that looks up data from another source.

In this lesson, you add seven new fields to your PC Software table—one for training expense, one for employee number, one for employee's supervisor, and one each for the four Microsoft Office software applications. Try adding these fields now.

To Add Fields

① **With the PC Software table of the *training* database still displayed in Datasheet view, click the View button.**
Now the table is shown in ***Design view***, the view used to make modifications to the table design. Notice that the View button looks different in Design view than it did in Datasheet

To Add Fields

view. The icon on the View button indicates the view that will be displayed when you click it.

If you have problems...

If the Table Design toolbar is not showing, choose <u>V</u>iew, <u>T</u>oolbars, Table Design from the menu.

② Position the insertion point in the next blank row of the PC Software table.
This is the row in which you want to enter the first new field name. The ***row selector arrow*** should be displayed next to this row (see Figure 2.7).

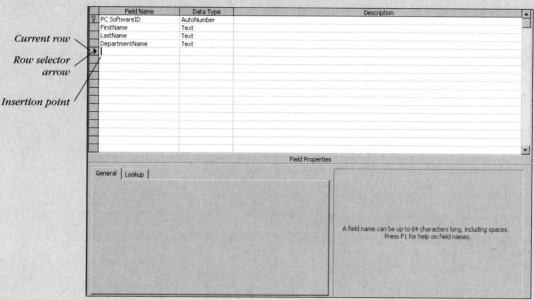

Figure 2.7

③ Type Cost and press ↵Enter.
Access enters the field name for this field. In the lower half of the window, Access displays the field properties you can set. Access moves the insertion point to the Data Type column so that you can choose the type of data you want the field to contain. The most common data type is Text, which is the default. You can click the down arrow (which is displayed when you move to the Data Type column) to display a drop-down list of data types. For now, leave the data type as the default.

④ Press ↵Enter.
The Text data type is accepted, and Access moves the insertion point to the Description column. If you include a description for a field, it is displayed in the status bar whenever you are in that field in Datasheet view or Form view. The information in the status bar provides the user with a more complete description of the purpose of the field.

(Continues)

To Add Fields (Continued)

⑤ Type Cost of training **and press** ↵Enter.
This is the description for the new field. When you press ↵Enter, Access moves the insertion point to the next row.

⑥ Type Employee Number **and press** Tab⇄ **three times.**
By pressing Tab⇄, you enter the name for this field, accept Text as the data type, and skip the Description column. Again, the insertion point is in position to add a new field to the table.

⑦ Type Supervisor **and press** ↵Enter **three times. Click the Maximize button to maximize the Design view window.**
Once again, you have added another new field to the table, accepting Text as the data type, skipping the description, and moving to the next row.

⑧ Type Word **and press** ↵Enter **three times. Use the same procedure to enter fields for** Excel, PowerPoint, **and** Access.
You have now added seven additional fields to the table. Your table should look similar to the one in Figure 2.8, although you may have to scroll up or down to see all of the fields.

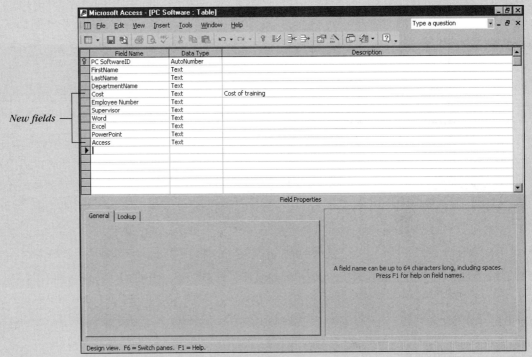

New fields —

Figure 2.8

⑨ Click the Save button to save your work, and leave both the PC Software table and the *training* database open.
The first time you save the table's design, you are prompted to assign a name. After you save and name the table the first time, it takes only a moment to save changes whenever necessary. If you make changes to the design, such as adding new fields, you must save the changes to the design.

In the next lesson, you learn another way to alter the structure of your PC Software table.

Lesson 4: Editing Fields

As you create your database, you may want to modify the structure. For example, you may want to change field names, choose a different data type, or edit or add descriptions. You make these changes in Design view.

Changing the field type may have an effect on the data in your table. For example, if you type text into a field and then change that field to a Yes/No field, you may encounter problems. Access prompts you to let you know when changes in the field type are made and when they might result in a loss of data. Be sure that you want to make the change before you confirm it.

In this lesson, you edit the name of a field, add a description, and change the field type.

To Edit Fields in a Table

1 **In the Design view of the PC Software table, position the pointer on the word *Cost* (the fifth field name) and double-click.**
This selects the word you want to change (see Figure 2.9). You may have to scroll up to get to this field.

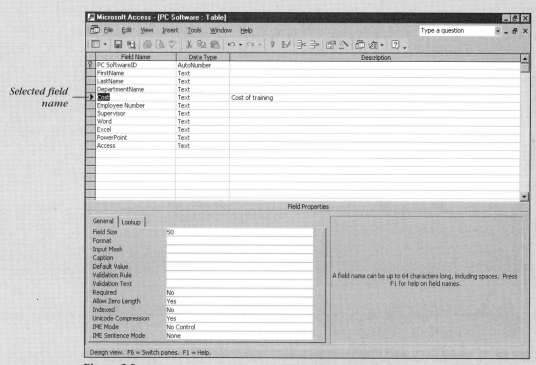

Figure 2.9

2 **Type Training Expenses.**
The existing highlighted text is replaced with the new text.

3 **Click in the Data Type column for the Training Expenses field.**
Notice that a list arrow is displayed, which indicates a list of data type options is available.

4 **Click the list arrow in the Data Type column.**
A list of choices is displayed (see Figure 2.10).

(Continues)

To Edit Fields in a Table (Continued)

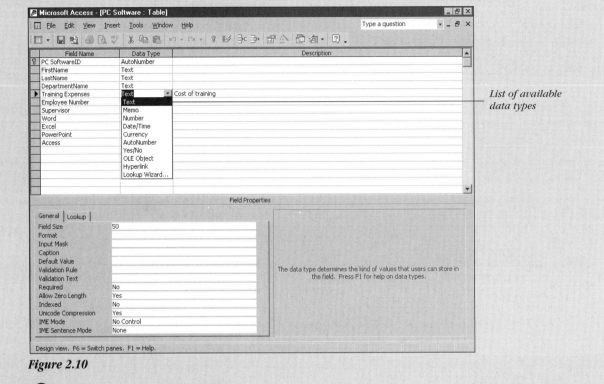

Figure 2.10

⑤ From the list, click *Currency*.
You have changed the data type to a type that is more appropriate for the information in this field. All data in this field is now displayed with a dollar sign, commas (if needed), and two decimal places.

⑥ Click in the Description column for the Supervisor field.
After moving the insertion point to this field, you can add a description.

⑦ Type Reporting Supervisor.
The description that you enter provides information about what is stored in this field.

⑧ Click the Save button on the toolbar to save your work.
Leave both the PC Software table and the *training* database open. In the next lesson, you learn how to move fields from one location in the table to another.

To extend your knowledge...

Quicker Selection of Data Type

If you know the name of the data type you want to enter in the Data Type column, you don't have to use the mouse to open the drop-down list. Instead, if the data type is highlighted, you can type the first letter of the data type you want. Access fills in the rest of the characters for you. By typing the letter **c**, for example, Access fills in *Currency*.

Changing a Field Name

Changing the field name or description does not have any effect on the data you already have entered in the table. Changing the field name may have an unintended effect, however; if any forms, queries, or reports refer to the field name, you may have to change the references manually to reflect the new name, depending on how your Access program is configured. Otherwise, these database objects will no longer work as they did before.

Lesson 5: Moving Fields

In addition to changing the name and data type of a field, you can change the order in which the fields are displayed in your database. When you enter records, you may want the fields in a different order. In the PC Software table, for example, you may find it easier to enter the employee's number immediately after you enter the employee's name. You may also want to move the ID (counter) field to the end, because you never have to enter anything in this field.

In this lesson, you first look at the table in Datasheet view—the view you use to enter records. You then change back to Design view to rearrange the fields.

To Move Fields in a Table

1 Click the View button on the toolbar to change from the current Design view to Datasheet view.
This changes your view of the database to Datasheet view (see Figure 2.11) where you can enter, sort, and edit the records in the database.

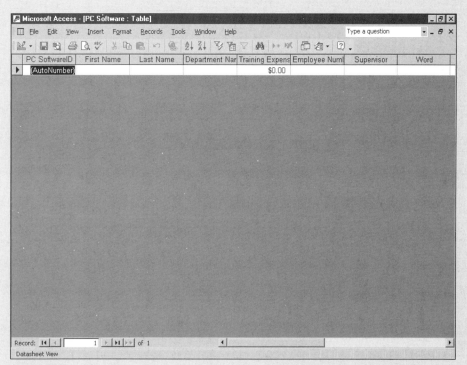

Figure 2.11

The datasheet you see is blank, except for the field names, because you haven't added any records yet. You learn how to work with records in Project 3, "Entering and Editing Data." In Datasheet view, you cannot make any changes to the structure of the table, although you will be able to change column widths.

2 Click the View button on the toolbar.
This returns you to Design view so that you can make changes.

(Continues)

To Move Fields in a Table (Continued)

3 **Click the row selector for the Employee Number field.**
This step selects the field you want to move. Notice that the entire row is highlighted (see Figure 2.12). You move this field so that it immediately follows the Last Name field.

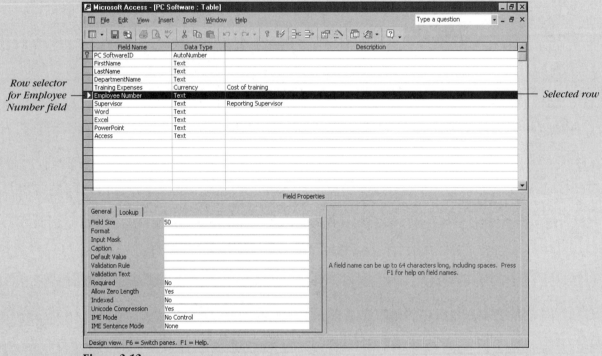

Row selector for Employee Number field

Selected row

Figure 2.12

4 **Click the row selector again, and hold down the left mouse button. Drag the row to its new position under LastName and then release the mouse button.**
As you drag, a small gray box appears under the mouse pointer, along with a horizontal line showing where the row will be placed. When you release the mouse button, Access places the row in its new spot.

If you have problems...

If the field you move is displayed in the wrong place after you drag and drop it, don't worry. Just move the field again.

If you see a double-headed arrow as you try to position the mouse, the mouse pointer isn't in the correct spot. If the double-headed arrow is displayed, Access thinks that you want to resize the row height or the Design view window.

If you accidentally resize rather than move your row, click the Undo button (or open the Edit menu and choose the Undo command). The Undo command reverses your most recent action, such as moving a row.

5 **Select the Training Expenses row, and drag it down to the first empty row of the table.**

To Move Fields in a Table

This step moves the Training Expenses field to the last position in the table. Next, try undoing the move.

6 **Click the Undo button.**
With Access, you can undo some of the changes you make to the database. In this example, however, you decide that you really do want the Training Expenses field at the end of the table.

7 **Click the Redo button.**
This moves the Training Expenses field back to the end of the table (see Figure 2.13).

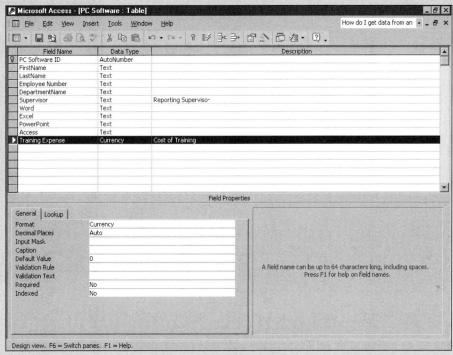

Figure 2.13

8 **Click the Save button to save your work. Keep both the *training* database and the PC Software table open in Design view.**
In the next lesson, you learn how to delete fields from your table structure.

Lesson 6: Deleting Fields

Another significant change that you can make to the structure of your PC Software table is to remove fields you no longer need. Suppose that you decide you don't really need a field for the supervisor. Instead of having it take up space in the table design, you can delete the field.

Keep in mind that deleting a field from your table also deletes all the data in that field. Because this may not be what you intended, Access displays a warning that asks you to confirm the change. Read the warning carefully and be sure that you want to delete all the data before you delete the field. If you have already created other database objects such as forms or reports that use this field, they will have to be revised individually.

To Delete Fields in a Table

1 **In the PC Software table of the *training* database, click the row selector for the Supervisor field.**
Access highlights the entire Supervisor row, showing that the Supervisor field is selected. This is the field you want to delete.

2 **Click the Delete Rows button to delete the row from your table.**
Access removes the field from the database table and deletes any data that was in that field (see Figure 2.14). If you had entered any data into this field in the Datasheet view, Access would warn you that the data would be lost.

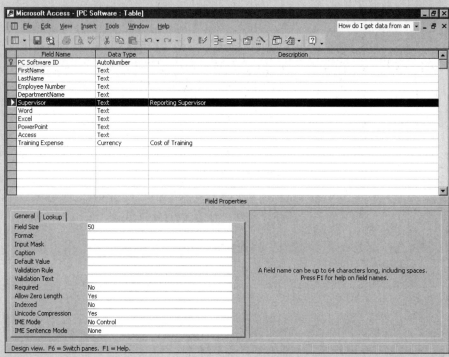

Figure 2.14

3 **Click the Save button to save your changes.**

4 **Click the View button.**
Notice how the records in the table have changed. The Supervisor field no longer exists (see Figure 2.15).

To Delete Fields in a Table

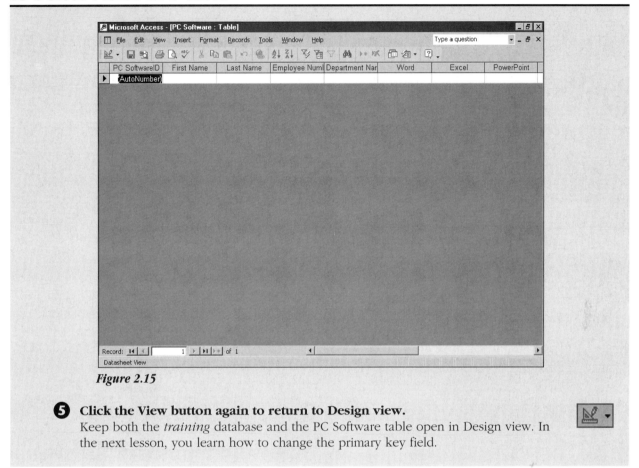

Figure 2.15

5 **Click the View button again to return to Design view.**
Keep both the *training* database and the PC Software table open in Design view. In the next lesson, you learn how to change the primary key field.

Lesson 7: Creating a New Primary Key

Assigning a primary key ensures that you won't enter the same information for the primary key field more than once in a table because it won't accept a duplicate entry. Because Access automatically builds an ***index*** for primary keys, it can easily search for information and sort tables based on the primary key field. An index is a location guide built by Access for all primary key fields that helps speed up searching and sorting for those fields. Indexes can also be created for other fields, as long as they are not OLE or Memo fields.

Examples of good primary key fields are things such as Social Security Numbers, student ID numbers, or automobile part numbers. You can use this feature to your advantage when you need to establish a ***relationship*** between one table and another. A relationship connects a field in one table to a field in a second table. Relationships enable you to draw information from more than one table at a time for forms or reports. This topic is discussed in much more detail in Project 7.

In this lesson, you change the primary key that Access assigned to a more appropriate primary key.

To Change the Primary Key Field and Save the Table Design

1 **Click the Row Selector for the Employee Number field.**
The Employee Number is a unique number assigned to each employee and is a perfect primary key field.

2 **Click the Primary Key button.**
The primary key field is indicated by the key symbol in the row selector (see Figure 2.16). Alternatively, you can open the <u>E</u>dit menu and choose the Primary <u>K</u>ey command. When you select a new primary key, the old primary key is removed.

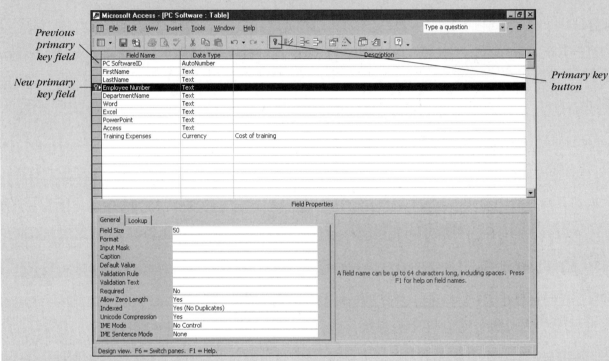

Figure 2.16

3 **Click the record selector of the PC SoftwareID field.**
Since you do not need the PC SoftwareID field, you can delete it.

4 **Click the Delete Rows button.**

5 **Click the Save button.**

6 **Click the View button to view the changes.**
The table is now shown in Datasheet view (see Figure 2.17). In the future, a record cannot be added that does not contain an Employee Number entry because it is the primary key.

To Change the Primary Key Field and Save the Table Design

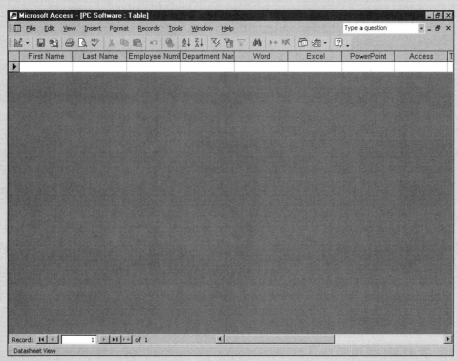

Figure 2.17

7 Close the PC Software table by clicking the Close button in the upper-right corner of the table window.

8 Close the *training* database by clicking the Close button in the upper-right corner of the database window.

If you are finished with your session at the computer, click the Close button in the upper-right corner of the Access window. Otherwise, continue with the "Checking Concepts and Terms" section.

Summary

In this project, you were introduced to some of the steps required to create a new database. You created your first table. You saved the new table and then went back into Design view to modify the structure of the table, adding, editing, moving, and deleting fields. You even changed the primary key field.

To expand your knowledge of the table creation process, use the Office Assistant to get more information about the different data types and in what situations each might be used. Type `datatype` in the index keyword box and click Search. Select *DataType Property* from the Choose a topic box.

Checking Concepts and Terms

Multiple Choice

Circle the letter of the correct answer for each of the following questions.

1. Which of the following is not a valid data type? [L3]

   a. Currency

   b. Yes/No

   c. Text

   d. Text & Numbers

2. If you let the program create a primary key for you, what type of field does it use? [L2]

   a. counter

   b. ID

   c. MDB

   d. primary

3. In Design view, how can you tell that a field is the primary key? [L7]

   a. The status bar displays text when you have the field selected.

   b. There is no way to tell in Design view.

   c. The field name is underlined.

   d. The key symbol appears on the row selector button.

4. Why is the Description entry in table Design view handy? [L3]

   a. It appears in the status bar when you enter data in the field in Datasheet view.

   b. It appears as a pop-up label when you place the mouse pointer on the field in Datasheet view.

   c. Access uses it to test data automatically that you enter into the field.

   d. It serves no purpose at all.

5. Which of the following is not a good example of a primary key field? [L7]

   a. birth date

   b. social security number

   c. employee ID

   d. part number

Screen ID

Label each element of the Access screen shown in Figure 2.18.

A. Primary key symbol

B. Primary key field

C. Primary key button

D. Properties area

E. View button

F. Row selector indicator

G. Save button

H. Delete Rows button

I. Undo button

J. Table name

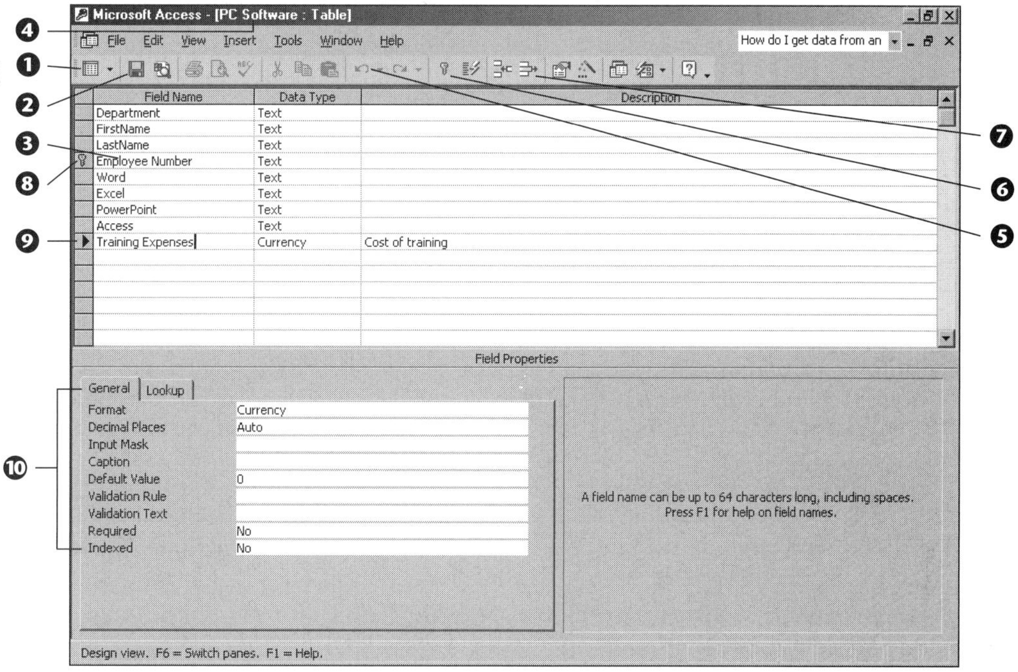

Figure 2.18

1. _____   6. _____

2. _____   7. _____

3. _____   8. _____

4. _____   9. _____

5. _____   10. _____

Discussion

1. If you wanted to create a table of people to send birthday cards to, what fields would you need to include? Could you get all of the information into one table, or would you need to split it up into two tables? Review the section on normalizing a database at the beginning of this project.

2. Assume you have been hired to set up a database for a small used bookstore. This bookstore prides itself on giving its customers great information. With each book that they sell, they also hand the customer a printout with the following information: author, name of the book, year of publication, number of pages, publisher, illustrator, author's nationality, and author's date of birth and death. How many tables would you set up for this database? Which fields would go in which table? What would be a good primary key field for each table?

3. In this project, you created a table that had the first name and last name in separate fields. What is the advantage of separating the first and last names? Why wouldn't it be just as good to have a single field for "Jane Smith"? How about "Smith, Jane"? What would be the advantage of creating a separate field for the middle name? It might help to think about how you would use the names if you were putting together an address list for a club or other organization.

Skill Drill

Skill Drill exercises reinforce project skills. Each skill reinforced is the same, or nearly the same, as a skill presented in the project. Each exercise includes a brief narrative introduction, followed by detailed instructions in a step-by-step format.

1. Keeping Track of Your Books

You are an avid reader and have been collecting books for years. You have also borrowed books from the library over the years, and sometimes you cannot remember whether you own the book or not. To make matters worse, you read a lot of mysteries, and you sometimes pick up a book and cannot remember whether you have read it. You decide it is time to create a database to keep track of your collection.

1. Launch Access, and select the Blank Database option.
2. Type `book collection` in the File name text box. Use the Save in drop-down list box to select the drive and/or folder in which you want to save your database. Click the Create button.
3. In the Tables object window, click the New button to create a new table. Select *Design view* and click OK.
4. Type `Author Last Name` in the Field Name column.
5. Press Tab↹. Accept Text as the Data Type.
6. Press Tab↹. Type `Last name of the author` in the Description column.
7. Add the following fields. Make them all Text fields and add a short description of each field in the Description column.

   `Author First Name`
   `Book`
   `Year Published`
   `Type of Book`
   `Publisher`
   `Pages`

8. Click the Save button. Name the table `Books` and then click OK.
9. Click Yes to enable Access to insert a primary key field.
10. Click the View button to look at your new table.

2. Adding and Deleting Fields

After some thought, you decide that you would like to make some changes to your database. You find that you are spending far more time typing than you would like, and the name of the publisher is the culprit. You cannot imagine a need for this field in the future, so you decide to eliminate it. You also realize that you should have included a field for whether or not you have read the book.

1. Click the View button to return to Design view. Place the insertion point in the first empty row in the list of fields.
2. Type `Read?` in the first blank row in the Field Name column.
3. Choose Yes/No as the data type.
4. Type `Check if the book has been read` in the Description column.
5. Click the row selector in the Publisher field.
6. Click the Delete Rows button to remove the field.
7. Click the Save button to save your changes to the structure of the table.

3. Editing the Data Type of Fields

Two of the fields, Pages and Year Published, are always going to be numerical. You decide that it would be a good idea to change the data type.

1. Click the Data Type column of the Year Published field.
2. Click the list arrow to display the drop-down menu.
3. Select *Number* from the list.
4. Highlight the data type in the Data Type column of the Pages field.
5. Type the letter n to change the data type to *Number*.
6. Click the Save button to save your changes to the structure of the table.

4. Moving a Field

After some more thought, you decide that you would like the Pages field to follow the Book field.

1. Click the row selector of the Pages field.
2. Click the row selector of the Pages field again, and drag the field up between the Book field and the Year Published field.
3. Click the View button to change to Datasheet view.
4. Click Yes to save your changes.
5. Check the order of the fields in Datasheet view to make sure the Pages field is in the right place.
6. Close the database, but leave Access open for the next exercise.

5. Creating a Database Using a Wizard

You have recently been transferred to the Public Relations department of Triple A Realty, a real estate sales and home construction agency. Your primary responsibility will be the scheduling of activities and events for Triple A and the tracking of employees assigned to staff the events. You know there is a database wizard that can help you create the database, but you cannot remember how to get started.

1. Activate the Office Assistant and type Create a database in the text box. Click the Search button.
2. Click the *Create an Access database* item from the menu that displays. Select the help item that relates to creating a database by using a database wizard.
3. Follow the steps listed to create a database using a database wizard. Use the database template for *Event Management*.
4. Type Triple A events in the File name text box. Select the location to save your data files from the Save in drop-down list and then click the Create button.
5. Close the Microsoft Access Help window by clicking the Close button on the Help window title bar. Read the information in the Database Wizard window about information that will be stored in the *Event Management* database and then click Next.
6. Select each item under *Tables in the database,* and review the fields for each table. Select the Information about employees table and then include the Email Name field by clicking the check box to add it to the list of fields chosen. Click the Next button.
7. Review the appearance of each screen display in the sample display by selecting each style name listed. When you complete the review, select the Stone style and click Next.
8. Review the styles available for printed reports by using the same procedure as step 7. Select the Corporate style and click Next.
9. Type Triple A events as the title of the database that appears on the main switchboard. Do not include a picture on your reports. Click Next.
10. Be sure there is a check in the box *Yes, start the database.* Click Finish.
11. The Database Wizard creates the database shell and related objects for use in the database, and then prompts you to enter your company name, address, and related information. Click OK. Enter the following information in the My Company Information table. Remember to press [Tab⇥] to move from field to field.

Company Name	Triple A Realty
Address	587 Boulder Boulevard
City	Ocean Springs
State/Province	MS
Postal Code	39564-0536
Country	USA
Phone Number	(228) 872-9032
Fax Number	(228) 872-9035

12. Click the Close button to close the My Company Information table and save the information.

13. The Main Switchboard window displays, listing options for working with the information in the database. Click the *Exit this database* button to close the *Triple A events* database. Leave Access open if you plan to complete additional exercises.

6. Creating a Table Using the Table Wizard

You have been named chairman for the Senior Prom for the local high school. Parents and students will need to be notified of dates and ticket information. You decide to use a table wizard to help you create a table quickly so that you can begin tracking this information for the prom.

1. Click the New button on the toolbar to create a new database. Click the Blank Database item in the task pane.

2. Enter `senior prom` in the File name text box. Select the location to save your data files from the Save in drop-down list, and click the Create button.

3. Double-click the icon beside *Create table by using wizard* in the Database window.

4. Select the Business category in the Table Wizard dialog box. Scroll down the listing of Sample Tables and select the Students table.

5. Move all fields from the Sample Fields list box into the Fields in my new table list box by clicking the Select All button. Click Next.

6. Name the table `Students and Parents`. Let the wizard set a primary key for you and then click Next.

7. Select the option button in the Table Wizard dialog box named *Enter data into the table using a form the wizard creates for me*. Click Finish to create the table and view the form created by the wizard.

8. Close the Students and Parents Form window by clicking the Close button on the title bar. Click Yes to save changes to the form design. Click OK.

9. Select the Tables object button in the *senior prom* database window. The Students and Parents table is listed.

10. Select the Forms object button to see the listing of the Students and Parents form. The icon beside the form name indicates the object type. Compare the form object icon to the table object icon.

11. Close the *senior prom* database and close Access, unless you are going to continue with the Challenge section.

Challenge

Challenge exercises expand on or are somewhat related to skills presented in the lessons. Each exercise provides a brief narrative introduction followed by instructions in a numbered step format that are not as detailed as those in the Skill Drill section.

1. Adding a Table to an Existing Database by Entering Data

You have decided to expand your Alaska database by adding tables that record other information about the Alaskan environment. The first table you want to add is about the wildlife you have seen in your travels.

1. Copy ea1-0201 to the drive and folder where your files are stored, remove the read-only status of the copied file, and rename it `Alaska environment`.
2. Open the *Alaska environment* database, and double-click *Create table by entering data*.
3. Enter `Black bear`, `Garbage dump`, `Seward`, `1995` in the first four fields, pressing ↵Enter after each entry.
4. Click the View button, and name the table `Wildlife I have seen`. Do not add a primary key field.
5. In Design view, name the four fields `Animal`, `Surroundings`, `Location`, and `Year`.
6. Add a new field called `ID`.
7. Make the data type of the new field AutoNumber.
8. Click the Primary Key button.
9. Close the table and save your changes.

2. Adding a Table to an Existing Database Using a Wizard

Now that you have added a wildlife table, you decide you need to have a table for plants you have seen. You know the common names, but decide you ought to leave a place for the scientific names when you get around to looking them up.

1. In the *Alaska environment* database, double-click *Create table by using wizard*.
2. Choose the <u>P</u>ersonal category and then select *Plants* from the Sample <u>T</u>ables options.
3. For fields, choose `CommonName`, `Genus`, `Species`, `LightPreference`, `TempPreference`, `Photograph`, and `Notes`.
4. Name your table `Plants I Have Seen`. Have the program set a primary key.
5. Do not relate this table to any other table.
6. Choose to enter information directly into the table.
7. Press Tab⇆ to enable the AutoNumber field to enter data automatically. Enter `Dandelion` as the Common Name, and type `Seen all over the place` for the Notes field. Leave all of the other fields blank.
8. Close the table.

3. Deleting More Than One Field at a Time

Looking at your Plants I Have Seen table, you realize that you are just doing this for fun, and the odds of you ever looking up the genus and species are very small. Therefore, you decide you want to remove these fields from your table.

1. In the *Alaska environment* database, select the Plants I Have Seen table, and open it in Design view.
2. Click the row selector for the Genus field, and hold the mouse button down.
3. Drag down and select the Species field as well.
4. Press Del. Click <u>Y</u>es to accept the deletion.
5. Close the table, and save your changes.

4. Add Check Boxes to a Table

You just saw a friend's database that has really neat check boxes for Yes/No fields and decide you would like to add one to one of your tables. The obvious choice would be a check box in the Geography table for places you have visited.

1. In the *Alaska environment* database, open the Geography table in Design view.
2. Add a new field called `Visited`.

3. Select Yes/No as the data type.

4. Click the View button, and save your changes.

5. Scroll to the right edge of the table.

6. Click the check boxes for the first two records.

7. Close the table.

5. Adding a Hyperlink Field

One of the data type options is called Hyperlink. You are not sure exactly what this is or how it can be used in an Access database.

1. Use the Office Assistant to figure out exactly what a Hyperlink field is and how it works. If you are still unsure, go online and check the Microsoft site (www.microsoft.com).

2. Open the Geography table in the *Alaska environment* database.

3. Go to the Web, and find a site about one of the cities listed in the table.

4. Add a new Hyperlink field called `Local Information`.

5. In the Local Information field in the datasheet, enter the URL (or Web address) that you found on the Web for an Alaskan city.

6. Test the URL.

7. Close the table.

6. Learning More About Field Names and Captions

Karen has created a database to track information on courses being offered at Waveburn Technical Institute. You and others in your office need to update the table by adding courses as they are scheduled. The field names that Karen used make it difficult to interpret the information in each field. You want to change the field names but know that if you do, the related objects already created in the database may not function properly.

1. Copy the ea1-0202 file, remove the read-only status of the copied file, and rename it `education`. Open the new database.

2. Open the Courses table in the *education* database.

3. Use Help to search for information on using captions to solve the problem of the column headings that display in Datasheet view.

4. Enter captions for each field that more clearly describes the information in the field. Suggestions for the field names are:

```
CID        Course ID#
CHRS       Course Hours
CDATE      Course Dates
CNAME      Course Name
```

5. Save the changes to the design of the Courses table.

6. View the changed headings in Datasheet view and then close the *education* database.

iscovery Zone

Discovery Zone exercises require advanced knowledge of topics presented in *essentials* lessons, application of skills from multiple lessons, or self-directed learning of new skills.

1. Creating a Lookup Wizard Field

The Lookup Wizard data type is unlike any of the other data types. It enables you to enter a code, which will fill in the field with information from another source.

Goal: Create a Lookup Wizard field that categorizes the animals listed in the Wildlife I Have Seen table.

Copy the ea1-0203 file, remove the read-only status of the copied file, and rename it **Alaska geology**.

Use the program's Help features and online help to figure out how to use a Lookup Wizard field. There are two different ways of using this type of field—you choose which one you want to use. You should create at least three categories for the wildlife types. For instance, one of your categories might be *Birds*.

2. Creating a Primary Key Field Using More Than One Field

Sometimes you want to use information in your database for your primary key field, but no one field is unique. Access offers you a way to use more than one field in combination as a primary key.

Goal: Create a primary key using two fields.

Use the Geography table in the *Alaska geology* database and create a primary key field out of the Latitude and Longitude fields. (Two places might have the same latitude or the same longitude, but no two places have both the same latitude and longitude.)

Hint: You will need to remove the primary key status from the existing primary key field before you can proceed.

3. Using a Database to Track Job Opportunities

You will soon complete your college degree in graphic design and want to start job hunting before graduation. You are willing to move, but want to stay within driving distance of your hometown of Tulsa, Oklahoma.

Create a database and an appropriate table for tracking information on job opportunities in graphic design. Add a hyperlink field to the table and include the URLs for at least two job listings. Name your database **job hunt**.

Entering and Editing Data

Objectives

In this project, you learn how to

- ✔ Add Records
- ✔ Move Among Records
- ✔ Edit Records
- ✔ Insert and Delete Records
- ✔ Adjust Column Widths and Hide Columns
- ✔ Find a Record
- ✔ Select Records Using Filter by Selection
- ✔ Select Records Using Filter by Form
- ✔ Sort Records

Key terms introduced in this project include

- ❑ Clipboard
- ❑ current record indicator
- ❑ Filter by Form
- ❑ Filter by Selection
- ❑ pencil icon
- ❑ record selector

Why Would I Do This?

After you create a database and table, you want to be able to put them to work. For your database to be useful, you must enter data into the table (or tables). For example, you can keep track of your business contacts by entering their names, addresses, and phone numbers into the Contacts table of the *address book* database you worked with in Project 1. You can use the *training* database you created in Project 2 to keep track of training that your staff receives by entering information about the employees and the training they have received into the PC Software table. As you learned in Project 1, the set of information you enter for each row in a table is called a record.

One reason databases are so useful is that you can work with and modify the records after you enter them. With a paper filing system, you have to cross out, erase, or redo a record when the information changes. With database software, however, you can easily change a record in the table to correct a mistake or to update the information. You can delete records you no longer need, search for a particular record, and sort the records—all quickly and with little effort on your part.

In this project, you learn how to add records to your table, move around in the records within the table, and edit and delete records. You also learn how to search for a particular record, filter groups of records, and sort your records according to a system that you determine.

Visual Summary

When you have completed this lesson, you will have created a table that looks like Figure 3.1.

The table has been sorted on the Employee Number field

This field has been edited

Column widths have been adjusted

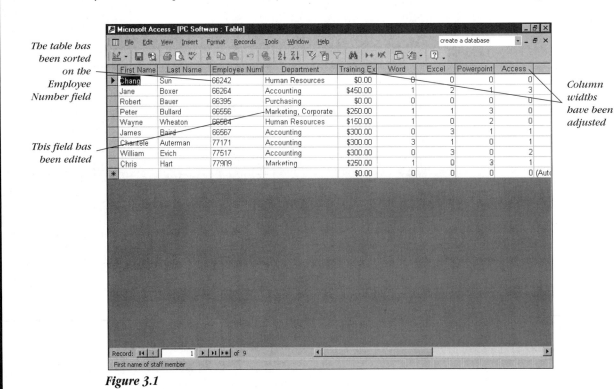

Figure 3.1

Lesson 1: Adding Records

In Design view, you can make changes to the fields in the table—change a field name, add a field, change the data type, and so on. Then, when you want to work with the data in the table, you switch to Datasheet view. In this view, you can add records or edit them.

In this lesson, you open a database, *employee training*. You switch to Datasheet view and then add records to the database.

To Add Records

1 **Launch Access. Click *More Files* in the Open a file section in the task pane.**

2 **Find the ea1-0301 file with the student files and then copy it to the drive and folder where your files are stored. Remove the read-only status from the copied file. Rename the new file employee training, and open the new database.**
The database should open with the Tables object button selected, and a PC Software table should be listed.

3 **Select the PC Software table in the Datasheet view and click the Open button.**
The PC Software table should be displayed onscreen in Datasheet view. Each of the field names appears along the top of the window. At this point, the table consists of one blank row. The insertion point is in the first field, and you see a small, black arrow next to the first field. This arrow indicates the current record (see Figure 3.2).

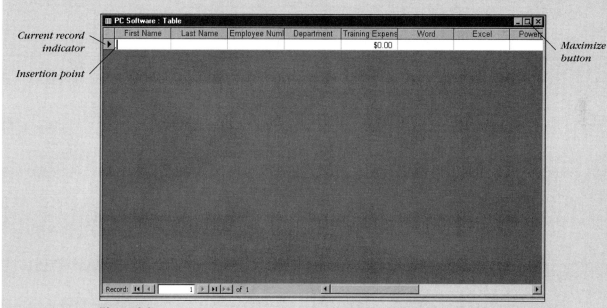

Current record indicator

Insertion point

Maximize button

Figure 3.2

4 **Maximize the Table window, type Chantele and press ↵Enter.**
As you type, Access displays a pencil icon in the ***record selector***, which is the shaded area to the left of the record. You can also use Tab↹ in place of ↵Enter when adding data to the table.

5 **Type Auterman and then press ↵Enter.**
The staff member's name is entered, and the insertion point moves to the Employee Number field.

(Continues)

To Add Records (Continued)

6 **Type 77171 and then press** ⏎Enter.

The employee number is entered, and the insertion point moves to the Department field.

7 **Type** `Accounting` **and then press** ⏎Enter.

The department is entered, and the insertion point moves to the Training Expense field.

8 **Type** `300.00` **and then press** ⏎Enter.

The expense for training this employee is entered, and the insertion point moves to the four fields for specific software training. Notice that Access formats the entry as currency.

9 **Type 3 and then press** ⏎Enter, **1 and then press** ⏎Enter, **0 and then press** ⏎Enter, **and finally 1 and then press** ⏎Enter.

The levels of classes taken are recorded in the four application fields. When you press ⏎Enter the last time, Access moves to the counter field, which has a value that was automatically entered when you started entering data in the first field.

10 **Press** ⏎Enter.

Access saves the record and moves to the next row so that you can add another record (see Figure 3.3). Whenever you move the insertion point off of the record you are editing, Access immediately saves the record or any changes you have made to the record.

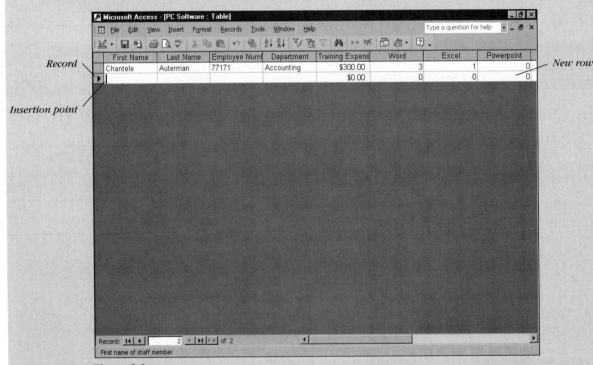

Figure 3.3

11 **Use the following list of data to add more records to the database table. (Because of the number of fields in each record, the items are separated by commas. Do not type the commas.) Save changes when done.**

```
Chang,Sun,66242,Human Resources,0,0,0,0,0

Jane,Boxer,66264,Purchasing,450,1,2,1,3

Robert,Bauer,66395,Purchasing,0,0,0,0,0
```

To Add Records

```
Peter,Bullard,66556,Marketing,250,1,1,3,0

James,Baird,66567,Accounting,300,0,3,1,1

Wayne,Wheaton,66564,Human Resources,150,1,0,2,0

Chris,Hart,77909,Marketing,250,1,0,3,1
```

Access adds these records to the database table. Keep the *employee training* database and the PC Software table open. In the next lesson, you learn how to move among the records in your table.

To extend your knowledge...

Automatic Dollar Signs

You do not need to enter the dollar sign ($) into a currency field. It will be added automatically by the program. Adding the dollar sign does not hurt anything, but if you learn to leave it off, it will save you a great deal of time if you have to enter large amounts of data. Also, if a dollar amount is a whole number, the program adds the .00 automatically, even if you don't type it.

Lesson 2: Moving Among Records

Earlier, you noticed that Access displays an arrow next to the current row. When you want to edit a field to change or update a record's information, you must first move to the row containing the record that you want to change. You can tell what row you have moved to because a black triangular arrow, called the **current record indicator**, is displayed in the record selector box to the left of the current row.

You can move among the records in several ways. If you can see the record you want on the screen, you can simply click it to select it. If you have numerous records in your table, however, you may have to scroll through the records until you can get to the one you want. To move to a particular record, you can use the vertical scrollbar, the navigation buttons displayed along the bottom of the window, or the arrow keys on the keyboard. Table 3.1 explains how these navigation buttons and keys work.

Table 3.1 Moving Among Records with the Navigation Buttons and Keys

To Move To	Buttons	Keyboard
First record in table	⏮	Ctrl + Home
Previous record in table	◀	↑
Next record in table	▶	↓
Last record in table	⏭	Ctrl + End
New record at end of table	▶✱	Ctrl + +

In this lesson, you move among the records in your table using each of these navigational methods.

To Move Among Records in a Table

1 With the PC Software table of the *employee training* database open, move the mouse pointer to the record selector at the left of the Wayne Wheaton record and click.

The record is selected.

2 Press Ctrl+Home. Access moves you to the first record in the database table. Notice the current record indicator arrow to the left of the active record (see Figure 3.4).

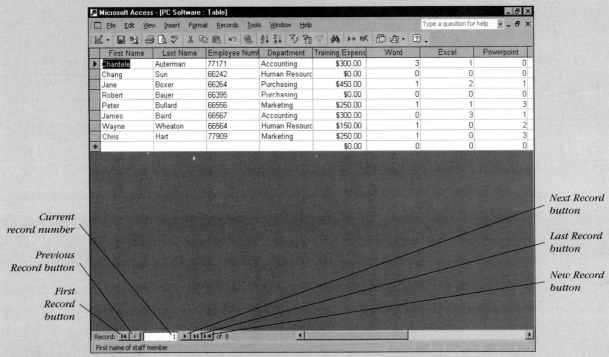

Figure 3.4

3 Press ↓.

Access moves you to the next record in the table.

4 Click the Last Record button.

Access moves you to the last record in the table.

5 Click the Previous Record button.

Access moves you to the previous record in the table.

6 Click the First Record button.

Access moves to the first record in the table.

7 Click the New Record button.

The pointer moves to the next empty record.

Now that you know how to move among the records in your table, the next lesson shows you how to make changes to the records. Keep the *employee training* database and the PC Software table open as you continue with Lesson 3.

If you have problems...

If you click a particular field in the table and enter the editing mode, the Ctrl+Home and Ctrl+End commands only move to the beginning and end of the current field. These commands move to the beginning and end of the table if a field or record is selected.

Lesson 3: Editing Records

As you work with the data in the database table, you find that you need to make changes from time to time. In your PC Software table, for example, you might want to correct a typing mistake or change other information. You can update or correct any of the records in your table while you are in Datasheet view.

The first step in editing records is to move to the record that you want to change. Next, you have to move to the field that you want to edit. To move among fields using the mouse, click in the field to which you want to move. When you click, Access places the insertion point in the field and does not select the entire text in that field.

You can also use the keys listed in Table 3.2 to move among fields. When you use these keys, Access moves to the specified field and selects all the text in that field.

Table 3.2 Moving Among Fields with the Keyboard

To Move To	Press
Next field	(Tab⇄) or (→)
Previous field	(⬆Shift)+(Tab⇄) or (←)
First field in record	(Home)
Last field in record	(End)

When you are in a field, you can add to, edit, or delete the current entry. Try moving among the fields and making changes now.

To Edit Records

❶ **With the PC Software table of the *employee training* database open, click after the word *Marketing* in the Department column of the record for Peter Bullard.**
The insertion point is placed where you are going to add new text in the field.

❷ **Type a comma (,), press** (Spacebar), **and type** Corporate.
As you begin typing, notice that Access displays a pencil icon in the record selector next to the record. This ***pencil icon*** reminds you that you are editing the record and that the change has not yet been saved (see Figure 3.5).

(Continues)

To Edit Records (Continued)

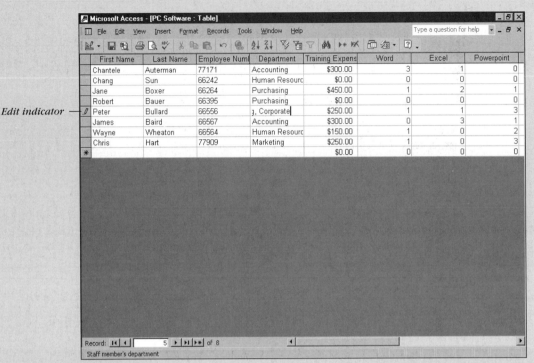

Edit indicator

Figure 3.5

❸ **Press ⬆ twice.**

This moves you to the Department field in the record for Jane Boxer. When you move to another record, Access automatically updates the record you just changed.

The text in that field is selected (see Figure 3.6). Anything you type replaces the selected text.

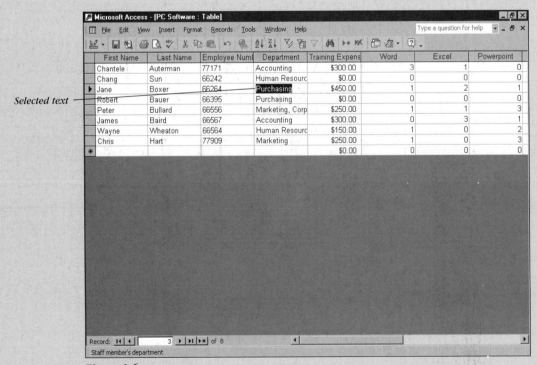

Selected text

Figure 3.6

To Edit Records

4 **Type** Accounting.
The record has been updated for this employee who has been transferred to a new department.

5 **Press** ⬇.
Access updates the record you just edited and moves to the next record.

Keep the *employee training* database and the PC Software table open. In Lesson 4, you learn how to insert new records and delete records you no longer need.

To extend your knowledge...

Undoing Changes

If you make a change by mistake, you can undo it by immediately clicking the Undo button, or by opening the Edit menu and choosing the Undo command. If you are editing a field and decide you don't want to save your edits, press Esc to ignore your changes.

Saving a Record

You can also save the change you make by pressing ⬆Shift+⏎Enter while still on the record you are editing. To save a record using the menu, choose the Records, Save Record command.

Lesson 4: Inserting and Deleting Records

When you first create your database table, you can't always predict exactly what information you'll want to include. As you use your database, you will most likely want to insert new records or delete outdated records.

With Access, you don't have to add all your records at one time. You can add a new record to the end of the table at any time. If you want to enter several records containing similar data, you can enter the data for one record, copy it, paste it into your table, and then edit the data in the new record.

You can delete a record by removing the row from the database table. In this lesson, you insert new records and delete a record you no longer need.

To Insert and Delete Records

1 **With the PC Software table of the *employee training* database open, click in the First Name field of the row marked by an asterisk.**
The insertion point is placed in the First Name field of the empty record where the new information will be added. The current record indicator arrow replaces the asterisk (see Figure 3.7).

(Continues)

To Insert and Delete Records (Continued)

First Name	Last Name	Employee Numl	Department	Training Expens	Word	Excel	Powerpoint
Chantele	Auterman	77171	Accounting	$300.00	3	1	0
Chang	Sun	66242	Human Resourc	$0.00	0	0	0
Jane	Boxer	66264	Accounting	$450.00	1	2	1
Robert	Bauer	66395	Purchasing	$0.00	0	0	0
Peter	Bullard	66556	Marketing, Corp	$250.00	1	1	3
James	Baird	66567	Accounting	$300.00	0	3	1
Wayne	Wheaton	66564	Human Resourc	$150.00	1	0	2
Chris	Hart	77909	Marketing	$250.00	1	0	3
				$0.00	0	0	0

Current record indicator

Figure 3.7

2 **Type the following data for your new record, pressing ⏎Enter after each entry. After the last entry, press ⏎Enter twice.**

William, Evich, 77517, Accounting, 300, 0, 3, 0, 2

Access adds the new employee record to the end of your table. You can also copy a record and add the copy so that you have two versions of the same record. You may want to do this if you have two or more similar records. This might be appropriate for an inventory database of computer hardware. To practice this skill, you can copy the record you just added.

3 **To copy the new record, click in the record selector to select the entire row.**
Clicking the record selector highlights the entire row.

4 **Click the Copy button.**
You won't notice anything different onscreen after you copy the record. At this point, you have just placed a copy of the selected record onto the *Clipboard*, a temporary storage location for whatever you have copied or cut from your document. Next, paste the copy of the record into your table.

5 **Click the record selector to highlight the empty record at the end of the table and then click the Paste button.**
Access adds the record to the end of the table. Now that you have the basic data in place, you can make any changes necessary for this particular record. Rather than edit this duplicate record just now, you are going to use it to practice deleting a record.

6 **Click the record selector next to the new record you just inserted.**
The record you just pasted is selected. You can also select the record by opening the Edit menu and choosing Select Record when the insertion point is anywhere in the record.

To Insert and Delete Records

7 **Click the Delete Record button.**
Access wants to be sure that you intended to delete the record, so you are prompted to confirm the deletion (see Figure 3.8). You cannot undo record deletions, so be absolutely sure that you want to delete a record before you confirm the deletion.

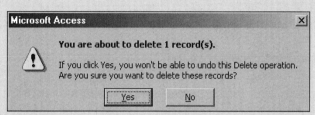

Figure 3.8

8 **Click the Yes button.**
Access deletes the record and saves the changes to the database table. Once a record is deleted, however, it cannot be undone.

Keep the PC Software table open. In Lesson 5, you learn how to change the width of the columns in your table and how to hide and unhide columns.

To extend your knowledge...

Copying Fields, Deleting and Adding Records

In addition to copying entire records, you can also copy an entry from one field to another. If you want to enter another record for someone from the Marketing Department, for example, you can copy *Marketing* from the Department field and paste it in the new record.

To copy an entry, move to the appropriate field, and select the text you want to copy by dragging across it. Then click the Copy button. Move to the location where you want to place the copied text, and click the Paste button. Access pastes the selected text.

You can also use shortcut keys: Ctrl+C for Copy and Ctrl+V for Paste.

To delete a record, you can select it and press Del, or place the insertion point anywhere in the record and choose Delete Record from the Edit menu.

To add a new record, you can click the New Record button on the toolbar.

Lesson 5: Adjusting Column Widths and Hiding Columns

By default, Access displays all the columns in your table with the same width. You can change the column width, making some columns wider so that you can see the entire entry, and making other columns narrower so that they don't take up as much space. The easiest way to adjust the column width is to use the mouse, but it can also be adjusted using Format, Column Width from the menu.

In addition to changing the column width, you can also hide columns you don't want displayed, such as the AutoNumber field, which is never used for data entry. Adjusting the column width does not change the field size.

To Adjust Column Widths and Hide Columns

1 **With the PC Software table of the *employee training* database open, place the mouse pointer on the line between the First Name and Last Name field selectors.**

The mouse pointer changes to a thick vertical bar with arrows on either side (see Figure 3.9). This pointer indicates that you can now move the column borders.

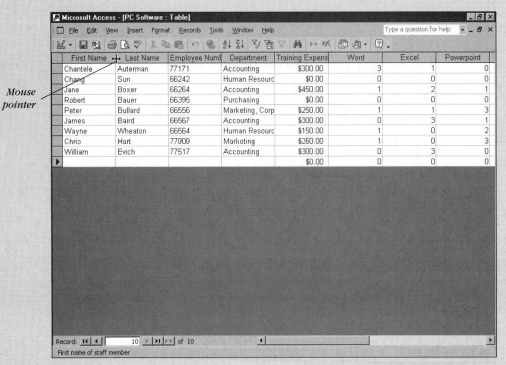

Mouse pointer

Figure 3.9

2 **Press and hold down the mouse button and drag to the left until you think the column is narrow enough and you can still see all the entries in the column. Release the mouse button.**

The new width is set. As you drag to the left, you make the column narrower. Notice that you can see the border of the column move as you drag. Don't worry if you cover up part of the field name.

If you have problems...

If you don't see the thick bar with the arrows, you don't have the pointer in the correct spot. Be sure that you are within the shaded area of the field selectors and that your pointer is sitting directly on the border separating the two columns.

3 **Move the mouse pointer to the border between the Department and Training Expense columns, and double-click the mouse button.**

Double-clicking is a shortcut method that automatically adjusts the column to fit the longest entry currently displayed onscreen in that column. This often creates a problem

To Adjust Column Widths and Hide Columns

when you use long field names, because double-clicking widens the column to show the whole field name if it is the longest entry in the column.

④ Drag across the field selectors for the Training Expense, Word, Excel, PowerPoint, Access, and ID fields. Use the horizontal scrollbar to view the selected columns.

When you drag across the headings, you select all six columns (see Figure 3.10). You can then adjust the widths of all six columns at one time.

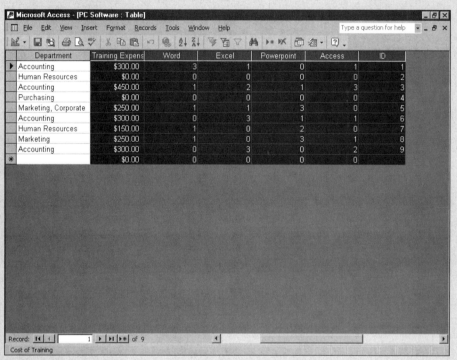

Figure 3.10

⑤ Drag the border on the right of the Training Expense column so that it is just big enough to hold the longest entry.

Notice that dragging one of the borders resizes all six columns.

⑥ Click anywhere in the table to deselect the columns.

⑦ Scroll to the left. Click in the field selector of the Employee Number field.

Now that you have selected this column, you can practice hiding it.

⑧ Open the Format menu, and choose the Hide Columns command.

Access hides the column you selected.

⑨ Open the Format menu, and choose the Unhide Columns command to unhide the column.

Access displays the Unhide Columns dialog box (see Figure 3.11). If the column has a check mark next to its name, the column is displayed. If there is no check mark, the column is hidden.

(Continues)

To Adjust Column Widths and Hide Columns (Continued)

Unhide Columns

Column:

☑ First Name
☑ Last Name
☐ Employee Number
☑ Department
☑ Training Expense
☑ Word
☑ Excel
☑ Powerpoint
☑ Access
☑ ID

[Close]

A check mark indicates that the column is displayed

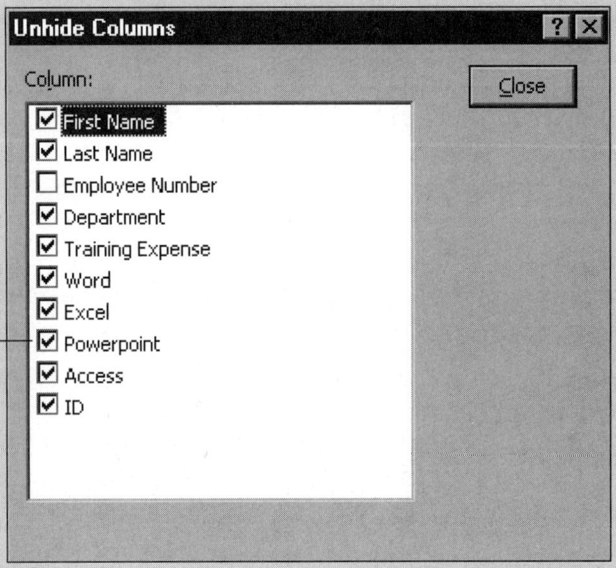

Figure 3.11

🔟 **Click the Employee Number checkbox and then click the Close button.**

Access closes the Unhide Columns dialog box. The Employee Number column reappears on the screen.

Save your work, and keep the PC Software table open.

To extend your knowledge...

Other Ways to Adjust and Hide Columns

You can also use the menus to adjust the column width. Move the insertion point to the column you want to adjust. Then open the Format menu and choose the Column Width command. Type a new value (the width of the column in points). Click the OK button.

You can also hide multiple columns by first selecting them and then selecting the Hide Columns command from the Format menu. In addition, you can use the Unhide Columns dialog box to hide columns. In the list displayed in the dialog box, click the checkbox next to a column to deselect it. This hides the column.

Lesson 6: Finding Records

In a table with many records and fields, it may be time-consuming to scroll through the records and fields to find a specific record. Instead, you can search for a specific field entry in order to find and move quickly to a record.

For example, if you want to find the *Wayne Wheaton* record, you can search for *Wheaton*. It is always faster to select the field you want to use for your search and then search just that field, but you can also search for text in any field in the table. In this lesson, you find a record by first searching a single field and then by searching all fields.

To Find a Record

❶ With the PC Software table of the *employee training* database open, click in the Last Name field.

It doesn't matter what row in which you click. Clicking anywhere in the field tells Access that you want to search for a particular record using the Last Name field only. The field with the insertion point is searched by default.

❷ Click the Find button.

Access displays the Find and Replace dialog box (see Figure 3.12). Here you tell Access what you want to find and where you want to look.

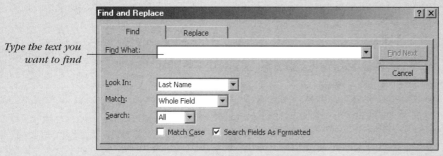

Figure 3.12

❸ Type Wheaton in the Find What box, and then click the Find Next button.

Access moves to the first match, and the dialog box remains open. You can continue to search by clicking the Find Next button until you find the record you want.

If you cannot see the match because the dialog box is in the way, move the dialog box by dragging its title bar.

❹ Drag across the text in the Find What text box to select it, then type Resources.

This is the next entry you want to find. Since you have the insertion point in a field, the Find option will only look in the selected field by default. You must change the search options.

❺ Click the list arrow in the Look In drop-down list box, and select *PC Software : Table*.

Instead of restricting the search to just the current field, you are now telling Access to look in all fields.

❻ Click the list arrow in the Match drop-down list box, and select *Any Part of Field*.

The text you want to find (Resources) won't be the entire entry; it is only part of the field. For this reason, you have to tell Access to match any part of the field. Figure 3.13 shows the options you have requested for this search.

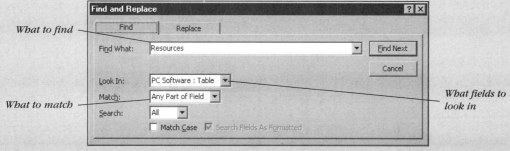

Figure 3.13

(Continues)

To Find a Record (Continued)

7 **Click the Find Next button.**

Access moves to the first occurrence and highlights *Resources* in the Department field in the record for Wayne Wheaton. Notice that the search starts from the currently selected record.

8 **Click the Find Next button.**

Access moves to the next occurrence and highlights *Resources* in the Department field in the record for Chang Sun (see Figure 3.14).

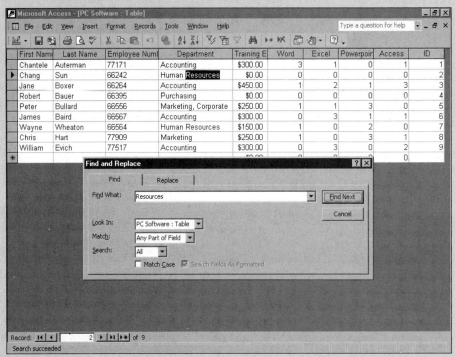

Figure 3.14

9 **Click the Cancel button.**

This step closes the Find and Replace dialog box. The last record found remains selected.

Keep the PC Software table open for the next lesson.

 ## To extend your knowledge...

Searching Before the Current Record

If you see a message telling you that Access has reached the end of the records and asking whether you want to start searching from the beginning, click the Yes button. By default, Access searches from the current record down through the database. The record you want may be located before the current one.

If you see another message telling you that Access reached the end of the records, Access did not find a match. Try the search again. Be sure that you typed the entry correctly. You may need to change some of the options.

Lesson 7: Selecting Records Using Filter by Selection

A quick method that can be used to examine data in a table is to select an entry in one of the fields and click the **Filter by Selection** button. A matching filter is immediately applied to the table and only those records that have the same value in that field are shown.

In this lesson, you learn how to use the Filter by Selection feature to display the records for employees who do not have any Access training.

To Filter Records Using a Selected Value

❶ In the PC Software table, maximize the datasheet window, if necessary. Click the Access field in Record 2.

The second record has a zero in the Access field, meaning that there has been no Access training for this employee. Before using the Filter by Selection option, you must first select a field entry that represents the records you want to filter.

❷ Click the Filter by Selection button.

A filter is applied that limits the display to four records (see Figure 3.15).

Filter by Selection button

Field to filter by

Number of records filtered

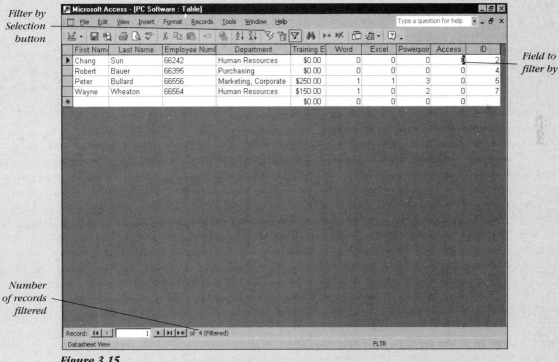

Figure 3.15

❸ Click the Remove Filter button.

The filter is removed and all nine records are displayed.

Keep the PC Software table open for use in the next lesson.

Lesson 8: Selecting Records Using Filter by Form

Another quick method that can be used to examine data displayed in tables, queries, and forms is to use a form filter. The ***Filter by Form*** feature gives you a blank copy of the form and enables you to type desired field entries in one or more fields at a time. A form filter provides more options than using Filter by Selection. Although it is not as flexible as a query and is not generally saved, the form filter technique can give you a quick and easy way of limiting data.

In the following steps, you learn how to use the Filter by Form feature to display the records of all Accounting employees who have completed all levels of Excel training (represented by a "3").

To Use Filter Criteria in More Than One Field

1 **Click the Filter by Form button. Press** Del **to erase the filter criteria from the last lesson, if necessary.**

2 **Click the Department field, click the drop-down arrow, choose** Accounting, **and press** ↵Enter.
Notice that quotation marks are automatically added to the name. This is typical of criteria for a text field.

3 **Type 3 in the Excel field.**
The number 3 in any of the software fields indicates completion of all three levels of training in that subject. This field is a number data field and quotation marks are not used. These two criteria will be used to filter the records to display those that match (see Figure 3.16)

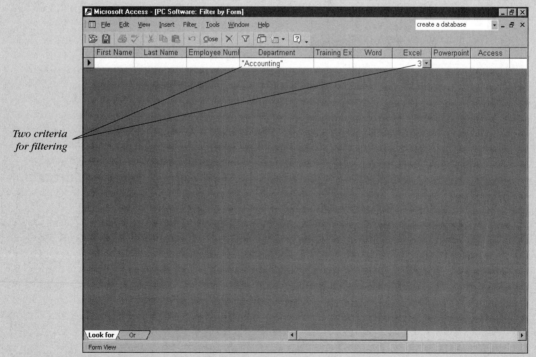

Two criteria for filtering

Figure 3.16

4 **Click the Apply Filter button.**
A list of two employees is displayed (see Figure 3.17).

To Use Filter Criteria in More Than One Field

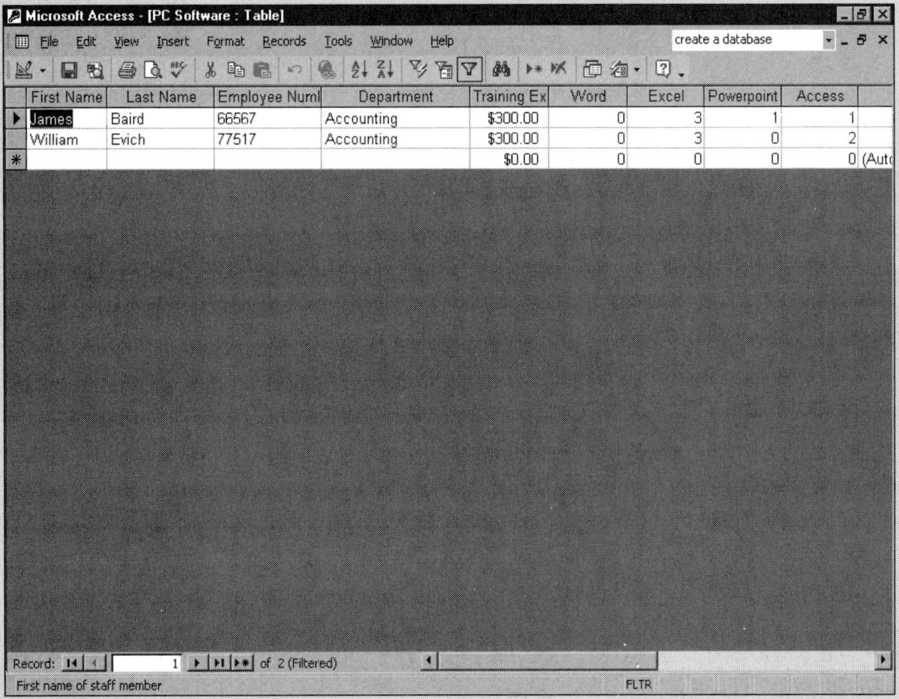

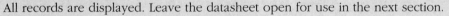

Microsoft Access - [PC Software : Table]
File Edit View Insert Format Records Tools Window Help
create a database
First Name | Last Name | Employee Numl | Department | Training Ex | Word | Excel | Powerpoint | Access
James | Baird | 66567 | Accounting | $300.00 | 0 | 3 | 1 | 1
William | Evich | 77517 | Accounting | $300.00 | 0 | 3 | 0 | 2
$0.00 | 0 | 0 | 0 | 0 (Aut
Record: 1 of 2 (Filtered)
First name of staff member
FLTR

Figure 3.17

5 Click the Remove Filter button.
All records are displayed. Leave the datasheet open for use in the next section.

You can fill in several fields in the form filter. Records will have to match all of the entries to be displayed. In some cases, you may want to see all the records that meet two different sets of criteria.

To Filter Using Two Sets of Criteria

1 Click the Filter by Form button to reveal the design of the filter.
Notice that the previous conditions were not deleted. They still specify the Accounting employees who have completed the Excel training (see Figure 3.18).

(Continues)

To Filter Using Two Sets of Criteria (Continued)

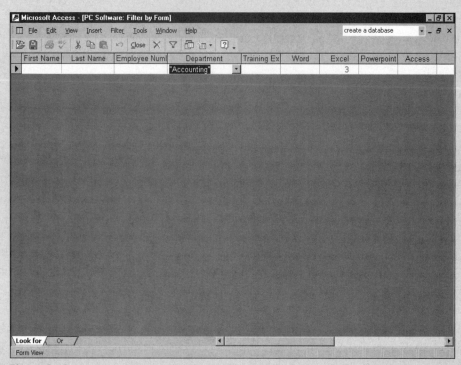

Figure 3.18

② **Click the *Or* tab at the bottom of the window.**
A second form displays in which you can enter a new set of criteria.

③ **Enter** Accounting **in the Department field and then enter 2 in the Access field.**
This criterion will show the employees who are fluent in Access by completing two levels of training.

④ **Click the Apply Filter button.**
The records are shown for Accounting employees who have completed all three courses (experts) in Excel and also the employees in the Accounting department who have completed two courses (fluent) in Access. There should be two records (see Figure 3.19).

To Filter Using Two Sets of Criteria

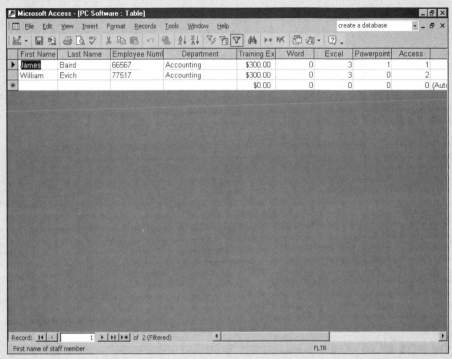

Figure 3.19

⑤ Click the Filter by Form button and then click the Clear Grid button.
The Clear Grid button removes all the criteria from the Filter by Form grid.

⑥ Click the Apply Filter button.
The empty criteria are applied. This is the method used to erase the criteria. Notice the Apply Filter button is dim, indicating that no filter criteria exist.

⑦ Save the changes.
Leave the table and database open for the next lesson.

To extend your knowledge...

If you create a filter, it is stored with the database object if you save the changes. When the table, query, or form is open, you can tell if a filter condition exists by looking at the Apply Filter button. If it does not have a square outline around the button, no filter condition exists. If it is active, a filter condition exists that may be removed by clicking the button. The name of the Remove Filter button may be misleading. It does not erase the filter conditions; it only removes the application of the filter.

Lesson 9: Sorting Records

Access displays the records in your table in an order determined by the primary key. If your table has no primary key, Access displays the records in the order in which they were entered.

If you use a primary key, Access sorts the entries alphabetically or numerically, based on the entries in that field. (If a counter field is your primary key, your records will be displayed in the order in which they were entered.) Fortunately, however, you aren't restricted to displaying your data only in the order determined by your primary key. With Access, you can sort the display by using any of the fields in the database table. You can also sort the display using multiple, adjacent fields.

In this lesson, you first sort your data on the Last Name field. You then use the toolbar to sort on the Employee Number field.

To Sort Records

1 **With the PC Software table of the *employee training* database open, click in the Last Name field.**
Clicking in this field tells Access that you want to base your sort on the Last Name field.

2 **Click the Sort Ascending button.**
Access sorts the records in ascending alphabetical order (A-to-Z) based on the entries in the Last Name field (see Figure 3.20).

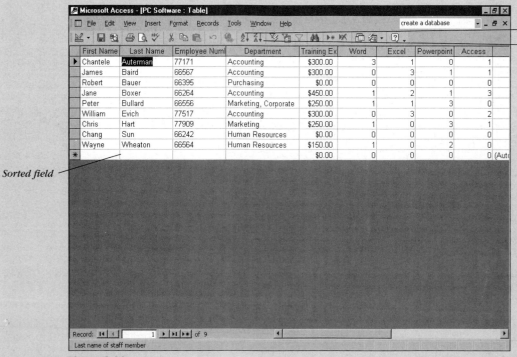

Figure 3.20

3 **Click in the Employee Number field.**
Clicking in this field tells Access that you now want to base your sort on the Employee Number field.

4 **Click the Sort Ascending button on the toolbar.**

To Sort Records

Access sorts the table by using the entries in the Employee Number field (see Figure 3.21). Keep in mind that the sort order displayed onscreen does not affect the order in which the records are actually stored.

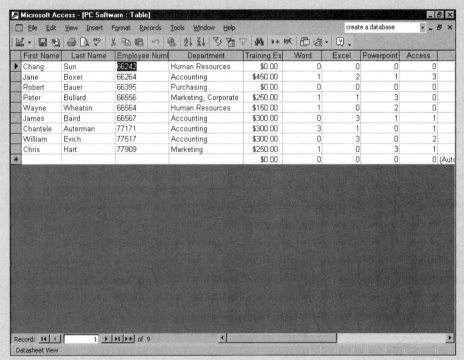

First Name	Last Name	Employee Num	Department	Training Ex	Word	Excel	Powerpoint	Access	
Chang	Sun	66242	Human Resources	$0.00	0	0	0	0	
Jane	Boxer	66264	Accounting	$450.00	1	2	1	3	
Robert	Bauer	66395	Purchasing	$0.00	0	0	0	0	
Peter	Bullard	66556	Marketing, Corporate	$250.00	1	1	3	0	
Wayne	Wheaton	66564	Human Resources	$150.00	1	0	2	0	
James	Baird	66567	Accounting	$300.00	0	3	1	1	
Chantele	Auterman	77171	Accounting	$300.00	3	1	0	1	
William	Evich	77517	Accounting	$300.00	0	3	0	2	
Chris	Hart	77909	Marketing	$250.00	1	0	3	1	
*				$0.00	0	0	0	0	(Aut(

Figure 3.21

⑤ Close the PC Software table.
A dialog box asks if you want to save your changes, which in this case were the changes in sort order.

⑥ Click the Yes button.
If you have completed your session on the computer, exit Access and Windows before turning it off. Otherwise, continue with the "Checking Concepts and Terms" section.

To extend your knowledge...

Another Way to Sort Records

You can also use the Records, Sort command from the menu and select the Sort Ascending or Sort Descending option. As with the buttons, you must first have the insertion point in the field you want to sort.

Sorting by Multiple Fields

To sort by multiple, adjacent fields (for example, last name then first name) select the field name for the first sort, hold down the (⬆Shift) key, and select the second field to sort (the second field must be adjacent and to the right of the first field). You can also click in the first field selector and drag to the right to select the second field. Click the Sort Ascending or Sort Descending button to perform the sort.

When you have completed a sort, if you wish to return records to their original order, choose Records from the menu, and click Remove Filter/Sort.

If the fields you want to sort on are not in the proper order (for example, your database *employee training* displays the first name field followed by the last name field), you can move the fields in Design view prior to the sort. By moving the field so that the last name column appears first in your table with the first name field as the next field immediately to the right, you can sort the table by last name, then by first name. You can also move a field by clicking the field selector, clicking on the field name, and then dragging the field to the desired location.

Summary

In this project, you worked with records in a table. You added, edited, inserted, and deleted records, and learned how to move around quickly in a table. You also used two of the more important features of a database—finding and sorting records. You also adjusted the widths of the columns to make the table more readable and learned to hide columns without deleting the field. Finally, you learned how to extract particular data in a table using the Filter by Form and Filter by Selection features.

You can expand your knowledge of tables by asking the Office Assistant how to design a table. Several topics about table design are available, and some of the basic design concepts are discussed in the topics on creating a table.

Checking Concepts and Terms

Multiple Choice

Circle the letter of the correct answer for each of the following questions.

1. If you want Access to search all fields in the table, which option do you select in the Find and Replace dialog box? [L6]

   a. Current Field
   b. Match Case
   c. Search Fields As Formatted
   d. none of the above

2. If you have a database of books that have been loaned out from a library, how can you show all of the books by a certain popular author? [L7]

   a. Place the cursor in the author field and use Filter by Selection.
   b. Place the cursor in the date field and use Filter by Selection.
   c. Scroll through the records using the navigation buttons and place a bookmark in each record that met the criteria.
   d. Print out the table and hand count the occurrences of the author's name.

3. Which method can you use to remove a filter permanently? [L7]

   a. Create a new empty filter and apply it to the form or query, then save the changes.

   b. Click the Delete button on the keyboard.

   c. Right-click on the filter and then click delete from the shortcut menu.

   d. Click the Remove Filter button.

4. Access automatically saves the data you enter to disk when you do which of the following? [L3]

   a. Press (Shift)+(Enter).

   b. Leave the field in which you entered the data.

   c. Choose Save Record from the Record menu.

   d. all of the above

5. Access identifies the record you are editing by which of the following? [L3]

   a. the arrow on the record selector

   b. the asterisk on the record selector

   c. the key symbol on the record selector

   d. the pencil icon on the record selector

Screen ID

Label each element of the Access screen shown in Figure 3.22.

A. First record button

B. Apply Filter button

C. Next Record button

D. Sort Ascending button

E. Editing Record indicator

F. New Record button

G. Filter by Form button

H. Previous Record button

I. Filter by Selection button

J. Last Record button

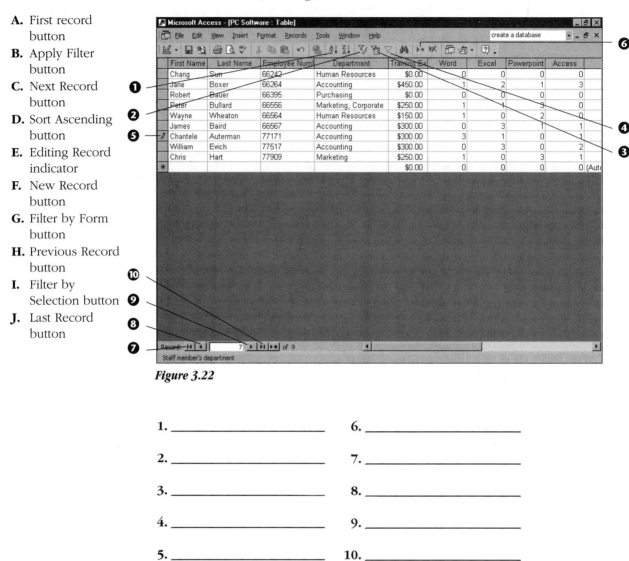

Figure 3.22

1. _____   6. _____

2. _____   7. _____

3. _____   8. _____

4. _____   9. _____

5. _____   10. _____

Discussion

1. Assume that you are designing a database table for automobile parts to use in a store. This table will be used by both the sales personnel at the counter and by the customers at a self-help computer. The table will contain the make of the car, part name, description, number sold year-to-date, quantity in stock, retail price, sale price, and cost. Which, if any, of the fields would you hide? Why?

2. In this project, you learned about several different methods of moving around in a table. When might it be preferable to use buttons? Keyboard shortcuts? The mouse?

3. Sorting records is often done in a database. Sorting by last name and first name is an example of sorting on more than one field at a time. What other instances can you think of when you might need to sort on two fields at once? Would there ever be a reason to sort on three fields? What are those reasons?

Skill Drill exercises reinforce project skills. Each skill reinforced is the same, or nearly the same, as a skill presented in the project. Each exercise includes a brief narrative introduction, followed by detailed instructions in a step-by-step format.

You are working for a company that does research for other companies. Your current project is to conduct a survey for a cable TV company to find out how subscribers feel about five of the channels offered in their basic cable package. You are just starting out and testing your survey with a small number of families. You have set up a preliminary survey and are recording the results in an Access database.

1. Adding Records

You have decided you need ten families for your trial run, so you will need to add two more families to your survey.

    1. Copy the ea1-0302 database file, remove the read-only status of the copied file, and name it **television survey**. Open the *television survey* database. Open the Questionnaire table.

    2. Click the View button to switch to Design view and read the Description column to see what each of the categories means. Click the View button again to return to Datasheet view.

    3. In Datasheet view, click the New Record button. Use either the one on the toolbar or the one included with the navigation buttons.

    4. Enter the following information into the Questionnaire table. (*Note:* You can enter checks in the check boxes by clicking on them with the mouse button or pressing Spacebar.)

Adults	Children	Use	Hours	#1	#2	#3	Doing	Comments
4	0	N	8	Discovery	CNN	SciFi	Great	More nature shows
1	2	Y		Disney	SciFi		Good	More cartoons!!!

    5. Close the table, but leave the database open.

2. Editing, Inserting, and Deleting Records

While looking over the paper survey forms you have received, you find that you made a couple of mistakes while entering the data. After discussing your sample data with a representative from the cable company, you find that they feel every household must have at least one of the five channels being tested in their list of favorites. This means that you have one record that needs to be deleted, and you need to find another one to take its place.

    1. Open the Questionnaire table in the *television survey* database. Make sure you are in Datasheet view.

    2. Move down to the 8th record (the one that has only CNN in the favorite channel fields).

    3. Highlight *CNN*, and type **TNT**.

    4. Move to the Improve field, and type **No opinion**.

    5. Click the record selector next to the record with no favorite channels listed. This should be the fourth record.

    6. Press Del to remove the record and click Yes to confirm the deletion.

    7. Click the New Record button.

8. Add the following information:

Adults	Children	Use	Hours	#1	#2	#3	Doing	Comments
2	2	Y	2	TNT	CNN	DISCOVERY	Good	Would like more news & nature shows

9. Save your changes. Leave the table open for the next exercise.

3. Adjusting Column Widths and Hiding Columns

You would like to be able to see more of your survey information onscreen at one time. The best way to do that is to reduce the width of several columns and hide the ID column.

1. In the *television survey* database, click the field selector of the ID field, and drag across until you have selected the ID, Adults, Children, Use, and Hours fields.

2. Grab the column separator between any two of the fields, and reduce the column width to the smallest size needed to show all of the data. You will cut off part of the field names.

3. Place the insertion point in the ID field.

4. Choose Format, Hide Columns from the menu.

5. Leave the table open for the next exercise.

4. Finding a Record

Although this is a small sample, you want to be prepared to find data when the full survey is completed.

1. In the *television survey* database, place the insertion point in the Improve field of the ninth record (the Disney Channel record you added in Exercise 1).

2. Click the Find button on the toolbar, then type **Nature** in the Find What box.

3. Select *Any Part of Field* from the Match drop-down list.

4. Click the Find Next button. If the first instance is hidden, move the Find and Replace dialog box out of the way. Notice that the first record found is the last record in the table.

5. Click the Find Next button again. A second match is found.

6. Click the Find Next button. When no more matches are found, click OK, and close the Find and Replace dialog box.

7. Leave the table open for the next exercise.

5. Filtering Records

You want to see how many households have children who answered the survey. You also want to see how popular CNN really is with your viewers. You decide to filter your records to find out.

1. In the *television survey* database, click in the #1 Channel field for the third record (this should be *Discovery*).

2. Click the Filter by Selection button. Four records should be listed.

3. Click the Remove Filter button.

4. Click the Filter by Form button and then click the Clear Grid button to remove the criteria from the previous steps.

5. Click in the Children field and type >0. Click the Apply Filter button. Six records should be listed.

6. Click the Filter by Form button again and then click the Clear Grid button.

7. Click in the #1 Channel field, click the drop-down arrow, and choose *CNN*.

8. Click the *Or* tab at the bottom of the screen. Click in the #2 Channel field, click the drop-down arrow, and choose *CNN*.

9. Repeat step 8 to include the #3 Channel in the filter. Click the Apply Filter button. There should be seven records.

10. Click the Remove Filter button and save your changes to the table. Leave the table open for the next exercise.

6. Sorting and Printing Records

Your client wants to see the sample survey data in two different orders.

1. In the *television survey* database, place the insertion point in the Children field, and click the Sort Descending button.
2. Select File, Page Setup, and move to the Page tab.
3. Select Landscape orientation and then click OK.
4. Click the Print button to print the table.
5. Click the *Use* field selector and then click the Sort Ascending button. You could print this table if necessary, although it is not necessary to do so at this time.
6. Close the table and save your changes. Close the database and close Access, unless you will be moving on to the Challenge section.

Challenge exercises expand on or are somewhat related to skills presented in the lessons. Each exercise provides a brief narrative introduction followed by instructions in a numbered step format that are not as detailed as those in the Skill Drill section.

The table you will be working with in the Challenge section is a list of your CDs in a database called *CD collection*. This table has fields for the artist, title, year, label, serial number, and category.

1. Freezing Columns

You may have to use the horizontal scrollbar to scroll back and forth to look at all of the fields for a record. When you scroll to the right, the name of the artist disappears from view. You would like to keep the name of the artist and title onscreen at all times.

1. Copy the ea1-0303 database file, remove the read-only status of the copied file, and rename it **CD collection**. Open the *CD collection* database.
2. Open the CD Collection table in Datasheet view.
3. Select both the Artist/Group and the CD Title fields.
4. Choose Format, Freeze Columns from the menu.
5. Scroll to the right to make sure the first two columns don't move off the screen.
6. Close the table, and save your changes.

2. Finding and Replacing Data

When you show a friend a printout of your CD collection, she points out that you misspelled the name of classical composer Gustav Holst, which you spelled "Holzt." You can scan the entire 371 records and try to make sure you find all of the misspelled words, or you can use the Find and Replace feature to do the hard work for you. You decide to try the latter.

1. In the *CD collection* database, open the CD Collection table in Datasheet view.
2. Highlight the CD Title column.
3. Choose Edit, Replace from the menu.
4. Type **Holzt** in the Find What box and **Holst** in the Replace With box. Make sure that you match any part of the field and look in only the CD Title field.
5. Click Find Next to find the first instance of the misspelled word. Replace it with the correct spelling. You will not be able to undo this action.
6. Click Replace All to find the rest of the misspelled words and click Yes to confirm.
7. Close the table and save your changes, if necessary.

3. Copying and Pasting Records

Sometimes you have a CD to enter into the table that is very similar to another one you have already entered. Try copying and pasting a record to save work.

1. In the *CD collection* database, open the CD Collection table in Datasheet view. Use the Find button to find the CD Title "Too Long in Exile" by Van Morrison. (*Hint*: you can just type the first couple of words in the Fi<u>n</u>d What box.)
2. Click the record selector to select the whole record.
3. Use the Copy button to copy the record.
4. Click the New Record button, and click the record selector to select the whole record.
5. Click the Paste button to paste the whole record you copied.
6. Change the CD Title field to `Days Like This`. Change the Year field to **1995**. Change the Serial number field to **31452 7307 2**.
7. Close the table.

4. Removing Sorts

You just noticed that there is a command to remove a sort, and you wonder how it works. Does it remove only the previous sort, sort of like the Undo option, or will it go back to the original order even after two sorts? Will it work after you have saved your changes and left the table? Look at the first three records so you can remember which records came first.

1. In the *CD collection* database, open the CD Collection table in Datasheet view. Place the insertion point anywhere in the Artist/Group column, and sort in ascending order.
2. Now sort on the Label field in descending order.
3. Choose <u>R</u>ecords, <u>R</u>emove Filter/Sort from the menu. Notice that the records are back in their original order.
4. Sort by Artist/Group, again in ascending order, and then close the table and save your changes.
5. Open the CD Collection table again, and notice that the sort on Artist/Group is still in effect.
6. Choose <u>R</u>ecords, <u>R</u>emove Filter/Sort from the menu. Did the records go back to their original order?
7. Close the table, and save your changes.

5. Changing Column Widths Using the Menu

The column widths are not quite right in the CD Collection table. Try the menu option to change the column widths.

1. In the *CD collection* database, open the CD Collection table in Datasheet view. Select the Year column.
2. Choose F<u>o</u>rmat, <u>C</u>olumn Width from the menu.
3. Click the <u>B</u>est Fit button to narrow the column.
4. Select the Serial number field and then choose F<u>o</u>rmat, <u>C</u>olumn Width from the menu.
5. Select the <u>S</u>tandard Width check box, and click OK.
6. Select the Artist/Group field and then choose F<u>o</u>rmat, <u>C</u>olumn Width from the menu. Notice that the <u>C</u>olumn Width is shown as 22.5. Change the number to **30**, and click OK.
7. Use the Access Help option to find out exactly what the numbers in the <u>C</u>olumn Width box are. Could they be points? Eighths of inches? Some other measurement?
8. Use what you found out from the Help source to make the CD Title column exactly 3" wide.
9. Close the table, and save your changes.

6. Formatting Text in a Table

You have seen text formatting on text in word processing programs and spreadsheets, and you wonder if the same thing can be done with text in Access.

1. In the *CD collection* database, open the CD Collection table in Datasheet view.

2. Use Access help to find out how to turn on the formatting toolbar in Datasheet view.

3. Change the background color to a pale blue (or other light background color of your choice).

4. Change the text to a very dark blue (or other dark font color of your choice).

5. Highlight any CD Title, and click the Italic button. Notice that all of the text in the datasheet is italicized. When you format anything in a datasheet, everything else in the datasheet is formatted the same way.

6. Close the table, and save your changes.

Discovery Zone exercises require advanced knowledge of topics presented in *essentials* lessons, application of skills from multiple lessons, or self-directed learning of new skills.

In these exercises, you will be using the *CD collection* database you used in the Challenge exercises. If you didn't do the Challenge exercises, copy ea1-0303 to a disk as **CD collection**.

1. Sending a Database to the Desktop as a Shortcut

You buy CDs all the time, and you find that you are opening this database several times a week. It would be a good idea to place an icon representing the database right on your desktop. That way, you will be able to boot your computer and double-click the CD Collection icon to move directly to the database, saving several steps!

Goal: Create, test, and delete a desktop shortcut to a specific database.

Use the available help to learn how to create a shortcut. Create a desktop shortcut for your *CD collection* database, test it, and then delete it from your desktop.

Hint: There are two ways to do this: one within Access and one using Windows. Try to figure out both of them.

2. Using Access Tools

Access has all sorts of tools available to help you enter data more quickly and proofread information when you are finished. The most commonly used tool is the spelling checker, which can be very important to people who are weak in this area. A second, lesser-known tool can be of at least as much help. This is the AutoCorrect feature.

Goal: Use the spelling checker to check spelling and add words to the dictionary, and the AutoCorrect tool to simplify the entry of long text entries.

The spelling checker

- Find two ways to activate the spelling checker.
- Check the spelling of several words in the CD Title column.
- Add one of the words to your dictionary.

The AutoCorrect tool

- Have the program automatically capitalize the first letter of a sentence if it is not turned on.
- Turn on the feature that changes the second letter of two capital letters to lower case, then make an exception for CD.
- Create a shortcut that enables you to type `ASMF` and have it replace those letters with `Academy of St. Martin-in-the-Fields (Sir Neville Marriner)`.
- Test the three features you just worked with.
- Look at some of the other tools available to use with your table.

3. Analyzing Your Table

When you look at your fields in the CD Collection table, you notice that the names of the artists are repeated frequently. Knowing that this probably isn't good database design, you'd like to have the table analyzed. You've heard that Access has a procedure to analyze tables.

Goal: Discover how to have Access analyze your table and then run the analysis option.

Use Help to find out where the table analysis tool is located. Run the analyzer to see whether the program feels your table should be split into two tables. If Access suggests splitting the table, read why, but do not actually go through with it.

Querying Your Database

PROJECT 4

| Objectives |

In this project, you learn how to

- ✔ Create a New Query using the Simple Query Wizard
- ✔ Edit a Query
- ✔ Change Field Order and Sort a Query
- ✔ Match Criteria
- ✔ Save a Query with a New Name and Open Multiple Queries
- ✔ Create a Calculated Field
- ✔ Format the Results of a Calculated Field

Key terms introduced in this project include

- ❑ column selector
- ❑ criteria
- ❑ criterion
- ❑ crosstab query
- ❑ design grid
- ❑ dynaset
- ❑ query
- ❑ Select query

Why Would I Do This?

The primary reason you spend time entering data into a database is so that you can easily find and work with the information. In your *address book* database, for example, you may want to display all of your contacts in Indiana. To do so, you would create a query. A *query* asks a question of the database, such as, "Which records have IN as the state?" and then it pulls those records from the database into a subset of records, called a *dynaset*. You can then work with or print just those records selected by your query.

You can also create queries that display all of the records but only show selected fields. For example, you can display only the Last Name and Employee Number fields in the *employee training* database. You can create a query that searches for values in one field, such as the Indiana example just given, but displays only selected fields in the result. You can also create more complex queries. For example, you can query your *employee training* database to display all staff members who have received training in either Microsoft Excel or PowerPoint. Queries are created and saved so that they can be used repeatedly.

In this project, you create, save, edit, and use a query.

Visual Summary

When you have completed this project, you will have created a query that looks like Figure 4.1.

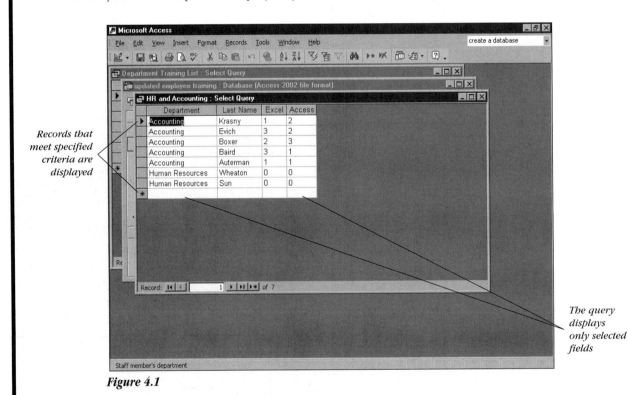

Records that meet specified criteria are displayed

The query displays only selected fields

Figure 4.1

Lesson 1: Creating a New Query Using the Simple Query Wizard

A table is the most common type of object you can include in a database, but there are several other types of objects. A query is another object you can create in a database.

In this lesson, you work with the data in the PC Software table of your *employee training* database. The PC Software table on your student disc that you copy and use in this project includes the records you entered in Project 3, "Entering and Editing Data," as well as some additional records. The headings in the revised table have been modified slightly to adjust the size of each column, allowing more information to appear onscreen. You start the procedure by creating a query and adding the table(s) with which you want to work. You create a query that contains only the Last Name and Department fields from the PC Software table. This list might be handy if you need to know who has received training in each department.

To Create a New Query

❶ Launch Access. Click *More Files* in the task pane to open an existing file.

❷ Copy the *ea1-0401* file, remove the read-only status of the copied file, and rename the file updated employee training. **Open the new database.**
The database should open to the Tables object button, and a PC Software table should be listed.

❸ Click the Queries object button.
The Queries list displays no queries, because you haven't created and saved any queries yet (see Figure 4.2).

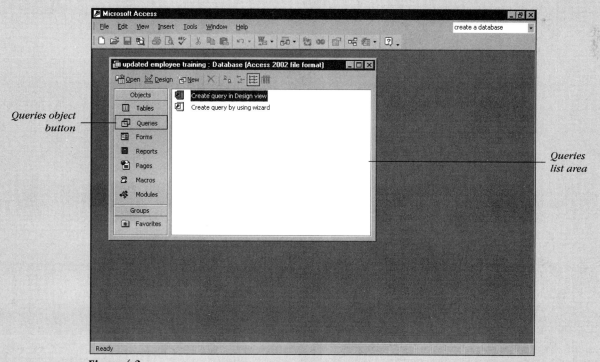

Figure 4.2

(Continues)

To Create a New Query (Continued)

4 **Click the New button.**
The New Query dialog box is displayed. You can create a query in Design view or you can use one of the Query Wizards to create a query. The simplest type of query, and the one you will probably use most often, is the **Select query**, which displays data that meet conditions you set. This method works best for specific kinds of queries, such as finding duplicate records.

5 **Click Simple Query Wizard and then click OK.**
The Simple Query Wizard walks you through several steps to determine which fields you want to include in the query.

6 **Click the Last Name field in the Available Fields list and click the Select button to move the field to the Selected Fields list.**

7 **Repeat step 6 to add the Department field. Click Next.**
The Selected Fields list should now include the Last Name and Department fields (see Figure 4.3).

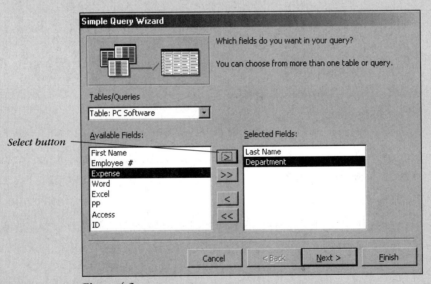

Figure 4.3

8 **Type** Department Training List **for the query name. Be sure the *Open the query to view information* option button is selected. Click Finish.**
As with any object you add to a database, you must save and name the object if you want to keep it. This is the name you want to assign the query. You can type up to 64 characters, including numbers, letters, spaces, and special characters. When you save a query, you save the structure of the query, not the dynaset. The dynaset is the result of running the query, which can be different each time it is run, because it is based on the data in your table. If the records in the table have changed, the resulting dynaset will reflect those changes.

If you have problems...

If Access will not accept your filename, it means that you have used one of the forbidden characters. Also, you cannot include leading spaces in the query name. If you use a restricted character in a filename, a message box appears telling you that the name you have entered is not valid. You can

To Create a New Query

> click OK and rename the file, or click the Help button for further information.

Notice that the title bar displays Select Query to remind you that you are viewing a dynaset, not the actual table (see Figure 4.4). The difference between a table and a dynaset is that the table consists of all the records with all of the fields; the dynaset consists of a subset of the records. Keep the query window open for the next lesson.

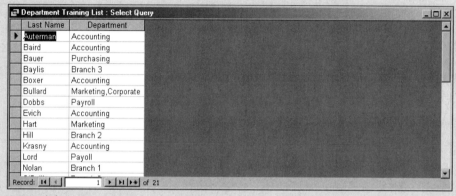

Figure 4.4

To extend your knowledge…

Using the Menus to Change Views

If you would rather use the menus, you can open the View menu and select the Datasheet View or the Design View command, instead of clicking the toolbar View button.

Running a Query

When you switch from Design view to Datasheet view, you are actually running your query. Instead of switching views, you can open the Query menu and select the Run command, or click the Run button on the toolbar.

Closing or Saving a Query

You don't have to save the query if you're sure you won't use it again. Just close the query window without saving. When Access prompts you to save, click the No button.

If you decide to save the query, you can do so by clicking the Save button, by choosing File, Save from the menu, or by pressing Ctrl+S.

Lesson 2: Editing the Query

Creating a query takes some practice and a little trial and error. You choose some fields, view the query, make some changes, view the query again, and so on, until you get the results you want.

You can edit the query to add or delete fields. In this project, you add three fields and then delete a field.

To Edit a Query

①   With the Department Training List query window displayed, click the View button on the toolbar.

When you opened the query in the preceding lesson, it was displayed in Datasheet view. To make changes, you first have to switch to Design view. You see a window divided into two parts. The top half of the query window displays a scroll box containing a list of the fields from the table you selected. Notice that the primary key field appears in bold type. The bottom portion of the window is the ***design grid***, where fields are selected, criteria are set, and functions are assigned.

②   Click the Excel field in the field list (you may have to scroll down to find it) and drag this field to the third column of the design grid.

As you drag, a small field box is displayed. When you release the mouse button, Access displays the field name in the Field row, and the table name in the Table row (see Figure 4.5). The Show row in this column displays a check mark in the check box, indicating that this field will be displayed in the query.

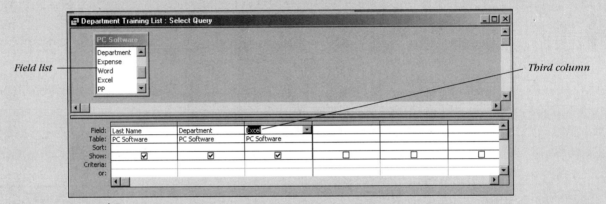

Figure 4.5

There are occasions when you may want to use a field but not display its contents. In that case, you would click on the Show box to deselect it.

③   Click the PP field in the field list, and drag this field to the third column of the design grid, the same column that currently contains the Excel field.

Access adds this field as the third column and moves the Excel field over one column to the right. You now have four fields in the query.

If you have problems...

If the PP field appears in the wrong location, drag across the PP name in the column where it appears, and press [Del]. Repeat step 3. If it is necessary to fill an empty column, click in the Field row of the empty column, click on the drop-down arrow and select the appropriate field for that column from the drop-down field list.

④   Double-click Access in the field list.

Access is added in the next empty field. You now have five fields in the query. In your window, you may not be able to see part, or even any, of the fifth column, depending on the size and settings of your computer monitor. Use the horizontal scrollbar to view the field you just added, if necessary.

To Edit a Query

You can add fields to the query by clicking the list arrow in the Field row of the query design grid and then choosing the field name, or by typing the field name in the Field row of the design grid.

5 **In the design grid, click the column selector over the PP column.**

When your pointer is in the *column selector* (the thin gray bar just above the field names), you see a black downward arrow for the mouse pointer. When you click the mouse button, the entire column is selected (see Figure 4.6). After you select a column, you can move it or delete it. Try deleting this column.

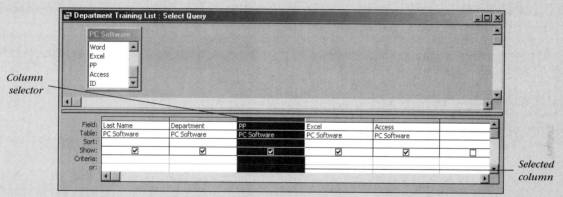

Column selector

Selected column

Figure 4.6

6 **Press** Del.

You can also open the Edit menu and choose the Delete Columns command. Access removes the field from the design grid.

7 **Click the Save button on the toolbar.**

Access saves the query with the changes you made. Keep the Department Training List query open in Design view. In the next lesson, you rearrange the order of the columns in your query.

To extend your knowledge...

Adding Several Fields at Once

You can select several fields from the field list and add them all at once. If the fields are listed next to each other, click the first field in the field list, hold down ⬆Shift, and click the last field in the field list. Access selects the first and last fields and all fields in between. You can also select fields that aren't listed next to each other. Click the first field you want to select, hold down Ctrl, and click the next field you want to select. Continue pressing Ctrl while you click each subsequent field. After you have selected all the fields you want, drag them to the design grid, and place them in the first empty space in the Field row. This will add all of the selected fields to the query.

Replacing a Deleted Column

You cannot use the Undo command to undo the deletion of a column. If you delete a column by mistake, simply add it again by dragging the name from the field list, double-clicking the field name in the field list, or using the drop-down list in the design grid.

Lesson 3: Changing Field Order and Sorting the Query

The way your query results are arranged depends on two factors. First, the order in which the fields are displayed is determined by the order in which you add them to the Field row in the design grid. If you don't like the order, you can rearrange the fields.

Second, the primary key determines the default order in which the records are displayed. You can change the query's sort order by using the Sort row in the design grid.

To Change Field Order and Sort a Query

❶ In the Department Training List query Design view, click the column selector above the Department field.
The entire column is selected. After you select a column, you can move it or delete it.

❷ Place the pointer on the column selector, and drag Department until it is the first column in the design grid.
A dotted box is displayed as part of the pointer to signify that you are dragging the column (see Figure 4.7). A dark vertical line also is displayed to indicate the insertion point for the selected column. When you release the mouse button, Access rearranges the columns in the new order.

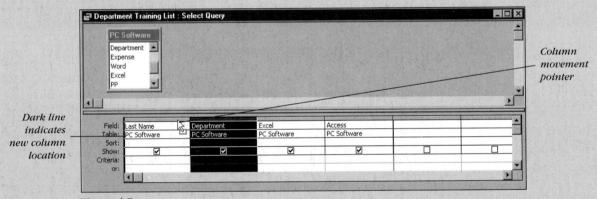

Figure 4.7

❸ Click in the Sort row of the Department field.
In this example, you want to sort the query by Department. When you click in the Sort box, Access displays a list arrow.

❹ Click the list arrow.
Access displays a drop-down list of sort choices (see Figure 4.8).

To Change Field Order and Sort a Query

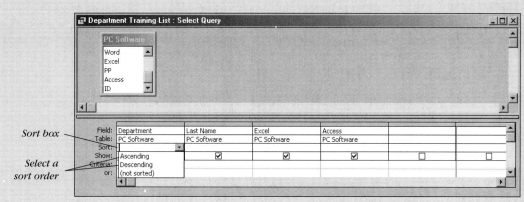

Figure 4.8

5 Click Ascending.
This selects the sort order (a-to-z) you want to use. You can check the query by changing to Datasheet view.

6 Click the View button on the toolbar.
You can see the results of your query in the Datasheet view (see Figure 4.9).

Figure 4.9

7 Click the View button on the toolbar again.
The query is once again displayed in Design view.

8 Click the Save button on the toolbar.
This saves the changes you made to the query. Keep the Department Training List query open in Design view as you continue with the next lesson.

Lesson 4: Matching Criteria

So far, the query you have created displays all of the records contained in the *updated employee training* database, but only shows the fields you selected. You can also use a query to display only certain records—records that match certain criteria. *Criteria* are a set of conditions that limit the records included in a query. A single condition is called a *criterion*.

You can match a single criterion, such as the last names of staff members who have received training in Excel, or you can match multiple criteria, such as staff members in the Marketing or Human Resources departments who have received training in Access or Excel. In this lesson, you practice using the various types of criteria.

To Match Criteria

❶ In the Design view of the Department Training List query, click in the Criteria box in the Department column.
The insertion point is moved to this location on the design grid. Here you can type the value that you want to match.

❷ Type Human Resources, and press ⏎Enter.
Access automatically adds quotation marks around the criterion that has been entered (see Figure 4.10). However, in some cases, such as when entering values that contain any punctuation marks, you must type the quotation marks.

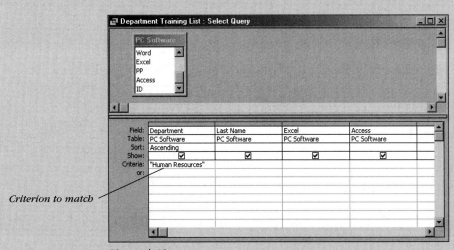

Figure 4.10

❸ Click the View button.
You see the results of the query. Notice that the dynaset now includes only the staff members in the Human Resources department (see Figure 4.11).

To Match Criteria

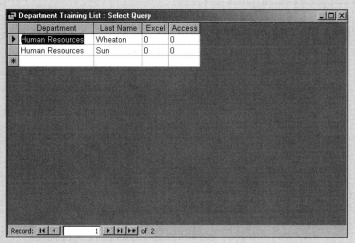

Figure 4.11

4 **Click the View button again.**
This returns you to the design grid so you can make a change to the query.

5 **Move to the box immediately below the Criteria box where you previously typed *Human Resources*. This is the *or:* row. Click this box.**

If you have problems...

If the window for the dialog box is not large enough to display more than one line of criteria, the list may scroll automatically. This results in some of the criteria disappearing from view. Maximize this window before proceeding, if necessary.

If you want to match more than one condition, use this row to specify the second value. For this example, you might want to specify staff members in Human Resources or Accounting who have received training.

6 **Type `Accounting`, and press [↵Enter].**
When the entry you want to match is one word and contains no punctuation, as in this example, you don't have to type quotation marks. Access adds them automatically.

7 **Click the View button.**
You see the results of the query. Notice that the dynaset now includes trained staff members from Human Resources and Accounting (see Figure 4.12). Keep the Department Training List query open. In the next lesson, you save the query with a new name.

(Continues)

To Match Criteria (Continued)

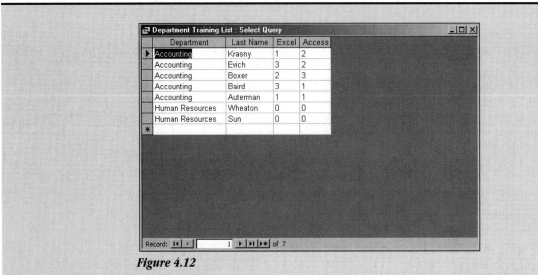

Figure 4.12

To extend your knowledge...

Resolving Query Errors

If you see a blank dynaset when you switch to Datasheet view, it means that Access found no matching records. Be sure that you typed the value you are trying to match exactly as you entered it in the database table. For example, you can't type "**Humans Resources**" to match "**Human Resources**." Check your typing, and try again.

If Access displays a syntax error message when you are entering text into the Criteria rows to make a match, it means that you did not type the entry in the correct format. Remember that if the text entry contains punctuation, you must supply quotation marks.

Other Query Types and Criteria

Access has many types of queries you can use. For example, you can match a range of values, as you would if you asked Access to display all staff members who received training in Excel at a level 2 or above. You can also create other types of queries, such as a query to display all duplicate records in a table.

There are other types of criteria that may be used besides a direct match. You can use comparisons such as <, which means less than, or >, which means greater than. If you use < to make a comparison in a text field, it uses alphabetical order. For example, if your criteria was *<Jones*, you would get all the names that came before Jones in the alphabet. Similarly, if you use *<1/1/95* in a date field, you would get all the dates before January 1, 1995. For more examples of different criteria, use the Access Help index to look up help for *Criteria*; then explore some of the different categories.

Lesson 5: Saving the Query with a New Name and Opening Multiple Queries

In some cases, you might modify a query and then want to keep both versions of the query—the original and the modified query—for future use. In this lesson, you learn how to save a query with a new name.

You can also open a query from the database window, and you can have more than one query window open at a time. This lesson explains how to open multiple queries.

To Save the Query with a New Name and Open Multiple Queries

❶ **In the Department Training List query, open the File menu and choose the Save As command.**
The Save As dialog box is displayed, with the current name listed in the *Save Query 'Department Training List' To:* text box (see Figure 4.13).

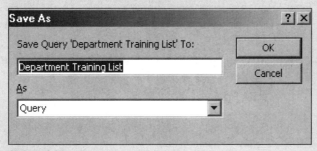

Figure 4.13

❷ **Type** HR and Accounting.
This is the name you want to use for the new query. Accept *Query* in the *As* text box.

❸ **Click the OK button.**
Access saves the query with the new name, and the new name is displayed in the title bar. The original query remains unchanged in the database.

❹ **Click the Close button in the query window.**
This returns you to the database window. The Queries object button should be selected. The two queries are displayed in the Queries list (see Figure 4.14).

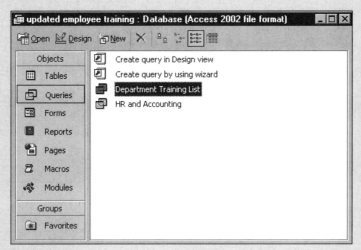

Figure 4.14

❺ **Select the Department Training List query, and click the Open button.**
This step opens the query. Notice that the query displays all departments, not just the ones for Human Resources and Accounting, because you did not save the criteria.

❻ **Click the Database Window button on the toolbar.**

❼ **Select and open the HR and Accounting query.**

(Continues)

To Save the Query with a New Name and Open Multiple Queries (Continued)

This opens your modified query. Now both queries are open onscreen as well as the database window.

⑧ Open the Window menu and choose Cascade.
This step arranges the windows so that you can see which windows are currently open (see Figure 4.15). You can work on more than one query at a time by moving between windows.

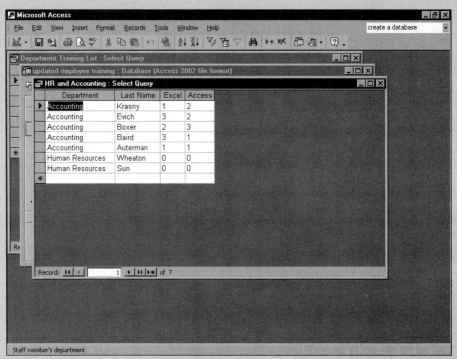

Figure 4.15

⑨ Close both query windows.
Leave the database open for the next lesson where you learn how to create a calculated field.

To extend your knowledge...

Copying and Opening a Query

You can also make a copy of a query in the database window by selecting the query, clicking the Copy button, and then clicking the Paste button. A Paste As dialog box opens so you can give the query copy a new name.

Once a query has been saved, you can open it in Design view instead of in Datasheet view. To open a query in Design view, click the query to select it, and then click the Design button.

Lesson 6: Creating a Calculated Field

A query can contain a field that is created from a calculation. These calculations, however, are not stored in the query, just the expression. So each time the query is run, the calculation is rerun. In this example, the company decides to give each employee a bonus for course completion. Employees who complete a course will receive $10 for their participation. The company tries to encourage computer training to better the customer service and productivity of all staff.

In this lesson, you create a calculated field to determine how much bonus pay each employee has earned.

To Create a Calculated Field

① **Select the Department Training List query, and click the Design button.**

② **Click in the first blank column in the Field Name row.**
This column should be the one immediately to the right of the Access field.

③ **Type BonusWord:[Word]*10, and press ⏎Enter.**
The text to the left of the colon is the field name for this field. When using an existing field in a calculation, the field name must be enclosed in square brackets. When you press ⏎Enter, the equation is added to the query and the insertion point moves to the next column (see Figure 4.16).

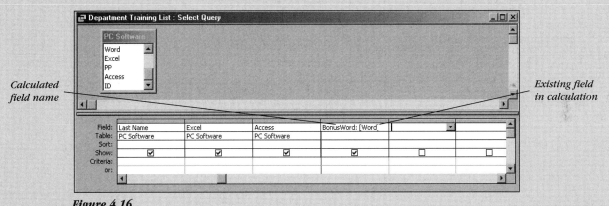

Calculated field name

Existing field in calculation

Figure 4.16

④ **Type BonusExcel:[Excel]*10, and press ⏎Enter.**
An equation must be created for all software courses.

⑤ **Type BonusPP:[PP]*10, and press ⏎Enter. Type BonusAccess:[Access]*10, and press ⏎Enter.**

⑥ **Click the View button to display the results of the calculated fields.**
When the records are displayed, each field contains a 0, 10, 20, or 30, depending on how many courses each employee completed (see Figure 4.17). Also notice that the field names are the same as the text that you typed to the left of the colon in Design view. You now want to total all bonuses for each employee.

(Continues)

To Create a Calculated Field (Continued)

Calculated fields

Department	Last Name	Excel	Access	BonusWord	BonusExcel	BonusPP	BonusAccess
Accounting	Krasny	1	2	10	10	10	20
Accounting	Baird	3	1	0	30	10	10
Accounting	Boxer	2	3	10	20	10	30
Accounting	Evich	3	2	0	30	0	20
Accounting	Auterman	1	1	30	10	0	10
Branch 1	Rowland	2	0	10	20	0	0
Branch 1	Rhodes	1		10	10		
Branch 1	Nolan	2	1	20	20	0	10
Branch 2	Hill	3	2	0	30	20	20
Branch 2	Steinberg	3	0	0	30	10	0
Branch 3	O'Sullivan	3	0	0	30	0	0
Branch 3	Roberts	2	2	10	20	10	20
Branch 3	Baylis	2	0	10	20	0	0

Record: 1 of 21

Figure 4.17

? If you have problems...

If you did not type the expression exactly as shown, you will receive an error message about syntax. Double-check your typing carefully.

7 **Click the View button to return to Design view.**

8 **Click in the next available Field box. Type**
`Total:[BonusWord]+[BonusExcel]+[BonusPP]+[BonusAccess]`, **and press** `↵Enter`.
This expression will add the results of the four calculated fields you added previously.

9 **Click the View button to switch to Datasheet view.**
The Totals field is the sum of all the individual class bonus fields (see Figure 4.18).

Last Name	Excel	Access	BonusWord	BonusExcel	BonusPP	BonusAccess	Total
Krasny	1	2	10	10	10	20	50
Baird	3	1	0	30	10	10	50
Boxer	2	3	10	20	10	30	70
Evich	3	2	0	30	0	20	50
Auterman	1	1	30	10	0	10	50
Rowland	2	0	10	20	0	0	30
Rhodes	1		10	10			
Nolan	2	1	20	20	0	10	50
Hill	3	2	0	30	20	20	70
Steinberg	3	0	0	30	10	0	40
O'Sullivan	3	0	0	30	0	0	30
Roberts	2	2	10	20	10	20	60
Baylis	2	0	10	20	0	0	30

Record: 1 of 21

Total field

Figure 4.18

10 **Click the Save button.**
Leave the query open for the next lesson where you learn how to format a calculated field.

To extend your knowledge...

Using the Expression Builder

You can also use the Expression Builder to create a calculated field if you are unsure of the structure. To do so, right-click the Field cell where you want the calculated field, and click Build from the shortcut menu. Use Microsoft Access Help if you need assistance with the Expression Builder.

Using a Variety of Calculations

There are several types of calculations that can be used in a query. This lesson only provides the simplest of calculations. There are also aggregate functions, custom calculations, text calculations, and update queries. Use Microsoft Access Help to learn more about calculations.

Lesson 7: Formatting the Results of a Calculated Field

Once a field has been calculated, it is usually a good idea to show the results with an appropriate format. In this example, the results should be displayed as currency.

To Format the Results of a Calculated Field

1 **Click the View button to switch to Design view.**

2 **Right-click the *Total* calculated field.**
A shortcut menu appears for the Total field (see Figure 4.19).

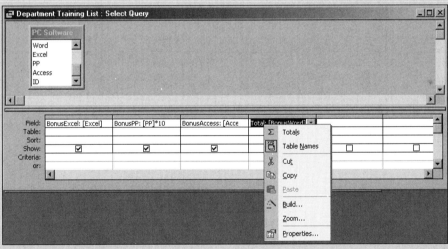

Figure 4.19

3 **Click the Properties option on the shortcut menu.**
A properties box appears with only a few options. These properties can be modified and will only be changed in this query.

4 **Click in the Format text box, then click the drop-down arrow that appears.**

5 **Scroll down the drop-down list, and choose Currency (see Figure 4.20).**

(Continues)

To Format the Results of a Calculated Field (Continued)

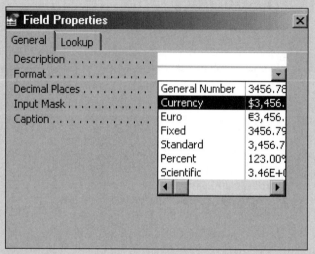

Figure 4.20

6 Click the Close button on the Properties box.

7 Click the View button to see the format change in the Total field.

The Totals field now has a dollar amount rather than a simple number in each record. After looking at the results of the query, you realize that the individual class bonus fields are not necessary in the results of the query. Hiding each of these fields removes their entry in the query results.

8 Drag the field selector over the four calculated fields (BonusWord, BonusExcel, BonusPP, and BonusAccess)

9 Choose F**o**rmat, **H**ide Columns.

The initial calculated fields are no longer displayed; however, the total for the bonuses is shown in the query (see Figure 4.21).

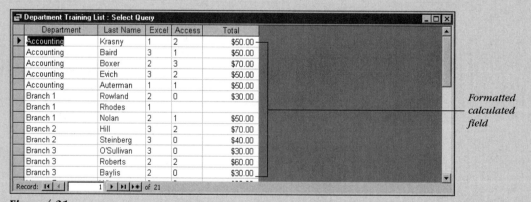

Figure 4.21

10 Click the Save button. Close the query and the database.

If you have completed your session on the computer, exit Access. Otherwise, continue with the "Checking Concepts and Terms" section.

Summary

This project focused on extracting a subset of information from a table. You learned how to create a query in Design view, select the appropriate fields, and save your query. You changed the fields and structure of the query and had the query display only records that met conditions that you set. You duplicated a query and saved it with a different name. Finally, you created and formatted a calculated field in a query.

You can expand your understanding of the use of queries by looking at the help available in the Office Assistant on some of the features that make queries more powerful. For example, you might want to type How do I enter criteria in the Office Assistant, look through the various help topics, and find examples of criteria expressions. These will give you a better idea of the many criteria features available in an Access query.

Checking Concepts and Terms

Multiple Choice

Circle the letter of the correct answer for each of the following questions.

1. Which of the following can you do to add a field to the query? [L2]

    a. Double-click the field name in the field list.

    b. Use the drop-down list in the Field row of the design grid.

    c. Drag the field name from the field list to the design grid.

    d. all of the above

2. What is the lower half of the query window called? [L2]

    a. field list

    b. design grid

    c. criteria box

    d. query area

3. How should you enter criteria for text fields if the criterion contains punctuation? [L4]

    a. in all uppercase

    b. in all lowercase

    c. in bold

    d. within quotation marks

4. Which of the following is not a way of creating another query? [L5]

    a. altering the current query and saving it with a new name

    b. selecting New on the Query dialog box and building a query from scratch

    c. selecting Duplicate from the Edit menu and saving the duplicate query with a new name

    d. copying the query in the database window and renaming the copy with a new name

5. When used in a calculated field, how should an existing field name appear? [L6]

    a. in quotation marks

    b. in square brackets

    c. in parentheses

    d. in front of a colon

Screen ID

Label each element of the Access screen shown in Figure 4.22.

A. Field list
B. View button
C. Calculated field
D. Sort order
E. Run button
F. Criterion
G. Source table of field
H. Field name
I. Column selector
J. Design grid

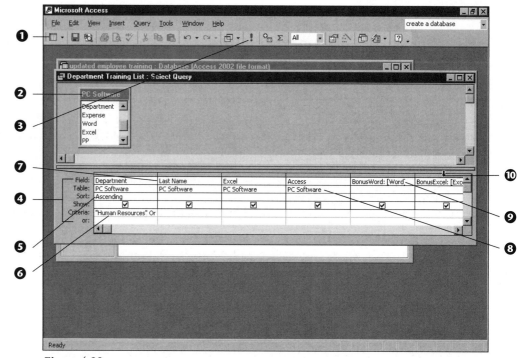

Figure 4.22

1. _____
2. _____
3. _____
4. _____
5. _____
6. _____
7. _____
8. _____
9. _____
10. _____

Discussion

1. You have created a home inventory using the following fields: room, category (for example, furniture, appliances, clothes), description, year purchased, serial number, and cost. What fields might you use queries on? Let's assume that some of your possessions are fairly valuable, and you want to submit a list of them to your insurance company. Which field would you set a criterion for, and which fields would you include in the query?

2. You have developed a table for an automobile parts store, containing fields for the make of the car, part name, description, number sold year-to-date, quantity in stock, retail price, sale price, and cost. You now want to create a query or queries that might be used repeatedly. What queries would you create, and what fields would each contain? What query can you think of that might include a field that you don't show in the dynaset (in other words, turn off the Show check box)?

3. You can sort data in either a table or a query using different procedures. Which procedure is easier if you are sorting on a single field? Which sort procedure is easier if you want to sort on multiple, non-adjacent fields?

Skill Drill exercises reinforce project skills. Each skill reinforced is the same, or nearly the same, as a skill presented in the project. Each exercise includes a brief narrative introduction, followed by detailed instructions in a step-by-step format.

You have created a database and table to store the information on your vast collection of history books. They are divided into four categories: United States, Ancient, World, and England & British Empire. There are fields for Author, Title, Year (either written or published), Pages, and Category. You would like to be able to sort your query and also view information by category.

1. Creating a Simple Query

You would like to create a query from which you can build other queries. First, you need to create a basic query.

1. Copy the *ea1-0402* database file, remove the read-only status from the copied file, and name it **history books**. Open the *history books* database. Select and open the History Books table, and look at the fields. Click the Close button to close the table.
2. Click the Queries object button, and click New to create a new query.
3. Choose Design View and then click OK. Click Add to add the History Books table. Close the Show Table dialog box.
4. Double-click the Author field to add it to the design grid.
5. Drag the Title field down to the design grid as the second field.
6. Add the Year and Category fields to the design grid, but do not add the Pages field.
7. Click the View button to see the results of your query.
8. Close the query, and save it as **All History Books**.

2. Editing Your Query

In your All History Books query, you have decided that you would really like to see the number of pages in the books, but don't care to see the Year of publication.

1. In the *history books* database, select the All History Books query and click the Design button.
2. Click the Pages field in the field box and drag it on top of the Year field. The Pages field should be between the Title field and the Year field.
3. Click the View button to view the results; then click the View button again to return to Design view.
4. Click the Show button for the Year field to hide the field in this query.
5. Click the View button to see the results of your change.
6. Close the query and save your changes.

3. Changing the Field Order in a Query

You have decided that you really should display the Year field, but you want to change the order of the fields.

1. In the *history books* database, select the All History Books query and click the Design button. Notice that the Year field has disappeared from the query, because it was not shown or used for anything (sorting or criteria).
2. Double-click the Year field to add it to the end of the fields in the design grid.
3. Click the Year column selector. Let go of the mouse button, click the column selector again, and then drag the field to the right of the Title field.

4. Use the same procedure to move the Category field to the first field position. The order of fields should now be: Category, Author, Title, Year, Pages.

5. Click the View button to view the new query layout. Close the query, and save your changes.

4. Sorting the Query and Saving with a New Name

You want to look at your history books in a couple of different orders. The query design grid makes it easy to do this.

1. In the *history books* database, select the All History Books query and click the Design button.

2. Click the Sort box for the Pages field in the design grid.

3. Click the list arrow in the Pages Sort box, and select Descending to look at your largest books first.

4. Click the View button to see a list of your books from largest to smallest.

5. Click the View button to return to Design view.

6. Click the list arrow in the Pages field to turn off the sorting on this field.

7. Click the list arrow on the Title field Sort box, and select Ascending order.

8. Click the View button to see a list of your books in alphabetical order by title.

9. Choose File, Save As from the menu. Save the query as `Sorted by Title`. Close the query.

5. Matching a Single Criterion

You have divided your history books into four categories, and you frequently want to look at the books by category. It would be good to have a query for each one.

1. In the *history books* database, select the All History Books query, and click the Design button.

2. Type `Ancient` in the Criteria box of the Category field.

3. Choose File, Save As from the menu. Save the query as `Ancient History Books`.

4. Delete Ancient from the Criteria box, and then type `United States` in its place. Choose File, Save As from the menu. Save the query as `United States History Books`.

5. Delete United States from the Criteria box and then type `World` in its place. Choose File, Save As from the menu. Save the query as `World History Books`.

6. Delete World from the Criteria box and then type `England & Empire` in its place. Choose File, Save As from the menu. Save the query as `England & British Empire History Books`.

7. Close the query. Highlight each of the four new queries, and open them to make sure you typed the Criteria information correctly. If one of the queries does not work, select it and then go to Design view to re-enter the criterion.

6. Creating a Calculated Field

As the marketing manager for a cable company, you are trying to assess the desires of the television market. You want to be certain who is watching television, what they are watching, and what additional comments they have about your cable company. Within the questionnaire, there are questions to answer how many adults are in the household as well as how many children. There is not a question about the total members in the household. You need this information to calculate totals. So, you add a calculated field to an existing query.

1. Copy the *ea1-0403* database file, remove the read-only status from the copied file, and rename it `television questionnaire`. Open the *television questionnaire* database.

2. Click the Query object button, select the Questionnaire Query query, and click the Design button.

3. Select the Use field column in the design grid.

4. Choose Insert, Columns.

5. In the field text box of the new column, type `Persons in Home:[Adults]+[Children]`. Press Enter.

6. Click the View button to see the results of the calculated field.

7. Close the query and save your changes. Close the database, but leave Access open if you are planning to move on to the Challenge section.

Challenge exercises expand on or are somewhat related to skills presented in the lessons. Each exercise provides a brief narrative introduction followed by instructions in a numbered step format that are not as detailed as those in the Skill Drill section.

The database you will be using for the Challenge section is a modified version of the same database of history books you used in the Skill Drill section.

1. Creating a Query Using a Wizard

You have decided to try some of the more advanced query features on your history books database, but just to be safe, you decide to create a second database with the same data. The first feature you want to try out is the Simple Query Wizard. Make sure you read each wizard screen and read the directions.

1. Copy the *ea1-0404* database file, remove the read-only status of the copied file, and rename it `history book collection` and open it. This is the same file you used in the Skill Drill section.

2. Select Simple Query Wizard from the New Query dialog box.

3. Select all of the fields for this query. Display all of the fields in the query.

4. Call your query `History Book Collection` and then close the query.

2. Sorting on Multiple Fields

It would be convenient to use a query to sort the data in the table on more than one field. In this case, you want to first sort by category, and then sort alphabetically by title within each category.

1. In the *history book collection* database, open the History Book Collection query in Design view.

2. Move the Category field to the first field in the design grid.

3. Move the Title field to the right of the Category field.

4. Sort the Category field in ascending order.

5. Sort the Title field in ascending order.

6. Save the query as `Sorted by Category and Title`. Close the query.

3. Limiting Records by Looking for Parts of Text Fields

For years you have been compiling a special collection of books on Michigan history. You have given them special titles—all of the titles begin with "Michigan:" followed by the title of the book or pamphlet. All of these special titles are saved in the United States category. You would like to create a query to separate the titles in your Michigan history collection from the rest of the United States history books.

1. In the *history book collection* database, open the History Book Collection query in Design view.

2. Use the available help features on your computer or online to find instructions on entering text criteria in a query.

3. In the Criteria box of the Title field, type in the expression used to find all titles that begin with *Michigan:*.

4. Run the query to make sure only the books beginning with "Michigan:" are included. (*Hint:* There should be 184 records in this query.)

5. Save the query as `Michigan History Books`. Close the query.

4. Limiting Records by Setting Limits to Numeric Fields

In the previous Challenge, you limited the records by setting a criterion that included only part of the Title field. It would also be nice to be able to set beginning and end limits to a numeric field, such as the Year field in the current database.

1. In the *history book collection* database, open the History Book Collection query in Design view.

2. Use the available help features on your computer or online to find instructions on entering number criteria in a query.

3. In the Criteria box of the Year field, type in the expression used to find all titles that were published between World War I and World War II. (*Note:* World War I ended in 1918 and World War II began for the U.S. in 1941. Your query should include books published between 1919 and 1940. Both 1919 and 1940 should be included.)

4. Sort on the Year field in ascending order.

5. Run the query to make sure only books published from 1919 to 1940 are included. (*Hint:* There should be a total of 59 books when you successfully set up the query.)

6. Save the query as `Books Published Between the Wars`. Close the query.

5. Including or Excluding Records by Searching for Words Anywhere in a Text Field

In an earlier Challenge, you found all of the titles beginning with "Michigan:." You might also like to be able to find words or phrases anywhere in a field. You might find it useful to be able to exclude all records with a certain word in the title. In this case, you look for the word "revolution" anywhere in the title.

1. In the *history book collection* database, open the History Book Collection query in Design view.

2. Use the available help features on your computer or online to find instructions on entering text criteria in a query.

3. In the Criteria box of the Title field, type in the expression that will find records that have the word "revolution" in them.

4. Run the query to make sure all of the books include the word "revolution." (*Hint:* There should be a total of 17 books when you successfully set up the query.)

5. Go back to your help source, and figure out how to exclude those 17 records that have the word "revolution" in them. Type in the expression to remove those 17 records from your list of books. (*Hint:* You should have 1,136 records that don't include that word.)

6. Change the Criteria box in the Title field back to include only those books with "revolution" in the title.

7. Save the query as `Books About Revolution`. Close the query, and close the database unless you are going to proceed to the Discovery Zone.

Discovery Zone exercises require advanced knowledge of topics presented in *essentials* lessons, application of skills from multiple lessons, or self-directed learning of new skills.

1. Creating a Crosstab Query

Crosstab Queries are powerful tools for summarizing data from large databases. They summarize the relationship between two or more fields. For example, if you sent out a survey with ten questions, you would enter each person's responses in a single record. If you got 1,000 responses, you would have 1,000 records, each with a numeric response (e.g., a 1-to-5 rating scale) to the ten questions. Counting the number of times each response was given for each question would take a long time. A crosstab query can give you a table of responses in seconds.

Goal: Create a crosstab query that counts the books published each year by category of book, and then sort the crosstab in descending order.

Use the *ea1-0402* file to create a new database called `history books analysis` on your disk. Use help from your computer or online to understand how crosstab queries work and how they are built. Save the query as `Category by Year Crosstab`.

Hint #1: Put the years from the Year field down the left side of the crosstab table, and use the categories from the Category field as column headers. If you do it the other way, it will be extremely difficult to read.

Hint #2: Have the program count the instances, not add them up!

Hint #3: You will not perform the sort until you have built and run the crosstab.

2. Using Queries to Delete Records from Tables

Queries can be used for more than just creating dynasets of tables. They can also be used to directly affect the information in tables. They can be used to append records to existing tables, to update the information in tables, and even to delete records in tables. These must be used with care! Any time you are going to use one of these special query types, always back up your database first, just in case you change more than you intended.

Goal: Use a query to delete records from a table.

Use the *history books analysis* database you used in the first Discovery Zone exercise. (If you did not do the first exercise, copy *ea1-0402* and create a new database on your disk.) Create and run a Delete Query that removes all titles beginning with "Michigan:" from the History Books table. Do not save the query.

Hint #1: Look for the Query Type button on the Design view toolbar.

Hint #2: Use what you learned in the Challenge section to identify those records that begin with "Michigan:."

Hint #3: Run the query from the Design view window.

Hint #4: You will know you are on the right track when you run the query, and the program warns you that you are about to permanently and irrevocably delete 184 rows.

Creating and Using Forms

Objectives

In this project, you learn how to

- ✔ Create an AutoForm
- ✔ Enter and Edit Data Using a Form
- ✔ Save, Close, and Open a Form
- ✔ Create a New Form Using the Form Wizard
- ✔ Add Fields to Forms
- ✔ Move and Resize Fields in Forms
- ✔ Add a Form Header and Label

Key terms introduced in this project include

- ❑ AutoForm
- ❑ control
- ❑ field label
- ❑ field text box
- ❑ form
- ❑ Form Detail
- ❑ Form Footer
- ❑ Form Header
- ❑ label
- ❑ move handle
- ❑ section
- ❑ selection handles
- ❑ tab order

PROJECT 5

Why Would I Do This?

When you enter records in a table, each record is displayed in a row, and all records are displayed. If the table has many fields, you may not be able to see all of the fields in the table onscreen, and you might find it difficult to find the record you want with all the records displayed. A ***form*** is generally used to display one record at a time, and you can place the fields anywhere on the screen. Even if a record has many fields, you may be able to see them all on one screen. You can move the fields around and add text to the form so that it resembles paper forms that are already in use. It is often easier for people to transfer data from paper forms to a form on the screen that looks the same.

Using a form offers the following advantages:

- You can select the fields you want to include in the form, and you can arrange them in the order you want.
- You can display only one record at a time, which makes it easier to concentrate on that record.
- You can make the form more graphically appealing.

Access provides an ***AutoForm*** that you can create quickly without a great deal of work. The Auto-Form is a wizard that sets up an input screen that includes all of the fields in the table. If this form isn't what you need, you can edit the form in Design view. In this project, you use both methods to create forms.

Visual Summary

When you have completed this project, you will have created a form that looks like Figure 5.1.

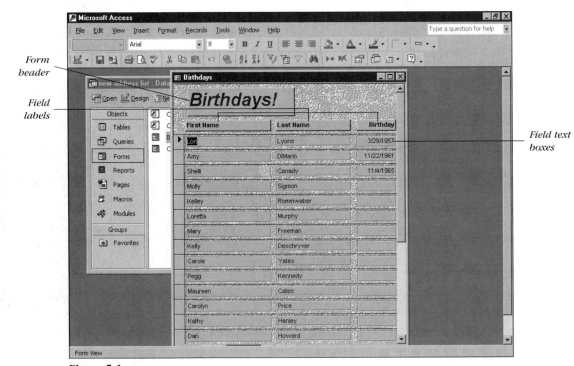

Figure 5.1

Lesson 1: Creating an AutoForm

If you want a simple form that lists each field in a single column and displays one record at a time, you can use one of the Access Form Wizards to create an AutoForm. The Form Wizards look at the structure of your database table and then create a form automatically. You simply choose the commands to start the Wizards.

To Create an AutoForm

1 **Launch Access. Click *More Files* in the task pane to open an existing file.**

2 **Copy the *ea1-0501* file, remove the read-only status of the copied file, and rename the file `new address list`. Open the new database.**
You should see the Database window that lists the Contacts table.

3 **Click the Forms object button.**
No forms are listed because you have not yet created or saved any (see Figure 5.2).

Forms object button

Figure 5.2

4 **Click the <u>N</u>ew button.**
The New Form dialog box is displayed. This dialog box is used to select a table to use with the form and then you decide whether you want to use one of the Form Wizards or start with a blank form.

5 **Click the down arrow in the box labeled *Choose the table or query where the object's data comes from.***
A list of the tables and queries available in the database displays (see Figure 5.3). You can base a form on either a query or a table. You must select the Contacts table, even though it is the only table or query available.

(Continues)

To Create an AutoForm (Continued)

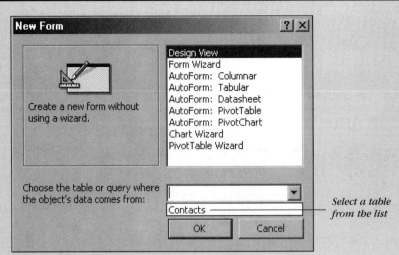

Figure 5.3

6 **Click *Contacts*.**

7 **Click the *AutoForm: Columnar* option and then click OK.**

The Form Wizard creates the form. This step may take several seconds. The status bar displays the progress so that you can see that Access is working. After the AutoForm is built, Access displays the table's first record. Notice that the fields are displayed in a column in the form. Your screen may not have the same background settings. The navigation buttons are displayed at the bottom of the form to enable you to move through the records (see Figure 5.4). Keep this form onscreen as you continue to the next lesson, where you learn more about the navigation buttons.

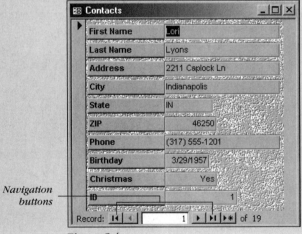

Figure 5.4

To extend your knowledge...

Other Ways to Create a New Form

You can also create a new form by clicking the drop-down arrow to the right of the New Object button on the toolbar in the Access window. When you are in the table Datasheet view, you can click the New Object list button and select either the Form button or the AutoForm button to create a new form.

Lesson 2: Entering and Editing Data Using a Form

Forms often make it easier to enter and edit data. Before you save the form, you may want to try some data entry to be sure that you like the structure of the form. If you don't like how the form is set up, you can change it or create a new one, as you learn later in this project.

You can use the same tools to enter, find, sort, and display records in a form that you use in a table. In this lesson, you will add and edit a record using a form.

To Enter and Edit Data Using a Form

1 **The AutoForm based on the Contacts table should still be onscreen from the previous lesson. Click either of the New Record buttons.**
New Record buttons are located both on the toolbar and with the navigation buttons on the bottom of the form window. This step adds a new record, and a blank form is displayed (see Figure 5.5).

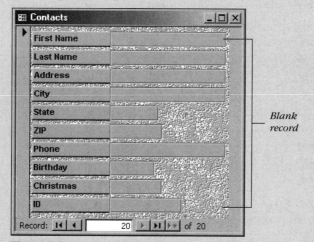

Figure 5.5

2 **Type the following data, pressing** Tab⇥ **after each entry to move to the next field.**

Janet

Eisenhut

455 Sheridan

Indianapolis

IN

46204

(317) 555-6588

3/29/60

Yes

(Continues)

To Enter and Edit Data Using a Form (Continued)

Notice that when you type the phone number, Access automatically provides parentheses around the area code, moves you over so that you can type the exchange, and provides a hyphen after the exchange.

You may have to scroll down to see all the fields in the form. When you reach the last field—the ID field—you do not have to enter a value, because it is a counter field. Also, remember that when you move to another record, Access automatically saves the record you just entered. Keep in mind that the record is saved in the underlying Contacts table. You don't have to worry about updating the table separately.

3 **Click the First Record button.**
This moves you to the first record in the table.

4 **Click the Next Record button to scroll through the records until you see the record for Shelli Canady.**
This is the record you want to edit. Notice that the Birthday field is blank.

If you have problems...
If you can't find the record that you want to edit by scrolling, you can open the Edit menu and use the Find command. (Refer to Project 3, "Entering and Editing Data," for more information on searching records.)

5 **Click in the Birthday field.**
This action moves the insertion point to the field you want to edit.

6 **Type 11/4/65.**
This enters a birthday for Shelli.

7 **Click the First Record button.**
This moves you back to the first record and saves the change to the record you just edited. Keep the form open onscreen as you continue to the next lesson.

To extend your knowledge...
Undoing Editing Changes
If you make an editing change and then want to undo it, open the Edit menu and choose the Undo command, or press the Undo button. This will undo your last change.

Keyboard Navigation
Besides using the navigation buttons, you can use the keyboard to move among records and fields. Press Tab↹ or ↓ or → to move to the next field; ⬆Shift+Tab↹ or ↑ or ← to move to the previous field; PgUp to scroll to the previous record; and PgDn to scroll to the next record. Ctrl+Home will move the insertion point to the first field in the first record and Ctrl+End will move the insertion point to the last field in the last record.

Lesson 3: Saving, Closing, and Opening a Form

If you use the form and like how it is organized, you can save the form so that you can use it again later. If you try to close the form without saving, Access reminds you to save. You don't have to save the form; you should save it only if you intend to use it again. If you accidentally close the form without saving it, you can simply re-create it (follow the steps in Lesson 1 of this project).

As with the other objects you have created, you are prompted to type a name the first time you save the form. You can type up to 64 characters, including spaces. After you have saved the form, you can close it and open it again when you want to use it.

To Save, Close, and Open a Form

❶ The AutoForm that uses the Contacts table should still be open onscreen. Click the Save button.
The Save As dialog box is displayed (see Figure 5.6). The default name, Contacts, is the name of the table on which the form is based.

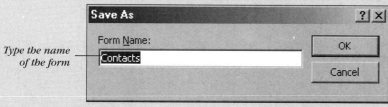

Type the name of the form

Figure 5.6

❷ Type `Contacts AutoForm` **and then click the OK button.**
Access saves the form.

❸ Click the Close button in the upper-right corner of the form window to close the form.
The form window closes, and you see the Database window again. Notice that your new form is now included in the Forms list (see Figure 5.7).

New form

Figure 5.7

❹ Double-click *Contacts AutoForm* **to open it.**

(Continues)

To Save, Close, and Open a Form (Continued)

Access displays the first record in the table on which the form is based. You can add, modify, or delete records. When you are finished working in the form, close it again. As you move from field to field, Access automatically saves any changes you make.

5 **Click the Close button to close the form.**
Access closes the form. Keep the *new address list* database open and continue to the next lesson.

To extend your knowledge...

Other Ways to Save a Form

You can choose File, Save from the menu or press Ctrl+S to save the form instead of using the Save button.

Lesson 4: Creating a New Form Using the Form Wizard

When you create a form for the first time, starting from scratch can be confusing. Fortunately, Access provides a Form Wizard to assist you. A form consists of several different elements. Each part of the form is called a **section**. The main, or **Form Detail**, section is the area in which records are displayed. Each record can have two parts: the **field text box**, which is the data within the field, and the **field label**, which is the name of the field within the form. You can also add **Form Headers** (top of form) or **Form Footers** (bottom of form). Anything you include in the section will be displayed onscreen in Form view when you use the form. You can also add page headers and page footers, which are not visible onscreen in Form view but will appear if you print the form.

The rest of this project covers some of the common features you can use when you create a form using the Form Wizard. Keep in mind, however, that Access offers other form features, such as drop-down lists, groups of option buttons, graphic objects, and much more.

You decided it would be a good idea to send birthday greetings to your customers to help maintain good relations. You added a birthday field to your Contacts table, but you have entered only the birthdays of contacts who are your customers. To make sure that birthday greetings are sent to your customers, you want to create a simple form that lists just the person's name and his or her birthday.

To Create a New Form Using the Form Wizard

1 **In the *new address list* Database window, click the Forms object button (if necessary); then click the New button.**
The New Form dialog box is displayed (see Figure 5.8). Before you choose whether you want to use the Form Wizard or start with a blank form, you should select the table you want to use for the form.

To Create a New Form Using the Form Wizard

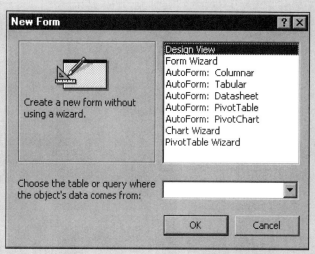

Figure 5.8

2 Click the down arrow in the box labeled *Choose the table or query where the object's data comes from.*

In the New Form dialog box, you are given a list of all tables and queries in the open database. You must select the table or query you want to be in the form.

3 Click *Contacts.*

You may use more than one table or query, if available, but you must first select the main table or query.

4 Select the Form Wizard option from the top of the list, and click OK.

The Form Wizard starts.

5 Click the First Name field from the <u>A</u>vailable Fields list, and click the Select button to move it to the <u>S</u>elected Fields list.

This is the first of two fields in the form that you add in this lesson (see Figure 5.9).

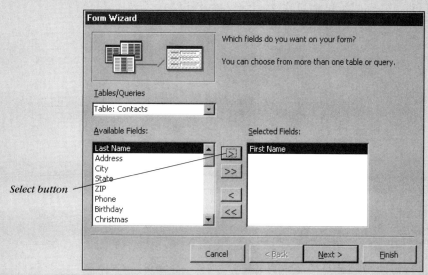

Figure 5.9

(Continues)

To Create a New Form Using the Form Wizard (Continued)

6 **Click the Birthday field from the Available Fields list and then click the Select button to move it to the Selected Fields list. Click Next.**
There are six form layouts from which to choose. The right form layout depends on the data within the form.

7 **Select the Tabular option, and click Next.**
You are next asked to choose a background for the form. It is a personal preference option.

8 **Select Stone, and click Next.**
The final dialog box of the Form Wizard suggests a title for the form.

9 **Type Birthdays, and click Finish.**
The Birthdays form is created (see Figure 5.10).

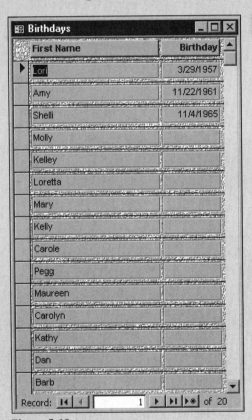

Figure 5.10

To extend your knowledge...

Creating a Form Using Design View

Sometimes the Form Wizards do not create exactly the form you want. When that happens, you can start from a blank form and create one that better suits your needs. The form can include any text, fields, and other controls you want to incorporate. ***Controls*** are any objects selected from the toolbox, such as text boxes, check boxes, or option buttons. Many times, it is simpler to create a form using the Form Wizard and then making modifications in Design view.

Controls Tied to the Table Fields

Some controls are bound to the fields in the table. If you create a text box for a field and enter data in the field in the form, for example, the field in the table is updated. Other controls are not tied to the table but, instead, are saved with the form. For example, you may want to add a descriptive title to the form. This type of text is called a ***label*** and is not bound to the underlying table.

Lesson 5: Adding Fields to Forms

When you want to set up or change the structure of a form, you must use Design view. Access includes the following items to help you design the form:

- **Toolbar**. Use the toolbar to access some form design commands. You can click the Save button to save the form, the View button to view the form, and so on. If you place the pointer on a button, the button name appears directly under the button.
- **Toolbox**. Use the toolbox to add items, such as labels or images, to the form. As with the toolbar, you can place the mouse pointer over a toolbox button to see its name. The Toolbox may not be displayed when you create a new form. If it is not, click the Toolbox button to display it.
- **Field list**. Use the field list to add fields to the form. The field list box may not be displayed when you create a new form. If it is not, click the Field List button in the toolbar.
- **Rulers**. Use the rulers to help position controls on the form.

You use the field list to add fields to the form. The new form you are creating for the Contacts table should still be on your screen from the preceding lesson. Try adding fields to the form now.

To Add Fields to a Form

❶ **Click the View button to switch to Design view. Maximize the form. Move the toolbox and field list box to the right side of the screen, if necessary.**

 If you have problems...

If the Design view does not display the Field List box, click the Field List button on the Forms Design toolbar. If the Toolbox does not appear, click the Toolbox button. If the Ruler does not appear, choose View, Ruler from the menu bar. Drag the boxes to the right of the Form Design window to optimize your working space.

❷ **Click the Birthday field text box in the Detail section, press** ⟨⬆Shift⟩**, and select the Birthday field label in the Form Header section.**

❸ **Drag to the right and drop the field so that its left edge is at approximately the 3 1/4″ mark on the horizontal ruler.**

As you drag, your pointer displays box borders. You can use this to help place the field onscreen. The field text box, which holds a place for the contents of the field you have selected, is placed where you release the box.

This places the field text box and field label, which is the field name, on the form (see Figure 5.11). The label box will be placed to the left of the text box, so you need to leave space for it.

(Continues)

To Add Fields to a Form (Continued)

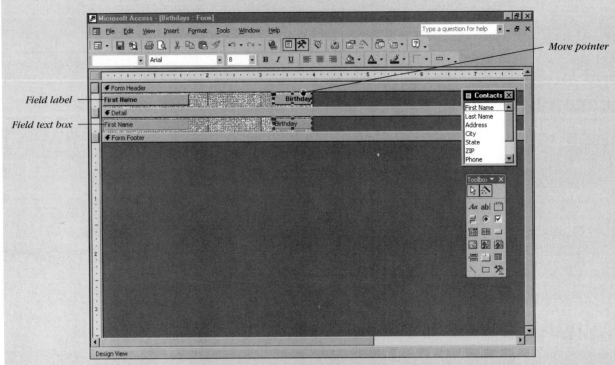

Field label

Field text box

Move pointer

Figure 5.11

④ **Drag the Last Name field from the field list box to the Detail section of the form. Place this field to the right of the First Name field at the 1 3/4″ mark horizontally and the same position vertically as the other fields.**

This step adds a third field to the form. As you drag and drop the field, try to align the field with the field above it. Make sure that you leave enough room between the two fields—don't drop the fields on top of one another. You now need to move the label to the Form Header section.

⑤ **Click anywhere in the form to deselect the fields.**

To move the label to the Form Header section, you must cut the label from the Detail section, then paste it in the Form Header section. Access does not allow dragging between the sections.

⑥ **Click the Last Name field label in the Detail section and then click the Cut button.**

Be sure that only the field label box is selected.

? **If you have problems...**

If you accidentally delete both field text box and field label, click the Undo button. Click just the field label and redo step 5.

---

⑦ **Click in the Form Header section and click the Paste button.**

Your form now includes three fields (see Figure 5.12). You can save and name the form so that these changes won't be lost. In the next lesson, you will move the field label box, which currently overlaps another label box.

To Add Fields to a Form

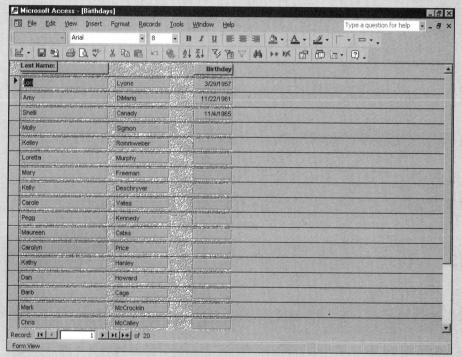

Overlapping field labels

Figure 5.12

❽ Click the Save button.
The changes are saved to the form.

❾ Click the View button on the toolbar.
The edited form is displayed (see Figure 5.13). You can see whether you need to make any adjustments to the form, such as moving a label, adding a new label, or resizing the fields. Keep the Birthdays form open, and continue with the next lesson.

Figure 5.13

To extend your knowledge...

Creating Other Forms; Modifying Forms

In addition to creating a blank form, you can use the Form Wizard to create other types of forms, such as columnar, tabular, charts, and pivot tables.

To modify an existing form, click its name in the Database window; then click the Design command button. Alternatively, you can open the form and change to Design view by clicking the View button.

Using Selection and Move Handles

Selection handles are small squares that appear at the corners and on the sides of boxes that are used to change the size of a box. In the Detail area of a form, selecting either the field label or field text box allows you to move them together, even though handles appear all the way around only the box on which you click. Both the label and text box have a large handle in the upper-left corner, called the **move handle,** which is used to move either box independently.

Lesson 6: Moving and Resizing Fields in Forms

When you create your form, you may find it difficult to get the fields in the right place the first time. That's okay; you can move or resize the fields after you have added them to the form. You can drag and place them visually, using the ruler as a guide. Otherwise, you can have Access align the fields with an underlying grid—making them an equal distance apart.

In this lesson, you move the Last Name field label next to the First Name field and lengthen the Last Name field label and text box.

To Move and Resize Fields in Forms

1 **In the Birthdays form, click the View button to return to Design view.**
To make changes to the form design, you must return to Design view. You cannot make changes in Form view.

2 **Click the Last Name field label.**
Selection handles appear around the borders (see Figure 5.14).

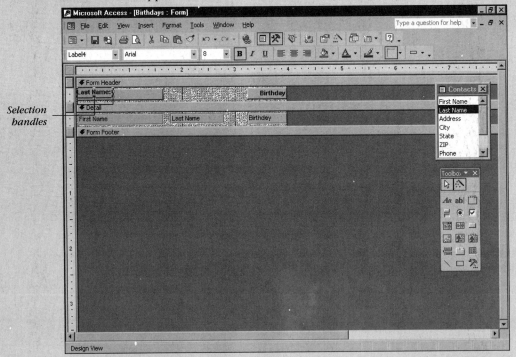

Selection handles

Figure 5.14

3 **Place the mouse pointer on one of the borders of the Last Name field label, but not on one of the handles.**
When the pointer is in the correct spot, it should resemble a small hand (see Figure 5.15). If you see arrows rather than the hand, the pointer isn't in the correct spot. Move it around until you see the hand.

To Move and Resize Fields in Forms

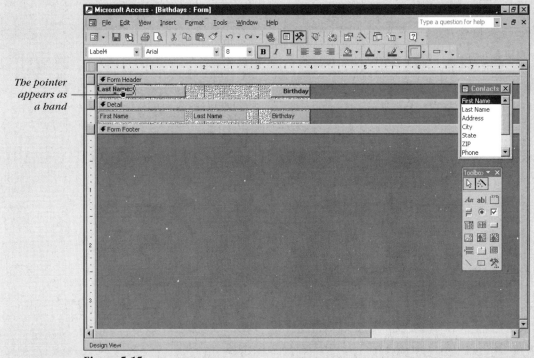

The pointer appears as a hand

Figure 5.15

4 **Drag the Last Name field label to the right of the First Name field label, and place it so that the left edge of the Last Name field label is at approximately the 1 3/4″ mark on the horizontal ruler.**
Now the field label is directly above the field text box.

5 **Move the pointer to the right side of the Last Name field label, and place it on the center handle. The pointer turns into a two-headed arrow (see Figure 5.16).**

(Continues)

To Move and Resize Fields in Forms (Continued)

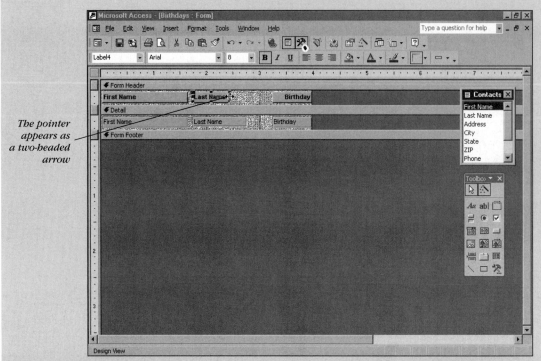

The pointer appears as a two-headed arrow

Figure 5.16

The Last Name field label and Last Name field text boxes are shorter than necessary, so you are going to change their sizes to approximately 1 1/2″ wide.

6 Make the field larger by dragging the right side of the field to the right. Stop at the 3 1/8″ mark on the horizontal ruler so that the field is about 1 1/2″ wide.

7 Select the Last Name field text box, and repeat step 6 to lengthen it.

8 Select the Last Name field label. Click again inside the label to edit it. Delete the colon at the end of the text.

9 Click the View button to return to Form view to view the edited form (see Figure 5.17).

To Move and Resize Fields in Forms

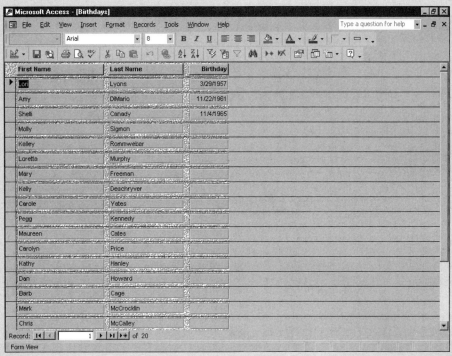

Figure 5.17

🔟 **Click the Save button.**

This step saves the form with the changes you just made. Keep the Birthdays form open. In the next lesson, you add a Form Header to the form.

If you have problems...

If you see arrows in the form and begin to drag, you will resize the field. If you resize by accident, click the Undo button to undo the change.

When you want to move a field, be sure to place the pointer on the edge of the field and wait until it changes to a hand. Don't place the pointer on one of the selection handles.

To extend your knowledge...

Moving the Label Box or Text Box

If you want to move the label box separately from the text box, point to the move handle. When the pointer turns into a pointing finger, you can click and drag the label box to a new location. The text box can move independently from the label box by using the same technique. Point to the larger box in the upper-left corner of the text box until the pointer turns into a pointing finger; then click and drag the text box to the desired location.

Changing Tab Order

When you enter data into a form, the insertion point jumps from one box to the next each time you press (Tab). This is called the ***tab order***. When you move fields around in a form, you may need to change the tab order. In Design view, select <u>V</u>iew, Ta<u>b</u> Order from the menu and a list of fields will be displayed. Click the button to the left of the field to select the one that you want to move and then click and drag it to the desired position on the list. You can also click the <u>A</u>uto Order button, which often (but not always) sets the tab order the way you want it.

Lesson 7: Adding a Form Header and Label

The final step for this form is to add a Form Header that will appear at the top of the form and to include a label showing the name of the form. Form Headers show up at the top of every form. Form Footers are similar to Form Headers, but they appear at the bottom of every form.

In this lesson, you first add a new section to the form—the Form Header section—and then you add a label to the form. In addition to adding the label, you can change the font and font size of the text so that the form label stands out.

To Add a Form Header and Label

1 **Click the View button to return to the Design view of the Birthday form.**
You want to include the form label in the header, but the section is too small. Therefore, you need to adjust the size of the section (see Figure 5.18).

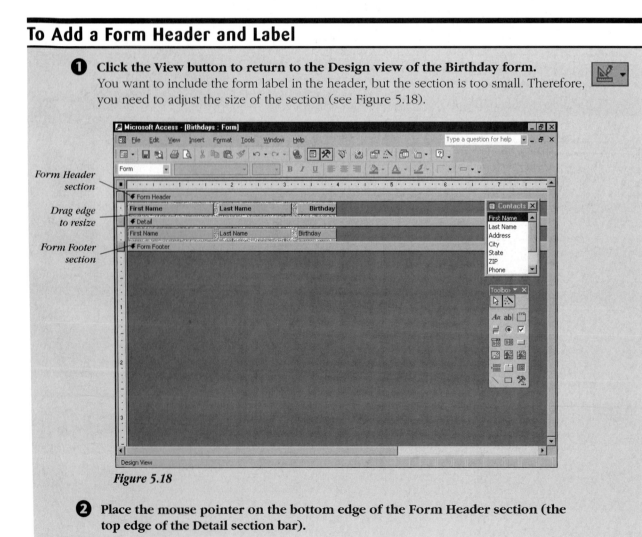

Figure 5.18

2 **Place the mouse pointer on the bottom edge of the Form Header section (the top edge of the Detail section bar).**

To Add a Form Header and Label

The pointer should change to display a thick horizontal bar with a two-sided arrow cross-bar (see Figure 5.19). This pointer shape indicates that you are about to resize this section.

The pointer appears as a two-sided arrow

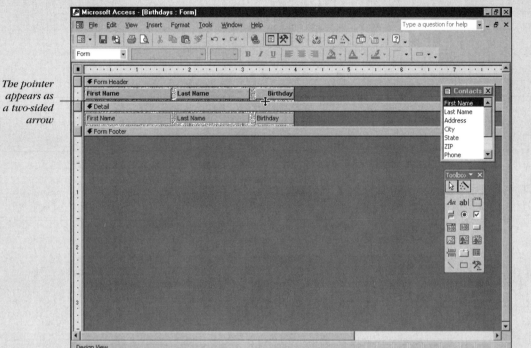

Figure 5.19

3 **Drag down until the Form Header is about 1″ tall.**

You can use the rulers along the left edge of the form's Design view to gauge the size of the section. Don't worry if the size isn't exact. Now that the header is a little bigger, you can move the existing labels and add a new label to the form.

4 **Press ⬆Shift), and click each of the three labels in the Form Header. With the hand pointer, drag them down to the bottom of the Form Header section.**

5 **Click the Label button in the toolbox.**

The Label button has an uppercase and lowercase "A" on it. Remember that you can place your pointer on a button to see its name.

6 **Position the crosshairs of the pointer near the upper-left corner of the Form Header section. Drag to the right and down to draw a box. Make the box approximately 2″ wide and 1/2″ tall.**

The pointer should appear as a small crosshair with an "A" underneath while you are positioning it (see Figure 5.20). When you release the mouse button, you see a label box with the insertion point inside.

(Continues)

To Add a Form Header and Label (Continued)

The Label pointer

Figure 5.20

? If you have problems...

If you make the label box too small, you can always resize it. Click the box to select it; then place the pointer on one of the selection handles and drag to resize.

---

7 **Type** Birthdays!
This is the text you want to include as the label. As you can see, the text is fairly small, but you can change it.

8 **Click outside the text area to end the text-editing mode.**

9 **Click inside the box to select it.**
Notice that the formatting toolbar displays the font and font size in the Font and Font Size drop-down lists. You can use these lists to change the font and the font size (see Figure 5.21).

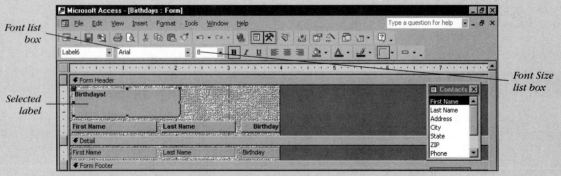
Font list box
Selected label
Font Size list box

Figure 5.21

10 **Click the down arrow next to the Font Size box. Click 24 (or the next largest size available on your system).**
This changes the font in the label box to 24-point type. You don't have to change the actual font, but you can make the text italic.

11 **Click the Italic button on the toolbar.**
Access makes the text italic.

12 **Click the Save button on the toolbar.**
The form is saved with the changes you have made.

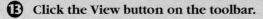

13 **Click the View button on the toolbar.**

To Add a Form Header and Label

This switches you to Form view so that you can see the form you just created (see Figure 5.22).

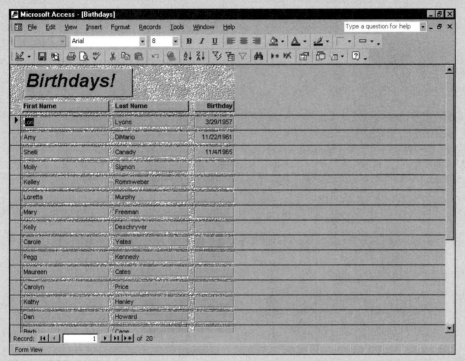

Figure 5.22

 Close the Birthdays form and then close the *new address list* database.
If you have completed your session on the computer, exit Access and Windows before you turn it off. Otherwise, continue with the "Checking Concepts and Terms" section of this project.

 ## To extend your knowledge...

Printing Forms and Selected Records

The purpose for creating forms is to make it easy for users to input and read data onscreen. Should you need to print a form, you can view it first by clicking the Print Preview button. If you click the Print button, all records in the database will be printed in a continuous form. If you want to print one record per page, click the Page Break button in the Toolbox and drag the small Page Break symbol onto the form.

If you want to print a selected record, move to that record and select File, Print to open the Print dialog box. Choose the Selected Record(s) option button. Choosing this option prints the current record.

Summary

This project focused on the use of the various form features built into Access. You learned how to create an AutoForm from a table and how to create a new form using the Form Wizard. You entered and edited information in a form and modified the form structure by adding fields, moving and resizing fields, and adding form headers and labels.

To enhance your ability to create effective forms, look for help on adding page headers and footers. Pay particular attention to the procedure for adding current information, such as the date, time, or page numbers to headers and footers.

Checking Concepts and Terms

Multiple Choice

Circle the letter of the correct answer for each of the following questions.

1. How do you create a new record using a form? [L2]

   a. Scroll to the last record and then edit it.

   b. Edit the first record displayed.

   c. Click the New Object button on the toolbar.

   d. Click the New Record button on the Navigation bar and then enter data into the empty form.

2. Which type of section includes the record information? [L4]

   a. Detail

   b. Page Header

   c. Page Footer

   d. Form Header

3. What should the pointer look like to move a field? [L6]

   a. a hand

   b. a white cross

   c. a two-headed arrow

   d. a crosshair

4. Which of the following is a fast way to create a form based on the current table? [L1]

   a. Use the QuickForm.

   b. Use an AutoForm.

   c. Open a blank form and then drag the fields onto it from the Field List window.

   d. Click NewForm on the Toolbox.

5. You can generate all the following by using the Form Wizard, except what? [L5]

   a. columnar forms

   b. charts

   c. pivot tables

   d. spreadsheets

Screen ID

Label each element of the Access screen shown in Figure 5.23.

A. Label pointer
B. Toolbox
C. Field text box
D. Label button
E. Toolbox button
F. Font list box
G. Field list button
H. Field label
I. Font size list box
J. Field list

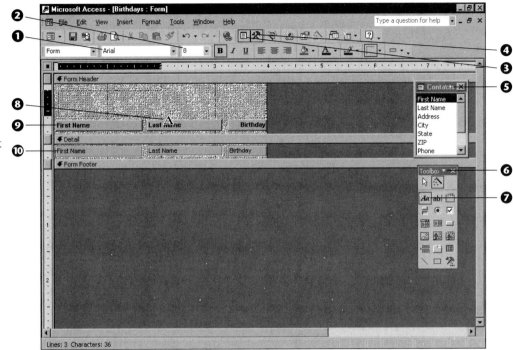

Figure 5.23

1. _____
2. _____
3. _____
4. _____
5. _____

6. _____
7. _____
8. _____
9. _____
10. _____

Discussion

1. In Project 3, you answered a question about when you might use forms and when you might want to enter data directly into the table. Now that you have some experience with forms, has your opinion changed? Why? Do you think you will use forms or tables (or some combination) for data entry into tables you anticipate using in the future? How will you do this?

2. If you have a table with a few fields (fewer than 10), what would be the advantage of using one of the form wizards to create a columnar or tabular form? What would be the advantage, if any, to creating the form in Design view?

3. You can add form headers, form footers, page headers, and page footers. When would you use page headers & footers? When would you use form headers and footers?

Skill Drill

Skill Drill exercises reinforce project skills. Each skill reinforced is the same, or nearly the same, as a skill presented in the project. Each exercise includes a brief narrative introduction, followed by detailed instructions in a step-by-step format.

The database you will be using for these exercises contains two tables, one with information about short story books, and the other with information about the authors of these books.

1. Creating an AutoForm

Entering the data into the Book information table is not easy, because the fields scroll off the screen to the right. It would be a good idea to create a form to make data entry easier. You decide to use the AutoForm feature to create the new form.

To create an AutoForm, complete the following steps:

1. Copy the *ea1-0502* database file, remove the read-only status of the copied file, and name it `short story books`. Select and open the Book information table; then look at the fields. Click the Close Window button to close the table.
2. Click the Forms object button, and click <u>N</u>ew to create a new form.
3. Select the Book information table from the drop-down list.
4. Select the *AutoForm: Columnar* wizard, and click OK.
5. Close the Form, select <u>Y</u>es to save the form, and type `Book information data input`.

2. Adding Data to the Form

You just found a short story book at the local used bookstore and cannot wait to try out the new form you just created.

To add data to the form, complete the following steps:

1. In the *short story books* database, select the *Book information data input* form, and click the <u>O</u>pen button.
2. Click the New Record button on the toolbar.
3. Press ⏎Enter to skip the BookID field, which is entered automatically.
4. Enter `Rinehart, Mary Roberts` in the Author field.
5. Enter `Affinities and Other Stories` in the Title field. Press Tab↹.
6. Enter `1920` for the Year field, `282` for the Page field, and `Review of Reviews` for the Publisher field.
7. Close the form.

3. Editing Data in the Form

When looking more carefully at the book you just entered, you find that the publisher you listed was just a reprint house, and that the original publisher was George H. Doran. You also find out that the date of publication for *Auld Licht Idylls,* by J. M. Barrie (also the author of the children's classic *Peter Pan*) was written in 1888. You need to go into your form and change this information.

To edit data in the form, complete the following steps:

1. In the *short story books* database, select the *Book information data input* form and then click the <u>O</u>pen button.
2. Place the insertion point in the Title field, and click the Find button.

3. Type `Affinities` in the Fi_n_d What drop-down list box and then select Start of Field from the Mat_ch_ drop-down list box.

4. Click _F_ind Next. Move the Find and Replace dialog box, if necessary, and change Review of Reviews to `George H. Doran` in the Publisher field.

5. Place the insertion point in the Title field, and type `Auld` in the Fi_n_d What drop-down list box.

6. Click _F_ind Next. Type `1888` in the Year field.

7. Close the Find and Replace dialog box and then close the Book information form.

4. Creating a New Form in Design View

Now that you have created a form for the Book information table, you decide that you also want one for the Author information table.

To create a new form in Design view, complete the following steps:

1. In the _short story books_ database, click the Forms object button; then click _N_ew to create a new form.

2. Select the Author information table from the drop-down list.

3. Select Design View, and click OK.

4. Maximize the Form window. Click the Toolbox and Field List buttons if they are not turned on. Select _V_iew, _R_uler to turn the rulers on, if necessary.

5. Drag the Author field onto the form about 1/4″ down and 3/4″ to the right of the left edge.

6. Drag the DOB field to the 3″ mark. Line it up to the right of the Author field.

7. Place the Birth City, State, and Birth Country fields under the Author field, about 1/4″ apart. Use the hand pointer to adjust the field locations, if necessary.

8. Click the View button to see your form.

9. Close the form, and save it as `Author information data input`.

5. Moving and Resizing Fields

You decide that you do not like the look of the form. You would like the last three fields to line up across the screen.

To move and resize fields, complete the following steps:

1. In the _short story books_ database, open the _Author information data input_ form in Design view.

2. Grab the State field, and move it just to the right of the Birth City field.

3. Grab the Birth Country field, and move it to the right of the State field. Don't worry if the field overlaps the edge of the work area—the work area will widen automatically.

4. Click the View button to see your form.

6. Deleting Field Labels and Adding a Label

Your form still does not look right. It would look much better without the field names and with a single label describing all three fields.

To delete field labels and add a label, complete the following steps:

1. In the _short story books_ database, click the View button to return to Design view.

2. Click the Birth City field label. Handles should appear around the label on the left, but not around the field text box (which should have one large handle in the upper-left corner).

3. Click Del to remove the Birth City label.

4. Select and then delete the field labels for the State and Birth Country fields.

5. Select all three fields in the second row, and move them down about 1/2″ and over to the left edge of the form. (_Note_: Click the Birth City field, hold down ⬆Shift, and click the State and Birth Country fields.)

6. Click the Label button, and click and drag the crosshair pointer to place a text box above the three fields you just moved.

7. Type `Place of Birth:` in the text box.

8. Click outside the text box and then click it again to select it. Click the Bold button. Resize the text box if necessary. Your Design window should look like Figure 5.24.

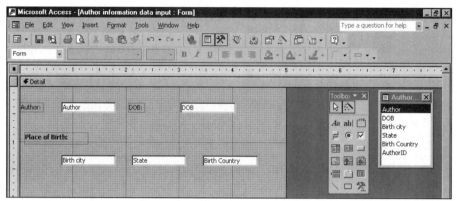

Figure 5.24

9. Click the View button, and click the Next Record button a few times to see how your form works. The fourth and fifth records should contain data in all five fields.

10. Close the form, and save your changes.

Challenge exercises expand on or are somewhat related to skills presented in the lessons. Each exercise provides a brief narrative introduction followed by instructions in a numbered step or bulleted list format that are not as detailed as those in the Skill Drill section.

The database you will be using for the Challenge section is the same database of short story books and authors you used in the Skill Drill section. The Book information data input form has been modified. Before you start the Challenge exercises, spend a little time looking at the form in Form view; then look at it in Design view. Notice how it has been laid out and how some of the field labels have been deleted and replaced by other labels.

1. Adding the Date and Time to the Form Header

You have decided to make your Book information data input form more user-friendly. Because you expect to print single forms frequently, you would also like to make the forms more informative. The first thing you want to do is to add the current date to the Form Header.

To add the date and time to a Form Header, complete the following steps:

1. Copy the *ea1-0503* database file, remove the read-only status of the copied file, and rename it `revised short story books`.

2. Open the database and open the Book information data input form in Form view. Maximize the form window and examine the form layout.

3. Move to Design view and examine the layout of the form.

4. Use the Insert menu to place the date (in the 12/31/99 format) and the time (in the 11:59 PM format) in the form.

5. Click the View button. If the date and time are not in the upper-left corner of the Form Header, return to Design view, and move them to that location.

6. Close the form, and save your changes.

2. Adding a Page Number to a Page Footer

You have added the date and time to the Form Header; now you want to keep track of the page numbers.

To add the page number to a Page Footer, complete the following steps:

1. In the *revised short story books* database, open the *Book information data input* form in Design view. Maximize the form window.

2. Scroll down until you can see the Form Footer area, if necessary.

3. Use the Insert menu to place the page number (in the Page N of M format).

4. Place the page number at the bottom of the page, and center align it.

5. Notice that the program has added Page Header and Page Footer sections. The page number is in the Page Footer section.

6. Click the View button to look at the page number. Notice that the page number does not appear. Use your Help menu to find out why it does not show up here and what possible use this feature might be. (*Hint*: Use the Contents tab and the Forms topic. The Creating Forms subtopic is helpful.)

7. Close the form, and save your changes.

3. Adding an Image to a Page Header

You have added the date and time to the Form Header and the page number to the Page Footer. Now you want to improve the appearance of your form. The first thing you want to do is to add a small graphic image to the Form Header.

To add an image to a Page Header, complete the following steps:

1. In the *revised short story books* database, open the *Book information data input* form in Design view. Maximize the form window.

2. Use the Help menu or online help to figure out how to add the books.bmp image file— included with your student files—to your form.

3. Move the image to the top of the right side of the Form Header.

4. Click the View button to see how the image looks on the form.

5. Close the form, and save your changes.

4. Customizing the Look of the Form

You have added an image to the form. Now you would like to make some changes to the overall form design. You decide to try to change the background color of the Detail area, and give the field labels and field text boxes a special effect.

To customize the look of a form, complete the following steps:

1. In the *revised short story books* database, open the *Book information data input* form in Design view. Maximize the form window.

2. Find the Fill/Back Color button, and change the background color to a pale blue.

3. Select all of the field labels and field text boxes. (*Hint*: You can move the pointer to the vertical ruler near the top of the Detail area. It changes to a right arrow. Click and drag down below the last row of fields, and release the mouse button. All of the field labels and field text boxes are selected.)

4. Use the right mouse button on any one of the selected field labels or field text boxes. Find the option that will enable you to customize these boxes, and select the third option on the first row.

5. Click the View button to see how your changes look on the form. Your form should look like Figure 5.25.

6. Close the form, and save your changes.

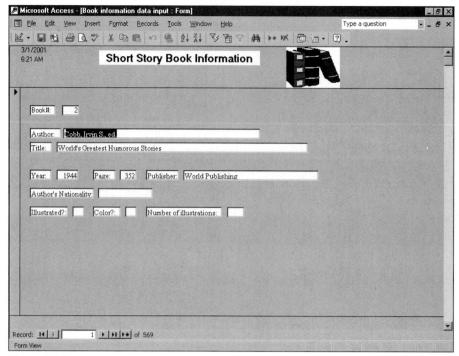

Figure 5.25

5. Inserting a Page Break and Printing a Form

The forms will print continuously if you don't add an artificial page break in form Design view.

To insert a page break and print a form, complete the following steps:

1. In the *revised short story books* database, open the *Book information data input* form in Design view. Maximize the form window.
2. Find and click the Page Break button on the Toolbox.
3. Move the new pointer and click about 1/4" under the last row of fields.
4. Click the View button to move to Form view.
5. Choose File, Print from the menu.
6. Make sure the correct printer is selected and the printer is turned on.
7. Choose the Selected Record(s) option to print only the current record and then click OK.
8. Close the form, and save your changes.

6. Copying a Form and Basing It on a Query

Your collection includes books by a number of different publishers, but you specialize in books published by Scribner's. You would like to create a query that would show just Scribner's books, and then use the new query as the source for a copy of the form on which you have been working.

To copy a form and base it on a query, complete the following steps:

1. In the *revised short story books* database, create a query in Design view. Add all of the fields from the Book information table. Use Scribner's as the Criteria in the Publisher field and then sort on Author and Title. Save the query as `Scribner's Books`.
2. Move to the Forms window. Use the Access help resources to find out how to make a copy of the Book information data input form, and paste it as `Scribner's information`.

3. Switch to the Scribner's information form in Design view. Use the Access help resources to view the Properties box for the entire form. (*Hint*: If you want to use the shortcut menu, the ruler must be turned on. If you want to use the menus, the whole form must be selected.)

4. Change the Record Source from the Book information table to the Scribner's Books query.

5. Switch to Form view, and scroll through a few records to make sure the only books shown are the ones published by Scribner's.

6. Close the form, and save your changes.

Discovery Zone exercises require advanced knowledge of topics presented in *essentials* lessons, application of skills from multiple lessons, or self-directed learning of new skills.

1. Adding a Drop-Down List to a Field in a Form

In many cases, you will have fields in tables that have a limited number of possible entries. An example would be a field that asks for the name of a state or a department in a company. Access has a feature that enables you to create a drop-down menu that you can use to choose from a list of choices. These drop-down menus are called combo boxes.

Goal: Create a combo box in the Publisher field that enables you to select from a list of the most common publishers.

Use the *eaA1-0504* file to create a new database called **short story books with a combo box** on your disk. Use help from your computer or online to understand how combo boxes are set up. Go to the Book information data input Form Design view and change the Publisher field text box to a combo box. Include the following publishers in the list:

```
Century

Colliers

Dodd, Mead

Grosset & Dunlap

Harpers

Scribner's
```

Hint #1: A shortcut menu option will help determine the type of field text box.

Hint #2: The Properties box for the Publisher field text box will be used to determine where the information for the combo box comes from. You can create a table to use as the source, or you can type the Value List in another box in the Properties box.

Hint #3: A Value List is usually best when you are working with only a few items, whereas a table is best for a larger number of items.

Your combo box should look like Figure 5.26.

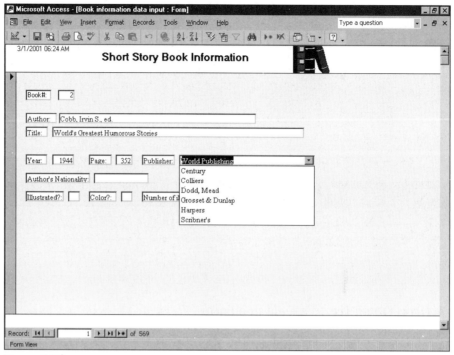

Figure 5.26

2. Using Multiple Pages with Tabs on a Form

When there are a large number of fields in a table, or if the table can be easily divided into more than one category, Access includes a feature that enables you to divide a form into pages. These pages have tabs at the top, and all you have to do to move between pages is to click on a tab.

Goal: Create two tabbed pages on a form based on a table showing the number of cars and trucks by location in the United States.

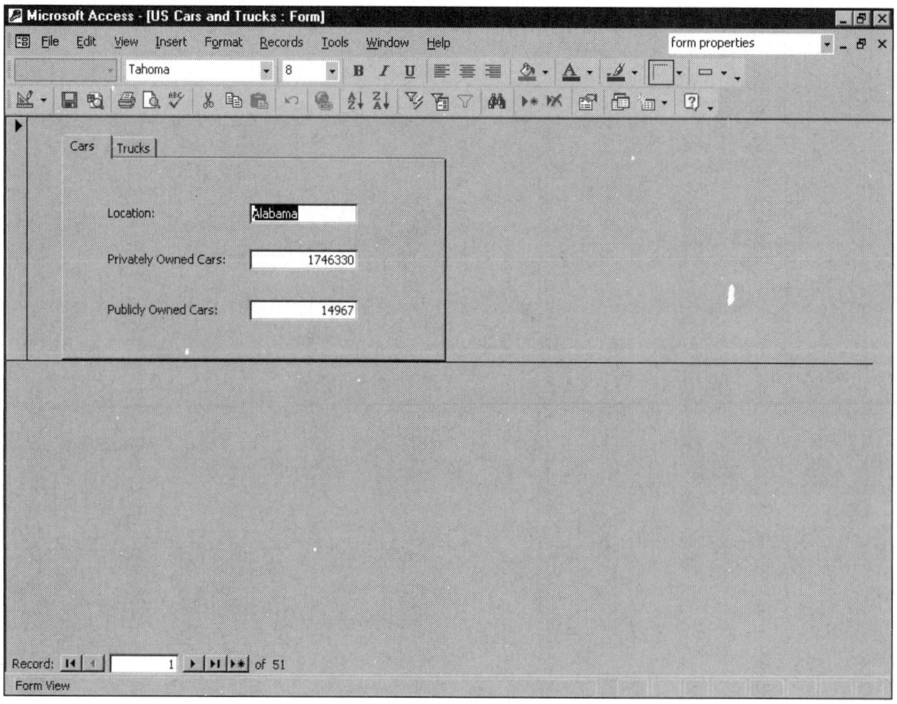

Figure 5.27

Use the *eaA1-0505* file to create a new database called **US Motor Vehicle statistics** on your disk. Use help from your computer or online to understand how Tab Control works. Create the new form in Design view, and save it as **US Cars and Trucks**. Your form should have the following:

- Two pages, with the tabs labeled **Cars** and **Trucks**.
- The Location, Privately Owned Cars, and Publicly Owned Cars fields on the Cars tab.
- The Location, Privately Owned Trucks, and Publicly Owned Trucks fields on the Trucks tab.
- Identical field labels for both occurrences of the Location field. (*Hint*: You will need to change the field name on one of them.)

Hint #1: This is much easier than it sounds! Look in the toolbox to get started.

Hint #2: Most of your time will be spent resizing the field labels and the field text boxes and lining them up.

Your tabbed form should look like Figure 5.27.

Creating and Printing Reports

Objectives

In this project, you learn how to

- ✔ Print the Data in a Table
- ✔ Create a Report Using a Report Wizard
- ✔ Print and Rename a Report
- ✔ Modify a Report Design
- ✔ Save a Report with a New Name
- ✔ Add Labels to Reports

Key terms introduced in this project include

- ❑ AutoReport
- ❑ expression
- ❑ landscape orientation
- ❑ portrait orientation
- ❑ report
- ❑ section

Why Would I Do This?

The information in your database can be displayed in several ways. You can print a form or print copies of tables or queries. These printouts are limited in format and flexibility. To produce flexible printouts from tables or queries, you need to learn how to use reports. **Reports** are database objects that are designed to print and summarize selected fields. They are divided into **sections** that can contain controls, labels, formulas, and even images. In this project, you learn the fundamental tasks involved in creating, modifying, saving, and printing a simple report.

Before you create a report, think about why you need the printed data. Do you want to check the entries to make sure they are correct? Do you need an address list or phone list? Do you need to pass the information along to someone else? If so, what information does that person need and in what order? If you spend a few moments determining the purpose of the report, you can design one that truly meets your needs.

Access provides many tools for creating a report—you can create an AutoReport, use the Report Wizards to create other common report types (single-column report, mailing labels, and so on), or create a blank report that you add information to later. You can also change the layout of an existing report design and add report labels to help make the report more self-explanatory. This project shows you how to use the report tools included with Access.

Visual Summary

When you have completed this project, you will have created a report that looks like Figure 6.1.

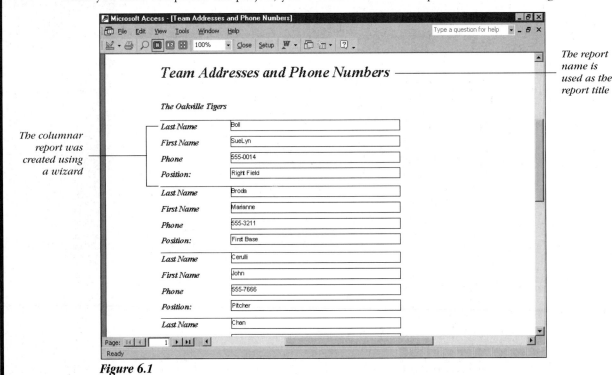

The columnar report was created using a wizard

The report name is used as the report title

Figure 6.1

Lesson 1: Printing the Table Data

If all you need is a printout of the entire table or query, it is faster to simply print the table without using a report. For example, you may want to print the data in a table so that you can check the accuracy of the records. In this case, you don't have to create a report.

To Print the Table Data

1 **Launch Access. Click *More files* in the task pane to open an existing file.**

2 **Copy the *ea1-0601* file, remove the read-only status of the copied file, and rename the file `softball team`. Open the new database.**
The *softball team* database includes a table of team members and a table of game information. After you open the *softball team* database, you should see the two tables displayed in the Tables list. In this project, you work with the Team table.

3 **Click the Team table, and then click the Open button to open the Team table. Maximize the Table window.**
This table is opened in Datasheet view. You may want to scroll through the table to see how it is set up. The table includes fields for the first and last name of each player along with his or her position, phone number, address, and dues. You can print this information, but before you print, preview the printout so that you have some idea of what the printed list will look like.

4 **Click the Print Preview button.**
A preview of the printed list is displayed (see Figure 6.2). The structure of the printout is fairly simple; each record is displayed as a row in a grid. The navigation button that enables you to scroll to the next page is active, which indicates that the printout will be more than one page. This means that all of the table columns will not fit on one page width when the report is printed.

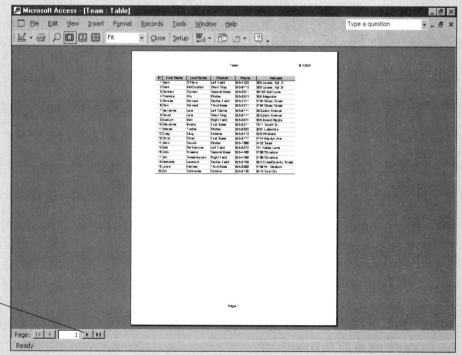

An active Next Page button means there is at least one more page

Figure 6.2

(Continues)

To Print the Table Data (Continued)

⑤ Click the Next Page button, which is the same as the Next Record button in a form or table.
This step displays the second page of the printout, which shows the remaining column. This presents a problem with printing all the fields in the table. If the table is too wide by just a few columns, you can still get a usable printout by changing the orientation of the page so that Access prints across the long edge of the page, rather than down the page. Using this landscape orientation, you can fit more columns across the page.

⑥ Click the Setup button on the Print Preview toolbar.
The Page Setup dialog box lists options for setting margins and page layouts.

⑦ Make sure the margins are all 1″ and then click the Page tab to display the page orientation (see Figure 6.3).

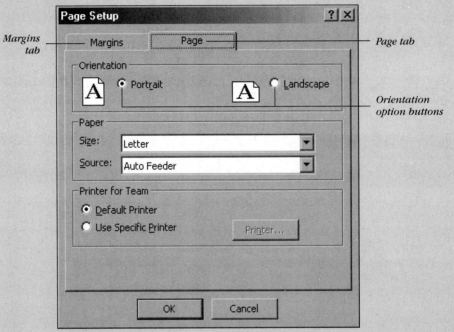

Figure 6.3

⑧ In the Orientation area, click the Landscape option button and then click OK.
This step changes the orientation of the page to *landscape*, which is the horizontal orientation of a page. The standard vertical positioning of a page is called *portrait orientation*. When you print the report now, all the columns fit on a single page.

⑨ From the File menu, choose Print.
The Print dialog box is displayed (Figure 6.4). Here you can control which pages are printed, how many copies are printed, and select other options. The default settings are already appropriate for this one-page printout. You can use the Print button when the default settings are appropriate.

To Print the Table Data

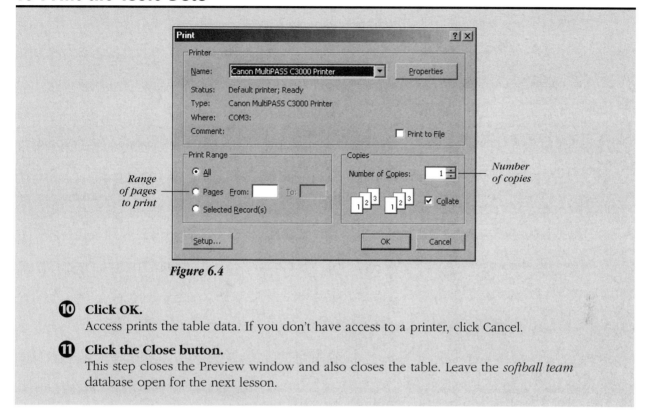

Figure 6.4

🔟 **Click OK.**
Access prints the table data. If you don't have access to a printer, click Cancel.

⑪ **Click the Close button.**
This step closes the Preview window and also closes the table. Leave the *softball team* database open for the next lesson.

 To extend your knowledge…

Previewing the Printout

You don't have to preview the printout, but previewing is a good idea. You can print directly from Datasheet view. Simply click the Print button on the toolbar or open the File menu and choose the Print command. Access then prints the table. The keyboard shortcut for the Print command is (Ctrl)+(P).

Fitting Data on the Page

If the data doesn't quite fit on the page, there are several things you can do to make them fit. You can reduce the width of the columns. If this cuts off some of the data, you can reduce the font size using Format, Font from the menu.

Lesson 2: Creating a Report Using a Report Wizard

Simple table printouts are limited in what they can do. Access provides several reporting options to make it easy to create more sophisticated reports. Using the New Report feature, you can create the reports described in Table 6.1.

Table 6.1 | Common Report Creation Options

Type of New Report	Description
Design View	Opens a design window where you can add fields or text. This option does not use the wizards.
Report Wizard	Guides you through the process of creating a report. The Report Wizard has several options for the layout and grouping of data.
AutoReport: Columnar	Places all the fields in a table in a single-column report.
AutoReport: Tabular	Places all the fields in the table in a row-and-column format similar to the layout of a spreadsheet.
Chart Wizard	Guides you through the process of selecting fields that you want to summarize in a graphical form. The Chart Wizard enables you to choose from several chart types, such as pie, line, and bar.
Label Wizard	Enables you to set up and print mailing labels in more than 100 different label styles.

A report wizard leads you step-by-step through the process of creating a report, asking you which fields to include in the report, which sort order to use, what title to print, and so on. After you make your selections, the wizard creates the report.

In this lesson, you create a columnar report for your Team table in the *softball team* database. This report works well as an address list.

To Create a Report Using a Report Wizard

❶ **Click the Reports object button.**
No reports are listed, because you haven't created any at this point (see Figure 6.5).

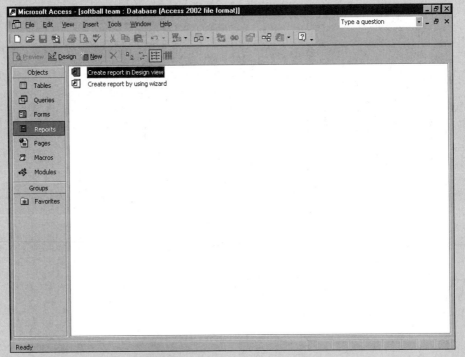

Figure 6.5

❷ **Click the New button.**

To Create a Report Using a Report Wizard

The New Report dialog box is displayed (see Figure 6.6). You will need to select the method of creating the report and the table or query on which you want to base the report. This is exactly the same procedure you used to create a form.

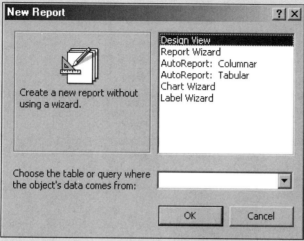

Figure 6.6

❸ Select Report Wizard, and choose the Team table from *Choose the table or query where the object's data comes from* drop-down list. Click OK.

❹ Click the First Name field in the Available Fields list and then click the Select button.

The Wizard removes the field from the Available Fields list and places the field in the Selected Fields list (see Figure 6.7). The fields will appear in the report in the order you select them. The First Name field, for example, will be the first field listed in the current report.

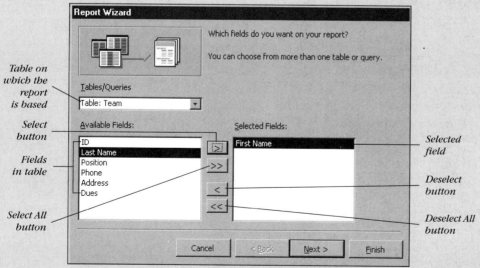

Figure 6.7

(Continues)

To Create a Report Using a Report Wizard (Continued)

5 **Highlight and add the Last Name, Address, and Phone fields to the Selected Fields list.**
Your report now includes four fields. They are all the fields you want to include for this lesson.

6 **Click the Next button.**
The second Report Wizard dialog box is displayed. You could use this step to group similar records together, such as grouping the team by position played. In this example, however, we have not included any fields that need to be listed together as a group.

7 **Click Next again.**
The third Report Wizard dialog box enables you to sort the data on one or more fields.

8 **Click the down arrow next to the first sort selection to reveal the available fields. Select Last Name to sort on. Click Next.**
The fourth Report Wizard dialog box enables you to select the layout, orientation, and fit (see Figure 6.8).

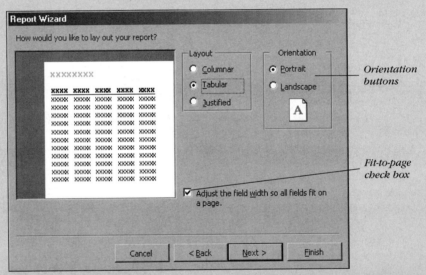

Figure 6.8

9 **Select a Columnar layout, Portrait orientation, and the check box labeled** *Adjust the field width so all fields fit on a page.* **Click the Next button.**
The fifth Report Wizard is displayed. In this dialog box, you select a report style.

10 **Select the Corporate style report and then click the Next button.**
The final Report Wizard dialog box is displayed. In this screen, you enter the title for the report. By default, the Wizard uses the table name as the title, unless you change it.

If you have problems...

If you make a mistake or change your mind about an option anywhere in the Wizard, you can back up by clicking the Back button in the Wizard dialog box.

11 **Type** Team Addresses and Phone Numbers **to change the title of the report and then click the Finish button.**

To Create a Report Using a Report Wizard

A preview of the report is displayed (see Figure 6.9) showing the title you entered. You can print, zoom, and save the report, as you learn in the next lesson. Keep the report open for the next lesson, where you print and rename a report.

The report name is used as the default label

Use navigation buttons to move among report pages

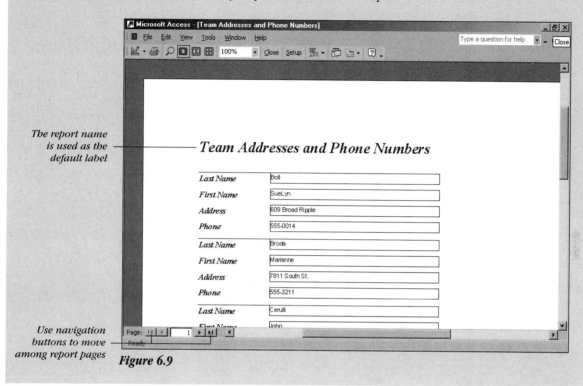

Figure 6.9

To extend your knowledge...

Using AutoReport Wizard

You can also create an AutoReport using the Report Wizards. An ***AutoReport*** includes all the fields from the table in the report. The report is in either a one-column or tabular format with as many records on the page as possible. The report also includes a header with the table name and current date, and a footer with the page number. To create this type of report from the Reports page, choose one of the two AutoReport options in the New Report dialog box.

Lesson 3: Printing and Renaming a Report

The next step is to print your report. Before you print, however, it's always a good idea to preview the report. In the Print Preview mode, you can use the navigation buttons to check for unexpected additional pages, check the font, the font size, and the actual data in the report. If you click the Zoom button on the toolbar, you can then view the entire report to determine how the printed report will look on the page. If you do not like how the report is set up, you can make changes before you print it. This strategy can save you some time and paper.

You can also rename a report in the Database window to ensure that it is not confused with other database objects with the same name.

To Print and Rename a Report

① **With the Preview window still active, click the pointer anywhere on the report.**
Access displays a full-page view of the report, so that you can see the entire page (see Figure 6.10).

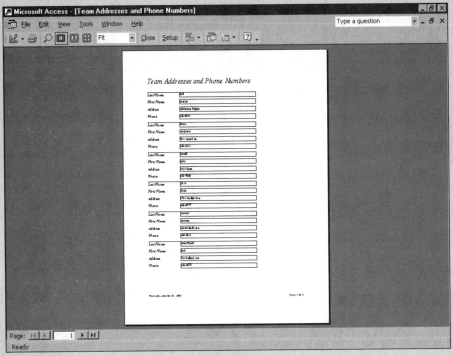

Figure 6.10

② **Click the report again.**
Access zooms in so that you can read the text of the report. It will center on the spot you clicked, so you may need to use the scrollbars to get back to the section you want to see. Now you are ready to print.

③ **Click the Print button on the toolbar.**
Access prints the report. If you do not have access to a printer, skip this step.

 If you have problems...
This report is three pages long. If you are restricted to printing one page, select File, Print from the menu, and choose to print from pages 1 to 1 in the Print Range section.

④ **Click the Close button on the toolbar to close the Preview window.**
The program returns to the report Design view.

⑤ **Click the Close button to close the report.**
The new report is shown in the Database window under the Reports list. You may decide that the name you gave the report could be improved.

⑥ **Right-click on the Team Addresses and Phone Numbers report, and select Rename from the shortcut menu.**
The name changes to Edit mode, in which it can be changed.

To Print and Rename a Report

7 Type the name Team Roster.

8 Press ⏎Enter or click outside the name box to save the change.

The report name is now *Team Roster*. Keep the database open for the next lesson, where you modify a report design.

Lesson 4: Modifying a Report Design

Once you have created a report, you may decide that you want to modify it. The finished report may not be exactly what you intended. Rather than start over with a wizard or a blank form, you can modify the report design so that the report includes the information you want.

When you look through the report in Design view, you will notice some unusual things in the Page Footer. These are **expressions**, which are predefined formulas that perform calculations, display built-in functions, or set limits. Access provides many expressions that you can include in reports.

Suppose that you need a phone list in addition to the team roster. You can modify the Roster report to create this new report. Start by deleting the Address field, which you don't need in your phone list. You can then add the position field so you have a list that includes the name, phone number, and position played by each member of the team.

To Modify a Report Design

1 **Select the Team Roster report and open it in Design view.**

The report is displayed in Design view (see Figure 6.11). This view is similar to the Design view you used when you modified a form. The same tools are available onscreen. You can use the ruler to place items on the report, the toolbox to add controls, and the field list to add fields.

(Continues)

To Modify a Report Design (Continued)

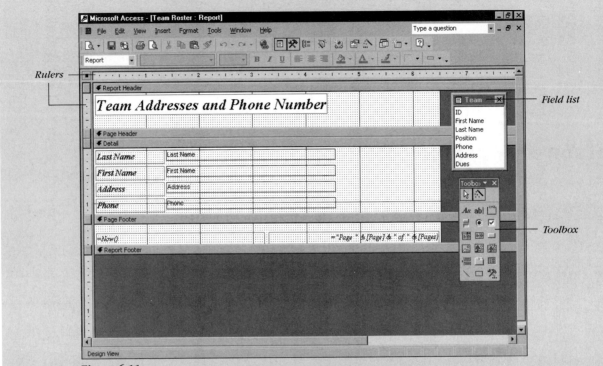

Figure 6.11

2   **Click the scroll arrows to scroll through the report and see how it is structured.**
Notice that the report includes a Page Footer with the date and page number. The expression **=NOW( )** inserts the current date (see Figure 6.12).

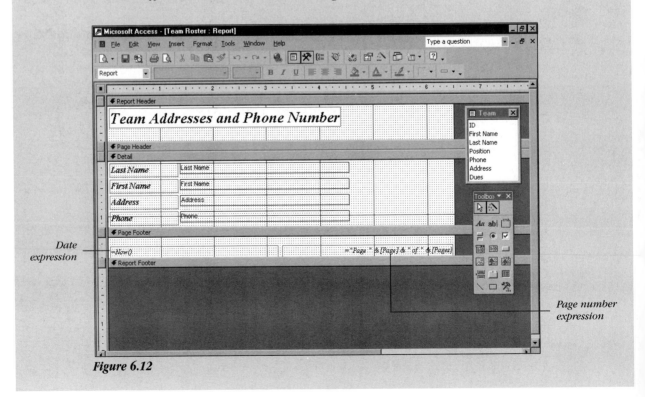

Figure 6.12

To Modify a Report Design

The expression **="Page" & [Page] & "Of" & [Pages]** on the right side of the Page Footer prints the current page and the total number of pages. Remember that you placed this expression in the form in Project 5, "Creating and Using Forms."

The Detail section includes four fields: First Name, Last Name, Address, and Phone.

❸ Maximize the window, if necessary, and click the Address field text box.
The field label is on the left, and the field text box is on the right. If you click on the Address field text box, handles will appear at the sides and corners of the field text box and in the upper left corner of the field label box.

❹ Press Del.
Access removes the field and its label from the report. Now you have a gap between two of the fields. To fix this gap, you can move the Phone field up.

❺ Click the Phone field text box to select it.
Position the pointer on the field so that it turns into an open hand.

❻ Drag the Phone field so that it is directly under the First Name field.
The Phone field is now closer to First Name. Now you will add the position field to the report.

❼ In the field list box, click the Position field and drag it to the detail section of the report, directly below the Phone field text box, and release the mouse.
The pointer turns into a small field box when you are dragging the field onto the report. As soon as you release the mouse, the field text box is positioned under the Phone text box and the field label for the new field is added to the left of the field (see Figure 6.13). Next, you need to format the new field to match the ones on the report.

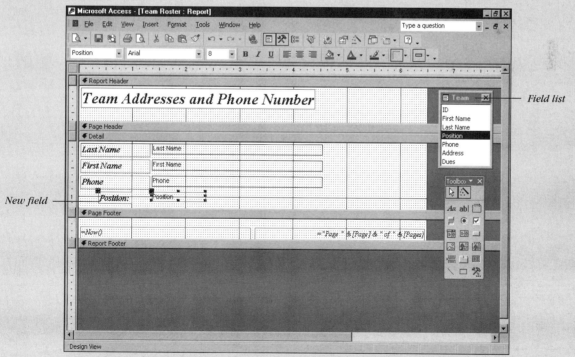

Figure 6.13

(Continues)

To Modify a Report Design (Continued)

8 Point to the Phone field text box above the new Position text box. Hold down ⬆Shift) and then click. The Phone and Position boxes should both be selected.

9 Choose F**o**rmat, **S**ize, To **W**idest to match the length of the two boxes.

10 Choose F**o**rmat, **S**ize, To **T**allest to match the height of the two boxes.

11 Choose F**o**rmat, **A**lign, **L**eft to match the alignment of the two boxes.

12 Click in an unused space in the Detail area to deselect the boxes.

13 Select the field label box for Position. Grab the center handle on the left edge of the field label box, and drag to the left until it is lined up with the left edge of the Phone field label box.

14 Click the Print Preview button on the toolbar.
The new field should now match the other boxes in size and alignment. However, the other field text boxes have a border. Next you add the border to the Position text box.

15 Click the View button to return to Design view, then click the Position field text box to select it.

16 Click the down arrow to the right of the Line/Border Width button on the Formatting toolbar (see Figure 6.14).

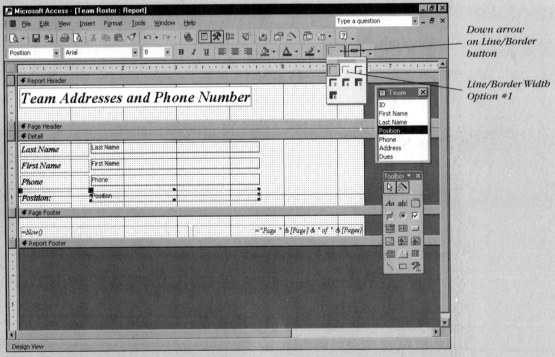

Figure 6.14

17 Select border option #1. Click the View button to look at the new design. Choose **F**ile, **S**ave to save your changes. Keep this report open for the next lesson.

To extend your knowledge...

Formatting Report Titles Using Size to Fit

When editing a label, the text may appear truncated if the new text length is greater than the original text. When the title is entered using the wizard, the program automatically applies the size to fit the format for this label. You can test this by selecting the title label, and choosing Format, Size, To Fit from the menu. The size of the label box remains the same because it is large enough to enable the title to print.

Modifying Wizard Reports

The Report Wizards are used to give you all of the necessary elements of a report and to place these elements in their proper locations. The wizards will save you time, but will seldom provide finished reports. You will almost always need to modify field lengths, add or format labels, modify the spacing between fields, and change locations of some of the elements. If you are asked to create a report using a wizard, make sure you use the Print Preview feature to scan through the data and look for fields that may have been cut off and need to be modified.

Lesson 5: Saving the Report with a New Name

As you modify a report, you may decide that you want to keep the original report as well as your modified version. If this is the case, you can save the modified report with a new name. Doing so enables you to use both reports.

In addition to saving the report with a new name, you should change the Report Header so that it reflects the purpose of the new report.

To Save the Report with a New Name

1 **With the Team Roster report still onscreen, click the View button to switch to Design view. Choose File, Save As from the menu.**
The Save As dialog box is displayed with the original name listed (see Figure 6.15).

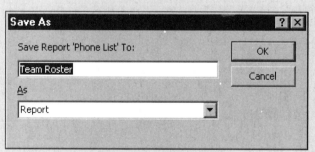

Figure 6.15

2 **Type Phone List, and click OK.**
The report is saved with a new name.

3 **Click the label box in the Report Header section.**
You can replace the existing text with a more descriptive title.

4 **Drag across the existing text to select it, and type Phone List.**
The new text replaces the selected text.

5 **Click the Save button.**

(Continues)

To Save the Report with a New Name (Continued)

This step saves your changes to the Phone List report by writing over the report with that name. Keep the Phone List report open and continue to the next lesson, where you add labels to a report.

To extend your knowledge...

Another Way to Copy a Report

You can also create a duplicate report from the database window. With the Reports tab selected, right-click on the report name and select Copy from the shortcut menu. Right-click again in an open area of the window and select Paste from the shortcut menu. Give the duplicate report a new name when prompted.

Lesson 6: Adding Labels to Reports

When you create a report using a wizard, the labels tend to be short and non-descriptive. Once you have modified the report, as you did in Lesson 4, you will often find that additional labels are necessary to explain exactly what is on the report. Access gives you an easy way to add labels to either the Report Header or the Page Header. Labels added to the Report Header will show up on the first page of the report, whereas labels added to the Page Header area will appear on the top of every page. In this lesson, you add the team name to the Page Header area.

To Add Labels to Reports

1 **With the Phone List report open in Design view, point to the top edge of the Detail section divider. When the mouse pointer changes to a two-headed arrow, click and drag down to make the Page Header area about 1/2″ high.**
You will use this space to place the new text label.

2 **Click the Label button in the Toolbox.**
When you move the pointer over an open area of the design window, the pointer turns into a large "A" with a crosshair attached.

3 **Click at the upper left corner in the Page Header section and drag down and to the right until you have a text box about 2″ wide and 1/4″ high.**
This label box is where you enter your text (see Figure 6.16).

To Add Labels to Reports

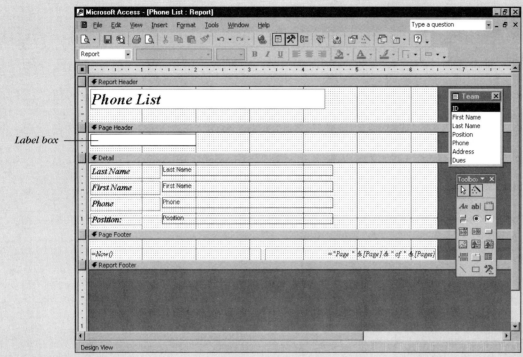

Figure 6.16

④ **Type** The Oakville Tigers **in the label box.**
If the text is too long for the box you created, you can select the box and resize it to fit.

⑤ **Click in an open area of the Page Header.**
This will turn off the text edit.

⑥ **Click the Print Preview button.**
The original title and the new title you just added are displayed at the top of the report
(see Figure 6.17).

(Continues)

To Add Labels to Reports (Continued)

Figure 6.17

❼ **Click the Close button on the Print Preview toolbar.**

❽ **Click the Save button; then close the report and close the database.**
If you have completed your session on the computer, exit Access and Windows before you turn off the computer. Otherwise, continue with the "Checking Concepts and Terms" section of this project.

To extend your knowledge...

Where Header and Footer Labels Appear

Remember, labels that are placed in the Report Header area will only appear on the first page, and labels that are placed in the Report Footer area will only appear on the last page of the report. Labels added to the Page Header and Page Footer areas will appear on every page of the report.

The main output component of Access is the report. Although you can print a table, as you did in this project, reports are designed to be printed for presenting information to others. In this project, you created a report using the Report Wizard. You printed the report and renamed it after it had been created. You then learned some of the techniques that can be used to modify a report, including how to add and resize fields. After modifying a report, you saved it with a new name using the Save As command. Finally, you used the label tool to add a label to the report.

Several different report styles and options can be used, as you noticed when you used the wizard. To expand your knowledge, create a report and explore the different options that are displayed in the wizard to see what alternatives are offered. Use Help and read the topic, *About reports,* including all the related topics. If Web access is available, use the Office on the Web help to locate examples of reports. Continue with the exercises at the end of this project to practice creating and modifying reports.

Checking Concepts and Terms

Multiple Choice

Circle the letter of the correct answer for each of the following questions.

1. Which of the following choices is not one of the selections when you select New from the Reports window? [L2]

   a. Report Wizard

   b. Double-column

   c. AutoReport: Tabular

   d. AutoReport: Columnar

2. Which report design tool helps you precisely position controls on the report? [L4]

   a. the toolbox

   b. the toolbar

   c. the field list

   d. the ruler

3. What do you click in Print Preview to switch between a full-page view and a close-up view of the report? [L3]

   a. the PageUp button

   b. anywhere on the report

   c. the View button

   d. the Full Page button

4. An AutoReport includes which of the following? [L2]

   a. all non-automatic fields in the table

   b. all fields in the database

   c. the fields you designate in the third dialog box

   d. all fields in the source table

5. Finished reports include all the following except what? [Intro]

   a. labels

   b. find buttons

   c. sections

   d. controls

Screen ID

Label each element of the Access screen shown in Figure 6.18.

A. Expression
B. Label button
C. Field label
D. Ruler
E. Field list box
F. Print Preview button
G. Field List button
H. Toolbox button
I. Field text box
J. Label

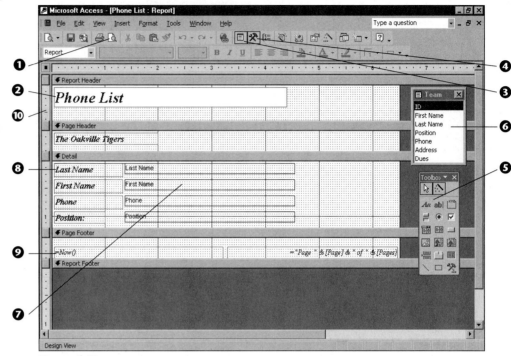

Figure 6.18

1. _____   6. _____

2. _____   7. _____

3. _____   8. _____

4. _____   9. _____

5. _____   10. _____

Discussion

1. Why do companies produce reports? What are some of the goals or purposes of reports that are created from databases? In databases that you use, what reports are produced? How are they organized? How are they sorted?

2. What formatting has been applied to reports you use that make them easier to read and understand? What techniques have you seen in

Access reports that are comparable to the formatting in the reports you use?

3. If you were to redesign a report that you currently receive, how would you organize the information? Think about bank statements, utility bills, and other bills you receive. These statements are reports to customers. Look for an example of a report that you think is well done and share it with class members, pointing out what makes this easy to use.

Skill Drill

Skill Drill exercises reinforce project skills. Each skill reinforced is the same, or nearly the same, as a skill presented in the project. Each exercise includes a brief narrative introduction, followed by detailed instructions in a step-by-step format.

The database you will be using for these exercises contains tornado data for the state of Arizona. These records cover a 45-year time span, and include all of the confirmed sightings during that period. The records are an abbreviated form of records produced by the National Oceanic and Atmospheric Administration (NOAA). The fields included in this sample table include the year, date, time of day, number of people killed, number of people injured, a damage scale, the county, and the F-scale (a measure of tornado intensity). Many of the fields are blank because there were no casualties or damage, or because the F-scale was not recorded.

1. Printing Data from a Table

You just want a quick printout of the tornadoes in Arizona over the past 45 years. The layout is not important, and because there are not a lot of fields, you decide to print out the information directly from the table.

To print data from a table, complete the following steps:

1. Copy the *ea1-0602* database file, remove the read-only status from the copied file, and name it `Arizona tornadoes`. In the *Arizona tornadoes* database, click the Tables object button. Select and open the Arizona Tornadoes table, and examine the fields. Notice that the records are displayed in chronological order.
2. Click the Print Preview button to make sure the fields will fit across the page in portrait orientation.
3. Click the drop-down arrow on the View button and select Datasheet view.
4. Select File, Print from the menu.
5. Print only the second page.
6. Close the table.

2. Creating a Report Using the Report Wizard

Printing directly from the table allowed you to scan the data quickly but did not give you any real control over the final product. You decide to use the Report Wizard to build a more useful, attractive report.

To create a report using the report wizard, complete the following steps:

1. In the *Arizona tornadoes* database, click the Reports object button.
2. Click the New button.
3. Select the Arizona Tornadoes table, and choose the Report Wizard.
4. Select all of the fields.
5. Group on the County field.
6. Sort on the Year field first. Sort on the Date field second.
7. Choose the Block layout.
8. Select the Soft Gray style.
9. Accept the default report title, Arizona Tornadoes. Click Finish.
10. Maximize the print preview window, and scroll down to look at your new report. Leave the report open for the next exercise.

3. Modifying a Report

The form you created using the wizard looks pretty good, but the title is not terribly descriptive. You decide to add the period of time covered by the report.

To modify a report, complete the following steps:

1. In the *Arizona tornadoes* database, click the View button to move to the report Design view.
2. Click once on the title in the Report Header to select it.
3. Grab the center handle on the right edge of the title and drag it to the 6″ mark. (If your rulers are not turned on, choose <u>V</u>iew, <u>R</u>uler from the menu.)
4. Modify the title so that it reads `Arizona Tornadoes, 1951–1995`.
5. Click the View button to see your changes.
6. Close the report and save your changes.

4. Changing Character Formatting in a Report

The report is looking better and better, but a few more changes would make it really easy to read. First, the text in the Detail area is a little small, and second, the names of the counties could be emphasized a little more.

To change character formatting in a report, complete the following steps:

1. In the *Arizona tornadoes* database, open the Arizona Tornadoes, report in Design view.
2. Move the pointer to the ruler to the left of the Detail area until it changes to an arrow pointing right.
3. Click once to select all of the fields in the detail section.
4. Click the down arrow next to the Font Size list box, and change the font size from 11 points to 12 points.
5. Click in an open area to deselect the fields, and click the County field to select it.
6. Click the Bold and Italic buttons to add character formatting to the county names.
7. Click the View button to see the changes to your report. Leave the report open for the next exercise.

5. Adding a Label to a Report

One last thing is needed to finish the report—a subtitle to show where the information came from. It is always good form to give your sources, even when the sources are public domain.

To add a label to a report, complete the following steps:

1. In the *Arizona tornadoes* database, click the View button to return to Design view.
2. Click the Label button and draw a label box about 1/4″ high and 3″ wide just below the title in the Report Header.
3. Type `National Oceanic and Atmospheric Administration (NOAA)` in the text box. Notice what happens when you get to the end of the text box.
4. Click in an open area to deselect the label, and click the label box to select it again. Handles should appear around the label.
5. Click the Italic button.
6. Click the Font/Fore Color button and select white to change the color of the font to match the title.
7. Click the View button to see the results of your changes. Your report should look like Figure 6.19.

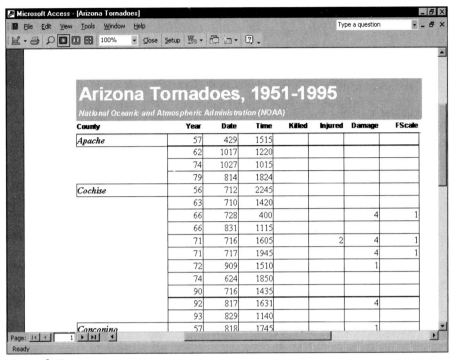

Figure 6.19

6. Finalizing and Printing a Report

Reports are created with one thing in mind—publishing, to either paper or the Web. You decide you would like to see how your report looks on paper. As you look at your report, you notice that the subtitle is truncated. You fix it and then print the report.

To finalize and print a report, complete the following steps:

1. In the *Arizona tornadoes* database, click on the preview window to see the whole page. Click the View button to go to Design view.

2. Click the subtitle to select it.

3. Choose F<u>o</u>rmat, <u>S</u>ize, To <u>F</u>it.

4. Click the Preview button to see if the subtitle fits. Click in the report once to show the full report, if necessary.

5. Choose <u>F</u>ile, <u>P</u>rint from the menu. Print page 1 only of the report.

6. Close the report and save your changes.

Challenge exercises expand on or are somewhat related to skills presented in the lessons. Each exercise provides a brief narrative introduction followed by instructions in a numbered step or bullet list format that are not as detailed as those in the Skill Drill section.

The database you will be using for the Challenge section is a modified version of the one you used in the Skill Drill section, including the changes you made.

1. Creating a Report Using the AutoReport: Columnar Option

You have not yet tried several other ways to create reports. You decide to experiment with a couple of them just to see what they look like. The first one you try is the AutoReport: Columnar option.

To create a report using the AutoReport: Columnar option, complete the following steps:

1. Copy the *ea1-0603* database file, remove the read-only status from the copied file, and rename it `AR tornadoes`. Open the *AR tornadoes* database.
2. Switch to the Reports window and create a new report.
3. Create an *AutoReport: Columnar* report based on the Arizona Tornadoes table.
4. Scroll down and look at the layout of the report. Move to Design view and examine the structure of the report.
5. Close the report, and save it as `Column Report`.

2. Creating a Report Using the AutoReport: Tabular Option

You have tried the AutoReport: Columnar option and cannot figure out how you would ever use it. Maybe the AutoReport: Tabular option will produce better results.

To create a report using the AutoReport: Tabular option, complete the following steps:

1. Create a new report in the *AR tornadoes* database.
2. Create an *AutoReport: Tabular* report based on the Arizona Tornadoes table.
3. Scroll down and look at the layout of the report. Move to Design view and examine the structure of the report. Which of the two AutoReports do you think would be most useful the majority of the time?
4. Close the report and save it as `Tabular Report`.

3. Summarizing Data in a Report

As you create reports in the future, you will often want to summarize the data grouped in a field. Access enables you to print all of the data along with summaries, or just the summaries themselves. In this exercise, you create a report that summarizes tornado data by county.

To summarize data in a report, complete the following steps:

1. In the *AR tornadoes* database, create a new report based on the Arizona Tornadoes table using the Report Wizard.
2. Select all of the fields and group by county. Don't sort the records; instead, click the Summary Options button on the sorting page of the wizard.
3. In the Summary Options dialog box, choose to Sum the Killed and Injured fields, and Avg (average) the Damage and FScale fields.
4. In the same dialog box, choose to display the Summary Only.
5. Use the Outline 2 layout and the Portrait orientation. Select the Bold style.
6. Name the new report `County Summaries`. Notice that some of the categories are empty, and some are shown with seven decimal places. A part of the second page is shown in Figure 6.20.
7. Leave the report open for the next exercise.

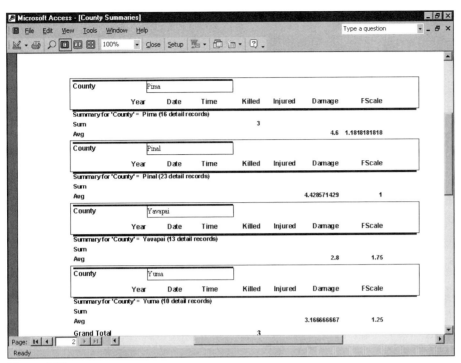

Figure 6.20

4. Formatting the Numbers on Reports

The numbers of decimal places in the Damage and FScale fields are inconsistent. You would like to fix them so that both fields display the results to one decimal place.

To format the numbers in a report, complete the following steps:

1. In the *AR tornadoes* database, display the County Summaries report in Design view, if necessary. Select both the Damage and the FScale summary fields in the County Footer area.
2. Click the Properties button in the Report Design toolbar.
3. Use the Help menu to figure out how to set the numbers to a fixed format and the decimal places to 1.
4. Click the View button to make sure you set both formatting options.
5. Close the report and save your changes.

5. Changing the Report Sort Order

The Tornado data has been grouped by county, and sorted by year and date. You decide that you would like to change it to sort on the FScale field in descending order.

To change the report sort order, complete the following steps:

1. In the *AR tornadoes* database, open the Arizona Tornadoes report in Design view.
2. Locate and click the Sorting and Grouping button.
3. Use the help options available to you to help you delete the Year and Date fields from the sorting area. Add the FScale field, and sort in descending order.
4. Look at a preview of your report.
5. Save the report as `Arizona Tornadoes by County and FScale`. Close the report.

6. Draw Lines in a Report

Looking at the report entitled Tabular Report that you created earlier in this Challenge section, you decide that you would like to try adding a line under the title.

To draw lines in a report, complete the following steps:

1. In the *AR tornadoes* database, open the Tabular Report in Design view.
2. Click the Line button and draw a straight line under the title in the Report Header. (*Hint*: To draw a straight line, hold down ◆Shift) while you click and drag the line.) Notice that the line is thin.
3. Use the available help to figure out how to change the attributes of a line. (*Hint*: The line style is a property of the line.)
4. Change the line width to 2.
5. View your changes; then close and save the report.

Discovery Zone exercises require advanced knowledge of topics presented in *essentials* lessons, application of skills from multiple lessons, or self-directed learning of new skills.

1. Changing the Grouping of Report Data and Keeping the Groups Together

When you finally get your report finished, you may decide that you want to change its focus. You might also consider copying and pasting the report to save the work of creating another one. You can then use this copy to display the data in a different manner. For example, in the Arizona Tornadoes report you grouped the data on the County field and sorted on the Year and Date fields. Suppose you also wanted to be able to examine the data by year, and you wanted to make sure the tornadoes of one year did not overlap from one page to the next.

Goal: Change the grouping field in an existing report and have the report keep the data from the grouped field together (on the same page) in the report.

Use the *ea1-0604* file to create a new database called **Arizona tornadoes by year** on your disk. Use help from your computer or online to understand how to change the grouped field and how to keep the data together for each of the grouped items. You will modify the Arizona Tornadoes report. To modify this report, you should:

- Change the grouping to the Year field, rather than the County field.
- Change the sort field to the Date field only.
- Change the character formatting to bold for the Year field and remove the bold formatting from the County field.
- Swap the location of the County field and the Year field.
- Have the county name show in every record; however, the year should be displayed only when it changes (that is, each year should be displayed only once).

Hint #1: There is a button on the Report Design toolbar that will lead you to a way to make several of the changes.

Hint #2: You can eliminate duplicate years in the Properties box.

Your report should look like Figure 6.21.

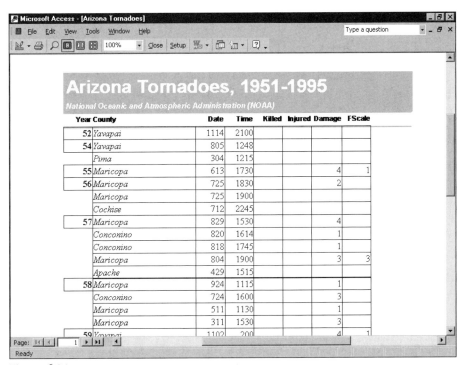

Figure 6.21

2. Creating Mailing Labels Using the Label Wizard

If you are creating a database for a business, church, or organization, one of the most common reports will be used to create mailing labels. Mailing labels are usually printed on special sheets that contain ready-to-use labels in various sizes. The Avery company specializes in making labels that fit every need, from folder labels to nametags. Each of the different types of labels have their own "Avery number." When you set up your mailing label, you will need to know which Avery label you are using. The wizard asks for the Avery number and then automatically sets the page up for you.

Goal: Create a report using the Label Wizard that will generate mailing labels from a table of addresses.

Use the *ea1-0605* file to create a new database called `address labels` on your disk. Read through the Access help on mailing labels to understand how the wizard works. Also, carefully read the help provided on each of the wizard screens. Use the following guidelines:

- The report should use Avery #5160 labels.
- The font should be normal (no special character formatting) and 10 point.
- The first row should contain the First Name and Last Name fields with a space between them.
- The second row of each label should contain the Address field.
- The third row of each label should contain the City field, followed by a comma and a space; then the State field and a space; and finally, the ZIP field.

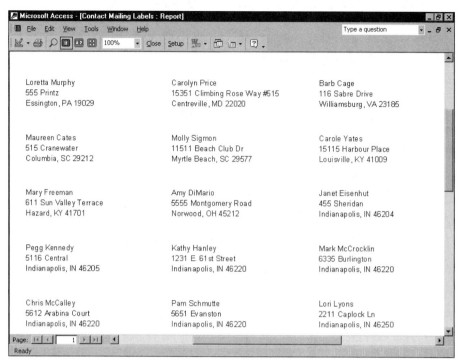

Figure 6.22

- Sort by the ZIP field.
- Name your report `Contact Mailing Labels`.

Preview the page and then print the labels. Your report should look like Figure 6.22.

Customizing Fields and Tables

| Objectives |

In this project, you learn how to

- ✔ Modify a Table Design
- ✔ Enter a Default Value
- ✔ Change a Field Type and Select a Format
- ✔ Change a Field Size
- ✔ Work with More Than One Table
- ✔ Create Table Relationships
- ✔ Create a Multiple Table Query

Key terms introduced in this project include

- ❑ combo box
- ❑ enforce referential integrity
- ❑ Input masks
- ❑ join
- ❑ list box
- ❑ one-to-many
- ❑ one-to-one

Why Would I Do This?

Access provides many features to help you customize your database table. You can select the field size, enter a default value, or select how data in that field is displayed.

When you first create a database, you may not be sure which of these options you want to use. After you have entered several records, however, you may find that you need to make changes, and you can make them by modifying the table design. You can add fields to the table or delete fields. You can also change the field properties, which are the defining attributes of a field, of the table entries. In this project, you learn how to modify a table design and change some of the field properties.

Another way you can customize tables is by connecting two or more tables together. Access is a relational database, which means that data is stored separately in tables and then connected or related by common fields in each table. Connecting tables enables you to set up a sophisticated database system and makes managing the information easier.

The connection between the two tables is called a relationship. The most common type of relationship is called a ***one-to-many*** relationship. If two tables have a one-to-many relationship, it means that each record in the first table can be related to more than one record in the second table. Records in both tables must share a field that can be used to relate them. Other types of relationships are possible. For instance, in a ***one-to-one*** relationship, one record from a table is related to one record in another table through a common field.

The advantage of using two tables can be demonstrated by a database designed for a small company. The company sells supplies to 20 different retail outlets. Each month, the company sends several orders to each outlet. The company wants to record the mailing address of each of the outlets and information about each order. If a single table is used with all the fields in it, the company will have to enter all of the address information of the outlet every time an order is sent. If the database is designed with two tables, the mailing address information can be entered once for each outlet in one table, and the specific order information can be entered in a second table.

This project examines some of the relational features of a database.

Visual Summary

When you have completed this project, you will have created a query that looks like Figure 7.1.

Fields from one table →

Date	Team	Last Name	First Name	Field
6/23/2002	First National Bank	O'Hara	Jean	Pittsfield
6/30/2002	B&B Manufacturing	McCrocklin	Mark	Allmendinger
7/6/2002	Banfields Bar & Grill	Connor	Denney	Eberwhite
7/13/2002	T & E Corp.	Wu	Thomas	Vets Park
7/20/2002	City Hospital	Howard	Denise	Pittsfield
7/20/2002	City Hospital	Howard	Dan	Pittsfield
7/27/2002	Computer Tech	Klug	Greg	Vets Park
8/3/2002	Ball Bearing Co.	Cerulli	John	Eberwhite
8/10/2002	CompuAid	DeSchryver	Bob	Allmendinger
8/17/2002	Murry's Department Store	Greene	Vicki	Vets Park
8/24/2002	Corner Drug Store	Smeehuyzen	Jim	Pittsfield

Location and Equipment Manager : Select Query

Record: 1 of 11

→ Fields from a second table

Figure 7.1

Lesson 1: Modifying a Table Design

It is a good idea to spend some time planning your database structure—thinking about which fields to include and in which order. If you had only one chance to get the database table right, however, you probably would get frustrated quickly, because it is difficult to anticipate all of the features that need to be included in a table.

Fortunately, Access lets you make changes to a table design even after you have created the table. Consequently, you can add fields, delete fields, or modify field properties as the need arises.

If the field already contains data and you make a change to the field, the data will be affected. Sometimes the change doesn't cause any problems. For example, if you have already entered numbers in a field and then decide you want to format them as currency, you won't lose any data.

However, if you enter a note in a field and then change that field type to a Yes/No field, you will lose most of the data in the field when Access reformats it to the new type. Just be sure that you understand the changes you are making and that you realize how they will affect your data. Back up your database before you change data types.

You begin this lesson by modifying the Team table of the Softball database by adding a few new fields.

To Modify a Table Design

❶ Launch Access. Click *More files* in the task pane to open an existing file.

❷ Copy the ea1-0701 file, remove the read-only status of the copied file, rename the file softball coach, and open the new database.
The *softball coach* database includes a table of team members and a table of game information. After you open the *softball coach* database, you should see the two tables displayed in the Tables list.

❸ Click the Team table, and then click the Design button. Maximize the Design window.
The Team table opens in Design view so that you can make changes (see Figure 7.2). When you first created the table, you didn't include the city, state, or Zip code for the players, because most of them live in the same city; you didn't think you needed to track this information.

(Continues)

To Modify a Table Design (Continued)

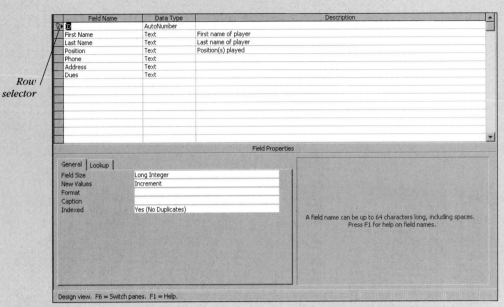

Figure 7.2

After using the database for some time, however, you have decided that you want to include the city, state, and Zip code in the table so that you can have complete addresses for mailings. Now you want to add these three fields to the table and then place them after the address field.

❹ Click the row selector next to the Dues field and click the Insert Rows button three times.

Access inserts three rows in which you can enter the City, State, and Zip code fields. You can also insert a row by selecting the Insert menu and choosing the Rows command.

❺ Click in the first empty Field Name column box, and type City. Press Tab⇆ three times.

This enters the field name, accepts Text as the field type, skips the Description column, and moves you to the next row.

❻ Repeat this step to enter the State and Zip fields.

When you have finished, you will have inserted three new fields (see Figure 7.3).

To Modify a Table Design

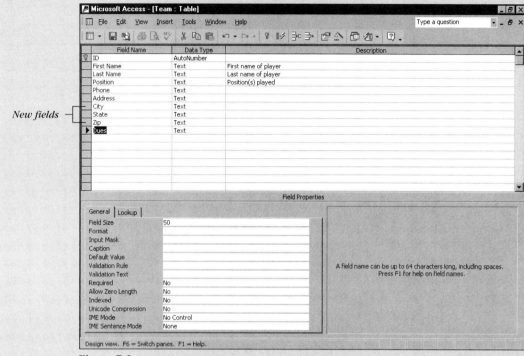

New fields

Figure 7.3

7 Click the Save button on the toolbar, and close the table. Leave the *softball coach* database open.

The Team table is saved with the modifications you have made.

8 Click the Games table to select it and then click **D**esign.

Notice that the table has a counter field that is used as the primary key. Because the team never plays more than one game on any given day, the Date field can serve as the primary key field.

9 Click the row selector for the Date field and then click the Primary Key button on the toolbar.

The primary key icon is now displayed on the row selector button next to the Date field.

10 Click the row selector button for the ID field, and press the Delete Rows button on the toolbar.

A warning message will appear that tells you all data in this field will be deleted permanently (see Figure 7.4).

(Continues)

To Modify a Table Design (Continued)

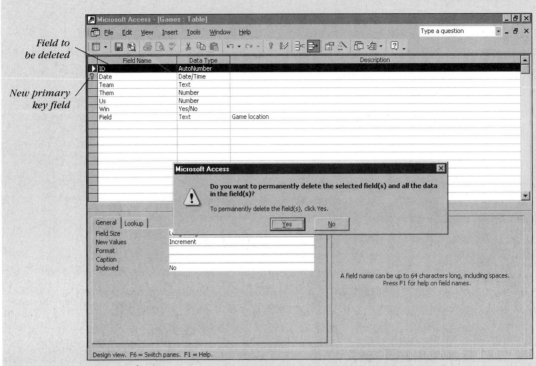

Field to be deleted

New primary key field

Figure 7.4

⑪ **Click** **Yes** **to confirm the deletion of the fields. Close the table and save your changes.**

Keep the database open for use in the next lesson, where you learn to enter a default value.

Lesson 2: Entering a Default Value

At times, you may want a particular value to appear in a specific field for most of the records in your table. In the three new fields you entered in the preceding lesson, for example, you want to use the same city, state, and Zip code for nearly all the records. You can type the entry over and over again for each record, or you can enter a default value.

When you enter a default value, Access automatically uses that field entry for all new records. (All records you entered previously, however, are not affected.) If you are entering a record with a different value, simply type over the default value.

To Enter a Default Value

❶ **Select the Team table and click** **Design. Click in the record selector next to the City field.**

This step selects the field you want to modify. When a field is selected, you see the appropriate field properties for that field type in the lower half of the window. The available properties vary, depending on the data type. In this area, you can enter a default value (see Figure 7.5).

To Enter a Default Value

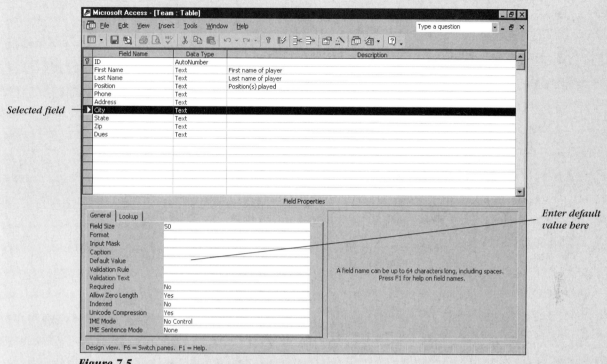

Figure 7.5

② **Click the Default Value property box in the Field Properties area. Type** Ann Arbor **and then press** ⏎Enter.

Notice that Access has placed quotation marks around the default value. They are automatically added to all text entries.

All records you add to the table from here on will default to Ann Arbor in the City field. Typing in the city name will overwrite this field.

If you have problems...

In some cases, you must surround the default value with quotation marks, or Access may display an error message if the entry is mistaken for a command. For example, when you type only **IN** as the default value for the state field, Access thinks you are creating an expression (formula) rather than entering a default value for Indiana. Quotation marks indicate to Access that this is not an expression.

If you see a syntax error message, it means that you forgot to type the quotation marks around the default value in the table design. Click the OK button and then edit the entry in Design view to include the quotation marks.

---

③ **Click in the row selector next to the State field.**

This selects the next field you want to modify.

④ **Click the Default Value property box for this field, and type** MI.

Here is where you enter the value you want to use for all new records.

(Continues)

To Enter a Default Value (Continued)

5 **Click the row selector next to the Zip field.**
This selects the Zip field and displays its properties.

6 **Click the Default Value property box for this field and type 48103.**

7 **Click the Save button.**
This saves the changes you have made to the table design. Now try adding a new record.

8 **Click the View button on the toolbar. Then click the New Record button.**
This switches you to Datasheet view, and moves the insertion point to a new row so that you can enter a new record.

9 **Press** Tab⇆ **to skip the Counter field; then type the following entries, pressing** Tab⇆ **after each one.**

Steve

Rasche

First Base

555-8177

8409 Evanston

Notice that when you get to the City, State, and Zip fields, the values have already been entered (see Figure 7.6).

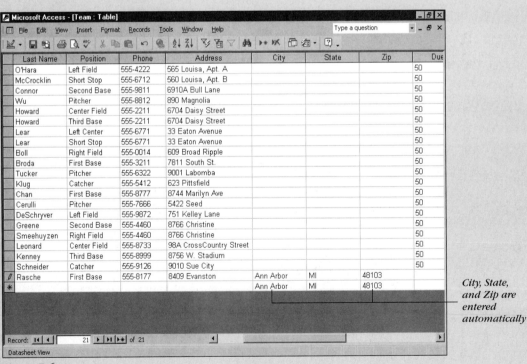

Last Name	Position	Phone	Address	City	State	Zip	Due
O'Hara	Left Field	555-4222	565 Louisa, Apt. A				50
McCrocklin	Short Stop	555-6712	560 Louisa, Apt. B				50
Connor	Second Base	555-9811	6910A Bull Lane				50
Wu	Pitcher	555-8812	890 Magnolia				50
Howard	Center Field	555-2211	6704 Daisy Street				50
Howard	Third Base	555-2211	6704 Daisy Street				50
Lear	Left Center	555-6771	33 Eaton Avenue				50
Lear	Short Stop	555-6771	33 Eaton Avenue				50
Boll	Right Field	555-0014	609 Broad Ripple				50
Broda	First Base	555-3211	7811 South St.				50
Tucker	Pitcher	555-6322	9001 Labomba				50
Klug	Catcher	555-5412	623 Pittsfield				50
Chan	First Base	555-8777	8744 Marilyn Ave				50
Cerulli	Pitcher	555-7666	5422 Seed				50
DeSchryver	Left Field	555-9872	751 Kelley Lane				50
Greene	Second Base	555-4460	8766 Christine				50
Smeehuyzen	Right Field	555-4460	8766 Christine				50
Leonard	Center Field	555-8733	98A CrossCountry Street				50
Kenney	Third Base	555-8999	8756 W. Stadium				50
Schneider	Catcher	555-9126	9010 Sue City				50
Rasche	First Base	555-8177	8409 Evanston	Ann Arbor	MI	48103	
				Ann Arbor	MI	48103	

City, State, and Zip are entered automatically

Record: 21 ▶ ▶I ▶* of 21

Datasheet View

Figure 7.6

10 **Press** Tab⇆ **three times to move past the three fields that have default values and then type 50 in the Dues field. Press** Tab⇆ **to move back to the first field.**
This record is saved when you press Tab⇆ to move to the next record. Keep the Team table open, and continue with the next lesson.

To extend your knowledge...

Creating Small Database Fields

One of the rules of database design is to create the smallest usable fields. In this table, the Address field contains the street number and the street name. This practice reduces the number of fields in the table but it also reduces your options for sorting the data. For example, if you wanted to sort the addresses by street name, it would be difficult because the street number comes first in the field.

Another illustration would be to use a single field for a person's name. If you entered names with the last name followed by a comma and the first name (Preston, John), they would sort properly, but you would have trouble when you wanted to print mailing labels, because the last name would always be listed before the first name. Once again, two fields are best.

In general, do not group two types of data into the same field unless you are confident that the need to use them separately is unlikely to occur. It is difficult to change this decision once the data has been entered.

Lesson 3: Changing a Field Type and Selecting a Format

In addition to adding fields to the table, you can also modify existing fields. Suppose that when you first added fields to your table, you were unfamiliar with the other data types, so you used Text as the data type for all your fields. A Text field type is the most common type and works well in many cases.

Now you have a better understanding of the various field types, and you want to change a particular field type so that it more accurately reflects the format of the data being entered. In this case, you can modify the table design and change the field type.

In this lesson, you change the Dues field to a Number data type and then select a format to display the number as currency. The format controls how the data in that field is displayed and what kind of data can be entered.

To Change a Field Type and Select a Format

❶ With the Team table still open, click the View button to return to Design view.
Remember that you can't make changes to the structure of the table in Datasheet view; you must switch to Design view.

❷ Click in the Data Type column of the Dues field.
This is the field you want to change. You see a down arrow, and the field properties for this field are listed in the lower half of the window. This field currently has a Text field type, but you have entered numbers in this field. You can change it to a Number field.

❸ Click the down arrow.
A drop-down list appears, showing the available data types (see Figure 7.7).

(Continues)

To Change a Field Type and Select a Format (Continued)

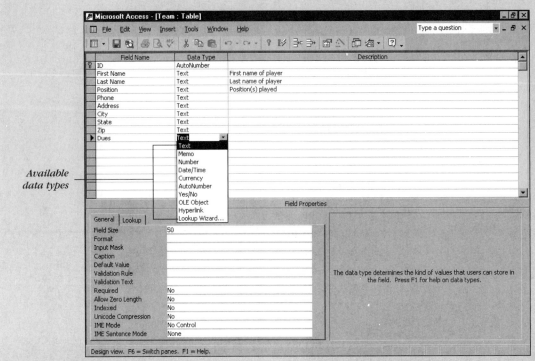

Available data types

Figure 7.7

❹ Click Number in the list.

This selects Number as the data type. You could have selected Currency; however, this method will show you several other options for formatting numbers as well as currency.

❺ Click the Format property box in the Field Properties area.

A down arrow is displayed in the text box.

❻ Click the down arrow.

A drop-down list appears showing the available display formats (see Figure 7.8). The listed formats vary depending on the data type of the selected field.

To Change a Field Type and Select a Format

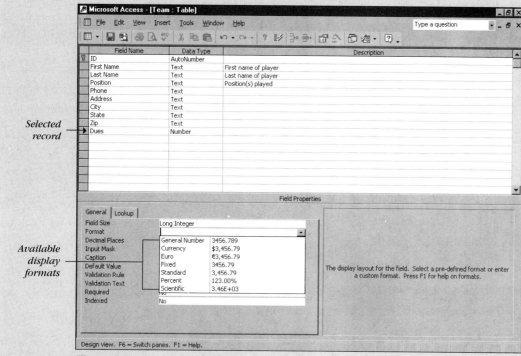

Selected record

Available display formats

Figure 7.8

❼ Click Currency in the list.
This selects Currency as the display format for the selected field.

❽ Click the Save button on the toolbar.
This saves the changes you have made to the table design. To take a look at how these changes affected your table, switch to Datasheet view.

❾ Click the View button on the toolbar.
Scroll to the Dues column and notice how the data is now formatted (see Figure 7.9). Keep the Team table open, and continue to the next lesson, where you learn how to change a field size.

(Continues)

To Change a Field Type and Select a Format (Continued)

Position	Phone	Address	City	State	Zip	Dues
Left Field	555-4222	565 Louisa, Apt. A				$50.00
Short Stop	555-6712	560 Louisa, Apt. B				$50.00
Second Base	555-9811	6910A Bull Lane				$50.00
Pitcher	555-8812	890 Magnolia				$50.00
Center Field	555-2211	6704 Daisy Street				$50.00
Third Base	555-2211	6704 Daisy Street				$50.00
Left Center	555-6771	33 Eaton Avenue				$50.00
Short Stop	555-6771	33 Eaton Avenue				$50.00
Right Field	555-0014	609 Broad Ripple				$50.00
First Base	555-3211	7811 South St.				$50.00
Pitcher	555-6322	9001 Labomba				$50.00
Catcher	555-5412	623 Pittsfield				$50.00
First Base	555-8777	8744 Marilyn Ave				$50.00
Pitcher	555-7666	5422 Seed				$50.00
Left Field	555-9872	751 Kelley Lane				$50.00
Second Base	555-4460	8766 Christine				$50.00
Right Field	555-4460	8766 Christine				$50.00
Center Field	555-8733	98A CrossCountry Street				$50.00
Third Base	555-8999	8756 W. Stadium				$50.00
Catcher	555-9126	9010 Sue City				$50.00
First Base	555-8177	8409 Evanston	Ann Arbor	MI	48103	$50.00
*			Ann Arbor	MI	48103	$0.00

Field with Currency display format

Record: 1 of 21

Datasheet View

Figure 7.9

To extend your knowledge...

Setting Decimal Places and Currency Signs

The Field Properties area is also the place to choose the number of decimal points to use for a number field. The default is *Auto*, which works well if you are using currency with two decimal places. If you wanted a field displaying dollar signs and commas every third number, but with no cents, you would use the drop-down menu in the Decimal Places box and choose 0.

Lesson 4: Changing a Field Size

Another property of your table that you may want to change is the field size. When a field is added to a form or report, the size of the field's text box is determined by the field size. Setting field sizes in the table for fields such as State will reduce the modifications you will have to make to forms and reports later.

Be careful that you do not choose a field size that is too small; doing so limits what you can enter in that field. In the State field, for example, you want to type the two-letter state abbreviation. You can change the field size and then add a description to the field so that anyone who uses this table is aware of this restriction.

To Change a Field Size

1 **With the Team table still open onscreen, click the View button.**
This switches to Design view, which is where you have to be to change the table.

2 **Click the Description column for the State field.**
This is the field you want to change. The field properties for this field are listed in the lower half of the window.

3 **Type Enter two-letter abbreviation.**
This description will appear in the Status bar in Datasheet view when the insertion point is in the State field.

4 **Click the Field Size property box in the Field Properties area.**
The default for text fields is 50, which will be too long for many fields.

5 **Delete *50*, and type 2.**
The new field size is large enough for a two-letter abbreviation for the state (see Figure 7.10).

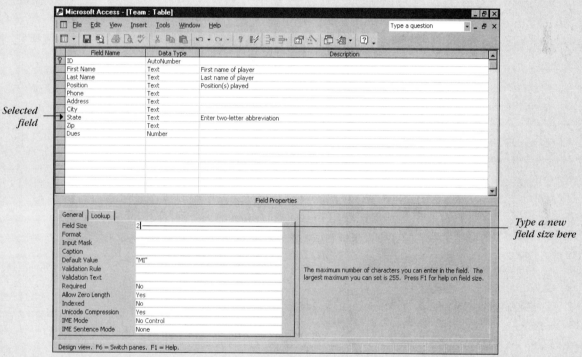

Figure 7.10

6 **Click the Save button.**
Access prompts you to let you know that you may lose some data by reducing the field size (see Figure 7.11). In this case, none of the entries is longer than two characters, so it is safe to proceed.

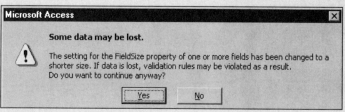

Figure 7.11

(Continues)

To Change a Field Size (Continued)

❼ Click Yes to confirm the change in field size.
Now when you enter a state in the table, you will be able to type only two characters. Keep the Team table open, and continue with the next lesson, where you work with more than one table.

To extend your knowledge...

Effect of Column Width on Field Size

Remember that changing the column width in Datasheet view has no effect on the field size. To change the field size, you must change the field property.

Lesson 5: Working with More Than One Table

Rather than lumping all the information you want to maintain in your Access database into one large table that may be difficult to manage, you can keep your data in more than one table. You can create separate tables and connect them by setting relationships.

To be able to relate tables, the tables must share at least one common field. The data type for the common field must be the same for both tables. You cannot, for example, relate a Text field to a Date/Time field. Once the relationship is established, you can take advantage of it by creating queries that use data from several tables at the same time.

In the rest of this project, you first add a common field you can use to relate two tables; then you enter the data, set the relationships, and use the two tables to create a query.

For this lesson, you want to relate the Games table to the Team table to see who is responsible for the equipment at each game. So that one person doesn't have to be responsible for the equipment all season, the job is rotated to a new player for each game. Start by adding a new field called *Equipment Date*. This field shows the date on which a specific player acts as equipment manager. This date field will then be related to the date field in the Games table.

To Work with More Than One Table

❶ With the Team table still open onscreen, click in the row selector next to the Dues field. Click the Insert Rows button.
Access inserts a new row in which you can enter the new field information.

❷ Click in the Field Name column, and type Equipment Date. **Press** `Tab⇄`.
The field name is entered, and Access moves you to the Data Type column.

❸ Click the down arrow.
A drop-down list appears, showing the available data types.

❹ Click Date/Time in the list.
This selects a Date data type for the Equipment Date field (see Figure 7.12).

To Work with More Than One Table

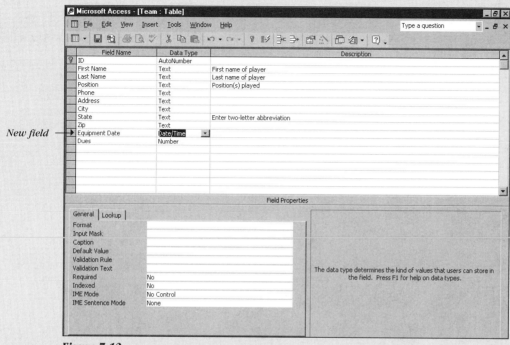

New field →

Figure 7.12

5 **Click the Save button.**

This saves the changes you have made to the table design. Next, you need to enter values in the field you just added.

6 **Click the View button.**

Access displays the table in Datasheet view so that you can enter values into the new field.

There is a problem with entering the Equipment Dates. The new field is several columns away from the column with the players' names.

7 **Point to the field selector for the first column. Click and drag across the first three columns (ID, First Name, and Last Name) to select them.**

8 **Select Format, Freeze Columns from the menu.**

This will keep these columns onscreen while you scroll through the other columns.

9 **Click anywhere in the table to deselect the columns, and scroll the table columns until you can see the name columns and the Equipment Date column at the same time (see Figure 7.13).**

(Continues)

To Work with More Than One Table (Continued)

Heavier line indicates that columns are frozen

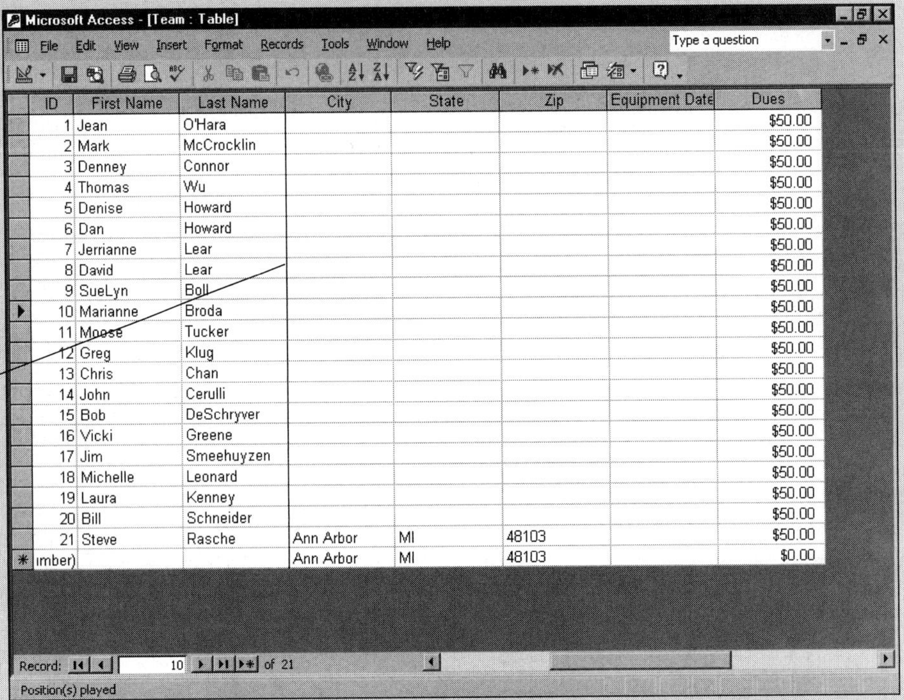

Figure 7.13

10 **Enter the following dates for the appropriate team players.**

Player	Equipment Date
O'Hara	6/23/02
McCrocklin	6/30/02
Connor	7/6/02
Wu	7/13/02
Howard, (Denise)	7/20/02
Howard, (Dan)	7/20/02
Klug	7/27/02
Cerulli	8/3/02
DeSchryver	8/10/02
Greene	8/17/02
Smeehuyzen	8/24/02

These dates match the dates in the Date field of the Games table. Notice that Dan and Denise Howard are sharing the responsibility on July 20 because they ride to the game together (see Figure 7.14). Access saves your entries automatically as you type an entry and move to the next row.

To Work with More Than One Table

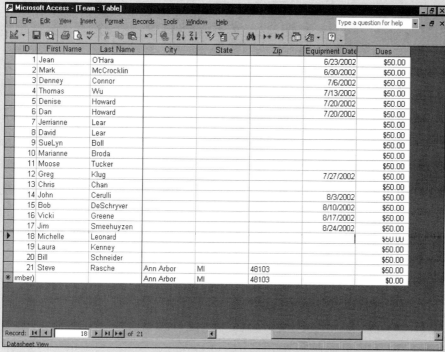

Figure 7.14

⓫ **Close the table by clicking the Close button in the upper right corner of the table window (not the Access window).**
Confirm that you want to save your changes to the layout. This preserves the Freeze Columns feature.

The table closes and the Database window is displayed. From this window, you can set the relationship between the tables, which you do in the next lesson.

To extend your knowledge...

Relating a Number Field to a Counter Field

There is a possibility that the two fields that are used to relate the tables may be different. When the primary key in one table is a counter field and it is used as one of the related fields, it must be related to a number field stored as a long integer in the other table. Counter fields are actually stored as long integers, so this exception still conforms to the "same data type" rule, but it isn't obvious.

Creating Common Fields Among Tables

Setting up common fields among tables that you want to relate is an idea you should consider when you are creating a new database. You can always edit the table to include a linking field, if necessary, and you can use an existing field if it is an appropriate data type.

Lesson 6: Creating Table Relationships

When you want to relate two tables, you choose a field in each table that contains the same values. For example, in the Team table, you now have a list of game dates in the Equipment Date field. These are the same dates contained in the Date field of the Games table.

Often the fields have the same name, but that isn't a requirement for establishing a relationship between the two. The fields must, however, be the same data type.

You can create various types of relationships. In this lesson, you create a one-to-many relationship between the dates in the Games table to the dates in the Team table. A one-to-many relationship requires that the field in the table on the "one" side of the relationship does not contain any duplicate values. The Date field that is used as the primary key for the Games table has this property. The field that will be on the "many" side of the relationship may use the same date more than once. In this example, Dan and Denise Howard are both assigned to take care of the equipment on the same game date.

To Create Table Relationships

1 **Click the Relationships button on the Database toolbar.**
You can also select the Tools menu and choose the Relationships command. The Show Table dialog box is displayed (see Figure 7.15). The first step in the process is to choose the tables you want to relate.

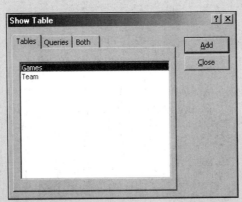

Figure 7.15

 ### If you have problems...
In some cases, such as after you have deleted relationships, the Show Table dialog box will not be displayed when you click the Relationships button. If this happens, click the Show Table button in the Relationship toolbar.

2 **Click the Games table and then click the Add button.**
Access adds the table to the Relationships window; the dialog box remains open.

3 **Click Team and then click the Add button.**
Access adds the Team table to the Relationships window. (The Team table will probably be hidden behind the Show Table dialog box.)

4 **Click the Close button in the Show Table dialog box.**
This closes the dialog box and displays both tables listed in the Relationships window.

To Create Table Relationships

⑤ **Place the pointer on the bottom border of the Team field list and drag down until all the fields are visible (see Figure 7.16). Do the same thing to the Games field list.**

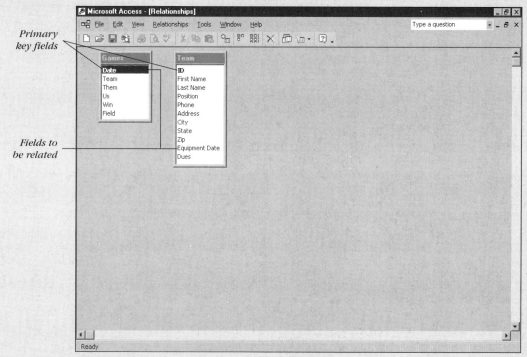

Figure 7.16

The primary key fields of each table are displayed in boldface type.

⑥ **Click the Date field in the Games table, and drag it to the Equipment Date field in the Team table.**

When you release the mouse button, the Edit Relationships dialog box is displayed (see Figure 7.17). In this dialog box, you can confirm that the relationship is correct. You can also set other options, such as the type of relationship you want. For this lesson, the default settings are acceptable.

(Continues)

To Create Table Relationships (Continued)

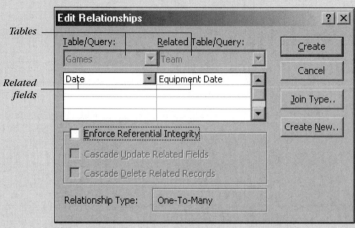

Figure 7.17

❼ **Click the Create button.**
Access creates the relationship. A line connects the two fields (see Figure 7.18).

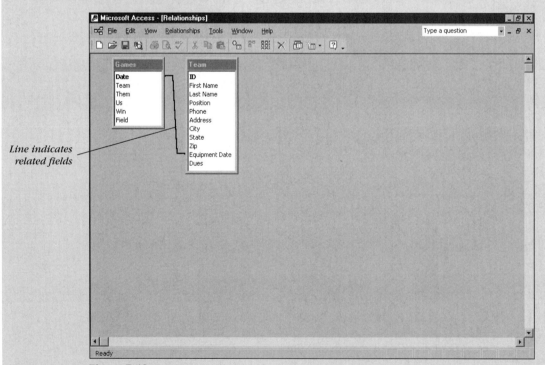

Figure 7.18

❽ **Click the Save button on the toolbar.**
This saves the relationship you just created; the Relationships window remains open.

❾ **Close the Relationships window.**
You return to the Database window. Keep the *softball coach* database open as you continue to the next lesson, where you create a multiple-table query.

To extend your knowledge...

Referential Integrity

When you create a one-to-many relationship, you can elect to **enforce referential integrity**. This is used to ensure that each record in the related table is connected to a record in the primary table. This helps prevent orphan records. It also prevents you from adding records that are not connected to an existing record in the primary table.

Deleting or Changing a Relationship

To delete a relationship, click the line connecting the two tables and press Del. Access prompts you to confirm the deletion. Click the OK button. Once the relationship has been deleted, the relationship can be re-created by dragging the field name from one table onto the field name in the second table.

If you want to change the relationship options, right-click on the line, then choose Edit Relationship from the shortcut menu. This option is also available in the Relationships menu choice.

Changing the Field Size of a Joined Field

You cannot change the field size of a field that is part of a relationship. If you want to change the field size of a field in a relationship, you need to remove the relationship first.

Lesson 7: Creating a Multiple-Table Query

After you have established a relationship between tables, you can create forms and queries using data from both tables. When you have defined a relationship, Access automatically knows how to relate the data in the two tables and creates a ***join***.

When you create a query that involves two or more tables, Access gives you a choice of three types of joins. The most commonly used join includes only those records with matching values in the common field in both tables. For example, your Games table includes the dates for all the Softball matches. Access uses these dates to create the join and pulls only the records with matching date entries from the Equipment Date field of the Team table. The other two types of joins include all the records from one table and just the matching records from the other table.

In this lesson, you create a query that lists three fields from the Games table: Date, Team, and Field; and one field, Equipment Manager, from the Team table.

To Create a Multiple-Table Query

❶ Click the Queries object button in the *softball coach* Database window, and click the New button.
The New Query dialog box is displayed, showing the different query design options.

❷ Select Design View and click OK.
The Show Table dialog box is displayed with the Query window in the background.

❸ Click the Games table and then click the Add button.
This adds the Games table to the query window.

❹ Click the Team table and then click the Add button.
This adds the Team table to the query window.

❺ Click the Close button.

(Continues)

To Create a Multiple-Table Query (Continued)

Notice that the relationship between the two tables is displayed. Also displayed are field lists for each table; you will need to scroll the list of Team fields to see the related field (see Figure 7.19).

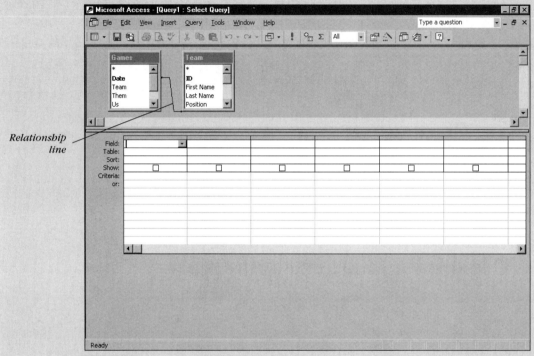

Figure 7.19

❻ **From the Games field list, drag the Date field to the first column in the design grid; then drag the Team field from the Games field list to the second column.**
The Date and Team fields are added to the query.

❼ **Drag the Last Name field from the Team field list to the third column in the design grid.**
The Last Name field is added to the query.

❽ **Drag the First Name field from the Team field list to the fourth column in the design grid.**
The First Name field is added to the query.

❾ **Drag Field from the Games field list to the fifth column of the design grid.**
You may have to scroll down the field list and scroll to the right to find the fifth column. You now have added all the fields you want to include in the query (see Figure 7.20). Check the results of the query.

To Create a Multiple-Table Query

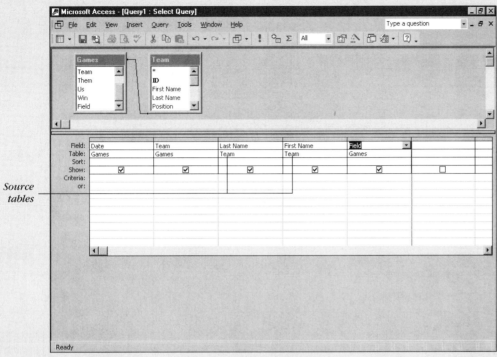

Figure 7.20

⓾ Click the View button on the toolbar.
The results of your query are displayed (see Figure 7.21). The query lists the game date, team played, equipment manager's last and first name, and playing field location. You can save this query.

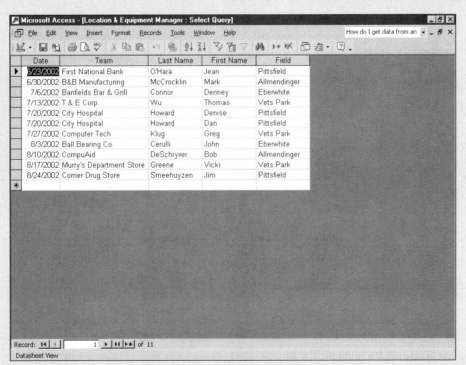

Figure 7.21

(Continues)

To Create a Multiple-Table Query (Continued)

⓫ Click the Save button.
The Save As dialog box is displayed.

⓬ Type Location & Equipment Manager **and click the OK button.**
This step saves the query with the name Location & Equipment Manager.

⓭ Close the query so that you are back in the *softball coach* **Database window and then close the database.**
If you have completed your session on the computer, exit Access. Otherwise, continue with the "Checking Concepts and Terms" section in this project.

To extend your knowledge...

Removing Joins Between Tables in a Query

You can also remove the joins between tables in a query. To do this, click on the line that joins the field lists. The line becomes much thicker, indicating that the relationship has been selected. Press Del. The line (and the relationship) is removed. This does not affect any relationships between the tables other than in this one query.

Summary

You can use the field properties in a table to help control the data that is entered. In this project, you learned how to modify a table by changing the field size, type, and format. You also learned how to work with more than one table by creating a relationship between tables and by using more than one table in a query.

To expand your knowledge, examine some of the other property options in the table Design view. Notice how the properties that are available depend on the data type of the field that is selected. Use Help to look for information on table field properties. Use the Field Properties Reference page, select a property that is of interest to you, and read how it works. Some of the properties are set in the table; others are set in a form or report.

Checking Concepts and Terms

Multiple Choice

Circle the letter of the correct answer for each of the following questions.

1. Which button do you use to insert a new field into a table in Design view? [L1]

   a. Insert Rows

   b. Insert Fields

   c. New Record

   d. Field Design

2. How are related tables displayed in the relationship or query window? [L6]

   a. Related fields are in boldface.

   b. Related fields are underlined.

   c. Related fields are connected by a line.

   d. Related fields are aligned next to each other.

3. When you define a default value for a field, how or when is that value used? [L2]

   a. for all existing records

   b. only for new records

   c. only for records that contain a blank field

   d. only when you select a special command

4. Why must you be careful about how you designate the information you use as default values? [L2]

   a. You can't use default values.

   b. The information must be used for every new record that follows.

   c. Even though you designate the information, you must Paste it each time you are in that field.

   d. Some words are reserved for Access commands and must be enclosed by quotation marks.

5. Where are default values entered? [L2]

   a. in the dialog box that appears when you select the Properties button on the toolbar

   b. in the Default Value box in the Field Properties area of the table Design view window

   c. in the Default Value box next to the Data Type box in the field definition area of the Table Design view window

   d. in the dialog box that appears when you select Default Values from the Edit menu

Screen ID

Label each element of the Access screen shown in Figure 7.22 and Figure 7.23.

A. Insert Rows button

B. Delete Rows button

C. Field selector indicator

D. Primary key indicator

E. View button

F. Source tables

G. Relationship line

H. Primary key field

I. Show Table button

J. Table name

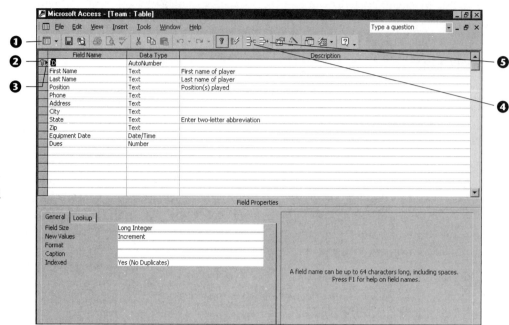

Figure 7.22

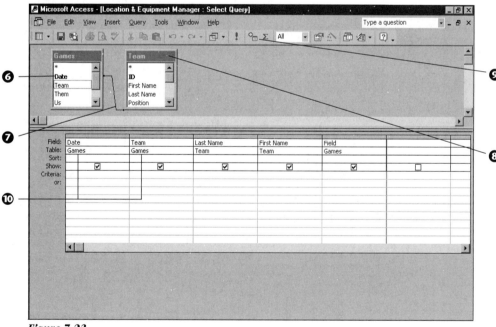

Figure 7.23

1. _____   6. _____

2. _____   7. _____

3. _____   8. _____

4. _____   9. _____

5. _____   10. _____

Discussion

1. In the databases with which you are familiar, how is data integrity maintained? What steps and procedures are used? Are there controls that restrict the type of data that can be entered in each field? How does this help to ensure that good data is entered? What are some of these controls?

2. When would it make sense to use a default value for a field? When would you not use a default for a field?

3. If you were a sales representative for a company and you had an assigned list of customers you were responsible for, what kind of information would you want to maintain about your customers? How might the company use a relational database to keep track of their sales force and their customers? How would these two sets of records be related?

Skill Drill exercises reinforce project skills. Each skill reinforced is the same, or nearly the same, as a skill presented in the project. Each exercise includes a brief narrative introduction, followed by detailed instructions in a step-by-step format.

The database you will use in the Skill Drill exercises contains a short table of suppliers for a small swimming pool, spa, and sauna company. It also contains a table containing a list of swimming pool parts.

1. Adding a Field to a Table

For billing purposes, you find that you need the tax number of your suppliers. There is no field for a tax number, so you will need to create one. It will need to go between the Phone field and the Billing field.

To add a field to a table, complete the following steps:

1. Copy the ea1-0702 database file, remove the read-only status of the copied file, and name it **pool store**. Open the new database. Select the Parts Suppliers table and click the Design button.
2. Click anywhere in the Billing field and click the Insert Rows button to insert a row between the Phone field and the Billing field.
3. Add a new field called **Tax Number**.
4. Accept Text as the Data Type.
5. Close the table and save your changes.

2. Adding a Default Value

There is a field in the Parts Supplier table that contains billing data. The various suppliers give you 30, 45, or 60 days to pay for your orders. Most of the suppliers use 30-day billing, so to save time, you decide it would be a good idea to add a default value to the field.

To add a default value, complete the following steps:

1. In the *pool store* database, select the Parts Supplier table and click the Design button.
2. Click anywhere in the Billing field.
3. Click in the Default Value box in the Field Properties area.
4. Enter "**30 Day**" for the Billing default value.
5. Close the table and save your changes.

3. Changing the Field Type

Because both the Price and Sale Price fields are dollar amounts, you would like to add dollar signs and decimal places to the fields. The easiest way to do this is to change the field types.

To change the field type, complete the following steps:

1. In the *pool store* database, select the Pool Parts Inventory table, and click the Design button.
2. Move to the Data Type column of the Price field.
3. Click the drop-down arrow, and select Currency from the drop-down list.
4. Move to the Data Type column of the Sale Price field.
5. Click the drop-down arrow, and select Currency from the drop-down list.
6. Click the View button to switch to Datasheet view. Save your changes when prompted. Look at the two fields you just changed.
7. Close the table.

4. Changing the Field Size

All of the fields in the Parts Supplier table are text fields, and most of them are too large.

To change the field size, complete the following steps:

1. In the *pool store* database, select the Parts Suppliers table, and click the Design button.
2. Click anywhere in the Contact field.
3. Delete the Field Size in the Field Properties area, and type **30** to change the field size to 30 characters.
4. Repeat the above procedure to change the field size of the City field to 20 characters.
5. Change the Phone, Zip, and Billing fields to 10 characters and the State field to two characters.
6. Close the table and save your changes. Click Yes to confirm that data could be lost.

5. Creating Table Relationships

You want to eventually be able to create a query that shows the contact person for each of the pool parts. The first step in this process is to create a relationship between the tables. The only fields that contain the same information are the Name field in the Parts Supplier table and the Distributor field in the Pool Parts Inventory field.

To create table relationships, complete the following steps:

1. In the Database window of the *pool store* database, click the Relationships button. If the Show Table dialog box is not displayed, click the Show Table button.
2. Select the Parts Suppliers table, and click the Add button.
3. Select the Pool Parts Inventory table, and click the Add button.
4. Click the Close button to close the Show Table dialog box.
5. Click the Name field in the Parts Suppliers field list, and drag it on top of the Distributor field in the Pool Parts Inventory field list.
6. Click the Create button to create the relationship.
7. Close the Relationships window, and save your changes.

6. Creating a Multiple-Table Query

You want to be able to print out a list of pool parts along with the names and telephone numbers of the contact person at the company that sells the parts. To do this, you need to create a query that is based on both tables in the *pool store* database.

To create a multiple-table query, complete the following steps:

1. In the *pool store* database, click the Queries object button and then click the Design button.
2. Select the Parts Suppliers table in the Show Table dialog box, and click the Add button.

3. Select the Pool Parts Inventory table, and click the <u>A</u>dd button.

4. Click the <u>C</u>lose button to close the Show Table dialog box.

5. Click the Contact field from the Parts Suppliers field list, and drag it into the first empty field of the query design table.

6. Click and drag the Phone field from the Parts Suppliers field list into the next empty field.

7. Click and drag the Part Name field from the Pool Parts Inventory field list into the next empty field.

8. Click and drag the Description field from the Pool Parts Inventory field list into the next empty field.

9. Click the View button to see the results of your query in Datasheet view.

10. Close the query, and save it as `Contacts and Parts`.

Challenge

Challenge exercises expand on or are somewhat related to skills presented in the lessons. Each exercise provides a brief narrative introduction followed by instructions in a numbered step or bulleted list format that are not as detailed as those in the Skill Drill section.

You will be using two databases for the Challenge exercises. The first is a modified version of the one you used in the Skill Drill exercises. The two tables could benefit from a few modifications, such as lists and drop-down boxes for fields with common entries. They could also use an input format for telephone number entry.

The second database contains information with which you are becoming familiar—tornado data. You will use this database to link three tables together. You will also create both a report and a form that draw information from more than one table.

1. Formatting Fields Using Input Masks

Input masks are special formatting features that make data entry easier. For example, when typing in a phone number, it helps to have the various parts set up in a (999)000-0000 format. Other types of data that can benefit from input masks are Social Security numbers, 9-digit Zip codes, dates, and time. In the Parts Suppliers table, the phone number has been entered as a long string of numbers. You will add an input mask to the Phone field.

To format a field using an input mask, complete the following steps:

1. Copy the ea1-0703 database file, remove the read-only status from the copied file, and rename it `pool store data`.

2. Open the *pool store data* database, and open the Parts Suppliers table in Design view.

3. Select the Phone field, and click in the Input Mask box of the Field Properties area.

4. Click the Build button (the one with three dots) on the right edge of the Input Mask box.

If you have problems...

You may get a message that Access can't start this wizard. This feature is not installed as part of the standard installation. You will be asked if you want to install it now. Check with your instructor for directions if you are in a computer lab. If you are using your own machine, insert the CD-ROM that came with your software and choose <u>Y</u>es.

5. Select the Phone Number input mask from the Input Mask Wizard dialog box.
6. Accept the defaults in the other wizard dialog boxes.
7. Switch to Datasheet view to look at the results of your new input mask.
8. Close the table.

2. Creating a List Box

When there are only a few choices that can be made in a field, you can place a list on the screen from which the user can choose. This is called a *list box*. List boxes have the advantage of making sure that data that is entered is entered consistently and with no typographical errors. Nothing can be entered into the field except those items shown in the list box. List boxes can also be added to forms.

To create a list box, complete the following steps:

1. In the *pool store data* database, open the Parts Suppliers table in Design view.
2. Click anywhere in the Billing field, and click the Lookup tab in the Field Properties area.
3. Use the Display Control drop-down arrow to select List Box.
4. Select Value List from the Row Source Type drop-down menu.
5. In the Row Source box, type "30 Day";"45 Day";"60 Day" exactly as shown. The quotation marks identify each item in the list, and the semicolons separate the list items.
6. Switch to Datasheet view to observe the results of your changes.
7. Close the table.

3. Creating a Drop-Down (Combo) Box

A second useful list type is called a *combo box*. This creates a list arrow and a drop-down list of choices for a field. The advantages of combo boxes are that they take up no more room than a standard field text box, and you can type in an item that is not included on the list. Combo boxes can also be added to forms.

To create a combo box, complete the following steps:

1. In the *pool store data* database, open the Pool Parts Inventory table in Design view.
2. Select the Distributor field, and click the Lookup tab in the Field Properties area.
3. Change the Display Control to Combo Box.
4. Change the Row Source to the Parts Suppliers table.
5. Switch to Datasheet view, and click in the Distributor field in the empty record at the end of the table.
6. Click the drop-down arrow to see your combo box.
7. Close the table and then close the *pool store data* database.

4. Linking Three Tables Together

It is possible to link more than two tables at a time. The database you will be working with in the next three exercises contains three tables—one with county names, one with state names, and one with tornado data and codes for the county and state names. The last two exercises involve creating queries and reports using all three tables. The first thing you must do is to create a relationship between the three tables.

To link three tables together, complete the following steps:

1. Copy the ea1-0704 database file, remove the read-only status from the copied file, and rename it five year tornado data. Open the database.
2. Open the Relationships window and then show the list of tables.
3. Add all three tables to the Relationships window.
4. Increase the size of the 5 Year US Tornado field list so that you can see all of the fields.
5. Move the field lists around in the Relationships window so that the 5 Year US Tornado field list is in the middle.

6. Create a relationship between the CountyID field in the 5 Year US Tornado table and the CountyID field in the County Names table.

7. Create a relationship between the StateID field in the 5 Year US Tornado table and the State field in the County Names table.

8. Close the Relationships window, and save your changes.

5. Creating a Query Using Fields from Three Tables

Now that you have created a relationship between the three tables, you can create a query that eliminates the code numbers for the counties and states and replaces them with the actual county and state names. This will make the data easier to read and understand.

To create a query using fields from multiple tables, complete the following steps:

1. Use the available help features to create a query containing fields from all three tables in the *five year tornado data* database. Use the Simple Query Wizard.

2. Include all of the fields from the 5 Year US Tornadoes table except the StateID, CountyID, and County fields.

3. Include the State Name field from the State Names table.

4. Include the County Name field from the County Names table.

5. Save the query using the default name.

6. Move the State Name field so that it is displayed in the first column, and display the County Name field in the second column.

7. Sort on four fields in the following order: State Name, County Name, Year, and Date. Preview your query.

8. Close the query, and save your changes.

6. Creating a Report Using Fields from Multiple Tables

A report can be produced in two ways. You can base it directly on the tables that contain the data, or you can base it on a query, where the work of selecting the tables, fields, criteria, and sort order has already been done.

To create a report using fields from multiple tables, complete the following steps:

1. Use the available help features to create a report based on the 5 Year US Tornadoes query in the *five year tornado data* database. Use the Report Wizard.

2. Accept all of the defaults. Name the report `Tornadoes`.

3. Fix any labels or data that are cut off.

4. Put your name in the center of the page footer and then print page 70 of the report.

5. Close the report. Close the database, and exit Access unless you are going to try the Discovery Zone exercises.

Discovery Zone exercises require advanced knowledge of topics presented in *essentials* lessons, application of skills from multiple lessons, or self-directed learning of new skills.

1. Creating Your Own Input Mask

Access has pre-set input masks for phone numbers, Social Security numbers, 9-digit Zip codes, and several other common data structures. You may have a data structure that is common in your business. Perhaps you would like to create an input mask for that data. You added a Tax Number field to the Parts Suppliers table in the *pool store* database earlier in this project. This field could use an input mask to aid in data entry, because all tax numbers have the same structure.

Goal: Create a new input mask and add it to the list of input masks available in Access.

Use the ea1-0705 file to create a new database called **pool inventory** on your disk. Use any available help from your computer or online to understand how to add an input mask to the Tax Number field. There should be a dash after the second character in the tax number and a dash before the last character. For example, the tax number for the Compaq Spa and Pool should read 2A-436234-C. Your input mask should:

- Require the entry of the two letters as letters.
- Require the entry of the seven numbers as numbers (0 through 9).
- Automatically change any letters entered into the input mask to uppercase.
- Insert a dash after the second character and before the last character.
- Use the underscore character as a placeholder for blanks while data is being entered.
- Store the dashes along with the letters and numbers.
- Show the Compaq Spa and Pool tax number (2A-436234-C) as the sample number in the Input Mask wizard.
- Save the new input mask so that you can use it in future databases.

Hint #1: You can make the input mask work by typing it into the Input Mask box in the Field Properties area of the Tax Number field, but in order to do the last two steps, you will need to use the Tax Number Build button.

Hint #2: You do not want to replace an existing input mask. When you are creating the input mask, no input mask should be displayed.

Enter a new record with the following data (these are in the order of the fields in your Parts Suppliers table): `Twinhead Chemicals, William McMahon, 4722 Edison Lane, Port Huron, MI, 48060, (810) 986-0000, 1B-7536222-Z, 30 Day.` When you enter the tax number, enter lowercase letters to see if the program automatically changes them to uppercase.

2. Creating Validation Rules and Validation Error Messages

All of your suppliers come from Michigan or northern Ohio, which means that all of the Zip codes you enter will begin with the number 4. You are also using just the five-digit Zip code rather than the nine-digit Zip code. To help avoid typographical errors in the future, you would like to have the program automatically detect when an incorrect Zip code is added, and include a message on the screen to help the user.

Goal: Create a validation rule for a Zip code field and add an error message to be displayed when an incorrect number is entered.

Use the *pool inventory* file that you created in the first exercise of the Discovery section. If you did not do the first exercise, use the ea1-0705 file to create a new database called **pool inventory** on your disk. Read through the Access help on validation rules and validation text to understand how validation works. Use the following guidelines:

- The validation rule should restrict entry to five-digit numbers beginning with the number 4.
- The error message that appears when an incorrect entry is made should say `The Zip code must be a 5-digit number beginning with the number 4.`

Hint #1: The Zip field is a text field, but that does not matter in this case. The procedure would be the same for a text field containing numbers or a numeric field.

Hint #2: You will need to build an expression for the validation rule so that you test the entry to make sure it is between two numbers.

Add a new record, and try to type in a number that does not meet your conditions to make sure your validation rule and validation text work the way you want.

3. Designing a Table for Employee Records

You have been asked to create a database for tracking employee information for Jackson Water Service. The business has not had a database system for this purpose, and the owner is depending on you to set up a database based on some general guidelines that he provides. Use your knowledge of creating a database, and of customizing tables and fields to create a database for Jackson Water Service.

Mr. Jackson, the owner, needs to track his employees' names and addresses for mailing purposes as well as a contact number for emergency situations. He also needs to know to which department they are assigned, their salary, overtime salary, and date hired. Beginning hourly salary is $15; beginning hourly overtime salary is $22.50.

Each employee has an ID assigned when they are hired that uses the following format—AC0001— where AC represents the first two letters of the department name to which the employee is assigned, followed by four numeric characters. Each employee ID is unique.

Create a database that contains at least two tables for tracking the necessary employee information. Add any input masks and formatting you think necessary for ease of data input and adjust all field sizes for the most appropriate size. Save the database as **Jackson Water Service** and use table names of your choice.

Enter the information for the following new employee to test your tables. If you have additional fields for which information is not given here, add your own information in those fields. James Saxon was hired today to work in the Marketing Department. His address is 327 Mercury Lane, Southfield, CA 89675-2145 and his emergency contact number is 695-967-8565.

When completed, close the database and then exit Access.

Integrating Access with Other Sources of Data and the Internet

Objectives

In this project, you learn how to

✔ Convert a Database from a Previous Version of Access

✔ Link an Access Table to a Form Letter in Word

✔ Merge an Access Table with a Form Letter

✔ Import a Table from Excel

✔ Create a Data Access Page Using the Page Wizard

✔ Use a Browser to Interact with the Database

Key terms introduced in this project include

❑ browser
❑ data access page
❑ delimiter
❑ import
❑ mail merge

Why Would I Do This?

As you have seen, the data in a database may come from another source—another database, a spreadsheet, or even the Internet. The files you interact with may be on your computer or on a computer anywhere in the world. The *tornado information* database that you used in an earlier project, for example, was obtained over the Internet from the U.S. Storm Data Center. You can also use the power of Access in combination with Microsoft Word to produce form letters that can send information to people individually.

The reports, queries, and forms you create may need to be seen by others. Access is capable of placing information on the World Wide Web so that it can be accessed from anywhere in the world.

Visual Summary

When you have completed this project, you will have created a document that merges data from a table of addresses, imported a table of data from a non-Access source, and set up the database for use on the Internet. The merged document, the imported table, and a form as a Web page look like Figures 8.1, 8.2, and 8.3.

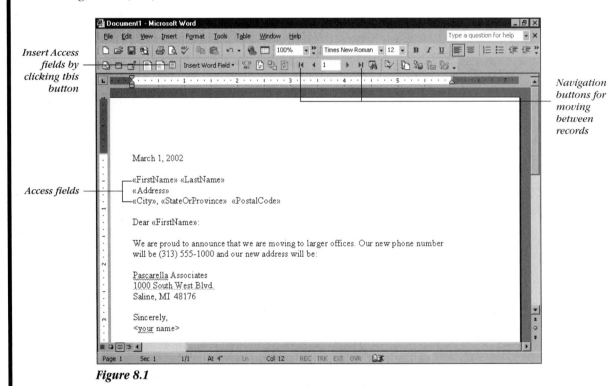

Figure 8.1

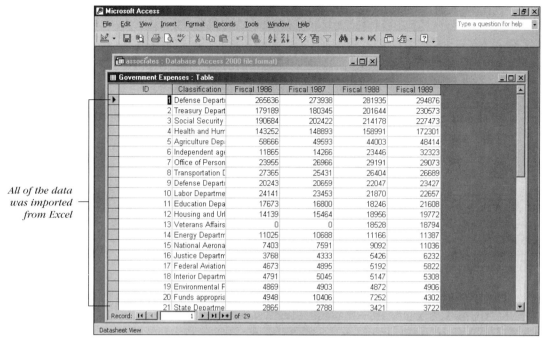

All of the data was imported from Excel

Figure 8.2

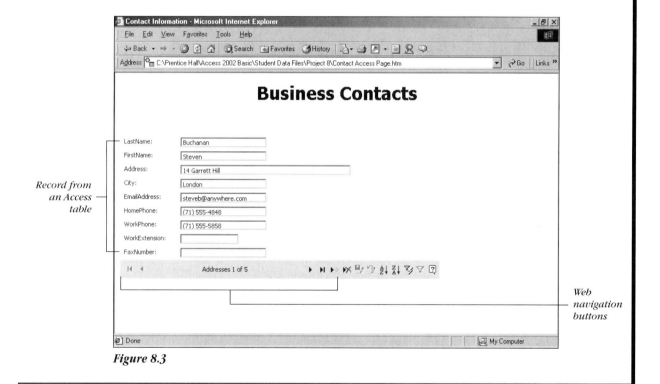

Record from an Access table

Web navigation buttons

Figure 8.3

Lesson 1: Converting a Database from a Previous Version of Access

Access has changed its basic file structure to conform to an international standard that supports several languages. Databases stored using previous versions of Access will be converted automatically to the new version. Older versions of Access cannot read this data structure, and there is no program provided at this time to convert entire Access 2002 databases into older versions of Access. Access does not have a Save As option like the other Office products.

In this lesson, you convert a database from an older version of Access to the Access default file format.

To Convert a Database from a Previous Version of Access

❶ **Launch Access. Click *More files* in the task pane to open an existing file.**

❷ **Find and select the ea1-0801 file in the student data files. Click O͟pen.**
The Convert/Open Database dialog box is displayed (see Figure 8.4).

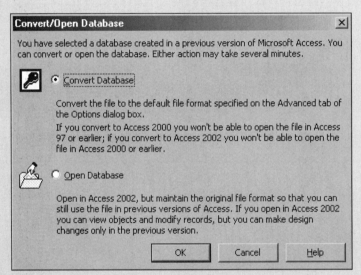

Convert/Open Database   ⊠

You have selected a database created in a previous version of Microsoft Access. You can convert or open the database. Either action may take several minutes.

⊙ Convert Database

Convert the file to the default file format specified on the Advanced tab of the Options dialog box.
If you convert to Access 2000 you won't be able to open the file in Access 97 or earlier; if you convert to Access 2002 you won't be able to open the file in Access 2000 or earlier.

○ Open Database

Open in Access 2002, but maintain the original file format so that you can still use the file in previous versions of Access. If you open in Access 2002 you can view objects and modify records, but you can make design changes only in the previous version.

OK   Cancel   Help

Figure 8.4

❸ **Select the C͟onvert Database option button and click OK.**
The *Convert Database Into* dialog box is displayed.

❹ **Choose the drive and folder in which you store your files in the Save i͟n drop-down list box. Change the name to associates in the File n͟ame text box (see Figure 8.5).**

To Convert a Database from a Previous Version of Access

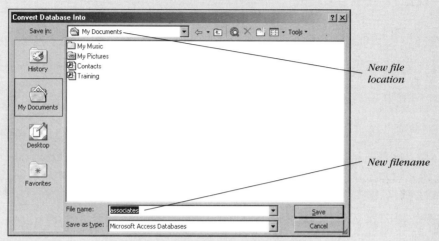

New file location

New filename

Figure 8.5

5 **Click Save.**

The file is converted and placed on your disk. The process may take a while, depending on the speed of your computer. When it is done, a caution box appears (see Figure 8.6).

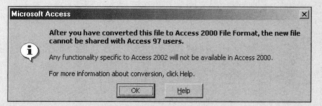

Figure 8.6

6 **Click OK.**

The file will open automatically. Leave the *associates* database open to use in the next lesson.

 ## To extend your knowledge...

Opening an Older Database Without Converting

The Convert/Open Database window also enables you to use the database without updating it to Access 2002. If you want to open the database without converting it, choose the Open Database option button. This is particularly important if you are sharing the database with someone who is still using an older version of the program. The limitation is that you cannot change the design of any of the objects in the database using Access 2002 until the database has been converted to this version. If structural changes are to be made, they have to be done by the person using the older version.

Lesson 2: Linking an Access Table to a Form Letter in Word

Databases that contain names and addresses can be merged with Microsoft Word documents to create a series of documents in which each document contains data that is unique to that individual. This feature is known as **_mail merge_**. We have all received mail that has a label attached with our names and addresses on it, and most of us have received letters that have our names, birthdays, addresses, or phone numbers embedded in the text. These are examples of how an organization can communicate with its members. Such mailings are not limited to postal services—you can also create mailings for fax or e-mail.

In this lesson, you create a letter to notify your business associates that you are moving and will have a new address and phone number.

To Link an Access Table to a Form Letter in Word

1 **If it is not already highlighted, select the Addresses table in the Database window. Click the list arrow to the right of the OfficeLinks button on the Standard toolbar.**
A list of links to other Microsoft Office programs is displayed.

2 **Select <u>M</u>erge It with Microsoft Word.**
The Microsoft Word Mail Merge Wizard dialog box is displayed (see Figure 8.7).

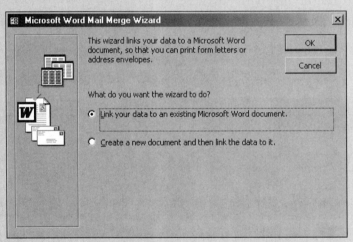

Figure 8.7

3 **Click the option button labeled _Create a new document and then link the data to it_. Click OK.**
Microsoft Word is launched and a new document opens. Notice that the Mail Merge toolbar is displayed (see Figure 8.8).

To Link an Access Table to a Form Letter in Word

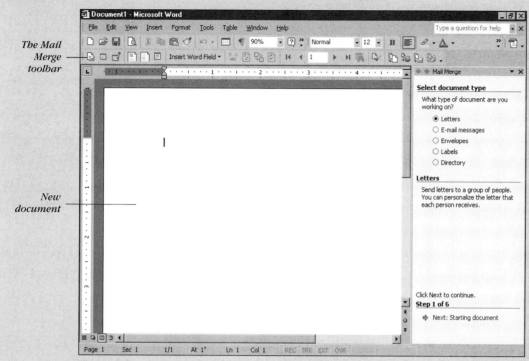

Figure 8.8

 If you have problems...

The Mail Merge toolbar should open. It may be above or below the formatting or standard toolbar. If it does not open, you can open it by choosing View, Toolbars from the menu and then click Mail Merge to open the toolbar.

④ Maximize the Word window, change the Zoom to 100%, and set the Font Size to 12, if necessary. Close the task pane.

⑤ Type today's date in the first line, and press ⏎Enter twice.
Notice that when you begin typing the date, Word automatically suggests the month, then the date. You can press ⏎Enter to accept the month, then press Spacebar. Press ⏎Enter again when today's date appears and the date will be completed for you. Press ⏎Enter twice more to move the insertion point down two lines.

⑥ Click the Insert Merge Fields button on the Mail Merge toolbar.
The Insert Merge Field dialog box displays a list of fields from the Addresses table in the *associates* database. You select one field at a time from this list to create the inside address for a letter.

⑦ Select the Database Fields option button, if necessary.

⑧ Click FirstName, click the Insert button, and then click Close. Press Spacebar.

(Continues)

To Link an Access Table to a Form Letter in Word (Continued)

The name of the field is placed in the document and is followed by a space.

9 **Click the Insert Merge Fields button again, and click LastName. Click Insert and then click Close.**
The LastName field is placed after the FirstName field.

10 **Press ⏎Enter to move to the next line of the address. Refer to the Figure 8.9 to create the rest of the document.**

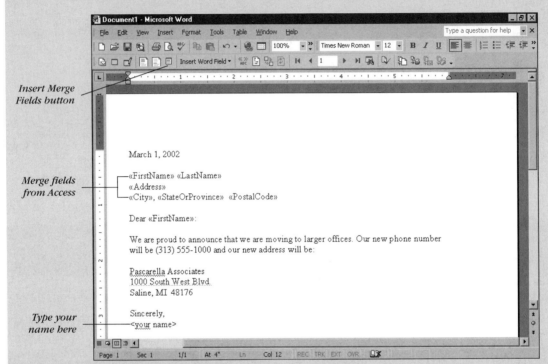

Insert Merge Fields button

Merge fields from Access

Type your name here

March 1, 2002

«FirstName» «LastName»
«Address»
«City», «StateOrProvince» «PostalCode»

Dear «FirstName»:

We are proud to announce that we are moving to larger offices. Our new phone number will be (313) 555-1000 and our new address will be:

Pascarella Associates
1000 South West Blvd.
Saline, MI 48176

Sincerely,
<your name>

Figure 8.9

Type your name in the last line rather than *<your name>*. Be sure to include the comma after the City field and spaces as appropriate. If the Office Assistant opens, just click Cancel to close it.

? If you have problems...

The font size on your letter may revert to 10 point or whatever default font is set for your computer. If this happens, don't worry about it. The goal of this lesson is to show you how to merge a database file with a Word document, and the formatting of the letter is not critical to this purpose.

11 **Click the Save button.**
The Save As dialog box opens.

12 **Type associates in the File name text box, and use the Save in drop-down list box to select the disk drive and folder that you are using for your files.**

13 **Click Save.**
The document is saved as *associates* for later use. Leave the document and the database open for use in the next lesson.

To extend your knowledge...

Using a Query-Based Mail Merge

You can also use the mail merge feature with a query. This is useful when you need to include a calculated field in the letter, restrict the mailing to clients who meet a certain criteria, or use fields from more than one table.

Naming an Access Database to Match a Word Document

Microsoft Word documents are automatically saved with a file extension of .doc, and Access databases are saved with an .mdb extension. You can use the same name for the Word document and the Access database, because they will have different extensions, even though the extensions may not appear onscreen.

Lesson 3: Merging an Access Table with a Form Letter

Once you have linked the database field names into a Word document, you can create a series of documents that each contain the data from a record in the database table. This process creates a file of the merged, personalized letters. You also print a few of the letters to ensure that they do not contain errors before you send the rest of them to the printer.

In this lesson, you merge the database file into the letter and print two of the documents.

To Merge an Access Table with a Form Letter

❶ Click the View Merged Data button on the Mail Merge toolbar in Word.
The data from the first record in the Addresses table is inserted into the document (see Figure 8.10).

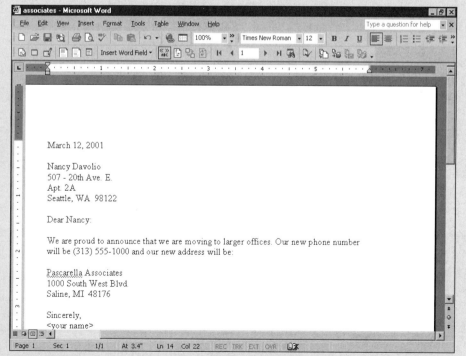

Figure 8.10

(Continues)

To Merge an Access Table with a Form Letter (Continued)

2 **Click the Next Record button.**
The data from the second record is displayed. Notice that the address of the first person takes two lines, whereas the second person's address takes only one line. Word adjusts for multiple line addresses and for empty fields.

3 **Click the Merge to New Document button on the Mail Merge toolbar.**
The Merge to New Document dialog box appears with options much like the Print dialog box. You must specify which records to merge (see Figure 8.11).

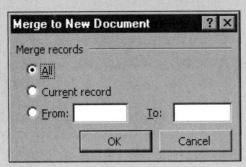

Figure 8.11

When merging, you have the choice of output. You can print to a new document, a printer, e-mail, or fax.

4 **Choose From and then type 1. Press Tab⇆ to move to the To box and then type 5. Click OK.**
Only the first five records are merged. You are now ready to print a couple of records to make sure the merge codes are placed correctly. Figure 8.12 shows two of the five records that matched.

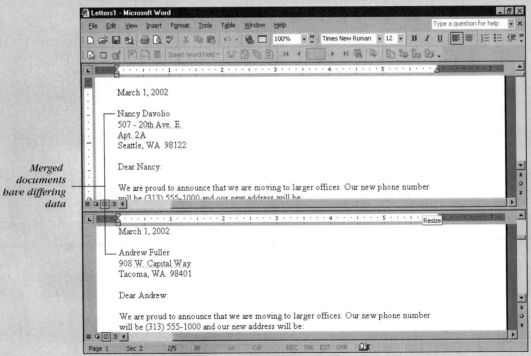

Merged documents have differing data

Figure 8.12

To Merge an Access Table with a Form Letter

⑤ Choose File, Print. Print only pages 1 and 2.
The first two letters are printed.

⑥ Close the merge document without saving changes. Close the *associates* Word document.
Save any changes when prompted. Close Microsoft Word. Leave the *associates* database open for use in the next lesson.

 ## To extend your knowledge...

Creating the Main Document Using Word

The mail merge process can start with Word rather than Access. You can open Word, use the mail merge procedures for Word to create a document, and then tie it to the Access database that contains the records of the names and addresses for your letter.

Lesson 4: Importing a Table from Excel

Excel has some database management features, such as the capability to sort and filter data. Therefore, many people use Excel as a simple database management program. Often, however, the amount of data that needs to be maintained becomes too cumbersome to do effectively in Excel. When this happens, you will need to ***import*** data that is stored in an Excel spreadsheet and use it with an Access database. When you import data, the rows of data are treated as records and are copied into Access. Each column of information in Excel is identified as a field in Access.

In this lesson, you will import an Excel spreadsheet that contains budget information for the U.S. Government into the *associates* database that is open from the previous lesson. The *associates* database is being used for convenience—the information being imported in the next three lessons is not related to the address table in the database.

To Import a Table from Excel

❶ Launch Excel and open ea1-0802. Scroll down the rows, and examine the data.
Notice that each row is a record of a type of government expense. The column headings will become field names (see Figure 8.13).

(Continues)

To Import a Table from Excel (Continued)

Column headings

	A	B	C	D	E
1	Classification	Fiscal 1986	Fiscal 1987	Fiscal 1988	Fiscal 1989
2	Defense Department (military)	265,636	273,938	281,935	294,876
3	Treasury Department	179,189	180,345	201,644	230,573
4	Social Security	190,684	202,422	214,178	227,473
5	Health and Human Services Department	143,252	148,893	158,991	172,301
6	Agriculture Department	58,666	49,593	44,003	48,414
7	Independent agencies	11,865	14,266	23,446	32,323
8	Office of Personnel Management	23,955	26,966	29,191	29,073
9	Transportation Department	27,365	25,431	26,404	26,689
10	Defense Department (civil)	20,243	20,659	22,047	23,427
11	Labor Department	24,141	23,453	21,870	22,657
12	Education Department	17,673	16,800	18,246	21,608
13	Housing and Urban Development Department	14,139	15,464	18,956	19,772
14	Veterans Affairs Department	0	0	18,528	18,794
15	Energy Department	11,025	10,688	11,166	11,387
16	National Aeronautics and Space Administration	7,403	7,591	9,092	11,036
17	Justice Department	3,768	4,333	5,426	6,232
18	Federal Aviation Adm	4,673	4,895	5,192	5,822
19	Interior Department	4,791	5,045	5,147	5,308
20	Environmental Protection Agency	4,869	4,903	4,872	4,906
21	Funds appropriated to the President	4,948	10,406	7,252	4,302
22	State Department	2,865	2,788	3,421	3,722
23	Commerce Department	2,083	2,156	2,279	2,571
24	Legislative Branch	1,665	1,812	1,852	2,094
25	The Judiciary	1,069	1,178	1,337	1,493
26	Bureau of the Census	0	217	333	557
27	Executive Office of the President	107	109	121	124

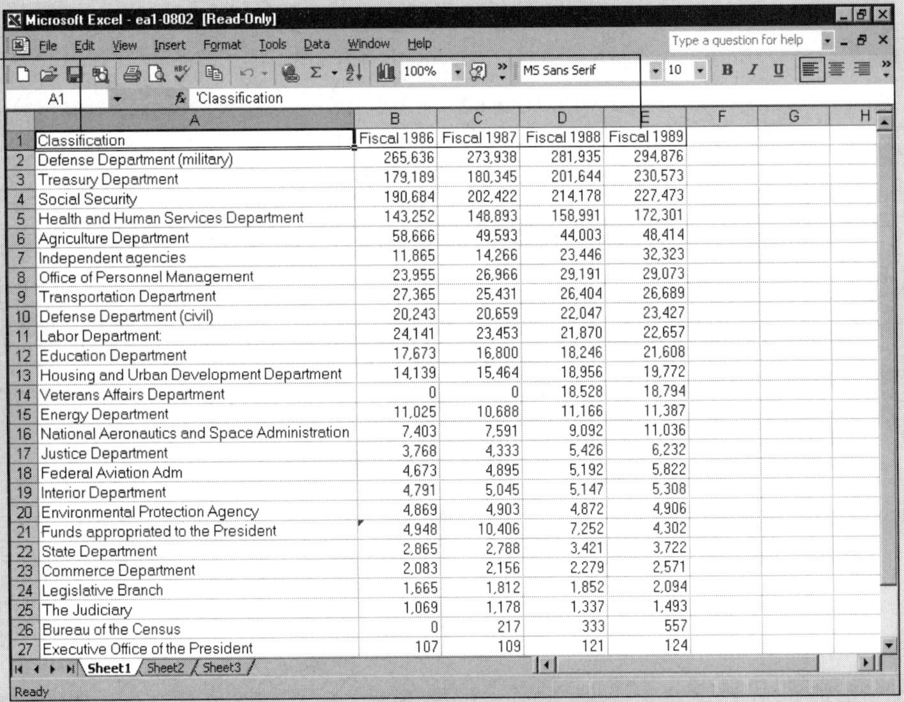

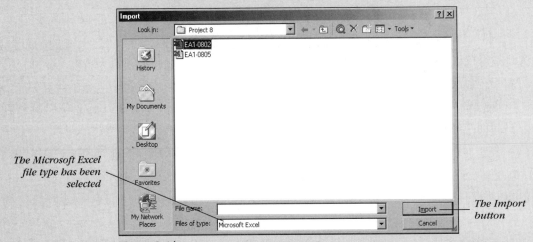

Figure 8.13

2. **Close the file and then close Excel.**
   Switch to Access and the *associates* database.

3. **Choose File, Get External Data, Import.**
   The Import dialog box is displayed.

4. **Click the list arrow next to the *Files of type* drop-down list box, and select Microsoft Excel. Locate and select the ea1-0802 Excel file with the student data files.**
   Your Import dialog box should look like Figure 8.14.

The Microsoft Excel file type has been selected

The Import button

Figure 8.14

5. **Click the Import button.**

To Import a Table from Excel

The Import Spreadsheet Wizard dialog box is displayed. Make sure the Show Worksheets option button is selected and that Sheet1 is highlighted. Notice that the column headings in the first row are displayed as data (see Figure 8.15).

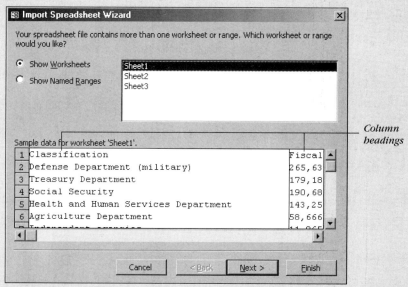

Figure 8.15

6 **Click Next. Click the check box next to *First Row Contains Column Headings*, if necessary.**

The row that contains the words Classification and Fiscal is converted to headers, which will appear as field names in the database table (see Figure 8.16).

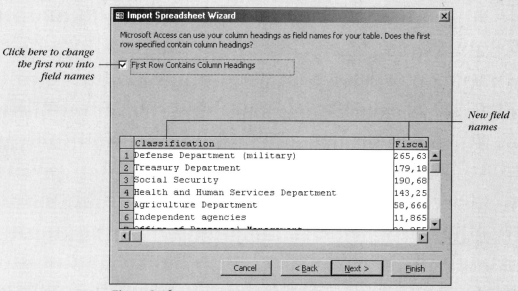

Figure 8.16

(Continues)

To Import a Table from Excel (Continued)

7 **Click Next. Make sure that the *In a New Table* option button is selected.**

8 **Click Next.**
Do not add indexes to any of the fields.

9 **Click Next. Select *Let Access add Primary Key*, if it is not already selected.**
In this case, there are no unique fields, so you can let Access add a field that gives each row a unique number.

10 **Click Next. Type Government Expenses in the *Import to Table* text box.**

11 **Click Finish. Click OK when Access prompts that the import is finished.**
The Government Expenses data is added to the database as a new table.

12 **Click the Open button in the Database window.**
The Government Expenses table is displayed (see Figure 8.17).

Primary key field

III Government Expenses : Table					_ □ ×
ID	Classification	Fiscal 1986	Fiscal 1987	Fiscal 1988	Fiscal 1989
1	Defense Depart	265636	273938	281935	294876
2	Treasury Depart	179189	180345	201644	230573
3	Social Security	190684	202422	214178	227473
4	Health and Hum	143252	148893	158991	172301
5	Agriculture Dep:	58666	49593	44003	48414
6	Independent age	11865	14266	23446	32323
7	Office of Person	23955	26966	29191	29073
8	Transportation [	27365	25431	26404	26689
9	Defense Depart	20243	20659	22047	23427
10	Labor Departme	24141	23453	21870	22657
11	Education Depa	17673	16800	18246	21608
12	Housing and Url	14139	15464	18956	19772
13	Veterans Affairs	0	0	18528	18794
14	Energy Departm	11025	10688	11166	11387
15	National Aerona	7403	7591	9092	11036
16	Justice Departm	3768	4333	5426	6232
17	Federal Aviation	4673	4895	5192	5822
18	Interior Departm	4791	5045	5147	5308
19	Environmental F	4869	4903	4872	4906
20	Funds appropria	4948	10406	7252	4302
21	State Departme	2865	2788	3421	3722

Record: 14 ◄ 1 ► ►I ►* of 29

New field names

Figure 8.17

13 **Click the Close button.**
This table is now available to use. Leave the *associates* database open for the next lesson.

To extend your knowledge...

Preparing to Import a Spreadsheet

A spreadsheet must be set up like a database table if you are going to import it successfully. Check to make sure that the Excel data is arranged in rows and columns. Each column should be a field type, and each row should be a record. If necessary, copy the data to a new spreadsheet. Remove blank rows or rows that contain decorative characters, such as long rows of dashes set up to look like a line.

Lesson 5: Creating a Data Access Page Using the Page Wizard

Access 2000 is capable of saving forms as interactive Web pages. To save an interactive Web page, save your object as a ***data access page***, which is a special type of Web page that has been designed for viewing and working with data from the Internet. You can place a database on a Web server and interact with it using an interactive Web page. To view an interactive Web page, you must have a browser that supports this feature, such as Internet Explorer 5.0.

In this lesson, you create a Web page that would allow your sales people to look up contact information.

To Create a Data Access Page Using the Pages Wizard

❶ In the *associates* Database window, click the Pages object button and then click New.
The New Data Access Page dialog box is displayed.

❷ Select Page Wizard, choose the Addresses table in the *Choose the table or query where the object's data comes from* drop-down list and then click OK.
The first page of the Page Wizard is displayed.

❸ Use the Select button to select the following fields: FirstName, LastName, Address, City, EmailAddress, HomePhone, WorkPhone, WorkExtension, and FaxNumber.
Your dialog box should look like Figure 8.18.

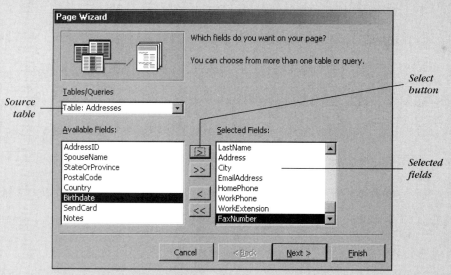

Figure 8.18

❹ Click Next.
The second Page Wizard dialog box is displayed. Do not use the grouping option at this time.

(Continues)

To Create a Data Access Page Using the Pages Wizard (Continued)

5 **Click Next.**
The third Page Wizard dialog box is displayed (see Figure 8.19). This page is used to sort the records.

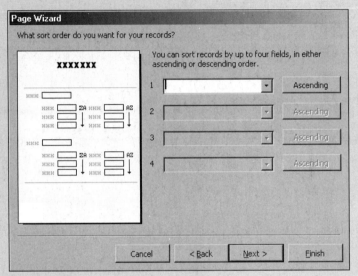

Figure 8.19

6 **Click the list arrow next to the first sorting box, and select LastName. Click Next.**
The fourth Page Wizard dialog box is displayed, asking you for a title for the page.

7 **Type the title** Contact Information **and then click Finish.**
The wizard creates the Contact Information data access page. It is opened in Design view.

8 **Click in the *Click here and type title text* area, and type** Business Contacts.
You could also type introductory text above the data area (see Figure 8.20).

To Create a Data Access Page Using the Pages Wizard

Figure 8.20

9 **Click the View button to switch to Page view. Maximize the window.**
The title is displayed at the top of the page and the first record is shown. A set of navigation buttons is displayed below the data (see Figure 8.21).

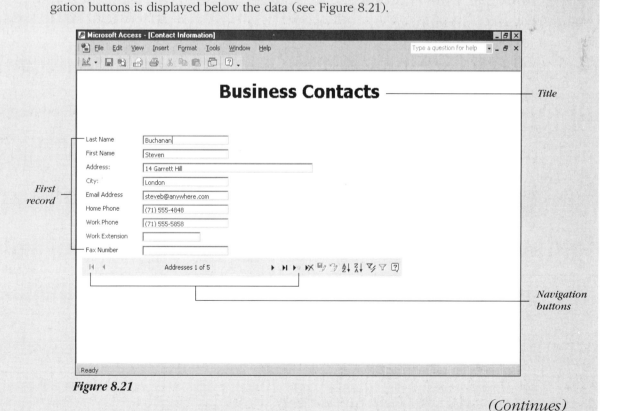

Figure 8.21

(Continues)

To Create a Data Access Page Using the Pages Wizard (Continued)

10 Use the navigation buttons at the bottom of the page to scroll through the records.

11 Close the page and choose <u>Y</u>es to save the changes.
The Save As Data Access Page dialog box opens.

12 Type `Contact Access Page` in the File <u>n</u>ame text box. Click <u>S</u>ave to save the data access page.
Make sure the Save in box displays the location of your database. In addition to saving this in the database, the page is also saved separately with an .htm extension in the same location as your database. In this case, the filename is Contact Access Page.htm.

 If you have problems...

An error message may appear about the connection string. If so, your computer is either not currently online or you must update the location in the ConnectionString property in the data access page's properties. Click OK and check your connection.

13 Close the *associates* database, and close Access.
In the next lesson you will view the data access page as you would on the Internet.

 To extend your knowledge...

File Structure of Data Access Pages

When you create a data access page, it is saved as a separate file that you can view as you would a Web page on the Internet. Microsoft Access automatically creates a shortcut to the file, which is what you see in the Database window. The process of creating a data access page is similar to creating forms or reports; however, there can be several different ways a page can be used. The design of the page is influenced by its ultimate purpose. For more information about designing a data access page, open Help and review the topic *About data access pages*.

Lesson 6: Using a Browser to Interact with the Database

If the database table and a related interactive Web page are placed on a Web server (or in a shared folder on a local area network), then others can use the database with a Web browser. A ***browser***, such as Internet Explorer or Netscape Navigator, is a program that enables you to view Web pages on the Internet. When you interact with the table on the Web, you can browse through the data. You can also sort and filter the data using any field. You can even change the data.

In this lesson, you use Internet Explorer to interact with the database on your disk as if it were placed on a Web server.

To Use a Browser to Interact with the Database

❶ Launch Internet Explorer and then connect to the Internet.
You must have Internet Explorer 5.0 or greater to run the Web page you created in Lesson 5.

❷ Click in the Address box, type the disk location and name of your Web page (for example, A:\Contact Access Page.htm), and then press ⏎Enter.
As you type, the program will automatically start to search for the file. A list of files that have been accessed previously by your computer may be displayed. The arrow at the end of the address box opens and closes this list.

The browser displays the page and a toolbar (see Figure 8.22).

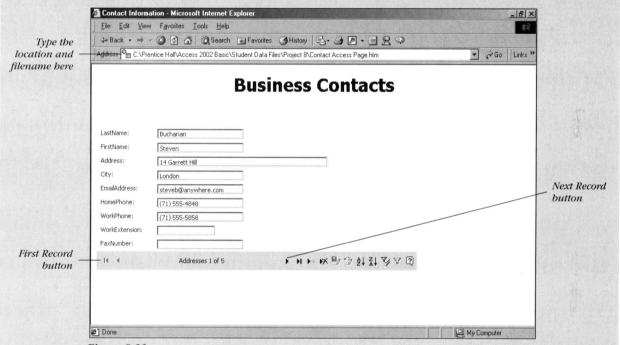

Type the location and filename here

First Record button

Next Record button

Figure 8.22

 If you have problems...
If you have saved your file to a folder, the folder may be opened and icons for the various files will be displayed. Click the file with the Explorer icon and the name Contacts Access Page.htm. to view your data access page.

❸ Click the Next Record navigation button to scroll through the records.

❹ Click the navigation button at the far left of the navigation bar to return to the first record.
Notice that the area codes for the two phone numbers are incorrect.

❺ Edit these two phone numbers to change the area code to (717).

❻ Click in the LastName field and then click the Sort Descending button.

(Continues)

To Use a Browser to Interact with the Database (Continued)

Scroll through the records using the navigation buttons. Notice that the records are displayed in reverse alphabetical order by last name.

7 **Close the browser.**
Notice that the Access program was not running during this lesson.

8 **Launch Access, and open the *associates* database.**

9 **Open the Addresses table, and scroll to the right until you can see both telephone numbers.**
Both area codes that you changed in the Web page are changed in the database table (see Figure 8.23).

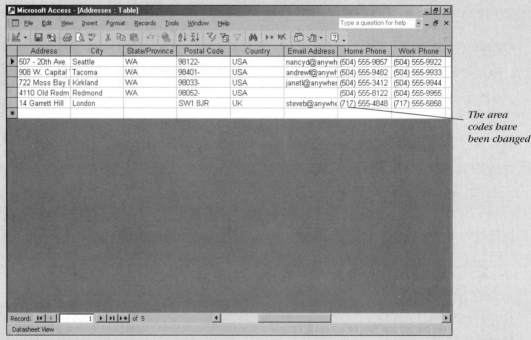

The area codes have been changed

Figure 8.23

10 **Close the table, and close the database.**
If you have completed your session on the computer, exit Access and Windows before you turn off the computer. Otherwise, continue with the "Checking Concepts and Terms" section of this project.

To extend your knowledge...

Entering Addresses in Internet Explorer

When you are typing the address in Internet Explorer, once it has determined that you are typing a drive name, it will offer you a drop-down menu. For example, after you type A: (if your page was saved on drive A:), a drop-down menu is displayed, showing all the files available on that drive.

Summary

In this project, you were introduced to some of the tools and techniques that enable you to work with information from other sources and to publish Access files for use as Web pages. Specifically, you learned to convert an existing Access database to the current version, Access 2002. You also imported data from an Excel spreadsheet into Access. You then created a data access page and viewed it using a Web browser.

To learn more about the capability of Access to import data from other sources, go to Help and look at the topic *Data sources you can import or link*. Also, examine the links on the *About data access pages* page. This will expand your knowledge about the design consideration when you want to make your database accessible using a Web browser.

Checking Concepts and Terms

Multiple Choice

Circle the letter of the correct answer for each of the following questions.

1. What can you do with a database created using an older version of Access? [L1]

   a. Enter data with Access 2002, but do not change any objects.

   b. Convert it to Access 2002.

   c. Share the database with people using different versions of Access.

   d. All of the above.

2. By what method can you send a mail merge document? [L3]

   a. a fax

   b. a printer

   c. e-mail

   d. All of the above

3. Your company has just changed to Access 2002. What must you do to be able to add a field to a table in an Access database created in an earlier version? [L1]

   a. You must use the earlier version to change the database.

   b. Open the database in the earlier version, and choose the save as command to save it to the newer version.

   c. Convert the database to Access 2002 and use Access 2002.

   d. Open the database in Access 2002 but do not convert it.

4. When you import data from Excel into Access, how does Access interpret the data? [L4]

   a. Rows of data are interpreted as records, and columns are interpreted as fields.

   b. Columns of data are interpreted as records, and rows are interpreted as fields.

   c. Access does not make any assumptions, and asks you to identify the records.

   d. You enter the names of the fields in the Import Wizard.

5. Which of the following is not true about merging data from Access into a Word document? [L2]

   a. You can begin the merge process by first opening Word and using the Word merge procedures.

   b. You can base the merge on a query or a table.

   c. You can use each field in the table only one time in the Word document.

   d. You can include calculated fields in a merged document.

Screen ID

Label each element of the Access screens shown in Figure 8.24 and 8.25.

A. Merge field

B. Returns to first record on a Web page

C. Sort descending button

D. Displays next record on a Web page

E. Places an Access field in a Word document

F. Press to start mail merge to a new document

G. Displays next merged record

H. Mail Merge toolbar

I. View merged data button

J. Data access page title

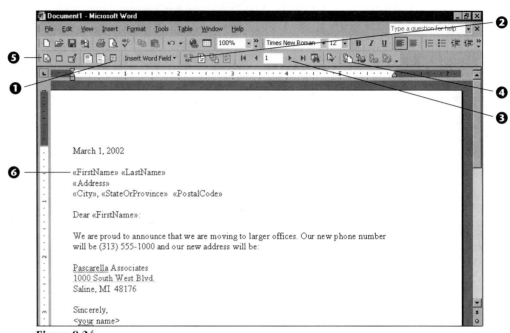

Figure 8.24

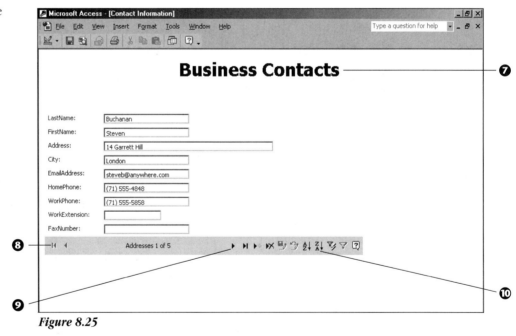

Figure 8.25

1. _____   6. _____

2. _____   7. _____

3. _____   8. _____

4. _____   9. _____

5. _____   10. _____

Discussion

1. What methods have been commonly used in the past for sharing files and information between co-workers? What was done before people used personal computers? What was done before people used networks and the Internet?

2. How has the communication technology used today impacted businesses? How does it affect the way we work? How can it make businesses more successful?

3. Of the various forms of communications technology that are used today, which do you think has had the greatest impact? Why?

Skill Drill exercises reinforce project skills. Each skill reinforced is the same, or nearly the same, as a skill presented in the project. Each exercise includes a brief narrative introduction, followed by detailed instructions in a step-by-step format.

1. Open a Database Created in an Older Version of Access

To practice converting databases from older versions of Access, convert this database of Michigan Tornadoes and give it a new name.

To open a database created in an older version of Access, follow these steps:

1. Launch Access.

2. Find and select the file ea1-0803 in the student data files.

3. Click the Convert Database option button.

4. Give the file a new filename of `Michigan tornadoes`.

5. Choose to save the file on drive A:.

6. Open the Michigan Tornadoes—Last Decade table to make sure the file translated properly.

7. Close the table, and close the database.

2. Creating a Memo Using Mail Merge

Your company is going to have a summer picnic. You have already invited all of your employees, but you decide it would also be a nice gesture to invite your contacts. You will use a new version of the *associates* database you worked with throughout this project to create a quick memo to send to the people in the Addresses table.

To create a memo using mail merge, do the following:

1. Copy the ea1-0804 database file, remove the read-only status from the copied file, and rename it `business contacts`. Open the new database and select the Addresses table and then click Open.

2. In record 5, enter `a guest` in the empty spouse field.

3. Click the OfficeLinks button (select the database window to activate the Database toolbar), and select *Merge It with Microsoft Word*. Select the option to create a new document in Word, and link data to it.

4. Create a mail merge memo announcing a company picnic. Invite each person by name. Also invite their spouse by name. Use Figure 8.26 as a guide.

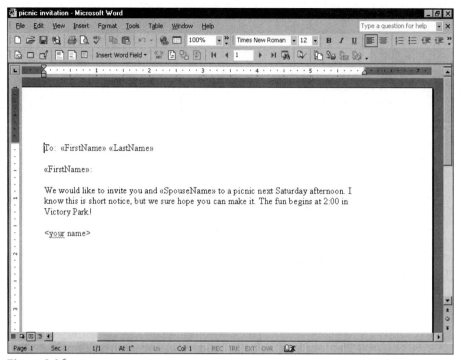

Figure 8.26

5. Use your name at the bottom of each letter where it says *<your name>*.

6. Save the document as `picnic invitation`. Leave it open for the next exercise. Leave the *business contacts* database open.

3. Merging and Printing a Mail Merge Document

Now that you have created the mail merge document to invite your contacts to the company picnic, it is time to make sure it works properly, and then print the memos.

To merge and print a mail merge document, here are the steps:

1. In Word, click the View Merged Data button to test your mail merge document.

2. Scroll through the records to make sure the text of the record you edited flows smoothly.

3. Click the Merge to Printer button.

4. Print the letters for records 1 and 5. To do this in one step, type **1,5** in the Pages box, and click OK.

5. Close the *picnic invitation* document, but leave the *business contacts* database open.

4. Importing a Table from Excel

Your company's sales are based on population growth, so you would like to have some population forecasts available to make long-range sales projections. One of the marketing people has put the information into an Excel worksheet. You want to move it into your Associates database.

To import a table from Excel, follow these steps:

1. In Access with the *business contacts* database open, choose File, Get External Data, and Import from the menu.

2. Specify Microsoft Excel in the Files of type box.

3. Find the ea1-0805 Excel file, and Import the first sheet.

4. Specify that the first row contains column headings. Create a new table.

5. Select the *Choose my own primary key* option button, and select the Year column as the primary key.

6. Name the table `Population Projection`.

7. Open the table, and review it to make sure it translated properly.

8. Print the table and then close it.

9. Leave the database open to use in the next exercise.

5. Creating a Data Page to Use on the Web

You want to put the government budget information on a Web page. The first step is to create the data page and decide what information you want to include.

To create a data page to use on the Web, do the following:

1. In the *business contacts* database window, click the Pages object button, and click <u>N</u>ew.

2. Select Page Wizard, and choose the Government Expenses table.

3. Select the Classification, Fiscal 1987, Fiscal 1988, and Fiscal 1989 fields. You will not be using the ID and Fiscal 1986 fields.

4. Sort by Classification.

5. Call the data page `Government Budget`.

6. In Design view, add a title called `U.S. Government Budget`.

7. Close the Data Access Page design window. When prompted, save the page with the name `Government Expenses`, and then close the *business contacts* database.

6. Opening a Data Page Using a Web Browser

Now that you have created a data access page, you need to open it using an Internet browser to make sure it is working properly.

To open a data page using a Web browser, do the following:

1. Launch Internet Explorer or another browser (make sure you are online), and enter the location and name of the Government Expenses.htm file you just created. Press `↵Enter` (If you have trouble locating the file, use <u>F</u>ile, <u>O</u>pen, B<u>r</u>owse and locate the file in the Microsoft Internet Explorer window.)

2. Use the navigation buttons to scroll through the records. What could you do to improve the quality of this page?

3. Close the Internet Explorer.

Challenge exercises expand on or are somewhat related to skills presented in the lessons. Each exercise provides a brief narrative introduction followed by instructions in a numbered step or bullet list format that are not as detailed as those in the Skill Drill section.

1. Opening and Adding Data to an Older Version of Access

You and your sister have been collecting CDs for years, and entering the information into a database. She has a computer that uses Access 97, whereas you have upgraded to Access 2002. You still want to keep up the database, so you have to open the old version without converting it. You would also like to add another field to help keep track of who owns which CD.

To open and add data to an older version of Access, do the following:

1. Copy the ea1-0806 file, remove the read-only status of the copied file, and change the name to CD collection.
2. Open the *CD collection* database. Choose the <u>O</u>pen Database option, not the <u>C</u>onvert Database option.
3. Open the CD Collection table, and add the following record

    Rollins, Sonny
    Saxophone Colossus
    1956
    Prestige
    OJCCD-291-2
    Jazz/Big Band

4. Go to Design view, and scroll to the first empty field.
5. Add a text field called *Whose?*.
6. Click the View button to switch back to the datasheet. What happens? Why?
7. Close the table. Close the *CD collection* database.

2. Importing a Table from an Old dBASE III Database

A common database for personal computers in the 1980s was dBASE III. Many database records from that decade are stored in that format, as are many data sources on the Web. In this exercise, you import data from a 1987 database that shows statistics about retail establishments and their employees in Michigan by postal code. (Sales and Payroll figures are in 1000s.)

To import a table from an old dBASEIII plus database, here are the steps:

1. Create a new database, and call it Michigan retail statistics.
2. Choose <u>F</u>ile, <u>G</u>et External Data, and <u>I</u>mport from the menu.
3. Specify that you are looking for dBASEIII file types, and select the ea1-0807.dbf file.
4. Import the file, and then close the Import dialog box. Rename the new table Retail Statistics. If you do not remember how to do this, use Help.
5. Open the Retail Statistics table. Click the record selector to the left of the first record. Press (⬆Shift) and click the record selector for the tenth record (Zip code is 48010) to select the first ten records.
6. Choose <u>F</u>ile, <u>P</u>rint, Selected <u>R</u>ecord(s), and print the first ten records.
7. Close the table, and close the database.

3. Importing a Text File

Data is frequently found in text files where the fields are separated by tabs, commas, spaces, or some other character. These data separators are known as ***delimiters***. If fields are separated by tabs, for example, the file is referred to as tab-delimited. Access can import such files using the Import wizard.

To import a text file, follow these steps:

1. Find the ea1-0808.txt file in your student data files. Open it in Microsoft Word to find out what kind of delimiter is used. Click the Show/Hide button, if necessary. Close the file.
2. Create a new database called hardware supplies.
3. Check the available Microsoft Help to figure out how to import a text file into a table. Import the text file, allowing Access to add a primary key field.
4. Name the new table Plumbing. Print the table.
5. Close the table, and close the database.

4. Creating a Data Access Page Based on a Query

You can base a data access page on a query as well as a table. This gives you the ability to use query features, such as criteria, to restrict the information you place on the Web. In the following three challenges, you use the *CD collection* information that you worked with in the first exercise in the Challenge section.

To create a data access page based on a query, do this:

1. Copy the ea1-0809 database, remove the read-only status of the copied file, and rename it `new CD collection`. Open the new database.
2. Create a new query based on the CD Collection table. Include all of the fields. Call the query `The 80's`.
3. Set the criteria so that the query only shows CDs between years 1980 and 1989.
4. Create a new data access page based on The 80's query. Do not group or sort.
5. Add a title that says `CDs of the 80's`.
6. Save it with the name `Music of the 80's`.
7. Close the database, and preview your Web page on your browser.

5. Editing an Existing Data Access Page

You will often look at your new Web page and decide that there should be some changes made. You can always go back to Access and edit your work.

To edit an existing data Access page, do the following:

1. Open the *new CD collection* database, and click the Pages object button, if necessary.
2. Select the Music of the 80's page, and open it in Design view.
3. Add `From the Collection of <your name>` as body text (type in your name for <your name>).
4. Use the available help to figure out how to add a clip art image to the page. Insert the music.jpg file included with the student data files. Place it to the right of the title.
5. Close the page, and save your changes.
6. Go to the Windows Explorer or My Computer and look at the file you just saved. There should be a new folder that contains a copy of the image you placed in the page. This folder needs to be kept with the page file.
7. Close the database, and close Access.

6. Sorting and Filtering Information on a Data Page

When you open a data access page on the Web, Access gives you some control over the data. You can sort on any field, and you can filter the data by category. This restricts the records in the list to the ones that match the filter you have applied. Applying a filter is like using criteria in a query to limit the records to the ones that match the criteria.

To sort and filter information on a data page, do this:

1. Open the Music of the 80's.htm page in the browser. Click in the Artist/Group field.
2. Click on the Sort Ascending button on the toolbar at the bottom of the screen. The records are sorted in ascending order by the Artist/Group field.
3. Scroll to the first record listed as Classical and then click in the Category field.

4. Click the Filter by Selection button that is near the right end of the toolbar at the bottom of the screen. To the right of the title in the scrollbar, it should display 1 of 34. This indicates that there are 34 classical selections in this list of CDs. Scroll through a few records to make sure that the filter worked.

5. Click the Remove Filter button to turn the filter off. All 131 records should be listed in the navigation bar as shown in Figure 8.27.

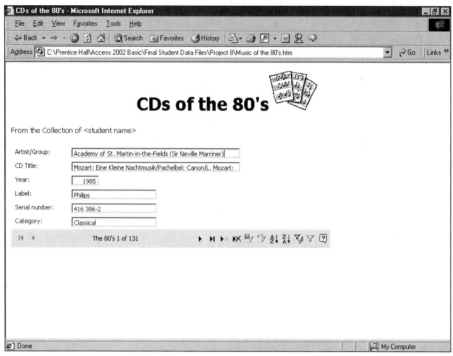

Figure 8.27

6. Close your browser.

Discovery Zone exercises require advanced knowledge of topics presented in *essentials* lessons, application of skills from multiple lessons, or self-directed learning of new skills.

1. Copying Part of a Table to a Word Document

A convenient way to transfer data from a database table to a document is a simple copy and paste. This results in creating a table in Word that can be formatted in a variety of styles. Try this procedure with the data from the Addresses table in the *associates* database that you worked with earlier in this project.

Goal: Copy columns of data from an Access table to a table in Word.

An associate has requested a list of names and addresses from you. Launch Word; then write a short note to your coworker that tells him or her that this is the list of names that was requested. Make sure you include your name at the end of your brief note.

Open the ea1-0804 database as **addresses**, and use the Addresses table. In your memo, you should include first and last name, and home and work phone numbers. To copy these fields to Word, they need to be next to each other so they can be copied as a group. (*Hint*: Do not make this a permanent change to the structure of the table; move the fields in Datasheet view.)

Select and copy the First Name, Last Name, Home Phone, and Work Phone fields, then switch to Word and paste it. Format the table by choosing T<u>a</u>ble, Table <u>A</u>utoFormat from the menu. Choose a format that you like. (*Hint*: Be sure to select the column headings when you are selecting the information to copy.)

Print the document and save it as **addresses**. Close the Word document, but leave the database open to use in the next exercise.

2. Updating a Table by Pasting Cells from a Spreadsheet

You may want to send a table of data for someone to work on who does not have the Access program, but who does have Excel. To do this, you can export the data to Excel.

Goal: Export a table to Excel, make changes to it in Excel, and then paste the new cells back into the Access table.

To ensure that you keep the original data intact, you want to make a copy of the table and export the copy to Excel. Make a copy of the Addresses table and name the copy **Address Updates**. (*Hint*: right-click on the table and use the shortcut menus.)

Export the table to Excel. Name it **address updates**. (*Hint*: The <u>E</u>xport command is on the <u>F</u>ile menu. When you name it, be sure to change the Save as <u>t</u>ype box to *Excel 97-2002*.)

Launch Excel and open the *address updates* file. Scroll to the right and add comments to the Notes field in the Excel sheet. Don't be concerned about the width of the columns.

Now you want to transfer this new information back to the original Access table. Copy the updated cells in the Excel sheet but do not include the heading. Open the Addresses table in Access. Click the Notes column selector and paste the entries from the Excel sheet. The information that was entered in Excel now is entered in the original Access table. Close the database and then close Excel.

PowerPoint

LINDA BIRD

PART

IV

Getting Started with PowerPoint

Objectives

In this project, you learn how to

- ✔ Explore the PowerPoint Window
- ✔ Create a Blank Presentation
- ✔ Create a Presentation Using a Design Template
- ✔ Enter and Edit Text
- ✔ Save a Presentation
- ✔ Print a Presentation
- ✔ Get Help
- ✔ Close Your Presentation and Exit PowerPoint

Key terms introduced in this project include

- ❑ Ask a Question box
- ❑ AutoLayout
- ❑ Content Layouts
- ❑ dialog box
- ❑ editing mode
- ❑ electronic slide show
- ❑ full menu
- ❑ grayscale
- ❑ hyperlink
- ❑ Navigation pane
- ❑ Normal view
- ❑ Notes pane
- ❑ Office Assistant
- ❑ output
- ❑ placeholders
- ❑ presentation
- ❑ presentation graphics program
- ❑ pure black and white
- ❑ Random Access Memory (RAM)
- ❑ ScreenTip
- ❑ short menu
- ❑ shortcut menu
- ❑ slide layout
- ❑ Slide pane
- ❑ task panes
- ❑ templates (design templates)
- ❑ Text Layouts

Why Would I Do This?

Microsoft PowerPoint is a powerful ***presentation graphics program***. Presentation graphics software such as PowerPoint helps you structure, design, and present information to an audience so that it's both catchy and visually appealing.

A ***presentation*** is simply a series of slides that contain visual information you can use to persuade an audience. Using PowerPoint, you can effectively and efficiently create professional-looking handouts, overheads, charts, and so on. Whether you're developing a marketing plan, reporting progress on a project, or simply conducting a meeting, PowerPoint can help you quickly create powerful presentations. And after you initially develop a presentation, you can jazz it up by adding and modifying text, charts, clip art, and drawn objects.

You can deliver PowerPoint presentations in various ways—by using printed handouts, 35MM slides, or overhead transparencies. Probably the most popular way to show a presentation, however, is to display it as an ***electronic slide show***. An electronic slide show is a predetermined list of slides that are displayed sequentially. You can show the list onscreen, via the Web, or by using a projection system to cast the image from your computer onto a large screen. As you learn PowerPoint, you'll probably think of many ways that you can use the program to communicate information effectively to others.

In this project, you get a jump-start on working with PowerPoint. You learn the basics of starting PowerPoint and of creating new presentations. You also see how to find help by using the ***Office Assistant***, PowerPoint's online Help system, so that you can learn the program quickly and easily.

Visual Summary

To get you up and running with PowerPoint, you'll start the program and find your way around the PowerPoint window. You'll also create a new, blank presentation and use Normal view to enter text. Additionally, you'll learn how to use PowerPoint's ***task panes*** to quickly execute commands. (A task pane is a small window within a program that gives you quick access to commonly used commands.)

When you finish developing the sample presentation, it will look similar to the one shown in Figure 1.1.

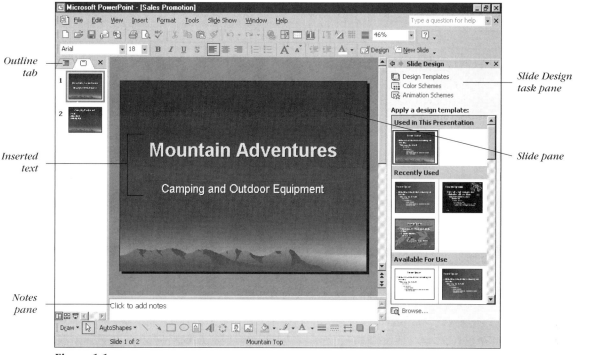

Figure 1.1

It's easy to communicate effectively when you use PowerPoint presentations. So grab your mouse and let's get going!

Lesson 1: Exploring the PowerPoint Window

Most people like choices. Luckily, Microsoft offers you a variety of methods that you can use to start PowerPoint. One of the most straightforward ways is to click the Windows Start button and then choose Microsoft PowerPoint from the <u>P</u>rograms menu. In this lesson, you start PowerPoint by using this method and then explore the PowerPoint application window.

To Explore the PowerPoint Window

1 **Move the mouse pointer to the Start button at the left edge of the Windows taskbar, and click the left mouse button.**
The Start button's popup menu displays.

2 **Move the mouse pointer to the <u>P</u>rograms menu item.**
A listing of available programs displays. Don't panic if the ones shown on your system don't match those on other computers, however. The exact programs listed just reflect the ones installed on each individual system.

(Continues)

To Explore the PowerPoint Window (Continued)

If you have problems...
If you don't see Microsoft PowerPoint on the Programs submenu, move the mouse pointer over the Microsoft Office folder; then, click the Microsoft PowerPoint icon from the Microsoft Office submenu.

3 **Move the mouse pointer to Microsoft PowerPoint and then click the left mouse button.**
PowerPoint is loaded into the computer's working area —Random Access Memory—and displays on your screen (see Figure 1.2). *Random Access Memory (RAM)* is the temporary storage space that a computer uses for programs that it's currently working on.

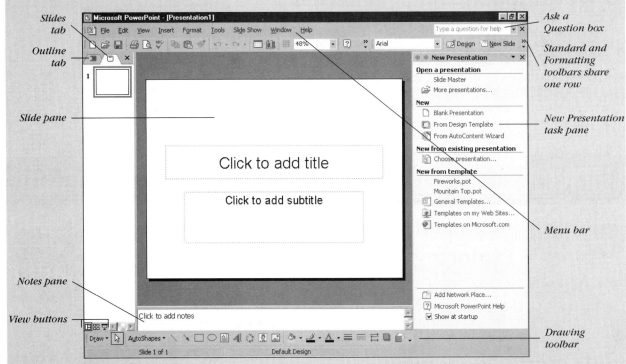

Figure 1.2

As you scan the PowerPoint window, you probably notice that many screen components are similar to other Windows programs. For example, the menu bar, title bar, and toolbars look similar to other programs that you may have used. However, there are a number of screen elements specifically related to using PowerPoint, such as the Slides tab and the Outline tab.

4 **Compare your application window with that shown in Figure 1.2.**
The main part of the application window is reserved for the presentation. Currently, the presentation is shown in *Normal view*. This view includes three main sections, or panes, that you can use to work with your presentation: a *Slide pane*, a *Notes pane*, and a tabbed section. Each of the three sections represents a way to work with your presentation. You use the Slide pane to see how each slide appears and to add text, graphics, or other objects to the slide. You use the Notes pane to develop speaker notes. Finally, you use the Outline and Slides tabs to organize the content of the entire presentation. Now, try working with PowerPoint's toolbar buttons.

To Explore the PowerPoint Window

5 **Rest your mouse pointer over any toolbar button on the Standard, Formatting, or Drawing toolbars.**

As you rest your mouse pointer over a button, a ***ScreenTip*** displays that names the button (see Figure 1.3). ScreenTips are a handy way to become familiar with the toolbar buttons.

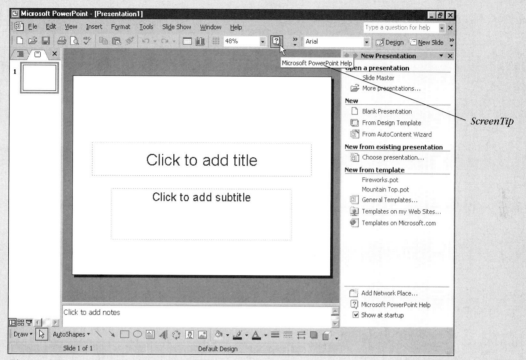

Figure 1.3

If you have problems...

If the ScreenTips don't appear, it's possible that their display has been turned off. Choose Tools, Customize and then click the Options tab. Check the box for Show ScreenTips on toolbars, and click OK.

Now try using the ScreenTips to identify the View buttons.

6 **Rest your mouse pointer over each of the View buttons, located in the lower left corner of the application window.**

A ScreenTip displays for each View button. In a later lesson you'll switch between PowerPoint's views. For now, you'll just use Normal view.

Next, set PowerPoint's display options so your screen matches those used in this book's figures. As you do so, you'll learn a little about working with toolbars and menus.

7 **Click Tools on the menu bar and then choose Customize from the pull-down menu.**

(Continues)

To Explore the PowerPoint Window (Continued)

The Customize dialog box is displayed (see Figure 1.4). A **dialog box** is a small window that is activated by a command. It usually presents you with options from which you can choose—and the Customize dialog box is no exception.

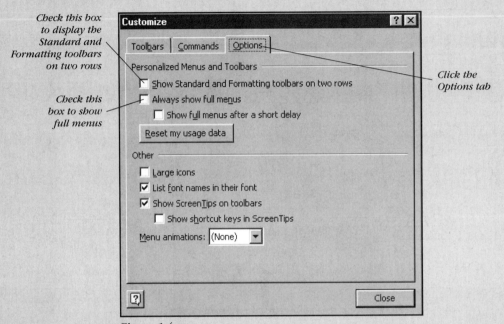

Check this box to display the Standard and Formatting toolbars on two rows

Check this box to show full menus

Click the Options tab

Figure 1.4

8 **Click the Options tab, if necessary.**

9 **Check the box for Show Standard and Formatting toolbars on two rows.**

10 **Check the box for Always show full menus and then click Close.**
The Customize dialog box closes, and PowerPoint's Standard and Formatting toolbars display on separate rows (see Figure 1.5). This helps you quickly access each of their buttons.

To Explore the PowerPoint Window

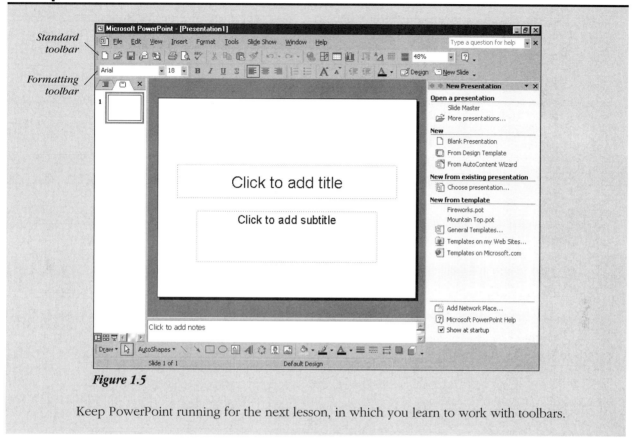

Figure 1.5

Keep PowerPoint running for the next lesson, in which you learn to work with toolbars.

 ## To extend your knowledge...

Working with Menus

PowerPoint, like other Office programs, includes both ***short menus*** and ***full menus***. By default, the shortened version is displayed first and includes the most commonly used commands. In contrast, the full menu includes all of PowerPoint's commands.

Even though the shortened menus display when you initially click a main menu command, you can easily display the full menu by double-clicking the menu command. Alternately, rest your mouse pointer on the double-down arrows at the bottom of the pull-down menu until the full menu is shown. Additionally, you can also customize the settings so that full menus always display (just as you did in the previous exercise).

Also, you can quickly access context-sensitive menu commands via a ***shortcut menu***. You do this by right-clicking an object or screen element.

Starting PowerPoint

If a shortcut icon for PowerPoint is displayed on your Windows desktop, you can start PowerPoint by double-clicking it. Alternately, right-click the icon to display a shortcut menu, and choose Open from the displayed menu to start PowerPoint.

Many systems are also set up to automatically display the Microsoft Office Shortcut Bar on the Windows desktop. This bar contains buttons that you can use to launch Microsoft Office programs, including PowerPoint.

Lesson 2: Creating a Blank Presentation

Now that you've launched PowerPoint, the stage is set for creating your first presentation! The New Presentation task pane provides three options for quickly creating a presentation: using the Auto-Content Wizard, using a design template, or starting completely from scratch with a blank presentation. Happily, you can find these options easily in the New section of the New Presentation task pane.

In this lesson, you'll learn how to create a new presentation from the ground up. Try creating a blank presentation from scratch now.

To Create a Blank Presentation

1 **Verify that the New Presentation task pane is still displayed onscreen.**

If you have problems...

Don't despair if you accidentally closed the New Presentation task pane or if it didn't display when you launched PowerPoint. Just choose File, New from the menu to display it, and continue with step 2 of the tutorial.

2 **In the New section of the New Presentation task pane, click Blank Presentation.**
A blank slide displays in the Slide pane area of the application window, complete with *placeholders*. Placeholders are designated areas on a slide in which you can insert text or other objects. Additionally, the Slide Layout task pane is displayed (see Figure 1.6). For now, you'll close this task pane.

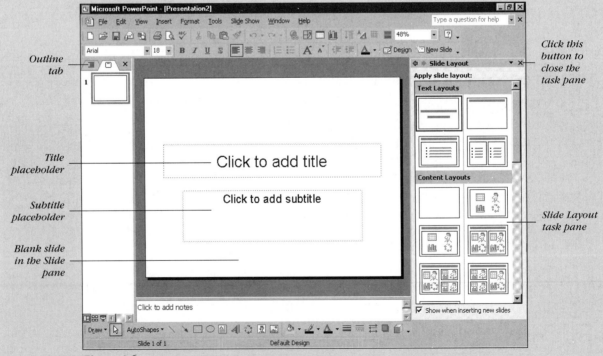

Figure 1.6

3 **Click the Close button in the Slide Layout task pane.**
Now you're ready to enter text in your presentation. As you develop your presentations, you will probably use the Normal view to enter text and graphics, as well as to quickly

To Create a Blank Presentation

scan the presentation's entire flow and content. Because of this versatility, Normal view is a handy all-purpose view.

4 **In the Slide pane, click in the title placeholder (the upper placeholder).**
The title placeholder is activated in *editing mode* and appears with a rope-like border. When a placeholder is in editing mode, it simply means that you can enter or edit text in the placeholder.

5 **Type** Training Proposal.
Your text is entered in the title placeholder. Don't panic if you make a mistake as you enter the text. You can make corrections as you do in a word processing program—just press Del or +Backspace.

6 **Click in the subtitle placeholder (the lower placeholder) and then type** By, **followed by** your name.

If you have problems...

If a red squiggly line appears beneath a word (such as your name), don't worry. PowerPoint flags possible typos or misspellings with the red line so that you can correct them. In this case, PowerPoint just doesn't recognize your name—so you can safely ignore the red line.

---

7 **Click the Outline tab. (Refer to Figure1.6, if necessary.)**
Notice that the text you entered on the slide was simultaneously placed on the Outline tab.

8 **Click the Slides tab.**
Notice that your presentation appears as a slide miniature on the tab.

9 **Click in the Slide pane outside of the subtitle placeholder.**
The placeholder is deselected and is no longer in editing mode. Congratulations! You just developed your first presentation. To build the presentation further, you could add more slides and text. For now, however, you'll close the presentation without permanently saving it.

10 **Choose File, Close from the menu.**
A message box displays, asking if you want to save the presentation.

11 **Choose No.**
Keep PowerPoint running for the next lesson, in which you learn how to create a presentation based on a design template.

Lesson 3: Creating a Presentation Using a Design Template

PowerPoint includes a number of predesigned *templates* (sometimes called *design templates*) upon which you can base your presentation. You can think of a template as a blueprint that PowerPoint uses to create slides. The template includes the formatting, color, and graphics necessary to create a particular "look."

Professional graphic artists have created these templates. Because of this, you can create a presentation based on the templates and be assured that your presentation has a consistent, well-designed look.

Using a template is helpful because you can concentrate on content rather than spending your efforts on design issues.

You can choose a template when you initially create a presentation, or apply one to an existing presentation any time you're working on it. In Project 4 you'll learn to apply different templates to an existing presentation. For now, you'll focus on developing a new presentation based on a design template. Try working with design templates now.

To Create a Presentation Using a Design Template

1 **Choose File, New from the menu bar.**
The New Presentation task pane is displayed.

2 **In the New section of the task pane, click From Design Template.**
The Slide Design task pane is displayed (see Figure 1.7). This task pane includes a number of thumbnails, or icons, that help you preview which designs are available.

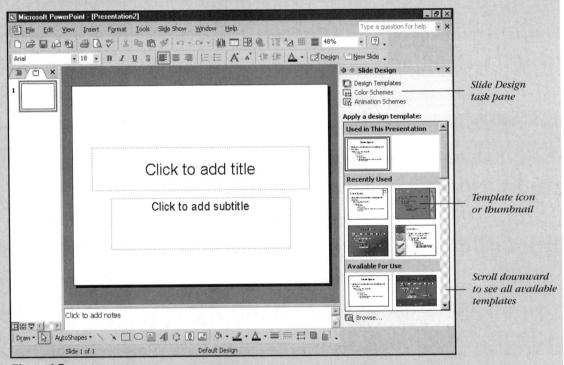

Figure 1.7

3 **Click the arrow at the bottom of the vertical scrollbar until you can see most of the templates in the category entitled, "Available For Use."**

 If you have problems...

Don't worry if the templates listed on your system look a bit different than the listing shown in this book—you probably just have "leftover" templates from previous versions of PowerPoint or ones that were customized and saved by another user. Count yourself lucky—this just means that you have more templates from which to choose!

Additionally, most of PowerPoint's templates are installed the first time you use them, so chances are high that they're already on your system. However, if not, see your instructor for help.

To Create a Presentation Using a Design Template

4 **Rest your mouse pointer over any template icon.**

A ScreenTip displays, identifying the name of the template (see Figure 1.8).

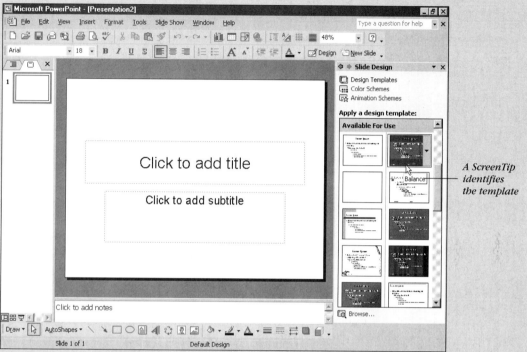

A ScreenTip identifies the template

Figure 1.8

5 **Use the ScreenTips to locate the Balance design template and then click it.**

PowerPoint applies the template's color, patterns, and 'look' to the presentation (see Figure 1.9).

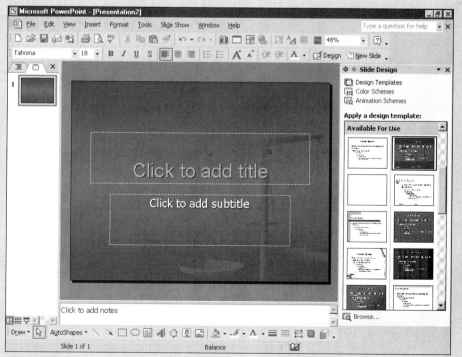

Figure 1.9

(Continues)

To Create a Presentation Using a Design Template (Continued)

You can choose a design template to use when you initially create a presentation, or apply the template to an existing presentation. PowerPoint's capability to change the 'look' of a presentation at any time during development gives you great flexibility. Try applying a different template now.

6 **In the Slide Design task pane, click the Mountain Top template.**

PowerPoint applies the new template to your presentation (see Figure 1.10). If you want, click several different design templates to apply them to your presentation. When you're finished experimenting, reapply the Mountain Top design template. Keep the presentation open for the next lesson, in which you learn more about entering and editing text.

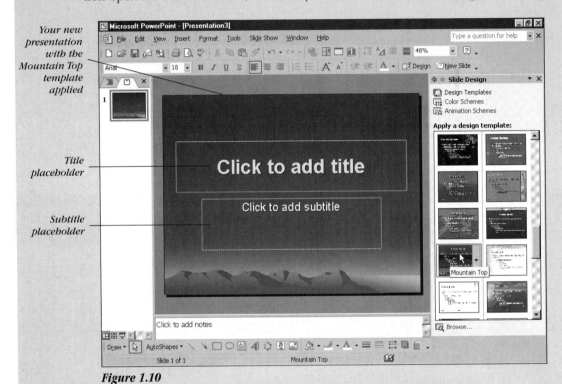

Your new presentation with the Mountain Top template applied

Title placeholder

Subtitle placeholder

Figure 1.10

Lesson 4: Entering and Editing Text

Creating a presentation—whether from scratch or via a design template—doesn't do much good unless you can use it to communicate your thoughts effectively. In this lesson, you learn the basics of entering and editing text in a slide's placeholders so that you can share your ideas. You also learn how to further develop a presentation by adding a slide to it.

To Enter and Edit Text

1 **Verify that your newly-created presentation (with the Mountain Top template applied) is open.**

2 **Click in the title placeholder and then type** Mountain Adventures **(refer to Figure 1.10, if necessary, to identify the title placeholder).**

To Enter and Edit Text

3 **Click in the subtitle placeholder and then type** `Camping and Outdoor Supplies` **(refer to Figure 1.10, if necessary, to identify the subtitle placeholder).**
You enter text in the placeholders, just as you did when you created a presentation completely from scratch. To delete text, you can use the ⟨◆Backspace⟩ and ⟨Del⟩ keys.

4 **Press the** ⟨◆Backspace⟩ **key as many times as necessary to erase the word** *Supplies.*

5 **Type** `Equipment.`
Now try adding a slide to your presentation—one with a placeholder you can use to quickly develop a bulleted list.

6 **Click the <u>N</u>ew Slide button on the Formatting toolbar.**
The Slide Layout task pane is displayed (see Figure 1.11). You can choose a ***slide layout*** (sometimes called an ***AutoLayout***) from this task pane. Each slide layout includes a different arrangement and placeholders, so that you can develop various types of slides. For example, you can add slides with ***Content Layouts*** that accommodate charts, clip art images, and diagrams. For now, however, you can just use the most commonly used type of slide layout in the ***Text Layouts*** category—the Title and Text layout. This type of layout includes a slide with placeholders for a title and a bulleted list. In fact, Power-Point assumes that this is usually the type of slide you want to add, and already applied this slide layout to your new slide.

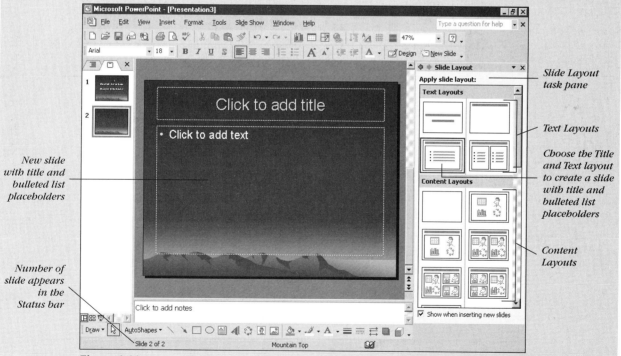

Figure 1.11

7 **Click in the title placeholder for Slide 2, and type** `Camping Equipment.`

8 **Click in the bulleted list placeholder, and type** `Tents.` **Press** ⟨◆Enter⟩.
The text for the first bulleted point is entered on your slide. Additionally, when you pressed ⟨◆Enter⟩, a new bullet was automatically created.

9 **Type** `Cook Stoves` **and then press** ⟨◆Enter⟩.

(Continues)

To Enter and Edit Text (Continued)

⑩ Type Sleeping Bags. **(Because you've completed the list, don't press ⏎Enter again or you'll create an extra bullet.)**

⑪ Click on the slide outside of the placeholders.
Your completed slide should appear similar to the one shown in Figure 1.12.

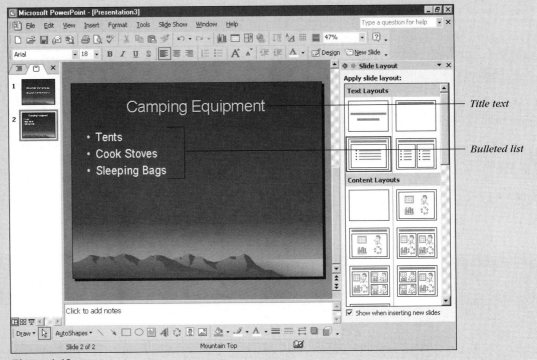

Figure 1.12

In other lessons you'll learn how to further revise your presentation. For now, however, keep the presentation open for the next lesson, in which you learn how to save it.

To extend your knowledge...

Using Undo

If you accidentally delete too much text (or have second thoughts about a modification) you can use the Undo feature to reverse your action. To do this, click the Undo button or press Ctrl+Z. In fact, you can click the Undo button multiple times to reverse up to 150 of your most recent actions.

Lesson 5: Saving a Presentation

So far the presentation you developed exists only in Random Access Memory (RAM)—the working area of the computer. RAM only retains its contents as long as power is supplied to your computer. Therefore, if power is interrupted to your computer, you'll lose everything it contains.

However, when you save the presentation from RAM to one of the computer's permanent storage areas (the floppy disk, the hard drive, a Zip disk, or a network drive), you have a stored copy. This saved file can be opened, used, and revised at a later time.

You use the File, Save or File, Save As commands to save a presentation. Use File, Save As when you first save a presentation, or when you change the name, drive, or folder of a saved presentation. You use File, Save to quickly update a file that was previously saved. (Alternately, you can click the Save button on the Standard toolbar.)

When you initially save a file, you must tell PowerPoint the name and storage location for the presentation—just as you label a file before placing it in a filing cabinet.

In this lesson, you save the sample presentation to your floppy disk—drive A, so make sure you have a disk in this drive before starting the tutorial.

To Save a Presentation

1 **With your presentation still open, choose File, Save As.**
The Save As dialog box is displayed (see Figure 1.13). You use this handy dialog box to indicate the name and location for your file.

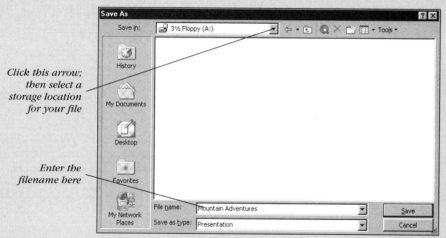

Click this arrow; then select a storage location for your file

Enter the filename here

Figure 1.13

2 **Click the Save in drop-down list arrow (refer to Figure 1.13 if necessary).**
PowerPoint displays a listing of available storage locations for your computer. This list may vary from computer to computer, depending on which drives are installed and whether or not your computer is on a network.

If you have problems...

It's possible that your instructor has another file location in mind for you to save your presentation—such as a subfolder in the My Documents folder on your hard drive. If you're unsure where to save the presentation, ask your instructor.

3 **Click 3½ Floppy (A:).**
Drive A is selected as the storage location for your presentation.

4 **Move the mouse pointer to the File name text box area.**
The pointer changes to an I-beam, indicating that this is an area that can accept text. However, before you can enter text, you must set the I-beam.

5 **Click in the File name text box and then drag over the default filename (*Mountain Adventures*).**

(Continues)

To Save a Presentation (Continued)

The default filename is selected. When text is selected, you can quickly replace it simply by typing in new text. As you enter the new text, the original text is replaced.

6 **Type** Sales Promotion **and then click the Save button near the bottom right corner of the dialog box.**

That's all there is to it! Your presentation is saved as *Sales Promotion* on the floppy disk. If you're observant, you'll also notice that the name appears in the title bar. You now have a permanent copy of your presentation stored for later use (and you're safe from losing data to power outages, surges, and so on).

However, if you make changes to the presentation (either now or later) you should choose File, Save or click the Save button on the Standard toolbar to update the stored file. When you do, the presentation is automatically updated using the same filename and location. In other words, the existing file is replaced rather than creating a second copy of it.

Keep your saved presentation open for the next lesson, in which you learn how to print it.

To extend your knowledge...

Creating folders for storing presentations

To keep everything tidy and organized on your computer, you'll probably want to group similar presentations together—such as those related to a particular client or topic. Luckily, you can create electronic folders from within the Save As dialog box. To do so, click the Create New Folder button. In the New Folder dialog box, enter the name for your new folder and then click OK.

Lesson 6: Printing a Presentation

One common way to ***output***, or produce, a presentation is to print it. You can print your entire presentation, including the slides and outline, in color, ***grayscale***, or ***pure black and white***. Grayscale includes shades of white, gray, and black. In contrast, when you choose the pure black and white option, PowerPoint converts all gray areas to black or white.

Besides the type of contrast you use, you can choose which presentation elements you want to print. For example, you can print an outline to see the overall flow and sequence of the presentation. Because the main purpose of the outline is to view the content, the printout shows only the text you've entered—no graphics are shown.

On the other hand, you can print the presentation as a series of slides. Of course, your slides show graphical elements as well as text. In this lesson you learn how to preview your presentation in grayscale, and how to print outlines and slides. Try your hand at printing now.

To Print a Presentation

1 **In the *Sales Promotion* presentation, choose File, Print.**

The Print dialog box is displayed (see Figure 1.14). You can use this dialog box to make choices about the type of output (slides vs. outline, for example), the number of copies, and the print range.

To Print a Presentation

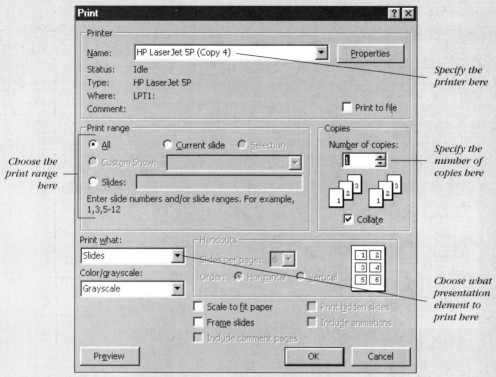

Figure 1.14

If you have problems...

Don't be fooled into thinking that you can access the Print dialog box by clicking the Print button on the Standard toolbar. Clicking the Print button automatically sends the current presentation to the printer with no further confirmation from you. Instead, make sure to choose File, Print from the menu so that you can display the Print dialog box.

2 **Click the drop-down arrow to the right of the Print what text box.**
A drop-down list displays the various ways that you can print your presentation.

3 **Select Outline View.**

4 **In the Number of copies text box, make sure that the number of copies is set to 1.**

5 **In the Print range area, make sure that the All option button is selected and then click OK.**
This accepts the print settings and prints the outline.

You can also print your presentation as slides. However, unless you have access to a color printer, it's a good idea to see how your presentation will look in grayscale (shades of black, gray, and white) before printing it.

Additionally, if you want to just print one slide (rather than the entire presentation) it's easiest to move the insertion point to the slide you want so that PowerPoint can identify it as the current slide. With those concepts in mind, try printing an individual slide now.

(Continues)

To Print a Presentation (Continued)

6 **In the open presentation, press** Ctrl+Home **to move the insertion point to the first slide—the Title slide.**
Moving the insertion point to this slide makes it the current slide. Now try displaying this slide in grayscale so that you can see how it will print.

7 **Click the Color/Grayscale button on the Standard toolbar.**
A drop-down list of color and black and white options is displayed.

8 **Choose Grayscale on the list.**
The slide displays in grayscale so that you can get an idea of how it will look when printed. Additionally, a Grayscale View toolbar is shown (see Figure 1.15).

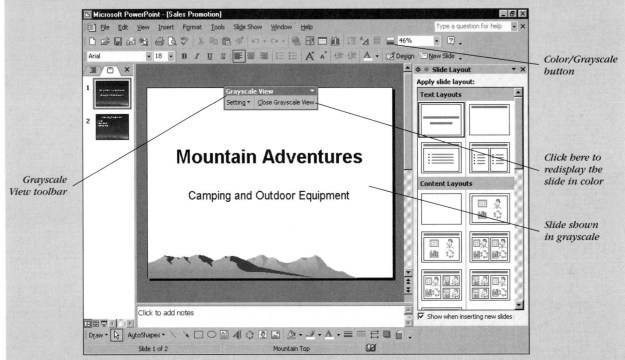

Figure 1.15

Now change options in the Print dialog box so that the slide prints properly.

9 **Press** Ctrl+P. **In the Print range section, click the Current slide option button so that only one slide will print.**
Next you need to confirm that you are printing slides, and that they will print in grayscale—not color.

10 **Make sure Slides is selected in the Print what text box, and confirm that Grayscale is selected in the Color/grayscale box. (If necessary, click the Color/grayscale drop-down list arrow and then choose Grayscale from the list.)**
Printing in grayscale optimizes the look of color slides for printing on black and white printers.

11 **Click OK to print the current slide.**
Now switch the display of your slide back to color.

12 **Click Close Grayscale View on the Grayscale View toolbar.**

13 **Choose File, Save.**

To Print a Presentation

The changes you made to the presentation (such as modifying the print settings) are saved. Keep the presentation open and PowerPoint running for the next lesson, in which you find ways to get help.

To extend your knowledge...

Using Print Preview

Because it's a graphical, visual program, you can usually tell how a slide will look when printed just by glancing at the Slide pane. However, you can see a full-screen version of the slide by choosing File, Print Preview. You learn more about using Print Preview in a later lesson.

Lesson 7: Getting Help

As you're learning new software, it's handy to have help at your fingertips. Of course, the best situation is having your own personal computer trainer standing by your side. In the absence of a real, flesh-and-blood person, however, you can tap into PowerPoint's extensive Help system. You can use the Office Assistant or the Help dialog box to display a list of subjects. For an even quicker path into the world of Help, you can use PowerPoint's ***Ask a Question box***.

To Use Help

 Choose Help, Microsoft PowerPoint Help, or click the Microsoft PowerPoint Help button.

The Office Assistant displays a message balloon. You can enter a question in the text box area of the balloon, and then have the Office Assistant find all the information related to your inquiry (see Figure 1.16). This balloon also sometimes includes a list of Help topics related to whatever features you used most recently. (If the Office Assistant is already displayed on your screen, just single-click it to display the balloon.)

(Continues)

To Use Help (Continued)

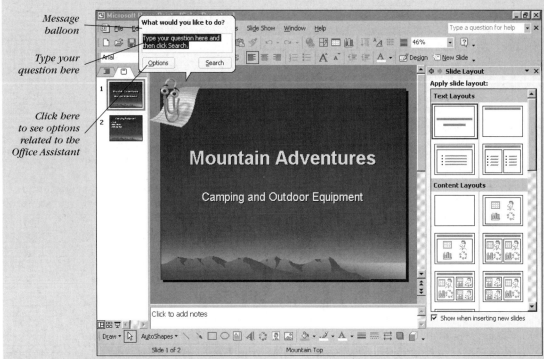

Figure 1.16

If you have problems...

If the Microsoft PowerPoint Help window displays instead of the Office Assistant, close the Help window and then choose Help, Show the Office Assistant from the menu. You can then click the Office Assistant to display the balloon.

2 **Type** How can I print slides? **in the message balloon, and then click Search.**

A list of related topics displays (see Figure 1.17). You can click the topic you want to display help about or you can click the See more... button to view additional topics.

To Use Help

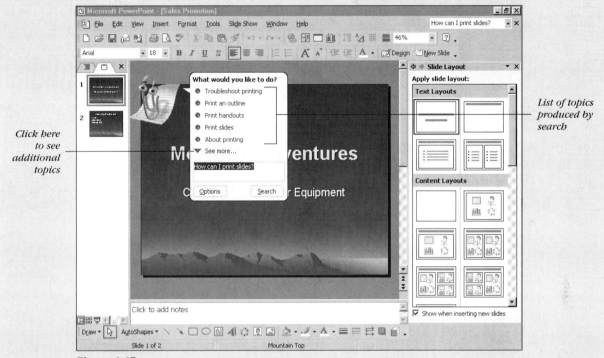

Click here to see additional topics

List of topics produced by search

Figure 1.17

❸ From the list, click *About printing*.

The Microsoft PowerPoint Help window for this topic is displayed (see Figure 1.18). Don't be concerned that the Help window displays on top of your PowerPoint application window and that the screen looks a bit cluttered. When you eventually close the Help window, PowerPoint will display your presentation in the Normal view again. The ***Navigation pane*** is shown on the left side of the window and is used to browse between Help topics.

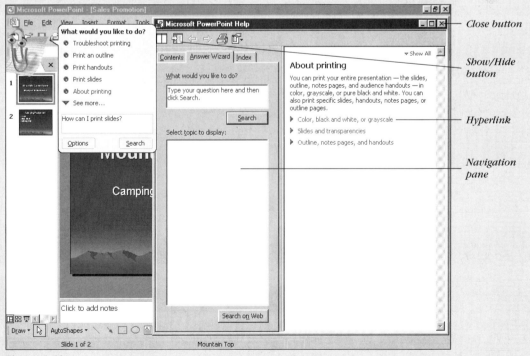

Close button

Show/Hide button

Hyperlink

Navigation pane

Figure 1.18

(Continues)

To Use Help (Continued)

If you have problems...

If your Help window doesn't appear similar to the one shown in Figure 1.18, click the Show button in the Help window toolbar to split the window into two panes.

Also, if the Office Assistant is displayed on top of the Help window, just drag it out of the way.

You can read the information included in the topic or view related topics. You can also click a *hyperlink* in the window. Hyperlink text is underlined and shown in a contrasting color. A special "helping hand" pointer displays whenever you move the mouse pointer over the hyperlink text. You can click a hyperlink to display related information. Try using a hyperlink now.

4 **Move your mouse pointer over the** Color, black and white, **or** grayscale **hyperlink in the right pane until the hand pointer displays and then click.**
The Microsoft PowerPoint Help window displays information related to the hyperlink. If you'd like, click other hyperlinks in the Help window. When you're finished, proceed with the lesson.

5 **Click the Microsoft PowerPoint Help window's Close button.**
The Help window closes.

6 **Right-click the Office Assistant and then choose** <u>H</u>ide.
Now try using a different method of tapping into PowerPoint's resources—the Ask a Question feature.

7 **Click in the Ask a Question box, located in the upper-right corner of the application window.**

8 **Type** Add text **and then press** ⏎Enter.
PowerPoint displays a listing a related topics (see Figure 1.19).

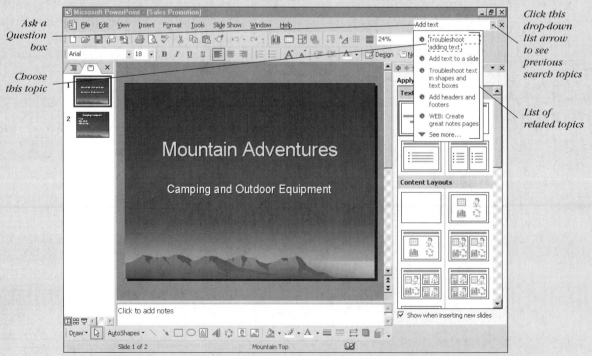

Figure 1.19

To Use Help

⑨ On the list of displayed topics, click *Troubleshoot adding text.*
The Microsoft PowerPoint Help window again displays, and shows a list of hyperlinks related to the topic at hand (see Figure 1.20). You can click any of these hyperlinks to display related information.

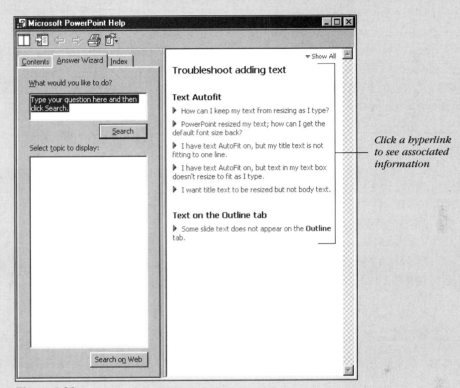

Figure 1.20

⑩ Click the hyperlinks shown in the right pane, and read the associated data. When you're finished, close the Microsoft PowerPoint Help window.
The presentation redisplays in Normal view. Keep the presentation open for the next lesson, in which you learn how to close a presentation and exit PowerPoint.

To extend your knowledge...

Finding Help on the Web

If you're like most users, you'll probably rely heavily on PowerPoint's built-in Help system to find ways to work more effectively with the program. If you absolutely can't find the information you need within PowerPoint, however, you have another option. You can tap into the resources available on the World Wide Web.

If you have Internet access, you can choose Help, Office on the Web. Perform whatever steps you usually do to connect to the Web (such as entering your password). PowerPoint automatically displays Microsoft's Web site for PowerPoint. After you're connected to the Web, you can use hyperlinks to move between Web sites. When you finish cruising the Web, disconnect from it and continue working in PowerPoint.

Lesson 8: Closing Your Presentation and Exiting PowerPoint

Now you're ready to close your presentation and exit PowerPoint. Closing a presentation and clearing it from memory is similar to clearing your desk at school or work to make room for another project. And if closing a presentation is similar to clearing off your desk, exiting the entire program is like leaving your office.

This lesson covers how to properly exit the PowerPoint program. You can exit PowerPoint in a couple of ways: by clicking the Application Close button or by choosing File, Exit from the menu. Try closing your presentation and exiting PowerPoint now.

To Close Your Presentation and Exit PowerPoint

❶ With the *Sales Promotion* presentation displayed, choose File, Save.
Even though you probably didn't make any changes to your presentation since you last saved it, it's a good habit to resave any document before you close it. (Of course, the exception to this rule is when you're sure you *don't* want to save the modifications.)

❷ Choose File, Close.
The presentation is cleared from the computer's memory and PowerPoint's application window. Now you're ready to exit the program.

❸ Choose File, Exit from the menu, or click the Application Close button.
The PowerPoint program closes and the Windows desktop (or another open application) redisplays.

It's also important to properly exit Windows before turning off the computer. The best way to do this is to use (ironically enough) Windows' Start button.

Be sure you close all other open applications before proceeding. If you don't know if another program is running or not, see your instructor for help.

❹ Click the Start button and then choose Shut Down from the menu.
The Shut Down Windows dialog box displays. You use this dialog box to control how to shut down or restart Windows.

❺ Make sure that the Shut down option is chosen and then click OK.
Windows closes temporary files and clears from memory. This process generally takes a few seconds, so be patient during the process. It's important to wait until Windows indicates that you can turn off the computer.

❻ Wait until the *It's now safe to turn off your computer* message displays.
After you receive confirmation, turn off your computer. (Some computers automatically turn off after you shut down Windows. If you have questions, ask your instructor.)

❼ If necessary, turn off your computer's main unit, monitor, and any other hardware (such as speakers or a printer).

Summary

Congratulations! In this project, you learned the basics of getting around in PowerPoint. You also created presentations using two methods: developing a blank presentation from scratch and creating a presentation by using a design template. You also tried your hand at entering and editing text and even added a slide to a presentation. You also saved and printed your work.

Additionally, you navigated the program's toolbars and menus. You acquired skills for researching Help topics by using the Office Assistant and the Ask a Question box. Finally, you learned how to close a presentation, properly exit PowerPoint, and shut down Windows.

To expand on your knowledge, spend a few minutes exploring Help on these topics. Additionally, complete some of the Skill Drill, Challenge, and Discovery Zone exercises.

Checking Concepts and Terms

Multiple Choice

Circle the letter of the correct answer for each of the following.

1. Which of the following elements are displayed in PowerPoint's Normal view? [L1]

   a. Outline tab
   b. Slide pane
   c. Notes pane
   d. All of the above

2. Which of the following describes a method that you can use to create a presentation? [L2, L3]

   a. typing `Create a Presentation Now` in the Ask a Question box
   b. clicking the From Design Template hyperlink in the New Presentation task pane
   c. clicking the New Slide button on the Standard toolbar
   d. All of the above

3. Which of the following are options that you can set in the Print dialog box? [L6]

   a. the number of copies to print
   b. which presentation item, such as Slides or Outline, that you want to print
   c. whether to print in color or grayscale
   d. All of the above

4. Which of the following is true regarding saving a presentation? [L5]

   a. The first time you save the presentation you must specify a filename and location.
   b. Presentations exist only in memory until they are saved.
   c. You can quickly update changes to a file by clicking the Save button.
   d. All of the above

5. How can you properly exit PowerPoint? [L8]

   a. simply turn off the computer
   b. choose File, Close
   c. click the Application Close button
   d. press Esc

Screen ID

Label each element of the PowerPoint application window shown in Figure 1.21. [L1]

A. Standard and Formatting toolbars

B. Menu bar

C. Ask a Question box

D. Title bar

E. New Presentation task pane

F. Drawing toolbar

G. View buttons

H. Slide pane

I. Notes pane

J. Outline tab

K. Slides tab

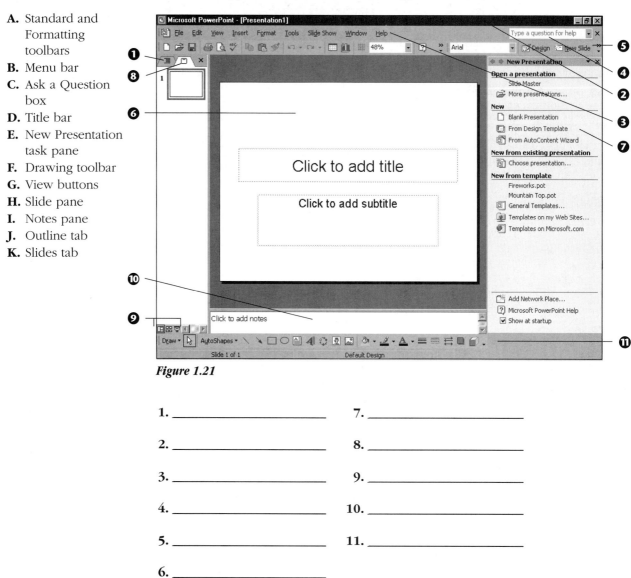

Figure 1.21

1. _____   7. _____

2. _____   8. _____

3. _____   9. _____

4. _____   10. _____

5. _____   11. _____

6. _____

Discussion

1. Discuss how a PowerPoint presentation can help communicate information with others. Give several examples of how presentations can be used in academic, business, and personal settings.

2. Compare and contrast the two main ways to create presentations that you've learned so far (blank presentation and design templates). List pros and cons for using each method and designate when you might want to use each.

3. Think about presentations, talks, and lectures that you've attended. List the elements that helped make a talk effective, and those that detracted from it. Discuss how the same elements can improve or detract from a PowerPoint presentation. What are pros and cons for giving an electronic presentation, such as the type you can develop with PowerPoint? In what settings would a traditional (non-electronic) presentation be more effective? In what settings would an electronic presentation be better?

Skill Drill exercises *reinforce* project skills. Each skill reinforced is the same, or nearly the same, as a skill presented in the project. Detailed instructions are provided in a step-by-step format.

1. Creating a New, Blank Presentation

You need to produce a flyer for a company picnic. Because it's quick and easy to create a presentation in PowerPoint, you decide to use the program to make the flyer.

1. Start PowerPoint, if necessary. In the New Presentation task pane, click Blank Presentation.
2. Confirm that a Title slide (with title and subtitle placeholders) is displayed in the Slide pane.
3. In the Slide pane, click in the title placeholder. Type `Company Picnic!`
4. Click in the subtitle placeholder. Type `Carolina Creek Park`.
5. Press `↵Enter` to move the insertion point to the next line of the subtitle. Type `June 12` and press `↵Enter`.
6. Type `5:00 P.M.-9:00 P.M.`
7. Click outside of the placeholders.
8. Choose <u>F</u>ile, <u>P</u>rint to display the Print dialog box.
9. Make sure Slides is selected in the Print <u>w</u>hat section, and that the Num<u>b</u>er of copies is set to 1. Click OK.
10. Choose <u>F</u>ile, <u>C</u>lose, and click <u>N</u>o to clear the presentation without saving it.

Keep PowerPoint running if you plan to continue working on exercises.

2. Exploring the PowerPoint Application Window and Using Help

Your computer instructor has hired you part-time to assist other students during an open lab. You're new to PowerPoint, however, and are worried that you won't remember the toolbar buttons' functions. To brush up on the program's commands, you spend a few minutes using ScreenTips.

1. In PowerPoint, rest your mouse pointer over each toolbar button on the Standard, Formatting, and Drawing toolbars until a ScreenTip displays. Note the name of each button.
2. Press `⇧Shift`+`F1` to activate the What's This? pointer. Click on the New button on the Standard toolbar. Read the ScreenTip associated with the button and then click the ScreenTip to remove it from the screen. Repeat the process for at least five other toolbar buttons.
3. Click in the Ask a Question box and then type `Creating Presentations`. Press `↵Enter`.
4. Read the information associated with each of the hyperlinks and then close the Microsoft PowerPoint Help window.
5. Click the Microsoft PowerPoint Help button. In the Office Assistant bubble, type `Saving Presentations`. Press `↵Enter`.
6. Click the hyperlink for *Troubleshoot saving.*
7. In the Microsoft PowerPoint Help window, click the hyperlinks to display related information. When you're finished, close the Microsoft PowerPoint Help window.

Keep PowerPoint running if you plan to continue working on exercises.

3. Using a Design Template to Create a Presentation

You're in charge of publicity for a local pet store. To help publicize an upcoming sale, you decide to develop a flyer using PowerPoint's design templates. Because PowerPoint has so many interesting templates, you spend a couple of minutes applying them to the presentation until you find just the right one.

1. In PowerPoint, choose File, New (if necessary) to display the New Presentation task pane.
2. In the New section of the task pane, click From Design Template.
3. Scroll downward in the Slide Design task pane until you can view the templates in the Available For Use category.
4. Use the ScreenTips to identify the names of several of the templates.
5. Click any of the templates in the Available For Use section to apply the design to your presentation.
6. Apply at least four other template designs to your presentation to see how they look. When you're finished, choose the Fireworks template. (If this template isn't available on your system, choose another one.)
7. Verify that the presentation slide's layout includes a title placeholder and a subtitle placeholder. (If you're unsure, choose Format, Slide Layout to display the Slide Layout task pane. Click the Title Slide icon in the Text Layouts section.)

Keep the presentation open and PowerPoint running for the next exercise.

4. Entering Text, Saving and Printing a Presentation

To finish developing your sales flyer, you enter text, save, and then print your presentation.

1. In the open presentation, click in the upper (title) placeholder. Type `Rebecca's Pet Store`.
2. Click in the lower (subtitle) placeholder. Type `Spring Sale!` Click on the slide outside the placeholders.
3. Choose File, Save As to display the Save As dialog box.
4. In the Save As dialog box, click the Save in drop-down list arrow. Choose the drive and folder in which you want to save the presentation.
5. Drag over to select the text in the File name text box. Type `Pet Store Sale`. Click Save.
6. Print your flyer by choosing File, Print from the menu. Make sure Slides is selected in the Print what section, and that the Number of copies is set to 1. Click OK.
7. Click the Save button to update any changes you made to the presentation.
8. Clear the presentation from memory by choosing File, Close.

Keep PowerPoint running if you plan to complete the Challenge and Discovery Zone exercises.

Challenge exercises expand on or are somewhat related to skills presented in the lessons. Each exercise provides a brief narrative introduction followed by instructions in a numbered step format that are not as detailed as those in the Skill Drill section. Each exercise is independent of the others, so that you may complete the exercises in any order.

1. Researching Help Topics

One of the Help Desk employees for your company is on vacation, and you've been asked to cover for him. To answer questions that some of your coworkers ask about PowerPoint, you rely on PowerPoint's Help system.

1. Choose <u>H</u>elp, Show the <u>O</u>ffice Assistant to display the Office Assistant (if necessary) and then use the Office Assistant to research the following topics:
   - How to create a new presentation
   - How to print a presentation
   - How to save a presentation
   - How to open an existing presentation
   - Which slide layouts are available in PowerPoint
   - How to format text with bold or italic
   - What views are available in PowerPoint
   - How to create speaker notes
   - How to insert clip art on a slide

2. Write down the steps to performing at least two of these actions and then try out the steps in PowerPoint.

3. Explain verbally to another user the steps involved in performing two other actions you researched. If possible, have the user complete the steps on a computer as you "talk" him or her through the actions.

Keep PowerPoint running if you plan to continue working on exercises.

2. Creating and Printing New Presentations

Your boss wants you to create some motivational and safety flyers to post around your building. To quickly create the flyers, you decide to develop a series of one-slide presentations in PowerPoint.

1. If necessary, use the Office Assistant to brush up on how to create a new blank presentation. Use Help to find out how to print a presentation slide.

2. Create a new blank presentation. Choose the Title Slide layout for the first (and only) slide. Enter `Don't Forget!` in the slide's title placeholder and then type `Safety is our #1 priority!` in the subtitle placeholder. Print the slide, and close the presentation without saving it.

3. Using the previous step as a guide, create another flyer. Enter `If You Don't Know... Ask!` in the title placeholder. Print the slide, and close the presentation without saving it.

4. Create a third flyer. In the title placeholder enter `We're part of the same team!` Print the slide, and close the presentation without saving it.

Keep PowerPoint running if you plan to continue working on exercises.

3. Developing a New Presentation

You work for the registrar's office at a local college. To get ready for fall registration, your boss wants you to develop signs to help direct students to the various college departments.

1. Create a new blank presentation. Choose the Title Slide Layout for the first (and only) slide. Enter `Accounting Department` in the slide's title placeholder. Type `Room 100` in the subtitle placeholder. Print the slide, and close the presentation without saving it.

2. Using the previous step as a guide, create a slide for each of the following departments. Print each slide, and close the presentation without saving it.

Enter in title placeholder:	Enter in subtitle placeholder:
Business Department	Room 112
Computer Science Department	Room 120
Drafting Department	Room 125
Industrial Technology Department	Room 132
Nursing Department	Room 145
Production Control Department	Room 154

Keep PowerPoint running if you plan to continue working on exercises.

4. Researching Help on the World Wide Web

You're writing a paper for your Computer Science class on PowerPoint and you exhausted the Help information included in the program. To obtain more data, you decide to get some help from Microsoft's Web sites.

1. Make sure that you have Web access and that your equipment is set up to connect to the Web. (If you have questions, see your instructor.)
2. Choose <u>H</u>elp, Office on the <u>W</u>eb. Complete whatever steps are necessary on your system to connect to the Web.
3. Explore Microsoft's Web sites for PowerPoint. (If you're having trouble locating the correct site, try entering `www.microsoft.com` to access Microsoft's homepage; then click the link(s) for PowerPoint.)
4. Research and write down at least five tips and tricks for working with PowerPoint that you didn't know.
5. Disconnect from the Web; then try out the new tips in PowerPoint.
6. Share the information you learned with at least one other person in your class. If you want, write a short paper or create a presentation on what you learned.

Keep PowerPoint running if you plan to work on the Discovery Zone exercises.

Discovery Zone exercises require advanced knowledge of topics presented in *essentials* lessons, application of skills from multiple lessons, or self-directed learning of new skills. Each exercise is independent of the others, so that you may complete the exercises in any order.

1. Creating and Printing Presentations

As you worked with PowerPoint in this project, you probably thought of several presentations that you want to create using the program. Use the knowledge you gained to develop and print at least three single-slide presentations. You can create each presentation as a blank presentation, or use one of PowerPoint's design templates. Use the Title Slide layout for each presentation.

With those guidelines in mind, create one of each of the following types of presentations:

- A presentation to use in a business setting
- A presentation to promote an upcoming event
- A sign to direct people to a certain location in your business

If you forget how to perform a particular action in PowerPoint, use the Office Assistant or the Ask a Question feature to brush up on the concepts. Print each presentation and then close it without saving it.

Keep PowerPoint running if you plan to continue working on exercises.

2. Getting Help Using the Office Assistant and on the Web

Think of three topics in PowerPoint you want to know more about. Research all the information about the topics that you can by using the Office Assistant. Write down what you learn. Next, connect to the World Wide Web to find out supporting data for your topics. If necessary, go to Microsoft's homepage (www.microsoft.com) to find hyperlinks to PowerPoint. If you are familiar with performing a search on the Web, you can also look for other PowerPoint Web sites.

Organize the information you find in outline form and share the information with at least one other person. If you are particularly ambitious, create a presentation that includes the information you found. (Hint: You'll probably want to add slides based on the Title and Text layout.) Print the presentation and then close it without saving it. Exit PowerPoint, and close Windows.

Creating and Modifying Presentations

Objectives

In this project, you learn how to

- ✔ Create a Presentation Using the AutoContent Wizard
- ✔ Add, Demote, and Promote Text
- ✔ Select, Move, and Copy Text
- ✔ Change Text Appearance
- ✔ Use the Format Painter
- ✔ Change the Text Alignment and Set Tabs
- ✔ Add, Remove, and Modify Bullets

Key terms introduced in this project include

- ❑ AutoContent Wizard
- ❑ bullets
- ❑ character attributes
- ❑ Clipboard
- ❑ demoting
- ❑ font
- ❑ footer area
- ❑ formatting
- ❑ horizontal text alignment
- ❑ points
- ❑ promoting
- ❑ select
- ❑ typeface
- ❑ wizards

Why Would I Do This?

The more tools you have in your PowerPoint arsenal, the better equipped you are to use the program effectively. In Project 1, "Getting Started with PowerPoint," you learned two methods for creating a new presentation: developing it totally from scratch and using a design template. PowerPoint also includes another way for easily creating a new presentation: relying on the AutoContent Wizard. After you initially create your presentation—no matter which method you choose—you can tap into a variety of ways to work with the presentation's text. In this project you create a presentation using the AutoContent Wizard and then learn efficient methods to enter, copy, move, align, and format text.

Visual Summary

In this project you learn how to use the AutoContent Wizard to quickly develop a presentation with the sample content and formatting already in place (see Figure 2.1). You also learn how to replace the sample content with your own data, and how to promote and demote text.

The AutoContent Wizard provides a quick way to create a presentation with sample content

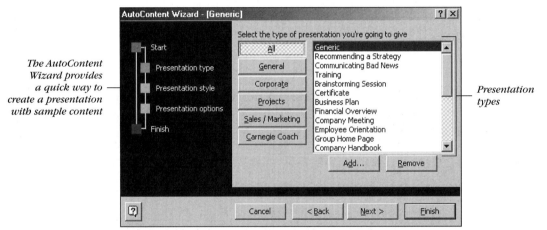

Presentation types

Figure 2.1

After you create the presentation, you can change its ***formatting***, which is the way that your presentation (including text, alignment, bullets, margins, and so on) is set up to display. For example, you can change your text color, size, alignment, or overall appearance. After you get the text formatting just the way you want it, you can quickly copy your formatting to other text by using the Format Painter. The fastest way to format your text usually involves using buttons on the Formatting toolbar (see Figure 2.2).

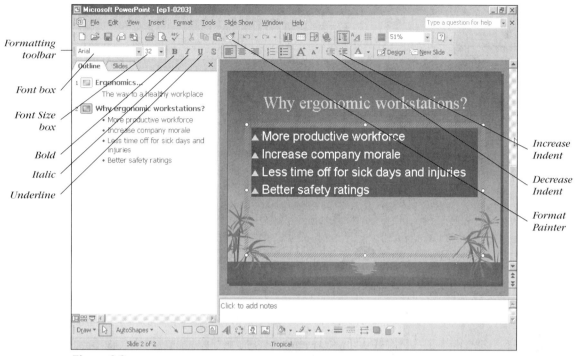

Formatting toolbar
Font box
Font Size box
Bold
Italic
Underline
Increase Indent
Decrease Indent
Format Painter

Figure 2.2

Finally, you can use various types of ***bullets***, the markers that help delineate your ideas (see Figure 2.3).

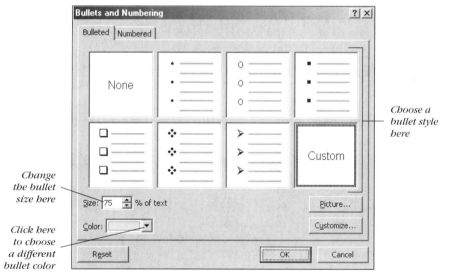

Choose a bullet style here
Change the bullet size here
Click here to choose a different bullet color

Figure 2.3

It's easy to refine and hone your presentation by using these features—and in this project you'll learn how.

Lesson 1: Creating a Presentation Using the AutoContent Wizard

You can use the AutoContent Wizard to quickly create a presentation. The **AutoContent Wizard** is a tool that helps you create presentations that include sample content as well as an underlying template. Microsoft's **wizards** are interactive tools that guide you step-by-step through a process that would otherwise be complicated or awkward—and the AutoContent Wizard is no exception. Just like other Microsoft wizards, you make choices on each page. You then click Next to advance to the subsequent page, Back to display the previous page, or Finish to quickly complete the process. (You can also click Cancel at any time to ditch the entire process.)

You can use the AutoContent Wizard to quickly create presentations on recommending a strategy, conducting training, reporting progress, and so on. In the following tutorial, you use the AutoContent Wizard to create a presentation showing the status of your latest project—upgrading your organization to Office XP.

To Create a Presentation Using the AutoContent Wizard

1 **Start PowerPoint, if necessary, and choose File, New.**
The New Presentation task pane is displayed.

2 **Click From AutoContent Wizard in the New Presentation task pane.**
The AutoContent Wizard dialog box displays, as shown in Figure 2.4. Notice that the chart on the left side of the dialog box helps track your progress as you create a presentation. The buttons at the bottom of the dialog box help you move between AutoContent pages (or even cancel) the wizard.

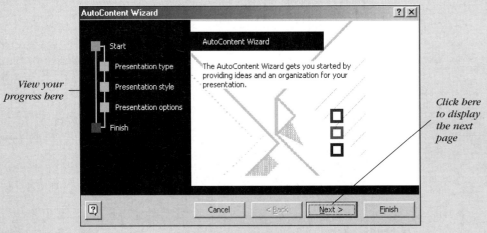

Figure 2.4

 ## If you have problems...
If the Office Assistant automatically displays when you launch the AutoContent Wizard, just choose *No, don't provide help now.* Clear the Assistant by right-clicking on it and choosing Hide.

3 **Click the Next button.**
The Presentation type page of the AutoContent Wizard displays. You can use this page to determine the type of presentation that best fits your needs.

To Create a Presentation Using the AutoContent Wizard

4 **Click the All button to display the entire list of predesigned presentations.**
All presentation types are shown in the list box on the right side of the dialog box (see Figure 2.5). You can limit the type of presentation listed by clicking one of the category buttons.

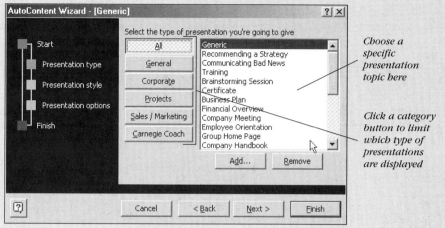

Figure 2.5

5 **Click several of the category buttons to see what sample presentations they include. When you finish experimenting, choose the Projects button.**

6 **Click Reporting Progress or Status, and then choose Next.**
The Presentation style page is displayed. You can use this page to choose the general type of output you want. For example, if you're running a brainstorming session or meeting, you can choose the On-screen presentation option. In contrast, if you want to publish the presentation to the World Wide Web, choose Web presentation.

If you have problems...

Some templates are "install on first use" features—which means that you'll be prompted to install it if it's never been used before. If this happens, see your instructor for help.

7 **Make sure the On-screen presentation option button is selected and then choose Next.**
The Presentation options page of the AutoContent Wizard dialog box displays. You use this page to add a title to your presentation. You can also add items to the ***footer area***— the place at the bottom of each slide. For example, you can add your company name or a slide number to each slide.

8 **Click in the Presentation title text box, and type** Upgrade Office XP.

9 **Click in the Footer text box, and type** By the Information Technology Team.

10 **Verify that the boxes are checked for Date last updated and Slide number, and click Next.**
The final page of the AutoContent Wizard displays.

(Continues)

To Create a Presentation Using the AutoContent Wizard (Continued)

⑪ Read the displayed information and then choose Finish to view your presentation.

The AutoContent Wizard creates the presentation and displays it in Normal view, as shown in Figure 2.6. As you recall from Project 1, this tri-pane view includes a Slide pane, a Notes pane, and Outline and Slide tabs. Additionally, the information you entered is included in the title slide. The remainder of the presentation is created as a series of slides with major topics and subtopics. These suggested topics serve as a blueprint for your presentation.

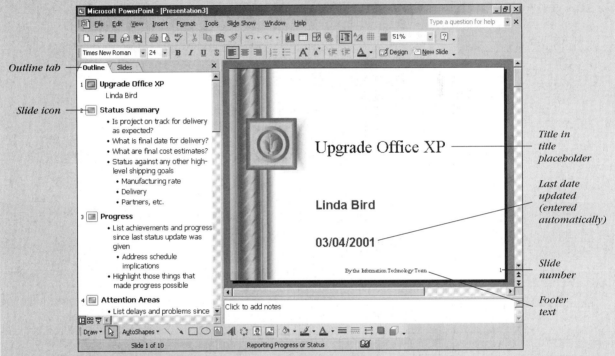

Figure 2.6

Keep this presentation open for the next lesson, in which you learn how to add, demote, and promote text.

Lesson 2: Adding, Demoting, and Promoting Text

When you first create a presentation using the AutoContent Wizard, you have a framework for adding text and graphics. The AutoContent Wizard also provides sample content to get you started on your presentation. In this lesson you'll replace the sample content with your own. You'll also learn how to add, demote, and promote text. **Demoting** text simply means to indent it more on an outline, indicating information that is a subpoint of a main point. Subpoints are usually less important than the main points, and may lend supporting facts to it. **Promoting** text simply means to indent it less on an outline, raising it to a higher level of importance. Try adding, demoting, and promoting text now.

To Add, Demote, and Promote Text

❶ If necessary, click the Outline tab.
You can edit text in the Slide pane or on the Outline tab. For now you'll use the Outline tab.

❷ On the Outline tab, click the first bullet, *Is project on track for delivery as expected?* **on Slide 2.**
The information associated with the first bullet is selected (see Figure 2.7). When you begin to type, the existing text is replaced with whatever you enter.

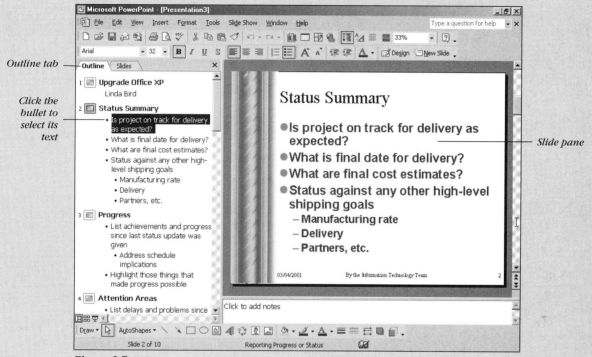

Figure 2.7

❸ With the text for the first bullet point selected, type Project is two weeks behind schedule.
The new text is entered simultaneously on the Outline tab and in the Slide pane.

❹ Click at the beginning of the next bulleted point on Slide 2, press and hold ⤊Shift)**, and click at the end of the last bulleted point. Release the** ⤊Shift) **key.**
The text and bullets are selected so that you can delete them, as shown in Figure 2.8.

(Continues)

To Add, Demote, and Promote Text (Continued)

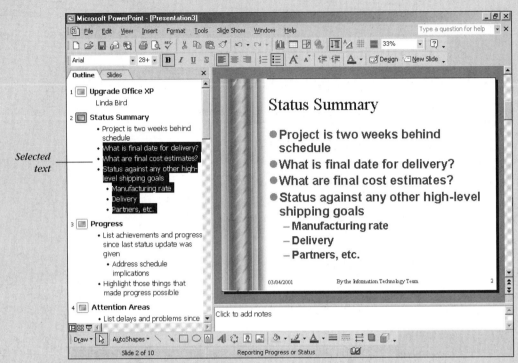

Figure 2.8

5 **Press** (Del).

The selected text is deleted. A faint bullet on the Outline tab shows the location for your next point. You can enter another main point at this outline level, or create subpoints for your main idea (that the project is two weeks behind). You create subpoints by demoting text. You can do this by pressing (Tab⇆) or clicking the Increase Indent button on the Formatting toolbar.

6 **Click the Increase Indent button on the Formatting toolbar and then type**
`Shipments of new computers were late.` **Press** (↵Enter).
Whenever you press (↵Enter), PowerPoint creates a bullet point at the same outline level as the previous one.

 ### If you have problems...

By default, PowerPoint displays both the Standard and Formatting toolbars on one row—which means that you can't see all the available buttons. To quickly show all the buttons for each toolbar, right-click the menu bar and then choose <u>C</u>ustomize. On the <u>O</u>ptions page, check the box for *Show Standard and Formatting toolbars on two rows* before choosing Close.

---

7 **Type** `Sarah Stone will check into this` **and then press** (↵Enter).
Now you're ready to enter another main point. You can move the bullet point to a higher outline level by pressing (⇧Shift)+(Tab⇆) or clicking the Decrease Indent button.

8 **Verify that the insertion point is displayed next to the last bullet on Slide 2 and then click the Decrease Indent button.**
The bullet is indented less so that you can enter another main point on your outline.

9 **Type** `Cost is running 10% over estimates.`
When you're finished, Slide 2 should appear similar to the one shown in Figure 2.9.

To Add, Demote, and Promote Text

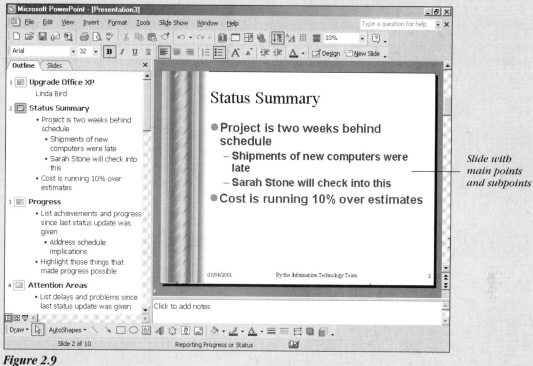

Figure 2.9

⑩ Choose File, Save As.
The Save As dialog box is displayed. You used this dialog box in Project 1 to save a presentation.

⑪ Make sure the correct folder and drive is chosen in the Save in box. (If you're unsure where to save your presentation, ask your instructor.)

⑫ Type Status Report in the File name box and then click Save.
Keep your Status Report presentation open for the next lesson, in which you learn how to select, move, and copy text.

To extend your knowledge...

Promoting and Demoting Existing Text

You don't have to promote (or demote) a bullet before you enter text. Instead, you can select one or more existing bulleted points and then click the Increase Indent or Decrease Indent buttons. Also, if you accidentally move the text too many outline levels, you can just choose Edit, Undo.

Lesson 3: Selecting, Moving, and Copying Text

To work more effectively with your presentation text, you'll usually need to select it. When you *select* text, you highlight it so you can subsequently move, copy, delete, or format it. You can select a single character, a word, one or more lines, or all the text on a slide.

After you select text, you can perform operations on it, such as copying and moving. After you copy text, the selected text appears in two places. In contrast, moving text removes it from the original location and places it in a new location. The most straightforward way to copy or move text is to use the Copy, Cut, and Paste buttons on the Standard toolbar.

Because the ability to select, copy, and move text is important, try your hand at it now.

To Select, Move, and Copy Text

❶ Verify that Slide 2 of the Status Report presentation from the previous lesson is displayed in Normal view.

❷ Click in the title placeholder in the Slide pane and then drag over the word *Status.*
The word is selected. Now try an even quicker method of selecting a word.

❸ Double-click the word *Summary* **in the title placeholder.**
You can also click a bullet in a text placeholder to select its text. When you select a bullet, you also automatically select all the associated subpoints.

❹ In the Slide pane, click the bullet point for *Project is two weeks behind schedule.*
The bulleted point and all subpoints are selected, as shown in Figure 2.10. Now try copying text.

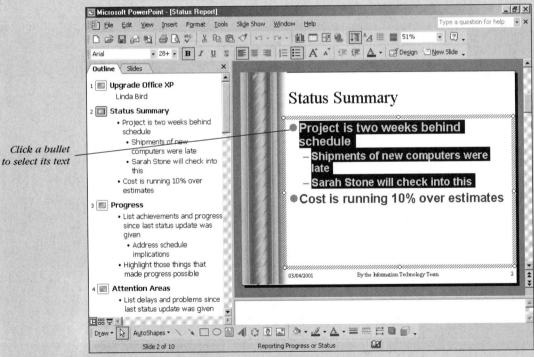

Click a bullet to select its text

Figure 2.10

❺ Click the bullet for *Sarah Stone will check into this* **and then click the Copy button on the Standard toolbar.**

To Select, Move, and Copy Text

The selected text is copied to a temporary area in memory reserved for copying and moving data, called the **Clipboard**.

6 **Click at the end of the bulleted point, *Costs are running 10% over estimates* and then press** ⏎Enter.
Before you paste information from the Clipboard, you need to position your insertion point where you want the data to appear.

7 **Click the Paste button on the Standard toolbar.**
The data is pasted from the Clipboard to the new location.

8 **If necessary, press** ⌫Backspace **to delete the extra bullet.**
Now try moving data.

9 **Click outside the placeholder on Slide 2 and then press** Ctrl+Home **to display Slide 1 in the Slide pane.**

10 **Double-click the word *Upgrade* to select it.**

11 **Click the Cut button on the Standard toolbar.**
The selected data is moved to the Clipboard.

12 **Click immediately after the word "XP" in the title placeholder and then click the Paste button.**
The selected text is moved to the new location.

13 **Click the Save button to update your changes to the Status Report presentation.**
Keep your presentation open for the next lesson, in which you learn how to change the appearance of your text.

To extend your knowledge...

Using Keyboard Commands to Cut, Copy, and Paste

As an alternative to using the toolbar buttons for copying and moving, you can use keyboard shortcuts. To copy selected text, press Ctrl+C; to cut selected text, press Ctrl+X. To paste information that's been moved or copied to the Clipboard, press Ctrl+V.

Lesson 4: Changing Text Appearance

The font that displays on a slide depends on the template you used to create it and the placeholder. A **font** is a collection of characters (letters, numbers, and special symbols) that have a specific appearance. Other terms for font are **typeface** and font face.

You can modify a font by adding **character attributes** such as bold, italic, or underline. You can also modify the text's font face, size, or color. Try enhancing a presentation by formatting its text now.

To Change Text Appearance

① **In your open Status Report presentation, press `PgDn` to display Slide 2.**

② **Double-click the word *Summary* in the title placeholder.**
This selects the word so that you can change the formatting.

③ **Click the Italic, Bold, and Underline buttons on the Formatting toolbar.**
Italic, bold, and underline effects are added to the selected word.

④ **Click the Undo button two times.**
Each time you click the Undo button, you reverse the most recent action. Since you reversed the last two actions, the word should still be formatted using italic.

⑤ **In the Slide pane, drag over the text for the first bulleted point, *Project is two weeks behind schedule.***
Notice that the Font and Font Size boxes on the Formatting toolbar indicate that this text is currently Arial 32 points (see Figure 2.11). Font size is measured in *points*, which is a unit of measurement used to designate character height. The larger the point size, the larger the text. Most slide text should be at least 18 points (or 1/4″) to be readable—especially if you plan to show the presentation by using an overhead projection system.

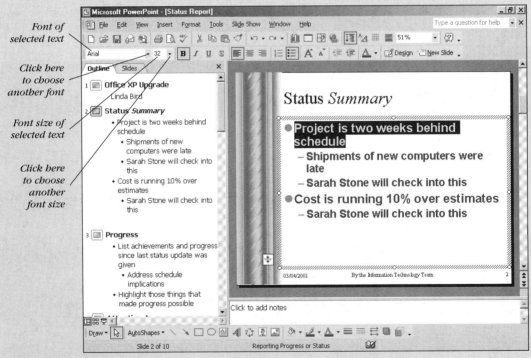

Figure 2.11

Now try using the Formatting toolbar's button to change text size.

⑥ **Click the drop-down arrow to the right of the Font Size box on the Formatting toolbar, scroll down, and then click *36* to select it as the new point size.**
The selected text changes to the larger point size.

Now modify the typeface's appearance.

To Change Text Appearance

7 **With the text for the first bulleted point still selected, click the Font box drop-down arrow.**

A graphical listing of fonts displays, which you can use for your presentation (see Figure 2.12).

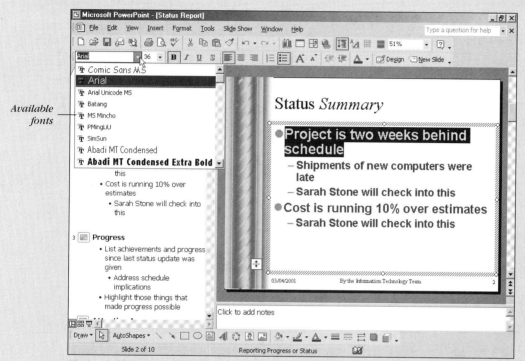

Available fonts

Figure 2.12

? If you have problems...

Don't panic if the fonts on your system don't match those as seen in Figure 2.12. The exact fonts available depend on which programs (and printers) are installed on your system. Additionally, the most recently used fonts display at the top of the list.

---

8 **Scroll down on the list and then click Comic Sans MS (if Comic Sans MS is not available, select another font).**

The new font is applied to the selected text.

Besides changing the font size and appearance, you can modify the font color. Try using the Font dialog box (instead of a toolbar) to make this change.

9 **With the text for the first bulleted point still displayed, choose F_ormat, _Font.**

The Font dialog box is displayed. This dialog box includes a number of ways to format text (see Figure 2.13). Notice that some of the formatting options (such as those listed in the Effects area) are not available on the Formatting toolbar. Because of this, it's handy to know how to use this dialog box.

(Continues)

To Change Text Appearance (Continued)

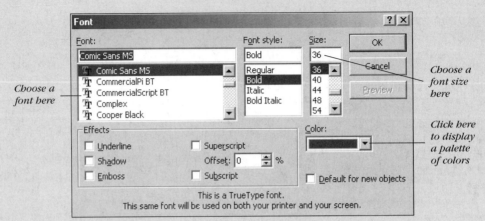

Figure 2.13

⑩ Click the Color drop-down list arrow.

PowerPoint displays eight colors on a color palette. The colors displayed are those most compatible with your particular template's color scheme. Just as an artist uses a palette to paint, you can pick and choose which colors you think will dress up your presentation.

⑪ Click the eighth color from the left and then click OK to close the Font dialog box.

Don't be surprised if the text doesn't appear the color you chose. When text is selected (and shown in reverse video), the colors don't look the same as they do when the text isn't selected. However, you can easily see the color change just by deselecting the text.

⑫ Click outside the placeholder in the Slide pane to deselect the text.

When the text is deselected, you should be able to more easily see the new font color.

⑬ Click the Save button to update your changes to the Status Report presentation.

Congratulations! You now know how to wield the basic tools for text formatting. In the next lesson, you learn how to copy formatting by using the Format Painter, so keep the Status Report presentation open.

To extend your knowledge...

Formatting Tips and Tricks

You can also add character effects by using keyboard shortcuts. For example, you can press Ctrl+B for bold, Ctrl+I for italic, and Ctrl+U for underline.

If you're in a hurry, you can change font size quickly by selecting text; then click the Increase Font Size or Decrease Font Size buttons on the Formatting toolbar repeatedly until the font is the size you want.

Lesson 5: Using the Format Painter

If you want to use the same combination of font, color, and size throughout your presentation, you don't have to laboriously create it from scratch each time. Instead you can just copy the formatting from one section of text to another. This is an efficient method of formatting text because you can create the font and color combination you want just once, and then copy it.

How do you actually "paint" formatting? By using the Format Painter! Think of the text with the formatting you want to copy as a paint can. When you click the Format Painter button, you dip your paintbrush into the can. You then "paint" the formatting to other text by dragging over it—just as you paint a wall by dragging a paintbrush over it.

Try using this timesaving feature now.

To Use the Format Painter

❶ In your open presentation, select the text for the first bulleted point, *Project is two weeks behind schedule*.

It's crucial to select the text from which you want to copy formatting by selecting it *before* you click the Format Painter button. Don't forget this step!

❷ Click the Format Painter button on the Standard toolbar.

The mouse pointer changes to the Format Painter I-beam pointer. This pointer appears (interestingly enough) as a miniature paintbrush, as shown in Figure 2.14. Now you can apply the formatting to other text.

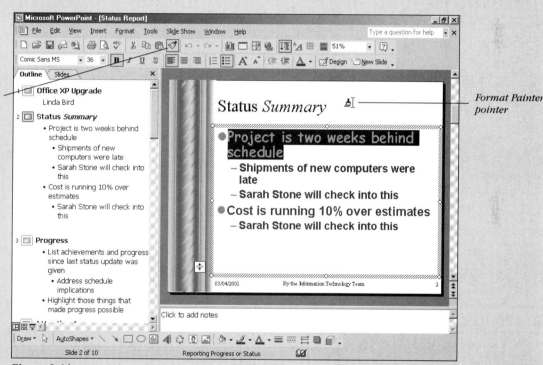

Figure 2.14

❸ Click and drag the pointer over the text for the second major bullet point, *Cost is running 10% over estimates*.

The formatting styles associated with *Project is running two weeks behind schedule* are applied to *Cost is running 10% over estimates* and the Format Painter is automatically turned off.

❹ Click outside the placeholder.

By deselecting your text, you can better see your changes.

❺ Double-click the word *Summary* in the title (upper) placeholder.

❻ Double-click the Format Painter button.

(Continues)

To Use the Format Painter (Continued)

By double-clicking the Format Painter button, you keep the Format Painter feature active so that you can format multiple text sections.

7 **Drag over the word *Status* in the title (upper) placeholder.**
The formatting is copied to the selected word and the Format Painter is still active. You apply the formatting to other text on the current slide (or even another slide).

8 **Press PgUp to display Slide 1.**

9 **Click and drag over the words *Office XP Upgrade* in the title placeholder.**
The formatting is applied to the selected text. To turn off the Format Painter, you can click its button a second time or simply press Esc.

10 **Click the Format Painter button.**
The Format Painter is turned off.

11 **Save your changes to the Status Report presentation.**
Keep the Status Report presentation open for the next lesson, in which you change text alignment.

Lesson 6: Changing the Text Alignment and Setting Tabs

In addition to changing the text appearance on slides, you can change ***horizontal text alignment***, which is simply the way the text displays horizontally in the placeholder (or other object). The way that the text displays in a placeholder—left justified, centered, or right justified—depends on the template that you use. Most commonly, however, title and subtitle text is centered; bulleted list text is usually left justified.

You can easily change text in *any* placeholder to left, center, or right alignment. The easiest way to do this is to use the alignment buttons on the Formatting toolbar. Try your hand at changing the alignment in the Status Report presentation now.

To Change the Text Alignment

1 **Display Slide 1 of the Status Report presentation in Normal view, if necessary.**

2 **Click in the text in the title placeholder *Office XP Upgrade*.**
Notice that the Align Left button on the Formatting toolbar is selected, indicating that it is turned on. When you choose another alignment, left alignment will be turned off.

3 **Click the Center button on the Formatting toolbar.**
The text in the placeholder becomes centered.

4 **Press PgDn to display Slide 2.**

5 **Starting at the beginning of the first bulleted line, drag over all the bulleted text in the lower placeholder to select it.**
You can apply formatting to multiple paragraphs, but you must first select them.

6 **Click the Align Right button on the Formatting toolbar.**
All the lines you selected are lined up on the right side of the placeholder (see Figure 2.15).

To Change the Text Alignment

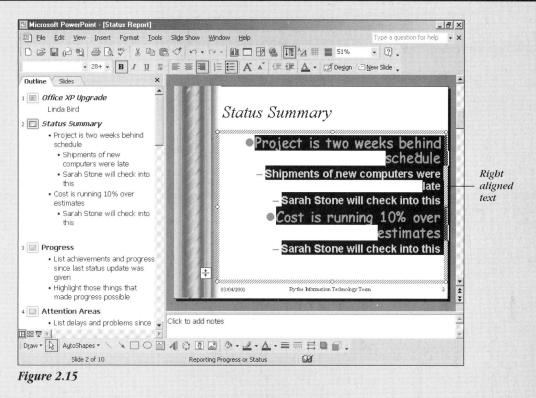

Figure 2.15

7 **With the text in the lower placeholder of Slide 2 still selected, click the Align Left button.**
The text is lined up on the left side of the placeholder.

8 **Save the changes to your Status Report presentation.**
Keep the presentation open for the next lesson, in which you add and remove bullets.

 ## To extend your knowledge...

Working with Tabs

You can set tabs in PowerPoint, just as you can in a word processing program. PowerPoint includes four tab types you can use. Left tabs line up the text at the left edge of the stop; right tabs line text up at the right edge of the stop. Of course, center tabs are great for centering text under the tab stop. Finally, decimal tabs line up numbers on the decimal point and are especially handy to use when you're working with numbers. By default, PowerPoint sets left aligned tabs every inch.

To set your own tabs, first choose View, Ruler to display the horizontal and vertical rulers. Click inside the placeholder that contains the text for which you want to set tabs. Click the tab type box on the left end of the horizontal ruler to choose which tab type (left, center, right, decimal) that you want. On the horizontal ruler, click where you want to set a tab. To move a tab, drag it to the left or right on the ruler; to remove the tab, drag it into the PowerPoint application window before releasing the mouse button. To use the tab, position the insertion point where you want to set the tab, and then press Tab↹.

Lesson 7: Adding, Removing, and Modifying Bullets

In PowerPoint, bullets are markers that make a list of items more readable. A bullet is an object, such as a circle or square. By default, PowerPoint displays bullets as circles, diamonds, squares, and so on. Bullets are also usually combined with indentation so that the related text wraps properly.

PowerPoint makes it easy to add bullets to a slide because it automatically includes them as part of the lower (text) placeholder on the most common type of slide—the Title and Text layout.

Because it's easiest to add and remove bulleted items in the Slide pane in Normal view, you'll use that pane for this lesson. Try working with bullets now.

To Add, Remove, and Modify Bullets

❶ In the open Status Report presentation, press `PgDn` to display Slide 3, *Progress*.
This slide contains a text placeholder with bullets. You can easily remove the bullets by selecting the associated text, and then clicking the Bullets button. First, however, delete the subpoint.

❷ Click the bullet for the subpoint *Address schedule implications* and then press `Del`.
Now select the remaining bullets.

❸ With your insertion point positioned within the lower (text) placeholder, press `Ctrl`+`A`.
All the bulleted text within the placeholder is selected. Now you can remove the bullets.

❹ Click the Bullets button.
Bullets are removed from all the paragraphs you selected. You can also add bullets by clicking the Bullets button again.

❺ With the paragraphs still selected, click the Bullets button again.
Bullets are added to the selected paragraphs.

Now, try changing the bullets to numbering. You generally use numbers instead of bullets when you want to emphasize the order or sequence of the items listed. For example, it's appropriate to use numbers if you want to show the steps involved in placing an order or maintaining a machine.

❻ With the paragraphs in the text placeholder still selected, click the Numbering button.
The bullets are replaced by numbering (see Figure 2.16).

To Add, Remove, and Modify Bullets

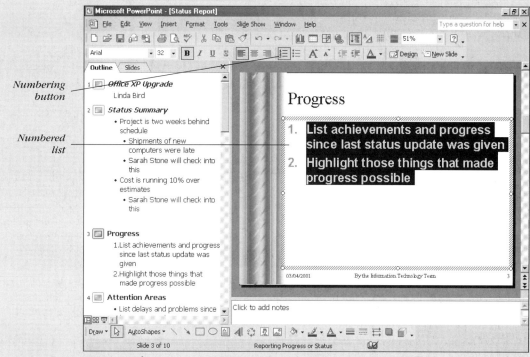

Numbering button

Numbered list

Figure 2.16

Now try reapplying bullets to your list.

7 **With the text in the lower placeholder still selected, click the Bullets button.**
The sequential numbers are replaced by bullets. You can also modify the appearance of your bullets.

8 **With your text in the lower placeholder still selected, choose F_ormat, _Bullets and Numbering.**
The Bullets and Numbering dialog box is displayed (see Figure 2.17). You can choose a different bullet style in this dialog box.

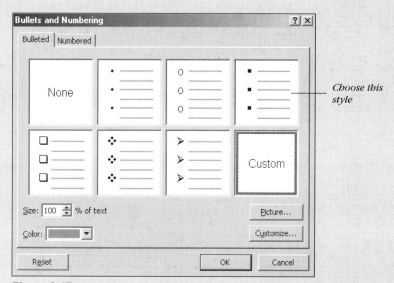

Choose this style

Figure 2.17

(Continues)

To Add, Remove, and Modify Bullets (Continued)

9 **Click the filled square box style (the rightmost style in the top row) and then click OK.**
The filled square bullet style is applied to the selected text.

10 **Save the Status Report presentation and then close it.**
Keep PowerPoint running if you plan to complete the end of chapter exercises.

To extend your knowledge...

Checking Your Spelling

One of the last steps before printing or giving a presentation is to make sure it's error-free. Besides manually proofreading the presentation, you can spell-check it. To do this, click the Spelling button on the Standard toolbar, or choose Tools, Spelling. PowerPoint searches your presentation for typos and misspelled words and displays them in the Spelling dialog box. You can choose Ignore to skip over the word, Change to replace it with another word, or Add to place the word in the dictionary. When PowerPoint is finished spell-checking your presentation, it displays a message box. Click OK to close the message box, and you're on your way to an error-free presentation!

In this project you greatly expanded your knowledge of working with PowerPoint. You used the AutoContent Wizard to create a presentation and replaced its sample content with your own. You also saw how easy it was to copy, move, demote, promote, align, and format text. You gained efficiency by using the Format Painter to quickly apply existing formats to other sections of text. Finally, you learned how to add, remove, and modify bullets and numbers.

To expand on your knowledge, spend a few minutes exploring Help on these topics. Additionally, complete some of the Skill Drill, Challenge, and Discovery Zone exercises.

Checking Concepts and Terms

Multiple Choice

Circle the letter of the correct answer for each of the following.

1. What does promoting a point mean? [L2]

   a. That you are making the text larger

   b. That you are selecting a subpoint

   c. That you are indenting the point less

   d. That you are indenting the point more

2. Where is text sent when it is cut or copied? [L3]

   a. To the Outboard

   b. To the Office Assistant

   c. To the Clipboard

   d. To the Explorer

3. How can you change character attributes, such as bold, italic, and underline? [L4]

   a. by using the Font dialog box

   b. by clicking toolbar buttons

   c. by pressing keyboard shortcuts, such as Ctrl+B for bold

   d. all of the above

4. Which of the following is true regarding the Format Painter? [L5]

   a. You must first select the text that contains the formatting you want to copy.

   b. You can change text appearance only for a text placeholder (not a title placeholder).

   c. Changes are made to the underlying template.

   d. All of the above

5. Which of the following is true about bullets? [L7]

   a. They are usually combined with indentation so that the related text wraps properly.

   b. They can be added or removed.

   c. They can be modified.

   d. All of the above

Screen ID

Label each button or screen element shown in Figure 2.18.

A. Font Size box
B. Font box
C. Bullets button
D. Numbering button
E. Align Right button
F. Center button
G. Align Left button
H. Underline button
I. Italic button
J. Format Painter button

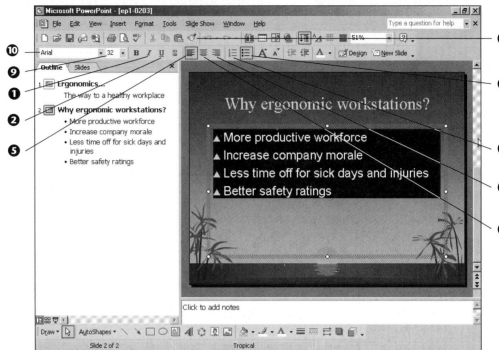

Figure 2.18

1. _____   6. _____

2. _____   7. _____

3. _____   8. _____

4. _____   9. _____

5. _____   10. _____

Discussion

1. In general, bullets and numbers are used for different types of lists. Describe two examples when bullets are more appropriate to use and then describe two examples of when numbers should be used instead of bullets. [L7]

2. In this project you learned how to use the AutoContent Wizard to initially create a presentation. In comparison to your other two methods (starting with a blank slide and starting with a template), what are the advantages of using this wizard? What are the disadvantages? [L1]

Skill Drill

Skill Drill exercises *reinforce* project skills. Each skill reinforced is the same, or nearly the same, as a skill presented in the project. Detailed instructions are provided in a step-by-step format.

1. Using the AutoContent Wizard

Because you recently attended a PowerPoint class, everyone in your department now considers you a PowerPoint expert. For this reason, your co-workers want you to convince management to buy the "latest and greatest" computers for them. You decide to use PowerPoint to present your ideas at a staff meeting to show that purchasing new computers would be cost-effective. Because you need to prepare the presentation by tomorrow, you decide to use the AutoContent Wizard.

1. In PowerPoint, choose File, New to display the New Presentation task pane. Choose From AutoContent Wizard.
2. Click Next to advance past the opening page of the wizard.
3. On the second page of the wizard, click All to display the entire list of presentations. Scroll down the list and choose *Selling Your Ideas*. Click Next.
4. On the third page, make sure that the On-screen presentation option is selected and then click Next.
5. On the fourth page, enter **Improving Productivity** as the presentation title. Enter **By** and then type your name in the Footer text box.
6. On the same page, make sure that the Date last updated and the Slide number boxes are checked. Click Next.
7. Click Finish to create the presentation, and display it in Normal view.
8. Choose File, Save As to display the Save As dialog box. Save the presentation as **New Computers**, and close it.

Keep PowerPoint running for the next exercise.

2. Changing Text Appearance

You work for a company that conducts seminars. One of your most popular seminars is "How to Give Exciting Presentations," but frankly, you think that the publicity materials used for this seminar are not very exciting. To jazz them up, you decide to use PowerPoint's formatting features.

1. Use Help to research how to open existing PowerPoint files.
2. Choose File, Open to display the Open dialog box. Click the *ep1-0201* file and then click the Open button. (If you have trouble locating or opening this file, see your instructor.)
3. Choose File, Save As to display the Save As dialog box. In the File name box, type **ABC Training** and then click Save. (This saves the original file using a different name.)
4. If necessary, press Ctrl+Home to display Slide 1 of the presentation. Also choose View, Normal to make sure the presentation is shown using Normal view.
5. Select the text in the title placeholder in Slide 1. Click the Font drop-down list arrow and then choose Impact from the list. (If this font isn't available on your system, choose another font.)
6. With the text still selected, click the Font Size drop-down list arrow and choose 48 from the list.
7. Press Ctrl+B and Ctrl+I to apply bold and italic to the title text.
8. Choose Format, Font to display the Font dialog box. Click the Color drop-down list arrow and then choose the red color (the seventh color box from the left on the top row). Click OK.
9. Click outside the placeholder to deselect your text and view your changes.

10. Double-click the word *How* in the subtitle placeholder to select it, and then click the Bold and Italic buttons on the Formatting toolbar.

11. With the word *How* still selected, double-click the Format Painter button. Drag over the remaining text in the subtitle placeholder to apply the formatting to the text.

12. Press Esc to turn off the Format Painter.

13. Click the Save button to update your changes to the *ABC Training* presentation. Keep it open for the next exercise.

3. Working with Bullets

To further modify your *ABC Training* presentation, you change the bullets in the presentation. Because you're not sure which bullet appearance you want, you experiment by using different bullet symbols before you finally settle on one.

1. Make sure that the *ABC Training* presentation you worked with in the previous exercise is displayed in Normal view.

2. Press PgDn to display Slide 2. Select all the bulleted text in the lower placeholder.

3. Click the Bullets button to remove the bullets from the slide and then click the Bullets button again to add bullets.

4. Choose Format, Bullets and Numbering to display the Bullets and Numbering dialog box. Click the open circular bullets (the third bullet symbol from the left on the top row) and then click OK.

5. Repeat step 4 to apply each of the different bullet symbols shown in the Bullets and Numbering dialog box.

6. With the text in the lower placeholder still selected, redisplay the Bullets and Numbering dialog box. Choose the square bullet symbol (the first bullet symbol from the left on the second row).

7. In the Bullets and Numbering dialog box, click the Color drop-down list arrow, and choose the red color box (the second box from the right in the first row). Click OK.

8. Click outside the placeholder to deselect your text and view your bullets.

9. Print Slide 2 as a slide.

10. Save and close the *ABC Training* presentation.

Keep PowerPoint running if you plan to complete additional exercises.

4. Modifying Bullets and Changing Alignment

You work part-time in a sports store near campus. To help recruit quality workers, you've put together a presentation that shows the company's commitment to their employees. To add interest to the presentation, you decide to modify bullets. You also decide to space and align the bulleted points so that they are more readable.

1. Choose File, Open to display the Open dialog box. Click the *ep1-0202* file and then click the Open button. (If you have trouble locating or opening this file, see your instructor.)

2. Choose File, Save As to display the Save As dialog box. In the File name box, type **Sports Store** and then click Save. (This saves the original file using a different name.)

3. Press PgDn to display Slide 2, *Our Commitment to Employees*, in Normal view. Select all the text in the lower placeholder.

4. Choose Format, Line Spacing to display the Line Spacing dialog box. Enter **1.25** in the Line spacing box and then click OK.

5. With the text still selected, click the Center button on the Formatting toolbar.

6. With the text still selected, choose Format, Bullets and Numbering. Click the check mark symbol (the last symbol on the second row).

7. Click the Color drop-down list arrow. Choose More Colors from the palette to display the Colors dialog box. Click a turquoise color in the dialog box and then click OK to close the Colors dialog box.

8. Click OK to close the Bullets and Numbering dialog box and then click outside the placeholder to deselect the text.

9. Save the *Sports Store* presentation and then close it.

Keep PowerPoint running if you plan to complete additional exercises.

Challenge exercises expand on or are somewhat related to skills presented in the lessons. Each exercise provides a brief narrative introduction followed by instructions in a numbered step format that are not as detailed as those in the Skill Drill section.

1. Using Formatting Features

You previously created a presentation to promote your company, which sells ergonomic products. To enhance it, you use some of the formatting features PowerPoint provides.

1. Open *ep1-0203* and save it as `Ergonomics`.

2. Use PowerPoint's Help to find out ways to format text, including how to use the Shadow button.

3. Display Slide 1 in Normal view and then format the word *Ergonomics* with italic, bold, and shadow features. Increase the point size for *Ergonomics* to 60 points, and change the text color to orange.

4. Use the Format Painter to apply the formatting from *Ergonomics* to the word *healthy* on Slide 1.

5. Display Slide 2, and select all the bulleted text in the lower placeholder. Center the text horizontally.

6. Save and then close the *Ergonomics* presentation.

Keep PowerPoint running if you plan to complete additional exercises.

2. Formatting a Presentation

Because you learned PowerPoint so well, you freelance by revising presentations for various businesses. You're currently working on a production report for one of your clients. You decide to spice it up by using PowerPoint's formatting features.

1. Open *ep1-0204* and save it as `Production Report`.

2. Improve the appearance of the title text on Slide 1 by changing it to another color (such as salmon) and font. Also increase the font size for the title to at least 54 points. Using the Format Painter, copy the formatting from the Slide 1, *Production Report* to the titles on Slides 2–4. (Hint: Double-click the Format Painter to keep it active.)

3. Apply italic to the subtitle text on Slide 1.

4. Change the bullet color on Slide 2 to match that of the slide title and then change the bullets to right-pointing triangles.

5. Using Slide 2 as an example, change the bullets on Slides 3–4.

6. Print the presentation as a series of slides.

7. Save the *Production Report* presentation and then close it.

Keep PowerPoint running if you plan to complete additional exercises.

3. Using Numbering and Bullets

You're about to graduate from college, and you're handing over the responsibilities of running the student council and the Sports Club to other students. To train them in leadership skills (including giving presentations), you develop a speech. Because numbers are more appropriate than bullets to use on some of the slides, you revise your presentation to include numbers.

1. Open *ep1-0205* and save it as **Presentation Guidelines**. Revise the presentation as follows:

- ○ Remove the bullet from Slide 3.
- ○ Change the bullets on Slide 4, *Key Topic*, to numbers. Also make the numbers the same size as the text (100%). (Hint: If you're unsure how to do this, consult Help.)
- ○ Change the color for the numbers on Slide 4 to dark blue. (Hint: Use the Numbered page of the Bullets and Numbering dialog box.)
- ○ Change the bullets on Slide 5, *Goals and Problems*, to drop shadow square symbols.
- ○ Change the bullets on Slide 6, *Solutions and Opportunities*, to a bullet of your choice.
- ○ Change the bullets on Slide 8, *Close*, to numbered steps. Change the color to dark blue and make the size 75% of text. (Hint: Use the Bullets and Numbering dialog box.)

2. Save your presentation, and then close it.

Keep PowerPoint running if you plan to complete additional exercises.

4. Formatting Text and Bullets

As the outgoing president of the University Biking Club, you develop a presentation to help the new club officers learn how to facilitate meetings. To make the presentation more appealing, you change bullet and text appearance by using PowerPoint's formatting features.

1. Open *ep1-0206* and save it as **Facilitating a Meeting**. Make the following changes to the presentation, using what you know about PowerPoint.

2. Change the font for the Slide 1 title to Comic Sans MS, 48 point text. Add shadow to the text, and change the color to turquoise. Using the Format Painter, copy this formatting to the titles of the other slides in the presentation.

3. On Slide 3, *Opening*, change the bullet's symbol for the four subpoints to right-pointing triangles.

4. Modify Slides 4—6 so that the bulleted points display similar to the bullets on Slide 3.

5. Print the presentation and then save and close it.

Keep PowerPoint running if you plan to complete the Discovery Zone exercises.

Discovery Zone exercises require advanced knowledge of topics presented in *essentials* lessons, application of skills from multiple lessons, or self-directed learning of new skills. Each exercise is independent of the others, so that you may complete the exercises in any order.

1. Creating Various Types of Presentations

Think of two school, community, or business organizations (or clubs) with which you are currently affiliated. Develop a presentation for each one, highlighting the purpose, officers, membership requirements, upcoming events, and so on. Use the AutoContent Wizard to develop the presentations, and delve into Help when necessary.

Add, demote, and promote text, using techniques covered in this project. Additionally, format the text so that the presentation has a pleasing appearance.

Spell-check your presentations. If directed by your instructor, save the presentations using a name of your choice. Close the presentations, but keep PowerPoint running if you plan to complete the other Discovery Zone exercises.

2. Developing and Modifying Presentations

You're the marketing director for an office products store that primarily sells computer hardware, software, and related supplies. You're slotted to give a presentation to the local retail merchant's association about the products and services you can offer, and want to develop a whiz-bang presentation. You decide to use PowerPoint's features to do so.

Use an appropriate AutoContent Wizard to develop a presentation that highlights your store's products. Cruise the Web to glean ideas of what type of products an office products store might offer; then replace the suggested text in your presentation with information that you find. Add, demote, and promote text as needed. Format the text and then spell-check the presentation and correct any errors.

If directed by your instructor, save the presentation using a name of your choice. Close the presentation but keep PowerPoint running if you plan to complete additional exercises.

3. Changing Alignment and Spacing

You're the head of the research and development department in your company. Because you are experienced at giving presentations, your boss has asked you to give a short talk to share your tips and tricks with other employees. To enhance the presentation, you change text alignment and paragraph spacing.

Open *ep1-0207* and save it as **Presenting a Technical Report**. Make the following changes to the report:

- Left-align the bulleted text on each slide.
- Adjust the line spacing for the bulleted text on each slide so that the points display evenly in the placeholders. (Hint: If you're unsure how to do this, consult Help.)
- Display Slide 6, *Close*. Delete the text *And, if applicable*. Change the remaining bullets to numbers.
- Change the bullets on Slides 3–5 to check marks.

Save and close the presentation; then exit PowerPoint.

Viewing and Restructuring Presentations

Objectives

In this project, you learn how to

- ✔ Open an Existing Presentation
- ✔ Navigate Among Different Views
- ✔ Move Among Slides in Normal View
- ✔ Run an Electronic Slide Show
- ✔ Use the Slide Show Shortcut Keys
- ✔ Add and Delete Slides and Change Slide Layout
- ✔ Change Slide Order

Key terms introduced in this project include

- ❏ context sensitive
- ❏ drag-and-drop
- ❏ keyboard shortcuts
- ❏ popup menu
- ❏ thumbnails
- ❏ views

Why Would I Do This?

Creating the framework of a presentation, as you did in the previous two projects, is a good start on the road to success with PowerPoint. However, any presentation that you create from scratch, with the AutoContent Wizard, or from a template, is really just a springboard for further revisions. As you develop your thoughts, you'll want the flexibility of adding or removing slides as well as revising text.

Luckily, it's easy to modify an existing presentation—and in this project we'll show you how! First, you learn how to open an existing presentation and save it using a new name. Next you focus on quick methods of adding and deleting slides, and changing slide order.

We'll also show you how to use the various perspectives, or **_views_**, which PowerPoint provides to work more effectively with a presentation. You'll learn how to switch between these views and choose the most appropriate one as you modify your presentation. You also see how to move among slides in both Normal and the Slide Show views.

Visual Summary

In this project, you learn proven methods of modifying a presentation. First, you see how to locate a presentation quickly by using the Open dialog box (see Figure 3.1). You also find out how to save the presentation using a new name (or location).

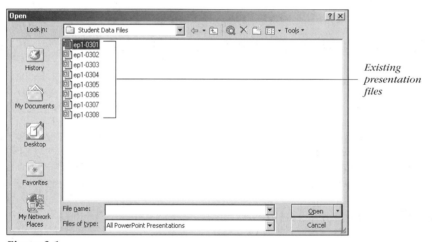

Existing presentation files

Figure 3.1

After you open a presentation, you learn how to work with your presentation using PowerPoint's various views. One of the best views to use when you want to add, delete, and rearrange your slides is Slide Sorter view (see Figure 3.2).

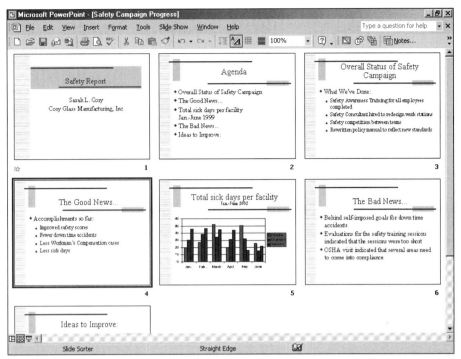

Figure 3.2

You'll also run your presentation as an electronic slide show. So come along and get a handle on the tools that you need to modify and view your presentations.

Lesson 1: Opening an Existing Presentation

When you want to use a paper file in your office, you probably get it from a file cabinet, make a copy, and then put it on your desk so that you can work on it. In the same way, opening an existing presentation in PowerPoint simply creates a copy from one of the computer's storage areas and places it in memory so that you can work with it.

This is handy because it allows you to revise existing presentations instead of having to create new ones from scratch. Think of how time-consuming it would be to re-create every presentation you want to use!

After you open a file, it's also sometimes advantageous to immediately create a "clone" of the file by saving it with a new name. When you do this, you can work with the copy but still keep the original file intact. You will use this method for the lessons in this book.

Now, try opening an existing presentation.

To Open an Existing Presentation

❶ Start PowerPoint, if necessary.

❷ Choose File, Open.

(Continues)

To Open an Existing Presentation (Continued)

Alternately, you can click the Open button on the Standard toolbar or press Ctrl+O from the keyboard. But no matter which method you choose, the Open dialog box displays, as shown in Figure 3.3. This dialog box shows the folders and files on your computer. And, just as a file cabinet in your office might contain many documents, an electronic folder might contain several presentations.

Click here to view possible file locations

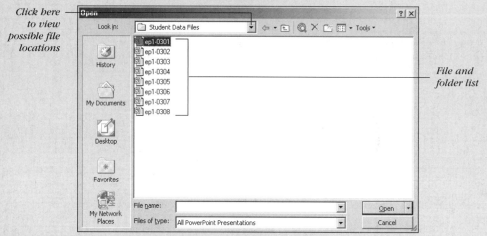

File and folder list

Figure 3.3

If you have problems...

If the list of folders on your system doesn't match that shown in Figure 3.3, don't worry. Because the folders on each computer can be set up to match your work habits, it's unlikely that you'd have exactly the same ones as those shown in the book. However, the My Documents folder is designated (by Microsoft) as the central location to save all your work.

3 **Click the Look in drop-down list arrow, and select the drive that contains your student data files from the list. (If you're unsure where to look, refer to the "How to Use the Student Data Files" section in the front of this book, or ask your instructor for help.)**

4 **If necessary, double-click the folder that includes your student data files.**
A listing of files you need to complete Project 3 is displayed.

5 **Click to select *ep1-0301*, if necessary.**

6 **With *ep1-0301* still selected, click the Open button.**
PowerPoint opens the selected file and displays it in Normal view. To help you quickly identify which presentation is open, PowerPoint displays the presentation's name in the title bar.

Now that the file is opened in memory, you can use the Save As dialog box to copy and rename the file. This keeps the original file unaltered.

7 **With the *ep1-0301* presentation onscreen, choose File, Save As.**
The Save As dialog box displays (see Figure 3.4). In the Save As dialog box, you can enter a new name for the file and choose Save. This effectively creates a copy of the original file with a new name.

To Open an Existing Presentation

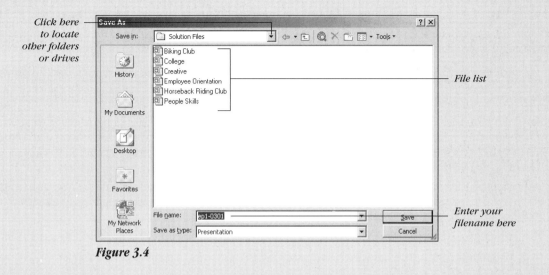

Click here to locate other folders or drives

File list

Enter your filename here

Figure 3.4

8 **In the File name text box, type** Quality Training **and then click the Save button.**

The *ep1-0301* file is copied and renamed *Quality Training* simultaneously. Notice that the title bar displays the new name. You'll work with this presentation in the next lesson, so leave it open.

To extend your knowledge...

More About Opening Presentations

You also can open a presentation from the New Presentation task pane. Here's how: Display the task pane by choosing File, New. If you've recently used the presentation, it will appear toward the top of the Open a presentation section; if not, click the More presentations link to quickly display the Open dialog box.

Lesson 2: Navigating Among Different Views

After you open (or create) a presentation, you can view it in a number of different ways: Normal view, Slide Sorter view, Notes Page view, or as an electronic Slide Show. Additionally, you can use the Slides and Outline tabs that display on the left side of the window in Normal view.

You can also resize the various panes in the Normal view window. For example, if you want to see your presentation's content, you can click the Outline tab and then resize its pane. The following table describes the best uses for each view or tab:

Table 3.1 | PowerPoint's Views

Use	To
Normal view	Get an overview of your entire presentation; work with the outline, notes, or individual slide elements.
Slides tab	Display the presentation as a series of slide thumbnails, or miniatures, on the Slides tab in Normal view. You can also click a slide miniature to view the associated slide in the Slide pane.
Outline tab	Work with the text in traditional outline form while still displaying Normal view.
Notes pane	Develop notes in Normal view.
Slide Sorter view	Display miniatures (thumbnails) of all slides, including text and graphics. Use this view to change the slide order, add transitions, and set timings for electronic slide shows.
Notes Page view	Display a page in which you can create speaker notes for each slide.
Slide Show	Display your presentation as an onscreen electronic slide show.
Slide view	Work with one slide at a time using the entire screen. This view is handy for adding or changing text or graphics.

You change to a different PowerPoint view by clicking the View buttons or by using the View menu. In this lesson, you use both methods to change the view. Try practicing these techniques now.

To Navigate Among Different Views

1 **In the open *Quality Training* presentation, rest the mouse pointer on any of the View buttons (see Figure 3.5).**

Figure 3.5

To Navigate Among Different Views

In a second or two, a ScreenTip displays, indicating the View button's name. Additionally, notice that the presentation is currently displayed using PowerPoint's Normal view. This view includes the Slide pane, a Notes pane, and the Outline and Slides tabs.

2 **Rest the mouse pointer over each of the three View buttons.**
A ScreenTip identifies each button.

3 **Click the Slide Sorter View button (or choose View, Slide Sorter from the menu).**
Your presentation displays as a series of miniature slides (see Figure 3.6). These miniatures are sometimes called ***thumbnails***. The Slide Sorter view is an excellent view to use to add, delete, or rearrange slides. (You learn to add, delete, and reorder slides later in this project.)

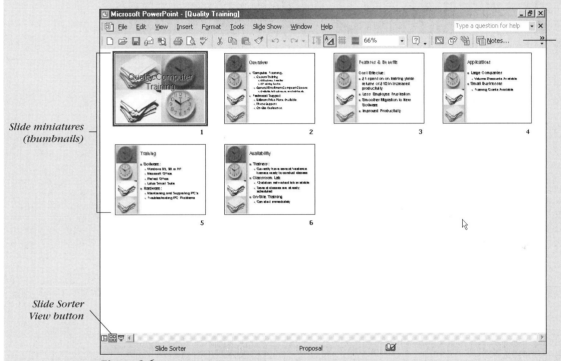

Slide Sorter toolbar

Slide miniatures (thumbnails)

Slide Sorter View button

Figure 3.6

 ### If you have problems...
Don't worry if your screen displays a different arrangement of slides than that shown in Figure 3.6. The number of slides displayed in Slide Sorter view depends on many factors, including monitor size.

4 **Click the Normal View button.**
The presentation again displays in Normal view. Now try using options on the View menu.

5 **Click the View menu.**
Notice that four options—Normal, Slide Sorter, Slide Show, and Notes Pages—display on this menu.

6 **Choose Notes Page from the View menu.**

(Continues)

To Navigate Among Different Views (Continued)

The presentation displays in Notes Page view (see Figure 3.7). This view includes a slide image, along with a notes box area. You can use this view to create and print speaker notes that help you remember key points.

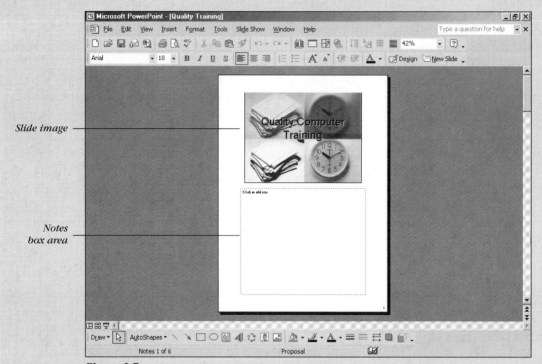

Slide image

Notes box area

Figure 3.7

7 **In Notes Page view, double-click the slide image.**
The presentation is redisplayed in Normal view. (You can also double-click a slide miniature in Slide Sorter view to redisplay the presentation in Normal view.)

Now try closing the Slides and Outline tabs so that you have more screen area to work with the current slide. This view is called Slide view.

8 **Click the Close button in the upper right corner of the Slides and Outline tabs (refer to Figure 3.5, if necessary).**
The presentation slide displays full-screen.

9 **Choose View, Normal (Restore Panes).**
The Slides and Outline tabs again display. You can switch between these tabs to show the associated pane. You can also resize the panes.

10 **If necessary, click the Slides tab.**
The presentation is shown as a series of miniature slides on the Slides tab (see Figure 3.8).

To Navigate Among Different Views

Outline tab

Slides tab

Figure 3.8

⓫ Click the Outline tab.
The presentation's outline is displayed on the Outline tab (see Figure 3.9).

Outline tab

Splitter bar

Figure 3.9

(Continues)

To Navigate Among Different Views (Continued)

Now try resizing the tabs by dragging the border (sometimes called the splitter bar) between the tabs and the Slide pane.

12 **Rest your mouse pointer over the splitter bar (refer to Figure 3.9) until a double-headed arrow displays.**

13 **Drag the splitter bar to the left about half the width of the Outline pane and then release the mouse button.**
The tabs are resized and the words at the top of the Slides and Outline tabs no longer display.

14 **Drag the splitter bar to the right until the original width of the pane is displayed. Release the mouse button.**

15 **Press Ctrl+S to save changes to your *Quality Training* presentation.**
Keep this presentation open for the next lesson, in which you learn how to move among slides in Normal view.

To extend your knowledge...

Some of PowerPoint's views are listed on the <u>V</u>iew menu but don't have a corresponding View button. For example, you can display your presentation in Notes Page view only by using the <u>V</u>iew, Notes <u>P</u>age command. Luckily, the most popular views (such as Normal and Slide Sorter views) are accessible using either the View buttons or the <u>V</u>iew menu.

Lesson 3: Moving Among Slides in Normal View

After you create a presentation, you need to know how to move around it efficiently. For example, you may need to quickly move to the first or last presentation slide, or "page through" the presentation slide by slide. To get you up to speed on how to move around within a presentation, we'll show you some efficient methods. First, you'll be guided through using ***keyboard shortcuts***, which are simply the keys you can press on the keyboard to perform an action. You'll then see how to perform the same actions with the mouse. As you work more and more with PowerPoint, you'll probably find which method best complements your work habits. Try experimenting with these methods now.

To Move Among Slides in Normal View

1 **Verify that the open presentation is displayed in Normal view and then press Ctrl+Home.**
The first slide in your presentation is displayed in the Slide pane.

2 **Press PgDn.**
The second presentation slide is displayed. You can press PgDn to quickly move through a presentation slide by slide; you can press PgUp to display the previous slide.

3 **Press PgUp.**
The first presentation slide is redisplayed. Now try displaying the last presentation slide.

4 **Press Ctrl+End.**

To Move Among Slides in Normal View

The last presentation slide is displayed in the Slide pane. Notice that the last slide is simultaneously selected on the Outline tab.

Now that you are familiar with some common keyboard shortcuts, try your hand at performing similar actions with the mouse. To move among slides using the mouse, you can use buttons on the vertical scrollbar in the Slide pane (or to the right of the Outline tab). For example, you can click the Next Slide or the Previous Slide button at the bottom of the Slide pane's vertical scrollbar. Alternately, you can drag the scroll box on the vertical scrollbar to move to the relative location within your presentation (see Figure 3.10).

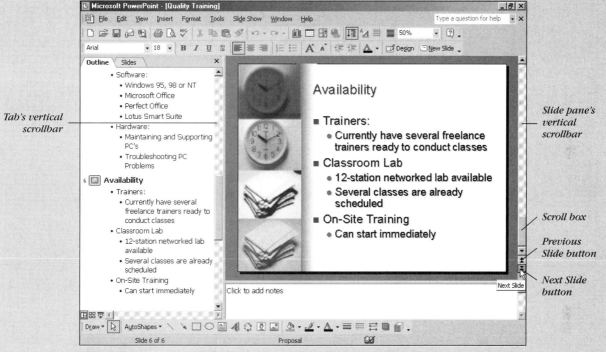

Figure 3.10

5 **Click the Previous Slide button at the bottom of the Slide pane's vertical scrollbar (refer to Figure 3.10).**

6 **Click the Next Slide button at the bottom of the Slide pane's vertical scrollbar.**
The last presentation slide redisplays. Now try using the scroll box to move to a relative location in your presentation. For example, if you want to display the fourth slide in an eight-slide presentation, you would drag the scroll box approximately halfway down the vertical scrollbar.

7 **Click the Slide pane's vertical scroll box; then drag it up and down slowly.**
A ScreenTip displays to the left of the scrollbar. This is a handy feature because the ScreenTip shows the slide number, total number of slides, and current slide title (see Figure 3.11). Furthermore, when you release the mouse button, the slide indicated by the ScreenTip displays.

(Continues)

To Move Among Slides in Normal View (Continued)

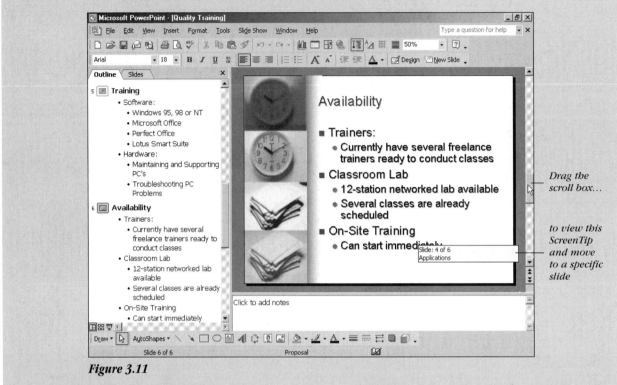

Figure 3.11

8 **Stop at Slide 4, *Applications*, and release the mouse button.**
The slide shown in the ScreenTip becomes the active slide and is shown in Normal view.
Now try moving to a different slide by selecting a slide icon on the Slides tab.

9 **Click the Slides tab; then scroll up (if necessary)_and click the icon for Slide 1,**
Quality Computer Training.
The first presentation slide is selected on the Slides tab, and it displays concurrently in
the Slide pane.

Keep the presentation open for the next lesson, in which you run an electronic slide
show.

Lesson 4: Running an Electronic Slide Show

As you work with PowerPoint, you soon discover that one of the most popular and effective means
of displaying a presentation is as an electronic slide show. You can run a slide show as a handy
method of checking the presentation's content and flow, or to actually show the presentation to an
audience using an overhead projection system. You can also create an onscreen, self-running presentation for use at trade shows, via your company's intranet, or even on the World Wide Web. In this
lesson, you learn the basics of running an electronic slide show.

To Run an Electronic Slide Show

1 **Make sure that Slide 1 in the *Quality Training* presentation is displayed in**
Normal view.

2 **Click the Slide Show button (or choose View, Slide Show).**

To Run an Electronic Slide Show

The electronic slide show begins. (You might see a black screen momentarily before the first slide is shown.) Notice that the first slide displayed is the one that was active when you began the show—Slide 1. Because of this, you can click the Slide Show button to start an electronic slide show from virtually any slide.

③ Click the left mouse button.
The next slide in the presentation displays.

④ Press PgDn.
The next slide in the presentation is shown.

⑤ Press PgUp.
The previous slide in the presentation is shown. Now practice some other ways to jump between slides in a slide show. One easy way is to use the shortcut menu (sometimes called a *popup menu*). Shortcut menus are displayed by right-clicking the mouse, and are *context sensitive*. Context sensitive means that the menu displays the commands that are related to the area of the screen that you right-click.

⑥ Click the right mouse button.
The Slide Show shortcut menu displays (see Figure 3.12). This menu includes commonly used commands that help you control a running slide show. Although you activate the shortcut menu by pressing the right mouse button, you choose commands with the left mouse button.

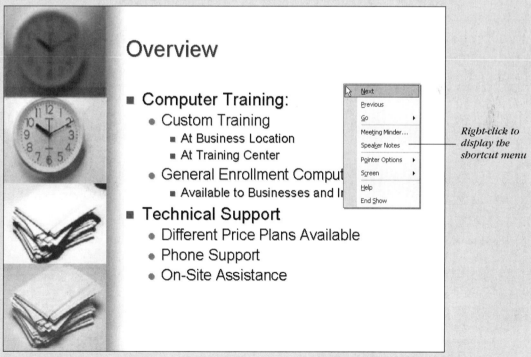

Figure 3.12

⑦ Choose Previous from the shortcut menu.

(Continues)

To Run an Electronic Slide Show (Continued)

Slide 1 is displayed. (You can also move forward in a presentation by choosing Next from the shortcut menu.)

8 **Right-click the mouse to display the shortcut menu; then choose Go, Slide Navigator.**

The Slide Navigator dialog box displays (see Figure 3.13). Because this dialog box shows all the slide titles, you can use it to quickly move to any slide in your presentation.

Double-click a slide to quickly display it

Figure 3.13

9 **Double-click Slide 5, *Training*.**

Slide 5 is displayed.

10 **Right-click the mouse and then choose End Show from the shortcut menu.**

PowerPoint displays the presentation in Normal view—the view you used most recently before you started the electronic slide show.

11 **Press** Ctrl + Home **to display the first presentation slide.**

Keep this presentation open for the next lesson, in which you learn even more tips and tricks for navigating within an electronic slide show.

To extend your knowledge...

Displaying the Slide Show Shortcut menu

You can also display the Slide Show shortcut menu during an electronic slide show by pressing Shift + F10, or by clicking the control icon that appears in the lower left corner of any slide in a slide show.

Lesson 5: Using the Slide Show Shortcut Keys

When you present your slide show to an audience, it's useful to know as many ways as possible to move among your slides. For example, you may want to quickly display a slide that includes production or sales figures—even if it's not the next slide in the sequence.

In Lesson 4, you learned how to launch an electronic slide show and some basic ways to move among the slides. In this lesson, you build on that knowledge by learning keyboard shortcuts. You can use keyboard shortcuts to move between slides in a presentation or to blank out the current slide so that the audience's attention is redirected to you. Try using some of these keyboard shortcuts now.

To Use the Slide Show Shortcut Keys

1 **In the open presentation, press** F5.
F5 is a keyboard shortcut you can use to launch a slide show, beginning with the first slide. Now try viewing the keyboard shortcuts that are available when you run a slide show.

2 **Press** F1.
The Slide Show Help dialog box displays, showing a list of available shortcut keys to help you get around the slide show (see Figure 3.14).

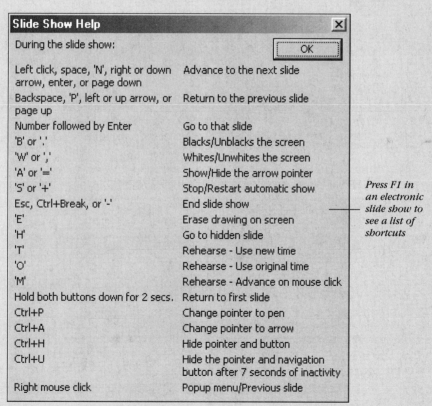

Press F1 in an electronic slide show to see a list of shortcuts

Figure 3.14

3 **Click OK to close the Slide Show Help dialog box and then press** N.
The next slide displays. In a similar fashion, pressing P displays the previous slide.

4 **Press** P.
PowerPoint displays the previous slide in your electronic slide show.

(Continues)

To Use the Slide Show Shortcut Keys (Continued)

You can also seamlessly display a particular slide by typing the slide's number and pressing ⏎Enter. This method is quicker than using the Slide Navigator, and your audience doesn't see the command onscreen. Try using this method to move to another slide now.

5 **Type 4 and then press ⏎Enter.**
The presentation displays Slide 4, *Applications*.

Now try using some of the other functions associated with keyboard shortcuts. For example, you can use keyboard shortcuts to clear the screen so that it doesn't distract the audience during your presentation. To do this, you can press B to blacken the screen or W to white it out. The screen remains blank until you press B or W a second time to redisplay the screen. Try using this helpful feature now.

6 **Press B to blacken the screen and then press B again.**
The display toggles between the screen and blackened views. (If you want, try pressing W twice—the first time to white out the screen and the second time to redisplay it before continuing with the tutorial.)

Now try a quick and easy way to end your slide show.

7 **Press Esc.**
The slide show ends and the presentation again displays in Normal view.

8 **Press Ctrl+Home, and save the *Quality Training* presentation.**
Keep this presentation open for the next lesson, in which you add and delete slides.

To extend your knowledge...

Running Slide Shows

When you click the Slide Show button, you launch the electronic slide show beginning on whichever slide is currently displayed. In contrast, if you press F5 or choose View, Slide Show, you'll begin the slide show starting with Slide 1—no matter which slide is displayed when you launch the show.

Hiding Slides

You can hide, or suppress the display of a slide during a slide show. For example, you might want to develop a slide with documentation or statistics you can use 'just in case' a question arises on the topic during your presentation—but you normally don't expect to use it. To hide the slide, first display the presentation in Slide Sorter view. Select the slide and then click the Hide Slide button. Press H during the slide show to display the hidden slide.

Lesson 6: Adding and Deleting Slides and Changing Slide Layout

No matter how carefully you initially craft your presentation, it's likely that you'll eventually need to make some revisions. For example, you might need to add slides that reflect the most recent sales or production figures.

You may also want to change the layout for a slide—without altering the slide's contents. In this lesson you learn fast methods of making these changes to your presentation.

First, to provide you with a handy reference, the following table lists the methods you can use to add or delete a slide.

Table 3.2 Inserting and Deleting Slides	
To	**Do This**
Add a slide	• Choose Insert, New Slide from the menu bar. • Click the New Slide button on the Formatting toolbar. • Press Ctrl+M.
Delete a slide	• In Slide Sorter view, click to select the slide, and then press Del. • Click the slide icon on the Slides tab or the Outline tab and then press Del. • Choose Edit, Delete Slide in any view.

Now that you have an idea of the ways in which you can add and delete slides, try your hand at it.

To Add and Delete Slides and Change Slide Layout

1 **Display the *Quality Training* presentation in Normal view and click the Slides tab, if necessary.**

2 **On the Slides tab, click the icon for Slide 3, *Features & Benefits*.**
You can instantly select an entire slide by clicking the icon on either the Outline or Slides tabs.

3 **Press Del.**
The selected slide, Slide 3, is deleted from the presentation, and the remaining slides are renumbered. You can reverse this deletion, however, by using a handy feature that PowerPoint provides to annul your last action—Undo.

4 **Click the Undo button on the Standard toolbar.**
Slide 3 is reinserted into the presentation.

You can also delete slides in Slide Sorter view. This is a good view to use when deleting, adding, or rearranging slides because you can easily see the effect of your action on the presentation as a whole.

5 **Click the Slide Sorter View button and then click Slide 4, *Applications*.**
The presentation is shown in Slide Sorter view with a double border surrounding Slide 4. This indicates that it is the selected slide (see Figure 3.15).

(Continues)

To Add and Delete Slides and Change Slide Layout (Continued)

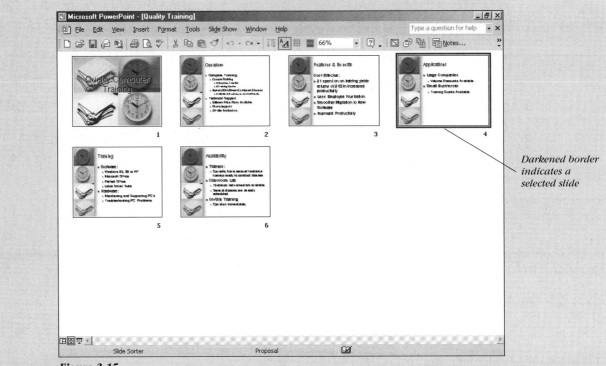

Darkened border indicates a selected slide

Figure 3.15

6 Press Del.
The selected slide is deleted. The black, vertical line between Slides 3 and 4 indicates that the insertion-point location is between the two slides. This is where you want to add a new slide. Luckily, you can create a specific type, or layout, for each new slide.

7 Choose Insert, New Slide.
PowerPoint displays the Slide Layout task pane and inserts a new, blank slide into your presentation at the designated location. Additionally, PowerPoint automatically chose the Title and Text layout for your slide, indicated by the border around that layout in the Slide Layout task pane (see Figure 3.16).

To Add and Delete Slides and Change Slide Layout

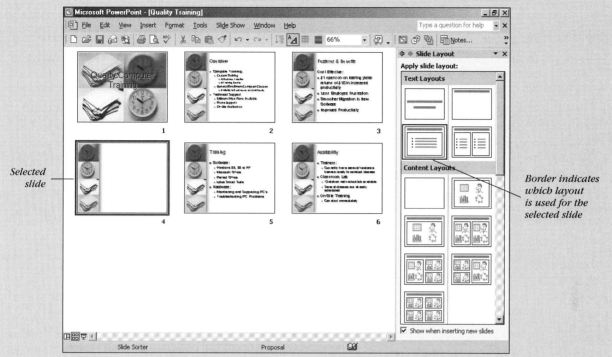

Figure 3.16

Most of the time you'll stick with the layout you chose when you initially created the slide. However, if you later change your mind about how you want your slide set up, you can quickly apply a different slide layout to an existing slide. Try displaying the slide in Normal view and changing the slide layout now.

8 **Double-click Slide 4—the new slide you inserted into your presentation.**
The slide displays in Normal view. Double-clicking a slide in Slide Sorter view is a quick way to switch to Normal view. Now try changing the slide layout.

9 **Click the Title Slide layout in the Slide Layout task pane.**
Placeholders for a title slide are shown on the slide.

10 **Click the Title and Text layout in the Slide Layout task pane.**
The Title and Text layout is reapplied to your slide. Remember that you can change the slide layout for any slide "on the fly" using the Slide Layout task pane. Now try inserting another slide.

If you have problems...

If you accidentally closed the Slide Layout task pane, you can redisplay it by choosing Format, Slide Layout.

11 **In the Slide Layout task pane, rest your mouse pointer over the Title and Text layout until a drop-down arrow displays, and then click the arrow.**

(Continues)

To Add and Delete Slides and Change Slide Layout (Continued)

A drop-down list displays (see Figure 3.17).

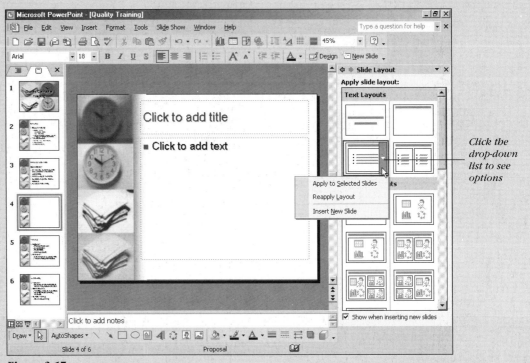

Click the drop-down list to see options

Figure 3.17

⑫ Choose Insert New Slide from the drop-down list.
A new slide is inserted immediately after the displayed slide, using Title and Text slide layout. You can quickly determine the new slide's location by looking at the Slides tab (see Figure 3.18).

To Add and Delete Slides and Change Slide Layout

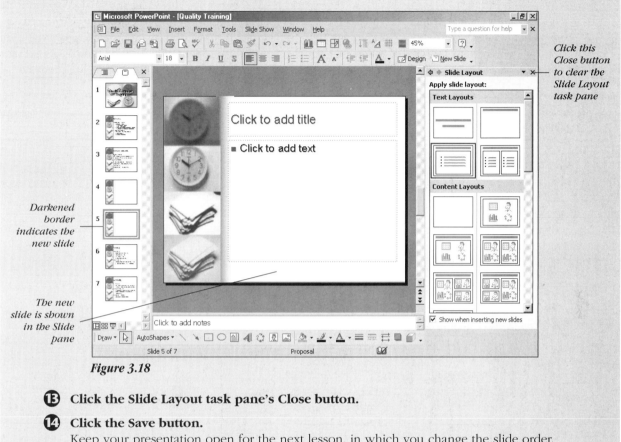

Darkened border indicates the new slide

The new slide is shown in the Slide pane

Figure 3.18

13 **Click the Slide Layout task pane's Close button.**

14 **Click the Save button.**
Keep your presentation open for the next lesson, in which you change the slide order.

To extend your knowledge...

Deleting Multiple Slides

Using the Slides or Outline tabs (or Slide Sorter view), you can delete several slides simultaneously. Click the first slide you want to delete, press ⬆Shift, and click the last slide—which selects all the intervening slides. You can also select non-adjacent slides by pressing Ctrl while clicking the slides you want. After you select the slides, press Del to remove them all.

Changing the Slide Layout for Multiple Slides

You can quickly change the slide layout for multiple slides. Select the slides and then click the layout in the Slide Layout task pane.

Lesson 7: Changing Slide Order

Even with the best planning, it's likely that you'll need to rearrange the slides in your presentation to create a more logical sequence. The easiest view to use for reordering slides is Slide Sorter view because you immediately see the move's effect on the presentation. To move a slide in this view select the slide and then drag it to the new location before releasing the mouse button. This method is sometimes referred to as *drag-and-drop.* Try rearranging your presentation slides using this technique now.

To Change Slide Order

1 **With the *Quality Training* presentation open, click the Slide Sorter View button.**
This is a good view to use to rearrange slides. Before you move a slide, though, you must first select it.

2 **Click Slide 6, *Training*, to select it.**
A double border surrounds Slide 6, indicating that it is selected.

3 **Move the mouse pointer to the middle of the selected slide and then drag the line indicator to the space between Slides 2 and 3.**
The new location for the slide is indicated by the inserted line between Slides 2 and 3 (see Figure 3.19).

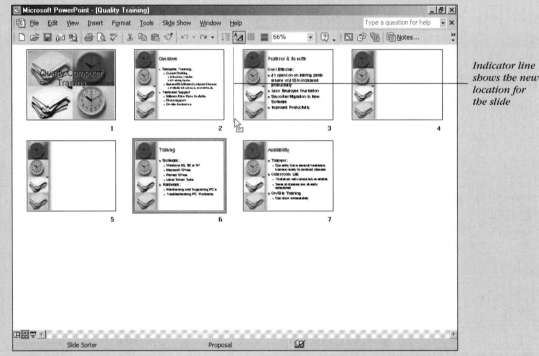

Indicator line shows the new location for the slide

Figure 3.19

4 **Release the mouse button.**
The selected slide is moved to the position between Slides 2 and 3. PowerPoint also renumbers the remaining slides to line up with their new positions.

Now try using the Cut and Paste buttons to move a slide.

5 **Click Slide 7, *Availability*, and click the Cut button.**
The selected slide is placed in the Clipboard. (As you probably recall from Project 2, the Clipboard is the area in memory where items that are cut or copied are placed.)

To Change Slide Order

6 **Click the mouse between Slide 4 and Slide 5.**
The blinking insertion point indicates the location where you want to paste the slide.

7 **Click the Paste button.**
The slide is pasted in the new location. Now delete the blank slides.

8 **Click Slide 6, press and hold the ⬆Shift key while you click Slide 7. Release the ⬆Shift key.**
Both slides are selected, as indicated by darkened borders.

9 **Choose Edit, Delete Slide from the menu.**
The slides are removed from your presentation.

10 **Your completed presentation should appear as shown in Figure 3.20.**

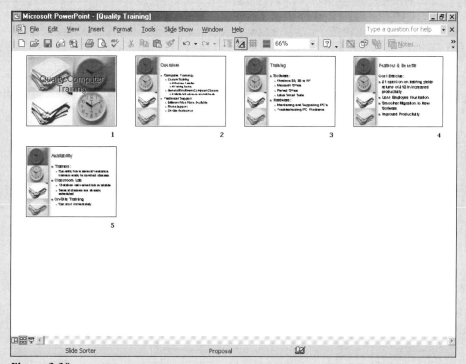

Figure 3.20

11 **Save your *Quality Training* presentation, and then close it.**
Keep PowerPoint running if you plan to complete the end of chapter exercises.

To extend your knowledge...

More About Reordering Slides

Although it's a bit tricky, you can select and move slides on the Outline and Slides tabs. Click a slide's thumbnail to select it and then drag the slide to the new location (indicated by a horizontal line) before releasing the mouse button.

Summary

As you worked through this project, you refined your PowerPoint skills. First, you opened an existing presentation and saved it using a new name. You explored PowerPoint's views and switched between them. You saw how to navigate among slides in Normal view. You also launched a slide show and used keyboard shortcuts to move around in the show. Finally, you modified and restructured your overall presentation by adding, deleting, and reordering slides.

Checking Concepts and Terms

Multiple Choice

Circle the letter of the correct answer for each of the following.

1. How do you save an existing presentation file using a new name or location? [L1]

   a. Click the Save button.

   b. Choose File, Save.

   c. Choose File, Save As.

   d. All of the above

2. How can you delete a slide? [L6]

   a. Click the Move Out button.

   b. Display the presentation in Slide Show view and then press (Esc).

   c. Select the slide in Slide Sorter view and then press (Del).

   d. Double-click a slide on the Slides tab.

3. How can you add a slide to your presentation? [L6]

   a. Click the Slide Sorter View button and then press (↵Enter).

   b. Press (PgDn) in Normal view.

   c. Click the Get a New Slide button.

   d. Click the New Slide button.

4. What happens when you delete a slide? [L6]

   a. PowerPoint automatically renumbers the remaining presentation slides.

   b. PowerPoint prompts you before removing the slide.

   c. The presentation automatically displays in Normal view.

   d. All of the above

5. Which of the following views is best to use when reordering the slides in your presentation? [L7]

   a. Slide Sorter view

   b. Notes Page view

   c. Slide Show view

   d. Rearrange view

Discussion

1. PowerPoint provides a number of views you can use while developing your presentation. What is the main purpose for each of the following? Normal view, Slide Show view, Slide Sorter view, Notes Page view. [L2]

2. How do PowerPoint's slide layouts help you quickly develop a presentation? [L6]

3. Discuss several situations where you might want to use Slide Show view. In what ways is an electronic slide show superior to the traditional methods of presenting information (such as using overhead transparencies or a slide projector)? [L4-5]

kill Drill

Skill Drill exercises *reinforce* project skills. Each skill reinforced is the same, or nearly the same, as a skill presented in the project. Detailed instructions are provided in a step-by-step format.

1. Navigating Among Views and Slides

One of your co-workers has developed a presentation that he wants you to look over. To get a better idea of the presentation's content, you decide to switch between views and move between slides.

1. Start PowerPoint, if necessary.
2. Open *ep1-0302* and save it as **Creative**.
3. Using information presented in this project, review the purpose for each of the views. Display a ScreenTip for each of the View buttons; then click each of the View buttons.
4. Make sure that the presentation is open in Normal view.
5. Display the presentation in each of the available views using the <u>V</u>iew menu. When you're finished, click the Normal View button.
6. Press Ctrl+Home to display the first presentation slide.
7. Press PgDn as many times as necessary to completely advance through your presentation. Press PgUp three times to move back in your presentation by three slides.
8. Click one of the slide icons on the Outline tab. Notice that the corresponding slide displays simultaneously in the Slide pane. Repeat the process with the other icons on the Outline tab.
9. Press Ctrl+Home to display the first presentation slide. Press Ctrl+End to show the last presentation slide.
10. Drag the scroll box in the Slide pane's vertical scrollbar upward until Slide 4 displays in the ScreenTip. Release the mouse button to display Slide 4.
11. Click the Next Slide button to advance to the next presentation slide. Click the Previous Slide button to show the previous slide.
12. Press Ctrl+Home to show the first presentation slide and then close the presentation.

Keep PowerPoint running for the next exercise.

2. Opening, Saving, and Restructuring a Presentation

You were recently promoted at your company and one of your new responsibilities involves running the new employee orientation sessions. In preparation for the next orientation session, you decide to modify the overall structure of the presentation you use for the session, as well as some of the text.

1. Choose <u>F</u>ile, <u>O</u>pen to display the Open dialog box. Display the folder where your student data files are located; then double-click *ep1-0303* to open it.
2. Choose <u>F</u>ile, Save <u>A</u>s to display the Save As dialog box. In the File <u>n</u>ame text box, type **Employee Orientation**. Click <u>S</u>ave.
3. Click the Slide Sorter View button to display the presentation in Slide Sorter view. Click Slide 3, *History of Company*, and then press Del. Repeat the process to delete the (new) Slide 3, *Who's Who*.
4. Click Slide 6, *Required Paperwork*, to select it. Drag the slide to between Slide 2 and Slide 3. Release the mouse button.

5. Double-click Slide 4, *Benefits Review*, to display it in Normal view. Make the following changes to the text using the Slide pane:
   - The fitness center has closed down, so it is no longer a benefit. Eliminate the point associated with it.
   - Change the text to show that you now get 3/4 sick day per month instead of 1/2.
   - Move the point for the 401(k) plan to just below the point for the two-week vacation benefit. (Hint: You can use cut and paste.)

6. Press F5 to run the presentation as an electronic slide show.

7. Click the mouse as many times as necessary to completely advance through the presentation. If necessary, press Esc to redisplay your presentation in Normal view.

8. Click the Save button to save your changes and then close the presentation.

Keep PowerPoint running for the next exercise.

3. Reordering Slides

You're a sales manager for a company and you want to present a short pep talk to your sales force about how to work with different types of people. To prepare for the talk, you revise a previously created presentation.

1. Open *ep1-0304* and save it as **People Skills**.

2. Choose View, Slide Sorter to display the presentation in Slide Sorter view.

3. Click Slide 3, *Summary*, and drag the slide to move it between Slide 1 and Slide 2.

4. With the new Slide 2, *Summary*, still selected, press Del to remove the slide from the presentation.

5. Click the Undo button twice to reverse the previous two actions.

6. Double-click Slide 2, *Skills*, to display it in Normal view.

7. Click the slide icon on the Outline tab for Slide 1 to display the first presentation slide.

8. Choose Format, Slide Layout. In the Slide Layout task pane, click the Title Slide layout to apply this layout to the slide. Clear the Slide Layout task pane by clicking its Close button.

9. Click the Slide Show button to view your presentation as a slide show.

10. Press N as many times as is necessary to completely advance through the presentation. When you're finished, press Esc to redisplay the presentation in Normal view.

11. Save your changes to the *People Skills* presentation; then close it.

Keep PowerPoint running for the next exercise.

4. Running a Slide Show

You're a college student who loves working with computers and software. Unfortunately, you spent too much time surfing the World Wide Web this term and your grades have suffered as a result. To communicate this news to your parents, you've developed a presentation for them. Because you're sure you'll be nervous when you show the presentation to your parents, you decide you'd better brush up on ways to navigate the presentation.

1. Open *ep1-0305* and save it as **College**.

2. Click the Normal view button to display the presentation in Normal view. Click the Slides tab and then click the Outline tab.

3. Practice using the mouse and keyboard shortcuts to move among presentation slides in Normal view. (If you need a refresher on these methods, see Lesson 3.)

4. Press F5 to run your presentation as an electronic slide show.

5. Press F1 to display the Slide Show Help dialog box and look over the shortcuts listed. If necessary, write down the methods you plan to use to move among slides.

6. Close the dialog box and then practice various ways to move around the slide show, using your list (or the Slide Show Help dialog box) as a guide.

7. Right-click the mouse in the slide show to display the slide show shortcut menu. Choose End <u>S</u>how from the menu.

8. Press <kbd>Ctrl</kbd>+<kbd>S</kbd> to save any changes you've made to the presentation and then close it.

Keep PowerPoint running if you plan to complete the Challenge and Discovery Zone exercises.

Challenge exercises expand on or are somewhat related to skills presented in the lessons. Each exercise provides a brief narrative introduction followed by instructions in a numbered step format that are not as detailed as those in the Skill Drill section. Each exercise is independent of the others, so that you may complete the exercises in any order.

1. Saving and Modifying an Existing Presentation

As president of the University Biking Club, you must present information to prospective members. You decide to revise an existing presentation in order to do this effectively.

1. In PowerPoint, open *ep1-0306* and save it as `Biking Club`.

2. Display the presentation in Slide Sorter view. Move Slide 3, *Officers*, to between Slide 1 and Slide 2.

3. Switch to Normal view. Move the bulleted subpoint on Slide 3, *Trip to watch Virginia Race of Champions*, up two lines. (Hint: It should display immediately beneath the *Coming Events* main point.)

4. Add a new slide after Slide 3. Choose the Title and Text slide layout for your new slide.

5. Add the following text on the newly inserted slide:
   Title placeholder: `How to Join`
   Text placeholder: `Fill out membership form`
   `Fill out proof of insurance form`
   `Pay dues to Grace S. Hank (Treasurer)`

6. Display your revised presentation in each of the views offered by PowerPoint.

7. Run your presentation as an electronic slide show. Practice using the various slide show shortcut keys to move among the presentation slides.

8. Save and close your *Biking Club* presentation.

Keep PowerPoint running if you plan to complete additional exercises.

2. Saving and Modifying a Presentation

As the events coordinator for the College Horseback Riding Club, you're in charge of an upcoming horse show. To publicize the event, you decide to revise an existing presentation to show during the next club meeting.

1. Open *ep1-0307* and save it as `Horseback Riding Club`.

2. Make the following changes to Slide 2:
   Demote the three points listed beneath *Classes*.
   Move the location (*Indoor Arena*) to the first line in the text placeholder so that it is the first bullet on the slide. (Hint: Use drag-and-drop or the Cut and Paste buttons.)

3. Add a slide at the end of the presentation using the Title Slide layout. Enter the following information:

Title placeholder: `How to enter:`
Subtitle placeholder: `Bring proof of club membership`
`Sign up for classes at entry stand`
`Pay club treasurer`

4. After looking over the last presentation slide, you decide that a different slide layout would display this information more clearly. Apply the Title and Text layout to this slide.

5. Use Help to find out how to copy slides from another presentation into an open presentation.

6. Open *ep1-0308*. Copy both slides from this presentation. Paste them between Slide 1 and Slide 2 in the *Horseback Riding Club* presentation. Close *ep1-0308*.

7. Display the first slide of your presentation in Normal view. Spell check your presentation and correct any errors you find.

8. Save and close your presentation.

Keep PowerPoint running if you plan to complete additional exercises.

3. Finding Out More About Electronic Slide Shows

You're the president of a local civic group and would like to use PowerPoint to conduct meetings. However, you're (admittedly) a novice computer user. To find out more about running electronic slide shows effectively, you use Help.

1. Make sure PowerPoint is running. Using the Ask a Question box (or online Help), research the following topics. (Make sure to take notes.)
   - Slide show shortcut keys
   - Onscreen presentations
   - Run a presentation on two monitors
   - Mark up slides during a slide show
   - Create action items
   - Self-running presentations

2. Using the information you gleaned from Help, experiment with various features related to running an electronic slide show.

3. Write down the most important and interesting features you've learned and then develop a PowerPoint presentation that outlines those features.

4. View your newly developed presentation using each of PowerPoint's views.

5. Run your presentation as a slide show. (Don't forget to practice using the slide show shortcut keys shown in the Slide Show Help dialog box.)

6. If possible, give your presentation to at least one other person.

7. Print the presentation; then, unless instructed otherwise by your teacher, close the presentation without saving it.

Keep PowerPoint running if you plan to complete additional exercises.

4. Setting Up a Slide Show

The "PowerPoint guru" at your office is on vacation. Your boss desperately needs you to help him get ready for a presentation he's giving at the company's annual meeting. He plans to meet with you later this afternoon to find out some of the options available for giving a PowerPoint presentation. You decide to spend some time researching commands on PowerPoint's Slide Show menu and then develop a snazzy presentation based on what you learn.

1. Create a blank presentation. Choose Slide Show, Set Up Show from PowerPoint's menu bar to display the Set Up Show dialog box.

2. Click the Help button in the Set Up Show dialog box (represented by the question mark in the upper right corner of the dialog box) and then click the first option in the Show type section. Read the ScreenTip. Clear the ScreenTip by clicking outside of it.

3. Repeat the sequence outlined in Step 2 to find out about each of the other options in the Set Up Show dialog box. Make sure to take notes about what you learn.

4. Using either the Help window or the Ask a Question box, find out about each of the other commands on the Slide Show menu. Write down what you learn.

5. Using your notes, develop a presentation that outlines ways you can give a presentation.

6. Display your presentation using each of PowerPoint's views, including Slide Show view.

7. Give the presentation to at least one other user. Get their feedback and revise your presentation as necessary.

8. Unless directed by your instructor, close the presentation without saving it.

Keep PowerPoint running if you plan to work on the Discovery Zone exercises.

Discovery Zone exercises require advanced knowledge of topics presented in *essentials* lessons, application of skills from multiple lessons, or self-directed learning of new skills. Each exercise is independent of the other, so that you may complete the exercises in any order.

1. Creating and Viewing Presentations

You're the secretary of the University Bicycling Club. To get ready for an upcoming meeting, you develop the following presentations:

• A one-slide flyer that announces the meeting time and location. (Hint: Use a template for this flyer.)

• A presentation that introduces a speaker for the meeting. (Hint: Use the AutoContent Wizard.)

• A presentation to motivate your team of club members. (Hint: Use the AutoContent Wizard.)

Enter appropriate information in each of the presentations. Switch between each of PowerPoint's views for each presentation. If the presentation contains multiple slides, use keyboard shortcuts and the mouse to move between the slides. (If you're particularly ambitious, use Help to find out how to add slide transitions and then add some to your multiple-slide presentations.)

Unless instructed otherwise by your teacher, print your presentations and then close them without saving them. Leave PowerPoint running if you plan to complete the final Discovery Zone Exercise.

2. Creating and Running a Presentation

One of the requirements for your business class is to give a speech on a software program. Because you're familiar with PowerPoint, you decide to create a PowerPoint presentation to supplement your talk.

Use the AutoContent Wizard and an appropriate presentation type to develop your talk. Research information on PowerPoint's main features. (Hint: Use this book's Table of Contents, PowerPoint's Help, or online Help.) Replace the sample content supplied by the AutoContent Wizard with your information.

Display your presentation in each of PowerPoint's available views. Also practice moving between slides in each view. Make sure to familiarize yourself with the slide show shortcut keys. Practice starting an electronic slide show on any slide. If possible, share the presentation with at least one other user. Print the presentation as an outline; then, unless instructed otherwise by your teacher, close the presentation without saving it. If you're finished your work session, close PowerPoint and shut down Windows before turning off your computer.

Changing a Presentation's Look

Objectives

In this project, you learn how to

- ✔ Use PowerPoint's Templates
- ✔ Customize a Template
- ✔ Use Color Schemes
- ✔ Change the Slide Background
- ✔ Modify the Slide Master
- ✔ Insert a Footer
- ✔ Insert Clip Art

Key terms introduced in this project include

- ❑ clip art
- ❑ clips
- ❑ color scheme
- ❑ footer
- ❑ gradient fills
- ❑ keywords
- ❑ master
- ❑ Master view
- ❑ rotation handle
- ❑ selection handles
- ❑ slide background
- ❑ slide master
- ❑ slide-title master pair
- ❑ title master

Why Would I Do This?

PowerPoint includes a wide variety of ways you can change the look of your presentation, each designed to enhance your presentation's content. For example, by adding a splash of color, a picture, or even a completely different background or design, you can strengthen the impact of your presentation. Luckily, PowerPoint includes a number of ways that you can enhance your presentation's appearance.

Visual Summary

PowerPoint includes a variety of built-in design templates and color schemes that you can use for your presentation. In Project 1, "Getting Started with PowerPoint," you saw how to apply a single template to your presentation. In this project you'll learn how to apply multiple templates to a presentation. You'll also learn how to customize templates for your needs (see Figure 4.1).

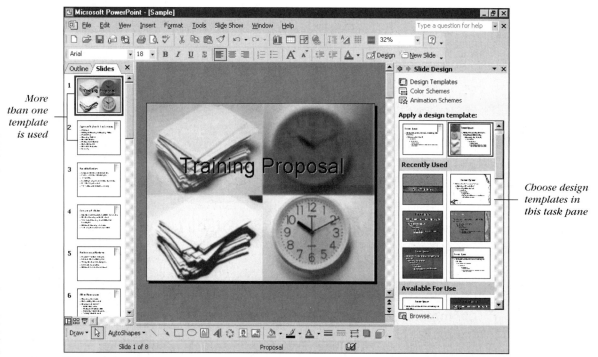

Figure 4.1

You'll also work with color schemes. A ***color scheme*** is a set of eight balanced colors that you can apply to a template. Another way to use color and design elements effectively is to change the ***slide background*** for selected (or all) slides in your presentation (see Figure 4.2).

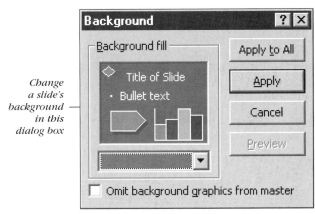

*Change
a slide's
background
in this
dialog box*

Figure 4.2

Additionally, you can modify the appearance of your entire presentation by making changes to the presentation's **master**. The master is a formatting feature in PowerPoint that works hand-in-hand with the template to control which elements appear on each slide. You use the master to quickly add or change design elements—such as date, slide number, or company logo—to all slides in your presentation. You can also quickly change the appearance of bullets or fonts throughout a presentation by making the modification to the master.

Any object you add to the master—such as a picture—appears in the corresponding location on all presentation slides. While PowerPoint includes four masters (title, slide, handout, and notes), you'll work with the two most widely used masters—the slide master and the title master (see Figure 4.3).

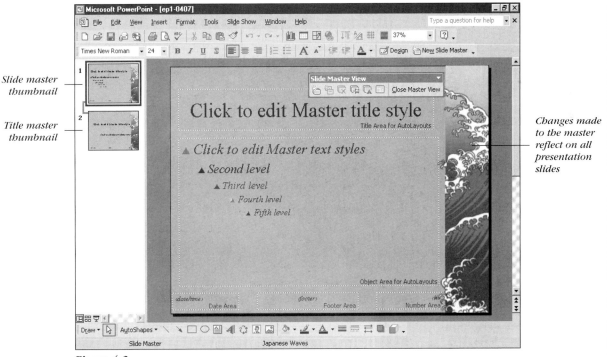

*Slide master
thumbnail*

*Title master
thumbnail*

*Changes made
to the master
reflect on all
presentation
slides*

Figure 4.3

Finally, you can jazz up almost any presentation by inserting **clips** that emphasize your information. While clips can be images, photographs, video, or movies, most people think of clips in terms of **clip art**, or electronic pictures (see Figure 4.4).

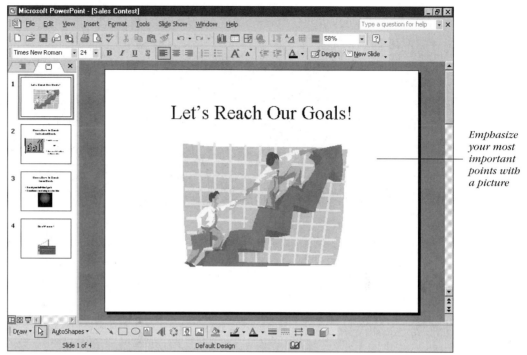

Emphasize your most important points with a picture

Figure 4.4

You can combine these features to quickly and easily produce an impressive, eye-catching presentation, so come along and learn how.

Lesson 1: Using PowerPoint's Templates

PowerPoint provides an extensive group of predesigned templates (also called design templates) that you can use for your presentation. A template is a "blueprint" that PowerPoint uses to create slides, including the formatting, color, and graphics necessary to create a particular "look." Because professional graphic artists created these templates, they can help you create a presentation with a consistent, well-designed look. Using a template allows you to concentrate on content rather than on layout and design.

In Project 2, "Creating and Modifying Presentations," you learned how to choose a template when you initially created a presentation. In this project you learn how to change templates for an existing presentation. This is handy if you've already developed a presentation, but aren't entirely satisfied with the design. You can simply apply different templates until you find one you like. You also see how to apply more than one template to a presentation. Try working with templates now.

To Use PowerPoint's Templates

❶ Start PowerPoint, if necessary, and then click the Open button.

❷ Locate and open the *ep1-0401* file, and save it as Company.
This presentation is based on a specific template, *Blends*, which dictates how the bullets, fonts, and objects appear. Try applying another template now to this presentation. The easiest way to do this is to choose the template in the Slide Design task pane.

To Use PowerPoint's Templates

3 **Choose Format, Slide Design (or click the Design button on the Formatting toolbar).**
The Slide Design task pane is displayed (see Figure 4.5).

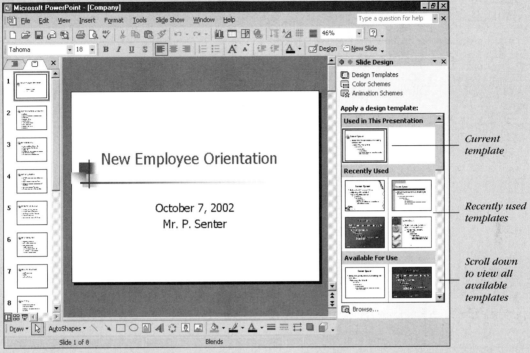

Figure 4.5

4 **Scroll down in the Slide Design task pane until you can view templates in the Available For Use section.**

5 **Rest your mouse pointer over any of the templates in the task pane.**
A ScreenTip displays, identifying the template by name.

6 **Using the ScreenTips, identify and then click the Capsules template.**
By default, PowerPoint applies whatever template you choose to the entire presentation. (You can tell this if you look at the thumbnails on the Slides tab.) However, you can use more than one template for a presentation just by selecting the slides before applying the template.

7 **On the Slides tab, click Slide 1; then press and hold ⬆Shift while clicking Slide 3. Release the mouse button.**
All three slides are selected, as shown by the darkened border around each.

8 **Click the Balance template in the Slide Design task pane.**
The Balance template is applied to the selected slides (see Figure 4.6).

(Continues)

To Use PowerPoint's Templates (Continued)

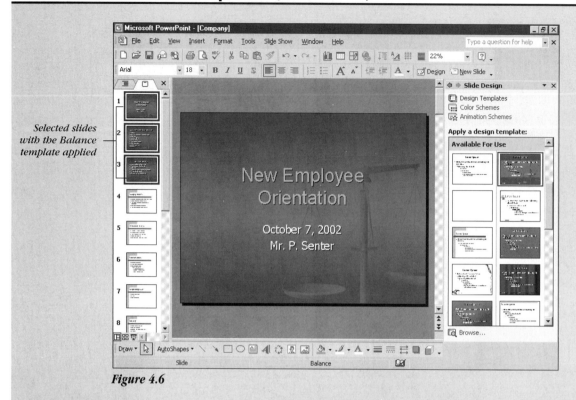

Figure 4.6

⑨ **Click the Slide Design task pane's Close button.**

⑩ **Save your changes to the *Company* presentation and then close it.**
Keep PowerPoint running for the next lesson, in which you customize a template.

Lesson 2: Customizing a Template

Tired of using the built-in templates PowerPoint provides? If so, you can create a custom template, and then apply it to other presentations. For example, imagine you design a presentation that includes your company's corporate colors and logo. You can save this presentation as a template and then apply it to other existing or new presentations. This helps create a consistent 'look' for your presentations. Try creating a custom template and applying it to a new presentation now.

To Customize a Template

❶ **In PowerPoint open *ep1-0402*, and save it as Corporate.**
This presentation will serve as the basis for your custom-designed template. There are already a number of design elements that have been changed for this presentation. Before you save the presentation as a template, you'll make additional modifications to its design.

❷ **Choose F̲ormat, Background.**
The Background dialog box is displayed (see Figure 4.7). You can use this dialog box to change the background color used for some or all presentation slides.

To Customize a Template

Figure 4.7

3 **Click the drop-down list arrow in the Background dialog box.**
A palette of colors that coordinate with the template are displayed.

4 **Choose the third color box from the left on the top row (dark gray) and then choose Apply to All.**
The background color is changed to gray (from green) for all slides. Now try changing the font used in your presentation.

5 **Select the text in the title placeholder on Slide 1 and then choose Comic Sans MS from the Font drop-down list. (If this font isn't available on your system, choose another.)**
Changes you make to the slide's formatting (and content) can be saved as a template.

6 **Choose File, Save As.**
The Save As dialog box is displayed. You usually use this dialog box to save your slides as a presentation, but you can also save your formatting, design (and even content) as a template.

7 **Click the Save as type drop-down list arrow and then choose Design Template from the list.**
PowerPoint automatically saves any templates in Office's Templates folder (see Figure 4.8). This is handy because all custom templates you create are placed in this folder, where they're available whenever you create a new presentation.

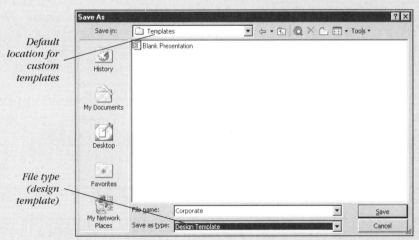

Figure 4.8

(Continues)

To Customize a Template (Continued)

8 Enter Money **in the File** **name** **text box and then click** **Save.**
The presentation is saved as a template. Even though the template is saved on your drive, it's not shown in the Slide Design task pane until you exit and restart PowerPoint.

9 **Close the presentation; then exit and restart PowerPoint.**
When PowerPoint restarts, a blank presentation is automatically created. Additionally, the New Presentation task pane displays. (If it doesn't display, choose File, New.)

10 **In the New Presentation task pane, click From Design Template and then scroll down to view the templates in the Available For Use section.**
The templates on your system are shown in alphabetical order in this section (see Figure 4.9). Now you're set to apply your custom template to the displayed presentation.

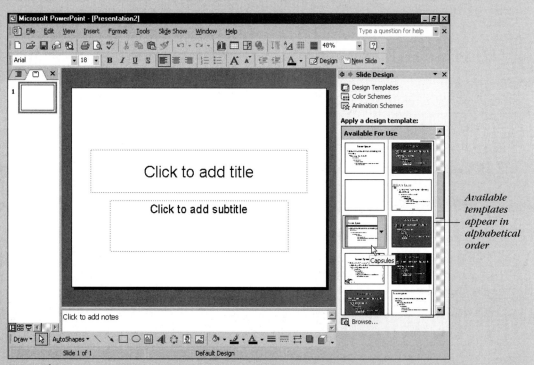

Available templates appear in alphabetical order

Figure 4.9

11 **Use the ScreenTips to identify the Money template (if necessary) and then click it.**
The Money template is applied to your new presentation (see Figure 4.10).

To Customize a Template

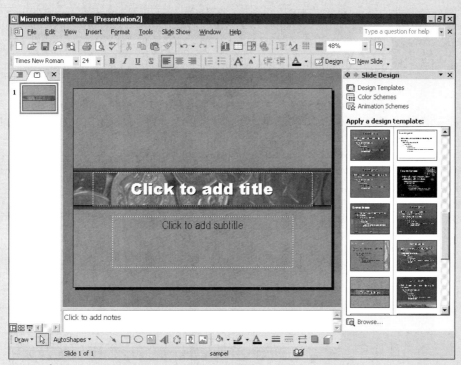

Figure 4.10

⑫ Close the Slide Design task pane.

⑬ Close the presentation without saving it.

Remember, your customized design template is still available so you can apply it to other presentations—even though you closed this presentation without resaving it as a presentation.

Keep PowerPoint running if you plan to complete additional exercises.

To extend your knowledge...

Adding Templates to the AutoContent Wizard

You can save custom-designed templates to the AutoContent Wizard so that they're available each time you launch the wizard. Choose File, New, to display the New Presentation task pane and then click the From AutoContent Wizard link. Advance to the second page in the AutoContent Wizard. Choose in which category you would like to save the template and then choose Add. Double-click the template you want in the Select Presentation Template dialog box and then click OK. Click Finish.

Lesson 3: Using Color Schemes

A color scheme is the underlying set of eight coordinated colors used by each template. PowerPoint's templates include color schemes to ensure that any new objects you create (or modify) will match those already in place. Knowing a little about color schemes is useful for the following reasons:

- **It helps ensure that text or objects that you recolor will match the underlying scheme.** When you change font color, the colors displayed on the top row of the palette are from the underlying color scheme.
- **You can change the color scheme for all slides in a presentation.** Why? Well suppose that you're planning to do a presentation on the road, and the overhead projection system or computer screen doesn't have the same contrast as your office computer. Being able to change the color scheme can create a better contrast and literally save your presentation (or job)!
- **To help you keep track of your presentations.** You may also have similar presentations, but have added customized slides for different audiences; one set for sales, one for marketing, one for advertising, and so on. By keeping the template the same but changing the color scheme used for each audience, you can instantly tell if you are running the correct version of your presentation.
- **You can change the color scheme for just one slide to emphasize certain information.** For example, you can highlight a new proposal or agenda. Changing color schemes for the slide that introduces the proposal is a subtle, but effective attention-grabber.

Try customizing the color scheme of an existing presentation now.

To Use Color Schemes

① **Open** *ep1-0403* **and save it as** Hickory.
Color schemes are most commonly applied in Normal view so you can quickly see the result on the slide thumbnails on the Slides tab. Slide Sorter view is also commonly used because you can see many presentation slides at once.

② **Click the Slide Design button on the Formatting toolbar.**
The Slide Design task pane is displayed.

③ **Click the Color Schemes link (towards the top of the task pane).**
The color schemes available for this presentation are displayed (see Figure 4.11). Notice that the underlying design elements remain the same no matter which color combination you choose.

To Use Color Schemes

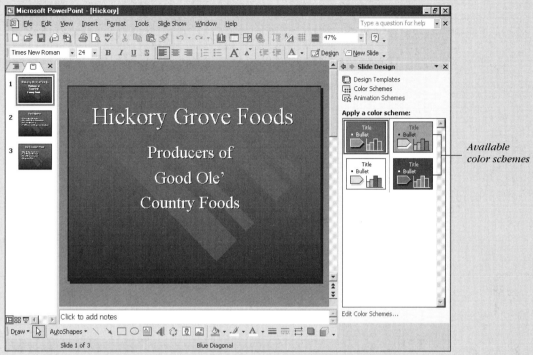

Figure 4.11

In general, you should select a scheme with a light background and dark text for over-heads. Select a dark background with light text for onscreen display and 35MM slides. Try selecting a color scheme for onscreen display now.

4 **Rest your mouse pointer over the dark maroon color scheme and then click the drop-down list arrow that automatically displays.**

5 **Choose Apply to All Slides.**
The presentation is shown with the dark maroon color scheme applied to all slides, as you can see by glancing at the Slides tab. However, you can also just change the color scheme for selected slides.

6 **Verify that Slide 1, *Hickory Grove Foods*, is selected on the Slides tab.**

7 **Rest your mouse pointer over the light purple color scheme in the Slide Design task pane until a drop-down list arrow displays.**

8 **Click the arrow and then choose Apply to Selected Slides.**
The color scheme is only applied to the selected slide—Slide 1 (see Figure 4.12). Notice that the slide elements—such as the graphics and font style—remain consistent on all slides (because they are created by the underlying template), but that the color combinations are different.

(Continues)

To Use Color Schemes (Continued)

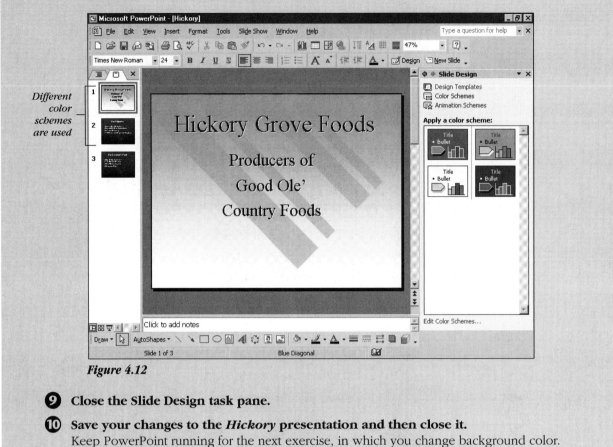

Different color schemes are used

Figure 4.12

⑨ **Close the Slide Design task pane.**

⑩ **Save your changes to the *Hickory* presentation and then close it.**
Keep PowerPoint running for the next exercise, in which you change background color.

Lesson 4: Changing the Slide Background

Want to make your presentation unique and grab your audience's attention? Simply spiff up your slide background by adding shadow effects, textures, and patterns. Changing the slide background differs from modifying the entire color scheme of eight colors because you modify only the slide's background.

One of the most popular effects is to apply a textured fill to the presentation's background, but other types of customization, such as adding ***gradient fills*** (colors that fade from one color to another) and patterns are also available. Try changing the background for your slides now.

To Change the Slide Background

① **Open *ep1-0404* and save it as** `Logging Company`.

② **Display Slide 1, *Business Overview*, in Normal view and then choose F̲ormat, Background.**
The Background dialog box is displayed (see Figure 4.13). In Lesson 2 you used this dialog box briefly to customize a template. Now you'll get a chance to work more completely with the feature.

To Change the Slide Background

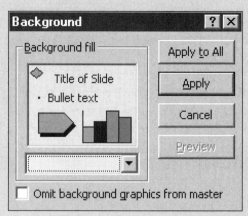

Figure 4.13

3 **In the Background fill section of the dialog box, click the drop-down list arrow and then choose Fill Effects.**

The Fill Effects dialog box is displayed (see Figure 4.14). You can use this dialog box to choose a variety of background styles.

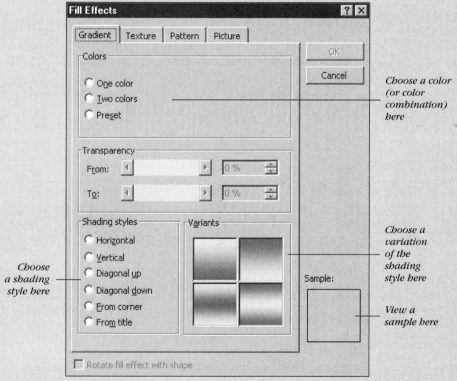

Figure 4.14

4 **Click the Gradient tab, if necessary, and then click the Preset option button (in the Colors section).**

PowerPoint displays a preset color combination (*Early Sunset*). Now explore other preset color combinations you can use for your slide's background.

(Continues)

To Change the Slide Background (Continued)

⑤ Click the Pr̲eset colors drop-down list arrow, and choose *Ocean* from the list.
The Ocean color combination displays in the Sample area. The Sample area gives you an idea of the way that the color combination will look when you apply it to your slide's background.

⑥ In the Shading styles section, click the Fro̲m title option button.
The effect displays in the Sample section of the dialog box. Now apply the fill effect to your slide's background.

⑦ Choose OK in the Fill Effects dialog box; then choose Apply t̲o All in the Background dialog box.
The new background style is applied to your slides.

PowerPoint also provides a number of textures that you can use for a slide's background. Take a look at these textures now.

⑧ Right-click in the slide pane area (but not within a placeholder) on Slide 1 to display the shortcut menu; then choose Bac̲kground.
The Background dialog box is displayed.

If you have problems...
Make sure to right-click on the background area of your slide (and not in a placeholder) so that the correct shortcut menu displays.

⑨ Choose F̲ill Effects from the drop-down list of available backgrounds.

⑩ In the Fill Effects dialog box, click the Texture tab.
The Texture page displays with a number of natural-looking backgrounds, such as wood and stone (see Figure 4.15).

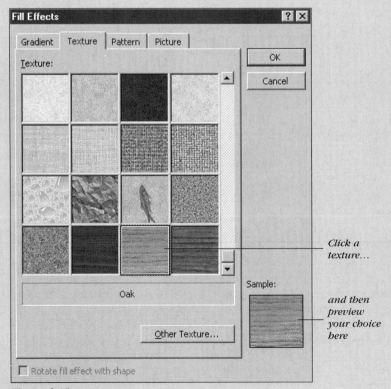

Figure 4.15

To Change the Slide Background

⑪ **Scroll down the list of Textures, choose *Oak* (the third box in the bottom row), and click OK to close the Fill Effects dialog box.**

⑫ **Choose Apply to All in the Background dialog box.**
The textured wood background is applied to your presentation slides (see Figure 4.16).

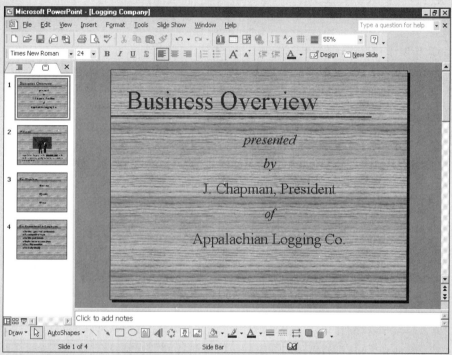

Figure 4.16

⑬ **Save your changes to the *Logging Company* presentation and then close it.**
Keep PowerPoint running for the next exercise, in which you work with the slide and title masters.

Lesson 5: Modifying the Slide Master

Every design template automatically includes masters that you can use to control how objects, text, and other items display in a presentation. The most commonly used master is the ***slide master***, which controls how objects on all presentation slides display (except the title slide). For example, you can use the slide master to dictate which fonts and bullet style used. Whenever you want to make a global change to all of your slides, you can make the change on the slide master and PowerPoint automatically updates all existing slides. Additionally, any new slides you add automatically include the changes.

While you use the slide master to control how items look on most presentation slides, you use the ***title master*** to change items on the title slide itself. The title master and slide master for a design template are called the ***slide-title master pair.*** Whenever you display the ***Master view***, both masters appear as thumbnails at the left side of the screen. You can click the thumbnail for the master you want to modify to display it in the Slide pane area.

To Modify the Slide Master

1 Open *ep1-0405* and save it as `Star Manufacturing`.

2 Display Slide 2 and then choose <u>V</u>iew, <u>M</u>aster, <u>S</u>lide Master.
The presentation appears in master view, and the slide master displays in the Slide pane. Additionally, thumbnails for both the slide master and title master appear at the left side of the screen (see Figure 4.17).

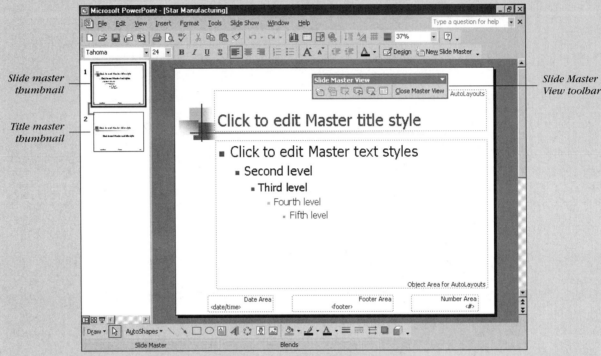

Figure 4.17

3 Click the object titled *Click to edit Master title style.*
The title placeholder is selected, as indicated by the thickened border. Try changing the formatting for this area—a change that will affect all title placeholders in your presentation.

4 Click the Italic button in the Formatting toolbar.
Italic is applied to the title placeholder text.

5 With the insertion point still positioned in the title placeholder, click the Increase Font Size button once.
The size of the text in this placeholder increases. Again, this change globally affects all slides because you're changing the slide master.

6 With the slide master still displayed in the Slide pane, click the text next to the first bullet level in the lower placeholder, *Click to edit Master text styles.*

7 Choose F<u>o</u>rmat, <u>B</u>ullets and Numbering.
The Bullets and Numbering dialog box is displayed (see Figure 4.18). You choose bullet (and numbering) styles in this dialog box.

To Modify the Slide Master

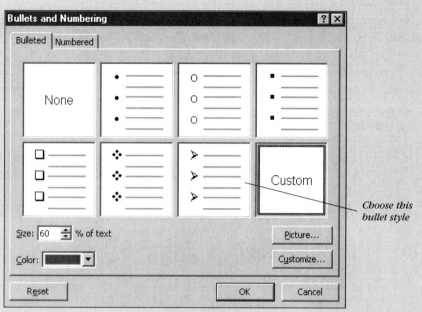

Choose this bullet style

Figure 4.18

8 **Double-click the right-pointing triangle style (refer to Figure 4.18, if necessary).**
The style is used for the first bullet level. Now make a change to the title master.

9 **Click the title master thumbnail (refer to Figure 4.17, if necessary).**
The title master displays in the Slide pane. Notice that the layout for this master is different than for the slide master (which included, among other things, bullets).

10 **Click in the upper placeholder, *Click to edit Master title style.***

11 **Click the Font Color drop-down list arrow and then choose Red from the palette.**
The text in the placeholder is shown using red. Now take a look at how your changes appear in the presentation.

12 **Click the Close Master View button on the Slide Master View toolbar, or choose View, Normal.**

13 **Scroll through your presentation to see the changes, noticing the modifications to the title slide and the other slides.**

14 **Save your changes to the *Star Manufacturing* presentation.**
Keep the presentation open for the next lesson, in which you insert footer information on your slides.

To extend your knowledge...

Revising the Title Master

Although you'll work the most often with the slide master, you can use the same type of process to revise the title master. The title master controls which elements display on the title slide.

Lesson 6: Inserting a Footer

You can include information—such as your name, department, or company name—at the top or bottom of every slide in your presentation. Data that appears at the bottom of each slide is called a *footer*. You can include the date, slide number, and text (such as your company's name) in the footer. You can insert a footer on a single slide, or all slides in a presentation. Try placing a footer in your presentation now.

To Insert a Footer

1 **Make sure Slide 1 of the *Star Manufacturing* presentation you worked with in the previous lesson is displayed in Normal view.**

2 **Choose View, Header and Footer.**
The Header and Footer dialog box is displayed (see Figure 4.19). You use this dialog box to choose which items you want to include in the footer. By default, the date appears on the left side of the footer, your text in the middle, and the slide number on the right.

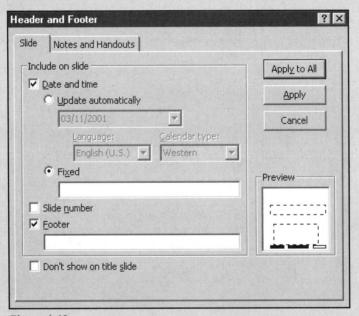

Figure 4.19

3 **Verify that the box for Date and time is checked and then click the option button for Update automatically.**
When you choose the Update automatically option, PowerPoint displays the current date and/or time. In contrast, if you choose the Fixed option in the Date area, PowerPoint will always show the date on which you created the presentation instead of updating it.

4 **Check the boxes for Slide number and Footer and then click the Footer text box.**

5 **Type By the Management Team in the text box and then click Apply.**
The footer information is added to the bottom of the current slide (see Figure 4.20).

To Insert a Footer

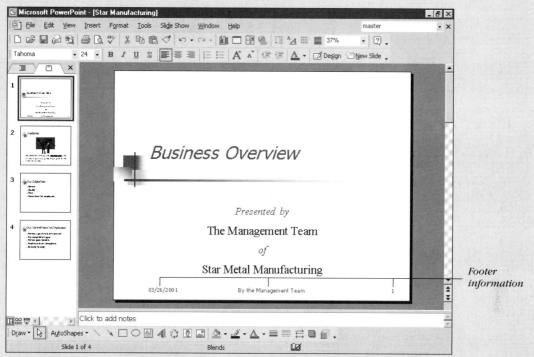

Figure 4.20

6 **Press** `PgDn` **three times to view the other presentation slides and confirm that they do not contain a footer.**
Now redisplay the Header and Footer dialog box so that you can apply the changes to all the slides in the presentation.

7 **Display Slide 1 in the Slide pane, if necessary. Redisplay the Header and Footer dialog box (by choosing View, Header and Footer) and then choose Apply to All.**

8 **Press** `F5`.
Your presentation displays as an electronic slide show so that you can better view your changes.

9 **Advance through the presentation until it again displays in Normal view.**

10 **Save and close the *Star Manufacturing* presentation.**
Keep PowerPoint open for the next exercise, in which you insert clip art.

To extend your knowledge...

Suppressing Footers on the Title Slide

Many people like to include a footer on all presentation slides *except* the title slide. To do this, make sure the *Don't show on title slide* box is checked in the Header and Footer dialog box.

Lesson 7: Inserting Clip Art

PowerPoint includes a good selection of electronic clip art (pictures) that you can use to enhance your presentation. Including clip art on a slide can help hold an audience's attention or reinforce key points. Luckily, PowerPoint includes a variety of pictures for personal and business use. For even more variety, you can download clips from the Web.

After clip art is placed on a slide, you can change its size, location, and appearance. Try your hand at using clip art now.

To Insert Clip Art

❶ In PowerPoint, click the New button on the Standard toolbar.
PowerPoint creates a new, blank presentation and displays the Slide Layout task pane. You can choose a content layout in this task pane. Content layouts include links so you can insert various types of objects, such as clip art (see Figure 4.21). You can identify which content layout is which by resting your mouse pointer over each one until a ScreenTip displays.

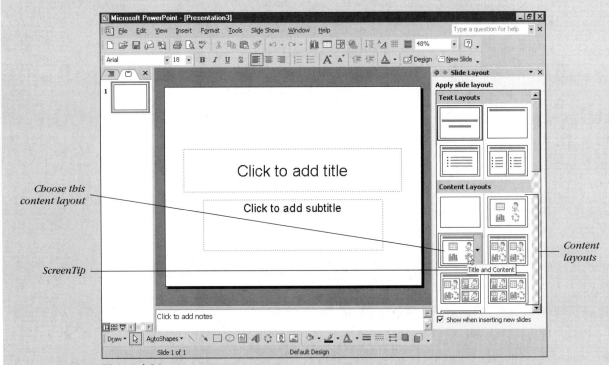

Figure 4.21

 If you have problems...

By default, PowerPoint displays the Slide Layout task pane whenever you create a new, blank presentation. However, if this option has been turned off on your system, choose Format, Slide Layout and then proceed with the next step.

❷ Using the ScreenTips, identify the Title and Content layout.

To Insert Clip Art

❸ Click the Title and Content layout.
The layout is applied to your slide (see Figure 4.22). The content icon in the middle of the slide includes links to six kinds of objects. You can identify each type of object by pointing to the object and viewing the ScreenTip.

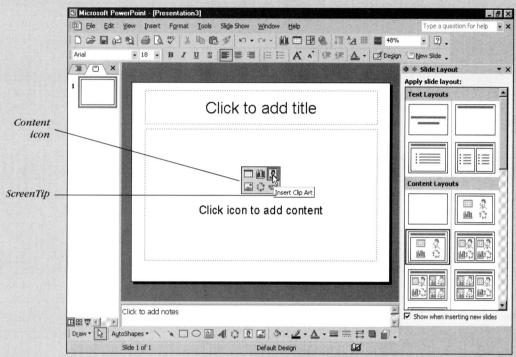

Figure 4.22

❹ Click the Insert Clip Art object on your slide.
The Select Picture dialog box is displayed (Figure 4.23). This dialog box includes all the clips available on your system. You can narrow the choices by searching for clips based on their *keywords*. Keywords are topical words that describe a clip. For example, a picture of a football might have keywords such as *sport* and *game* associated with it.

(Continues)

To Insert Clip Art (Continued)

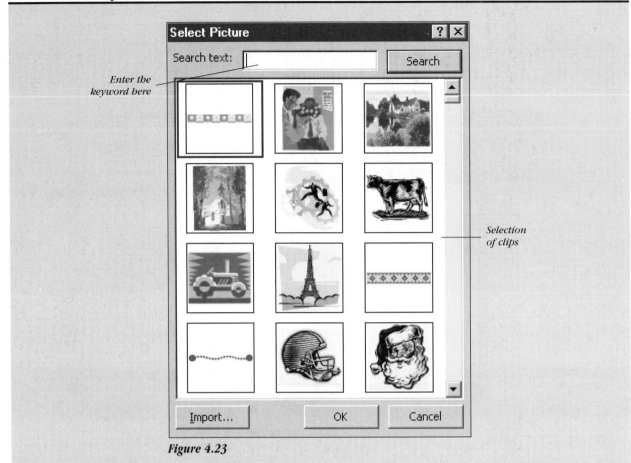

Enter the keyword here

Selection of clips

Figure 4.23

⑤ In the Search text box, type `animal` **and then press** ⏎Enter.
The clip art images that include the keyword *animal* are shown in the Select Picture dialog box (see Figure 4.24).

To Insert Clip Art

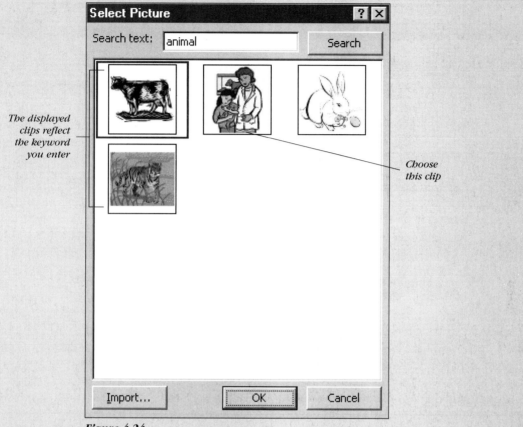

The displayed clips reflect the keyword you enter

Choose this clip

Figure 4.24

6 **Click the clip indicated in Figure 4.24 and then click OK.**

The clip is inserted in your slide (see Figure 4.25). Notice that the clip also includes **selection handles** and a **rotation handle**. You drag the selection handles to resize the clip; you drag the rotation handle to change the angle of the clip.

(Continues)

To Insert Clip Art (Continued)

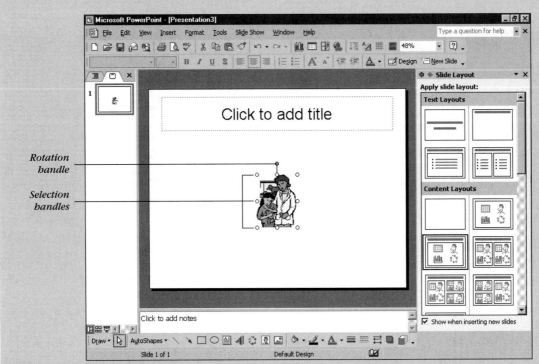

Rotation handle

Selection handles

Figure 4.25

7 **Rest your mouse pointer over the selection handle in the lower right corner of the clip until a two-headed arrow displays; then drag approximately 2″ down and to the right.**
The clip is resized. (If you have trouble, click the Undo button and start again.) Now move the clip. To do this, you drag the middle of a selected clip to the new location.

8 **Verify that the clip is still selected and that selection handles appear around the border of the object.**

9 **Move your mouse pointer to the middle of the clip so that a four-headed arrow appears; then drag the clip to the middle of the available white space on the slide.**
If you ever need to delete a clip, you can simply select it and then press ⒹⒺⓁ. For now, however, you'll deselect the clip and then finish your slide by adding some text to it.

10 **Click outside the clip to deselect it (and remove the selection handles).**

11 **Click in the title placeholder, type** Take Home a Shelter Pet Today!, **and then click outside of the placeholder.**
Your completed slide should appear similar to the one shown in Figure 4.26.

To Insert Clip Art

Figure 4.26

⓬ **Save your presentation as** Animal Shelter.

⓭ **Print your one-slide presentation and then close it.**
Keep PowerPoint running if you plan to complete the end of chapter exercises.

To extend your knowledge...

More About Inserting Clips

PowerPoint actually includes a number of ways that you can insert clip art into your presentation. For example, you can click the Insert Clip Art button on the Drawing toolbar, or choose Insert, Picture, Clip Art from the menu. Either way, the Insert Clip Art task pane will be displayed so that you can enter keyword(s) in the Search text box and click Search. PowerPoint will display thumbnails of all the clips that include the keywords. Click a thumbnail to insert it on your slide.

You can also look for clips on the Web that include the keyword(s). To do this, make sure your connection to the Web is active and then click the Clips Online link at the bottom of the Insert Clip Art task pane.

Finally, you can insert picture files (such as photographs) from your computer. To do this, choose Insert, Picture, From File. In the Insert Picture dialog box, double-click the picture file you want to insert in your presentation. After it's inserted, you can move and resize the picture file using the same techniques as you did for clip art objects.

Summary

In this project, you reached into PowerPoint's bag of tricks and pulled out ideas to help you develop a colorful, eye-catching presentation. You saw how to apply one or more design templates to a presentation and how to design and save a customized template. You experimented with various color schemes and slide backgrounds. You modified the slide master and added footer information. Finally, you inserted clip art on a slide.

To expand on your knowledge, spend a few minutes exploring Help on these topics. Additionally, complete some of the Skill Drill, Challenge, and Discovery Zone exercises.

Checking Concepts and Terms

Multiple Choice

Circle the letter of the correct answer for each of the following.

1. What is a good reason for changing color schemes? [L3]

   a. to change display contrast when using your presentation as an electronic slide show

   b. to emphasize a particular slide

   c. to keep track of similar, yet slightly different presentations that you created for different audiences

   d. All of the above

2. Which of the following is true about design templates? [L1-2]

   a. They are the same as a presentation's slide master.

   b. They are a "blueprint" that PowerPoint uses to determine the overall look of a presentation.

   c. They can't be changed once selected.

   d. None of the above

3. Which dialog box do you use to save a custom template? [L2]

   a. Apply Design Template

   b. Save a Template

   c. Save As

   d. None of the above

4. What do changes made to a presentation's slide master affect? [L5]

   a. only the displayed slide

   b. all presentation slides except the title slide

   c. all open presentations

   d. all presentations on your hard or network drive

5. Which of the following is true about clip art? [L7]

   a. You can use the selection handles to resize the clip.

   b. You can pull clips from the Web if you have an Internet connection.

   c. You can use clips to emphasize main points in your presentation.

   d. All of the above

Discussion

1. What are the differences between the following: slide master, design template, slide background, color schemes? In what ways are they similar? [L1-5]

2. What are some items that you can change on a slide master? Give examples of when you might want to change each item or object. [L5]

3. Which PowerPoint feature would you use for each of the following situations? Why? [L1-5]

- You want to display your company's logo on each presentation slide.
- You want to change the overall design and "look" of your presentation.
- You want to use the same design template for your presentation, but need more contrast for an onscreen display.
- You want to indicate a change of direction in your presentation, or introduce a new topic.

Skill Drill

Skill Drill exercises *reinforce* project skills. Each skill reinforced is the same, or nearly the same, as a skill presented in the project. Detailed instructions are provided in a step-by-step format.

1. Learning about Templates

As a middle manager for a company, you frequently give presentations. To learn more about working with design templates, you use the Help feature.

1. In PowerPoint choose Help, Microsoft PowerPoint Help. (If necessary, click the Show button to split the Help window into two panes.)
2. Click the Answer Wizard tab and then type `design template` in the *What would you like to do?* box. Press [↵Enter].
3. Click the first topic listed in the Select topic to display box. Read the associated information in the right pane of the Help window. Take notes on what you learn (or click the Print button at the top of the Help window to print the information).
4. Repeat step 3 for each of the topics listed in the Select topic to display box.
5. Close the Help window. Using your notes and the printed pages as a guide, try each of the commands related to working with templates.
6. Share what you learn with at least one other person. Alternately, develop a PowerPoint presentation that covers the various ways to use templates.

Keep PowerPoint running if you plan to complete additional exercises.

2. Using Templates and Color Schemes

Your boss asked you to revise a presentation that she previously created. Furthermore, she wants you to add some elements to jazz it up a bit. To do this, you decide to apply a different design template and color scheme. You also add clip art and text to the slide master.

1. Open *ep1-0406* and save it as **Financial Services.** Verify that Slide 1 of the presentation is displayed in Normal view.
2. Click the Design button to display the Slide Design task pane. In the task pane, click the following templates in turn to see how the presentation looks with each.
   - Blends
   - Compass

       ○ Crayons
       ○ Curtain Call
       ○ Digital Dots
       ○ Edge
       ○ Fading Grid
       ○ Maple
       ○ Ocean
       ○ Proposal
       ○ Stream

3. Click the *Balance* template.

4. Click the Color Schemes link in the Slide Design task pane.

5. Click each of the displayed color schemes to apply them to the presentation. When you're finished viewing the various color schemes, click the turquoise color scheme.

6. Close the Slide Design task pane.

7. Save your changes to the *Financial Services* presentation.

Keep the presentation open and PowerPoint running if you plan to complete the next Skill Drill exercise.

3. Adding a Footer to a Presentation

To make further revisions to the Financial Services presentation, you add a footer.

1. Verify that the *Financial Services* presentation you worked with in the previous Skill Drill exercise is open, and that the first presentation slide is displayed.

2. Choose <u>V</u>iew, <u>H</u>eader and Footer to display the Header and Footer dialog box.

3. In the <u>F</u>ooter text box, type `Report developed by B. Cory`.

4. Check the Slide <u>n</u>umber box so that a slide number will display on each slide.

5. Click the <u>U</u>pdate automatically option button so that the current date will always show in the presentation. Choose Apply to All.

6. Scroll through your presentation to view the changes. When you're finished, redisplay the first presentation slide in Normal view.

7. Save your changes to the *Financial Services* presentation.

Keep the presentation open and PowerPoint running if you plan to complete the next Skill Drill exercise.

4. Working with the Slide Master and Inserting Clip Art

Your boss wants you to add clip art to every slide in the presentation. Instead of adding the same clip manually to each slide, you decide to place it on the slide master. You also modify the font on the slide master to make the change globally.

1. Verify that the first slide of the *Financial Services* presentation is displayed in Normal view.

2. Choose <u>V</u>iew, <u>M</u>aster, <u>S</u>lide Master.

3. Click the *Click to edit Master title style* placeholder and then click the Italic button. Also click the Increase Font Size button once.

4. With the presentation still displayed in master view, choose <u>I</u>nsert, <u>P</u>icture, <u>C</u>lip Art. (If the Add Clips to Organizer dialog box displays, click the <u>L</u>ater button to close it.)

5. In the Insert Clip Art task pane, type `business` in the Search text box, and then click Search.

6. Insert an appropriate clip into your presentation by clicking it in the Insert Clip Art task pane.

7. With the presentation still displayed in master view, move the clip to the upper left corner of the slide, and resize the clip so that it doesn't cover any text.

8. Click the Normal View button to redisplay your presentation in Normal view. View your presentation on the Slides tab to confirm that the changes you made to the slide master display on each slide.

9. Press F5 to run your presentation as a slide show. Again, make sure the changes you made in master view are applied to the entire presentation.

10. Close the Insert Clip Art task pane, if necessary. Save and then close the presentation.

Keep PowerPoint running if you plan to complete the Challenge and Discovery Zone exercises.

Challenge exercises expand on or are somewhat related to skills presented in the lessons. Each exercise provides a brief narrative introduction followed by instructions in a numbered step format that are not as detailed as those in the Skill Drill section.

1. Finding Out About Masters and Clip Art

Because you've picked up PowerPoint so quickly, your instructor has asked you to serve as an assistant in the computer lab during open lab times. You eagerly agreed, but then realized that you feel "shaky" about some of the main features in PowerPoint, including working with the slide master and clip art. To get up to speed on these features, you spend a few minutes researching them via PowerPoint's Help feature.

1. Using the Ask a Question box, research the following topics:
   - Various methods of inserting clip art in a presentation
   - How to insert clip art from the Web
   - How to modify clip art
   - Troubleshooting clip art problems
   - How to modify the title, handout, and notes masters
2. Practice working with the features, using information from the Help system as a guide.
3. Create a presentation that covers the information and share it with at least one other user. Unless your instructor indicates otherwise, close the presentation without saving it.

Keep PowerPoint running if you plan to complete additional exercises.

2. Revising the Slide Master

You're developing a talk for your company's annual meeting. You modify the slide master so that the elements (such as your company's logo) appear on all slides.

1. Open *ep1-0407* and save it as **Tech Head Trends**.
2. Move to Slide 2 and then display the slide master. Make the following revisions to the master:
   - Change the first-level bullet style to large open squares.
   - Format the text in the title placeholder as italic.
   - Format the text for the bulleted points without italic.
   - Use the Insert, Picture, From File command to display the Insert Picture dialog box. Navigate to the folder (or Web site) that includes your student data files and then insert the Computer Disk file in your presentation. Move the clip to the upper left corner of the slide, and resize it approximately one-quarter of its original size.
3. Close the slide master and view your changes in Normal view and as a slide show. Make any necessary revisions.
4. Save and close your *Tech Head Trends* presentation.

Keep PowerPoint running if you plan to complete additional exercises.

3. Changing Color Schemes and Templates

As president of the University Biking Club, you're preparing for an upcoming meeting. To choose the best design template for your presentation, you preview several before choosing one. You also change the color scheme.

1. Open *ep1-0408* and save it as `Bicycle`. Display Slide 1 of the presentation in Normal view.
2. Apply each of PowerPoint's available design templates to the presentation. When you're finished, choose the Fading Grid template.
3. Display the color schemes for the Fading Grid template. Apply each of the color schemes to the presentation to view the effect. When you're finished viewing them, apply one color scheme to the title slide and a different one to the remainder of the slides.
4. Add an appropriate clip art image to the title slide. You can either choose from the clips available within PowerPoint or access those on the Web.
5. View your presentation as a slide show to see your changes.
6. Save your *Bicycle* presentation and then close it.

Keep PowerPoint running if you plan to complete additional exercises.

4. Using PowerPoint's Features to Change a Presentation's "Look"

You're working for the Computer Warehouse, a large store that sells computers and software. To get ready for an upcoming sale, your boss has asked you to develop a sales flyer. Before he decides on a final flyer, however, he wants to see several prototypes. To quickly develop several flyers that have the same information but a different "look," you decide to use PowerPoint's templates and clip art.

1. Open *ep1-0409* and save it as `Computer Warehouse`.
2. Insert a clip on the presentation. Resize and move the clip if necessary; then print the slide. After you print the slide, delete the clip. Use the same process to insert at least two other clips, printing the slide each time to show how it appears with the different clips.
3. Apply at least five design templates to the slide. Print the slide with each of the templates applied so that you can show your boss how they appear.
4. Save the presentation with your favorite template and clip art image in place. Close the presentation.

Keep PowerPoint running if you plan to work on the Discovery Zone exercises.

Discovery Zone exercises require advanced knowledge of topics presented in *essentials* lessons, application of skills from multiple lessons, or self-directed learning of new skills. Each exercise is independent of the others, so that you may complete the exercises in any order.

1. Combining PowerPoint Features

As sales manager for a mass-market kitchen cabinet factory, you develop and give a large number of presentations. Determine which PowerPoint feature you would use for each of the following situations.

- You want to display your company's logo on each presentation slide.
- You want to change the overall design and "look" of your presentation.
- You want to add a textured effect to the background of your presentation slides.

- You want to use the same design template for your presentation, but need more contrast for an onscreen display.
- You want to insert the date at the bottom of each presentation slide.

Use Help to research how to use each feature. Next develop a sample presentation (using the Auto-Content Wizard, if you want) and practice using each feature until you are confident that you can perform the steps automatically. Unless your instructor indicates otherwise, close your sample presentation without saving it.

Keep PowerPoint running if you plan to complete the final exercise.

2. Using and Creating Templates

You assist the president of a large tooling manufacturer. Since you have a strong knowledge of PowerPoint, he's asked you to help him develop a custom template for your company and then add it to the AutoContent Wizard.

Develop a new, blank presentation. Modify and format the presentation using what you know about design templates, color schemes, slide backgrounds, and slide masters.

Save the presentation as a template, using a name of your choice. Then add the template to the Auto-Content Wizard so that it displays each time you launch the Wizard.

Create a new presentation based on the template (Hint: Use the File, New command). Also create a presentation (based on your custom template) using the AutoContent Wizard. Unless your instructor indicates otherwise, close your sample presentation without saving it. When you're finished, close all open presentations and exit PowerPoint.

Working with Charts

Objectives

In this project, you learn how to

- ✔ Select an Appropriate Chart Type
- ✔ Create a Data Chart
- ✔ Edit Chart Data
- ✔ Resize, Move, and Change Chart Types
- ✔ Choose a Chart Subtype and Format a Chart
- ✔ Add Animation to a Chart
- ✔ Create and Format an Organization Chart

Key terms introduced in this project include

- ❏ activating
- ❏ animating
- ❏ cell
- ❏ cell pointer
- ❏ chart
- ❏ chart subtypes
- ❏ Custom Animation list
- ❏ data charts
- ❏ data series
- ❏ datasheet
- ❏ default
- ❏ embedded object
- ❏ object
- ❏ organization chart
- ❏ peripheral program

Why Would I Do This?

Have you ever longed for a way to convey complicated data in a clear, concise manner to business clients, stockholders, or colleagues? One of the best ways to do this is to present your data as a PowerPoint chart, or graph. A ***chart*** is simply a pictorial representation of data. You can use charts to emphasize your information or show it in a easy-to-understand manner.

Visual Summary

Charts are powerful tools in a presentation. Remember that people are usually more convinced by a well-presented chart than by endless words or explanations. Business users want to know the bottom line—so use PowerPoint's capability to create pictorial charts to your advantage. For example, Figure 5.1 shows information as text. Figure 5.2 shows the same information graphically as a data chart. By the end of this project, you'll learn how to change dull, hard-to-understand statistics into colorful, appealing charts such as that shown in Figure 5.2.

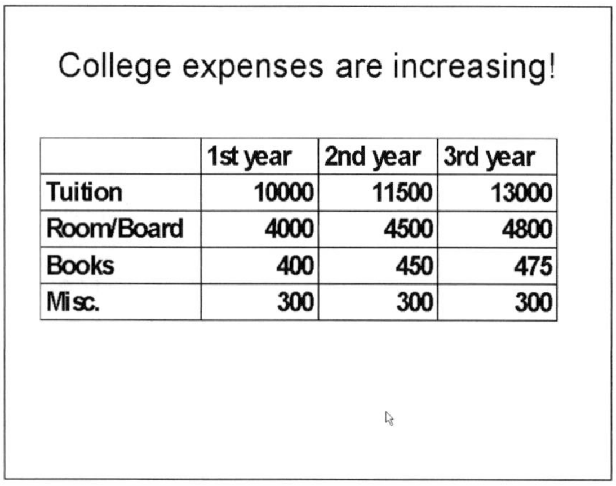

College expenses are increasing!

	1st year	2nd year	3rd year
Tuition	10000	11500	13000
Room/Board	4000	4500	4800
Books	400	450	475
Misc.	300	300	300

Figure 5.1

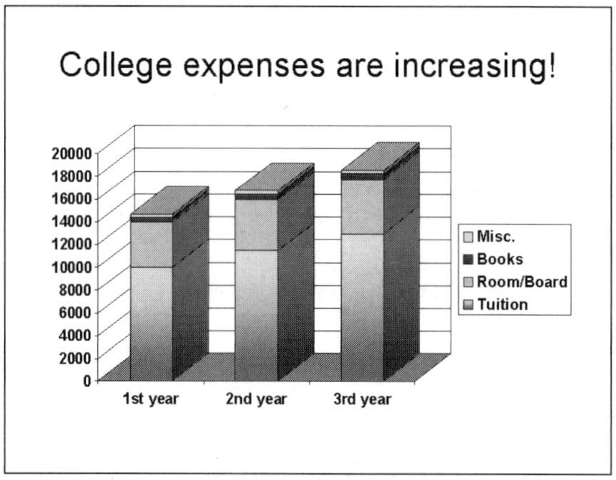

College expenses are increasing!

Figure 5.2

Fortunately, it's relatively easy to create and modify splashy charts in PowerPoint—charts that capture people's attention and emphasize your ideas. In this project, we'll show you the basics of creating and formatting ***data charts***. Data charts show numerical data in a pictorial manner much like the chart in Figure 5.3.

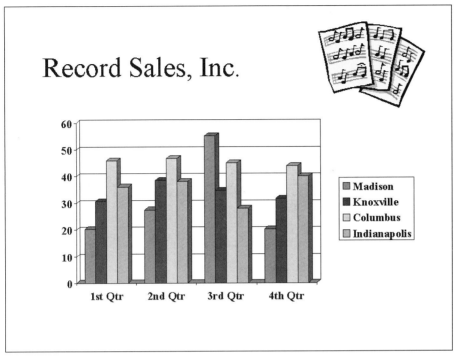

Figure 5.3

You'll also learn how to create and revise an organization chart—a chart that shows the hierarchical structure of an organization (see Figure 5.4).

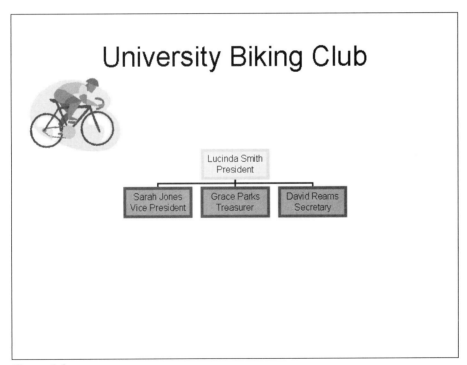

Figure 5.4

Before you begin, however, it's important to know which type of chart to use for your data. So come along as we explore the chart types, and learn when to use each.

Lesson 1: Selecting an Appropriate Chart Type

You can select from several standard chart types to present your data clearly and effectively. Additionally, each chart type includes several ***chart subtypes***—variations of each of the main chart types. As you develop your presentation, you'll want to set up your data using the best chart type for the information you're trying to convey. Because the most commonly used chart types are line, bar, column, pie, and organization, we'll guide you through how to use these types. However, so that you'll have a handy reference as you expand your charting skills, we've included Table 5.1, which lists all of the chart types used in PowerPoint.

Table 5.1 PowerPoint Chart Types

Chart Type	Main Use	Example
Column chart	Shows data changes over time or illustrates a comparison of items. The values are organized vertically, and categories are shown horizontally to emphasize variation over time.	Sales by quarter for the year.
Bar chart	Shows comparison of individual items. Categories are arranged vertically and values are arranged horizontally, placing more emphasis on categories than values.	Sales by region, with region on the vertical axis and sales on the horizontal axis.
Line chart	Shows trends in data at equal intervals.	Monthly production over a twelve-month period.
Pie chart	Illustrates the relationship of parts to the whole. Pie charts can show only one data series.	Market share held by your company versus your competitors.
XY (Scatter) chart	Shows the relationship between values in several chart series.	The relationship between quantity and price.
Area chart	Shows the magnitude of change over time.	Cumulative sales from several divisions.
Doughnut chart	Similar to a pie chart because it shows the relationship of parts to the whole. However, it can show more than one data series, with each "ring" representing a series.	Expenses broken down by category for several departments.
Radar chart	Shows frequencies of changes in data relative to each other and to a center point.	Analysis of how well several products did in comparison with each other.

(Continues)

Table 5.1	PowerPoint Chart Types (Continued)	
Chart Type	**Main Use**	**Example**
Surface chart	Shows where the result of combining two sets of data produces the greatest overall value.	A chart showing the greatest combination of cold and wind (wind chill).
Bubble chart	Shows data similar to a scatter chart, but also shows (by size of the bubble) the result of the data.	A chart showing the effect of temperature and humidity on soda sales.
Stock chart	Shows high, low, and closing values for stock.	A chart that shows stock performance for your company.
Cylinder, Cone, and Pyramid charts	Shows data similar to that in bar and column charts, but displays it as cylinders, cones, or pyramids.	A chart using pyramids to graphically show the height of peaks in the Great Smoky Mountains.

In addition to the chart types listed in Table 5.1, PowerPoint has the capability to produce *organization charts*, those that show how your business is structured. You'll learn how to create and format an organization chart in Lesson 7.

Lesson 2: Creating a Data Chart

PowerPoint has the capability to create different types of data charts so that you can illustrate your points effectively. Data charts are simply charts that include numerical data (as opposed to organization charts, which show how an organization is set up).

PowerPoint uses Microsoft Graph, a ***peripheral program,*** to create data charts. Peripheral programs are started every time you access a feature within the main program, and place an embedded object (such as a chart) on a slide. You can think of the embedded object as being a doorway leading to the peripheral program, giving you access to its features and commands. PowerPoint shares Microsoft Graph with other Office programs. This makes chart development more uniform and efficient when working with PowerPoint and the various Office products.

There are a couple different methods you can use to launch Microsoft Graph and insert a chart on a slide. You can use the Insert Chart button on an existing or new slide, or you can use the Insert Chart button on the Standard toolbar. After you start Microsoft Graph, a ***datasheet*** is displayed so that you can enter your information. A datasheet is a grid of columns and rows that enables you to enter numerical data into a PowerPoint chart. The intersection of a column and row is called a ***cell.*** Cells are always named by the column heading, followed by the row number (such as A1). If you're familiar with Excel, you'll feel right at home using a datasheet, since it's set up like a "mini" worksheet.

When you're finished entering your data in the datasheet, you close the peripheral program, and your chart is embedded as an object on your slide. An ***embedded object*** is an item that is created by one program, but inserted into a document created by another program. In this case, a chart object (created by Microsoft Graph) is placed on a PowerPoint slide.

Now that you know the terminology associated with data charts, try creating one.

To Create a Data Chart

① **Start PowerPoint if necessary. Open *ep1-0501,* and save it as** Bell Manufacturing.

② **Display Slide 3, *Revenue*, in Normal view and then choose Insert, New Slide.**
A new slide is inserted in your presentation. Additionally, the Slide Layout task pane automatically displays so you can choose a Content Layout (see Figure 5.5). Each of the Content Layouts includes an Insert Chart button (on the Content icon) you can click to launch Microsoft Graph.

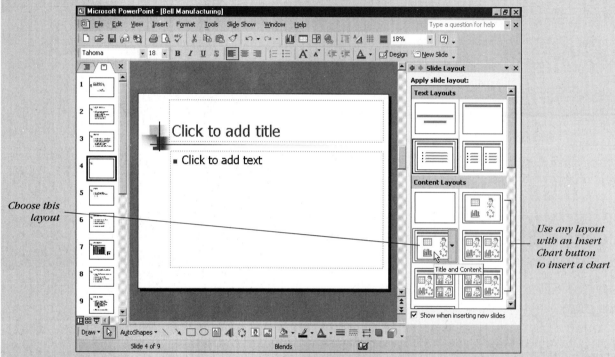

Choose this layout

Use any layout with an Insert Chart button to insert a chart

Figure 5.5

③ **Click the Title and Content layout (refer to Figure 5.5, if necessary).**
The Title and Content layout is applied to your slide. This slide layout includes a place-holder for the title as well as for various types of inserted objects—including charts (see Figure 5.6).

To Create a Data Chart

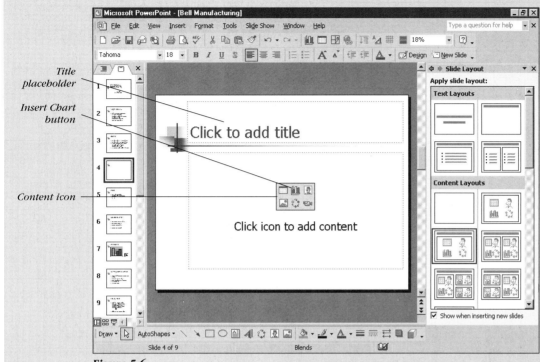

Figure 5.6

4 **Click in the title placeholder; then type** Revenues—2000 vs. 2001.
This is the title for the chart. Now you're ready to create the chart itself.

5 **Click the Insert Chart button on the Content icon.**
Microsoft Graph starts, and a datasheet is displayed with sample data. Additionally, because Microsoft Graph is the active program, the Microsoft Graph toolbar and menu bar are available so that you can easily access charting commands (see Figure 5.7).

(Continues)

To Create a Data Chart (Continued)

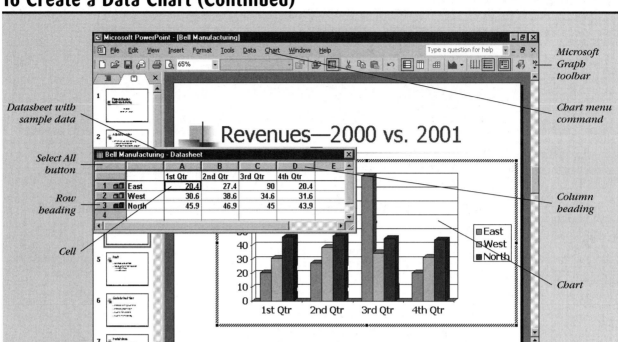

Figure 5.7

The sample data is simply a guide and is easily replaced with your own data. To enter your data, click the cell in the datasheet and then type your entry. When you're finished, press (↵Enter) or an arrow key to move to another cell. Try entering some data now.

6 Click the cell containing the word *East*.
A darkened border around the cell, called the ***cell pointer***, indicates that this is the active cell—ready for an entry.

7 Type 2000 and then press (↓).
This enters *2000* in the cell and moves the cell pointer down one cell. (You can also press (↵Enter) to move the cell pointer down one cell.)

8 Click in the row 3 heading (*North*).
The entire row is selected.

9 Press (Del).
The sample data from the entire row 3 is deleted.

10 Enter the data shown in Figure 5.8 into your datasheet.

		A	B	C	D	E
		1st Qtr	2nd Qtr	3rd Qtr	4th Qtr	
1	2000	3.4	2.7	4.2	3.7	
2	2001	4.2	3.2	4.7	3.9	
3						
4						

Bell Manufacturing - Datasheet

Figure 5.8

To Create a Data Chart

⑪ **When you finish entering the data, click the Close button in the datasheet's upper-right corner.**

The datasheet closes, and you can better see the column chart that is created. This is the *default* chart type, which means that PowerPoint automatically uses this type of chart unless you indicate otherwise. Additionally, the chart is embedded into the slide as an *object*. Black selection handles encompass the chart, indicating that it's still activated—Microsoft Graph is still active in memory (see Figure 5.9).

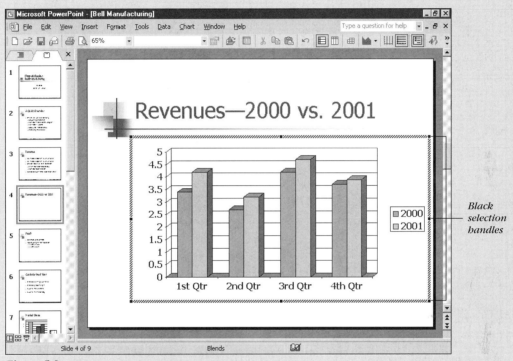

Figure 5.9

⑫ **Click outside the chart.**

The Microsoft Graph program is no longer active, and its associated menu bar and toolbar no longer display. However, white, circular selection handles still appear around the chart (see Figure 5.10). You can use these handles to move or resize the chart, just as you can any other object.

(Continues)

To Create a Data Chart (Continued)

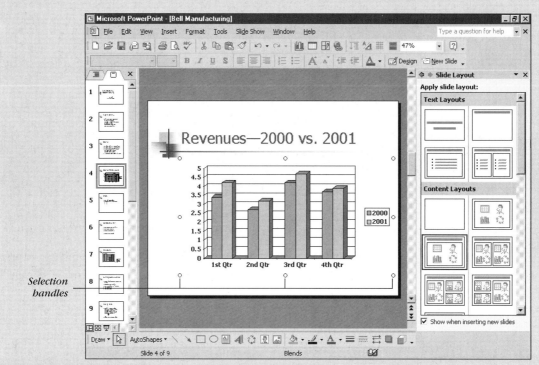

Figure 5.10

⑬ Click outside the chart object again.
The chart is completely deselected, and the selection handles are cleared.

⑭ Click the Slide Layout task pane's Close button.
The task pane is cleared so that you have more screen area to work with your slide.

⑮ Save the changes to the *Bell Manufacturing* presentation.
Keep the presentation open for the next lesson, in which you learn to edit chart data.

To extend your knowledge...

Selecting Information in a Datasheet

It's handy to know some efficient ways to work with information that you enter and edit in your datasheet. For example, you can click a column letter to select an entire column for deletion—just as you selected an entire row for deletion in the previous lesson. In a similar way, you can click the Select All button (at the intersection of the row numbers and column letters) to quickly select the entire datasheet and then press Del to delete all the sample data at once.

More About Creating Charts

Clicking the Insert Chart button on any Content Layout is an easy way to make a chart. However, if you want to place a chart on a slide without using a Content Layout, choose Insert, Chart or click the Insert Chart button on the Standard toolbar.

Lesson 3: Editing Chart Data

After you create a chart, you may want to edit its data. For example, you may want to update sales or production figures as they become available. In this lesson you learn how to make modifications to an existing chart.

Before you make changes to a chart, you must first activate it. However, there's a difference between selecting a chart object and ***activating*** it.

Clicking a chart object one time selects it and places white, circular selection handles around its border. In contrast, double-clicking the chart activates it and opens the Microsoft Graph peripheral program so that you can again use Microsoft Graph's commands and features. You'll see black selection handles and a rope-like border when the chart is activated.

Try activating your chart and editing its data now.

To Edit Chart Data

❶ In the open *Bell Manufacturing* presentation, double-click the chart object you created on Slide 4.

The chart is activated, as shown by the rope-like border and black selection handles (see Figure 5.11).

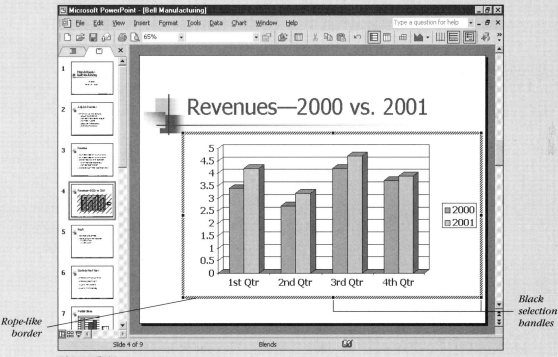

Rope-like border

Black selection handles

Figure 5.11

 ## If you have problems...

It's sometimes tricky to activate the chart, rather than simply select it. If your chart doesn't look like the one in Figure 5.11, double-click on the chart again. Make sure to click in fairly rapid succession and to hold the mouse steady between clicks. If you're really having trouble activating the chart by double-clicking, you can instead single-click the chart and then press ⏎Enter.

(Continues)

To Edit Chart Data (Continued)

② **Click the View Datasheet button on Microsoft Graph's Standard toolbar.**
The datasheet is displayed, enabling you to revise the data it contains.

③ **Click the Select All button in the upper-left corner of the datasheet.**
The entire datasheet is highlighted to show that it's selected (see Figure 5.12).

Click here to select the entire datasheet

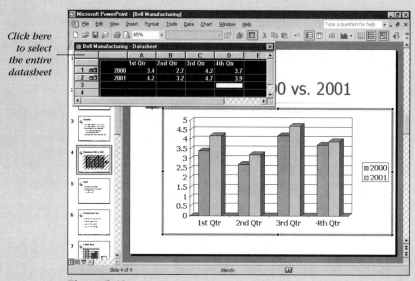

Figure 5.12

④ **Press Del.**
The datasheet contents are deleted. Now you can enter new data.

⑤ **Enter the information shown in Figure 5.13 into your datasheet.**

▦ Bell Manufacturing - Datasheet		A	B	C	D	E	
		2000	2001				
1	Projected	13.7	14				
2	Actual	14	16				
3							
4							

Figure 5.13

⑥ **When you finish entering the data, click the View Datasheet button.**
The datasheet closes, but the chart remains active.

Keep your *Bell Manufacturing* presentation open for the next lesson, in which you learn to change the chart type, and move and resize your chart.

Lesson 4: Resizing, Moving, and Changing Chart Types

You've created a chart and revised its data. However, besides these changes you can also move and resize your chart object on the slide. Furthermore, you can change the chart type to arrange your data differently. The easiest way to do this is to click the drop-down list arrow next to the Chart Type button. Keep in mind that the underlying data remains the same—the chart types simply display the data differently. Because you don't affect the data when you change the chart type, you can experiment freely to see which chart type best conveys your data.

Try resizing and moving your chart as well as changing the chart type now.

To Resize, Move, and Change Chart Types

1 **In the open *Bell Manufacturing* presentation, make sure the chart on Slide 4 is active.**
Black selection handles indicate that the chart is still active. (If your chart isn't displayed in this manner, double-click the chart object to activate it.)

Now hide the display of Microsoft Graph's Formatting toolbar. When you do this, you'll automatically "uncover" the Standard toolbar's buttons that you need to use.

2 **Choose <u>V</u>iew, <u>T</u>oolbars, Formatting.**
The Formatting toolbar's display is turned off so that only the Standard toolbar is visible. This toolbar includes the buttons that you'll use throughout the lesson. One of the most popular buttons is the Chart Type button, which includes a drop-down palette of chart types.

3 **On the Microsoft Graph Standard toolbar, click the Chart Type drop-down list arrow.**
The types of charts available on your system are displayed on a palette (see Figure 5.14). Notice that some of the charts are simply variations of other types. For example, the palette shows both 2-D and 3-D bar and column charts.

(Continues)

To Resize, Move, and Change Chart Types (Continued)

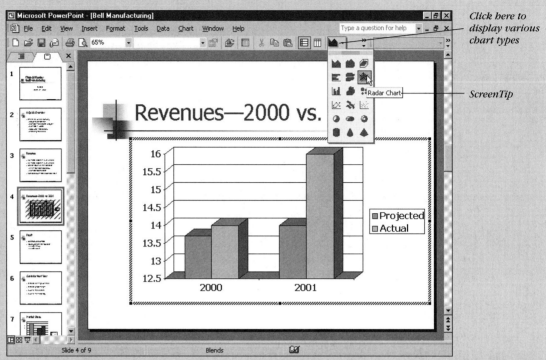

Figure 5.14

④ Rest the mouse pointer momentarily on any chart type on the palette.
A ScreenTip is displayed that identifies the type of chart.

⑤ Move the mouse pointer to the 3-D Bar Chart button on the palette; then click to select it.
The chart is displayed as a bar chart (see Figure 5.15). For practice, spend a few minutes changing to other chart types. When you're finished experimenting, choose the 3-D Bar Chart before continuing with the lesson.

To Resize, Move, and Change Chart Types

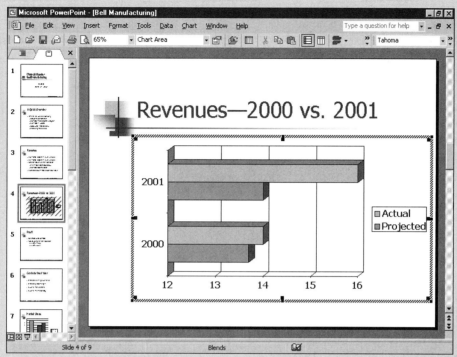

Figure 5.15

Besides changing the chart type, you can make other modifications to your chart. For example, you may want to resize or move the chart on your slide. Luckily, PowerPoint makes this task easy.

6 **Click outside the chart to close Microsoft Graph.**
White, circular selection handles appear around the chart, indicating that it is selected (but that Microsoft Graph is no longer active).

Now try resizing the chart object.

7 **Move the mouse pointer to the white selection handle on the upper-right corner of the chart so that the pointer displays as a two-headed resizing arrow.**

8 **Drag toward the middle of the chart until the chart is approximately half the original size; then release the mouse button.**
The object is resized on the slide. Now try moving the object to the middle of the available space.

9 **Move the mouse pointer to the middle of the chart object until a four-sided arrow is displayed.**

10 **Drag the chart object so that it is displayed in the middle of the slide; then release the mouse button.**

11 **Click outside the chart object to deselect it.**
The slide should now look similar to the one in Figure 5.16.

(Continues)

To Resize, Move, and Change Chart Types (Continued)

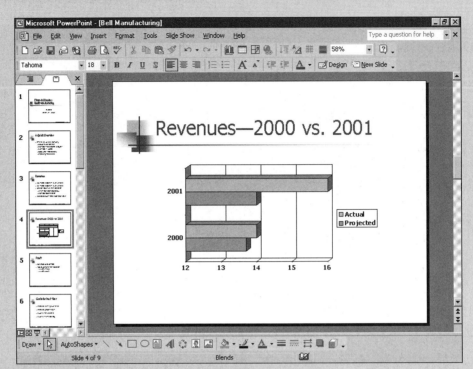

Figure 5.16

 Save the changes to your *Bell Manufacturing* presentation and then close it.
Keep PowerPoint running for the next lesson, in which you learn more about formatting a chart.

To extend your knowledge...

More on Modifying Your Chart

There are a number of other buttons on Microsoft Graph's Standard toolbar that help you display your data just as you'd like. For example, you can quickly switch how your data appears by clicking the By Row or By Column buttons. You can also add or remove a legend by clicking the Legend button. To find out more about working with charts, activate a chart and then choose Help, Microsoft Graph Help from the Microsoft Graph menu bar.

Lesson 5: Choosing a Chart Subtype and Formatting a Chart

So far in this project you've learned how to create charts and make some revisions. However, PowerPoint provides a number of tools you can use to make your charts even more readable and understandable—and in this lesson you'll learn how to wield them! For example, you'll learn how to choose a chart subtype and how to change a chart's text and color. You work with a safety campaign presentation, which includes a column chart. Try using some formatting options on this chart now.

To Choose a Chart Subtype

① Open *ep1-0502,* **and save it as** Safety.

② **Click Slide 4 on the Slides tab.**
The slide is shown in the Slide pane area.

③ **Double-click the existing chart on Slide 4,** *Total sick days per facility,* **and close the datasheet.**
Microsoft Graph is activated, as shown by the black handles around the chart. The chart is currently a column chart. For this presentation, however, you want to view the information in a stacked column chart. To change the chart's format to a different subtype, you can use the Chart Type dialog box.

④ **Choose Chart, Chart Type.**
The Chart Type dialog box is displayed (see Figure 5.17). You can use this dialog box to select a variation, or subtype, of the main chart type. (If you don't see the Chart command on the menu bar, most likely you haven't properly activated the chart. Just double-click the chart object to activate it.)

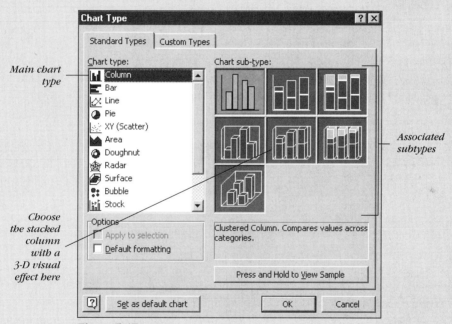

Figure 5.17

⑤ **Click on the** *Stacked column with a 3-D visual effect* **subtype—the middle chart in the second row.**
A description of the selected subtype appears below the chart subtypes. You can also preview how your data looks when displayed by the subtype by using the special preview button that PowerPoint provides.

⑥ **Move the mouse pointer to the Press and Hold to View Sample button. Click and hold down the mouse button for a few seconds before releasing it.**
PowerPoint displays your data with the selected chart's format. If you want, select and preview several other chart types (and subtypes). When you're finished, choose the *Stacked column with a 3-D visual effect* subtype before proceeding.

(Continues)

To Choose a Chart Subtype (Continued)

7 **Click OK in the Chart Type dialog box.**
The selected chart type is applied to your chart.

Keep your chart activated for the next exercise in this lesson, in which you explore some other methods of formatting your chart.

By now you're familiar with creating a chart, editing data, and changing chart types. Next we'll focus on working with individual elements in a chart. A chart is made up of several objects, such as the data series, graph walls, legend, and so on. You can format or delete any of these elements—but first you must select the object. The easiest way to select a chart object is to use the Chart Objects drop-down list on the Standard toolbar. Try selecting, formatting, and deleting chart objects now.

To Format a Chart

1 **In the activated chart, click the drop-down list arrow to the right of the Chart Objects box and choose Series "Danville."**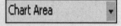
The data series that represents the Danville factory is selected. In fact, if you look carefully you can see selected handles displayed around the series to help you identify your selection. A **_data series_** is a collection of values that pertain to a single subject. Now format the data series.

2 **Choose For_mat, _Selected Data Series from the menu bar.**
The Format Data Series dialog box is displayed (see Figure 5.18). Notice that PowerPoint includes several formatting categories—such as Patterns and Shape—each on a separate, tabbed page.

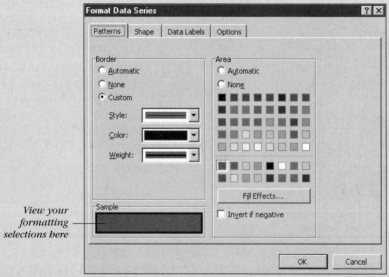

View your formatting selections here

Figure 5.18

3 **In the Area section of the Patterns page, click the white color box.**
The Sample box displays the result of your choice. Now try changing the pattern associated with the data series.

To Format a Chart

4 **Click the Fill Effects button.**
The Fill Effects dialog box is displayed (see Figure 5.19). You can choose a gradient, pattern, or texture for the data series.

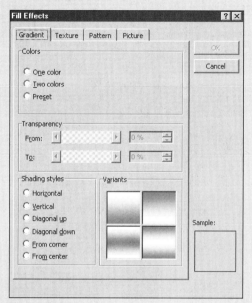

Figure 5.19

5 **Click the Texture tab to display its page and then click several fill textures.**
Each texture you choose is shown in the Sample box. Now try viewing available patterns.

6 **Click the Pattern tab and then choose the second pattern from the left on the second row.**
Your selected pattern is shown in the Sample box.

7 **Click OK in the Fill Effects dialog box and in the Format Data Series dialog box to accept your changes.**
The color and pattern you chose is applied to the data series. You can format any chart object in a similar way: Use the Chart Objects drop-down list to select an object; then choose the Selected (*name of object*) command from the Format menu.

You can also double-click a chart object to open an associated Format dialog box. Try using this method to change the legend's appearance now.

8 **Double-click the legend to display the Format Legend dialog box and then click the Patterns page (if necessary).**
You use this dialog box to modify the colors, font, and placement for the legend.

If you have problems...
Make sure you double-click the legend background, and not one of the legend entries (such as Danville).

9 **In the Area section of the Patterns page, choose red for your legend color and then click OK.**
The legend's background is formatted with the new color. You can also delete a chart object by selecting it and pressing ⌦. Try deleting a data series now.

(Continues)

To Format a Chart (Continued)

10 **Click the drop-down list arrow to the right of the Chart Objects box and then choose Series "Samville."**
The series is selected so that you can delete it.

11 **Press** Del**.**
The selected series is removed from the chart. Notice that the legend entry for Samville is deleted simultaneously (see Figure 5.20).

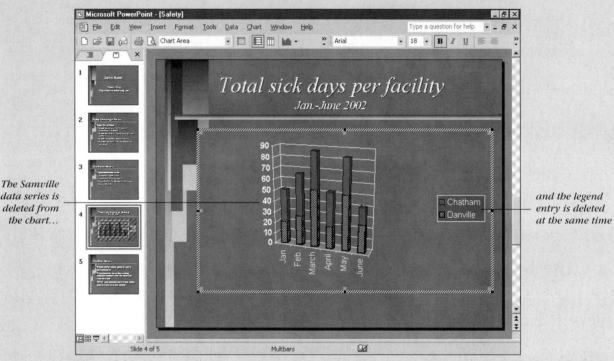

The Samville data series is deleted from the chart...

and the legend entry is deleted at the same time

Figure 5.20

Before you close Microsoft Graph, turn the display for the Formatting toolbar back on.

12 **Choose View, Toolbars, Formatting.**
The Microsoft Graph Formatting toolbar is visible again. Now embed the chart on your slide.

13 **Click outside the chart to embed it on the slide; then save and close the *Safety* presentation.**
Keep PowerPoint open for the next lesson, in which you add animation to a chart.

Lesson 6: Adding Animation to a Chart

You can animate almost any object on a PowerPoint slide, and a chart is no exception. *Animating* refers to displaying objects in sequence to produce the illusion of movement or to control the flow of information. For charts you can display data by element or by the entire data series. Try animating a chart now.

To Add Animation to a Chart

❶ Open *ep1-0503,* and save it as `Record Sales`.

❷ Click the title, *Record Sales, Inc.*, to select it.

❸ Choose Sli**d**e Show, Custo**m** Animation.
The Custom Animation task pane is displayed (see Figure 5.21).

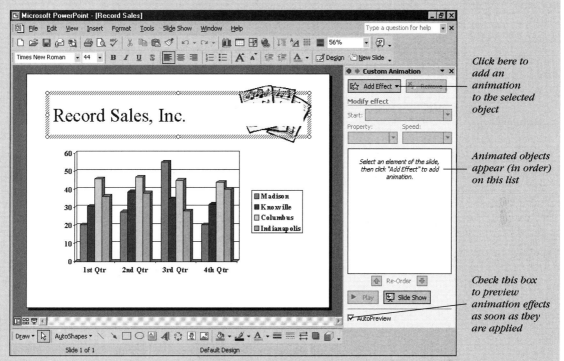

Click here to add an animation to the selected object

Animated objects appear (in order) on this list

Check this box to preview animation effects as soon as they are applied

Figure 5.21

❹ Click the Add Effect button; then point to **E**ntrance on the drop-down list.
A listing of ways that your chart title can initially display on your slide is shown (see Figure 5.22).

(Continues)

To Add Animation to a Chart (Continued)

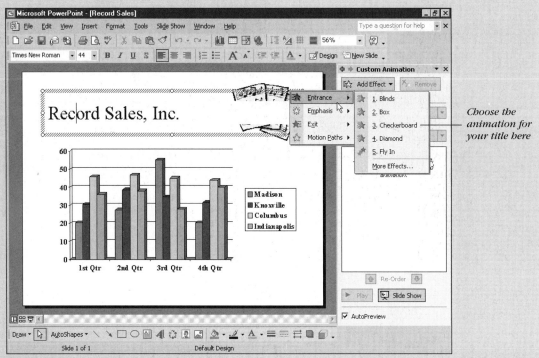

Figure 5.22

5 **Click *Fly In* from the list.**

The animation effect is applied to the selected object—your chart title, and a numbered tag appears beside the chart title. Additionally, the animation is shown on the slide and is added to your ***Custom Animation list***. This list shows the order of animation for a slide (see Figure 5.23).

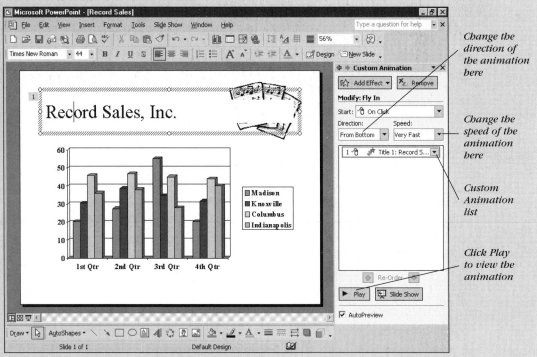

Figure 5.23

To Add Animation to a Chart

If you have problems...

The number of effects (and the exact ones shown on the Entrance list) change depending on which ones you've used most recently. Because of this, it's possible that *Fly In* may not appear on the list. If you don't see this effect, choose <u>M</u>ore Effects at the bottom of the list to display the Add Entrance Effect dialog box. Double-click the *Fly In* effect in the dialog box.

If you have problems...

By default, PowerPoint displays the custom animation effects as soon as you apply them to a slide. If the animation doesn't automatically play, check the AutoPreview box in the Custom Animation task pane.

6 **Verify that your chart title is still selected. In the Custom Animation task pane, click the Direction drop-down list arrow and then choose From <u>L</u>eft.**

7 **Click the Speed drop-down list arrow and then choose Medium.**
Now add animation to your chart. You can animate the chart as a whole, or animate the individual elements, such as categories in a series.

8 **Single-click the chart to select it and then choose Add Effect, <u>E</u>ntrance, *Blinds*.**
The effect is added to the chart. Additionally, the chart is added to the Custom Animation list and another numbered tag appears, beside the chart. These numbered tags indicate the order in which the chart objects will animate (see Figure 5.24).

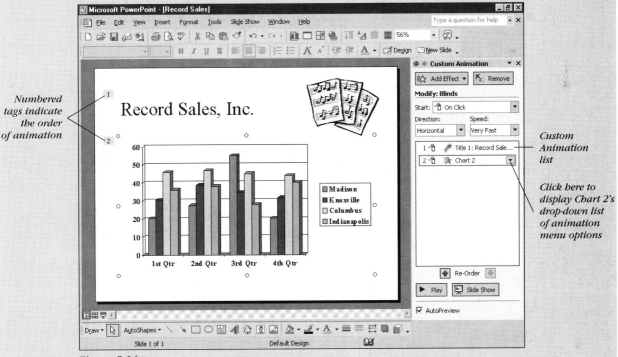

Figure 5.24

9 **With the chart object still selected, click Chart 2's drop-down list (on the Custom Animation list) and then choose <u>E</u>ffect Options.**
The Blinds dialog box is displayed.

(Continues)

To Add Animation to a Chart (Continued)

⑩ Click the Chart Animation tab and then click the <u>G</u>roup chart drop-down list arrow.

A listing of ways you can animate your chart is displayed (see Figure 5.25). Depending on the emphasis of your presentation, you can display your chart in a variety of ways (such as by each element in a series).

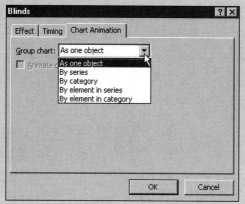

Figure 5.25

⑪ Choose *By element in category* and then click OK.

Now you can view the animation. While you can always see the animation by running a PowerPoint slide show, you can also preview the effects by simply clicking Play in the Custom Animation task pane.

⑫ Click Play in the Custom Animation task pane.

PowerPoint plays the animations you added to the slide so that you can preview them.

⑬ Click the Custom Animation task pane's Close button.

⑭ Save and close your *Record Sales* presentation.

Keep PowerPoint running for the next exercise, in which you learn how to create and format an organization chart.

To extend your knowledge...

More About Animating Objects

You can animate almost any object or text on a slide, including text, charts, drawn objects, and clip art. Luckily, the process you use is similar to how you animate a chart: Select the object and then choose options in the Custom Animation task pane.

After you initially add animation to an object, you can exert great control over the type, direction, and speed of the animation. You do this by choosing options from the Direction and Speed drop-down lists in the Custom Animation task pane. You can also change the order in which objects on a slide animate. To do so, click the object on the Custom Animation list that you want to reorder and then click the Re-Order up or down arrows. Finally, to delete an animation (but *not* the associated object), select it on the Custom Animation list and then click the Remove button.

As you've probably already guessed, PowerPoint includes a wealth of ways to animate your slide objects. To learn more about this method of enhancing your presentation, type `custom animation` or `animate charts` in the Ask a Question box.

Lesson 7: Creating and Formatting an Organization Chart

An *organization chart* shows the structure and relationship between people or functions within an organization. The easiest way to create an organization chart in PowerPoint is to click the Insert Diagram or Organization Chart button on the Drawing toolbar and then choose Organization Chart.

In this lesson you create an organization chart, enter text, and then format it. Try working with an organization chart now.

To Create and Format an Organization Chart

1 **Open *ep1-0504*, and save it as** Organization.

2 **Click the Insert Diagram or Organization Chart button from the Drawing toolbar.**
The Diagram Gallery dialog box is displayed (see Figure 5.26).

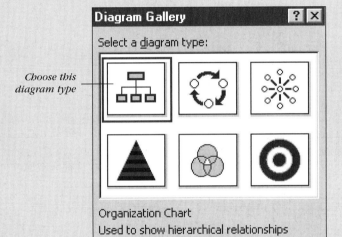

Choose this diagram type

Figure 5.26

3 **Click the Organization Chart diagram type and then click OK.**
PowerPoint creates an organization chart and displays it as an object on your slide (see Figure 5.27). By default, PowerPoint makes an organization chart with one manager box and three subordinate boxes. Additionally, the rope-like border indicates the entire chart is activated, while circular selection handles show that an individual box is selected.

(Continues)

To Create and Format an Organization Chart (Continued)

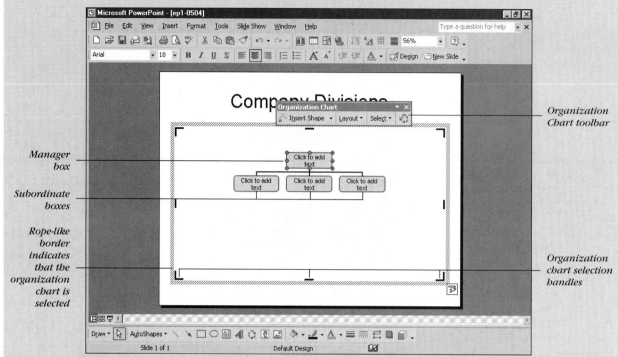

Figure 5.27

4 **Click in the Manager box and then type** Company Headquarters. **Press** ⏎Enter **and then type** Knoxville, TN.

Don't worry if the text extends beyond the borders of the box; PowerPoint will automatically resize the box to fit the text as soon as you click outside of it or select another object.

5 **Click in the leftmost subordinate box and then type** Morristown, TN.

6 **Enter** Greeneville, TN **in the middle subordinate box and** Kingsport, TN **in the rightmost subordinate box; then click outside the boxes (but within the chart) to better view your changes.**

Now try formatting your chart. You can select a box (or boxes) and then choose options on the Format menu or Formatting toolbar. Alternately, you can select the entire organization chart and then apply formatting to the entire chart at once.

7 **Verify that the rope-like border displays around the organization chart and then click the Bold and Italic buttons on the Formatting toolbar.**

Bold and italic is applied to all the text in the organization chart. Now try using the AutoFormat command.

8 **Click the Autoformat button on the Organization Chart toolbar.**

The Organization Chart Style Gallery is displayed (see Figure 5.28). You can use styles in this dialog box to quickly apply a set of formatting commands to create a particular "look."

To Create and Format an Organization Chart

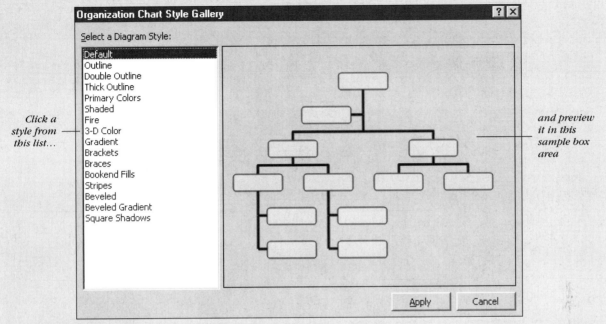

Figure 5.28

9   **Click various options on the Select a Diagram Style list, and preview them in the sample box area.**

10   **Click the Beveled Gradient style and then choose Apply.**
The style is applied to your organization chart (see Figure 5.29).

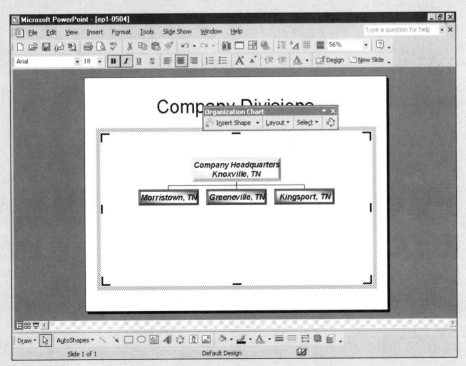

Figure 5.29

(Continues)

To Create and Format an Organization Chart (Continued)

11 Click outside your organization chart object to deselect it.

12 Choose **File**, **Print** and then click OK.
Your slide is printed so that you have a hard copy of the organization chart.

13 Save your changes to the *Organization* presentation and then close it.
Keep PowerPoint running if you plan to complete the end of chapter exercises.

To extend your knowledge...

More about Working with Organization Charts

In this lesson you saw how to create an organization chart by using the Insert Diagram or Organization Chart button on the Drawing toolbar. However, you can also choose a Content Layout that includes an icon for inserting an organization chart.

Also, you can resize, move, and delete the organization chart just as you can other objects: Select the chart and then drag the selection handles to resize it; drag the border of the selected object to move it; press (Del) to delete it. Finally, to modify an organization chart object, double-click it.

In this project you learned the basics of creating data and organization charts. First you learned how to select which chart is most appropriate for the data you want to display, and then you created several charts. After you initially developed the charts, you explored ways of formatting and revising them.

To expand on your knowledge, spend a few minutes exploring Help on these topics. Additionally, complete some of the Skill Drill, Challenge, and Discovery Zone exercises.

Multiple Choice

Circle the letter of the correct answer for each of the following.

1. Which of the following changes can you make to a data chart once it's created? [L2-6]

   a. Add animation

   b. Change the chart type

   c. Change the data itself

   d. All of the above

2. Which of the following chart types can you create with PowerPoint? [L1-7]

   a. Column chart

   b. Pie chart

   c. Organization chart

   d. All of the above

3. A pie chart is best used for showing which of the following? [L1]

   a. The relationship of parts to the whole

   b. Data changes over time

   c. Trends in data at equal intervals

   d. The magnitude of change over time

4. Which of the following is true regarding an organization chart? [L7]

   a. It is used to show changes over time.

   b. It is used to show stock prices in an organization.

   c. It shows comparisons of individual items.

   d. None of the above

5. Which of the following represents a method of selecting cells in a datasheet? [L3]

   a. Click the Select All button to select all cells.

   b. Click the column heading to select a column.

   c. Click a row heading to select a row.

   d. All of the above

Discussion

1. Imagine that you work for a company and need to develop charts for a variety of situations. Which of the following chart types would you use for each of the following: [L1]

- A chart to show your company's market share versus a competitor's market share.
- A chart that shows the structure of your business.
- A chart to show monthly sales amounts for the past year.
- A chart to show your company's stock prices for the last month.
- A chart to show daily production levels for the past month.

2. Think about how you create, modify, and format data charts and organization charts. How are the processes similar? How are they different? [L2-7]

3. In what ways are pie charts, radar charts, and doughnut charts similar? In what ways are they different? In what ways are column and bar charts similar? In what ways are they different? [L1]

Skill Drill exercises *reinforce* project skills. Each skill reinforced is the same, or nearly the same, as a skill presented in the project. Detailed instructions are provided in a step-by-step format.

1. Creating a Line Chart

You need to show your boss that the cost of living is constantly rising, while your wages (adjusted for inflation, of course!) are falling. Create a line chart to emphasize your point.

   1. In PowerPoint create a new, one-slide presentation.

   2. In the Slide Layout task pane click the Title and Content layout (in the Content Layouts section) to apply this layout to your slide.

   3. Click in the slide's title placeholder and then type `I need a raise!` as the title.

4. Click the Insert Chart button on the Content icon in the lower placeholder. Enter the following information in the datasheet that displays, and delete the remaining row and column containing sample data:

	January	February	March
Income	2000	1980	1967
Cost of Living	2000	2100	2150

5. Close the datasheet. The chart displays as a column chart.

6. Choose Chart, Chart Type to display the Chart Type dialog box.

7. Click Line in the Chart type list. Then choose the *Line with markers displayed at each data value* subtype (the first subtype on the second row). Click OK.

Keep the chart activated and your presentation open for the next exercise, in which you format the chart.

2. Formatting a Data Chart

After looking over your data chart, you decide that you need to spiff it up with some formatting.

1. Double-click the chart object (if necessary) to activate Microsoft Graph. Close the datasheet.

2. Click the Chart Objects drop-down list arrow and then choose Series "Income" from the list.

3. Choose Format, Selected Data Series from the menu bar. In the Line section on the Patterns page, click the Weight drop-down list arrow and then choose the thickest line available.

4. In the Format Data Series dialog box, click the Data Labels tab. Choose Value; then click OK.

5. Double-click the line that represents Series "Cost of Living" to display the Format Data Series dialog box. On the Data Labels page, choose Value.

6. Click the Patterns page of the Format Data Series dialog box. Click the Weight drop-down list arrow and then choose the thickest line available. Choose OK to close the Format Data Series dialog box.

7. Click outside the chart to embed it as an object on your slide.

8. Close the Slide Layout task pane as well as the Slides tab and Outline tab.

9. Print a copy of your slide.

10. Save the presentation as `Living Expenses`; then close it.

Keep PowerPoint running if you plan to complete additional exercises.

3. Creating an Organization Chart

As secretary for the University Biking Club you want to show how the club is structured. You decide to use an organization chart to do so.

1. In PowerPoint create a new, one-slide presentation. In the Slide Layout task pane, choose the Title and Content layout (in the Content Layouts section). Close the Slide Layout task pane.

2. Click in the slide's title placeholder and then type `University Biking Club`.

3. In the lower placeholder, click the Insert Diagram or Organization Chart button.

4. Verify that Organization Chart is chosen in the Diagram Gallery dialog box and then choose OK.

5. Enter the following data in the top-level (manager) box: `Lucinda Smith, President`

6. Enter the following data in the three lower-level (subordinate) boxes:
```
Heather Parks, Vice President
Grace Jones, Treasurer
David Reams, Secretary
```

7. Click outside the boxes (but within the organization chart object) to better view your data.

8. Save the presentation as `Club Organization`.

Keep the organization chart activated and your presentation open for the next exercise, in which you format the chart.

4. Modifying an Organization Chart

After looking over your organization chart, you decide to jazz it up a bit by formatting it.

1. Verify that your *Club Organization* presentation is still open and that the organization chart is selected. (Hint: You should see a rope-like border around the organization chart if it is selected.)

2. With your organization chart selected, click the Font Color button's drop-down list arrow. Choose the dark blue color box to apply that color to the entire organization chart's text.

3. With your organization chart still selected, click the AutoFormat button on the Organization Chart toolbar.

4. Preview several of the styles in the Organization Chart Style Gallery. When you're finished experimenting, click the 3-D Color style and then choose Apply.

5. Click the manager box (*Lucinda Smith, President*) to select it.

6. On the Organization Chart toolbar, click the Layout button and then choose Right Hanging from the list.

7. Verify that the manager box is still selected. On the Organization Chart toolbar, click the Insert Shape drop-down list arrow and then choose Subordinate from the list.

8. In the newly-added subordinate box, enter `Tracy Johnson, Publicity`.

9. Drag over the text (*Tracy Johnson, Publicity*) in the new subordinate box and then click the Font Color button to apply the dark blue color.

10. Click outside the organization chart.

11. Print a copy of your slide.

12. Save your changes to the *Club Organization* presentation;, then close it.

Keep PowerPoint running if you plan to complete additional exercises.

Challenge

Challenge exercises expand on or are somewhat related to skills presented in the lessons. Each exercise provides a brief narrative introduction followed by instructions in a numbered step format that are not as detailed as those in the Skill Drill section.

1. Creating a Data Chart

You need to create a presentation that includes sales data for your company. Because PowerPoint excels at creating good-looking charts, you decide to use it to develop the presentation.

1. Create a new, one-slide presentation. Use the Title and Content layout for the slide and then close the Slide Layout task pane.

2. Create a column chart with the title `Five Year Summary`, using the following data:

	1997	1998	1999	2000	2001
Sales	104	135	125	140	150
Expenses	65	89	67	60	88

3. Change the chart type to at least five other chart types. When you're finished, change the chart to a 2-D clustered bar chart.

4. Change the color for the Expenses data series to red. Change the color for the Sales data series to dark blue.

5. Save the presentation as **Sales Summary**.

6. Print one copy of your presentation (as a slide); then close it.

Keep PowerPoint running if you plan to complete additional exercises.

2. Creating and Formatting an Organization Chart

Your boss wants you to create an organization chart to share at an upcoming staff meeting. You decide to use PowerPoint to create this type of chart.

1. Create a new presentation. Apply the Title and Content layout to the first (and only) slide. Close the Slide Layout task pane.

2. Enter **Our Company** in the title placeholder of the slide.

3. Create an organization chart and then add the following data to the chart:
   Joseph Lowell, President
   Rebecca Cory, Sales
   Eugene Stegall, Production
   Sarah Jones, Marketing

4. Format the text for the manager box (*Joseph Lowell, President*) as bold and italic. Format the text in all the other boxes as italic (no bold).

5. Apply the Gradient style to your organization chart.

6. Change the layout for the chart to the <u>B</u>oth Hanging layout. (Hint: If you are unsure how to apply this layout, review Skill Drill Exercise #4 or research Help.)

7. Print your organization chart.

8. Save the presentation as **Company Structure**; then close it.

Keep PowerPoint running if you plan to complete additional exercises.

3. Changing Chart Types

You've previously created a stacked column chart that shows expenses as a percentage of income. To spiff up the chart, you decide to change colors and patterns.

1. Open *ep1-0505* and save it as **Income**.

2. Using the Chart Type drop-down list, change the chart to each of the following types:
   - Area Chart
   - 3-D Area Chart
   - 3-D Surface Chart
   - Bar Chart
   - 3-D Bar Chart
   - Radar Chart
   - Column Chart
   - 3-D Column Chart
   - Line Chart
   - 3-D Line Chart
   - (XY) Scatter Chart
   - 3-D Cylinder Chart
   - 3-D Cone Chart
   - 3-D Pyramid Chart

3. Change the chart to a 3-D Bar Chart and then display the Chart Type dialog box. Choose the *Stacked bar with a 3-D visual effect* type; then click OK.

4. Format the Income data series in blue. Choose a Gradient fill effect. (Hint: Click the Fill Effects button in the Format Data Series dialog box.) Choose a <u>V</u>ertical Shading style.

5. Format the Expenses data series in red, and apply a Gradient fill effect with the same <u>V</u>ertical Shading style you used for the Income data series.

6. Save, print, and close your *Income* presentation.

Keep PowerPoint running if you plan to complete additional exercises.

4. Working with a Pie Chart

You've created a chart that shows your company's percentage of market share. However, you want to modify the chart to emphasize how well your company is doing. To do so, you rely on Microsoft Graph's features.

1. Open *ep1-0506* and save it as `Market Share.`

2. Activate Microsoft Graph for the chart object; then close the datasheet.

3. Change the pie chart to 3-D and then format each of the slices as follows:
Bell Manufacturing—format with the White marble texture
Cory Manufacturing—format with the Paper bag texture
Hitt Manufacturing—format with Pink tissue paper texture
Lowell Manufacturing—format with Purple mesh texture

4. Drag the wedge that represents *Bell Mfg.* away from the rest of the pie chart to emphasize its data.

5. Format the chart's background (Chart Area) in a red that matches the template's color.

6. Format the Legend using a blue that matches the template's color.

7. Resize and move the chart area so that it takes up approximately 30% less room on the slide and is centered in the middle of the available space.

8. Print a copy of your slide.

9. Save the *Market Share* presentation; then close it.

Keep PowerPoint open if you plan to complete additional exercises.

Discovery Zone exercises require advanced knowledge of topics presented in *essentials* lessons, application of skills from multiple lessons, or self-directed learning of new skills. Each exercise is independent of the others so that you may complete the exercises in any order.

1. Finding Out More about Microsoft Graph

You're a newly-hired employee in the Information Systems Department at a company. Charts are extremely popular at your organization. So that you can do a better job of helping those in your company, you decide to research how to use Microsoft Graph more effectively.

Using the Help system, find out the following:

- How can you format data series using various fill effects?
- What options are available to format a legend?
- What options are available to format a chart's background?
- What options are available to format data walls and gridlines?
- How can you change a column chart to other shapes (such as pyramids)?
- How can you change one data series to a cone shape and another data series (on the same chart) to a cylinder shape?

- What is the purpose of a radar chart?
- How can you use a doughnut chart?
- What similarities are there between doughnut charts and pie charts? What differences are there between them?

Outline the information you find in a logical, easy-to-follow sequence. (If you're familiar with Word, consider entering this information in a Word document.)

Practice using each of the features you researched on a chart. Then present the information to at least one other user.

Keep PowerPoint running if you plan to complete additional exercises.

2. Finding Out More about Organization Charts

Several people in your business use organization charts. You decide to research how to create this type of chart more effectively.

Using the Help system, find out the following:

- Which options are available to format lines on your chart?
- Which options are available to format boxes on your chart?
- How can you change background color for your chart?
- How do you align text?
- What are different ways of selecting boxes?
- How can you use a different layout (or style) for your chart?
- How can you adjust the view to better see your chart?
- What drawing tools are available to create organization charts? How are they used?
- How can you change the default setup for a new organization chart so that only one box is initially displayed?

Outline the information you find in a logical, easy-to-follow sequence. (If you're familiar with Word, consider entering this information in a Word document.)

Practice using each of the features you researched on an organization chart; then present the information to at least one other user.

Keep PowerPoint running if you plan to complete additional exercises.

3. Developing a Data Chart

Due to rising costs, you need more money for college expenses. To illustrate this to your parents, you prepare a PowerPoint presentation to take with you on your next visit home.

Create a new presentation. Use the Title and Content layout for the first (and only) slide in your presentation. Close the Slide Layout task pane.

Enter `College expenses are increasing!` in the title placeholder. Then create a column chart to illustrate the following information:

	1st year	2nd year	3rd year
Tuition	10000	11500	13000
Room/Board	4000	4500	4800
Books	400	450	475
Misc.	300	300	300

View your column chart by row and by column. Add a Data Table, remove it, and then click the By Row button to view your data in that manner. (Hint: If you're unsure how to work with these features, check out Help.)

Display your chart using each of the chart types and subtypes available in Microsoft Graph. Develop two lists: one that lists which chart types are appropriate for the data, and one that lists which chart types are not appropriate.

Display your data using the *Stacked column with a 3-D visual effect* subtype. Format the chart using either textures or gradient effects. Also change the color for the Books data series to red.

Save the presentation as **Rising College Expenses**. Print your presentation; then close it.

Keep PowerPoint running if you plan to complete additional exercises.

4. Developing a Numerical Chart

As treasurer of the University Biking Club you track how club dues have been spent over the last two years. Because you want to share this information in an understandable way at your next meeting, you create and format a column chart using PowerPoint.

Create a new presentation. Use the Title and Content layout for the first (and only) slide in your presentation. Close the Slide Layout task pane.

Enter **Dues… where do they go?** in the title placeholder; then create a column chart to illustrate the following information:

	2000	2001
Club Activities	1200	1350
Newsletter	350	375
Advertisements	89	125
Contributions	500	500

View your column chart by row and by column. Add a Data Table, remove it, and then click the By Row button to view your data in that manner.

Display your chart using each of the chart types and subtypes available in Microsoft Graph. Finally, choose the *Stacked column with a 3-D visual effect* subtype. Format the chart using a different texture for each data series.

Save the presentation as **Club Dues**. Print your presentation; then close it.

Working with Electronic Slide Shows

Objectives

In this project, you learn how to

- ✔ Add Slide Transitions
- ✔ Use Animation Schemes
- ✔ Animate Objects
- ✔ Time the Slide Show Presentation
- ✔ Use the Annotation Pen
- ✔ Use the Meeting Minder

Key terms introduced in this project include

- ❏ action items
- ❏ animation schemes
- ❏ annotate
- ❏ annotation pen
- ❏ Meeting Minder
- ❏ multimedia
- ❏ rehearse timings
- ❏ slide transition
- ❏ triggering

Why Would I Do This?

When you're giving a presentation, you want to make the strongest possible impression. Although you want your content to be center stage, PowerPoint includes a number of techniques you can use to emphasize the content *and* command your audience's attention at the same time. In this project, you learn a variety of ways to automate your presentation. Each of the techniques can help focus your audience's attention on your ideas.

Visual Summary

One way to keep people's attention is to change the way one slide replaces another during an electronic slide show—the ***slide transition***. You can set transitions in the Slide Transition task pane (see Figure 6.1).

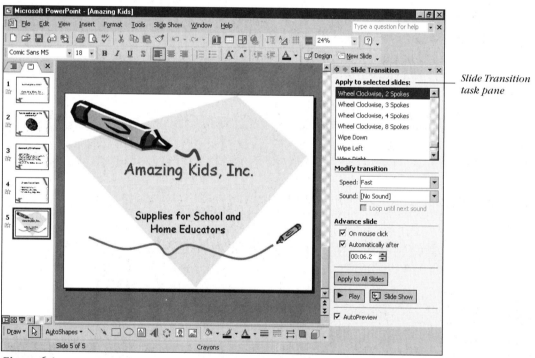

Figure 6.1

You can also use PowerPoint's built-in ***animation schemes***. These animation schemes include predesigned transitions that are categorized by the effect you want to achieve—such as subtle or exciting. Another way to create anticipation (and control the flow of information) is to animate the text so that your bullet points display one at a time. You can also animate objects to control the flow of information and redirect the audience's attention. In Project 5 you learned how to animate chart elements; you use a similar process and the Custom Animation task pane to animate objects (see Figure 6.2).

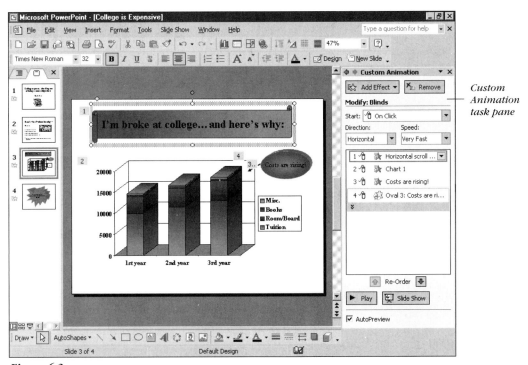

Custom Animation task pane

Figure 6.2

Finally, to help you keep track of ideas that pop up during a presentation, you can use the Meeting Minder. You use this feature to develop meeting minutes or action items onscreen. For example, when you enter information in the Meeting Minder dialog box, PowerPoint automatically creates a set of action items as a new presentation slide (see Figure 6.3). As a finishing touch for your presentation, you can even print this slide and hand it out to participants as they leave.

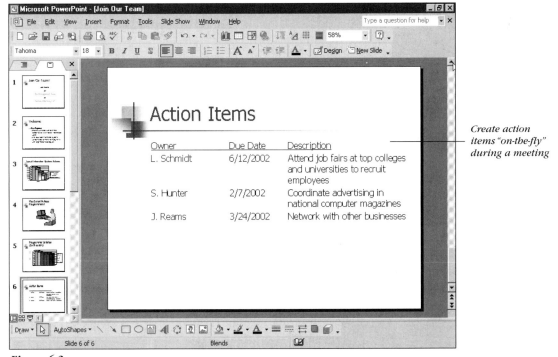

Create action items "on-the-fly" during a meeting

Figure 6.3

To make your presentations more compelling, attention getting, and professional, take a look at these techniques now.

Lesson 1: Adding Slide Transitions

In Project 3, "Viewing and Restructuring Presentations," you learned how to move through a presentation in Slide Show view. By now, you've probably run some other slide shows as well. As you ran the slide shows, you probably noticed that each new slide instantly replaced the previous one.

However, you'll be glad to know that you can change the way one slide moves to the next by using a slide transition. A slide transition is a visual effect that changes how one slide replaces another. Using PowerPoint's built-in slide transitions helps you make more of an impact during an onscreen presentation. For example, you can set up a slide to fade, wipe, or dissolve into another. Furthermore, you can set a slide transition for a single slide or for all slides in the presentation.

The easiest way to add transitions is to use the Slide Transition task pane. Try adding some transitions now.

To Add Slide Transitions

❶ Start PowerPoint, if necessary. Open *ep1-0601*, and save it as Creative Kids.
The presentation is displayed in Normal view. It's generally easiest to add slide transitions in Normal view (or Slide Sorter view) because you can see thumbnails of all the slides.

❷ Choose Slide Show, Slide Transition from the menu.
The Slide Transition task pane is displayed (see Figure 6.4).

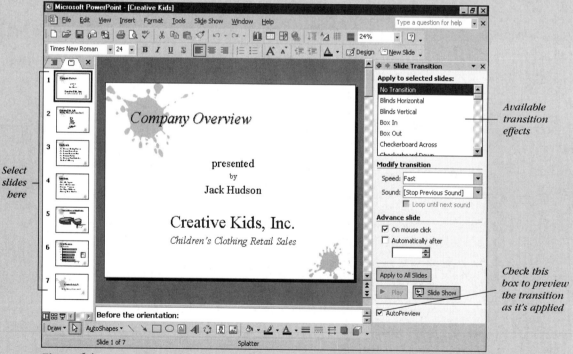

Figure 6.4

❸ Select Slide 1 on the Slides tab, and check the AutoPreview box in the Slide Transition task pane (if necessary).
You select a slide before applying a transition so that PowerPoint will add the transition to the correct slide.

❹ Click Checkerboard Across in the Apply to selected slides list.

To Add Slide Transitions

PowerPoint applies the slide transition to the slide and "plays" it so that you can preview the effect. In addition, an animation icon appears next to the slide on the Slides tab to indicate that it includes animation (see Figure 6.5).

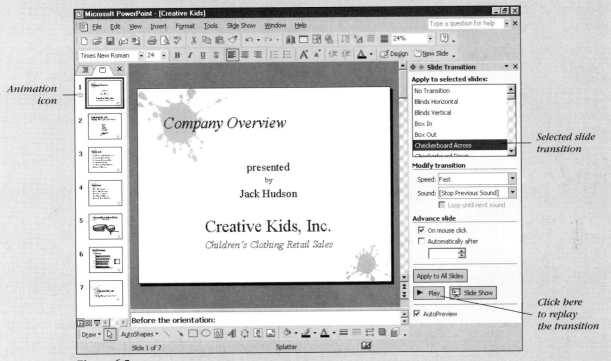

Figure 6.5

⑤   Click the Play button at the bottom of the Slide Transition task pane.

The slide transition replays so that you can again see it. Alternately, you can click the animation icon to preview the slide transition. (If you'd like, click several of the available slide transitions. When you finish experimenting, choose Checkerboard Across again.)

You can add different slide transitions to each individual slide in a presentation. However, it's less distracting for most audiences to use only a handful of transitions for a presentation. One way to do this is to apply the same transition to several slides at once.

⑥   On the Slides tab, click Slide 1, press and hold ⬆Shift and then click Slide 4.

All the intervening slides are selected, as shown by the dark borders around each (see Figure 6.6).

(Continues)

To Add Slide Transitions (Continued)

Figure 6.6

7 **In the Slide Transition task pane, scroll down through the list of available transitions and then click Dissolve.**
The transition is applied to all the selected slides, as indicated by the animation icons on the Slides tab. Now try applying a single slide transition to all the slides in the presentation.

8 **On the list of available slide transitions, click Fade Smoothly and then click the Apply to All Slides button in the Slide Transition task pane.**
The slide transition is applied to all the slides in the presentation. After you add slide transitions, it's handy to view your presentation as an electronic slide show.

9 **In the Slide Transition task pane, click the Slide Show button.**
The slide show begins.

10 **Click the left mouse button as many times as is necessary to completely advance through the slide show.**
The presentation redisplays in Normal view. Now try removing some of the slide transitions. To do so, first select the slides.

11 **Select Slides 2–3 on the Slides tab and then choose No Transition at the top of the Apply to selected slides list.**
The slide transitions (and the animation icons) are removed from the slides.

12 **Save your changes to the *Creative Kids* presentation.**
Keep the presentation open and PowerPoint running for the next lesson, in which you learn how to use animation schemes.

To extend your knowledge...

More about Slide Transitions

As you begin to use PowerPoint's slide transitions, you'll find a wealth of options you can use in the Slide Transition task pane. For example, you can control the speed of the slide transition or even add sound. To regulate the speed at which the slide transition plays, select the slide(s) and then choose an option from the Speed drop-down list. To make a sound play during a transition, select the slide(s) to which you want to add the sound and then choose options on the Sound drop-down list. Just make sure you don't add so many transition effects that they distract from your main message!

Lesson 2: Using Animation Schemes

An effective way to grab an audience's attention is to animate your text during a slide show so you can help them focus on important points, control the flow of information, or simply add interest to your presentation. For example, you can have your bullet points display one by one to prevent your audience from losing focus by reading ahead on a slide. The easiest way to animate text is to rely on PowerPoint's animation schemes. Animation schemes are pre-set visual effects that you can apply to text on slides. PowerPoint's animation schemes also include slide transitions, which replace any slide transitions you've previously applied. Try your hand now at applying animation schemes.

To Use Animation Schemes

1 **Make sure that the *Creative Kids* presentation is displayed in Normal view and then select Slide 3 on the Slides tab.**
Because Slide 3 has bullet points, you can apply an animation scheme so that PowerPoint will display, or build, them separately.

2 **Choose Slide Show, Animation Schemes.**
The Animation Schemes section of the Slide Design task pane is displayed (see Figure 6.7).

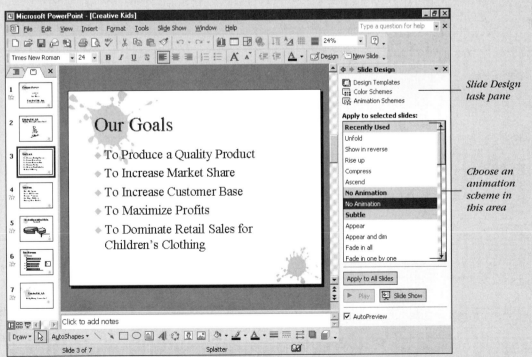

Figure 6.7

(Continues)

To Use Animation Schemes (Continued)

3 **Scroll up and down the Apply to selected slides list.**
Notice that PowerPoint includes a variety of animation schemes—ranging from mild (*Subtle*) to wild (*Exciting*). PowerPoint also places the most recently used animation schemes at the top of the list and includes an option for removing animation (*No Animation*).

4 **Confirm that the AutoPreview box in the task pane is checked.**
Checking this option will ensure that you can preview the animation schemes at the time they are applied.

5 **With Slide 3 still selected, click the *Fade in one by one* animation scheme (in the *Subtle* category).**
The animation scheme is applied to your slide.

6 **With Slide 3 still selected, click the *Big title* animation scheme (in the *Exciting* category).**

7 **With Slide 3 still selected, click the *Ascend* animation scheme (in the *Moderate* category).**
If you want, click several other animation schemes in the Slide Design task pane. When you're finished experimenting, choose *Ascend*.

8 **Select Slide 4 on the Slides tab and then click *Bounce* (in the *Exciting* category).**
Now try viewing your animations as a slide show.

9 **Press Ctrl+Home and then click the Slide Show button in the task pane.**

10 **Click as many times as is necessary to completely advance through the slide show and redisplay your presentation in Normal view.**
Now remove one of the animation schemes.

11 **Select Slide 4 on the Slides tab and then choose No Animation in the Slide Design task pane.**
The animation is removed from the selected slide.

12 **Save your changes to the *Creative Kids* presentation.**
Keep the presentation open and PowerPoint running for the next lesson, in which you animate objects.

To extend your knowledge...

Setting Custom Animation for Text

You can exert even more control over how text animates by setting custom animation. To do this, select the placeholder that includes the text you want to animate and then choose Slide Show, Custom Animation. In the Custom Animation task pane, click Add Effect and then choose options from the displayed menu.

Lesson 3: Animating Objects

In the previous lesson you learned how to work with animation schemes; in Project 5, "Working with Charts," you animated chart elements. Because of these previous experiences, you've probably already realized that you can animate almost any object on a slide, including clip art images, placeholders, and drawn objects. In this lesson you'll expand your previous knowledge as you learn how to add custom animation to slide objects. These effects will play in sequence during a slide show each time you click the mouse—an event known as *triggering* a sequence.

You can add animation to objects as they enter the slide by displaying the Custom Animation task pane and then choosing the Entrance option on the Add Effect menu. You can also add animation to objects that will display when the objects "leave" the slide by choosing the Exit option on the Add Effect menu. Finally, you can add animation, such as text that becomes larger, to a slide object without having it enter or exit the slide. You do this by choosing the Emphasis option on the Add Effect menu. Try adding some animation effects to objects now.

To Animate Objects

❶ Make sure the *Creative Kids* presentation is still open. Click Slide 2 on the Slides tab and then click in the title placeholder.
The placeholder is the first object that you want to animate.

❷ Choose Slide Show, Custom Animation.
The Custom Animation task pane is displayed. You can add animation effects to an object by selecting it and then clicking the Add Effect button.

❸ Verify that the title placeholder on Slide 2 is selected and then click the Add Effect button.
The Add Effect button's menu is displayed (see Figure 6.8). You can choose Entrance to add animation as the placeholder is initially displayed; choose Exit to make the object disappear (with animation) from the slide. Finally, you can choose Emphasis to add visual effects without making the object appear or disappear.

Animation will be applied to the selected object

The Add Effect button's menu options

Figure 6.8

❹ Click Entrance, More Effects.
The Add Entrance Effect dialog box is displayed (see Figure 6.9). Notice that this dialog box includes a wealth of effects, categorized as *Basic*, *Subtle*, *Moderate*, and *Exciting*.

(Continues)

To Animate Objects (Continued)

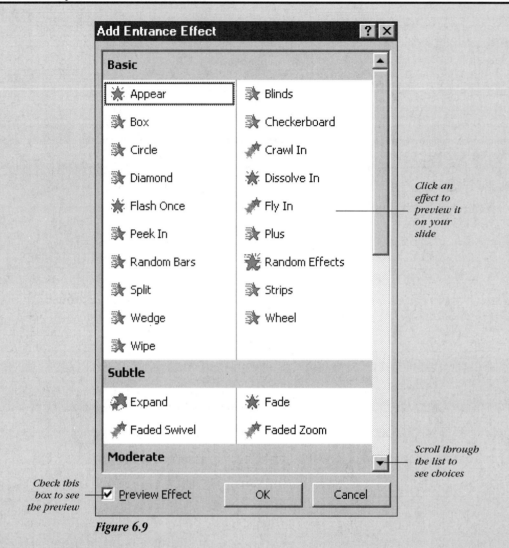

Figure 6.9

You can click an effect in this dialog box and then "preview" it on your slide.

5 **Verify that the Preview Effect box is checked; then click several effects in the Add Entrance Effect dialog box.**
Each effect you click is "played" on the slide.

6 **Click the Dissolve In effect in the Basic category and then click OK.**
Now try adding an animation effect to the clip art object on the slide.

7 **Click the clip art image to select it.**

8 **In the Custom Animation task pane, click Add Effect, Entrance, Fly In.**
The animation is applied to the selected object. Additionally, the order of animation is shown on the Custom Animation list and on the numbered tags (see Figure 6.10).

To Animate Objects

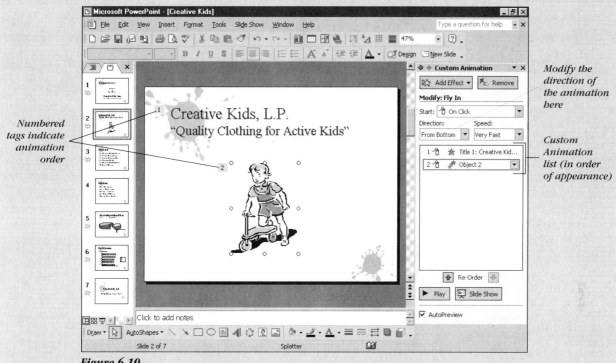

Figure 6.10

9 **With the clip art object still selected, click the Direction drop-down list arrow on the Custom Animation list.**

10 **Choose From Right.**
The clip art object appears to "fly in" from the right side of the slide.

11 **Click the Play button in the Custom Animation task pane.**
The animation for the slide plays.

12 **Press F5 and then click the mouse to advance through the slide show.**
Notice that each mouse click "triggers" an event, such as an animation or the display of a slide.

13 **When the slide show ends, close the Custom Animation task pane, and save the changes to the *Creative Kids* presentation.**
Keep the presentation open and PowerPoint running for the next lesson, in which you set slide timings.

To extend your knowledge...

More about Animation Schemes

You can apply animation schemes for several slides simultaneously by first selecting the slides and then choosing the animation scheme you want. You can also change the order that the animations appear by selecting an animation on the Custom Animation list and then clicking the Re-Order up and down arrows. Finally, you can delete an animation by selecting it on the Custom Animation list and then clicking the Remove button.

Lesson 4: Timing the Slide Show Presentation

PowerPoint includes a ***rehearse timings*** feature that you can use to time an electronic slide show. This helps you find out how long you're spending on each slide and tracks the presentation's overall length.

You can set up your slide show to display each new slide *automatically* after a certain number of seconds or change slides *manually* only when the left mouse button is clicked. If you plan to use the slide show as a self-running presentation (such as at a trade show or on the Internet), you'll probably opt for the former method. However, if you're presenting the show to a live audience, you'll definitely want control by using manual advance.

Even if you plan to use manual advance, you can rehearse your presentation by using the rehearse timings feature. This is a good way of measuring the overall length of the presentation. To do this, start the rehearse timings feature and then talk through your presentation as if you're giving it to a live audience. When you're finished, you'll have a good idea of the overall length of the presentation, as well as the time spent on each individual slide. Keep in mind that you don't want to spend so long on a slide that your audience loses attention, however. The general rule when using manual advancement is to allow a maximum of two–three minutes per slide.

In contrast, automatic advancement is great if you have an onscreen show that you want to run continually (at a trade show exhibit or on the Internet, for example). When using automatic advancement, you need to spend only as much time on a slide as the average person needs to read it. If the slide stays onscreen too long, people lose interest.

Keeping these benefits in mind, try using the rehearse timings feature now.

To Time the Slide Show Presentation

❶ Select Slide 1 of the *Creative Kids* presentation.
Before proceeding, read through steps 2–5 so that you have a good idea of how to set slide timings.

❷ Choose Slide Show, Rehearse Timings.
The slide show begins—but with a difference. A Rehearsal toolbar displays and keeps track of how many seconds you show each slide. This toolbar also records the overall length of the presentation (see Figure 6.11).

To Time the Slide Show Presentation

Next button

Pause button

Elapsed time for current slide

Elapsed time for entire presentation

Figure 6.11

③ After ten seconds, click the left mouse button to advance to Slide 2.

④ In slides 2–6, set timings of your choice (pause from 5–10 seconds for each bullet point or slide before clicking the mouse button to proceed).

When you finish going through the entire show, PowerPoint displays a message box so you can decide if you want to keep the timings as part of your presentation (see Figure 6.12).

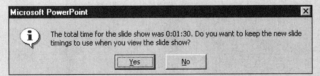

Figure 6.12

⑤ Choose <u>Y</u>es.

The presentation displays in Slide Sorter view. Additionally, the number of seconds used for each slide is shown (see Figure 6.13). Now view your electronic slide show with the new timings.

(Continues)

To Time the Slide Show Presentation (Continued)

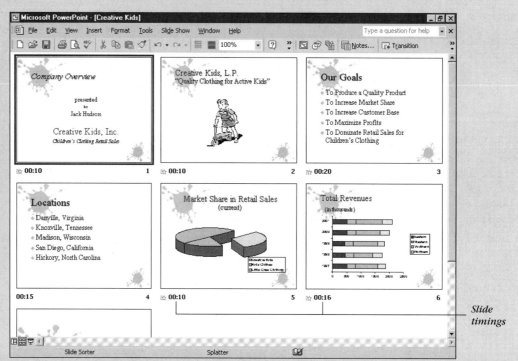

Figure 6.13

❻ **Click Slide 1 and then press** F5.
The show begins, and advances through the slides using the timings you specified.

❼ **When the slide show finishes and the black screen displays, click to exit the slide show.**
The presentation redisplays in Slide Sorter view.

If you have problems...

By default, PowerPoint ends each slide show with a black slide so that the audience redirects their attention to you. It's possible that this option may have been turned off for your system, however. If you like the effect, here's how to turn it back on: Choose Tools, Options, and then click the View tab. Check the *End with black slide* box, and click OK to close the Options dialog box.

❽ **Save the *Creative Kids* presentation and then close it.**
Keep PowerPoint open for the next lesson, in which you learn how to use the annotation pen.

To extend your knowledge...

Setting Up Self-Running Presentations

If you want to use your slide show as a self-running presentation (such as at a trade show), set your slide timings just as you learned in this lesson. Then choose Slide Show, Set Up Show to display the Set Up Show dialog box. Choose *Loop continuously until 'Esc'* and then click OK.

For even more control over a self-running presentation, you can choose *Browsed at a kiosk (full screen)* in the Set Up Show dialog box. This runs the slide show full-screen continuously and restarts the show after five minutes of inactivity. The audience can advance slides manually, but can't make changes to the presentation.

Finally, you can add **multimedia** effects, such as music, sound, and videos to your presentation. To find out how to enhance your presentation with these effects, enter *multimedia* in the Ask a Question box.

Lesson 5: Using the Annotation Pen

Have you ever wished that you could write or draw on a slide during a slide show? Perhaps you want to draw attention to specific information or recapture your audience's attention. Luckily, PowerPoint provides an **annotation pen**, which is an electronic pen that you use with the mouse to **annotate** the slide. Annotating is writing or drawing directly on the slide, and is an effective method of emphasizing information.

The comments you write are not permanent—when you display another slide, they're automatically erased. Alternately, you can erase the notations but continue to display the current slide.

For even more impact, you can change annotation pen colors. For example, you might use white for most of the points that you're trying to make, and then switch to orange for added emphasis. Try using the pen in a presentation now.

To Use the Annotation Pen

1 Open *ep1-0602,* **and save it as** Join Our Team.

2 **Display Slide 3 and then click the Slide Show button.**
The slide show begins. To use the pen, you must activate it by choosing Pen from the slide show shortcut menu.

3 **Right-click to display the shortcut menu and then choose Pointer Options, Pen.**
The pointer changes to an electronic annotation pen. You can use this pen to draw by holding down the left mouse button and dragging.

4 **Drag to draw an arrow emphasizing the salary progression from Systems Support to Systems Analyst (see Figure 6.14).**

(Continues)

To Use the Annotation Pen (Continued)

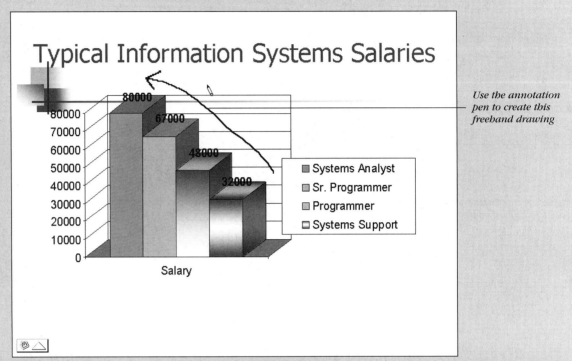

Use the annotation pen to create this freehand drawing

Figure 6.14

The annotation is automatically erased whenever you move to another slide. If you want to continue to display the current slide (but erase the drawing), press E. Try this now.

5 **Press E.**
The drawing is erased. Notice that your pen is still active so that you can write other comments; or you can activate the arrow, which automatically turns off the pen. The easiest way to turn off the pen is to press Esc.

6 **Press Esc.**
The arrow mouse pointer displays and the electronic pen is turned off.

Now try an alternative method of turning on the pen—by pressing Ctrl+P. This method is not only quicker, but also more popular because the audience doesn't see the shortcut menu. Try activating the pen by using this technique.

7 **Press Ctrl+P.**
The electronic pen is activated. Now try changing the pen color.

8 **Right-click to display the shortcut menu and then choose Pointer Options, Pen Color.**
A submenu displays with a list of available pen colors (see Figure 6.15).

To Use the Annotation Pen

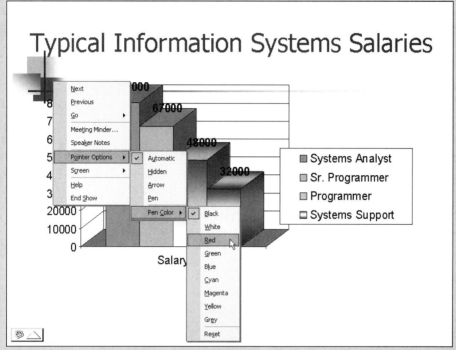

Figure 6.15

9 **Choose Yellow and then draw freehand on your slide to see the new pen color.**
The drawing displays, using the color you indicated. Now try using a keyboard shortcut to switch back to the arrow.

10 **Press Ctrl+A.**
The pen icon changes to an arrow mouse pointer.

11 **Press Esc to stop the slide show.**

12 **Save your *Join Our Team* presentation.**
Leave the presentation open and PowerPoint running for the next lesson, in which you use the Meeting Minder to take electronic notes during a presentation.

If you have problems...

When the annotation pen is active, clicking the left mouse button won't advance the slide show to the next screen or bullet. Instead, it just produces a dot on screen. Press Esc (or Ctrl+A) to change the annotation pen back to an arrow and then click.

Lesson 6: Using the Meeting Minder

The *Meeting Minder* is a PowerPoint feature that helps you take electronic notes during a presentation. You can use this tool to take meeting minutes or record action items. *Action items* are any items that you want to assign to people during a meeting. You can display these items on a new slide at the end of your slide show or even print them.

The Meeting Minder is especially useful during an informal presentation, such as a staff meeting or brainstorming session. Try using this feature now.

To Use the Meeting Minder

❶ In the open *Join Our Team* presentation, click Slide 4 on the Slides tab to select it.

❷ Click the Slide Show button.
This starts the presentation, beginning with the current slide.

❸ Right-click the mouse to display the shortcut menu and then choose Mee**t**ing Minder.
The Meeting Minder dialog box displays with two tabs: Meeting Minutes and Action Items.

❹ Click the Action Items tab.
The Action Items page is displayed (see Figure 6.16).

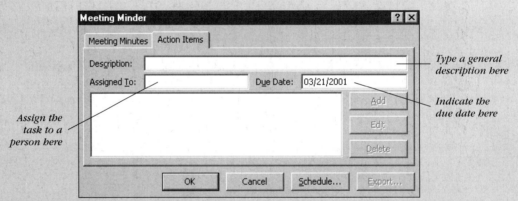

Figure 6.16

❺ In the Des**c**ription text box, type `Attend job fairs at top colleges and universities to recruit employees` and then press `Tab⇥`.
The text you typed is entered in the text box and the insertion point moves to the Assigned To text box.

❻ Type `L. Schmidt` and then press `Tab⇥`.
The insertion point moves to the D**u**e Date text box. By default, this text box displays the current system date.

❼ Enter `6/12/2002` to replace the current system date.
After you create the basic information for an action item, you add it to the list.

❽ Click **A**dd to place the item on the list.
The action item displays on the list, and the text boxes clear so that you can enter other tasks.

❾ Enter the following items in the Action Items page of the Meeting Minder dialog box:

To Use the Meeting Minder

Description	Assigned To	Due Date
Coordinate advertising in national computer magazines	S. Hunter	2/7/2002
Network with other businesses	J. Reams	3/24/2002

10 **Choose OK to close the Meeting Minder dialog box.**
PowerPoint automatically creates a slide with the action items you entered and places it at the end of the presentation.

11 **Press Esc to end the slide show and then press Ctrl + End.**
The slide show ends, and the last slide—your action items—displays, as shown in Figure 6.17. You can display the slide using an overhead projection system, or print it to give it to your participants.

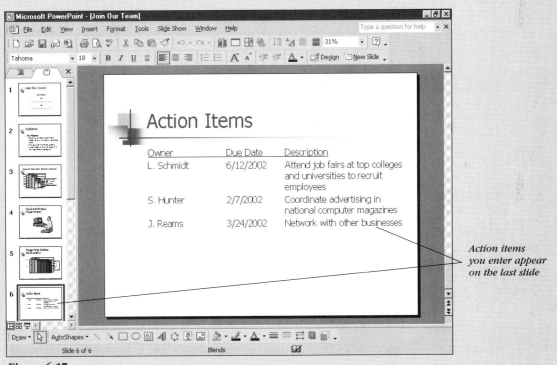

Figure 6.17

12 **With the Action Items slide displayed in Normal view, choose File, Print.**

13 **Make sure that Current slide is chosen in the Print range section and then choose OK.**

14 **Save the *Join Our Team* presentation and then close it.**
Keep PowerPoint running if you plan to complete the end of chapter exercises.

To extend your knowledge...

Exporting Your Meeting Minutes to Word or Outlook

You can export your meeting minutes (or action items) to Word or Outlook. To send the information to Word, click the Export button in the Meeting Minder dialog box. In the Meeting Minder Export dialog box, check the box to *Send meeting minutes and action items to Microsoft Word* and then choose Export Now.

To add the information from the Meeting Minder to your Outlook calendar, click Schedule in the Meeting Minder dialog box.

Summary

In this project you learned some methods for enhancing your presentation when you run it as an onscreen slide show. You learned how to add slide transitions and animations to your slides to control the flow of information and keep your audience's attention. You also rehearsed and timed a slide show, so you could check its overall length. Finally, you practiced using the annotation pen and creating action items with the Meeting Minder feature.

To expand on your knowledge, spend a few minutes exploring Help on these topics. Additionally, complete some of the Skill Drill, Challenge, and Discovery Zone exercises.

Checking Concepts and Terms

Multiple Choice

Circle the letter of the correct answer for each of the following.

1. Which of the following can you use to record action items? [L6]

   a. Minute Taker
   b. Rehearse Timings
   c. Meeting Minder
   d. Custom Animation list

2. For what is the annotation pen used? [L5]

   a. To highlight information during an onscreen presentation
   b. To create a list of action items
   c. To take meeting minutes
   d. To draw objects in Normal view

3. What happens when you use the Action Items feature? [L6]

   a. PowerPoint automatically prints your presentation as an outline
   b. An animation scheme is added to each slide
   c. An Action Items slide is automatically created
   d. Animation is added to all bullet points

4. What are Blinds, Checkerboard Across, and Box In all examples of? [L1]

   a. annotations

   b. action items

   c. meeting minutes

   d. slide transitions

5. Why might you want to add animation to your bullet points? [L3]

   a. To control the flow of information

   b. To keep your audience from reading ahead

   c. To increase interest

   d. All of the above

Discussion

1. Which PowerPoint feature would you use for each of the following situations? (Note: There might be more than one feature you could use for a couple of the situations.) [L1-6]

   ○ You are conducting a brainstorming session and want to create a list of "to-do" items.

   ○ You are running a staff meeting and want to generate some meeting minutes.

   ○ You need to emphasize information while running a slide show.

   ○ You want to prevent your audience from reading ahead on a slide.

   ○ You want to capture your audience's attention.

2. Discuss the pros and cons for using each of the following PowerPoint features in your presentation. Also discuss the pitfalls of overusing the feature. [L1-6]

   ○ Slide transitions

   ○ Animations

   ○ Annotation pen

   ○ Meeting Minder

3. Discuss the advantages of timing your presentation. Also discuss the differences between advancing a slide show manually and automatically. [L4]

Skill Drill exercises *reinforce* project skills. Each skill reinforced is the same, or nearly the same, as a skill presented in the project. Detailed instructions are provided in a step-by-step format.

1. Using Help to Find Out About Slide Shows

You conduct a lot of meetings for a volunteer organization. To help you run the meetings more effectively, you use PowerPoint's slide show feature. To learn more about electronic slide shows, you use Help.

   1. Start PowerPoint and then choose Help, Microsoft PowerPoint Help. If necessary, click the Show button to split the window into two panes.

   2. On the Contents page, double-click the icon for Microsoft PowerPoint Help.

   3. Double-click the Running Presentations icon; then double-click the subtopic, *Running a Presentation*.

   4. Click each of the subtopics listed and read about them. Also write down what you learn about running a slide show before advancing to the next topic.

   5. Close the Help window.

   6. Practice what you learned about running slide shows, using your notes as a guide.

   7. Share what you learn with at least one other user.

Keep PowerPoint running if you plan to complete additional exercises.

2. Adding Slide Transitions and Animations

You're scheduled to conduct a new employee orientation session, but you're concerned that your audience will be bored with the information. To make the meeting more interesting, you decide to add slide transitions and text animations.

1. Open *ep1-0603*, and save it as **Improved Orientation**. Display the presentation in Slide Sorter view, and select Slide 1.
2. Choose Slide Show, Slide Transition to display the Slide Transition task pane. Set the following slide transitions:
   - Choose Box In as the slide transition for Slide 1.
   - Select Slide 2 and choose Box Out as the slide transition.
   - Select Slides 3–4 and choose Checkerboard Across as the slide transition.
   - Select Slide 5 and choose Comb Vertical as the slide transition.
   - Select Slides 6–8 and choose Newsflash as the slide transition.
3. Close the Slide Transition task pane.
4. Select Slide 1, and click the Slide Show button to run your presentation as a slide show. When you're finished, make sure the presentation is displayed in Slide Sorter view.
5. Select Slide 1, and click the Rehearse Timings button on the Slide Sorter toolbar. Make each slide display for between 5–10 seconds.
6. In the Microsoft PowerPoint message box, choose Yes to accept the slide timings and then view the timings in Slide Sorter view.
7. Click the Slide Show button to automatically run the slide show with the slide timings you set.
8. In Slide Sorter view, click the Rehearse Timings button again and set new timings. Choose Yes to accept the new slide timings.
9. Run the slide show again; then save and close the presentation.

Keep PowerPoint running if you plan to complete additional exercises.

3. Using the Annotation Pen

You're trying to convince your parents that you need more money for college expenses. To do so, you give a presentation to them on college expenses, using the annotation pen to emphasize your main points.

1. Open *ep1-0604*, and save it as **College is Expensive**. Display the first presentation slide and then click the Slide Show button.
2. When Slide 1 displays in the slide show, press Ctrl+P to display the annotation pen. Use the pen to underline the word *successful* on the slide.
3. Press Esc (or Ctrl+A) to switch the pen to an arrow. Display Slide 3 in your slide show.
4. Right-click on the slide to display the slide show shortcut menu. Choose Pointer Options, Pen Color, Red.
5. Draw a line from the 1st year column to the 3rd year column to illustrate the increasing costs of college.
6. Use the annotation pen to circle the words *Costs are rising!*.
7. Press Esc (or Ctrl+A) to switch the pen back to a pointer.
8. Press ⏎Enter to display the last presentation slide. Use the pen to circle the word *ME*.
9. Press E to erase the annotation on the slide. Press Esc twice to end the slide show.
10. Save the *College is Expensive* presentation.

Keep the presentation open and PowerPoint running if you plan to complete additional exercises.

4. Adding Animations and Slide Transitions

To add excitement and interest to your presentation, you add animations and slide transitions.

1. Verify that the *College is Expensive* presentation is open from the previous Skill Drill exercise. (If it's not running, open *ep1-0604,* and save it as `College is Expensive`.)
2. Select Slide 1 on the Slides tab and then choose Sli<u>d</u>e Show, Slide <u>T</u>ransition.
3. Choose Blinds Horizontal in the Slide Transition task pane to apply that transition to Slide 1.
4. Click Slide 2 on the Slides tab to select it. Choose Dissolve in the Slide Transition task pane to apply that transition to Slide 2.
5. Select Slide 3 and then choose Box In for the slide transition.
6. In the Slide Transition task pane, click the Sound drop-down list arrow, and choose Cash Register from the list.
7. Click Slide 4 to select it, and choose Wedge for the slide transition.
8. Close the Slide Transition task pane.
9. Click Slide 1 on the Slides tab and then press F5 to run your presentation as a slide show. Press ↵Enter as many times as is necessary to completely advance through the slide show.
10. Save your *College is Expensive* presentation; then close it.

Keep PowerPoint running if you plan to complete the Challenge and Discovery Zone exercises.

Challenge

Challenge exercises expand on or are somewhat related to skills presented in the lessons. Each exercise provides a brief narrative introduction followed by instructions in a numbered step format that are not as detailed as those in the Skill Drill section.

Animating Objects

... re giving a short talk to the local Chamber of Commerce organization about your company's contrib... ns to the community. The meeting is during lunch, and you're concerned that people may get ...y ... er eating a big meal. To keep their attention focused on your presentation, you add some ...ati... ffects to your slides.

...pe ...1-0605, and save it as `Amazing Kids`.

...y ... Slide Transition task pane and then add the following transitions to the presen-

... Fa... Smoothly to Slide 1.

... Circle to Slide 3.

...eel ...ckwise, 2 Spokes to Slide 5.

...c ... Slide 5.

...ar... n from Slide 3.

...nati... schemes to the presentation:

...mation scheme to Slide 3.

...tion ...heme to Slide 4.

...u... s to Slide 2:

...de... ith Blinds as the <u>E</u>ntrance effect.

...ith Fly In as the <u>E</u>ntrance effect.

6. Preview the presentation as a slide show.

7. Save your changes to the *Amazing Kids* presentation and then close it.

8. Close the task pane.

Keep PowerPoint running if you plan to complete additional exercises.

2. Adding Slide Transitions and Animations

For your college speech class, you're presenting a talk on how to give presentations. To help hold the class's attention, you add slide transitions to your PowerPoint presentation.

1. Open *ep1-0606*, and save it as `Giving Presentations`.

2. Display the presentation in Normal view. Use the Slide Transition task pane to add a transition of your choosing to each slide in the presentation. (Hint: Try combining opposite effects, such as using Box In for one slide, and Box Out for the next one. Another example of a possible combination is Cover Down/Uncover Up.)

3. Click the animation icon next to each slide's thumbnail on the Slides tab to preview the transition effect.

4. Add animation schemes to each slide that has a bulleted list. (Choose a different animation for each slide.)

5. Set slide timings; then discuss each slide's information—just as you would for a live audience.

6. View the timings that you set in Slide Sorter view. Run the presentation as a slide show.

7. Set up the slide show to play continuously (loop). (Hint: Use PowerPoint's Help to find out how to do this, or refer to information presented at the end of Lesson 4 of this project.)

8. Run the slide show. When you finish viewing the show, press Esc to end it.

9. Close the task pane.

10. Save the *Giving Presentations* presentation.

Keep the presentation open and PowerPoint running if you plan to complete the next exercise.

3. Using the Annotation Pen

To focus your audience's attention, you decide to use the annotation pen during your speech class presentation. To prepare for the presentation, you practice using the pen.

1. Verify that the *Giving Presentations* presentation is open from the previous Challenge exercise. (If it's not running, open *ep1-0606* and then save it as `Giving Presentations`.)

2. Select Slide 1 and then run the presentation as a slide show.

3. Advance to Slide 4. Use the annotation pen to draw an arrow to each of the subpoints listed on the slide. Erase the drawing and then change the pen color to blue.

4. Practice using the keyboard shortcuts and the shortcut menu to switch between the arrow and the pen.

5. On a blank area of the slide, practice drawing the following items:

- arrow
- square
- circle
- your name (in cursive)
- your company or school name (in cursive)

6. Save your *Giving Presentations* presentation and then close it.

Keep PowerPoint running if you plan to complete additional exercises.

4. Learning More About Animations

You provide technical computer support for a large company. The middle managers (who need to conduct meetings) have asked you to conduct a special training session on usi animation features. To prepare for the training session, you spend a few minutes researching Power-Point's animation features.

1. Use the Ask a Question box to research the following topics:
   - How to set animations for objects
   - How to add sound to animations
   - How to display bulleted points one at a time
2. Use the <u>C</u>ontents page of Help to display all the subpoints in the Creating Presentations, Animating Text and Objects category. Write down what you learn.
3. Use PowerPoint to create a presentation (with a minimum of 20 slides) that outlines the main ways to animate slides and add slide transitions. Apply a design template of your choice. Make sure to also "practice what you preach" and add several slide transitions and animations to the presentation.
4. Share your presentation with at least one other user. Print a copy of the presentation; then, unless your instructor indicates otherwise, close the presentation without saving it.

Keep PowerPoint running if you plan to complete the Discovery Zone exercises.

Discovery Zone exercises require advanced knowledge of topics presented in *essentials* lessons, application of skills from multiple lessons, or self-directed learning of new skills.

1. Learning about Multimedia

You want to incorporate multimedia effects, such as music, sound, and video, in your presentation. Using PowerPoint's Help system and online resources, find out about the following topics:

- How to add music background to a slide
- The difference between adding a clip from the Gallery and adding a clip from a file
- How to add a sound to a slide transition
- How to add a sound when a slide object or chart element is introduced
- How to insert a video in your presentation
- How to resize and move a video

Write down what you learn and then develop a PowerPoint presentation that incorporates multimedia effects. (If you're familiar with Word, you can develop a table instead.) Use the knowledge you gain from the book to develop the best possible presentation. Print the presentation as a series of slides. Finally, give the presentation to your class. When you're finished, close the presentation without saving it.

2. Creating Presentations

Create each of the following types of presentations:

- A presentation you can use in a business setting
- A presentation you can use to promote a club, team, or organization
- A presentation you can use in a college class

Include the following elements in each presentation:

- A chart
- A bulleted list
- A clip art object

After you initially develop the content (and objects, such as clip art and charts) for the presentations, automate the presentations by using the following PowerPoint features:

- Slide transitions
- Animation schemes
- Multimedia clips (sound, music, or video)
- Chart animations
- Slide timings

Give your presentations to your class. Use the feedback that your classmates offer to revise and improve the presentations; then present the slide shows a second time.

Save all your presentations. When you finish working, close the presentations, and exit PowerPoint.

Producing Output

Objectives

In this project, you learn how to

✔ Add Speaker Notes
✔ Print Speaker Notes and Handouts
✔ Use Page Setup
✔ Use Advanced Print Settings
✔ Pack Up Your Presentation
✔ Use Web Page Preview
✔ Publish a Presentation to the Web

Key terms introduced in this project include

❑ frame
❑ handouts
❑ homepage
❑ Hypertext Markup
Language (HTML)
❑ Internet
❑ landscape
orientation
❑ notes box
❑ orientation

❑ Pack and Go Wizard
❑ portrait orientation
❑ PowerPoint Viewer
❑ slide image
❑ speaker notes
❑ upload
❑ Web browser
❑ Web Page Preview
❑ World Wide Web
(WWW)

Why Would I Do This?

You've spent considerable time creating and reworking that winning presentation. However, after you finally put the finishing touches on it, you probably want to tap into the various ways to output it. Outputting involves displaying and printing (or even converting to another format) the results of your hard work. While most people think of output primarily in terms of printing a presentation, there are in fact, a number of other ways to produce output. For example, you can create overhead transparencies or 35mm slides. You can also publish your presentation as a Web page.

Visual Summary

In this project you learn the nuts and bolts for creating various forms of output. You also learn how to use the Page Setup feature to "tweak" how the presentation will display and print (see Figure 7.1).

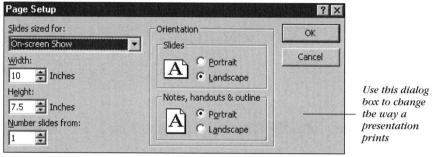

Use this dialog box to change the way a presentation prints

Figure 7.1

To bolster your skills even more, you find out how to print slides using a variety of formats and how to create speaker notes and handouts (see Figure 7.2). You can also output the presentation and take it with you using Pack and Go.

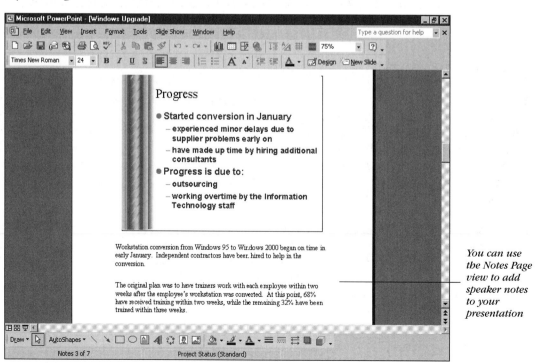

You can use the Notes Page view to add speaker notes to your presentation

Figure 7.2

Finally, one of the slickest things about PowerPoint is its tight, seamless integration with the Internet, especially the Internet's graphical, user-friendly side—the ***World Wide Web (WWW)***. For example, PowerPoint has built-in Web support, so that anyone who uses the Web can view your presentations. As a result, saving and publishing your presentation as a Web page allows you to share it with an extremely large audience—virtually everyone connected to the Internet. All they need to view your presentation is a Web browser, software you use to view Web pages. Popular examples of this type of software include Internet Explorer and Netscape Navigator. You can use the Publish as Web Page dialog box to save your presentation as a series of Web pages (see Figure 7.3).

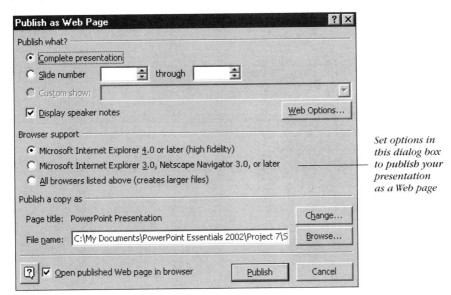

Set options in this dialog box to publish your presentation as a Web page

Figure 7.3

The ability to output your presentation using such a variety of methods will greatly increase how effectively you can use the program, so come along and learn new ways to output the presentation now.

Lesson 1: Adding Speaker Notes

Have you ever been in the middle of an important presentation, when your mind suddenly went blank? Or been asked a particularly tricky question by someone in your audience? In either case, if you had ***speaker notes*** to rely on, you probably got through the situation without too much trouble. Speaker notes are just what their name implies—supporting data, quotations, or illustrations that you can use when giving a presentation. Although you may have developed notes in the past by writing on a legal pad, PowerPoint includes a feature that helps you create the electronic equivalent—from right within the program.

In this lesson we'll help you learn how to quickly add speaker notes so that supporting data is right at your fingertips. Here's how it works: Each slide can have corresponding notes that you create. You can prepare speaker notes when you initially develop your presentation or you can add them later. You can use the Notes Page view to add your notes, or use the Notes pane in Normal view. Try using both methods of preparing notes now.

To Add Speaker Notes

1 **In PowerPoint, open** *ep1-0701* **and then save it as** Safety Campaign.
Now switch to Notes Page view—a view which provides a slide image and a notes box area.

2 **Make sure that Slide 1 is displayed and then choose** **View, Notes Page.**
The current slide is shown in Notes Page view (see Figure 7.4). This view shows a small-scale version of the slide, called a ***slide image***, as well as an area where you can enter your notes—the ***notes box***.

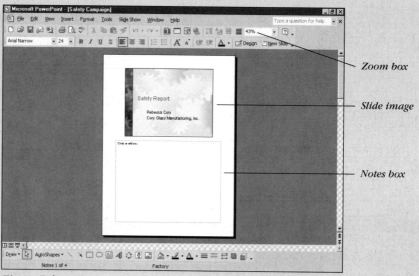

Figure 7.4

You've probably noticed that the notes box area is too small to reasonably view (or enter) text. Luckily, you can enlarge the view by using the Zoom box.

3 **Click the Zoom box's drop-down list arrow, and choose** **75%.**
The view is enlarged so that you can enter your notes (see Figure 7.5). Because the monitor size (and screen settings) vary from one computer to the next, don't be concerned if your screen looks slightly different from that shown in the figure.

To Add Speaker Notes

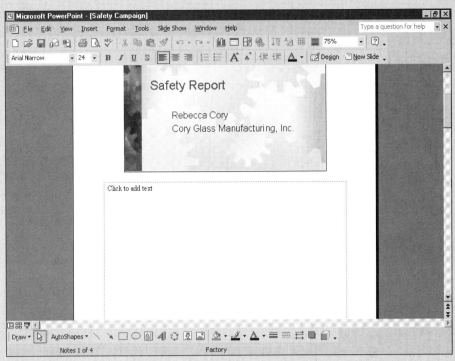

Figure 7.5

Now create your speaker notes. Remember that these notes are usually used as reminders for yourself—to keep you on track and to make sure you don't forget any critical information during a presentation.

4 **Click in the notes box and type the following:**
(Make sure to play Bach's Brandenburg Concerto #5 as people arrive, and then fade it out.)

"Welcome! I'm glad to be presenting this safety report to you today. Here at Cory Glass Manufacturing, we have some good news about our safety record, as well as some challenges ahead."

The text you type is entered in the notes box and becomes part of the slide. Even when you switch to another view, the notes are still attached to the slide.

Another method of entering notes is to use the Notes pane in Normal view. Try using this method now.

5 **Click the Normal View button and then press PgDn to display Slide 2.**
This is the slide to which you want to attach some notes. By default, however, the Notes pane is so small that it's hard to see your notes. To make it easier to enter (and view) your notes, it's a good idea to first resize the Notes pane.

6 **Move your mouse pointer over the horizontal divider that separates the Notes pane and Slide pane until a two-headed resizing arrow displays (see Figure 7.6).**

(Continues)

To Add Speaker Notes (Continued)

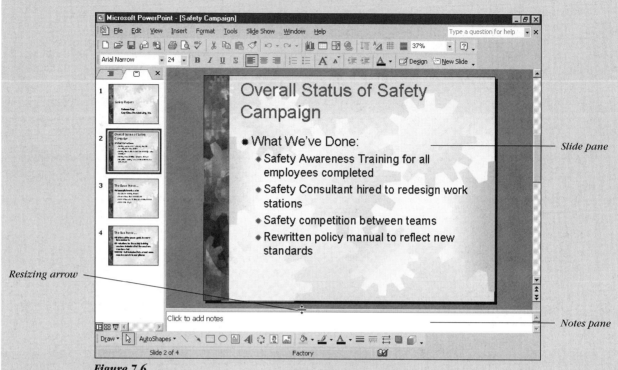

Figure 7.6

❼ **Drag the resizing arrow upward until the screen is evenly split between the Slide and Notes panes, and release the mouse button.**

The Notes and Slide panes are resized so that you can more easily see notes as you enter them (see Figure 7.7). Now try entering your notes.

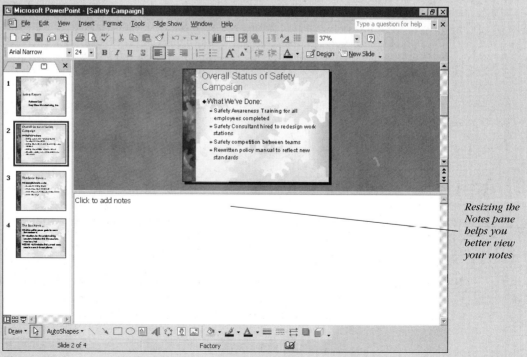

Figure 7.7

To Add Speaker Notes

8 **Click in the Notes pane and enter the following text:**

Safety Awareness Training: The 1-hour mandatory program was completed by all 275 employees during the last two months.

Safety Consultant: We used Safety Engineers, Inc. from Columbus, Ohio to work closely with employees and managers. The new workstations were designed with input from our employees, and surpass OSHA, state, and local regulations.

Safety Competition: We want to thank Lauren Clark for this idea! The competition is 2 months long, and measures safety criteria (lost time accidents, sick days, etc.) for the 3 teams involved. Each member of the winning team will receive an extra 1% salary bonus. The competition is still going on, and will finish at the end of the month.

Now resize your Slide and Notes panes back to their original sizes.

9 **Drag the horizontal divider between the Slide and Notes pane downward until each pane displays by using its original size; then release the mouse button.**
The slide appears in Normal view. Notice that the Notes pane automatically includes a vertical scrollbar that you can use to scroll through your notes whenever the notes don't completely display in the Notes pane.

10 **Save the *Safety Campaign* presentation.**
Keep the presentation running for the next lesson, in which you print the notes.

To extend your knowledge...

Entering Notes During a Slide Show

It's most common to enter and view notes in the Normal or Notes Page views. However, you can also view and enter notes during a running slide show. To do this, right-click your mouse to display the Slide Show shortcut menu and then choose Speaker Notes. View, enter, or modify the text in the Speaker Notes window that displays. When you finish working with the notes, click the Close button.

Formatting Speaker Notes

You can format speaker notes—but only in Notes Page view. Choose View, Notes Page and then use buttons on the Formatting toolbar to format the notes, just as you would for text on your slides.

Lesson 2: Printing Speaker Notes and Handouts

Your speaker notes would be of little value if you couldn't print them for a ready reference during your presentation. Luckily, printing your notes is straightforward and relatively easy. To print the notes, choose File, Print, and then choose Notes Pages in the Print what area of the Print dialog box.

You can also print **handouts** to give to your audience. By default, PowerPoint includes options to print one, two, three, four, six, or nine slides per page as handouts. In contrast to the notes pages, handouts include only the slide's contents, not the accompanying notes. You print handouts the same way you print notes—by specifying the type of output you want in the Print what area of the Print dialog box.

Try printing speaker notes and handouts for your presentation now.

To Print Speaker Notes and Handouts

❶ With Slide 2 in the open *Safety Campaign* presentation displayed, choose File, Print.

The Print dialog box is displayed (see Figure 7.8). You used this dialog box in Project 1 to print slides and outlines. In this lesson, you use it to print notes and handouts.

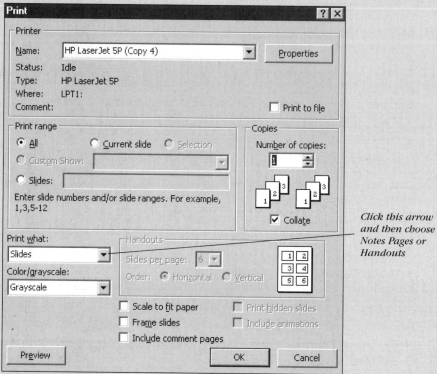

Figure 7.8

❷ Click the Print what drop-down list arrow and then choose Notes Pages from the list.

This specifies to PowerPoint that you want to print the speaker notes associated with the current presentation.

The notes generally print with a better appearance if you frame the slide image, notes box, and page. A *frame* is simply a border that surrounds the slide element you choose. You can add frames by checking the Frame slides box.

❸ Check the Frame slides box, if necessary.

You can print the current slide, print all presentation slides, or pick and choose just those that you want. You specify which slides PowerPoint should print in the Print range area of the dialog box.

❹ In the Print range area, choose the Current slide option button.

After selecting the options you want, you're ready to print.

❺ Make sure that your printer is turned on and then choose OK.

The notes for your current slide print. Now try printing audience handouts.

❻ Choose File, Print to redisplay the Print dialog box.

❼ Click the Print what drop-down list arrow, and choose Handouts from the list.

When you choose Handouts from the list, the Handouts section of the Print dialog box becomes active (see Figure 7.9). You use this section to designate how you want to set

To Print Speaker Notes and Handouts

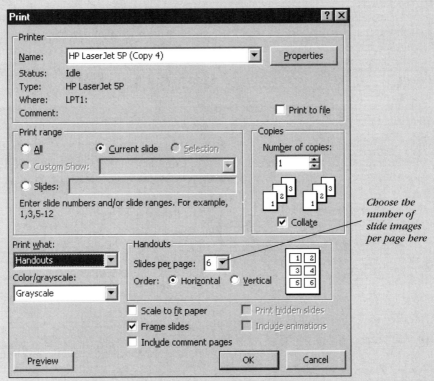

Figure 7.9

up your handouts. For example, you can click the Slides per page drop-down list arrow and choose a different number of slides.

8 **Click the Slides per page drop-down list arrow and then choose 4.**
This specifies that four slide images will print per page.

9 **Make sure the Frame slides box is checked, and that the Print range is set to All.**

 ## If you have problems...

If you don't want to print the presentation (or don't have access to a printer), click the Preview button in the Print dialog box instead of completing the next step. After previewing your file, click the Close button on the Preview window's toolbar and then continue with the lesson.

---

10 **Click OK to print your handouts.**

11 **Save the *Safety Campaign* presentation.**
Keep the presentation open for the next lesson, in which you use the Page Setup feature.

Lesson 3: Using Page Setup

You can use PowerPoint's Page Setup feature to change the slide size or ***orientation***. The orientation of a slide refers to rotation of the slide when viewing or printing it. ***Landscape orientation*** is the layout used where the width of the paper is greater than the height (see Figure 7.10). In contrast, ***portrait orientation*** is the layout used where the height of the page is greater than the width (see Figure 7.11). You can change the orientation of the slides as well as that of the note pages and handouts.

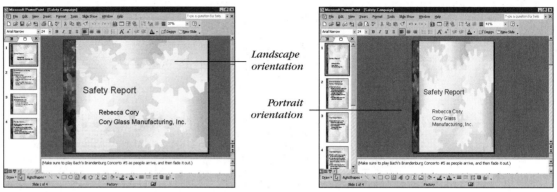

Landscape orientation

Portrait orientation

Figure 7.10   **Figure 7.11**

In this lesson you learn how to use Page Setup to make modifications in size and orientation to your presentation slides.

To Use Page Setup

❶ **Make sure Slide 1 in the *Safety Campaign* presentation is displayed in Normal view.**

❷ **Choose File, Page Setup.**
The Page Setup dialog box is displayed (see Figure 7.12). By default the slides are sized to fill the screen when used as an electronic slide show. Try choosing a different size instead.

Change slide size here

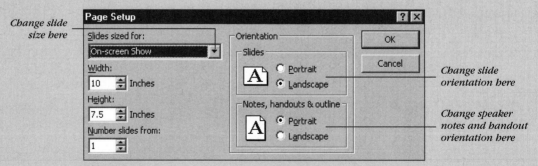

Change slide orientation here

Change speaker notes and handout orientation here

Figure 7.12

❸ **Click the *Slides sized for* drop-down list arrow, and choose Banner; then click OK.**
This setup automatically changes the slide size to 8″ wide by 1″ tall (see Figure 7.13). While this size might be appropriate if you want to print a slide as a banner, it doesn't work well for an onscreen show, so try making some other modifications to the slide size.

To Use Page Setup

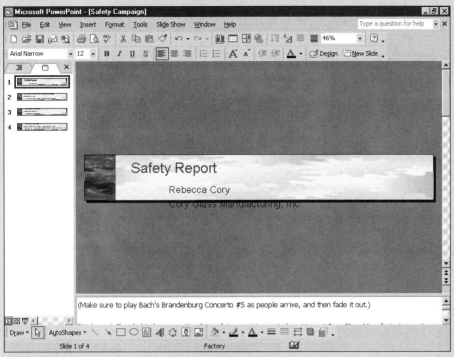

Figure 7.13

4 **Choose File, Page Setup to redisplay the Page Setup dialog box.**

5 **Choose Letter Paper (8.5x11 in) on the *Slides sized for* drop-down list.**
The Width and Height settings in the dialog box automatically change to reflect the new
size. (You can also change the width and height manually if you want custom-sized
slides.) Before closing the Page Setup dialog box, try changing the orientation.

6 **In the Orientation section of the dialog box, change the orientation of your
slides to Portrait; then click OK.**
The slides are resized and reoriented (see Figure 7.14). Now try printing a slide.

(Continues)

To Use Page Setup (Continued)

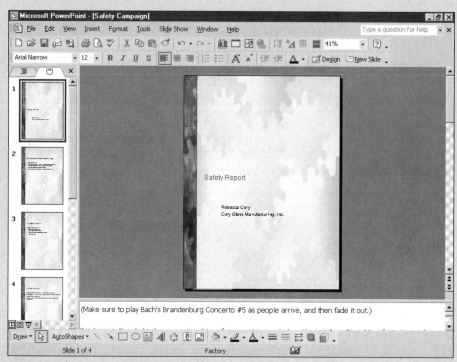

Figure 7.14

7 With Slide 1 of your presentation displayed, choose File, Print.

8 Choose Current slide in the Print range section of the dialog box. (If you're printing on a black-and-white printer, also make sure Grayscale is chosen in the Color/grayscale list.)

9 Click OK.
The slide is printed using portrait orientation. Now change the slide's orientation and size back to the original settings.

10 In the Page Setup dialog box, size the slides for an On-screen Show. Also change the slide orientation to Landscape; then choose OK.
The presentation displays using the default settings for a slide show.

11 Save the *Safety Campaign* presentation.
Keep the presentation open for the next lesson, in which you use advanced print settings to output your presentation using a variety of formats.

Lesson 4: Using Advanced Print Settings

As you've seen in previous projects, PowerPoint includes a number of ways that you can print your presentation. You saw how you could print the presentation as slides, an outline, or print the accompanying speaker notes and audience handouts. Additionally, you changed the size and orientation of the slides. In this lesson you explore a few more options for printing your slides.

To Use Advanced Print Settings

1 **Make sure Slide 1 in the *Safety Campaign* presentation is displayed in Normal view.**

2 **Choose File, Print.**
The Print dialog box displays. You can use this dialog box to indicate the number of slides you want to print, and how many copies of each you'd like.

3 **In the Print range section, click the Slides option button and then enter 1,3 in the Slides text box.**
Separating the slide numbers by commas lets you "pick and choose" which ones you want. (To pick adjacent slides, use a hyphen between the slide numbers.)

4 **Increase the Number of copies to 2. Click OK.**
Two copies of Slides 1 and 3 print. Now try changing the page size and orientation to 8 1/2″ x 14″ (legal size) before printing.

5 **Choose File, Page Setup.**

6 **Select the text in the Width text box and then type 8.5. Press** Tab⇆.
The new width for your slides is set to 8 1/2″.

7 **Enter 14 in the Height text box.**
The new height (14″) is entered in the Height text box, and PowerPoint automatically switched the orientation to Portrait (see Figure 7.15).

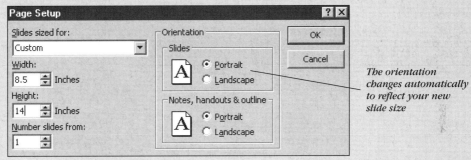

The orientation changes automatically to reflect your new slide size

Figure 7.15

8 **Click OK to apply the new slide size and orientation.**
Now you're ready to print your slides. (Before you continue, make sure you have 8 1/2″ x 14″ paper in your printer.)

9 **Choose File, Print.**

10 **In the Print dialog box, select Slides in the Print range area, enter 3-4 in the Slides text box, and then click OK.**
The slide range you indicated (Slides 3–4) is printed.

11 **Save your *Safety Campaign* presentation and then close it.**
Keep PowerPoint running for the next lesson, in which you use the Pack and Go feature.

To extend your knowledge...

Printing Slides as Overhead Transparencies

Much of the time you'll use your presentation as an onscreen slide show. However, if you don't have access to the equipment necessary to project the presentation electronically (or if the equipment fails), you'll be glad to know that you can instead create a series of overhead transparencies to use.

To print a slide as a transparency, choose File, Page Setup to display the Page Setup dialog box. Click the *Slides sized for* drop-down list arrow and then choose Overhead from the list. PowerPoint automatically resizes your slides to print as overhead transparencies.

Finally, before attempting to feed a transparency through your printer, make sure your model can handle this type of printing, or you'll have a gunky mess on your hands!

Lesson 5: Packing Up Your Presentation

You can use the **Pack and Go Wizard** to package all presentation files (including linked files and fonts) on a disk, so that you can run the presentation on another computer. Additionally, you have the option of packing the **PowerPoint Viewer**, which is a program used to run slide shows on computers that don't have PowerPoint installed on them. A wizard, as you probably recall from earlier projects, is an interactive help utility that guides you through each step of a multi-step operation. Wizards help automate processes that would otherwise be tricky or complicated to accomplish.

For this lesson, imagine that you work for a sports equipment company, and you hope to open a store in a town that is several hours from your home office. To promote your company in the new location, you're scheduled to give an overview of your company's products and goals to the Chamber of Commerce. Because the Pack and Go Wizard makes it easy to take your presentation "on the road," you decide to use it to package your presentation on a floppy disk.

To Pack Up Your Presentation

1 Open *ep1-0702*, and save it as New Store.

2 Choose File, Pack and Go.
The first page of the Pack and Go Wizard is displayed (see Figure 7.16). You can make choices on each page of the wizard and then click Next to proceed to the following page.

Figure 7.16

3 Click the Next button.
The second page of the wizard displays (*Pick files to pack*). This page gives you the choice of packaging the open presentation or another one.

4 Make sure that the Active presentation box is checked, and then click Next.

To Pack Up Your Presentation

The third page of the wizard is displayed (*Choose destination*), so you can specify where you want to store the packed presentation. In most cases, you'll accept the default option—placing the presentation on floppy disks. You can also place the presentation on your hard drive, a zip disk, or on another computer to which you are networked.

5 **Make sure the A:\ drive option button is selected and then click <u>N</u>ext.**
The Links page of the wizard displays (see Figure 7.17). You can include any linked files so that they're available on the destination computer. You can also choose to embed the fonts, which ensures that the text displays properly on the destination computer (even if the font isn't installed on it). Although linked files and embedded fonts take up more room on your disk, it gives you peace of mind to know that everything you need to give your presentation is included.

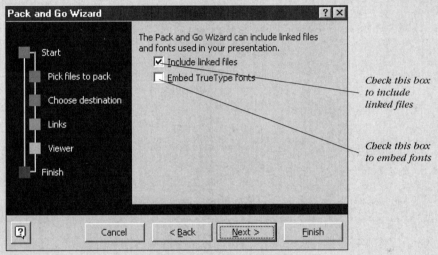

Figure 7.17

6 **Check both boxes on the Links page and then click <u>N</u>ext.**
The Viewer page of the wizard displays. Including the PowerPoint Viewer takes up room on your disk, but it ensures that you can give your presentation from virtually any computer—whether or not it has PowerPoint installed. For this lesson, however, you'll use the default setting (<u>D</u>on't include the Viewer).

7 **Make sure that the <u>D</u>on't include the Viewer option button is selected and then click <u>N</u>ext.**
The final page of the Pack and Go Wizard is displayed.

8 **Make sure that you have a blank, formatted disk in drive A; then click <u>F</u>inish.**

If you have problems...

The Pack and Go Wizard is an *install on first use feature*. This means that you're prompted (through use of a message box) to install the feature the first time you try to use it. If necessary, make sure the Office XP CD is inserted in the CD-ROM drive and then choose <u>Y</u>es in the message box. When the feature is installed, continue with the lesson.

(Continues)

To Pack Up Your Presentation (Continued)

PowerPoint packages your presentation (including the linked files and embedding the fonts) onto the floppy disk. How long should this process take? It depends on the size of your presentation (and the processing speed of your computer). You'll know that the presentation is "packaged" when your presentation redisplays in Normal view, however.

If you have problems...

If there's not enough room on the floppy disk for a presentation, Power-Point prompts you to insert another disk. Just pop the second disk into the drive and then press ⏎Enter.

❾ **Save the *New Store* presentation and then close it.**
Leave PowerPoint running for the next lesson, in which you preview how a presentation will look as a Web page.

To extend your knowledge...

Unpacking Your Presentation

So you packed up your presentation... but how do you unpack it? On the computer you plan to use for your presentation, display the contents of drive A. Double-click the pngsetup.exe file icon. In the Pack and Go Setup dialog box, specify the drive and folder location where you want to unpack the files and then click OK. When the presentation is successfully unpacked, a message box displays, asking if you want to display the presentation as a slide show. Choose <u>Y</u>es, and your show is off and running!

Lesson 6: Using Web Page Preview

You can publish presentations to your company's intranet or to the World Wide Web. Publishing a presentation refers to converting a copy of it to ***Hypertext Markup Language (HTML)*** format so you can use it on the Web. Before you use HTML to save the presentation, however, it's a good idea to see how it will actually look on the Web. To help you out, you can use PowerPoint's ***Web Page Preview***. This view helps you see how your presentation will display as a Web page by opening it in your Web browser. Try using this view now.

To Use Web Page Preview

❶ **Open *ep1-0703*, and save it as** Ergonomic Products.

❷ **Click on each of the slides on the Slides tab to view each page of the presentation.**
This presentation includes a number of hyperlinks to other locations. It's typical for Web-based documents to include hyperlinks to related information or Web sites. For example, Slides 2–6 include buttons that you can click to display the first slide. However, whether

To Use Web Page Preview

or not you've already developed hyperlinks in your presentation, hyperlinks are added in a frame at the left side of the window when you use Web Page Preview.

Now use Web Page Preview to see how your presentation will look on the Web.

③ Choose File, Web Page Preview.

The presentation displays in your browser, giving you a good idea of the way your presentation will look when you actually save it as a Web page (see Figure 7.18). Notice that the first page of your presentation is automatically used as the *homepage*. (A homepage, which is the opening page of a Web site, is usually devoted to the main topic for the site.) Additionally, a hyperlink for each slide appears on the left side of the window—making it easy to access a page by clicking its hyperlink.

Hyperlinks for each presentation slide appear in this frame

Click the Expand/ Collapse Outline button to display or hide the subpoints

Click here to close the browser window

Click the Next Slide button to scroll through your slides

Click here to view your presentation as a slide show

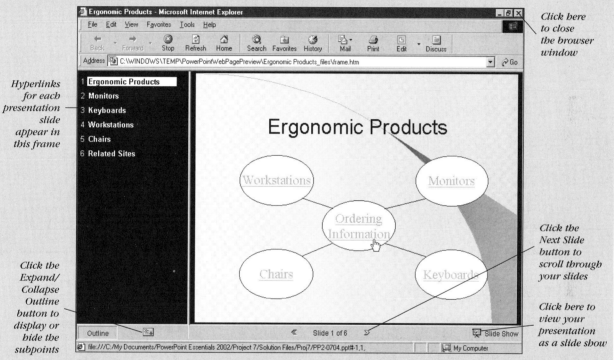

Figure 7.18

If you have problems...

Don't worry if your screen doesn't exactly match Figure 7.18, in which Internet Explorer is used as the browser. The way your screen appears depends on which Web browser you use. Additionally, if Internet Explorer isn't set up as the default browser, you may need to first save the presentation as a Web page before viewing it using Web Page Preview.

Additionally, you may need to maximize the browser window to better see the presentation.

Now try testing out the hyperlinks.

(Continues)

To Use Web Page Preview (Continued)

4 **Click the *Chairs* hyperlink in the frame (on the left side of the browser window).**
The Chairs page of the presentation displays. Now try to redisplay the homepage.

5 **Click the Home Page button in the lower right corner of the Web page.**
The first presentation slide (analogous to the homepage) redisplays. Remember: You can use either the hyperlinks that you create within the presentation or the ones in the frame to move between locations.

6 **Click the Next Slide button at the bottom of the browser window (refer to Figure 7.18 for the location of this button, if necessary).**
The next presentation slide is displayed.

7 **Click the Expand/Collapse Outline button at the bottom of the browser window (refer to Figure 7.18 for the location of this button, if necessary).**
The subtopics for each slide are displayed in the frame (see Figure 7.19).

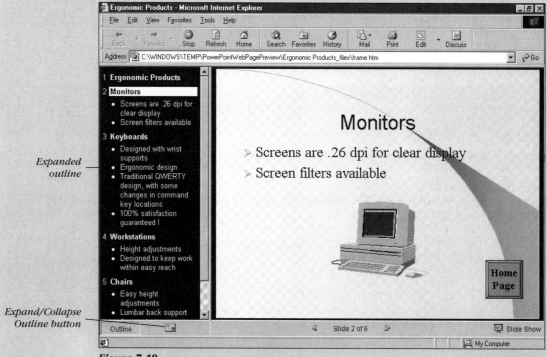

Figure 7.19

When you're satisfied that a presentation will work well for Web use and it includes the hyperlinks you want, you can close the browser window.

8 **Click the Close button in the upper-right corner of the browser window.**
The browser window closes and your presentation (in PowerPoint) redisplays.

9 **Save the *Ergonomic Products* presentation.**
Keep the presentation open and PowerPoint running for the next exercise, in which you save the presentation as a Web page.

To extend your knowledge...

Designing Presentations for the Web

When you are creating a presentation for the Web, keep a couple of things in mind. First, make sure you keep the text and graphics readable and interesting, but don't add so many graphics that your pages are sluggish to display. Many users will give up on your presentation rather than wait for poky pages to appear onscreen.

Also, keep in mind that some of PowerPoint's animation features (such as slide transitions, text builds, and so on) are not supported by some Web browsers. Unless you install the PowerPoint Animation Player (and can count on all viewers to do the same), your audience won't be able to see these enhancements.

Finally, make sure hyperlinks point to targets within your presentation (or on the network), or they won't work. For example, links to other presentation pages or Web sites generally work well, but not those to your hard drive.

Lesson 7: Publishing a Presentation to the Web

Have you ever been in front of a large audience? How about an audience of several million people? By placing your PowerPoint presentations on the Web, you can do just that! However, publishing to the Web can seem daunting for many people. Luckily, PowerPoint makes it easy to convert an existing presentation to a series of HTML files that Web browsers can recognize. Because of this, you don't have to jump through hoops to create a presentation to use on the Web.

In the previous lesson, you saw what your presentation would look like on the Web. You also tested the presentation's hyperlinks to make sure that they would work as expected in the Web environment.

Now you're ready to publish your presentation to the Web by saving the presentation in HTML format—as a Web page.

To Publish a Presentation to the Web

1 **In the open *Ergonomic Products* presentation, choose File, Save as Web Page.**
The Save As dialog box displays, but with some differences from the "run-of-the-mill" Save As dialog box that you typically use to save presentations (see Figure 7.20). For example, Web Page (HTML) is automatically chosen for the file format.

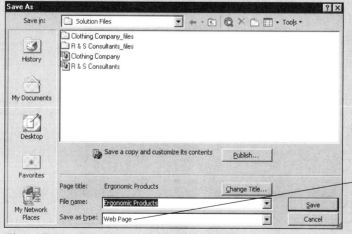

Web Page format (HTML) is automatically chosen

Figure 7.20

(Continues)

To Publish a Presentation to the Web (Continued)

Now specify where you want to save the Web pages you're about to create. Because literally tens (or even hundreds) of HTML files can be created for any presentation, you should carefully select an appropriate location. (If you're not sure where to place the HTML files, ask your instructor before proceeding with the next step.)

2 **Click the Save in drop-down list arrow and designate the location where you want to store your Web page files.**
Next, assign a name for the Web page file and folder you're about to create.

3 **In the File name box, enter** Company.
Now take a look at some of the additional settings that you can change when you save a presentation for Web use.

4 **In the Save As dialog box, click the Publish button.**
The Publish as Web Page dialog box is displayed (see Figure 7.21). This dialog box includes a variety of options that are related to saving your presentation in HTML format. For example, you can publish the entire presentation or choose a selected range of slides. You can also use the Change Title button to edit the information that appears in the title bar of the Web page.

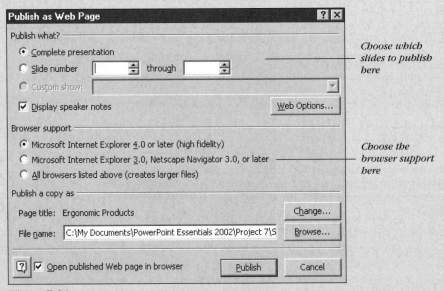

Figure 7.21

Now you're ready to create the HTML files.

5 **In the Publish as Web Page dialog box, click Publish.**
The presentation is saved as a group of HTML files. (If the presentation displays in your Web browser, close it.)

Since you're finished with the *Ergonomic Products* presentation itself, you can close it.

6 **Save and close the *Ergonomic Products* presentation.**
Now take a look at the HTML files that you created. A handy way to do this from within PowerPoint is to use the Open dialog box.

7 **Choose File, Open.**
The Open dialog box is displayed (see Figure 7.22). (If necessary, select the location where your Web page files are stored in the Look in drop-down list.)

To Publish a Presentation to the Web

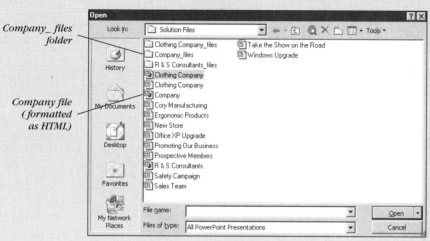

Company_ files folder

Company file (formatted as HTML)

Figure 7.22

Notice that both a *Company* file and a *Company_files* folder are shown. Try displaying the properties associated with the *Company* file to confirm that PowerPoint saved it by using HTML file format.

❽ Right-click on the *Company* file and then choose Properties from the shortcut menu.

The General page of the Properties dialog box displays (see Figure 7.23). Notice that this file uses the HTML format.

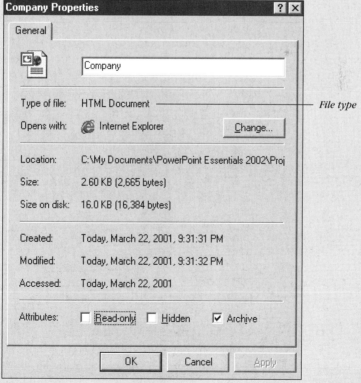

File type

Figure 7.23

(Continues)

To Publish a Presentation to the Web (Continued)

9 **Click OK to close the Company Properties dialog box and then double-click the**
_Company_files_ folder.
A listing of files created for your Web pages displays. You can confirm that each of these
files uses the HTML format by displaying the associated Properties dialog boxes.

10 **Display the Properties dialog box for several of the files listed.**
Each of the files shows HTML as the file type. After you _upload_ (copy files) to your Web
server, you're ready to appear—electronically speaking—before millions!

11 **Close any Properties dialog boxes that may be open.**

12 **Click Cancel to close the Open dialog box without opening any files.**
Keep PowerPoint running if you plan to complete the end of chapter exercises.

To extend your knowledge...

The Internet and World Wide Web

You almost can't go through a day without hearing about the _**Internet**_. Originally designed as a
way for government and university facilities to share information, the Internet has grown to become
a loose association of thousands of networks worldwide. The Internet is an electronic city of
sorts—by using it, you can access libraries, scientific, medical, or business information, and so on.

The World Wide Web (abbreviated WWW or simply known as the Web) is the graphical, user-
friendly way to explore the Internet. Using the Web is easy for most people because Web pages are
chock-full of hyperlinks that you can click to quickly jump to related information.

You can't put a document with just any kind of file format on the Web, however. Documents that
are used on the Web need to be saved by using Hypertext Markup Language (HTML) file format.
HTML controls the display of graphics, formatting, and hyperlinks that are the hallmarks of the
World Wide Web.

Others can view the HTML documents if they have a _**Web browser**_—software that helps you locate
and view Web pages by clicking hyperlinks to move from one Web page to another. Because so
many people can access the Web, businesses (and individuals) can greatly increase their marketing
leverage by publishing to it.

Summary

Congratulations! After completing this book, you're "up and running" with PowerPoint and are well
on your way to creating effective presentations for home, school, volunteer organizations, or business.

In this final project, you learned several ways to output presentations and use PowerPoint as a communication tool. First you created and printed speaker notes. You also learned advanced methods of
printing your presentation. You "packed up" your presentation so you could take it with you to other
locations. Finally, you learned how to interface PowerPoint with the Web or your company's intranet
by previewing and saving the presentation as a Web page.

To expand on your knowledge, spend a few minutes exploring Help on these topics. Additionally,
complete some of the Skill Drill, Challenge, and Discovery Zone exercises.

Checking Concepts and Terms

Multiple Choice

Circle the letter of the correct answer for each of the following.

1. Which of the following are ways that you can output a presentation? [L1-4]

   a. Printing handouts

   b. Printing speaker notes

   c. Printing an overhead transparency

   d. All of the above

2. Which of the following describes portrait orientation? [L3]

   a. The height of the slide is greater than the width.

   b. The width of the slide is greater than the height.

   c. Speaker notes automatically use the same orientation.

   d. Audience handouts automatically use the same orientation.

3. Which of the following is true regarding speaker notes? [L1]

   a. They provide supporting data or documentation during a presentation.

   b. They help you keep on track during a presentation.

   c. They help you remember quotations or anecdotes.

   d. All of the above

4. What two ways can you view and add speaker notes to your presentation? [L1]

   a. Notes Page view and the Notes pane

   b. Handout view and Notes Page pane

   c. Speaker Notes window and Handout view

   d. Speaker pane and Normal pane

5. Which of the following is true regarding a Web homepage? [L6-7]

   a. It usually contains a number of hyperlinks to other documents.

   b. It makes your computer display in *home mode*.

   c. It is the same as a Web browser.

   d. It is software that you use to post information to a Web server.

Discussion

1. What are the advantages of using the Web as a marketing or communication tool? [L6-7]

2. There are currently millions of Web sites in existence. What design elements can you include in a presentation that will help it stand out among all the sites? [L6-7]

3. What are some advantages for developing speaker notes? [L1-2]

Skill Drill exercises *reinforce* project skills. Each skill reinforced is the same, or nearly the same, as a skill presented in the project. Detailed instructions are provided in a step-by-step format.

1. Adding Speaker Notes

You're in charge of converting your company's network from Windows 95 to Windows 2000. To present your progress to management in an upcoming meeting, you prepare speaker notes.

1. Open *ep1-0704,* and save it as `Windows Upgrade`.
2. Press `PgDn` twice to display Slide 3, *Progress*. Choose View, Notes Page.
3. Click the Zoom drop-down list arrow, and choose *75%* from the list to enlarge the view.
4. Click in the notes box and then enter the following text:

   `Workstation conversion from Windows 95 to Windows 2000 began on time in early January. Independent contractors have been hired to help in the conversion.`

   `The original plan was to have trainers work with each employee within two weeks after the employee's workstation was converted. At this point, 68% have received training within two weeks, while the remaining 32% have been trained within three weeks.`
5. Click the Normal View button. Press `PgDn` twice to display Slide 5, *Costs.*
6. Type the following text in the Notes pane area of Slide 5:

   `Make sure to emphasize that no additional cost overruns are anticipated.`
7. Save the changes to your *Windows Upgrade* presentation.

Keep the presentation open if you plan to complete the next exercise on printing speaker notes and handouts.

2. Printing Slides, Speaker Notes, and Handouts

So that you'll have a ready reference when you give your *Windows Upgrade* presentation, you print your speaker notes. You also print handouts to give to your audience.

1. Verify that the *Windows Upgrade* presentation is open from the previous exercise.
2. Display Slide 3, *Progress*, in Normal view.
3. Choose File, Print to display the Print dialog box. Click the Print what drop-down list arrow and then choose Notes Pages.
4. In the Print range section, click Current slide so that you'll only print speaker notes for Slide 3. Click OK to print your speaker notes.
5. Now print your handouts. Choose File, Print to again display the Print dialog box. Click the Print what drop-down list arrow and then choose Handouts.
6. In the Handouts section, click the Slides per page drop-down list arrow and then choose 4.
7. Make sure that the Frame slides box is checked. Click OK to print your handouts.
8. Save the changes to your *Windows Upgrade* presentation and then close it.

Keep PowerPoint running if you plan to complete additional exercises.

3. Using the Pack and Go Wizard

You're scheduled to give an orientation meeting for employees at one of your company's offices. To make it easy to take your presentation along, you decide to use Pack and Go.

After you pack up the presentation, imagine that you arrive at the office where you plan to give the talk. To set up for the seminar, you unpack the presentation and then run it as a slide show.

1. Open *ep1-0705,* and save it as `Take the Show on the Road`.
2. With the presentation displayed onscreen, choose File, Pack and Go. Click Next to proceed past the opening page of the wizard.
3. Make sure that Active presentation is selected on the second page of the wizard and then click Next.
4. On the third page (*Choose destination*) make sure that A:\ drive is chosen and then click Next.
5. Check both boxes on the Links page of the wizard and then click Next.
6. On the Viewer page, choose Don't include the Viewer. Choose Next.
7. Read over the information on the final page of the wizard. Make sure that you have a blank disk in drive A and then click Finish. Click OK in the message box.
8. Close the *Take the Show on the Road* presentation, but keep PowerPoint running so you can practice unpacking the presentation.
9. Click PowerPoint's Minimize button to shrink PowerPoint to a taskbar button. On the Windows desktop, double-click the My Computer icon. In the My Computer window, double-click the 3 1/2 Floppy (A:) icon.
10. Double-click the pngsetup icon. In the Pack and Go Setup dialog box, enter `C:\Session` (or the location indicated by your instructor). Click OK.
11. Another Pack and Go Setup message box prompts you to create the directory. Click OK.
12. Another message box displays, indicating that the presentation was installed in C:\Session. Click Yes in the message box to run the slide show.
13. Press ⏎Enter as many times as is necessary to advance completely through the slide show.
14. Close the 3 1/2 Floppy window on your desktop; then click the Microsoft PowerPoint button on the taskbar to maximize the program window.
15. Now practice opening the presentation from within PowerPoint. In PowerPoint, display the Open dialog box. Locate and open the Session folder on drive C:.
16. Open the *Take the Show on the Road* file, run it as a slide show, and then close it.

Keep PowerPoint running if you plan to complete additional exercises.

4. Viewing a Presentation as a Web Page

You work for a company that produces children's clothing. You're the most computer-literate employee at your office, so your boss asked you to develop a Web site for the company. Because you don't know how to code in HTML, you decide to use a PowerPoint presentation as the basis of your Web site instead. To see how the presentation will look on the Web, you use Web Page Preview to see it; then you save the presentation as a Web page.

1. Open *ep1-0706,* and save it as `Clothing Company`.
2. Use Help to find out more about previewing and saving a presentation as a Web page.
3. Display the first presentation slide in Normal view and then choose File, Web Page Preview. Maximize the browser window.
4. Click the *Our Goals* hyperlink on the left side of the window to display that page.
5. Click the Home button in the lower left corner of the slide to redisplay the homepage for your presentation.
6. Repeat Steps 4–5 for each of the hyperlinks and buttons in your presentation.

7. Close the browser window. Now you're ready to save the presentation as a Web page.

8. Display the presentation in Normal view and then choose File, Save as Web Page. In the Save As dialog box, enter `Clothing Company` in the File name box. Indicate a file location and then click Publish.

9. In the Publish as Web Page dialog box, click the Change button. Enter `Active Kids` in the Set Page Title dialog box. Click OK to redisplay the Publish as Web Page dialog box.

10. In the Publish as Web Page dialog box, check the box for Open published Web page in browser, if necessary. Change the location in the File name box to the one used in your classroom (or specified by your instructor). Click Publish.

11. Maximize the browser window. Click each hyperlink and action button to test it.

12. Close the browser window. Save the *Clothing Company* presentation and then close it.

Keep PowerPoint running if you plan to complete the Challenge and Discovery Zone exercises.

Challenge

Challenge exercises expand on or are somewhat related to skills presented in the lessons. Each exercise provides a brief narrative introduction followed by instructions in a numbered step format that are not as detailed as those in the Skill Drill section.

1. Adding and Printing Speaker Notes

As publicity manager for an ergonomics company, you've been asked to give a presentation to a local business organization. Even though you feel this is a good opportunity to promote your company, you're a bit nervous about giving the presentation. To better help you prepare for the talk, you create and print speaker notes.

1. Open *ep1-0707*, and save it as `Promoting Our Business`.

2. Add the following speaker note to Slide 1:

   `Make sure to welcome the meeting attendees enthusiastically. Don't forget to play upbeat music as they arrive at the meeting.`

3. Add the following notes to Slide 3, *History of Our Company*:

   `Company was founded in 1990 to provide ergonomic computer equipment.`
   `Company has grown at a rate of 10% (average) per year.`
   `With increased interest in ergonomic workstation design, we anticipate continued growth.`
   `Our motto:"To make working with computers as comfortable as it is productive."`

4. Run your presentation as a slide show, starting with Slide 1. In the slide show, view your notes for both Slide 1 and Slide 3. (Hint: Use the Slide Show shortcut menu.)

5. Print speaker notes for your presentation and then print handouts (six slides per page).

6. Save the changes to your *Promoting Our Business* presentation; then close it.

Keep PowerPoint running if you plan to complete additional exercises.

2. Formatting Speaker Notes

As sales manager of your company, you conduct training for the sales team. To motivate your salespeople, you develop a presentation for an upcoming training session. To help you remember information, you add speaker notes to the presentation.

1. Open *ep1-0708*, and save it as `Sales Team`.
2. Add the following speaker note to Slide 1, *Motivating a Team*:

   `Make sure to have the sales awards displayed at the front of the room and to have upbeat music playing.`
3. Add the following speaker note to Slide 2, *Deliver an Inspirational Opening*:

   `"People tend to support what they help create."--Betsy Hudson`
4. Use Help to find out how to format your notes.
5. Display Slide 2, *Deliver an Inspirational Opening*, in Notes Page view. Zoom to *75%* to enlarge the notes box area.
6. Select the quotation (but not the name that follows it), and then click the Bold button on the Formatting toolbar.
7. Select the name (*Betsy Hudson*) in the notes box and then click the Italic button on the Formatting toolbar. Switch your presentation to Normal view.
8. Use Page Setup to change your speaker notes and handouts to <u>L</u>andscape orientation.
9. Print your speaker notes and then print handouts of your presentation (three slides per page).
10. Save your *Sales Team* presentation and then close it.

Keep PowerPoint running if you plan to complete additional exercises.

3. Previewing and Saving Your Presentation as a Web Page

As the head of Information Technology for your organization, you're in charge of upgrading all employees to Office XP. So that you can keep everyone up-to-date about the project's progress, you develop a presentation and save it as HTML so that you can put it on your company's intranet.

1. Open *ep1-0709*, and save it as `Office XP Upgrade`. View each slide of the presentation. Notice that each slide (except Slide 1) includes an action button.
2. Preview the presentation in Web Page Preview. Test each of the hyperlinks and buttons in the presentation. Close the browser window.
3. Save the presentation as a Web page, using the name `R & S Consultants` for the Page title and the filename. If necessary, change the location in the File <u>n</u>ame box to the one specified by your instructor.
4. Use Help to find out how to post the presentation on an intranet. If possible, actually complete the steps to post the presentation on your organization's intranet or the Internet.
5. Save the presentation and then close it.

Keep PowerPoint running if you plan to complete additional exercises.

4. Packing and Unpacking a Presentation

You work for a large company that manufactures steel ball bearings. As a regional safety manager, you periodically give Safety Report presentations at the corporate office. To make it easy to take your presentation with you, you use the Pack and Go Wizard to compress it. When you arrive at headquarters, you unpack and run it.

1. Open *ep1-0710*, and save it as `Cory Manufacturing`.
2. Use the Pack and Go Wizard to pack up the presentation on a floppy (or Zip) disk. Choose the following options in the Pack and Go Wizard dialog box:
    ○ <u>I</u>nclude linked files
    ○ <u>E</u>mbed TrueType fonts
    ○ <u>D</u>on't include the Viewer
3. Close the *Cory Manufacturing* presentation and PowerPoint.
4. Unpack the *Cory Manufacturing* presentation from the floppy (or Zip) disk to C:\Safety.
5. Run the slide show from the Pack and Go Setup dialog box.

6. Open PowerPoint. Locate the *Cory Manufacturing* presentation in the C:\Safety folder. Open the presentation and then run it as a slide show from within PowerPoint.

7. Close the presentation without saving any changes.

Keep PowerPoint running if you plan to complete the Discovery Zone exercises.

iscovery Zone

Discovery Zone exercises require advanced knowledge of topics presented in *essentials* lessons, application of skills from multiple lessons, or self-directed learning of new skills. Each exercise is independent of the others, so that you may complete the exercises in any order.

1. Outputting Your Presentation in a Variety of Ways

To document a recruitment talk that you are presenting to prospective members for the University Biking Club, you add speaker notes to a presentation. You also output the presentation in a variety of ways.

Open *ep1-0711,* and save it as **Prospective Members.** Add the following notes to the presentation:

- Slide 2: Mention that officers are elected every September.
- Slide 3: Mention that Greg Schmidt, famous bicyclist, will be at the Race of Champions.

Format the speaker note on Slide 3 as follows:

- Enlarge the font to **14** points.
- Add bold to **Greg Schmidt**.
- Italicize Race of Champions.

View your speaker notes in Normal view.

Change the orientation for your speaker notes to Landscape and then print the speaker notes for Slide 3.

Use Help to find out all the ways you can output your presentation, including how to print the presentation as overheads. Print the slides in the presentation as overhead transparencies, if you have a printer that can accommodate transparencies. Save changes to your *Prospective Members* presentation; then close it.

Keep PowerPoint running if you plan to complete the final exercise.

2. Working with the Notes Master

You're an old hand at creating and printing speaker notes. However, a friend recently told you that you could change how your notes are printed by modifying the notes master.

To find out more about using and modifying the notes master, use PowerPoint's Help. Specifically, find out the answers to the following questions:

- What is the notes master?
- What items are on the notes master?
- How can you delete, move, or resize the items on the notes master?
- Can you add a logo or other picture to a notes master?

Write down the answers to your questions. Open a presentation for which you've already developed speaker notes, and modify the notes master. Print your speaker notes. Unless your instructor specifies otherwise, don't save the presentation.

PART

V

Glossary

absolute cell reference Specifies that the row and/or column cell references in a worksheet do not change as a formula is copied (for example, copying the formula =$A$1*A5 in cell A6 to cells B6 and C6 results in the formulas =$A$1*B5 and =$A$1*C5, respectively). You can create an absolute reference by placing a dollar sign ($) in front of the part(s) of the cell reference that you do not want to change during the copy operation. *See also* **relative cell reference**

action Any task or change you make in a document.

action items Assignments that you give people during a slide show or meeting. You can use PowerPoint's Meeting Minder feature to create a list of these tasks on a slide.

activate To double-click an embedded object, such as a chart, so that the associated peripheral program is launched.

active document window The window that contains a document with the insertion point; the title bar is blue or another color.

Advanced Filter A list-management feature in Excel that allows you to specify more complex criteria and to copy filtered records to another location.

alignment The placement of text between the left and right margins in a document or the left and right edges of a cell. The default alignment is left.

AND search criteria Two or more search conditions, all of which must be met.

animating Displaying objects in sequence to produce the illusion of movement, or to control the flow of information.

animation schemes Pre-designed visual effects in PowerPoint that are categorized by the effect you want to achieve, such as subtle or exciting.

annotate To write or draw electronically on a slide during a slide show.

annotation pen A special mouse pointer that enables you to write or draw directly on a slide during an electronic slide show.

annuity An investment that provides fixed payments at equal intervals. The term appears in explanations of the arguments for several Excel functions, including the future value (FV) function.

argument A specific component in a function, such as a range of cells. For example, the function =SUM(B5:B20)

has one argument—the range of cells from B5 through B20. The function =IF(B5>B2,"Goal Met","Keep Trying") has three arguments within parentheses, separated by commas.

arithmetic operators Symbols in formulas that specify the type of calculation; symbols include +, –, *, and / (to add, subtract, multiply, and divide, respectively).

ascending order The order to follow when sorting A to Z, lowest to highest value, earliest to most recent date, and so on.

Ask a Question box A help feature that you can use to search an application's help system topically.

AutoComplete A feature that helps you complete entry in a file. For example, if you start typing today's date in a Word document, you see a ScreenTip that displays the entire date. Press ↵Enter to complete the date automatically. In Excel, the feature compares text you are typing into a cell with text already entered in the same column, and automatically completes the word or phrase if a match is found. You can accept the suggested entry or continue typing.

AutoContent Wizard A tool that helps you create presentations that include sample content as well as an underlying template.

AutoCorrect A feature that can correct common errors as you type, such as changing *adn* to *and*.

AutoFill A feature that allows you to automatically fill in a series of numbers, dates, or other items in a specified range.

AutoFilter Limits the display of records in a list, based on simple search conditions.

AutoForm A form created automatically by Access that includes all the fields in a table.

AutoLayout *See* **slide layout**

automatic page break Page break inserted by Word when you fill an entire page. These breaks adjust automatically when you add and delete text.

AutoReport A tool for creating an automatically formatted report from a database table or query.

AutoSum A feature that you can use to insert a formula that sums a range of cells automatically. Excel suggests a formula that you can accept or edit.

AVERAGE function A predefined formula that calculates the average of specified values.

bar tab   A tab marker that produces a vertical bar or line between columns when you press Tab.

border   A line style that surrounds text, table cells, or an object.

browser   A program that enables you to view Web pages on the Internet. Examples are Internet Explorer and Netscape Navigator.

bullet   A symbol, such as a circle or square, that is used to set off an item in a list.

bulleted list   An itemized list or enumeration that contains a bullet symbol at the left side of each item.

case   Capitalization style of text.

cell   The intersection of a column and a row in a datasheet, table, or worksheet.

cell address   Describes which column and row in a worksheet intersect to form the cell; for example, A1 is the address for the cell in the first column (column A) and the first row (row 1).

cell pointer   A darkened border around a PowerPoint datasheet cell, indicating that it is the active cell.

character attributes   Modifications to the font—color, bold, italic, underline, and so forth—that emphasize ideas and help improve readability and clarity. Also known as **character effects** or **character formats**.

character spacing   The amount of space between printed characters.

chart   A graphical representation of data that makes it easy to see trends and make comparisons.

chart subtypes   Variations of the main chart type.

Click and Type feature   In Word's Print Layout view, this feature lets you double-click in any area of the document and then type new text. Depending on where you double-click, Word inserts left tabs, centers the text, or aligns text at the right margin.

clip   An electronic picture, photograph, video, or sound file that you can insert in a presentation.

clip art   Graphic images, pictures, or drawings.

Clipboard   A temporary area in memory reserved for copying and moving data.

Clip Organizer   Gallery of clips—clip art, photos, sounds, and movies—stored on your hard drive. It has the capability to help the user organize clips, including from other sources.

close   The process of removing an open file or a dialog box from the screen.

clustered column chart   A chart that presents multiple data series as side-by-side columns.

color scheme   A set of eight balanced colors that you can apply to a PowerPoint template.

column   A group of table cells arranged vertically.

column chart   A chart in which each data point is reflected in the height of its column, in relation to the scale shown on the Y axis.

column headings   Text that appears at the top of table columns to identify the contents of each column.

column letter   Identifies a column in an Excel worksheet; lettered A through Z, AA through AZ, and so on through IV, up to 256 columns.

column selector   In Access, the thin shaded line above the field name in the query Design view. When you click the column selector, the whole column is selected.

column width   The horizontal measurement of a column.

combination chart   Includes two or more chart types, such as showing one data series as a column and another as a line. Create a combination chart if the values in the data series vary widely or you want to emphasize differences in the data.

combo box   A data entry drop-down list that looks up valid entries from a table, query, or source list.

comparison operator   Used to test the relationship between two items, such as finding out whether the items are equal (=) or if one is greater than (>) the other.

concatenation operator   The & symbol in a formula that joins one or more text entries to form a single entry.

conditional formatting   Used to accent a cell, depending on the value of the cell. Conditional formats return a result that is based on whether or not the value in the cell meets a specified condition. Formatting options include font style, font color, shading, patterns, borders, bold, italic, and underlining.

constants   Text values (also called labels), numeric values (numbers), or date and time values. Constants do not change unless you edit them.

Content Layouts   Preset slide layouts that include placeholders for objects, such as charts, clip art images, and diagrams.

context sensitive   Describes a shortcut menu that displays commands related to the area of the screen or the object that you right-click.

control   Any object selected from the toolbox or field list, such as a text box, check box, or option button that you add to a form or report.

copy   To make a copy of the selected text or object and place it temporarily in the Office Clipboard.

criteria   A test or set of conditions that limits the records included in a query or filter. A single condition is called a **criterion**.

crosstab query   A specialized query that summarizes the relationship between two or more fields.

current (or active) cell   The selected cell where the next action you take happens, such as typing. An outline appears around the cell to indicate that it is the current cell.

current record indicator   An arrow in the record selector that points to the currently active record.

Custom Animation list   A list that shows the order of animation for a slide.

cut   To remove text or an object from its location and place it temporarily in the Office Clipboard.

data   Unprocessed raw facts or assumptions that are stored in a document such as a worksheet or database.

data access page   A special type of Web page that has been designed for viewing and working with data on the Internet.

database   A collection of data that is organized in a way that provides for storage, retrieval, analysis, and output of large amounts of information.

Database window   A page that displays a list of the table, query, form, report, macro, and module objects that comprise an Access database.

data chart   A PowerPoint chart that shows numerical data in a pictorial manner.

data form   A dialog box that displays a list one record at a time. If you work with a large list, you may prefer to add and delete records by using this form, which shows all the fields in one record.

data series   A collection of values that pertain to a single subject.

datasheet   A mini-worksheet, made up of a grid of columns and rows, that enables you to enter numerical data into a PowerPoint chart.

Datasheet view   The row-and-column view you use when you enter or edit records in an Access table.

data type   A definition of the kind of data that can be entered into a field.

date or time field   A placeholder for a date or time that needs to change to reflect the current date or time when opened or printed.

default   A setting that a program uses unless you specify another setting.

delimiter   A character that separates fields in a text file. Common delimiters are tabs, commas, semicolons, and spaces.

demoting   To indent text more on an outline, indicating information that is a subpoint of a main point. Subpoints are usually less important than the main points, and may lend supporting facts to it. The opposite of promoting.

descending order   The order to follow when sorting Z to A, highest to lowest value, most recent to earliest date, and so on.

designer font   A special font used in creative documents, such as wedding announcements, fliers, brochures, and other special-occasion documents. Examples of designer fonts include Broadway BT, Comic Sans MS, and Keystroke.

design grid   The area used to define the conditions of a query. You can specify fields, sort order, and criteria to be used to search your database.

design template   *See* **template**

Design view   The view of the table you use when you are creating or changing fields. You see columns for the field name, data type, and description of each field.

desktop   A screen that provides a quick means to open and close programs and control the components of your computer system; consists of icons, a taskbar, and a Start button.

dialog box   A window that enables a user to input data or specify settings related to the current task.

Document Map   Displays a window that lists the structure of headings in your document.

document window   An area in which you type and format your documents.

double indent   Indenting text from both the left and the right margins.

double-space   Text that leaves one blank line between text lines.

drag-and-drop   A method of moving an object by selecting it, dragging it with the mouse to a new location, and then releasing the mouse button to drop the object in place.

dynaset   A subset of records created as a result of a query.

editing mode   A state in which you can enter or edit text in the cell, object, or placeholder.

electronic slide show   A predetermined list of slides that are displayed sequentially. You can show the list onscreen, via the Web, or by using a projection system to cast the image from your computer onto a large screen.

embed   To copy contents or an object so that the copied item does not update whenever that item changes in the source location.

embedded chart   A graphical representation of data created within the worksheet rather than as a separate worksheet.

embedded object   An item that is created by one program and then inserted into a document created by another program.

em dash   A dash the width of a lowercase m (—) that indicates a pause or change in thought.

en dash   A dash the width of a lowercase n that indicates a series; for example, pages 9–15.

end-of-document marker   A small horizontal line that indicates the end of the document in Word's Normal view.

enforce referential integrity   Ensures that each record in a related Access table is connected to a record in the primary table. This helps prevent orphan records, and it prevents you from adding records that are not connected to an existing record in the primary table.

exit   The process of closing an application, such as Word.

expression   A predefined or user-defined formula that performs calculations, displays built-in functions, or sets limits. You can include expressions in reports and other Access objects, such as macros.

field   A data item in each database record, such as order number or order date in a database that tracks catalog sales. In a table format, each field is set up in a column.

field label   The field name attached to a field text box in an Access form or report.

field text box   A placeholder for the contents of a field in an Access database. Field text boxes show the actual data that has been entered into a table.

file   A collection of data stored on disk that has a name, called a filename.

file extension   The last part of a filename; consists of three characters that represent the type of file.

filename   The name of a collection of data stored on disk.

fill   The shading color used within a cell, graphics object, drawing object, or text box.

fill handle   Displays as a small black square in the lower-right corner of the current (active) cell. You can drag the fill handle to copy cell contents to adjacent cells.

filter   To hide rows in a list, except those that meet specified criteria. This is a temporary view of your list. Canceling the filter operation displays all the records again.

Filter by Form   A search feature that finds all the records matching values that you type into one or more fields on a blank form.

Filter by Selection   A search feature that finds all of the records matching a value in a field that you select.

first line indent   Indents the first line of a paragraph.

folder   A category for organizing and storing files on a storage device, such as a data disk or hard drive.

font   Style, weight, and typeface of a set of characters.

font size   The height of the characters, typically measured in points, where 72 points equal one vertical inch.

footer   Document information, such as a filename or date, that appears at the bottom of every page.

footer area   Section at the bottom of each slide where you can display slide numbers or other text.

form   A type of object you can use to enter, edit, and view records. Think of a form as a fill-in-the-blanks screen.

format   To apply attributes to text or cells that alter the display of the text or cell contents. For example, you can italicize text and display a border around a cell or group of cells.

format (a disk)   A procedure that prepares a disk to store files. Formatting also identifies and automatically isolates any bad spots on the surface of the disk, and creates an area for a disk directory.

Format Painter   A feature that helps you copy existing formats to other locations.

formatting   The way that your file (including text, alignment, bullets, margins, and so forth) is set up to display.

formatting marks   Nonprinting symbols and characters in a Word document that indicate spaces, tabs, and hard returns. You display these symbols by clicking the Show/Hide ¶ button on the Standard toolbar. These symbols are useful when selecting text.

Formatting toolbar   Provides, in button form, shortcuts to frequently used commands for changing the appearance of data. The Formatting and Standard toolbars can share one row or display on two rows.

Form Detail   The main part of a form in which the records are displayed.

Form Footer   The area at the bottom of the form containing controls such as labels, dates, or page numbers. This appears at the bottom of each form page.

Form Header   The area at the top of the form containing controls such as labels, dates, or graphics. This appears at the top of each form page.

formula   Produces a calculated result, usually based on a reference to one or more cells in the worksheet. The results of a formula change if you change the contents of a cell referenced in the formula.

formula bar   Displays the contents of the current or active cell.

frame   A border that surrounds a slide element.

full menu   The pull-down menu that shows all commands. You display the full menu by pointing to the arrows at the bottom of the short menu.

Full Screen view   The view in which a Word document fills the entire screen. You do not see the title bar, toolbars, and other screen elements.

function   A predefined formula in Excel.

FV function   Calculates the future value of an investment based on fixed payments (deposits), earning a fixed rate of interest across equal time periods.

gradient fill   A pattern you can apply to objects where colors fade gradually from one shade to another.

graphical user interface (GUI)   A program interface, such as Microsoft Windows, that incorporates graphics to make the program easier to use.

grayed-out   The status of an option or a button that appears in gray and is not currently available.

grayscale   A way to view or print a presentation using shades of gray, black, and white.

gridlines   Horizontal and vertical lines that separate cells within a table or worksheet.

handouts   Printed output that includes only the slides' contents and not the accompanying speaker notes.

hanging indent   Paragraph format that keeps the first line of a paragraph at the left margin and indents the remaining lines from the left margin.

hard return   Defines the end of a line where you press ↵Enter.

header   Document information, such as a filename or date, that appears at the top of every page.

heading   Text between paragraphs or sections that helps identify the content of that section.

Help   Onscreen assistance or reference manual. It provides information about features, step-by-step instructions, and other assistance.

highlight   Places a color behind text, such as a highlighter pen, to draw attention to text.

homepage   The opening page of a Web site. It usually includes information on the main topic for the site and links to other pages.

horizontal scrollbar   An object at the bottom of a window that enables you to shift window contents left and right to view information that expands beyond the width of a window.

horizontal text alignment   The way the text displays between the left and right edges of a line, cell, or placeholder.

hyperlink   A link you can click to display another page or program.

hypertext links   Underlined words or phrases that appear in a different color. In Help, clicking a hypertext link displays another topic.

Hypertext Markup Language (HTML)   The type of programming language used to code Web pages. HTML controls the display of graphics, formatting, and hyperlinks.

icon   A small picture that represents a task, object, or program. For example, the Print icon looks like a printer.

IF function   A logical function used to perform one of two operations in a single cell, based on the evaluation of some condition being true or false.

import   To include data from a source outside of the existing file.

index   A location guide built by Access for all primary key fields that helps speed up searching and sorting for a particular field. Indexes can also be created for other fields, as long as they are not OLE or Memo fields.

information   Data transformed into a useful form; created when you select the data you need, organize the data in a meaningful order, format the data into a useful layout, and display the results—usually to the screen or a printer.

input mask   Special formatting features that make data entry in an Access database easier, such as when typing a phone number.

Insert Clip Art task pane   A window pane in which you search for and select clip art, photographs, movies, and sounds.

insertion point   A blinking vertical line that shows the current location in the document or in a dialog box text box.

Insert mode   A setting that shifts existing characters to the right when you type new characters.

Internet   Originally designed as a way for government and university facilities to share information; now a loose association of thousands of networks worldwide linking information of all kinds.

join   The manner in which the common fields between two Access tables are associated.

kerning   Automatically adjusts spacing between characters to achieve a more evenly spaced appearance.

keyboard shortcuts   The keys (or a key combination) you can press on the keyboard to perform an action.

keywords   Topical words that describe a clip. For example, a picture of a football might have keywords such as sport and game associated with it.

label   Text on an Access form or report that is not bound to the table.

landscape orientation   Produces a printed page that is wider than it is long.

launch   To run a Microsoft Office program.

leader   A tab option that produces a series of dots, a dashed line, or a solid line between tabulated columns in a Word document.

left indent   An indent format that indents a paragraph from the left margin.

legend   Displays the colors, patterns, or symbols that identify data categories in a chart.

line break   A marker that continues text on the next line, but treats the text as a continuation of the previous paragraph instead of as a separate paragraph. You insert a line break by pressing ⇧Shift+↵Enter.

line chart   Plots one or more data series as connected points along an axis.

line spacing   The amount of vertical space from the bottom of one text line to the top of the next text line. The default line spacing is single.

link   To copy cell contents or an object so that the copied item does update whenever that item changes in the source location.

list   An Excel database in which columns are fields and rows are records.

list box   A data entry list that looks up valid entries from a table, query, or source list, and does not allow the user to type new data.

long label   Text that exceeds the width of its cell. Overflow text displays if the adjacent cells are blank.

mail merge   A word processing feature that allows you to customize documents using information from a database table.

manual page break   A break you insert to immediately start text at the top of the next page.

margins   Amount of white space around the top, left, right, and bottom of text on a page.

master   A formatting feature that you can use to control which elements appear on each slide.

Master view   The view used when you make modifications to the slide or title master.

MAX function   Displays the largest value among specified values.

maximize   An action that resizes a window to occupy the entire screen.

Meeting Minder   A PowerPoint feature you can use to create action items, or record meeting minutes during a presentation.

menu   A list of commands.

menu bar   A bar that contains common menu names that, when activated, display a list of related commands. The File menu, for example, contains such commands as Open, Close, Save, and Print.

message box   A box that displays information—for example, that a procedure has been completed or an error has occurred—but does not provide an opportunity for the user to respond, except to close the box.

MIN function   Displays the smallest value among specified values.

minimize   An action that keeps a window open but removes it from the screen display.

mouse pointer   A small arrow on the display screen that moves as you move the mouse.

move handle   The large selection handle at the top-left corner of a field text box or a field label box; used to move the text box or label box independently from one another.

multimedia   Special effects you can add to a presentation, such as music, sound, and videos.

name box   Displays the cell address of the current cell, or the name of a cell or range of cells.

Navigation pane   A pane displayed on the left side of the Help window. The Navigation pane is used to browse among Help topics.

nonbreaking hyphen   A special type of hyphen that prevents hyphenated words from separating by the word-wrap feature. For example, you can insert hard hyphens to keep 555-1234 from word-wrapping.

nonbreaking space   A special type of space that prevents words from separating by the word-wrap feature. For example, pressing Ctrl+Shift+Spacebar inserts a nonbreaking space to keep October 16 from word-wrapping.

normalize   To apply a set of design rules to the tables in a database.

Normal view   The main working view in PowerPoint, which includes three sections, or panes: a Slide pane, a Notes pane, and a tabbed section. In Word, this view shows text without displaying space for margins, page numbers, headers, or other supplement text.

notes box   An area of a slide where you can enter speaker notes while using Notes Page view.

Notes pane   The area in PowerPoint's Normal view where you can enter speaker notes.

NOW function   A function that enters the serial number of the current date and time—numbers to the left of the decimal point represent the date, and numbers to the right of the decimal point represent the time.

object   In general, a nontext item, such as a clip art image. In Access, a term for components of a database, including tables, queries, forms, reports, pages, macros, and modules.

Object Linking and Embedding (OLE)   A set of standards that enables you to insert objects, such as pictures or charts, from one document created with one application into documents created with another application.

Office Assistant   A component of onscreen Help in the form of an animated graphics image that can be turned on or off; brings up a list of subjects related to a question you type.

Office Clipboard   An area of memory designed to store multiple items that you cut or copy from a document.

one-to-many   A relationship in which a record in one table may be related to more than one record in a second table.

one-to-one   A relationship in which a record in one table is related to one record in another table through a common field.

opening   The process of retrieving a document from storage, such as from a data disk, and displaying it onscreen.

operating system   A computer program that manages all the computer's resources, sets priorities for programs running at the same time, and has several built-in functions that manage files stored on a computer's disks.

order of precedence   The order in which Excel performs calculations. For example, multiplication and division take place before addition and subtraction.

organization chart   A chart that shows the hierarchical structure of an organization.

orientation   Refers to the rotation of a page or slide when viewing or printing it.

orphan   The first line of a paragraph that appears by itself at the bottom of a page.

OR search criteria   Two or more search conditions, only one of which must be met.

outline numbered list   A list that contains several levels of numbering in an outline format.

output   Producing a presentation electronically, converting it to another format (such as a Web page), or printing it.

Overtype mode   A setting that replaces existing characters when you type new characters.

Pack and Go Wizard   A PowerPoint feature you can use to package your presentation for use on another computer.

paragraph spacing   Controls the amount of space before or after the paragraph.

paste   To insert selected contents of the Office Clipboard in the insertion point's location.

Paste Options Smart Tag   An icon that appears when you paste text. When you click it, you can choose the formatting style for the text you paste.

pattern   Repeats an effect such as a horizontal, vertical, or diagonal stripe.

pencil icon   An icon that looks like a pencil. It is displayed in the record selector when you are editing an Access record in Datasheet view, and it indicates that the current changes have not yet been saved.

peripheral program   A program, such as Microsoft Graph, that is started every time you access a feature within the main program, and place an embedded object, such as a chart, on a slide.

pie chart   A circular chart in which each piece (wedge) shows a data segment and its relationship to the whole.

placeholders   Designated areas on a slide in which you can insert text or other objects.

PMT function   A function that calculates the payment due on a loan, assuming equal payments and a fixed interest rate.

point   A unit of measurement used to designate character height. One point is equivalent to 1/72″.

popup menu   The same as a shortcut menu, this is a context-sensitive menu that displays when you right-click an object.

portrait orientation   Produces a printed page that is longer than it is wide.

position   A font option that raises or lowers text from the baseline without creating superscript or subscript size.

PowerPoint Viewer   A program used to run slide shows on computers that don't have PowerPoint installed on them.

presentation   A series of electronic slides containing visual information you can use to persuade or inform an audience.

presentation graphics program   Software such as PowerPoint that helps you structure, design, and present information to an audience so that it's both catchy and visually appealing. Presentation graphics software generally creates information as a series of electronic slides that you can display or output in a variety of ways.

primary key   A field that contains a unique value for each record and is used to identify the record.

Print Layout view   The view that illustrates what the document will look like when it's printed. You see margins, page numbers, headers, and so on.

promoting   To indent text less on an outline, raising it to a higher level of importance. The opposite of demoting.

properties   The characteristics of a screen element. For example, a number has such properties as number of decimal places, format, font size, and others.

pure black and white   A printing option in which all gray tones are converted to either black or white.

query   A question posed to the database that determines what information is retrieved. A query can be used to restrict which fields are shown and what conditions the displayed data must meet. It can also be defined as one of the objects in a database.

Random Access Memory (RAM)   The temporary storage space that a computer uses for programs with which it's currently working.

range   One cell or a rectangular group of adjacent cells.

read-only   A file attribute that indicates a file can be opened but not changed.

record   A group of data pertaining to one event, transaction, or person. The categories of information in a record are called fields.

record selector   The shaded area to the left of a record. It indicates whether the record is selected or being edited. Clicking on it selects the whole record.

Redo   Reverses an undo action.

reference operator   Used to combine cell references in calculations. The colon (:), which connects the first and last cells of the range to be summed, is an example of a reference operator.

rehearse timings   A PowerPoint feature you can use to track the length of your presentation.

relational database   A database with two or more tables that are linked together.

relationship   The connection between two tables.

relative cell reference   Specifies that the row and/or column cell references change as a formula is copied. For example, copying the formula =A1+A2 in cell A3 to cells B3 and C3 results in the formulas =B1+B2 and =C1+C2, respectively. *See also* **absolute cell reference**

report   A database object that is designed to print and summarize selected fields.

restore   An action that automatically resizes a window to its size before being maximized.

Reveal Formatting task pane   A window pane that displays font characteristics, alignment, indentation, spacing, and tabs.

reverse text effect   An appearance that uses a darker background with a lighter text color. For example, a yellow text font on a blue background creates a reverse text effect.

right indent   Indents a paragraph a specified amount of space from the right margin.

rotation handle   A green marker that appears at the top of a selected object. You can drag the rotation handle to spin or rotate an object.

row   A group of table cells arranged horizontally.

row height   The vertical space from the top to the bottom of a row.

row number   Numbered 1 through 65,536 in an Excel worksheet.

row selector   The shaded area to the left of a field in the table Design view. Clicking a box in this area selects the entire row.

ruler   Shows the location of tabs, indents, and left and right margins.

sans serif font   A font that does not have serifs. This type of font is useful for headings, so they stand out from body text.

saving   The process of storing a document for future use.

scale   Increases or decreases the text horizontally as a percentage of its size.

ScreenTip   A small pop-up window that displays when you rest the mouse pointer over a toolbar button or other screen element. ScreenTips usually display the name of the button or screen element to help identify them.

scrollbars   Enable you to move the display within a window vertically and horizontally so that you can see other parts of the display.

scrollbox   An object within a horizontal or vertical scrollbar that you can drag to shift quickly the display within a window.

scrolling   The process of moving the insertion point through your document or shifting the display within a window.

section (form)   A division of a form, such as the Detail, Page Header, Form Header, Page Footer, or Form Footer, that can contain controls, labels, formulas, and images.

section (report)   A division of a report, such as the Detail, Page Header, or Page Footer, that can contain controls, labels, formulas, and images.

section break   A marker that divides a document into sections; section breaks allow you to have different formats, such as page numbering.

select   To highlight or click an item so you can subsequently move, copy, delete, or format it.

selection bar   The space in the left margin area where you see a right-pointing arrow, indicating that you can make a selection. For example, click once to select the current text line.

selection handles   Markers that appear around the border of a selected object (also known as **sizing handles**). You can drag a selection handle to resize an object.

Select query   Lists data in an Access database that meets conditions set by the user.

serif font   A font that displays tiny little lines or extensions at the top and bottom of most characters in the font. The serifs guide the reader's eyes across the text.

shading   A colored background, similar to highlight, except that the space within the area is also colored; it is also the background color within a table cell or group of cells.

sheet tab   A means to access each sheet in a workbook. Click a sheet tab to quickly move to that sheet.

shortcut   A fast keyboard method for performing a task. For example, the keyboard shortcut for bolding text is Ctrl+B.

shortcut menu   A context-sensitive menu that displays when you right-click an object. This is sometimes called a pop-up menu.

short menu   A pull-down menu from the menu bar (also known as an adaptive menu). When you first select from the menu bar, you see a short menu of the most commonly used tasks you use. The short menu adapts based on your usage of the features.

single-space   Text lines that are close together, one immediately above the other.

sizing handles   Small black squares at the corners and midpoints of a selected object. The handles indicate that the object can be moved and sized.

slide background   The background color and design of a slide.

slide image   A small-scale version of a slide shown in Notes Page view.

slide layout   Sometimes called an AutoLayout, this refers to the arrangement of placeholders for a slide.

slide master   A formatting feature in PowerPoint that works hand-in-hand with the template to control which elements appear on each slide. You use the slide master to quickly add or change design elements—such as the date, a slide number, or a company logo—to all slides in your presentation. You can also quickly change the appearance of bullets or fonts throughout a presentation by making the modification to the master.

Slide pane   The area in Normal view that you use to view and work with slide elements, such as text or objects.

slide-title master pair   The pair of masters that controls the elements and look of a presentation. These masters appear as a pair on the left side of the application window whenever you use Master view.

slide transition   The way one slide replaces another during an electronic slide show.

Smart Tag   An icon that displays options when you click it. It might display a note to enter a name in the Microsoft Outlook Contacts folder or provide options for pasting text.

soft return   Occurs when Word word-wraps text to the next line within a paragraph as you type it.

sort   To rearrange the records in a list, based on the contents of one or more fields.

sort field   The column you want a program to use in sorting (sometimes called a sort key).

spacing   A font option that controls the amount of space between two or more characters.

speaker notes   Supporting data, quotations, or illustrations that you can use when giving a presentation.

spelling checker   A feature that highlights words that are not in its dictionary and lets you change or ignore any highlighted word.

spreadsheet   A work area—called a **worksheet** in Excel—comprised of rows and columns.

stacked column chart   Displays multiple data series as stacked components of a single column instead of as side-by-side columns. The stacked column subtype is appropriate if the multiple data series total to a meaningful number.

Standard toolbar   Provides, in button form, shortcuts to frequently used commands including Save, Print, Cut (move), Copy, and Paste. The Formatting and Standard toolbars can share one row or display on two rows.

Start button   Pressing this button provides a menu approach to opening and closing programs, managing files and folders, getting onscreen Help about Windows, and controlling system components; it is located at the left end of the Windows taskbar.

status bar   A bar that provides information about the current operation or workspace, such as displaying *CAPS* if you set Caps Lock on.

subfolder   A folder created within another folder.

submenu   A second-level menu displaying a set of options activated by selecting a menu item. For example, choosing View, Toolbars displays the Toolbars submenu that lists specific toolbars.

suppress   Hides or removes something onscreen. For example, suppressing the page number prevents the number from displaying and printing on a page.

switchboard   A form that launches when a database is opened and makes access to the database objects easier for those persons who are less familiar with Access database structures.

synonym   A word that means the same as another word. Word contains a feature that helps you select appropriate synonyms for words.

table   One of the objects in an Access database. Tables store data in row-and-column format and are the foundation of the database. In Word, a series of rows and columns that organize data effectively.

table alignment   The horizontal position of a table between the left and right margins.

tab order   The order in which the insertion point jumps from field to field on a form.

tabs   Markers that specify the position for aligning text when you press Tab.

taskbar (Windows)   A bar that displays a button for each open file; generally located across the bottom of the Windows desktop. Use the taskbar to switch from one application to another.

task pane   A small window within a program that gives you quick access to commonly used commands. The task pane is usually displayed on the right side of the application window.

template (design template)   A blueprint that PowerPoint uses to create slides. The template includes the formatting, color, and graphics necessary to create a particular "look."

Text Layouts   Preset slide layouts that include placeholders for text.

thumbnail   A miniature representation. For example, a small picture of the first slide displays when you click the name of a PowerPoint presentation to open.

tight wrap   A wrapping style that lets text contour or wrap tightly around the outer edges of the image itself instead of the square border area that surrounds an image.

title bar   A bar that displays across the top of a window; provides the name of the open object and program at its left end, and a series of buttons at its right end. The buttons enable you to minimize, maximize or restore, and close the window respectively.

title master   The master that controls which items appear on the title slide of a presentation.

toolbar A bar containing a set of buttons; each button on the toolbar performs a predefined task.

triggering Playing animation effects in sequence during a slide show each time you click the mouse.

typeface A style of print such as Arial, Courier, or Times New Roman. *See also* **font**

Undo Reverses an action that you perform in the document. Actions are undone in reverse sequential order; that is, the last action performed is the first reversed.

upload To copy files to a server so that they can be viewed on the Web.

variable data Amounts that are subject to change, such as the interest rate or amount borrowed in a loan situation.

vertical alignment Positions text between the top and bottom edges on a page.

vertical scrollbar An object at the side of a window that enables you to shift window contents up and down to view information that extends beyond the height of a window.

view buttons Switches between different view modes, such as Normal, Web Layout, Print Layout, and Outline view.

views The various perspectives you can use to work with your presentation.

watermark A washed-out graphic object or text that typically appears behind text.

Web browser Software you use to locate and view Web pages.

Web Page Preview A PowerPoint feature you can use to see how your presentation will look as a Web site.

What's This? The Help feature that describes the functions of different parts of the screen.

widow The last line of a paragraph that appears by itself at the top of a page.

window An enclosed, rectangular area on the screen that enables you to see the output from a program.

windows, cascading An arrangement in which open windows display in a stack—each window slightly to the right of, and slightly below, the previous window.

windows, tiled An arrangement in which open windows display horizontally—each window to the right of the previous one—or vertically—each window below the previous one.

Windows A group of operating systems developed for personal computers by Microsoft.

Windows Explorer A utility program that enables you to access programs and documents, as well as copy, move, delete, and rename files.

wizard An interactive tool that guides you step-by-step through a process that would otherwise be complicated or awkward.

WordArt A feature that creates interesting shapes and designs for text.

WordPad A Windows utility program for creating small word-processing files in several formats.

word-wrap feature Continues text on the next line if it can't fit at the end of the current line.

workbook An Excel file that contains one or more worksheets.

worksheet Excel's term for a work area comprised of rows and columns; also known as a **spreadsheet**.

worksheet frame The row and column headings that appear along the top and left edge of the worksheet window.

worksheet model Generally contains labels and formulas, but the cells that hold variable data are left blank.

worksheet window Contains the current worksheet—the work area.

World Wide Web (WWW) The graphical, user-friendly part of the Internet. You can display different Web pages by clicking hyperlinks.

wrapping style Specifies the way text wraps around an object, such as a clip art image.

WYSIWYG Stands for "What You See Is What You Get." This means that your printout will look like what you see onscreen.

X axis The horizontal axis of a chart that generally appears at the bottom edge.

Y axis A vertical axis of a chart that usually appears at the left edge. Some chart types support creation of a second Y axis at the right edge of the chart.

zoom Specifies the magnification percentage of the way your document appears onscreen.

Index